COMPLEXITY'S EMBRACE

Centre for International
Governance Innovation

COMPLEXITY'S EMBRACE
The International Law Implications of Brexit

Editors
Oonagh E. Fitzgerald | Eva Lein

ISBN 978-1-928096-62-7 (cloth)
ISBN 978-1-928096-63-4 (paper)
ISBN 978-1-928096-64-1 (ePUB)
ISBN 978-1-928096-65-8 (ePDF)

Library and Archives Canada Cataloguing in Publication

Complexity's Embrace : The International Law Implications of Brexit / edited by Oonagh E. Fitzgerald and Eva Lein

Includes bibliographical references.
Issued in print and electronic formats.
ISBN 978-1-928096-62-7 (cloth).--ISBN 978-1-928096-63-4 (paper).--
ISBN 978-1-928096-64-1 (ePUB).--ISBN 978-1-928096-65-8 (ePDF)

1. European Union--Great Britain. 2. International and municipal law--Great Britain.
3. Commercial law--Great Britain. 4. Commercial law--European Union countries. 5. Civil law--Great Britain. 6. Civil law--European Union countries. 7. Environmental law--Great Britain.
8. Environmental law--European Union countries. I. Fitzgerald, Oonagh E., 1955-, editor II. Lein, Eva, editor III. British Institute of International and Comparative Law, issuing body IV. Centre for International Governance Innovation, issuing body

KD4015.C66 2018   342.41   C2018-901020-7
                                                 C2018-901021-5

Published by the Centre for International Governance Innovation (CIGI) in partnership with the British Institute of International and Comparative Law (BIICL).

Printed and bound in Canada on 100 percent post-consumer recycled paper (FSC®).

Cover and page design by Melodie Wakefield.

Centre for International Governance Innovation and CIGI are registered trademarks.

Centre for International Governance Innovation

British Institute of International and Comparative Law

Centre for International Governance Innovation
67 Erb Street West
Waterloo, ON Canada N2L 6C2

British Institute of International and Comparative Law
Charles Clore House, 17 Russell Square
London, WC1B 5JP, UK

www.cigionline.org

www.biicl.org

Contents

Foreword

Diana Wallis

As human beings, we tend to look for the way forward and to seek progression, yet despite the recent warm words of the UK foreign minister, it is hard to see the UK decision to leave the European Union in positive, progressive terms. However it is viewed, it involves "undoing," "repealing" and "re-enacting," and even the famous "taking back control" slogan in this sense has a regressive tone. All this, as elegantly put in the introduction to this volume, is counterintuitive to most international lawyers, who have seen our role as enablers of greater and simpler interaction and integration in an increasingly interconnected world. Suddenly we are asked to contemplate full reverse gear, but without any clear vision of what we are attempting to reach or, to put it positively, what is the nature of this new international order and, most particularly, the British place in it.

Sometimes images help. I will always recall, as a member of the European Parliament, a meeting with a senior US official from the Clinton administration. After we had finished our business, she was keen to see the Parliament and the plenary chamber. So off we went. As she entered the door and saw all the members' seats and the flags, she turned toward me and this very tough lady had tears in her eyes. The sight caught her off balance and she said, "It's like when I was a child, how I imagined a world Parliament!" Perhaps we British, at least, do not appreciate what we have created.

So how to dismantle, or rather disentangle, the United Kingdom from decades of closer legal engagement with our continental neighbours? For those of us who have been daily hoping for a vision or road map of future possibilities from the British government, this volume provides an excellent discussion of possibilities and, of course, the various difficulties they will entrain. It is helpful to examine in detail several sectors of law such as environmental or intellectual property rights. Of course, we all have our favourite subjects, but the problem with Brexit is that it seeps into every legal and regulatory activity where unknown consequences surface. It is hard to visualize the whole, which is probably partly why discussions revert to simplistic reliance on arguments about "sovereignty," which take us no further toward a vision of the future.

Personally, I always expected that the UK government would formulate some sort of "Switzerland-light" vision, in which the country keeps its internal democracy intact, freed from the Court of Justice of the European Union and attempts to establish an extensive set of "bilaterals" on key issues or sectors. Of course, the European Commission would hate it and it would be tough, but at least it would be some sort of substantial template. Instead, we seem to be veering toward a complete third-country relationship. In this respect, the thoughts from Canada within this volume are illuminating, both on dealing with referenda and coming to terms with a new order in international trade. However, in Canada, there appears to have been more reflection and coming together through society at large, which currently remains starkly absent in the UK debate. The implications of this debate, or rather divide, in Northern Ireland and Scotland threaten the very foundations of the United Kingdom.

Perhaps we were lulled into a false sense of security. I would have tended to characterize the British view of the European Union as akin to our relationship with the weather: something we talk and complain about endlessly, but ultimately just get on with. I did not imagine that my compatriots would get themselves into such a situation and then, some 18 months after making the decision, still lack a clear view of where we are heading. This volume will assist those who search for possible answers and outcomes. It may not be the old linear progress we assumed, but whatever else, Brexit (and US President Donald Trump) are ushering in a new and very dynamic era for international lawyers and law.

Acknowledgements

We are most grateful to the authors who contributed chapters to this book. We also thank former BIICL Director Robert McCorquodale, former ILRP Deputy Director Markus Gehring, and CIGI and BIICL's events team for their engagement in making the 2017 conference a success. We thank especially Susan Bubak, Sharon McCartney and Carol Bonnett from the CIGI publications team for their highly professional advice and meticulous editing, as well as Melodie Wakefield from the CIGI design team for her stylish layout of the series and book. We are indebted to Maziar Peihani and Nethmi Kulatilake for their careful work in helping to keep us on schedule and managing the peer review process. We acknowledge the helpful assistance of CIGI Counsel Sam Anissimov and Program Manager Scott Lewis in developing the publication partnership and the contributors' contracts. We thank the communications teams at CIGI and BIICL for their support in promoting the series and book through strategic placement of op-eds and commentaries by contributing authors.

Abbreviations and Acronyms

AD/CVD	antidumping and countervailing duties	B2B	business-to-business
AFTA	Atlantic Free Trade Area	BaFin	German Financial Supervisory Authority
AIFs	alternative investment funds	BATNA	best alternative to a negotiated agreement
AIFMs	alternative investment fund managers	BBIs	behind-the-border issues
AIFMD	Alternative Investment Fund Managers Directive	BCBS	Basel Committee on Banking Supervision
ANZCERTA	Australia-New Zealand Closer Economic Relations Trade Agreement	BEIS	Department for Business, Energy and Industrial Strategy
ASEAN	Association of Southeast Asian Nations	BGB	German Civil Code

BIICL	British Institute of International and Comparative Law	CRD IV	Capital Requirements Directive IV
BREFs	Best Available Techniques Reference Documents	CRR	Capital Requirements Regulation
		CSDs	central securities depositories
BRRD	Bank Resolution and Recovery Directive	CSDR	Central Securities Depositories Regulation
BVI	British Virgin Islands	CU	Customs Union
C-TPAT	Customs-Trade Partnership Against Terrorism	DEEU	Department for Exiting the European Union
CBIR	Cross-Border Insolvency Regulations	DEFRA	Department for Environment, Food and Rural Affairs
CCPs	central counterparties		
CEN	European Committee for Standardization	EAP	Environmental Action Programme
CET	common external tariff	EBA	European Banking Authority
CETA	Comprehensive Economic and Trade Agreement		
CFR	Charter of Fundamental Rights	EC	European Commission/ European Community
		ECA	European Communities Act
CFTC	Commodity Futures Trading Commission	ECB	European Central Bank
		ECHR	European Convention on Human Rights
CIGI	Centre for International Governance Innovation	ECJ	European Court of Justice
CIPA	Chartered Institute of Patent Attorneys	ECOWAS	Economic Community of West African States
CITMA	Chartered Institute of Trade Mark Attorneys	EEA	European Economic Area
CIWUD	Credit Institutions Winding Up Directive	EEC	European Economic Community
CJEU	Court of Justice of the European Union	EFTA	European Free Trade Association
CO2	carbon dioxide	EIA	environmental impact assessment
COMI	centre of main interests	EIR	European Insolvency Regulation
COP	Conference of the Parties of the UNFCCC	EMIR	European Market Infrastructure Regulation
CPTPP	Comprehensive and Progressive Agreement for Trans-Pacific Partnership	EP	European patents

EPC	European Patent Convention		IMF	International Monetary Fund
EPO	European Patent Office		INDCs	intended nationally determined contributions
ERC	European resolution college			
ESA	European Supervisory Authorities		InfoSoc	Information Society
			INR	initial negotiating rights
ESMA	European Securities and Markets Authority		IP	intellectual property
			IPPC	integrated pollution prevention and control
ETS	Emissions Trading System			
EU27	remaining 27 member states of the European Union		IPRs	intellectual property rights
			ISDS	investor-state dispute settlement
EUIPO	European Union Intellectual Property Office			
			KWG	German Banking Act
Euratom	European Atomic Energy Community		MAR	Market Abuse Regulation
			MEAs	Multilateral Environmental Agreements
EUSFTA	EU-Singapore Free Trade Agreement			
			MFN	Most Favoured Nation
FAST	Free and Secure Trade		MiFID	Markets in Financial Instruments Directive
FATF	Financial Action Task Force			
FCAs	future customs arrangements		MiFIR	Markets in Financial Instruments Regulation
FSB	Financial Stability Board			
FTA	free trade agreement		MNEs	multinational enterprises
G20	Group of Twenty		MRAs	mutual recognition agreements
GATS	General Agreement on Trade in Services			
			MtCO2e	million tonnes carbon dioxide equivalent
GATT	General Agreement on Tariffs and Trade			
			NAFTA	North American Free Trade Agreement
GHG	greenhouse gas			
GIs	geographical indications		NGOs	non-governmental organizations
GMOs	genetically modified organisms			
			OHIM	Office for Harmonization in the Internal Market
HRA	Human Rights Act			
HRBA	human-rights-based approach		PANEL	participation, accountability, non-discrimination and equality, empowerment and legality
HTS	harmonized tariff system			
IEEP	Institute for European Environmental Policy		PCO	protective costs order
			PDOs	protected designations of origin
IEM	internal energy market			

PGIs	protected geographical indications	TRQs	tariff rate quotas
PPMs	production and process methods	TTIP	Transatlantic Trade and Investment Partnership
PRA	Prudential Regulation Authority	UCITS	Undertakings for Collective Investment in Transferable Securities
PRIIPS	packaged retail and insurance-based investment products	UCITSD	Undertakings for Collective Investment in Transferable Securities Directive
PTAs	preferential trade agreements	UKELA	UK Environmental Law Association
REACH	Registration, Evaluation, Authorisation and Restriction of Chemicals	UKIPO	United Kingdom Intellectual Property Office
ROO	rules of origin	UKSC	UK Supreme Court
SADC	Southern African Development Community	UNCITRAL	United Nations Commission on International Trade Law
SCC	Supreme Court of Canada	UNECE	United Nations Economic Commission for Europe
SDGs	Sustainable Development Goals	UNFCCC	United Nations Framework Convention on Climate Change
SEA	Single European Act		
SIFIs	systemically important financial institutions	UP	unitary patent
SMEs	small- and medium-sized enterprises	UPC	Unified Patent Court
SPCs	supplementary protection certificates	WHO/FAO	World Health Organization/ Food and Agriculture Organization of the United Nations
SPS	sanitary and phytosanitary		
TBTs	technical barriers to trade	WIPO	World Intellectual Property Organization
TEU	Treaty on European Union		
TFEU	Treaty on the Functioning of the European Union	WTO	World Trade Organization
TPCE	Technical Platform for Cooperation on the Environment	WWF	World Wide Fund for Nature
TPP	Trans-Pacific Partnership Agreement		
TRIPS	Agreement on Trade-Related Aspects of Intellectual Property Rights		

Introduction

Oonagh E. Fitzgerald and Eva Lein

In June 2016, the United Kingdom voted in favour of leaving the European Union. The government's initial response to it has unleashed an unprecedented political, economic, social and legal storm, the full implications of which have been revealing themselves over the last year and a half.

From the perspective of international lawyers, the Brexit vote and its ramifications grab our attention. How can the United Kingdom extract itself from the European Union? What are the formal or mechanical steps to be taken at the international level? Which steps have to be taken from a domestic constitutional perspective? What are the implications for international trade and regulatory cooperation in global value chains, financial services, cross-border insolvency, intellectual property (IP) rights, environmental protection and environmental justice, human rights, democratic rights and the accommodation of minorities?

Trained to the view that international law's mission is to articulate global rules that contribute to enduring peace, harmony, prosperity, equity and sustainability, it is reflexive for international lawyers to think that more integration rather than less should be civilization's destiny. The Brexit

1

vote and the equally surprising election results in the United States have deeply destabilized that assumption and raised a myriad of new questions about the future of international law, in particular how to reverse the course of integration, how to unmake international law and how to create new international accords.

As the Brexit cases were being argued and adjudicated, international lawyers from the British Institute of International and Comparative Law (BIICL) and the Centre for International Governance Innovation (CIGI) decided to collaborate in holding a conference in London, England, to examine the international law dimensions of Brexit. At the time, the seriousness of Brexit's implications was belied by the dogmatic and simplistic discussion in large parts of the mainstream media, where any hint of critical thinking was being attacked as anti-British and anti-democratic. The one-day conference in February 2017, attended by UK, European and North American public servants, academics and practitioners, was a revelation to all participants as it was the first time that the full range of international law implications had been laid out for thoughtful public discussion.

Due to the positive response to the conference and the discussion of these important international law issues, BIICL and CIGI agreed to collaborate on the publication of papers flowing from the conference, first as an online series and then as this book. With contributions from the United Kingdom, Europe and North America, and both academic and practitioners' perspectives, the book examines the international and domestic law and governance implications of Brexit on a wide range of topics: international trade, financial services, cross-border insolvency, intellectual property rights, environmental law and human rights.

Although trade policy does not seem to have been among the main drivers of the vote to leave the European Union, Brexit's implications for the United Kingdom's trading arrangements are considerable. Four chapters explore the many unprecedented questions about the United Kingdom's future trading arrangements. In "Brexit and International Trade: One Year after the Referendum," Valerie Hughes notes that views differ as to whether, post-Brexit, the United Kingdom and the European Union could continue to exercise rights under the World Trade Organization (WTO) following bilateral renegotiations and adjustments, or whether they would each need to secure new WTO schedules. Given this uncertainty, Hughes suggests two recent legal decisions, one from the European Court of Justice on EU and EU member state competence, and the other from a WTO dispute-settlement panel discussing modification of WTO members' schedules, may provide useful guidance for trade negotiators and legal advisers going forward.

Armand de Mestral's chapter, "Squaring the Circle: The Search for an Accommodation between the European Union and the United Kingdom," examines, from a Canadian perspective, the options for a new economic relationship among the United Kingdom, the European Union and North America, and proposes that the United Kingdom launch an Atlantic free trade agreement to counterbalance the European Union, once it is legally able to do so.

In "Renegotiating the EU-UK Trade Relationship: Lessons from NAFTA," David A. Gantz assesses the UK government's range of choices for forging a new trading relationship with Europe to replace continued membership in the European Union's Single Market and/or Customs Union, which currently provides unrestricted trade. The choices of reversion to WTO rules, to a free trade agreement (FTA), or to a hybrid combination of FTA and customs union are considered, as well as lessons from the North American Free Trade Agreement (NAFTA). Gantz concludes that, given the Leave side's priorities of immigration control, regulatory autonomy and freedom from the European Court of Justice, an FTA like NAFTA may be the only legally feasible form of preferential trade.

In his chapter, "Trade Policy in the Age of Populism: Why the New Bilateralism Will Not Work," Thomas Cottier reviews the new UK trade policy announced by the Conservative government in October 2017. It is based upon WTO rules, plurilateral agreements and a wide new network of self-standing bilateral preferential agreements, and articulates a vision of the United Kingdom reassuming an independent and leading role in trade policy. Cottier notes that this new bilateralism will expose UK negotiators to diverging interests and power dynamics, such that the United Kingdom's freedom to chart its own course in international trade will be largely circumscribed by existing global trading relations.

With the United Kingdom being the financial services hub of the planet, inevitably there are important questions about what the impact of Brexit will be on the United Kingdom's competitive advantage in the financial sector. Two chapters examine the challenges for the United Kingdom's globally oriented and globally dominant financial services sector in a post-Brexit economy. In "Brexit and Financial Services: Navigating through the Complexity of Exit Scenarios," Maziar Peihani asks how to govern future relations between the United Kingdom and the European Union in the realm of financial services. He assesses the key legal and regulatory issues that may arise with the three primary scenarios that may govern the parties' future relationship: the European Economic Area, third-country equivalence and a bespoke agreement.

In their chapter entitled, "How Does It Feel to Be a Third Country? The Consequences of Brexit for Financial Market Law," Dirk Zetzsche and Matthias Lehmann analyze options in financial market law available to British issuers, credit institutions, insurance companies, securities firms, and asset and fund managers, considering that post-Brexit the United Kingdom will become a third country from the perspective of the European Union. They posit that whether London will continue to be the centre for European financial transactions will depend on its access to the Single Market and suggest that British companies will achieve market access via equivalence, by setting up a European subsidiary, through bilateral agreements and passively using the fundamental freedom of services. Thus, even after Brexit, British companies will have to obey certain European laws if they want to maintain access to the Single Market, and British law making will not be free from coordination with the Continent in order to ensure market access.

Coordination of cross-border insolvency resolution is an important issue in a country dependent on global trade and investment. Two chapters examine dimensions of this issue. Co-authors Christoph Paulus, Federico Mucciarelli, Howard Morris and Gabriel Moss in the chapter entitled "Cross-border Insolvencies after Brexit: Views from the United Kingdom and Continental Europe," express their dismay at the faulty reasoning of Leave supporters who naively hope that the United Kingdom will prevail in negotiations with the European Union and "have its cake and eat it too" without recognizing the deep interconnectedness of the UK economy with the EU Single Market. Such entanglement of EU and UK production means that the insolvency of firms active across national borders involves interests of stakeholders (creditors, employees and suppliers) situated in different member states, necessitating measures for mutual recognition and enforcement of insolvency procedures. The chapter examines the modes of recognition of foreign insolvency proceedings under British law and the likely impact of Brexit; the impact of Brexit on forum and law shopping; the reform proposal for British workout procedures; and the use of British workout procedures by EU companies.

Dorothy Livingston's chapter entitled "Failing Financial Institutions: How Will Brexit Impact Cross-border Cooperation in Recovery, Reconstruction and Insolvency Processes?" discusses issues of cross-border recognition and assistance related to processes affecting financial institutions arising from Brexit. The chapter examines whether Brexit represents a setback in efforts to create a robust approach to cross-border insolvency of systemically important financial institutions (SIFIs); how Brexit will affect the recognition of recovery, reconstruction and insolvency proceedings with a cross-border element affecting failure of a SIFI; whether the WTO General Agreement on Trade in Services has any bearing on the issues; and how far the courts can address any political and regulatory failures to preserve the existing levels of mutual recognition as between the United Kingdom and EU member states.

Other authors debate the impact of Brexit on the protection of IP rights in the United Kingdom and abroad, showing that continuity in the IP field is both more likely and more beneficial than radical change, such that even after leaving the European Union, there will be a compelling need to maintain harmonized IP rules. In "UK Patent Law and Copyright Law after Brexit: Potential Consequences," Luke McDonagh notes that although neither UK patent law nor copyright law is fully harmonized with the European Union, Brexit could nonetheless have a sizable impact on both sets of IP rights. For patents, Brexit could lead the United Kingdom to diverge from EU principles on biotechnology and supplementary protection certificates, and also puts the United Kingdom's role in the new Unified Patent Court system into doubt. In the area of copyright, the United Kingdom could use Brexit as an opportunity to move away from EU standards, including the key definitions of originality and parody. Nonetheless, McDonagh concludes that both the European Union and the United Kingdom will likely seek to retain a great deal of regulatory convergence and cooperation over IP.

In his chapter entitled "The Effect of Brexit on Trademarks, Designs and Other 'Europeanized' Areas of Intellectual Property Law in the United Kingdom," Marc Mimler observes that despite the uncertainty about Brexit, the effects on IP law in the United Kingdom will be profound because IP law represents the most Europeanized area of private law. He considers the Europeanization of UK laws of trademarks and designs over the last decades, as well as the development of the law of geographical indications, the doctrine of exhaustion and the interface of IP and competition rules as developed in the European Union, and discusses how different Brexit scenarios might affect them.

Four chapters on environmental law consider which international treaties will survive Brexit, how mixed or exclusive EU competency treaties will have to be renegotiated, and how the considerable challenges posed by Brexit for environmental law may provide an opportunity to improve implementation and enforcement arrangements and climate justice. First, in "Brexit and Environmental Law: The Rocky Road Ahead," Markus Gehring and Freedom-Kai Phillips observe that EU environmental law developed organically in areas where EU member states felt that common standards would be useful because differing standards would have a direct effect on the internal market. European environmental law has also been shaped by the United Kingdom through the introduction of market mechanisms into environmental legislation previously unknown to the administrative legal systems of civil law governing continental Europe. This chapter reviews legal and policy considerations underpinning Brexit in light of international environmental commitments, in particular relating to climate change. Although deregulatory pressures could threaten the dream of a greener Britain post-Brexit, EU environmental standards for imported products could, in most areas relevant for trade in goods, determine UK environmental law for the foreseeable future if the United Kingdom wishes to trade with the European Union.

Damilola S. Olawuyi, in his chapter entitled "Advancing Environmental Justice in a Post-Brexit United Kingdom," evaluates the possible implications of Brexit for achieving environmental justice, defined as being the need for countries to mitigate sources of environmental pollution and approach development in a manner that respects, protects and fulfills the human rights of all sectors of society, especially the most vulnerable. The possible loss of the EU policy "back stop" on environmental justice, post-Brexit, raises fundamental questions about whether, and how, a stand-alone United Kingdom could guarantee and protect public rights to environmental justice with the same commitment, consistency and vigour as the European Union. Olawuyi recommends a clear, committed and inclusive approach to environmental governance if the United Kingdom is to maintain and advance recent progress on environmental justice matters post-Brexit.

In "Brexit and International Environmental Law," Richard Macrory and Joe Newbigin note that the United Kingdom is party to more than 40 international environmental treaties (and over 100 international environmental agreements when protocols, amendments and so forth are also considered) and that the UK government has committed to remaining bound by its international environmental obligations in the interests of regulatory stability until an opportunity for re-evaluation arises. Post-Brexit, therefore, international environmental law could be seen to provide an important underpinning in terms of future national environmental obligations, rights and minimum standards. The authors observe that the European Union has developed sophisticated mechanisms for the enforcement of EU obligations against member states, including those arising from international agreements, and that it is questionable whether these will be replicated post-Brexit in relation to international agreements to which the United Kingdom is a party.

Stephen Tromans, in his chapter, "Brexit, Brexatom, the Environment and Future International Relations," observes that in the field of environmental protection, views differ sharply as to the benefits of EU membership, even though this was not fully canvassed during the Brexit debates. He examines the impact of EU law on UK environmental law and policy, and the possible implications of Brexit for the environment. He considers the question of future relations among the United Kingdom, the European Union and the wider international community in terms of any limits on the United Kingdom's autonomy to set its own environmental standards. Tromans explains that leaving the European Union will also entail leaving the European Atomic Energy Community, a separate legal entity that shares institutional features with the European Union.

The book is completed by three chapters discussing the potential human rights implications of Brexit. In "Lessons from Brexit: Reconciling International and Constitutional Aspirations," Oonagh E. Fitzgerald draws lessons from Canadian constitutional jurisprudence to shed light on the importance of taking an inclusive approach to minorities when making momentous constitutional change. The June 2016 vote, with its slim majority in favour of Brexit and its regionally divided outcomes, with strong Remain support in Northern Ireland and Scotland, presented the UK government with a quandary it seemed ill-equipped to manage: how to achieve Brexit without also dismantling the United Kingdom. The analysis of the recent UK decision in *Miller*[1] on the invocation of article 50 of the Treaty on European Union and the Canadian ruling in *Reference re Quebec Secession*[2] suggests that majority rule is only one of a collection of core conventions, principles and laws that operate together to sustain constitutional democracy in times of great crisis.

Colm O'Cinneide, in his chapter entitled "Brexit and Human Rights," reviews the plentiful commentary asserting that Brexit will open up a "vacuum" in rights protection, pose a "risk" to existing human rights protection, become a policy quagmire that erodes established human rights and civil liberties, and will undermine the human rights framework that forms a key element of the Northern Ireland peace settlement, laid out in the Good Friday Agreement of 1998. He also notes that other commentators have argued that these concerns are radically overstated, and that leaving the European Union offers an opportunity for the United Kingdom to develop superior standards of rights protection better reflecting "British values" than currently exist in British or European law. O'Cinneide carefully assesses the merits of these competing claims in order to clarify Brexit's potential impact on human rights in the near and medium term.

In "Brexit: Can the United Kingdom Change its Mind?", Helen Mountfield refers to the divisional court in *Shindler*[3] and the Supreme Court in *Miller* as reinforcing the long-established principle that British courts do not recognize "the will of the people" but only the will of the elected legislature, such that a referendum authorized by legislation is only advisory unless the legislation also provides for what will happen in the event of a particular result. Since Parliament has only authorized the prime minister to notify the European Council of Britain's current intention to withdraw from the European Union, and had not authorized withdrawal itself, there is no constitutional authority to leave the European Union. Mountfield asserts that if Parliament does not approve the deal negotiated by the prime minister, article 50 would permit, and the British constitution would require, that the prime minister inform the European Council that the United Kingdom's intention has changed, it withdraws its notice and decides to remain.

After decades of strengthening European integration and independence, the giving of notice under article 50 of the Treaty on European Union forces the UK government and the European Union to address the complex challenge of unravelling the many threads that bind them, and to chart a new course of separation and autonomy. This book, with its careful analysis of the many areas of international and domestic law potentially affected by Brexit, will help politicians, policy makers, practitioners and civil society actors determine whether the Brexit vote really should mean Brexit, and if so, at what cost to existing institutions of law and governance.

---

1   *R v Miller*, [2017] UKSC 5.

2   [1998] 2 SCR 217 (SCC).

3   *Shindler v Chancellor of the Duchy of Lancaster*, [2016] EWCA Civ 469, s 7.

Section One

TRADE

1

Brexit and International Trade: One Year after the Referendum

Valerie Hughes

Introduction

It has been just over a year since the people of the United Kingdom voted to leave the European Union.[1] The result of the referendum, which shocked many, both in the United Kingdom and abroad, raised numerous questions about the process for and implications of the United Kingdom's withdrawal from the union it joined in 1972. Several of those questions concern the United Kingdom's future trading arrangements, be they with the European Union and its remaining member states, or more broadly with members of the World Trade Organization (WTO). This chapter focuses on the legal landscape that informs what those future trading relationships might be.

Speaking to the World Trade Symposium held in London on June 7, 2016 — two weeks before the Brexit referendum vote was held — WTO Director-General Roberto Azevêdo observed that although the United Kingdom would remain a member of the WTO even if it were to leave the

---

1   The vote took place on June 23, 2016.

European Union, its terms of trade for goods and services were founded on the United Kingdom's membership of the European Union and, therefore, a United Kingdom outside the European Union would need to negotiate these terms anew with all WTO members. The director-general painted a rather daunting picture of the road ahead for the United Kingdom, explaining that there was "no precedent for this — even the process for conducting these negotiations is unclear at this stage." He pointed out that it would not be possible — as some had suggested — to simply cut and paste the commitments found in the European Union's terms of trade, noting that "no WTO member can unilaterally decide what its rights and obligations are." Azevêdo cautioned that "it could take quite some time before the UK got back to a similar position...in terms of its trading relationships with other countries," and observed that with respect to the United Kingdom's future trading relationships, "the only certainty is uncertainty."[2]

One year later, Azevêdo could probably recycle much of the language from that June 2016 speech were he to speak on the same subject today, for little has changed regarding the uncertainty surrounding the future of the United Kingdom's trading relationships.

Legal and Political Developments since June 2016

Legal Challenge to Initiating Brexit Process

There have, however, been a number of developments during the past year and a half that inform some of the issues that arose in light of the Brexit vote. We know now, for example, that by virtue of the United Kingdom's constitutional arrangements, the UK government was not entitled to rely on its prerogative powers to authorize it to trigger article 50 of the Treaty on European Union (TEU), which initiates the procedure for an EU member state to withdraw from the European Union. Rather, the Supreme Court of the United Kingdom determined that an Act of Parliament is required to authorize UK ministers to do so.[3] In making this decision, the court was asked by both sides in the case to assume that the exercise of the power to serve notice of withdrawal "cannot be given in qualified or conditional terms and that, once given, it cannot be withdrawn."[4] The court did not pronounce on the point of irrevocability, but proceeded on the basis that the assumption was correct and concluded that it "follows from this that once the United Kingdom gives Notice, it will inevitably cease at a later date to be a member of the European Union and a party to the EU Treaties."[5]

---

2   Roberto Azevêdo, "Trade and Globalisation in the 21st Century: The Path to Greater Inclusion" (Speech delivered at the World Trade Symposium, 7 June 2016), online: <www.wto.org/english/news_e/spra_e/spra126_e.htm>. The event was organized by the *Financial Times* and Misys.

3   *R (on the application of Miller and another) (Respondents) v Secretary of State for Exiting the European Union (Appellant); Reference by the Attorney General for Northern Ireland: In the matter of an application by Agnew and others for Judicial Review; Reference by the Court of Appeal (Northern Ireland): In the matter of an application by Raymond McCord for Judicial Review* [2017] UKSC 5, online: <www.supremecourt.uk/cases/docs/uksc-2016-0196-judgment.pdf>.

4   *Ibid* at para 26.

5   *Ibid.*

The requisite Act of Parliament was passed on March 16, 2017,[6] and notice under article 50 was served on March 29, 2017.[7] Thus, although there might be faint calls from time to time for an "exit from Brexit," there should be little doubt now that the United Kingdom will leave the European Union before April 2019.

British Election

What is less certain, however, is what the exit strategy will be. Until recently, it seemed fairly clear that the United Kingdom would pursue a "hard Brexit," such that remaining in the Customs Union or participating in the EU Single Market after Brexit were out of the question. Suggestions that the United Kingdom might follow the Norway[8] or Switzerland[9] models had also been rejected.[10] Prime Minister Theresa May committed to pursue a comprehensive free trade agreement (FTA) covering goods and services and a new customs arrangement governing trade in goods with the European Union, and she rejected the notion that the United Kingdom would be bound by the European Union's common external tariff.[11]

May had also served notice that the United Kingdom was prepared to walk away from the negotiating table if the trade deal was not "the best deal for Britain," asserting that "no deal is better than a bad deal for the UK."[12] At the same time, she had observed that "immediate stability" would be "ensure[d]" by "lodging new UK schedules with the World Trade Organization, in alignment with EU schedules to which we are bound whilst still a member of the European Union."[13] May also promised to achieve "continuity" in the United Kingdom's trading relationships with third countries covered by existing EU FTAs or preferential arrangements.[14] More specifically, the British prime minister undertook to "seek to replicate all existing EU free trade agreements."[15]

---

6   The bill was passed by Parliament on March 13, 2017, and received royal assent and became an Act of Parliament on March 16, 2017.

7   Letter from Prime Minister Theresa May to Donald Tusk, president of the European Council (29 March 2017), online: <www.gov.uk/government/publications/prime-ministers-letter-to-donald-tusk-triggering-article-50>.

8   Under the Norway model, the United Kingdom would have access to the EU Single Market. In exchange, the United Kingdom would contribute to the EU budget, accept the EU core principle of free movement of people, and follow certain EU laws in areas such as employment, the environment and consumer protection. The United Kingdom would be bound by EU legislation in those areas, but would not have any say in their development.

9   Under the Switzerland model, there is no general right of access to the EU Single Market; instead, market access is governed by bilateral agreements covering specific sectors. Switzerland has negotiated more than 100 bilateral agreements, mostly covering access to goods and very limited access in services. For example, the banking sector is not covered. Switzerland's contribution to the EU budget is less than that of Norway, but it must observe the freedom of movement of people and must comply with some EU laws. Like Norway, Switzerland has no say in the development of those laws.

10   UK, Department for Exiting the European Union, *The United Kingdom's exit from, and new partnership with, the European Union* (Policy Paper delivered at Parliament, 2 February 2017) at 35, online: <www.gov.uk/government/publications/the-united-kingdoms-exit-from-and-new-partnership-with-the-european-union-white-paper/the-united-kingdoms-exit-from-and-new-partnership-with-the-european-union--2>.

11   *Ibid* at 46. Although all EU member states are in the EU Customs Union, some countries outside of the European Union have customs arrangements with the European Union whereby they follow the common external tariff. For example, Turkey is not part of the European Union, but has formed a customs union with it pursuant to which it must apply the same external tariff as does the European Union.

12   Conservative Party, *Forward, Together: Our Plan for a Stronger Britain and a Prosperous Future, The Conservative and Unionist Party Manifesto 2017* at 36, online: <www.conservatives.com/manifesto> [*Conservative Party Manifesto*].

13   *Ibid* at 15.

14   *Ibid* at 51, 54–55. The United States is the United Kingdom's single biggest export market on a country-by-country basis: *ibid* at 51.

15   *Ibid* at 15.

Following the UK general election on June 8, 2017, however, when the Conservatives lost their overall majority, the prime minister's pursuit of a hard Brexit appeared to lose steam. At the same time, some UK Cabinet ministers are openly advocating to remain in the Single Market and Customs Union for a transition period of two to three years following the United Kingdom's exit from the European Union, followed by an implementation phase to allow a new UK-specific trade accord to be put in place.[16] Under the circumstances, there is still considerable uncertainty about the type and breadth of trading relationships the United Kingdom will have with the European Union (and hence with other countries) once it has left the European Union.

Of course, the United Kingdom is not the only player in the Brexit negotiations, and decisions about the United Kingdom's exit from the European Union will not be taken by the United Kingdom alone. The European Union will have to agree to any transition agreement, as well as to the terms of any future trade deal with the United Kingdom.

EU Negotiating Guidelines

Following the triggering of article 50 by the United Kingdom on March 29, 2017, the European Council adopted guidelines "defin[ing] the framework for negotiations under Article 50 TEU and set[ting] out the overall positions and principles that the Union will pursue throughout the negotiation."[17] The European Council stated that it "stands ready to initiate work towards an agreement on trade, to be finalised and concluded once the United Kingdom is no longer a Member State," and that "any free trade agreement should be balanced, ambitious and wide-ranging," but "cannot, however, amount to participation in the Single Market or parts thereof, as this would undermine its integrity and proper functioning."[18] In terms of coverage, the council indicated that it "must ensure a level playing field, notably in terms of competition and state aid, and in this regard encompass safeguards against unfair competitive advantages through, *inter alia*, tax, social, environmental and regulatory measures and practices."[19]

Importantly, the guidelines also provide that the negotiations will be conducted by a single block — the European Union — and that there will be no individual negotiations with member states. Specifically, the guidelines provide that "the Union will approach the negotiations with unified positions, and will engage with the United Kingdom exclusively through the channels set out in these guidelines and in the negotiating directives. So as not to undercut the position of the Union, there will be no separate negotiations between individual Member States and the United Kingdom on matters pertaining to the withdrawal of the United Kingdom from the Union."[20]

16 See e.g. Sarah Gordon & George Parker, "Philip Hammond seeks 'off-the-shelf' Brexit transition", *Financial Times* (27 July 2017), online: <www.ft.com/content/cc1dbf04-71fc-11e7-aca6-c6bd07df1a3c>; George Parker & Alex Barker, "'Status quo' Brexit transition plan reflects cabinet power grab", *Financial Times* (27 July 2017), online: <www.ft.com/content/df460e26-72b3-11e7-93ff-99f383b09ff9>. However, at the time of writing, there does not appear to be a consensus on this: Helen Warrell, "Liam Fox says free movement post-Brexit defies referendum result", *Financial Times* (31 July 2017), online: <www.ft.com/content/79132f52-7507-11e7-a3e8-60495fe6ca71>.

17 European Council, Press Release, "European Council (Art. 50) guidelines following the United Kingdom's notification under Article 50 TEU" (29 April 2017) at para 5, online: <www.consilium.europa.eu/en/press/press-releases/2017/04/29-euco-brexit-guidelines>.

18 *Ibid* at paras 19–20.

19 *Ibid* at para 20.

20 *Ibid* at para 2.

This statement refers to the entire set of negotiations necessary to secure the UK-EU "divorce," including with respect to security, crime prevention, immigration and the rights of EU nationals living in the United Kingdom. But it also covers trade, and as such brings to mind the difficulties that arose when Canada and the European Union sought to sign the Comprehensive Economic and Trade Agreement (CETA) in 2016, following seven years of negotiations. Although not required under EU law,[21] the European Union had undertaken to sign CETA only once all 28 EU member governments agreed to the treaty text. When the Parliament of the Federation of Wallonia, a region of Belgium, opposed the deal and prevented Belgium from giving its consent to signature, this almost scuttled the agreement. Eventually, Wallonia's agreement was secured and the treaty was signed in October 2016.[22]

It is not clear at this point whether the European Union will commit to the remaining 27 member states that they will have veto rights over signature of an eventual trade agreement with the United Kingdom. Even if it does not do so, however, it is possible that one or more of the EU member states will seek to have a say in the contents of the deal. Should this occur, it could have significant implications for the UK-EU trade agreement negotiations. It is reasonable to expect that any UK-EU FTA will cover a wide array of subject areas, including the import and export of goods, customs, anti-dumping, countervailing and safeguard measures, technical regulations, sanitary and phytosanitary (SPS) measures, investment, services including financial services, intellectual property, government procurement, competition, as well as institutional matters such as dispute settlement. The question arises as to whether all these subject areas fall within the exclusive competence of the European Union under the common commercial policy, whether any of them fall within the exclusive competence of the national governments of the member states, or whether any fall under shared EU/EU-member-state competence. A recent opinion of the European Court of Justice (ECJ) sheds much light on this complex legal issue.

Opinion of the ECJ on EU Competence in Concluding Wide-ranging FTAs

On July 10, 2015, the European Commission asked the ECJ to opine on whether the provisions of the FTA negotiated and initialed with the Republic of Singapore fall within the exclusive competence of the European Union, a competence shared between the European Union and the member states, or a competence of the member states alone.[23] In December 2016, Advocate

---

21 As explained by CIGI Senior Fellows Armand de Mestral and Markus Gehring in an article published in *The Globe and Mail* on October 21, 2016, "requiring unanimity for CETA's signature appears to be an entirely new practice, unheard of until very recently. Under the governing Treaty on the Functioning of the European Union (TFEU), Article 218.8 states that: 'The Council shall act by a qualified majority throughout the procedure.' The qualified majority is met when 55 per cent of states representing 65 per cent of their population vote in favour of a measure. Qualified majority voting has been gradually introduced into EU law to stop one country from blocking decisions....Mixed agreements [like CETA, which falls mostly within the European Union's competence but includes a few provisions falling within the competence of national governments] pose special problems in that, at least in the ratification stage, all countries need to agree. But so far unanimity has not been required for signing the treaty."

22 Both governments proceeded thereafter to enact implementing legislation. The European Parliament ratified CETA on February 15, 2017. Canadian implementing legislation received royal assent on May 16, 2017.

23 Request for an opinion pursuant to article 218(11) of the TFEU, made on July 10, 2015, by the European Commission. The EU-Singapore Agreement includes 17 chapters, as well as a protocol on rules of origin and understandings on taxation and other matters. The FTA covers trade in goods, trade and investment in renewable energy generation, trade in services, government procurement, investment including foreign direct investment, commercial and non-commercial aspects of intellectual property rights, competition, and labour and environmental standards.

General Eleanor Sharpston issued an opinion to the court,[24] advising it to decide that the FTA could be concluded only by the European Union and the member states acting jointly.[25]

Sharpston recognized the far-reaching implications a decision by the court along the lines of her advice would have on future trade negotiations to be conducted by the European Union. She understood that "a ratification process involving all the Member States alongside the European Union is of necessity likely to be both cumbersome and complex," and acknowledged that it could "involve the risk that the outcome of lengthy negotiations may be blocked by a few Member States or even by a single Member State." She conceded that this "might undermine the efficiency of EU external action and have negative consequences for the European Union's relations with the third State(s) concerned." Nevertheless, she reasoned that "the need for unity and rapidity of EU external action and the difficulties which might arise if the European Union and the Member States have to participate jointly in the conclusion and implementation of an international agreement cannot affect the question who has competence to conclude it. That question is to be resolved exclusively on the basis of the Treaties."[26]

Although opinions provided to the ECJ by the advocates general are non-binding, they are generally very influential, and the court usually follows them. In this case, however, the court did not do so. The court determined that the competence of the European Union is broader than that allowed by Sharpston, and found that the shared competence with the member states is much narrower than what the advocate general concluded.[27] The court concluded that all the provisions of the EU-Singapore FTA fall within the exclusive competence of the European Union, with the exception of provisions dealing with non-direct investment and investor-state dispute settlement (ISDS). Provisions addressing the latter two subjects, the court said, fall within the shared competence of the European Union and the member states.[28]

The court explained that under article 3(1)(e) of the TFEU, the European Union has exclusive competence in the area of common commercial policy. Article 207(1) of the TFEU indicates that the common commercial policy "shall be based on uniform principles, particularly with regard to changes in tariff rates, the conclusion of tariff and trade agreements relating to trade in goods and services, and the commercial aspects of intellectual property, foreign direct investment, the achievement of uniformity in measures of liberalisation, export policy and measures to protect trade such as those to be taken in the event of dumping or subsidies." The court reasoned that "it follows that only the components of the envisaged agreement that display a specific link, in

---

24 The European Court of Justice is assisted by advocates general who deliver independent opinions on cases before the court.

25 Advocate General Eleanor Sharpston, opinion delivered at the European Court of Justice (21 December 2016), Opinion Procedure 2/15, ECLI:EU:C:2016:992 at paras 558–562, online: <www.eur-lex.europa.eu>.

26 Ibid at paras 565–566.

27 Sharpston concluded that the European Union enjoys exclusive external competence with regard to provisions of the FTA dealing with trade in goods, trade and investment in renewable energy generation, trade in services and government procurement, except in relation to transport services, foreign direct investment, the commercial aspects of intellectual property rights (but not the non-commercial aspects of those rights), competition, and trade in rail and road transport services. She considered that the European Union's competence is shared with the member states in several areas, including with respect to trade in air transport services, maritime transport services, and transport by inland waterway, types of investment other than foreign direct investment, government procurement insofar as it applies to transport services, non-commercial aspects of intellectual property rights, and labour and environmental standards.

28 Advocate General Eleanor Sharpston, Opinion 2/15 of the Court (Full Court), opinion pursuant to article 218(11) TFEU, "Free Trade Agreement between the European Union and the Republic of Singapore" (16 May 2017), ECLI:EU:C:2017:376 at para 305, online: <www.eur-lex.europa.eu>.

the above sense, with trade between the European Union and the Republic of Singapore fall within the field of the common commercial policy."

Importantly, the court cautioned against taking too broad a view of what falls within the common commercial policy, noting that it is "settled case-law that the mere fact that an EU act, such as an agreement concluded by it, is liable to have implications for trade with one or more third States is not enough for it to be concluded that the act must be classified as falling within the common commercial policy." The court continued, observing that, "on the other hand, an EU act falls within that policy if it relates specifically to such trade in that it is essentially intended to promote, facilitate or govern such trade and has direct and immediate effects on it."[29] Thus the court established the following test for determining whether a provision falls within the sole competence of the European Union: "it must be established whether the commitments contained in that agreement are intended to promote, facilitate or govern such trade and have direct and immediate effects on it."[30]

This decision has significant implications for the future UK-EU trade negotiations, for there is now greater clarity about where the competencies lie with respect to subject areas and commitments one might expect to be included in an eventual UK-EU FTA. It suggests that the European Union will not be legally required to obtain agreement from the remaining 27 member states before committing to provisions governing trade in goods and services, trade remedies, SPS, competition and other areas, and would need approval only with respect to provisions dealing with ISDS and indirect foreign investment. Although the European Union may decide to offer a veto to all member states on the contents of the entire agreement, it does not appear to be obliged to do so under EU law. Thus the CETA experience of facing an unexpected eleventh-hour member state veto when it comes to signing an eventual EU-UK FTA is much less likely.

This assumes, of course, that the two sides will conclude an FTA prior to April 2019, or that a transitional arrangement governing trade is agreed upon by the time the United Kingdom exits the European Union. If there is no deal by that time, however, the UK-EU trading relationship will nevertheless be governed by WTO rules. Both the European Union and the United Kingdom are WTO members in their own right. WTO rules will also govern the trading relationship between the United Kingdom and non-EU countries that are WTO members, unless and until treaties are implemented between them stipulating otherwise. Any rights the United Kingdom has enjoyed under preferential trading arrangements that the European Union has with other countries will be lost upon the United Kingdom's exit from the European Union, and the United Kingdom will be obliged to negotiate its own such arrangements.

29 *Ibid* at para 36.
30 *Ibid* at paras 33–34, 37.

Default to WTO Rules

If the UK-EU trading relationship and the UK-non-EU member state trading relationship were to default to WTO rules, what would those relationships look like?

WTO obligations comprise general rules that apply to all members, and specific commitments made by individual members. The specific commitments are set out in documents called "schedules of concessions" or "schedules of commitments." Goods schedules reflect specific tariff concessions and other commitments, and usually consist of maximum tariff levels (referred to as "bound tariffs" or "bindings"). In the case of agricultural products, these concessions and commitments also relate to tariff rate quotas (TRQs[31]), limits on export subsidies and some types of domestic support. Services schedules reflect market-access commitments and exemptions on a number of services sectors.

The United Kingdom was a contracting party to the General Agreement on Tariffs and Trade (GATT) 1947 and as such was entitled to become an original member of the WTO upon meeting two conditions set out in article XI:1 of the Marrakesh Agreement Establishing the World Trade Organization.[32] The first condition was acceptance of the Marrakesh Agreement and the Multilateral Trade Agreements; this was met by the United Kingdom on December 30, 1994, and these agreements came into force for the United Kingdom on January 1, 1995.[33] The second condition was to have schedules of concessions and commitments for goods and services annexed to the GATT 1994 and the General Agreement on Trade in Services (GATS), respectively. The United Kingdom did not annex UK-specific schedules, but it nevertheless met the second condition by virtue of its coverage under the schedules annexed by the European Union, which apply to all EU member states.

Views differ as to what the legal situation of the UK schedules will be once the United Kingdom leaves the European Union. Some argue that the United Kingdom's rights and obligations set out in the schedules are contingent upon its status as a member state of the European Union, with the result that it would need to develop new WTO goods and services schedules of its own, while others suggest that Brexit will not change the United Kingdom's rights and obligations set forth in the existing EU schedules, but only which WTO member exercises them. In other words, according to the latter view, the United Kingdom does not need new schedules because its schedules already exist in the form of EU schedules, although some elements currently applicable to the European Union as a whole (such as the right to subsidize agricultural

---

31 A TRQ refers to the application of a reduced tariff rate for a specified quantity of imported goods. Imports above the specified quantity are subject to a higher tariff rate.

32 Article XI:1 of the *Marrakesh Agreement Establishing the World Trade Organization*, 15 April 1994, (entered into force 1 January 1995) states: "The contracting parties to GATT 1947 as of the date of entry into force of this Agreement, and the European Communities, which accept this Agreement and the Multilateral Trade Agreements and for which Schedules of Concessions and Commitments are annexed to GATT 1994 and for which Schedules of Specific Commitments are annexed to GATS shall become original Members of the WTO." See online: <https://www.wto.org/english/docs_e/legal_e/04-wto_e.htm>.

33 *Status of WTO Legal Instruments – 2015 edition*, at 11, 41, online: <www.wto.org/english/res_e/booksp_e/wto_status_legal_inst15_e.pdf>.

production at certain levels and the TRQ commitments) would have to be adjusted to reflect rights and obligations applicable only to the United Kingdom.[34]

The United Kingdom appears at this time to subscribe to the former view. The *Conservative Party Manifesto* of May 18, 2017, stipulates that the United Kingdom will lodge schedules with the WTO that will be "in alignment"[35] with the EU schedules. It can be assumed, therefore, that the United Kingdom will seek to replicate many of the tariff bindings found in the EU goods schedule. More difficult to "align" will be scheduled commitments related to TRQs, for they have been undertaken by the European Union with respect to imports into the European Union as a whole. The United Kingdom may not wish to commit to the same size quota applied by the European Union with respect to the entire union. Another challenge will be in the "alignment" of agricultural support commitments; determining the United Kingdom's share of the European Union's scheduled support commitments could be complicated.[36] Moreover, it cannot be assumed that the United Kingdom would wish to "cut and paste" the complete set of EU services commitments, which were negotiated by the European Union with the services industries of its entire membership in mind. The United Kingdom's services industries are naturally of a different order than those of the EU membership. What is clear, however, is that if the United Kingdom wishes to lodge new goods and services schedules as the Conservative Party has suggested it will do, or if it seeks instead to exercise its rights under the EU schedules, but subject to adjustments such as with respect to TRQs, agricultural support and certain services commitments, in either case all WTO members (including the European Union) must agree to the schedules submitted by the United Kingdom to the WTO. This is because "no WTO Member can unilaterally decide what its WTO rights and obligations are."[37]

Beyond the issues respecting its own schedules, there is also the question of the United Kingdom's right to access commitments found in other WTO members' scheduled concessions, which are currently accessed by the United Kingdom via the European Union. It can be anticipated that at least some WTO members (including perhaps the European Union) will assert that the United Kingdom's access is contingent upon the United Kingdom being a member of the European Union, which could trigger negotiations to determine new access rights specific to the United Kingdom.

Finally, the United Kingdom may wish to consider whether it needs to address its status with respect to certain other WTO instruments that were accepted on its behalf by the European Union.[38] For example, the Protocol Amending the Marrakesh Agreement Establishing the

---

34   See e.g. Lorand Bartels, "The UK's Status in the WTO after Brexit" (2016), online: SSRN <https://ssrn.com/abstract=2841747>; and Peter Ungphakorn, "Nothing simple about UK regaining WTO status post-Brexit" (27 June 2016), online: International Centre for Trade and Sustainable Development <www.ictsd.org/opinion/nothing-simple-about-uk-regaining-wto-status-post-brexit>.

35   *Conservative Party Manifesto, supra* note 12 at 15.

36   *Ibid* at 26. In the *Conservative Party Manifesto* of May 18, 2017, a promise is made to "commit the same cash total in funds for farm support until the end of parliament."

37   Azevêdo, *supra* note 2. See also *European Communities–Customs Classification of Certain Computer Equipment* (1998), WTO Docs WT/DS62/AB/R, WT/DS67/AB/R, WT/DS68/AB/R at para 84 (Appellate Body Report), online: <https://docs.wto.org>, where the Appellate Body explained that "Tariff concessions provided for in a Member's Schedule…are reciprocal and result from a mutually advantageous negotiation between importing and exporting Members."

38   Article X:7 of the *Marrakesh Agreement Establishing the WTO* stipulates that "Any Member accepting an amendment to this Agreement or to a Multilateral Trade Agreement in Annex 1 shall deposit an instrument of acceptance with the Director-General."

World Trade Organization, which inserted the Trade Facilitation Agreement into Annex 1A of the WTO Agreement, was accepted by the European Union, which notified the WTO of its acceptance "so that it shall be binding upon the European Union."[39]

Modifications of Schedules in the WTO

Beyond the questions surrounding *what* rights and obligations the United Kingdom will have post-Brexit under its UK-specific schedules is the question of *how* to go about reaching agreement with WTO members on the content of those schedules. While accession for new members is governed by article XII of the Marrakesh Agreement, and terms of accession are hammered out through bilateral and plurilateral negotiations and eventually agreed upon by the WTO Ministerial Conference, the United Kingdom's situation — as an existing member of the WTO but without goods and services schedules in its own name — is different. There is no prescribed procedure to follow.

Article XXVIII of the GATT 1994 provides for *modification* of goods schedules, while article XXI of the GATS provides for *modification* of services schedules. Given the unique situation presented by Brexit, it is not clear whether these provisions govern the negotiation and/or agreement by the United Kingdom and WTO members of UK-specific WTO schedules, for these provisions address the modification of *existing* schedules, but not the approval of new ones. As noted above, there are differing views as to whether the United Kingdom needs to develop new schedules, or if the EU schedules constitute the UK schedules subject to some adjustments.[40] In any event, if article XXVIII of the GATT 1994 and article XXI of the GATS do apply, or if members decide to follow them because there is no other practical means of approving the UK-specific schedules to be lodged by the United Kingdom, the process of reaching agreement with WTO members on the content of the UK schedules could be lengthy and complex.

Modification of Goods Schedules under Article XXVIII of the GATT 1994

According to article XXVIII of the GATT 1994, modification of goods schedules may be effected from time to time through negotiation and agreement with certain WTO members, namely those with whom the relevant concessions were "initially negotiated" (referred to as members with initial negotiating rights or INR) and any member that is determined to have a "principal supplying interest" (referred to as "principal suppliers") in the concession(s). In addition, consultations must be held (although no agreement is necessary) with members that are determined to have a "substantial interest" in the concession(s).[41]

---

39   *Protocol Amending the Marrakesh Agreement Establishing the World Trade Organization* (2015), WTO Doc WT/LET/1090, online: WTO <https://docs.wto.org>.

40   Bartels, *supra* note 34; Ungphakorn, *supra* note 34.

41   Additional details on some of the technical aspects of article XXVIII negotiations (such as the determination of which member has a principal supplying interest, time limits for steps in the process and data requirements) are found in the ad note to article XXVIII, the Understanding on the Interpretation of Article XXVIII of the General Agreement on Tariffs and Trade 1994 (which forms an integral part of the GATT 1994), and the Procedures for Negotiations under Article XXVIII, found in the *Analytical Index: Guide to GATT Law and Practice* (WTO, 1995) at 960–961.

The article XXVIII negotiations may include provision for compensatory adjustment.[42] In such negotiations, the members concerned "shall endeavour to maintain a general level of reciprocal and mutually advantageous concessions not less favourable to trade than that provided for [under the GATT] prior to such negotiations."[43] If agreement cannot be reached by a specified time, the modifying member can proceed with the modification, but member(s) determined to have INR, member(s) determined to be principal suppliers and member(s) determined to have a substantial interest will be entitled to withdraw "substantially equivalent concessions initially negotiated with the [modifying member]."[44] It is also possible to refer any disagreement about proposed modifications to the WTO membership for their examination, with a view to finding a resolution.[45]

If article XXVIII applies or is followed with regard to securing UK-specific goods schedules, the task of identifying which members hold INR, which are principal suppliers, and which have a substantial interest in the concessions is likely to be far from straightforward, given the unique circumstances presented by Brexit. Nor will it be easy to determine, in the context of negotiations on compensation, the "level of reciprocal and mutually advantageous concessions not less favourable to trade than that provided for...prior to such negotiations." Also challenging will be determining what constitutes "substantially equivalent concessions initially negotiated with the [modifying member]" that some members will be entitled to withdraw in the event of a failure to reach agreement. Those who maintain that the United Kingdom currently has an existing goods schedule in the form of the schedule exercised by the European Union might argue that these questions should be resolved in the same way they would be if the European Union were seeking to modify its goods schedule, but it is possible that this view will not be universally held across the WTO membership.

Changes in goods schedules "which reflect modifications resulting from action under...Article XVIII" of the GATT 1994 must be certified by the director-general of the WTO pursuant to the Procedures for Modification and Rectification of Schedules of Tariff Concessions, which were adopted by the WTO GATT Council in March 1980 (referred to as the "1980 Procedures").[46] Under these procedures, the director-general circulates a draft of the changes to all WTO members and, if no objection is raised by a WTO member within three months on the ground that the director-general's draft *does not correctly reflect the negotiated modifications*, the draft becomes a certification and the changes to the schedule are thereby certified.[47] If an objection is filed, the relevant WTO members enter into negotiations to resolve the problem. In such circumstances, certification will not proceed unless and until the objection is withdrawn. It is possible, therefore, for a single WTO member to block certification of a modification carried out pursuant to article XXVIII of the GATT 1994.

---

42 *General Agreement on Tariffs and Trade*, 14 April 1994, arts XXVIII:2, XXVIII:4(a) (entered into force 1 January 1995) [*GATT 1994*].

43 *Ibid*, art XXVIII:2.

44 *Ibid*, art XXVIII:3.

45 *Ibid*, art XXVIII:4(d).

46 *GATT*, 28 March 1980, L/4962 at para 1, online: <www.wto.org/gatt_docs/English/SULPDF/90970413.pdf>.

47 1980 Procedures at paras 1 and 3.

The legal implications of certification following article XXVIII negotiations are discussed in the next section of this chapter in light of a recent WTO panel report where this issue was addressed.

Amendments and Rectifications of a Purely Formal Character

The complex negotiations under article XXVIII of the GATT 1994 would not be necessary if WTO members considered that the changeover from coverage via the EU goods schedule to applying a UK-specific goods schedule did not alter the "scope" of concessions, or that the schedule changes amounted to rectifications of a "purely formal character." If that were the case, a simpler and (usually) faster procedure may be followed to give effect to a UK-specific goods schedule. The 1980 Procedures provide in paragraph 2 that: "changes in the authentic texts of Schedules shall be made *when amendments or rearrangements which do not alter the scope of a concession* are introduced in national customs tariffs in respect of bound items. Such changes and other rectifications *of a purely formal character* shall be made by means of Certifications."[48]

Similar to modifications made as a result of article XXVIII negotiations, a draft containing the changes to the schedule is communicated by the director-general to all members. The draft becomes a certification and the changes to the schedule are thereby certified, provided that no objection is raised by a member within three months on the ground that the proposed rectification is "not within the terms" of paragraph 2.[49]

If the United Kingdom lodges its goods schedule with a request that the director-general certify it pursuant to the procedures set forth immediately above, members will have to consider whether the UK-specific goods schedule reflects "amendments or rearrangements which do not alter the scope of a concession" or "other rectifications of a purely formal character." If any member considers that the goods schedule submitted by the United Kingdom does not meet one or more of these criteria (that is, if the member considers that the proposed rectification is not within the terms of paragraph 2 set forth above), it may file an objection to the change within three months of circulation by the WTO director-general of the draft certification. Negotiations would ensue between the United Kingdom and any objecting member(s) with a view to having the objection(s) withdrawn. Certification will not proceed unless and until any objections are withdrawn.[50] As with the certification process following action under article XXVIII, a single member can block the certification of an amendment or rectification addressed in paragraph 2 of the 1980 Procedures.

If, however, no member raises an objection within the three-month period, certification of the modification will be automatic. In other words, even if WTO members consider that the above criteria in the 1980 Procedures have not been met, they may choose not to object so that the UK-specific schedule can be certified by the director-general regardless of conformity with paragraph 2 of the 1980 Procedures.

---

48 *Ibid* at para 2 [emphasis added].

49 *Ibid* at para 3.

50 Only a small number (13, or three percent) of matters pursued under the 1980 Procedures have not been concluded for various reasons, some of which have been due to objections filed by members. See *Current Situation of Schedules of WTO Members* [*Current Situation*], online: <www.wto.org//english/tratop_e/schedules_e/goods_schedules_table_e.htm#>.

Modification of Services Schedules under Article XXI of the GATS

Regarding modification of services schedules, article XXI of the GATS provides that a member may modify or withdraw commitments in its services schedule upon notice to the Council for Trade in Services and subject to entering into negotiations with any "affected" member (defined as any member whose benefits under the GATS may be affected by the modification or withdrawal) "with a view to reaching agreement on any necessary compensatory adjustment."[51] Members concerned "shall endeavor" in such negotiations to "maintain a general level of mutually advantageous commitments not less favourable to trade than that provided for in Schedules of specific commitments prior to such negotiations."[52] If agreement on compensatory adjustment is not reached within a certain period of time, the "affected Member" can go to arbitration to determine the compensatory adjustment, and the modifying member cannot modify or withdraw the commitment until it has made compensatory adjustment in conformity with the arbitration findings.[53] If the modifying member proceeds with the modification or withdrawal and does not comply with the arbitration findings, any affected member "may modify or withdraw substantially equivalent benefits in conformity with those findings" with respect to the modifying member.[54]

Procedures governing modification of services schedules under article XXI were adopted by the Council for Trade in Services in 1999.[55] They are somewhat different from the procedures stipulated in the 1980 Procedures followed when modifying goods schedules under article XXVIII. For services schedule modifications, any member "which considers that its interests under the Agreement may be affected by the proposed modification" (the "affected Member") has 45 days following notification of the proposed modification to make a claim.[56] Thus, whether a WTO member is "affected" by the proposed modification in the services schedule is self-determined.

The member proposing to make the modification and the affected member must enter into negotiations, which may lead to the modifying member agreeing to pay compensation. If no agreement is reached in these negotiations by a certain time, the affected member has 45 days to request arbitration. In such case, the arbitration body examines the compensatory adjustments offered or requested and seeks to "find a resulting balance of rights and obligations which maintains a general level of mutually advantageous commitments not less favourable to trade than that provided for in Schedules of specific commitments prior to the negotiations." The schedule modification can proceed following the arbitration only if it is in accordance with the arbitration findings.[57]

---

51 *GATS*, arts XXI:1, XXI:2(a).

52 *Ibid*, art XXI:2(a).

53 *Ibid*, arts XXI:3(a), XXI:4(a).

54 *Ibid*, art XXI:4(b).

55 Procedures for the Implementation of Article XXI of the General Agreement on Trade in Services (GATS) (Modification of Schedules), adopted by the Council for Trade in Services on 19 July 1999, WTO Doc S/L/80, 29 October 1999, online: <www.wto.org/english/tratop_e/serv_e/sl80.doc> [Procedures for the Implementation of Article XXI].

56 *Ibid* at para 3.

57 *Ibid* at paras 4, 7, 9, 13, 15.

If, however, no member submits a claim that its interests may be affected by the proposed modification within the 45-day period, or if the "affected Member" does not request arbitration in a timely fashion following negotiations (i.e., within 45 days of completion of the negotiations), the modifying member can proceed with the proposed modification.[58]

If it is determined that article XXI of the GATS does apply to the circumstances of the United Kingdom post-Brexit, or if WTO members decide to follow article XXI because there is no other practical means of agreeing on a UK-specific services schedule, it may be difficult, given the unique set of circumstances brought about by Brexit, to determine in any negotiations with the United Kingdom the "general level of mutually advantageous commitments not less favourable to trade than that provided for in Schedules of specific commitments prior to such negotiations."

Modification of GATS schedules that result from action under article XXI take effect by means of certification. A draft schedule indicating the changes is communicated by the WTO secretariat to all members, who then have 45 days to raise an objection on the ground that "the draft schedule does not correctly reflect the results of the action under Article XXI."[59] If no objection is raised, the WTO secretariat issues a communication stating that the certification procedure has been completed and indicating the date of entry into force for the modification. If a timely objection is filed, the modifying member and the member who filed an objection must enter into consultations with a view to reaching a satisfactory solution. The certification procedure will be deemed concluded only upon withdrawal of the objection.[60] Similarly to the goods situation, certification of a modification to a services schedule can be blocked by a single WTO member.

As with goods schedules, it will be up to WTO members to determine whether they wish to actively exercise their rights under article XXI of the GATS and the procedures governing the modification of services schedules, or whether they would prefer to allow a UK-specific schedule lodged by the United Kingdom to be certified without objection. If they decide on the latter, the changeover from applying the EU services schedule to applying the eventual UK-specific services schedule could proceed relatively quickly.

Recent WTO Case Law Regarding Modification of Goods Schedules

Although there have been many negotiations regarding modifications of schedules conducted pursuant to article XXVIII of the GATT 1994,[61] much of the information about them remains classified information between the negotiating parties. Moreover, there is relatively little case law providing guidance on how to interpret the various elements of the provision. As such, there is little public information available to guide the United Kingdom in navigating its way through such negotiations, if that route is indeed followed. However, a recent panel report titled *European Union*

---

58   *Ibid* at paras 3, 8.
59   *Ibid* at para 20.
60   *Ibid* at paras 20–22.
61   *Current Situation, supra* note 50. There have been 41 requests to enter into renegotiations under GATT article XXVIII since the establishment of the WTO in 1995.

–Measures Affecting Tariff Concessions on Certain Poultry Meat Products,[62] adopted by the WTO Dispute Settlement Body on April 19, 2017, and not appealed, contains some useful insight on the article XXVIII process.

The dispute was brought by China, which challenged the European Union's modification of its tariff concessions on certain poultry products. China argued that the European Union failed to negotiate or consult with all WTO members that had a principal supplying interest or a substantial interest in those products, contrary to article XXVIII:1 of the GATT 1994. China further alleged that the tariff rates and TRQs agreed and implemented as a result of the European Union's modification negotiations with Brazil and Thailand failed to maintain a general level of reciprocal and mutually advantageous concessions not less favourable to trade than that provided for under the GATT 1994 prior to such negotiations, contrary to article XXVIII:2 of the GATT 1994.[63] China argued further that the European Union violated article II:1 of the GATT 1994 by adopting tariff rates that exceeded the bound tariff rates listed in the EU goods schedule as, China reasoned, the tariff rates and TRQs negotiated and implemented by the European Union under article XXVIII were "ineffectual" to replace the bound tariff rates listed in the EU goods schedule preceding the modification negotiations.[64] Finally, China maintained that the European Union acted inconsistently with the procedures for negotiations under article XXVIII and the 1980 Procedures because there was no notification for certification, no notification of the date on which the changes to the goods schedule came into force, and no notification of the draft modification of its schedule.[65]

The panel determined that the European Union had not acted inconsistently with articles XXVIII:1, XXVIII:2 or II:1 of the GATT 1994.[66] The decision is not binding, except with respect to the European Union and China, and the facts are not necessarily like those that may present themselves in the context of the United Kingdom's possible negotiation and establishment of its goods schedule. Nevertheless, certain findings of the panel may inform those future negotiations, should they take place.

Status of Procedures for Negotiations under Article XXVIII of the GATT 1994 and the 1980 Procedures

One such finding relates to the status of the Procedures for Negotiations under article XXVIII of the GATT 1994 and the 1980 Procedures. The panel agreed with the parties and third parties[67] to the dispute that these instruments, both of which were adopted in 1980 in the context of the GATT and prior to the establishment of the WTO in 1995, qualify as "decisions," "procedures" or "customary practices" within the meaning of article XVI:1 of the Marrakesh Agreement. It provides that "the WTO shall be guided by the decisions, procedures and customary practices followed by the CONTRACTING PARTIES to the GATT 1947." The panel therefore considered that it was "under a duty to take account of these procedures in [their] interpretation

---

62 *European Union–Measures Affecting Tariff Concessions on Certain Poultry Meat Products* (2017), WTO Doc WT/DS492 (Panel Report), [*EU–Poultry Meat (China)*].

63 *Ibid* at para 3.1.

64 *Ibid.*

65 *Ibid.* China also alleged that the European Union acted inconsistently with articles I and XIII of the GATT 1994. These claims are not discussed in this chapter.

66 *Ibid* at para 8.1.

67 Brazil, Canada, Russia, Thailand and the United States.

of the relevant provisions of the GATT 1994."[68] This suggests that members will look to apply both the Procedures for Negotiations under article XXVIII and the 1980 Procedures in any future schedule modification negotiations under article XXVIII of the GATT 1994.

Determination of Members with Principal and Substantial Supplying Interest

In rejecting China's complaint that the European Union had acted inconsistently with article XXVIII:1 of the GATT 1994 by failing to recognize China as having a principal supplying interest or supplying interest in the products subject to the tariff concessions being modified and failing to negotiate the modifications with China, the panel determined that the European Union had properly excluded China from the modification negotiations because the European Union was entitled to rely on *actual* import levels of the products in question and did not have to *estimate* what members' shares *would have been* in the absence of non-discriminatory SPS measures restricting poultry imports from China.[69] The panel also noted that both disputing parties agreed that for purposes of determining which member holds a substantial supplying interest, it is "more appropriate to examine import shares based on quantity, rather than value."[70]

Necessity to Reappraise Determination of Supplying Interest

Perhaps more relevant for an eventual UK process that might extend over a number of years, the panel also rejected China's contention that the European Union should have made a *redetermination* of which members had a principal supplying interest or supplying interest in the products in question based on actual imports from a more recent reference period rather than the reference period used by the European Union, given the length of time (i.e., three years) between the notification of intention to modify concessions and the conclusion of the negotiations. The panel observed that:

- the Procedures for Negotiations under Article XXVIII require a member seeking to modify concessions to send a notification to that effect for circulation to WTO members, which must include statistics on imports of the relevant products by country of origin over a preceding three-year period; and

- any member which considers that it has a principal or substantial supplying interest in the concession(s) to be modified should communicate its claim to the notifying member within 90 days of the circulation of the import statistics.

Based on these requirements, the panel considered that the identification of members having a principal or substantial supplying interest seemed to be a necessary precondition for opening the negotiations on modifications, suggesting that in such circumstances, reappraisal cannot be a requirement. The panel also thought that if there were a requirement to reappraise after a certain period of time, one would have expected the procedures to have made reference to it, but they do not do so. The panel also observed that GATT/WTO practice does not support China's

---

68 *EU–Poultry Meat (China), supra* note 62 at paras 7.25–7.26.
69 *Ibid* at para 7.205. The WTO consistency of the SPS measures were not at issue in the dispute.
70 *Ibid* at para 7.98.

contention that there is an obligation to reappraise which members hold principal or substantial supplying interests.[71]

Importantly, however, the panel also called attention to what it called a "balance between several competing objectives" struck in the rules regarding the determination of which members hold a supplying interest, and it pointed to the ad note to article XXVIII:1, which it said gives expression to that balance. The ad note explains that "the object" of providing for participation in the negotiations of any member with a principal supplying interest is to "ensure that a [member] with a larger share in the trade affected by the concession than a [member] with which the concession was originally negotiated [i.e., the member with the INR] shall have an *effective opportunity to protect the contractual right* which it enjoys" under the GATT 1994.[72] The ad note also provides "on the other hand" that "it is not intended that the scope of the negotiations should be such as to make negotiations and agreement under Article XXVIII *unduly difficult*."[73]

Given the silence regarding reappraisal and the need to strike a balance between the competing objectives in article XXVIII, and although the panel rejected China's claim for reappraisal in this dispute, the panel declined to formulate a general legal rule on whether a member is under a legal obligation, in all cases, to reappraise which members hold a principal or substantial supplying interest following the initiation of the negotiations.[74]

General Level of Reciprocal and Mutually Advantageous Concessions

Turning to article XXVIII:2 of the GATT 1994, whereby the members concerned "shall endeavour to maintain a general level of reciprocal and mutually advantageous concessions not less favourable to trade than that provided for [under the GATT] prior to such negotiations," the European Union considered this to be a "best efforts" obligation for which members were accorded a "wide margin of discretion" in negotiating the level of compensation. China, by contrast, pointed to the word "shall" and disagreed with the European Union regarding the discretion afforded by the provision. Both parties, however, agreed that this provision constitutes a legally binding obligation and considered that if the compensation were negotiated in accordance with the calculation set out in paragraph 6 of the Understanding on the Interpretation of Article XXVIII of the GATT 1994, it would be presumed to be compliant with article XXVIII:2. The panel agreed with the parties' view that this provision constitutes a legal obligation, observing that article XXVIII:2 provides no specific rules on determining compensation and that members approach such negotiations in "very different ways."[75] The panel determined that the European Union was not obliged under article XXVIII:2 of the GATT 1994 and paragraph 6 of the understanding to calculate overall compensation on the basis of import levels over the three-year period immediately preceding the conclusion of the negotiations and found, therefore, that China had not demonstrated that the European Union had acted inconsistently with article XXVIII:2 in calculating overall compensation.[76]

---

71 *Ibid* at paras 7.212–7.214, 7.227.
72 *GATT 1994, supra* note 42 at art XXVIII:1 [emphasis added].
73 *Ibid* at para 7.216 [emphasis added].
74 *Ibid* at para 7.218.
75 *Ibid* at paras 7.242–7.244.
76 *Ibid* at para 7.277.

Imports into More Recent EU Members

China also claimed that the European Union should have accounted for poultry imports into Romania, Bulgaria and Croatia in determining the level of overall compensation. Had it done so, China argued, compensation would have been higher when calculated in accordance with paragraph 6 of the understanding. The panel disagreed, observing that the negotiations on modification and the relevant import period notified both preceded those countries joining the European Union.[77]

Level of Compensation Allocated among Supplying Countries

Perhaps of particular relevance in any future UK negotiation under article XXVIII is China's challenge of the compensation allocated *among* supplying countries (as opposed to the overall compensation negotiated). China claimed that by allocating all or the vast majority of the replacement TRQs to Brazil and Thailand, leaving a relatively small "all others" share and no country-specific share for China, the European Union had acted inconsistently with article XXVIII:2 of the GATT 1994 and paragraph 6 of the understanding. The European Union countered that article XXVIII and paragraph 6 of the understanding regulate the *overall* value for all members of the compensation provided and apply only at the level of the total amount of each TRQ. According to the European Union, those provisions do not apply to the allocation of TRQs among supplying countries, which, it maintained, is addressed exclusively in article XIII of the GATT 1994 (which deals with the administration of quantitative restrictions). The panel, having conducted a textual analysis of article XXVIII:2 and of paragraph 6 of the understanding, and after considering the context of the provisions, determined that the provisions do not apply to the allocation of TRQ shares *among* supplying countries.[78]

Legal Effect of Certification Procedures

China further claimed that because the EU modifications had not yet been incorporated into the EU goods schedule through the certification procedure set forth in the 1980 Procedures, the modifications had no legal effect and did not replace the bound duties listed in the EU goods schedule. As a result, said China, by applying the new concessions rather than the tariff rates listed in its goods schedule, the European Union had acted inconsistently with article II:1 of the GATT 1994, which prohibits members from according to the commerce of other members' treatment less favourable than that provided for in the member's goods schedule.[79]

The European Union opposed China's view, arguing that certification under the procedures is not a legal prerequisite for giving effect to modifications agreed in article XXVIII negotiations.[80] The European Union indicated that the changes agreed with Brazil and Thailand had been communicated to members and that it had submitted for certification a first batch of modifications to its schedule on March 24, 2014, but that certification had not yet occurred.[81]

---

77 *Ibid* at para 283.

78 *Ibid* at paras 7.287–7.302.

79 *Ibid* at para 7.496.

80 *Ibid.*

81 Certification occurred on December 14, 2016, which was after the panel report was issued to the disputing parties, but before circulation to all WTO members. See *Schedules of Tariff Concessions to the General Agreement on Tariffs and Trade 1994*, (2016) WTO Doc WT/Let/1220, online: <www.wto.org>.

(The modifications negotiated with Brazil and Thailand were included in the modifications package negotiated in connection with the expansion of the European Union to 25 members.) The European Union explained that it had not yet submitted for certification the remainder of the modifications negotiated with Brazil and Thailand, but that it planned to do so when submitting the modification package associated with the expansion of the European Union to 27 members.[82]

The panel was thus required to determine whether certification is a legal prerequisite that must be completed before a WTO member modifying its concessions can proceed to implement the changes agreed upon in the article XXVIII negotiations at the national level without acting inconsistently with article II:1 of the GATT 1994. The panel ruled that certification is not required before implementing the negotiated changes.

The panel relied on the Appellate Body ruling in *EC–Bananas III (article 21.5–Ecuador II, article 21.5–US)* that modification of schedules does not require an amendment under article X of the Marrakesh Agreement, but "is enacted through a special procedure set out in Article XXVIII." The panel emphasized the Appellate Body's reference to the "special procedure" through which the modification "is enacted," which language suggested to the panel that the Appellate Body considered that article XXVIII provided the legal basis for modifying a schedule. The panel also found support for its view in the language of article XXVIII:3(a), which states that modifying members "shall be free" to modify the concessions if agreement between the relevant members cannot be reached, and in article XXVIII(b), which allows negotiating members to withdraw substantially equivalent concessions once the modifying member has taken such action in the face of the lack of agreement.[83] The panel reasoned that "insofar as the terms of Article XXVIII:3 imply that Members concerned are 'free' to withdraw or modify concessions prior to certification of changes to the Schedule in those situations, then we consider that such a right must exist *a fortiori* where, as in the present case, the modification has been agreed by the [relevant] Members."[84]

The panel also analyzed the provisions of the Procedures for Negotiations under Article XXVIII (which are different from the 1980 Procedures relied upon by China in this case), pointing out that paragraph 7 thereof provides that members "will be free to give effect to the changes agreed upon in the negotiations…*as from the date on which the conclusion of all the negotiations has been notified*" to the WTO and not as from the date of certification. The panel also called attention to the different terminology used in paragraph 8, which stipulates that "*Formal effect* will be given to the changes in the schedules by means of Certifications."[85]

Having analyzed the Procedures for Negotiations under article XXVIII, the panel also analyzed the provisions of the 1980 Procedures, noting that they address *how* changes in authentic text of a schedule are to be made. For the panel, these procedures "clarify that certification is the legal prerequisite to altering the authoritative text of a Schedule,"[86] but do not speak to whether

---

82 *EU–Poultry Meat (China)*, *supra* note 62 at paras 7.501–7.502.

83 *Ibid* at paras 7.514–7.515, 7.517.

84 *Ibid* at para 7.518.

85 *Ibid* at paras 7.523–7.524, 7.530 [emphasis added].

86 *Ibid* at para 7.538.

certification is a legal prerequisite to giving effect to concessions agreed upon in article XXVIII negotiations.

The panel took care to underline that its finding that certification is not a legal prerequisite to implementing changes negotiated to a goods schedule under article XXVIII does not suggest that the process for certification is meaningless. Indeed, the panel pointed to situations where the introduction of changes to the text of a goods schedule is a legal prerequisite for effecting a change in members' substantive rights and obligations. The panel referred to a proposed rectification to correct an error in a goods schedule (which change would not be effected through an article XXVIII process). The panel made clear that such change would have no legal effect until the proposed rectification was certified via the 1980 Procedures.[87] The panel also suggested that an agreement to reduce tariffs may not be enforceable through WTO dispute settlement procedures until the changes have been introduced through certification. The panel summed up its view stating that the "legal consequence of certification varies in different situations, and therefore must be analysed in relation to the particular situation at hand."[88]

The panel drew two important implications from its interpretation of the 1980 Procedures that could inform the United Kingdom's approach to negotiating and/or implementing its goods schedule. First, the panel observed that paragraph 3 of the 1980 Procedures permits members to object within three months to a proposed certification on the ground that it "does not correctly reflect the modifications" resulting from article XXVIII negotiations. For the panel, this implies that "the certification process does not confer a 'veto' right upon those Members which did not participate in the negotiations and who may not be satisfied with the compensation agreed." Second, the panel said that absence of an objection under paragraph 3 "cannot be construed as a Member 'acquiescing' or 'accepting' that the changes introduced into the authentic text of the Member's Schedule are consistent with the Member's obligations under the GATT."[89]

In light of these various conclusions reached by the panel, it rejected China's claim that the European Union had acted inconsistently with article II:1 of the GATT 1994 by giving effect to the changes agreed with Brazil and Thailand prior to certification of the modifications.[90]

Conclusion

As the director-general pointed out in his speech to the World Trade Symposium in June 2016, the United Kingdom is a member of the WTO and this will not change following the country's departure from the European Union. However, the United Kingdom will find itself in a unique situation post-Brexit, given that it is currently covered by the EU goods and services schedules and presumably will need to secure WTO members' agreement to UK-specific schedules (be they simply the adjusted EU schedules or newly negotiated ones) once it leaves the European Union.

---

87 The panel referred, in note 730 of its report, to paragraph 7.54 of the panel report in *Russia–Tariff Treatment* (WT/DS485), noting that the relevant schedule for purposes of that dispute was the original Russian schedule because the European Union and Japan had objected to a rectification proposed by Russia, resulting in the proposed change not being certified.

88 *EU–Poultry Meat (China), supra* note 62 at para 7.536.

89 *Ibid* at para 7.541.

90 *Ibid* at para 8.1.

There are no existing procedures in the WTO that precisely govern the situation in which the United Kingdom will find itself post-Brexit. The United Kingdom's future trading relationship with the European Union, the contours of which are still very much unknown, will of course inform the future UK-WTO trading relationship in any event. But in terms of securing agreed UK-specific schedules, the United Kingdom and other WTO members might need to look for additional guidance and inspiration to existing WTO procedures governing the modification of goods and services schedules found primarily in article XXVIII of the GATT 1994 and article XXI of the GATS. Nevertheless, even if members choose to rely on these provisions to address the UK schedules situation post-Brexit, they are unlikely to provide answers to many of the questions that will arise as the process unfolds.

Another complication in securing agreed post-Brexit UK-specific schedules is that there is a paucity of WTO case law to guide any such process, whatever it turns out to be. However, the recent findings in the panel report in *EU–Poultry Meat (China)*, which was not appealed, provide some guidance upon which the United Kingdom and other members may seek to rely.

Under the circumstances, the words of the director-general of the WTO spoken in June 2016 remain apt: "I don't have a crystal ball to assess the outcome of these various different negotiations — and nor does anybody else."[91]

Indeed.

Depending on your perspective, we are either fortunate or cursed to live in interesting times.

---

91 Azevêdo, *supra* note 2.

2

Squaring the Circle: The Search for an Accommodation between the European Union and the United Kingdom

Armand de Mestral

> And those behind cried "Forward!" And those before cried "Back!"
> (Thomas Babington, Lord Macaulay, "Horatius at the Bridge")

Introduction: Why Is Canada Interested?

Is Brexit Canada's problem? Why should Canada be interested? Does Canada's national experience have anything to say about the current crisis in the relations between the United Kingdom and its 27 partners in the European Union? Clearly, it does. First, Canada is very much the product of Europe and has had long-standing relationships with all EU countries. Constitutionally, it is in large measure the product of the United Kingdom.[1] Second, Canada has very close economic ties with the European Union. After the United States, the European Union

---

1   LW White & WD Hussey, *Government in Great Britain, the Empire, and the Commonwealth* (Cambridge, UK: Cambridge University Press, 2015).

is Canada's most important trading partner.[2] In the European Union, the United Kingdom is Canada's second-largest trading partner and its leading EU investor.[3] Third, in 2017, Canada entered into a major trading agreement with the European Union and wants to ensure that the advantages that will flow from this agreement will not be compromised by the departure of the United Kingdom. Finally, UK government representatives have said that the United Kingdom will seek to conclude a free trade agreement (FTA) with trading partners such as Canada as soon as the United Kingdom is legally able to do so.[4] Brexit is Canada's problem.

Does Canada have anything to offer to the resolution of the current difficulties in the negotiations between the European Union and the United Kingdom? Clearly, it does. As a result of US President Donald Trump's call to renegotiate the North American Free Trade Agreement (NAFTA),[5] Canada is in the process of realizing the destructive potential of the unravelling of a major trade agreement and is seeking to avoid a negative outcome of the negotiations. The first reflex of the Canadian government, the Canadian business community and the Canadian people has been to take stock of the close ties binding Canada to the United States and the vital necessity of not compromising those bonds. This is a process that has yet to fully begin in the United Kingdom. It is far better to consider in a sober fashion the elements that bind countries in a highly interdependent world, rather than stressing self-assertion and abstract visions of sovereignty. The United Kingdom might well consider how the Canadian government and industry have instinctively sought allies in the United States at the national, state and municipal levels in order to ensure that trade negotiators in the United States are aware of the domestic consequences of breaking existing alliances. The trading relationship between Canada and the United States may need to be updated and adjusted to fit political realities, but this process should not destroy all that has been built up to the advantages of citizens on both sides of the border.

Canada has lived through potentially divisive referenda in 1980 and 1995, concerning the call for the separation of Quebec. Canadians are aware of the difficulties posed by referenda: the uncertain meaning of questions and the uncertain public interpretations of the result. Both Quebec referenda were advisory and called for a mandate to negotiate, with the results of negotiations to be put to a second referendum. The UK government, in its haste, has not shown such caution. However, it may not be too late to tell the people of the United Kingdom that the final result will be put to a second referendum, rather than treating the ambiguous result of the close advisory referendum of 2016 as a clear and fixed outcome. What could be more democratic?

2   Christian Deblock & Michèle Rioux, "From economic dialogue to CETA: Canada's trade relations with the European Union" (2011) 66:1 Intl J 39.

3   Government of Canada, "Commercial and Economic Relations", online: <www.canadainternational.gc.ca/united_kingdom-royaume_uni/bilateral_relations_bilaterales/commercial-commerciales.aspx?lang=eng>.

4   Rachelle Younglai, "Britain keen to maintain trade with Canada after Brexit: U.K. negotiator", *The Globe and Mail* (26 January 2017), online: <https://beta.theglobeandmail.com/report-on-business/economy/britain-keen-to-maintain-trade-with-canada-after-brexit-uk-negotiator/article33786675/?ref=http://www.theglobeandmail.com&>.

5   *North American Free Trade Agreement Between the Government of Canada, the Government of Mexico and the Government of the United States*, 17 December 1992, Can TS 1994 No 2, 32 ILM 289, 605 (entered into force 1 January 1994) [*NAFTA*].

The Political and Legal Dimensions

Until and unless the notice of withdrawal from the European Union is rescinded, the government of the United Kingdom will seek to define and negotiate its future relationship with the European Union. The central question appears to be whether it is possible to find a formula that will allow the United Kingdom to continue to enjoy close economic ties with the European Union, while ceasing to be a member and subject to the many disciplines of membership in the European Union. This is both a legal and a political question, involving a calculus of the meaning of the narrowly decided referendum, the interpretation of central concepts of EU law, and the willingness of both the UK and EU negotiators to seek creative solutions to a highly volatile question.

A first question is strictly political and is found in the ambiguity of the referendum question and the response of voters to the question. Did voters unequivocally vote to leave both the European Union itself and the internal market? Does the referendum result require the government to seek a "hard" Brexit in the sense of abandoning essential elements of the EU internal market, as it is defined by the Treaty on the Functioning of the European Union (TFEU),[6] or does the government enjoy flexibility in defining the terms of a new arrangement with the European Union? Opinions continue to differ, with those concerned with the fate of the UK economy, its key financial sector, immigration and its impact on staffing in essential sectors such as the health service, pressing for the maintenance of a very high degree of integration with the European Union. Others, more concerned with asserting "sovereignty" (itself a multifaceted concept) and allowing the United Kingdom to be free in the future to chart an economic and social course different from that of continental Europe, assert the need to break ties with the European Union in many fundamental ways.

The issues can also be characterized in more strictly legal terms — in particular EU law. Is it possible to remain in the European Union's internal market while not being a member of the European Union? Some commentators also try to distinguish between the European Union's internal market and the Customs Union (CU) — an interesting avenue of speculation, but, ultimately, very difficult to sustain as a matter of EU law. The internal market of the European Union has developed over time from the original "common market" of the European Economic Community "based on a customs union," to the Single Market, and finally, the internal market complemented by a host of other policies, such as transportation, fisheries, the common commercial policy, the areas of freedom, justice and security, and a foreign policy. Successive treaties have moved the goal posts in legal, economic and political terms. The internal market today is clearly more than the sum of the right of free movement of goods, services, persons and capital. It reflects the definition of exclusive and shared competences both within and outside the European Union. A broad definition might lead to the conclusion that the internal market is the European Union itself. Does it include the area of peace, security and justice? Does it include the external policy and the common commercial policy? Is it essential that the Court of Justice of the European Union (CJEU) has the final say? Put this way, it is possible to assert a more limited and essentially economic definition of the internal market, as this chapter attempts to do.

---

6   *Consolidated version of the Treaty on the Functioning of the European Union,*13 December 2007, [2008] OJ, C 115/47 (entered into force 1 December 2009) [*TFEU*], online: <http://eur-lex.europa.eu/legal-content/EN/TXT/?uri=celex%3A12012E%2FTXT>.

In the end, there are legal constraints upon the type of arrangement to which EU negotiators can commit. Negotiators will certainly feel legally constrained. The CJEU may have the final word, and thus, the legal question of whether the United Kingdom might leave the European Union but remain in the internal market is a very difficult question. Is it possible to imagine a more limited CU falling short of remaining in the full internal market? As this appears to be the preference of many in the United Kingdom, including many leading political leaders, it may be the decisive legal and political question for both the United Kingdom and the European Union.

The limited Brexit, while not yet formally defined for the purposes of negotiating the future trading relationship between the United Kingdom and the European Union, appears to be the most palatable to the current government. This position would take the United Kingdom out of the European Union, while retaining most of the principal advantages of the current trading relationship. The focus appears to be essentially on maintaining a range of economic ties, while breaking away from many of the wider range of EU rules that govern political, social and environmental issues — and even escaping from a range of disciplines broadly linked to trade, but not deemed to be of the essence. This approach seems to focus in particular on trade in goods and matters clearly related to goods, such as the abolition of tariffs, customs facilitation issues, transportation and the access of goods to the other market, including common standards, as well as maintaining open trade in services and open capital and payments markets. Apparently excluded are matters relating to the movement of people, immigrants and refugees.[7] The agreement that might come closest to this position is the European Union-Turkey Customs Union of 1993.[8] Whatever is included in a CU moves freely and, for obvious reasons, this provides reassurance to all those who fear the consequences of breaking existing economic ties. Most closely comparable to this approach, but by no means identical, is the European Economic Area (EEA) Agreement[9] between the European Union and the European Free Trade Agreement (EFTA) countries.

Another broad approach, and the one that seems to be preferred by harder Brexit supporters, is that of an FTA.[10] Like a CU, FTAs are permitted by the General Agreement on Tariffs and Trade 1994, article XXIV,[11] on the condition that they cover substantially all trade and lead, on balance, to trade creation rather than trade diversion. The FTA leaves the parties entirely free to conclude trade agreements with other states and to maintain their own customs and trade rules, subject only to removing agreed barriers on an agreed range of goods and services and capital movements between the parties. Sovereignty is preserved, but in a context in which it is possible to remove a wide range of trade barriers with a view to maintaining a larger market and protecting supply chains between the parties. This is, in fact, the option chosen by

---

7   EC, Commission, "Negotiating documents on Article 50 negotiations with the United Kingdom", online: <www. ec.europa.eu/commission/brexit-negotiations/negotiating-documents-article-50-negotiations-united-kingdom_en?field_ core_tags_tid_i18n=351&page=1>.

8   *European Union-Turkey Customs Union*, 22 December 1995, [1996] OJ, L 35 [*EU-Turkey CU*], online: <www.avrupa.info. tr/sites/default/files/2016-09/Custom_Union_des_ENG_0.pdf>.

9   *Agreement on the European Economic Area*, 2 May 1992, [1994] OJ, L 1 (entered into force 1 January 1994) [*EEA Agreement*], online: <www.efta.int/media/documents/legal-texts/eea/the-eea-agreement/Main%20Text%20of%20the%20 Agreement/EEAagreement.pdf>.

10   Jack Maidment, "EU trade commissioner says bloc will do post-Brexit free trade deal with UK 'for sure'", *The Telegraph* (27 April 2017), online: <www.telegraph.co.uk/news/2017/04/27/eu-trade-commissioner-says-bloc-will-do-post-brexit- free-trade/>.

11   *General Agreement on Tariffs and Trade*, 15 April 1994, 1867 UNTS 187, 33 ILM 1153 art XXIV (entered into force 1 January 1995).

almost all states when they negotiate trade liberalization on the bilateral and regional levels. The European Union has concluded a large number of FTAs, often under the rubric of "association" agreements.

The most recent and far-reaching FTA that may be relevant to the current situation is the Canada-European Union Comprehensive Economic and Trade Agreement (CETA),[12] approved by both parties and currently awaiting the decision to bring it into force on a provisional basis. CETA offers a model of what can be done with an FTA and is an appealing prospect for many Brexit supporters.

An analysis of the more than 600 CUs and FTAs in existence today suggests that rights of access and guarantees of respect for the terms of the agreement exist on a continuum. It is extremely difficult to maintain very strict categories in the abstract. Much can be done under either a CU or an FTA. The European Union is one of the very few genuine CUs functioning today; its economic reach and supranational institutions make it, in some ways, qualitatively different from all the others. In many respects, it is comparable to a federation; hence, it is difficult to compare the European Union to an abstract model of a CU. CUs exist that fall far short of the European Union, and FTAs exist that are designed to promote a high degree of economic integration. FTAs exist in a great variety of shapes and sizes and can be designed to cover a wide range of issues. For example, the Australia-New Zealand Closer Economic Relations Trade Agreement (ANZCERTA) provides for a much higher degree of social and economic integration than the EU-Turkey Customs Union.[13]

The Spirit of the Negotiations: Search for a *Modus Vivendi*

How should one analyze the debate over the optimum outcome to the Brexit negotiations? Can one assert that some abstract concepts (CU, internal market, FTA) are immutable and not interchangeable, or should one approach the analysis from a strictly pragmatic standpoint? It is tempting to assert that the only possible approach is the pragmatic one. Flexibility and an open mind appear to be essential on both sides if the European Union and the United Kingdom are to agree on a trading regime that suits both. Clearly, much can be done with any ideal model of economic agreement, provided that the parties are united in their objectives. As so far this is not the case, the first hurdle is purely political. The UK government does not yet know what it is trying to achieve, while the European Union has already taken a firm stance on the order of negotiations and has published papers outlining various negotiating positions on the future trading relationship.

But the issue is not only political. As noted above, there are legal constraints. Even if the European Union and the United Kingdom are willing to approach negotiations on the future relationship in a very pragmatic fashion and to not argue as to whether the United Kingdom must adhere to some legalistic vision of the internal market or remain in a CU, the negotiators cannot forget the nature of the EU legal order and the rules and institutions that govern it. The

---

12 *Comprehensive Economic and Trade Agreement between Canada, of the one part, and the European Union [and its Member States...]*, 29 February 2016 [*CETA*], online: <http://trade.ec.europa.eu/doclib/docs/2016/february/tradoc_154329.pdf>.

13 *Australia-New Zealand Closer Economic Relations Trade Agreement*, 28 March 1983, (entered into force 1 January 1983) [*ANZCERTA*], online: <http://dfat.gov.au/trade/agreements/anzcerta/pages/australia-new-zealand-closer-economic-relations-trade-agreement.aspx>; *EU-Turkey CU, supra* note 8.

European Union is much more than a simple CU. Unlike an FTA, in which the parties can agree to liberalize their trading relationship under a defined set of rules that do not change over time, the European Union is an evolving institution. Legislation is constantly being introduced and debated; the treaties, regulations and directives are in a constant process of interpretation and application by the European Union, EU members and their courts, as well as by the CJEU. The European Union has become a process of integration, and it is not an entity that is fixed in time.

This makes the debate over the future role of the CJEU anything but academic. The European Union, on one side, cannot agree to set aside the future rulings of the court for the purposes of its future commitments to the United Kingdom, however much the United Kingdom might wish to escape from the CJEU. The future decisions of the CJEU will always be relevant to the ongoing interpretation of the meaning of the treaties and of legislation. The United Kingdom will have to accept this fact. The role of the court is an ongoing problem for the European Union as well; it should be noted that the role of the court vis-à-vis the European Court of Human Rights remains an unsolved riddle since 2009, despite a treaty command to ratify the European Convention on Human Rights.[14] Acceptance of the nature of the European Union, whether in an active or passive form, is a question that cannot be avoided by UK negotiators.

Models of Association Available to the Parties

Defining the UK Position

The position of the United Kingdom is still a work in progress. White papers were issued throughout the summer of 2017, defining the United Kingdom's position[15] in partial response to the European Union's position papers,[16] and the Great Repeal Bill[17] was introduced and hotly debated[18] in Parliament after the throne speech of June 2017. One can analyze these documents to understand their underlying premises. One can analyze the political statements of objectives by the prime minister and the responsible ministers. One can even go back to the statements made by various political figures during the referendum campaign in 2016. Overall, what emerges is a sense of unease in the United Kingdom at the direction that the European Union has taken over time, and a desire to be free of the political structures and supranational institutions of the European Union. A plan appears to be emerging at the domestic level concerning the kind of legislative framework that is intended by the current UK government. This involves putting an end to the application of the European Communities Act 1972;[19] ending the supremacy of EU law in the domestic UK legal order; freezing EU law as forming part of UK law at a fixed date to be determined, but not later than the date when the United Kingdom formally leaves the European Union; putting an end to the jurisdiction of the CJEU and subjecting the

---

14   Council of Europe, *European Convention for the Protection of Human Rights and Fundamental Freedoms, as amended by Protocols Nos. 11 and 14*, 4 November 1950, 213 UNTS 221, ETS 5 (entered into force 3 September 1953), online: <www.coe.int/en/web/conventions/full-list/-/conventions/treaty/005>.

15   United Kingdom, Department for Exiting the European Union, *The United Kingdom's exit from and new partnership with the European Union* (February 2017) [Brexit White Paper], online: <www.gov.uk/government/publications/the-united-kingdoms-exit-from-and-new-partnership-with-the-european-union-white-paper/the-united-kingdoms-exit-from-and-new-partnership-with-the-european-union--2>.

16   See EC, Commission, *supra* note 7 for a list of the EU position papers that were drafted.

17   Bill 5, *European Union (Withdrawal) Bill* [HC], 2017–2019 sess, 2017 (1st reading 13 July 2017).

18   Mikey Smith & Dan Bloom, "Brexit Repeal Bill debate recap: MPs clash furiously over Theresa May's 'power grab' law", *The Mirror* (7 September 2017), online: <www.mirror.co.uk/news/politics/brexit-great-repeal-bill-debate-11127253>.

19   *European Communities Act 1972* (UK), c 68.

determination of all legal issues in the United Kingdom to UK courts; and withdrawing from participation in all EU administrative and political bodies and, where necessary, replacing them with comparable institutions in the United Kingdom.[20]

The current UK plan is essentially legal and constitutional. The problem with it is that the economic consequences of Brexit and the consequences for, and future direction of, the UK economy are not spelled out. There is no economic plan for the future, only a legislative and constitutional framework.

What does the UK government want? Despite all that has passed, this is the maddening question for the European Union, as well as for the 60 million inhabitants of the United Kingdom. Citizens and other residents of the United Kingdom remain uncertain about what was decided, and remain almost equally divided as to how they wish the situation to evolve. The convinced sovereigntists who won the referendum seem to have largely disappeared. Almost half the population voted to remain and still wish to do so, even if they are resigned to leaving, and many of the other half appear to be having second thoughts about Brexit. The Conservative government is attempting to provide leadership, but in doing so appears ever more divided within itself, with some ministers openly contradicting each other, and some parts of the Conservative parliamentary majority also taking positions that are not compatible with those of the prime minister. British commercial and industrial leaders, after having assisted or remaining largely neutral during the referendum campaign, have now become alarmed at the prospect of failed negotiations and the consequences of the United Kingdom being ejected from the European Union without a comfortable fall-back position to protect their interests. On July 7, 2017, the assembled leaders of commerce and industry called on the Brexit minister to ensure that the United Kingdom remains in the internal market for the indefinite future, until such time as negotiations are fully completed and all is certain.[21]

Perhaps most distressing of all in mid-2017 is that the nature and objectives of the negotiations remain something of a mystery — at least so far as the UK government is concerned. The European Union has published a series of papers outlining its strategy. These papers focus in particular on the terms of the departure from the European Union, which they insist must be fully determined before beginning the negotiations on the future economic relationship with the United Kingdom. This appears to have been accepted by the UK government, which opened negotiations with an unsatisfactory offer in late June 2017 on the future of EU citizens in the United Kingdom.[22] On the broader question of the future economic relationship, EU leaders have shown a high degree of unity, but have restricted themselves to suggesting that the United Kingdom cannot leave the European Union while expecting to retain all the advantages of membership. It has also been made clear that the United Kingdom has no legal right to negotiate free trade arrangements with other states until it has actually left the European Union.

Insofar as any coherent position had been defined by fall 2017, it appears that the UK government's position remained close to what the European Union says is impossible. No clear negotiating position has been defined by the prime minister or by the Brexit minister.

---

20 Brexit White Paper, *supra* note 15.

21 Christopher Williams, "CBI: UK must stay in single market until EU deal done", *The Telegraph* (6 July 2017), online: <www.telegraph.co.uk/business/2017/07/06/david-davis-faces-calls-transitional-brexit-deal-chevening-summit1/>.

22 EC, Commission, *supra* note 7.

The chancellor of the exchequer indicated in early July 2017 that maintenance of existing economic ties, including remaining in the internal market, must be the fundamental goal of the negotiations, putting his position closer to the position of commerce and industry and further from some of his colleagues. One might say with Lucius Cassius before Phillipi: "The storm is up, and all is on the hazard."[23]

As no formal proposal has been made for the structure of future economic relations, it appears best to review the principal models currently available to both sides. Doubtless those responsible for developing the policy have been undertaking the same exercise.

The Internal Market

The internal market is a complex phenomenon not easily reduced to a unified concept separable from the rest of the treaty. Article 26 of the TFEU defines the internal market as "an area without internal frontiers in which the free movement of goods, persons, services and capital is ensured in accordance with the provisions of the Treaties."[24] Article 114 grants the European Union competence to legislate "for the achievement of the objectives set out in Article 26."[25] The internal market is defined by the two articles of title I of part 3 of the TFEU. The substances of the various freedoms of movement are defined at greater length by the subsequent titles of part 3, as well as by many other articles throughout the treaty, such as article 114. It is thus difficult to claim that the internal market is a legally finite concept defined as a single unit of the TFEU. This, in turn, makes it difficult to assert that there is a bloc of articles to which the United Kingdom could easily adhere, or insist that the internal market is separate from the titles of part 3 dealing with agriculture or transportation. What is the relationship of the internal market to the concept of the area of freedom, security and justice or the many articles defining EU economic competences?

Similar ambiguity exists with respect to the separation of the concepts of the internal market and the CU. Can they be separated, as some suggest, for the purposes of defining an ongoing UK relationship with the European Union? To confuse matters further, article 3(1) grants the European Union exclusive competence over the CU, along with tariffs, while competence over the internal market is described by article 4(2)(a) as being "shared."[26] This reflects the evolution of treaty language through several EU treaties since the Treaty of Rome,[27] which originally defined the European Economic Community (EEC) as "based on a customs union." At that point, the EEC was particularly focused on the free movement of goods, but, from the start, it also guaranteed the free movement of persons, services and capital. To assert that the United Kingdom must adhere to the internal market in its integrity, as the EU negotiating positions suggest, may not provide the degree of clarity necessary for a long-term renegotiation of the relationship of the parties, and it will be necessary to define the precise content of the future commitments of the United Kingdom in much greater detail.

---

23 William Shakespeare, *Julius Caesar*, (Oxford, UK: Oxford University Press, 2010), act 5, scene 1.

24 *TFEU, supra* note 6, art 26.

25 *Ibid*, art 114.

26 *Ibid*, arts 3(1), 4(2)(a).

27 EC, *Treaty Establishing the European Community*, 25 March 1957, OJ, C 325, online: <http://eur-lex.europa.eu/legal-content/EN/TXT/?uri=CELEX%3A12002E%2FTXT>.

A number of commentators and politicians have suggested that the United Kingdom should only commit to the EU CU. Like the concept of the internal market, the concept of the EU CU is not easily separated from all the other elements of the TFEU. In many respects, it has been incorporated into the broader concept of the Single Market and, subsequently, the internal market. It would seem that the only meaningful way to use the concept of the CU would be to define it as those parts of the TFEU that relate to the free movement of goods — and even that would require complex negotiations to reach a mutually satisfactory definition, as the treatment of goods is subject to a wide range of EU treaty duties and legislative competences. Remaining in the internal market or in a defined CU would require the negotiation of rules of origin covering all the elements encompassed by the agreement, whether they are applicable to an internal market or to a CU. The World Trade Organization (WTO) decision in the *Turkey – Textiles* case suggests that this might be legally possible.[28]

An equally important and perhaps very difficult issue would be the extent to which the United Kingdom might become free to conclude trade agreements with other states, as the UK government asserts it intends to do. Part of the declared strategy of leaving the European Union has been to allow the United Kingdom to conclude trade agreements with other states, such as Canada, China, Japan or the United States. Brexit supporters have asserted that these agreements would not only compensate for leaving the European Union, but would also provide even more interesting avenues for UK trade, thus making the United Kingdom again the great trading nation that it once was. President Trump has indicated support for this strategy and has suggested that a "very, very big deal" with the United States awaits a liberated United Kingdom.[29] Others have expressed skepticism regarding whether these FTAs could replace the advantages of EU membership.[30] The EU negotiating authorities have insisted that the United Kingdom must refrain from making any such trade agreements until Brexit is final, thus leaving the United Kingdom in the invidious position of being unable to pursue a new strategy to compensate for leaving the European Union until some indeterminate future date and certainly not in time to have these FTAs in place when it leaves the European Union. Equally frustrating is the uncertainty regarding the question of whether the United Kingdom could conclude FTAs while remaining in the internal market or in a reduced CU. Two precedents, examined below, suggest an answer that is somewhat positive, although subject to onerous conditions.

The EEA

The model most frequently cited is the agreement concluded with the members of the EFTA minus Switzerland, with which the European Union has made separate parallel arrangements to be discussed below. Iceland, Liechtenstein, Norway and Switzerland (the remaining countries of the EFTA founded in 1957), which for various reasons did not wish to join the European Union, nevertheless were eager to ensure maximum access to the EU market and concluded an agreement in 1993 for this purpose. Under the EEA Agreement,[31] EFTA goods, services, persons and capital have access to the EU internal market on terms equivalent to those of all EU members. The object

---

28 Notification of Mutually Acceptable Solution, 19 July 2001, WT/DS34/14, WTO, online: <www.wto.org/english/tratop_e/dispu_e/cases_e/ds34_e.htm>.

29 Anushka Asthana, "Trump expects trade deal with UK to be completed 'very, very quickly'", *The Guardian* (8 July 2017), online <www.theguardian.com/world/2017/jul/08/theresa-may-in-bid-to-boost-post-brexit-trade-with-g20-meetings>.

30 Steven Brakman, Harry Garretsen & Tristan Kohl, "Options for a 'Global Britain' after Brexit", *VOX* (11 May 2017), online: <http://voxeu.org/article/options-global-britain-after-brexit>.

31 *EEA Agreement, supra* note 9.

of this agreement is to maintain the "privileged relationship"[32] between EFTA countries and the European Union "based on proximity, long-standing common values and European identity."[33] The EFTA countries are not members of the European Union; the EFTA and individual EFTA countries remain free to conclude agreements with third states. However, the treaty guarantees that EFTA goods and services, citizens and capital have access to the European Union under terms defined by EU law. The price of this remarkable degree of access is that EFTA countries must implement standards and rules applicable to goods, services and capital that are identical to those governing the European Union. The European Union regularly informs the EFTA states of the relevant changes that are made to EU law, and it is the duty of the EFTA governments to adopt these regulations and directives without change or discussion. The EEA Agreement also provides for the integration of relevant social and environmental policies by the parties.

The great advantage of the EEA is that there is a very high degree of economic integration between the two groups, without the necessity of membership in the European Union. Iceland and Norway are thus able to maintain somewhat separate fisheries and agriculture and resource exploitation policies, which are the essence of their economies, while obtaining the immense advantage of full access to the EU internal market. On its face, the EEA model appears to give those who wish to leave the European Union and those who wish to retain all its advantages everything they want. However, it appears that in the eyes of the supporters of a hard Brexit, the price is too high, as it requires virtually total acceptance of EU law on commerce and competition as it exists from time to time. The agreement is governed by an EEA council and a joint committee of the parties. Decisions of the EEA council are binding on both parties. Disputes are to be settled by negotiation, and the work of the EFTA Court, national courts and the CJEU should proceed in harmony, but ultimately, any matter involving the interpretation of EU law is to be determined by the CJEU. EFTA members have to contribute to the EU budget, but have no say in determining the budget or its expenditure.

Is it possible to envisage the United Kingdom obtaining the same benefits by adhering to the EEA or joining the EFTA? This possibility has been raised by commentators in the United Kingdom both before and after the Brexit vote and remains a very serious hypothesis.[34] In July 2017, the suggestion was made that the United Kingdom might also obtain the benefits of the EEA by becoming an associate member of the EFTA,[35] as did Finland in the 1970s. All three options involve acceptance of the arrangement by the members of the EFTA and also of the European Union. So far, the European Union has not responded to any specific negotiating proposal on the subject. There are obvious questions to be asked. Is the EEA option, designed for a few small outlying countries, capable of application to one of the major economies of Europe? Would it suit the EFTA states to allow the United Kingdom (which was a founding member before it left to join the European Union) to rejoin and thus seriously complicate their relationship with the European Union? Would the EU negotiators not view this as an attempt to remain in the internal market while abandoning the broader responsibilities of EU membership? Perhaps not, as the EEA requires virtually complete unilateral adhesion to the

---

32 *Ibid*, Preamble.

33 *Ibid*.

34 Brexit White Paper, *supra* note 15.

35 Patrick Wintour, "UK considers potential shortcut on trade deals post-Brexit", *The Guardian* (2 July 2017), online <www.theguardian.com/politics/2017/jul/02/uk-shortcut-free-trade-post-brexit>.

European Union's internal market rules as they exist from time to time, as well as a contribution to the EU budget set by the European Union.

The EEA option would suit many in the United Kingdom who wish to leave the European Union, but also be firmly grounded in the internal market. The greatest objections would probably come from the hard Brexit faction in the United Kingdom, which would object to the maintenance of EU law, the jurisdiction of the CJEU and payment into the EU budget. By the autumn of 2017, neither side had put this option on the table, despite its being the most attractive to those who wish to leave the European Union but maintain maximum economic ties.

Swiss Bilateral Agreements

Following the referendum in which the Swiss electorate refused to join the EEA in 1992, Switzerland negotiated a series of agreements, first in 1999 and again in 2004 and 2010, building upon its 1972 FTA with the then EEC. These agreements, although not ensuring total elimination of tariffs and quotas, do make possible a very favourable regime of reciprocal free access to goods, services, persons and capital, as well as eliminating many border controls by allowing Switzerland to join the Schengen Area. As a counterpart, Switzerland has agreed, as with the EEA, to apply all relevant EU regulations and directives and to limit bank secrecy and make the regulation of EU banking rules much more effective in Switzerland. The movement of persons according to the EU standard was the object of a further referendum in 2015, and the Swiss government has attempted to deal with the call to end even EU immigration by maintaining the rule, subject to a principle that jobs may be offered to Swiss citizens on a priority basis.

The current regime is based on more than 100 bilateral agreements, all of which are deemed to be interrelated and subject to the threat that the violation of any one agreement could bring down the whole edifice. This system may appear to Brexit supporters to be a very appealing model, as it appears to allow for the negotiation of free movement in particular sectors without having to accept the full panoply of rights and duties of the internal market. However, there have been constant tensions between Switzerland and the European Union arising out of these bilateral agreements, and it is most unlikely that the European Union would be willing to envisage a similar approach with the United Kingdom. Furthermore, the sectoral regulation of trade is banned by the law of the WTO; the current regime can only be explained by the very particular place of neutral Switzerland, surrounded by the European Union, and by the fact that the interests of no other state appear to be offended by this violation of basic WTO law.

The EU-Turkey CU

The most obvious model of a CU to be considered is the CU that was first concluded with Turkey in 1993.[36] This CU provides for the free movement of goods of Turkish origin into the European Union. Goods imported from third-party states, such as textiles from India, do not enjoy the benefit of this CU, unless they undergo radical change or are incorporated into new products of Turkish origin. The CU covers only goods, although there have been discussions of extending it to other factors, and Turkish citizens enjoy visa-free access to the European Union, but not a full right of free movement of persons as defined by EU law. Under this CU, Turkey

---

36 *EU-Turkey CU, supra* note 8.

must apply the EU customs tariff, as it exists from time to time, to all goods. Turkish goods moving into the European Union enjoy the benefits of EU law and are subject to any relevant rulings of the CJEU. The CU has led to the movement of a very large volume of trade in goods between the parties, and the European Union is Turkey's principal trading partner.

One conclusion to be drawn from this agreement is that Turkey must refrain from concluding any trade agreement dealing with the movement of goods, as this is strictly covered by the terms of the CU and can only be negotiated jointly with the European Union. This would suggest a serious limitation on any intention of the United Kingdom to conclude trade agreements with third-party states on any matter covered by a future agreement with the European Union, either on access to the internal market or the CU.

FTAs

If maintenance of at least some rights under EU law or replication of the Turkish, EEA or Swiss models prove impossible, the other solution is to negotiate an FTA. The great advantage of the free trade model, and the reason why it is chosen by so many countries in their bilateral or regional trade relations, is that it is much less "invasive" than a CU; it generally focuses on goods and non-tariff barriers, and leaves the parties free to maintain different trade relations with third-party states. The supporters of limited legal ties between the United Kingdom and the European Union find this approach very appealing. The major problem with this model is that the existing degree of legal and economic integration of the United Kingdom into the European Union has gone light years beyond the requirements of the average FTA. To fall back to the FTA model is to opt for a much lower level of integration than currently exists in the European Union, resulting in the probable disruption of important trading patterns for UK goods and services and the virtually certain disruption of the movement of people in both directions. The FTA model is difficult to adapt to the presence of supranational rules and institutions and usually is characterized by limited institutional arrangements. An FTA is thus a serious step back from the degree of economic and legal integration currently existing in the European Union and could seriously disrupt the economy of the United Kingdom. A further problem is that recreating trading rules between the United Kingdom and the European Union in the form of a new FTA, rather than building on existing systems, will require a lengthy and very complex renegotiation of many basic issues. It is virtually certain that this is impossible within the article 50 time limit. It is also true that most FTAs in the past have been static, having little capacity to adapt to changing circumstances.

Despite the disadvantages of the FTA option, it must be noted that FTAs provide a flexible model, and some examples can be cited of complex and dynamic trading relationships that have been maintained within an FTA framework. To take two examples, NAFTA and ANZCERTA both demonstrate close economic integration under an FTA model. ANZCERTA, building on a previous FTA, has expanded over the years through frequent amendments to provide for virtually total free trade in goods, even agricultural commodities, as well as services and the movement of people. Considerable efforts have been made to enable the free movement of Australian and New Zealand citizens between the parties, as well as to facilitate the harmonization of laws and allow competition tribunals to have jurisdiction in both countries.

NAFTA, while not going quite as far on all points as ANZCERTA, does provide a framework for the integration of the three economies of Canada, Mexico and the United States.[37] Based on the elimination of tariffs, except on some agricultural commodities, national treatment of all goods and services, as well as unification of the key automobile industry, NAFTA has witnessed the tripling of trade among the three countries, making both Canada and Mexico the leading trading partners of the United States. NAFTA has also been the motor of a vast increase in foreign investment in the three countries. One of the principal successes of NAFTA is to ensure that the thousands of trucks and trains that cross the two borders every day do so in a matter of seconds rather than minutes or hours and, in general, NAFTA has provided a framework under which goods cross borders as expeditiously as possible.

Both these agreements are possible due to the neighbouring relationship, close pre-existing trade ties and considerable similarity of legal systems between Canada and the United States, although not with Mexico. NAFTA provides for no extraterritorial jurisdiction of courts, but does create a network of five systems of dispute settlement. On the other hand, the failure of the parties to provide methods for updating various chapters as they become outdated and the recent call by President Trump to scrap or renegotiate NAFTA highlight the fragility of the FTA model, which is subject to no supranational rules or institutions and is ultimately subject to the will of governments.

The paradoxical potential for deep integration and, at the same time, the vast difference existing between the European Union and the FTA model is displayed by the recently negotiated CETA between Canada and the European Union.[38] This is the most comprehensive FTA currently in existence, covering goods, services, capital and even the movement of certain persons. It deals with recognition of product standards and seeks to promote common approaches to regulation, as well as dealing with sensitive "non-trade" issues of human rights, labour and environmental standards. But to indicate the fundamental difference, CETA does not offer "free movement" in the sense of EU law, and each government remains ultimately free to take what steps it wishes. Unfortunately for the United Kingdom, the final stages of the approval of CETA have shown that it can be very difficult for the European Union to reach agreement on the adoption of an FTA if it is characterized as a "mixed agreement," which is how any broad agreement between the European Union and the United Kingdom would probably be legally characterized.

Thus, if the FTA model is the only one upon which the United Kingdom and the European Union can agree, it can be relied upon to provide a considerable degree of economic integration, but it will fall far short of the existing EU treaties. A great deal can be done with an FTA should both parties be willing to put water in their wine and make sensible pragmatic compromises. The European Union has shown itself willing to make remarkable compromises with the EFTA and Switzerland, on condition that these countries make equally remarkable unilateral concessions by agreeing to apply large parts of EU law and contribute to the EU budget. This is the obvious way for the United Kingdom to remain in the internal market. Whether the United Kingdom is willing to put itself in this position is not at all clear.

---

37 *NAFTA, supra* note 5.

38 *CETA, supra* note 12.

Can an FTA be designed that would provide the United Kingdom with all the benefits of the internal market? Given the role of supranational rules and institutions in defining and regulating the internal market, it is difficult to imagine how this could be accomplished to the satisfaction of both parties on the basis of their current positions. But it is not impossible. Speedy withdrawal of the article 50 notice is the preferable solution to this whole imbroglio.

The Atlantic Free Trade Area

Defenders of Brexit claim that they wish to make Britain the great trading nation it once was. Withdrawing from the most remarkable trade agreement in history for a much weaker level of economic integration seems a poor substitute for being a member of the European Union, even if the United Kingdom is ultimately able to negotiate a host of FTAs with other countries instead of the 50 FTAs that the European Union has already negotiated. However, there is one agreement that might be equal to achieving the objective of making Britain the great trading nation it once was. This is complete free trade between all of Europe and all of North America: in other words, an Atlantic Free Trade Area (AFTA).

We live in an age of "mega-regional" trade agreements (CETA; the Comprehensive and Progressive Agreement for Trans-Pacific Partnership [CPTPP];[39] the Transatlantic Trade and Investment Partnership [TTIP];[40] the Regional Comprehensive Economic Partnership,[41] consisting of the 10 member states of the Association of Southeast Asian Nations [ASEAN];[42] Mercosur;[43] the Economic Community of West African States [ECOWAS];[44] the Southern African Development Community [SADC][45] and so on). The ultimate mega-regional (short of a return to the WTO) would be an agreement providing for free trade between all the countries of Europe and North America. Rather than just pursuing an FTA with the European Union, if it is unprepared to make the sacrifice of remaining in the European Union and if the internal market is not on offer, the United Kingdom would be performing an immense service to the world in seeking to promote genuine free trade between Europe and North America. An AFTA would be the greatest trading bloc in the world. It would lead the world in opening markets and setting regulatory standards, which would then be the default standards for products and services in the global economy. Should the United Kingdom be willing to lead this charge, it would indeed be seen as capable of being the great trading nation it once was.

An AFTA should remove all tariffs on goods, including agricultural commodities. Common technical standards and the mutual recognition of standards for the regulation of safety of health and the regulatory environment could be enshrined in an AFTA, subject to a clear understanding of the right of each party to regulate these matters. Much could be done to promote the freedom to provide services throughout an AFTA, subject again to a clear understanding of the right to

---

39 *Comprehensive and Progressive Agreement for Trans-Pacific Partnership*, 23 January 2018, online: Global Affairs Canada <www.international.gc.ca/trade-commerce/trade-agreements-accords-commerciaux/agr-acc/tpp-ptp/index. aspx?lang=eng>.

40 EC, Commission, "Trans-Atlantic Trade and Investment Partnership", online: <http://ec.europa.eu/trade/policy/in-focus/ttip/documents-and-events/>.

41 ASEAN, "Regional Comprehensive Economic Partnership", online: <http://asean.org/?static_post=rcep-regional-comprehensive-economic-partnership>.

42 ASEAN, online: <http://asean.org/>.

43 EC, Commission, "Mercosur", online: <http://ec.europa.eu/trade/policy/countries-and-regions/regions/mercosur/>.

44 ECOWAS, online: <www.ecowas.int/>.

45 SADC, online: <www.sadc.int/>.

regulate. In particular, banking and financial services, including the non-banking sector, could be the object of standards based on the highest international standards. Movement of people would not be politically acceptable, but much could be done to promote the mutual recognition of professional standards, as has been done in CETA. A single approach to regulation of competition matters and the promotion and protection of foreign investment and related dispute settlement could also be provided in an AFTA.

Interestingly, much of the groundwork for an AFTA has already been laid. CETA has been negotiated, considerable efforts have been made to reach agreement between the European Union and the United States in the unfinished TTIP negotiations, and, despite President Trump, the CPTPP has shown what can be done between a large and heterogeneous group of states. Mega-regional agreements are possible and models exist. The United Kingdom has only to use these models creatively to promote an AFTA.

At a time when there is much uncertainty about the future of the global economy, when there are many tensions arising from conflicts in the Middle East or attendant on the emergence of a strong and assertive China, the emergence of an AFTA would provide a great island of stability, both for its own members and for the rest of the world. In all likelihood, the emergence of common standards in an AFTA would lead to these standards being transposed to upgraded trade agreements under the WTO. CETA and the unfinished TTIP negotiations have prepared the way. All that remains is for a great trading nation to take the lead.

Conclusion

As it searches for an accommodation with the European Union, the United Kingdom is learning that it has a wide variety of options to consider. The best option from an economic perspective is no doubt to remain in the internal market, but this may be politically distasteful to many in the United Kingdom. None of the other options reviewed in this chapter provide the same degree of integration and legal certainty that the internal market offers, but various models of CUs or free trade areas can be envisaged to provide at least some of the advantages that will be given up by the United Kingdom in leaving the European Union. Arguably, the most constructive approach would be for the United Kingdom to seek to put together a vast AFTA with the rest of Europe and the three countries of North America.

3

Renegotiating the EU-UK Trade Relationship: Lessons from NAFTA

David A. Gantz

Introduction

British Prime Minister Theresa May first proposed a "bold and ambitious free trade agreement" in a speech on January 17, 2017.[1] That objective was repeated in the United Kingdom's formal notice of the invocation of article 50 of the Treaty on European Union on March 29, beginning the two-year "Brexit" period until withdrawal.[2] In August, the UK government outlined what it hopes to achieve in a future customs arrangements (FCA) paper with the European Union.[3]

---

1   Letter from Prime Minister Theresa May to European Council President Donald Tusk (29 March 2017), online: <www.gov.uk/government/uploads/system/uploads/attachment_data/file/604079/Prime_Ministers_letter_to_European_Council_President_Donald_Tusk.pdf>. For a detailed discussion of the options, see "The six flavours of Brexit", *The Economist* (22 July 2017), online: <www.economist.com/news/britain/21725335-eu-offers-many-menus-norwegian-turkish-there-no-la-carte-option-six>. The article shows why the more trade-friendly options such as the Single Market and the Customs Union (CU) are not attainable.

2   May, *supra* note 1.

3   HM Government, *Future Customs Arrangements: A Future Partnership Paper* (15 August 2017) [FCA], online: <www.gov.uk/government/uploads/system/uploads/attachment_data/file/637748/Future_customs_arrangements_-_a_future_partnership_paper.pdf>.

This arrangement, a "customs partnership" that is still lacking detail, is both bold and ambitious. It envisions a future trade relationship that has elements of a CU mixed with elements of a free trade agreement (FTA), as discussed more fully below, beginning after a two- to three-year transitional period during which the United Kingdom would continue to participate in the EU CU (and be subject to EU budget contributions and to the jurisdiction of EU regulations and court decisions). More recently, on September 22, 2017, in Florence, Italy, May called for concluding something better and more creative than an "advanced free trade agreement" such as the Comprehensive Economic and Trade Agreement (CETA)[4] between the European Union and Canada, but offered little indication as to what form such an arrangement might take.[5]

The evolution from continued UK membership in the EU CU for the transitional period to permanent customs relations under a hybrid agreement is not fully explained in the FCA[6] paper (let alone in the Florence speech), but UK officials appear to recognize that under the future relationship, traders may be "required to demonstrate the origin of goods, as may be required under a future trade agreement between the UK and the EU,"[7] and will very likely have to deal with customs declarations and border inspections that are unnecessary at the present time. In other words, there is no assurance that the system proposed in August would provide less encumbered trade than a straight FTA with streamlined border procedures, as long as the United Kingdom insists on "taking back its borders," with legal structures, standards, immigration laws, trade policies and court review that are no longer part of the EU system.[8]

Why will the United Kingdom withdraw from membership in the European Union's Single Market and CU, either of which would provide many fewer obstacles to future UK-EU trade than an FTA or even a hybrid agreement? As discussed more fully in this chapter, an FTA is the only legally and politically feasible form of preferential trade relationship that could generally assure duty-free, quota-free exchange of goods between the United Kingdom and members of the European Union, given the prime minister's earlier articulated priorities: full UK control over immigration from the remaining 27 member states of the European Union (EU27), operation under the United Kingdom's own regulatory framework rather than under regulations and directives imposed by the European Union, the flexibility to conclude trade agreements with third countries and avoidance of the jurisdiction of the Court of Justice of the European Union (CJEU).[9] It remains to be seen how a hybrid combination of FTA and CU would be made legal under international trading rules, politically acceptable to both parties, operationally feasible and, perhaps most important, acceptable to both the European Union and the United Kingdom after any transition period.

4   *Comprehensive Economic and Trade Agreement*, European Union and Canada, 30 October 2016, (entered into provisional force 21 September 2017) [*CETA*], online: <http://trade.ec.europa.eu/doclib/docs/2016/february/tradoc_154329.pdf>.

5   Theresa May, "Theresa May's Florence speech on Brexit, full text", *The Spectator* (22 September 2017), online: <https://blogs.spectator.co.uk/2017/09/theresa-mays-brexit-speech-full-text/>.

6   FCA paper, *supra* note 3 at 11–12, paras 48, 52.

7   *Ibid* at 7, para 28.

8   See Joe Owen, Marcus Shepheard & Alex Stojanovic, *Implementing Brexit: Customs* (11 September 2017), online: Institute for Government <www.instituteforgovernment.org.uk/sites/default/files/publications/IfG_Brexit_customs_WEB_0.pdf> (detailing the "significant changes in the way the UK border operates" when the United Kingdom leaves the jurisdiction of the CJEU, takes control over immigration and pursues an independent trade policy).

9   Presumably, the FTA would be combined with an "economic integration agreement" under article V of the World Trade Organization's (WTO) General Agreement on Trade in Services.

It would be misleading to suggest that the UK government has created a consistent, comprehensive plan for negotiating the withdrawal of the United Kingdom and the creation of a new bilateral trade relationship. Rather, the period since the UK vote for Brexit on June 23, 2016, has been marked by confusion, uncertainty and general UK government incompetence, including historic miscalculations by then Prime Minister David Cameron in holding the referendum; internal conflicts among May, Boris Johnson, Liam Fox, David Davis and other members of the Conservative government; and repetition for months of two misleading and unhelpful slogans, "Brexit means Brexit" and "no agreement is better than a bad agreement."[10] Add to these the false promises (now mostly abandoned) by persons such as Johnson in October 2016 that the United Kingdom can "have its cake and eat it too";[11] May's decision on April 18, 2017, to call a snap election for June 8, resulting in the government's loss of a parliamentary majority; and the mistaken belief that the United Kingdom can leave the CU and Single Market but retain virtually all its benefits, or build a CU to achieve "frictionless trade," which are misconceptions that EU negotiator Michael Barnier has been quick to point out.[12]

As of October 2017, the uncertainty continues, even though the United Kingdom and the European Union formally began their Brexit discussions on June 19 and in August provided a general view of objectives for the future trade relationship in the FCA paper. The FCA paper suggests that those favouring a "softer" Brexit, such as UK Chancellor Philip Hammond, long a proponent of a "jobs-first Brexit," have gained greater influence.[13]

Only recently has the prime minister indicated that she understands the impact of a "hard" Brexit on the UK business community, despite a vague pledge that she "will not let companies fall over a Brexit 'cliff edge'" and instead will seek an "implementation phase" that would provide a transition period of two to three years after March 2019.[14] There finally appears to be some appreciation by the UK government of data that suggests a soft Brexit (such as an FTA) would still reduce future UK-EU trade by 20 to 25 percent, while a hard Brexit (such as reversion to WTO tariffs and other rules) could reduce trade by 40 percent.[15]

---

10 Theresa May, (Speech delivered at Lancaster House, London, UK, 17 January 2017), online: *Daily Telegraph* <www.telegraph.co.uk/news/2017/01/17/theresa-mays-brexit-speech-full/>. No agreement would be a disaster for the United Kingdom because it would mean reversion to WTO Most Favoured Nation (MFN) duties, which, even if they were the same as current MFN duties, would require the consensus of all other members of the WTO, and among other costs would subject UK auto imports to the European Union's (the United Kingdom's largest auto export market with 56 percent of total exports) 10 percent MFN duties on autos and 4.5 percent duties on most auto parts. See "17 year high for British car manufacturing as global demand hits record levels", Society of Motor Manufacturers and Traders (SMMT) (26 January 2016), online: <www.smmt.co.uk/2017/01/17-year-high-british-car-manufacturing-global-demand-hits-record-levels/>. See "Trade in goods and customs duties in TTIP", online: European Commission, <http://trade.ec.europa.eu/doclib/docs/2015/january/tradoc_152998.1%20Trade%20in%20goods%20and%20customs%20tariffs.pdf>.

11 See Rowena Mason & Anushka Asthana, "Philip Hammond on leaving EU: 'We can't have our cake and eat it'" *The Guardian* (29 March 2017), online: <www.theguardian.com/politics/2017/mar/29/philllip-hammond-on-leaving-eu-we-cant-have-our-cake-and-eat-it> (referring to both Hammond and Johnson).

12 Alex Barker, "Britain yet to face facts on Brexit, EU's Barnier Warns", *Financial Times* (6 July 2017), online: <www.ft.com/content/8404d08a-6221-11e7-91a7-502f7ee26895?mhq5j=e1>.

13 See Jim Brunsden, "Hammond refuses to confirm UK will leave EU single market", *Financial Times* (17 June 2017), online: <www.ft.com/content/bb16efbc-5291-11e7-bfb8-997009366969> (noting that Hammond's influence is likely to increase post-election).

14 See George Parker & Caroline Binham, "Theresa May pledges no Brexit 'cliff edge' for companies", *Financial Times* (20 July 2017), online: <www.ft.com/content/1afeb7aa-6d33-11e7-bfeb-33fe0c5b7eaa?segmentId=a7371401-027d-d8bf-8a7f-2a746e767d56> (reporting on a meeting with May's business council).

15 See "The six flavours of Brexit," *supra* note 1.

In October 2017, it seemed probable that the transition period advocated by the United Kingdom would continue until 2021 or 2022, the latter being the longest possible time before another UK election must be held.[16] Such a period might allow for the creation of a hybrid trade system along the lines proposed in the FCA for use post-2022, assuming of course that the European Union is prepared to accept a hybrid agreement in some form, which most likely will be far more similar to an FTA, as May foresaw in January 2017, than to the existing EU CU.

An FTA or hybrid CU and FTA would appear to be within the exclusive competence of the European Commission, European Council and European Parliament and thus would not require member parliamentary approval (risking a veto by any one of the approximately 38 national or regional parliaments). With CETA, for example, the agreement was subject to significant delays, largely because it contained investor-state dispute settlement (ISDS) provisions.[17] Fortunately for the future of EU trade agreements, including one with the United Kingdom, a recent CJEU decision relating to the EU-Singapore FTA states that with the exception of ISDS provisions, other chapters of modern FTAs are within the exclusive competence of the European Union, so that approval of individual parliaments is *not* required (assuming the agreement contains no ISDS provisions).[18]

The breadth and complexity of the Brexit issues could fill this and many other chapters. It is also much too early in the Brexit process to predict the detailed content of a future customs agreement or even whether one can be negotiated. That being said, the UK and EU negotiators have much to learn from the experience of Canada, Mexico and the United States operating under the North American Free Trade Agreement (NAFTA) for nearly 24 years.[19] In terms of the actual text of an agreement establishing a future customs relationship, the parties can be expected to look first and foremost to CETA,[20] since the European Commission, European Council and European Parliament have all provisionally approved this modern, "wide and deep" FTA. Still, CETA is different in at least two major respects:

---

16 See George Parker & Alex Barker, "'Status quo' Brexit transition plan reflects cabinet power grab", *Financial Times* (28 July 2017), online: <www.ft.com/content/df460e26-72b3-11e7-93ff-99f383b09ff9> (suggesting a growing consensus within the Cabinet for a transition period during which the United Kingdom would continue to be bound by the EU requirements on immigration and remain a member of the CU).

17 See e.g. David A Gantz, "The CETA Ratification Saga: The Demise of ISDS in EU Trade Agreements?" (2017) Arizona Legal Studies Discussion Paper No 17-10.

18 See Arthur Beesley, "EU Singapore ruling charts possible Brexit path", *Financial Times* (17 May 2017), online: <www. conservativehome.com/parliament/2016/04/theresa-mays-speech-on-brexit-full-text.html> (suggesting that the opinion means a UK-EU FTA could be approved by a qualified majority of the EU members if certain provisions are left out). This also bodes well for the recent conclusion in principle of the outlines of an "economic partnership agreement" between the European Union and Japan, even though final agreement on a text and entry into force are undoubtedly two or more years in the future.

19 *North American Free Trade Agreement*, Canada, Mexico and United States, 17 December 1992, (entered into force 1 January 1994) [*NAFTA*], online: <www.nafta-sec-alena.org/Home/Texts-of-the-Agreement/North-American-Free-Trade-Agreement>.

20 *CETA, supra* note 4. As summarized by the European Commission, the comprehensive CETA will remove customs duties; help make European firms more competitive in Canada; make it easier for EU firms to bid for Canadian public contracts (and vice versa); open up the Canadian services market to EU companies; open up markets for European food and drink exports; protect traditional European food and drink products (known as geographical indications) from being copied; cut EU exporters' costs without cutting standards; benefit small and medium-sized EU firms; benefit EU consumers; make it easier for European professionals to work in Canada; allow for the mutual recognition of some qualifications; create predictable conditions for both EU and Canadian investors; make it easier for European firms to invest in Canada; help Europe's creative industries, innovators and artists; support people's rights at work; and protect the environment. With CETA, the European Union and Canada pledge to ensure that economic growth, social issues and environmental protection go hand in hand. See European Commission, "CETA explained" (April 2017), online: <http://ec.europa.eu/trade/policy/in-focus/ceta/ceta-explained/>.

- Canada and the EU nations are more than 3,000 miles apart, so trade will move exclusively by ship or aircraft (reducing the disruption of customs entry procedures) rather than by truck across a land or narrow (North Sea) border; and

- no experience exists with regard to how CETA will function in practice, given that it entered into force provisionally only on September 21, 2017.[21]

Thus, the lessons of NAFTA (including some unfortunate aspects that could be avoided in a future UK-EU agreement), where goods primarily move by truck, and where the United States and Canada and the United States and Mexico share common land borders of approximately 3,000 miles and 2,000 miles, respectively, are the focus of the balance of this chapter. While it seems unlikely, it could also be hoped that if negotiators for the European Union and the United Kingdom both understood the disadvantages of an FTA with its rules of origin (ROO), they might be encouraged to develop a less potentially harmful arrangement, or at least to adopt many of the innovative approaches that the United States has implemented for trade with Canada and Mexico over the years, such as the Free and Secure Trade (FAST) for commercial vehicles and the Customs-Trade Partnership Against Terrorism (C-TPAT) mechanisms[22] for speeding up cross-border trade, as discussed later.

At the time of this writing, the United States is effectively forcing Mexico and Canada to engage in the renegotiation of NAFTA.[23] It is unclear whether the negotiations will ultimately result in a modernized NAFTA, a continuation of the status quo or the termination of NAFTA by the United States with regard to Mexico, Canada or both. Nor is it evident when the negotiations might be concluded.[24] There is more than a little irony in the fact that both the United Kingdom and the United States appear determined to risk damaging or destroying the two most successful regional trade agreements in history, the European Union and NAFTA, respectively. The assumption for the purposes of this chapter is that the NAFTA experience is relevant for the United Kingdom and the European Union even if NAFTA disappears in the future, despite the enormous risks such elimination would run for businesses that trade and invest within North America.[25]

This discussion of future negotiations between the European Union and the United Kingdom is limited to certain aspects of trade in goods. It does not consider trade in agriculture or services,

---

21 See Bengt Ljung, "Last-Minute Snag Threatens to Postpone EU-Canada Deal", (6 July 2017) 34 Int'l Trade Rep (BBNA) 962 (reporting that the July 1 deadline was to be missed because of a disagreement over trade in cheese and generic pharmaceutical products); see "EU, Canada agree start of free trade agreement", *Reuters* (8 July 2017), online: <www.reuters.com/article/us-canada-eu-trade/eu-canada-agree-start-of-free-trade-agreement-idUSKBN19T0PC>; see "The free trade agreement EU-Canada applied 'temporarily' on September 21", *The Siver Times* (8 July 2017), online: <https://sivertimes.com/the-free-trade-agreement-eu-canada-applied-temporarily-on-september-21/49321> (reporting on a joint statement by Canadian Prime Minister Justin Trudeau and European Commission President Jean-Claude Junker that CETA would enter into force on September 21).

22 US Customs and Border Protection, "FAST: Free and Secure Trade for Commercial Vehicles", (21 July 2017) [FAST], online: <www.cbp.gov/travel/trusted-traveler-programs/fast>.

23 See letter from US Trade Representative Robert E Lighthizer to Congress (18 May 2017), online: <https://ustr.gov/sites/default/files/files/Press/Releases/NAFTA%20Notification.pdf>, notifying the administration's intent to initiate negotiations on the "modernization" of NAFTA.

24 See Andrew Mayeda, "Trump's Trade Chief Says U.S. Won't Force Quick Deal on NAFTA", *Bloomberg* (22 June 2017), online <www.bloomberg.com/news/articles/2017-06-21/trump-s-trade-chief-says-u-s-won-t-force-quick-deal-on-nafta> (quoting Lighthizer as saying that there is no deadline to reach a deal on NAFTA).

25 See Shawn Donna, "Renegotiating NAFTA: 5 Points to Keep in Mind", *Financial Times* (23 January 2017), online: <www.ft.com/content/4c1594c6-e18d-11e6-8405-9e5580d6e5fb?mhq5j=e1>.

immigration, efforts to incorporate EU laws and regulations into UK law (no longer subject to the jurisdiction of the CJEU), or any of the other trade-related issues that will be subject to discussion and debate between the European Union and the United Kingdom over the next two to five years. The chapter is divided into five additional parts. The second part summarizes the legal constraints facing the United Kingdom's conflicting desires regarding a much higher level of national sovereignty over applicable laws, controls over EU immigration and the jurisdiction of the CJEU on the one hand, and duty-free, quota-free movement of goods and open trade in services, including financial services, on the other. The third section discusses the challenges of shifting from a common market/CU to an FTA, a reverse process that has not been attempted before. The fourth part focuses on several of the key lessons to be learned by both the United Kingdom and the European Union from the NAFTA experience. The fifth section discusses a key industrial sector in North America and in the European Union, the auto and auto parts industry, one that in both jurisdictions has benefited from duty-free trade, seamless supply chains and relatively open movement of auto parts, as well as finished vehicles. The sixth part provides commentary and conclusions, including a discussion of possible alternatives to an FTA and of the much-discussed FTA with the United States.

Constraints on Maintaining a Favourable UK-EU Trade Relationship

Continued Single Market Membership

Continued membership in the single market, as May confirmed again in the Florence speech,[26] is precluded unless the United Kingdom is willing to accept the jurisdiction of the European Commission and the CJEU, continued financial support for the European Union's budget and open immigration (the "Fourth Freedom") from the remaining EU member countries.[27] Membership in the existing or a new CU (as with Turkey) with all external UK tariffs determined by the European Union's common external tariff (CET) is not possible if the United Kingdom wishes to be able to negotiate its own trade agreements (including tariff elimination) with the United States, other third parties and the more than 50 nations with which the European Union currently has trade agreements in force.[28] Secretary of State for International Trade Liam Fox is currently tasked with negotiating such new bilateral agreements — even though the United Kingdom will not legally be free to do so until Brexit is complete and any transitional arrangements from March 2019 onward have been completed — and is not likely to be enthusiastic about negotiating himself out of a job. A divorce without a trade deal would leave the United Kingdom at the mercy of negotiation of tariff rates (including those relating to agricultural trade) with the WTO and its consensus requirements,[29] applicable to both third-party trade and trade with the EU27.

---

26 May, *supra* note 4.

27 See Chris Giles & Alex Barker, "Hard or soft Brexit? The six scenarios for Britain", *Financial Times* (23 June 2017), online: <www.ft.com/content/52fb4998-573f-11e7-9fed-c19e2700005f?mhq5j=e1> (outlining the options, ranging from remaining in the Single Market to a "divorce" with no new trade relationship).

28 *Ibid* at 9–11.

29 *Agreement Establishing the World Trade Organization*, 15 April 1994, art IX (entered into force 1 January 1995) (calling for decision making by consensus).

Replicating the Norwegian or Swiss Relationships

It does not appear that the Norwegian or Swiss relationships with the European Union could be replicated for the United Kingdom. Norway, as a member of the European Economic Area (EEA), along with Iceland and Liechtenstein, has agreed to follow EU single-market rules and to accept free movement of workers, as well as the other elements of the "Four Freedoms." As the European Commission notes, "the EEA agreement provides for a high degree of economic integration, common competition rules, rules for state aid and government procurement."[30] When changes are made in EU law, Norway and other EEA members must accept and implement them, even though Norway has no input or control over those changes. Norway was also required to become a member of the Schengen area to avoid passport controls with neighbouring Sweden, and to agree to cooperation with EU research, defence and anti-terrorism mechanisms. It is also subject, to some degree, to EU anti-competition laws.[31] For the United Kingdom, the attractions of membership in the EEA in order to maintain the equivalent of the single market with a different label would appear to pale in comparison with putting the United Kingdom in the position of having to accept EU regulation without any significant participation in the process, and the requirement to accept free movement of workers from the EU27. In other words, it is a complete non-starter, as the prime minister confirmed on September 22.[32]

The Swiss relationship with the European Union reflects similar disadvantages for a UK government determined to enhance its "sovereignty," in particular with regard to regulation of immigration. After Switzerland rejected EEA membership in 1992, Switzerland and the European Union agreed on a package of agreements (more than 100 to date) covering, *inter alia*, free movement of persons, technical trade barriers, public procurement, agriculture, air and land transport, participation in Schengen, and Swiss financial contributions to economic and social objectives.[33] It is also worth noting that the EU-Swiss relationship may well be altered as a result of a referendum in 2014 in which the Swiss population voted to strictly limit immigration from EU nations. The Swiss Parliament enacted a compromise immigration law at the end of 2016, but it is unclear whether the new law will permit Switzerland to maintain its current access to the Single Market for the longer term.[34]

Focusing on "Equivalence" under FCAs

In some other sectors, such as financial services, discussion has occurred as to whether "equivalence" in the regulatory structure could be substituted for the current financial regulation of UK financial institutions by the European Commission,[35] which might provide a basis

---

30 European Commission, "Countries and Regions: Norway", online: <http://ec.europa.eu/trade/policy/countries-and-regions/countries/norway/>.

31 "Norway's deal with the EU still holds lessons for Britain", *Financial Times* (2 February 2017), online: <www.economist.com/news/europe/21716039-sooner-or-later-britain-will-face-trade-offs-between-sovereignty-and-access-norways-deal>.

32 May, *supra* note 5.

33 European Commission, "Countries and Regions: Switzerland", online: <http://ec.europa.eu/trade/policy/countries-and-regions/countries/switzerland/>.

34 "Switzerland makes U-turn over EU worker quotas to keep single market access", *The Guardian* (16 December 2016), online: <www.theguardian.com/world/2016/dec/16/switzerland-u-turn-quotas-on-eu-workers-immigration>.

35 See British Bankers' Association, "Brexit Quick Brief #4: What is 'equivalence' and how does it work?" (2016), online: <www.bba.org.uk/wp-content/uploads/2016/12/webversion-BQB-4-1.pdf>.

for maintaining the status quo in future financial services relations, as long as UK banking regulations were considered equivalent to the EU regulations. A similar approach could apply to trade in goods through efforts to maintain equivalent product and safety standards in such sectors as automobiles, chemicals and pharmaceutical products, among others. Thus, for example, the safety standards for autos manufactured in the United Kingdom would be kept identical to those required in the European Union (and any future changes in EU regulations would be promptly incorporated into the separate UK regulations). Unfortunately, common regulatory requirements are only one part of the challenges facing traders between the European Union and the United Kingdom if the relationship is an FTA. The others, as discussed more fully later in the fourth section of this chapter, include compliance with ROO, various additional entry documents not required for trade within the Single Market and CU, and the need for border inspections to prevent abuses. That documentation would presumably include certification that the regulatory requirements for goods produced in the United Kingdom and being exported to the European Union were being met.

The FCA paper appears to be an attempt to maintain some aspects of the equivalency of the single market for trade between the United Kingdom and the European Union after the transition period, including participation in the European Union's CET for goods that enter the United Kingdom and are destined for re-export to the EU27, presumably including parts and components used in UK auto manufacturing. The idea is to accept the European Union's existing system for such goods, including equivalent border arrangements and expanded security and data sharing,[36] and common regulatory requirements such as those relating to auto, chemical and pharmaceutical safety. The United Kingdom would seek, and the European Union would grant, a continued waiver for submission of entry and exit documentation for UK-EU and EU-UK trade. As the FCA paper summarizes:

> By mirroring the EU's customs approach at its external border, we could ensure that all goods entering the EU via the UK have paid the correct EU duties. This would remove the need for the UK and the EU to introduce customs processes between us, so that goods moving between the UK and the EU would be treated as they are now for customs purposes. The UK would also be able to apply its own tariffs and trade policy to UK exports and imports from other countries destined for the UK market, in line with our aspiration for an independent trade policy. We would need to explore with the EU how such an approach would fit with the other elements of our deep and special partnership.[37]

Goods entering the United Kingdom for consumption in the United Kingdom would thus be treated separately. The advantage of this approach is to permit the United Kingdom to negotiate separate FTAs with third countries, such as the United States, and agree to set tariffs on such trade that are not consistent with the European Union's CET. However, several potential problems exist with this proposal. First, for the 40 percent of UK exports destined for the other EU member states, the regime would not have changed at all; the European Union would still determine tariff levels and standards, just as is the situation today, but without any formal UK input into the process, presumably with all the domestic political sensitivities that affect the

---

36 FCA, *supra* note 3 at 8–9, paras 30, 32, 34.
37 *Ibid* at 10, para 40.

alleged loss of sovereignty more broadly. Second, a massive tracing and potential circumvention risk would be created, whereby, for example, an automobile transmission imported into the United Kingdom (duty free), from a third country (duty free), under an FTA would, instead of being used by Nissan to assemble into a vehicle to be sold in the United Kingdom, be incorporated in a vehicle exported to Germany (without paying the CET of about 4.5 percent).

For those complying (UK producers, UK importers and foreign exporters under FTAs), the record-keeping would be complex and costly even if extensively automated.[38] ROO might be avoided on UK-EU trade, but the record-keeping requirements to assure no circumvention takes place might well be as onerous as dealing with traditional ROO. And ROO would be required for any FTAs between the United Kingdom and third countries. For all these reasons, it appears that while maintenance of equivalence of UK product standards with current and future EU standards would greatly facilitate the movement of goods from the United Kingdom to the European Union, it would not resolve the need for border documentation and customs inspections. Ultimately, the permanent FTA is much more likely to resemble an FTA than a hybrid FTA and CU, hopefully with an agreed mechanism for speeding border crossings for commercial vehicles, as with FAST and C-TPAT, but without the open border that characterizes intra-EU trade today.

It is also evident from the FCA paper that UK authorities realize their proposals may not be accepted, entirely or even in large part. Thus, it is asserted in the FCA, "The Government believes that the UK and the EU should also jointly consider innovative approaches that could support UK-EU trade outside of a CU arrangement, while still removing the need for customs processes at the border."[39] In other words, even if the hybrid CU and FTA approach suggested by the United Kingdom is not accepted, the parties should find a way to avoid (or at least minimize) customs oversight at the border. This statement recognizes the extreme desirability of avoiding the high cost of customs documentations for stakeholders, even if realistically it may be difficult or impossible to achieve. It also suggests implicitly that there may be other variations. For example, under a permanent trade agreement, the parties might agree to maintain operations under the EU CU for the auto and auto parts sector alone, using that sector as a test that could be broadened in a future agreement.

Costs and Complexities of an FTA Relationship

Even assuming that a successful FTA can be negotiated and concluded by the United Kingdom and the European Union, importing and exporting will be significantly changed. While manufactured goods should still trade duty free and tariff free, the documentary and logistical requirements for such trade are likely to become more time consuming and complex, including entry delays at Le Havre, France, at least initially, even if the United Kingdom and the European Union are able to agree on innovative mechanisms for streamlining the clearance process. Also, despite the FCA proposal, it is difficult to envision such an arrangement without the United

---

38 The FCA paper argues, perhaps over-optimistically, that a new Customs Declaration Service being implemented before Brexit "will be compliant with The EU's Union Customs Code to ensure continuity for business and will provide modern, digital customs technology, which will ensure HMRC [Her Majesty's Revenue & Customs] has the flexibility needed to deal with the outcome of the negotiations with the EU." See FCA, *supra* note 3 at 7, para 26.

39 *Ibid* at 9, para 38.

Kingdom being subject to some sort of common legal jurisdiction shared by Brussels and the United Kingdom over standards and perhaps more broadly.[40]

If an FTA can be achieved in the negotiations, major aspects include the following:

- Burdensome but necessary ROO, other documentary requirements such as customs declarations, border controls and delays for traders and vehicles, even for goods that may be subject to a hybrid CU, may threaten regional supply chains. The burden will fall most heavily on small- and medium-sized enterprises (SMEs), since large multinational enterprises (MNEs) have the internal staff to deal with such demands.

- The desirability of a system similar to FAST and C-TPAT, "a commercial clearance program for known low-risk shipments entering the United States from Canada and Mexico. Initiated after 9/11, this innovative trusted traveler/trusted shipper program allows expedited processing for commercial carriers who have completed background checks and fulfill certain eligibility requirements."[41]

- Potential difficulties faced by UK exports because of diverging product standards, in particular for autos, drugs and chemicals, because such standards will need to be addressed in the future under UK legislation rather than on the basis of common EU regulations and directives, unless the United Kingdom creates a system whereby new EU regulations are automatically incorporated into UK domestic law (without any formal UK participation in the drafting process in Brussels).

- The withdrawal of the United Kingdom from the Single Market and CU (even with a hybrid system in place) means loss of free trade benefits with the more than 60 countries covered by existing EU FTAs, until they are replaced by new bilateral or multilateral FTAs or their equivalent (which by some estimates could take 10 to 20 years to put into place).

- UK manufacturers face a loss of protection currently afforded by dozens of EU antidumping and countervailing (AD/CVD) orders, unless and until new UK AD/CVD orders are implemented after WTO-compliant investigations are initiated and concluded under new UK laws and regulations. This in turn will require the creation of a new, expert administrative unit with dozens or hundreds of expert government lawyers and investigators.

- Coverage of trade in services will almost certainly be less comprehensive than membership in the EU Single Market, leading to loss of "passporting" and potential difficulties in maintaining London as the principal clearing house for euro-denominated transactions, and the almost certain loss of some financial services jobs to Amsterdam, Dublin, Frankfurt, Luxembourg

---

40 James Blitz, "Theresa May's cabinet starts to split over Brexit", *Financial Times* (28 June 2017), online: <www.ft.com/content/db64f4ba-5b49-11e7-9bc8-8055f264aa8b>.

41 US Customs and Border Protection, "FAST: Free and Secure Trade for Commercial Vehicles" (21 July 2017), online: <www.cbp.gov/travel/trusted-traveler-programs/fast>. The European Union is in the process of streamlining trade transactions through a "new computerized transit system," designed for movement of goods within the European Union, which could conceivably be used in trade between the European Union and the United Kingdom, even if the latter is no longer part of the Single Market and the CU. See Langdon Systems, "New Computerised Transit System", online: <www.langdonsystems.com/ncts_overview.asp>. See FAST, *supra* note 22.

or Paris.[42] Free movement of professionals as well as students may also be restricted, with the former disadvantaging MNEs based in the European Union, and the latter adversely affecting the United Kingdom's many universities that encourage international students and engage in joint research with EU institutions of higher education.

- Shifting administration of thousands of laws and regulations from the European Commission in Brussels to the United Kingdom will require a dramatic increase in the necessary UK bureaucracy in regulatory areas now covered by the European Union, including a need for several hundred experienced trade agreement negotiators, not only for Brexit, but for future UK bilateral agreements with current EU FTA partners, as well as possible new ones, such as the United States and Japan.[43]

GATT Rules on CUs and FTAs

Perhaps the most significant exception to the MFN principle of the General Agreement on Tariffs and Trade (GATT) is for FTAs and CUs. Those arrangements that meet the strict (but poorly enforced) requirements of GATT article XXIV may deviate from MFN (non-discriminatory) treatment and apply preferential tariffs (usually zero) to other members of the FTA or CU. In both FTAs and CUs, the parties are required to eliminate internal tariffs on substantially all trade within a reasonable time (usually 10 years), to notify the GATT's Committee on Regional Trade Agreements of the negotiations and their results, and to assure that in the process of forming a CU or FTA, "the duties and other regulations of commerce" not be higher or more restrictive than the corresponding duties and other regulations of commerce existing in the same constituent territories prior to the formation of the free trade area.[44]

The major difference between a CU, such as the European Union, and an FTA, such as NAFTA, is that the CU applies a CET to all imports of a product from outside the region, regardless of which member country makes the importation, whereas in NAFTA, each of the three parties is permitted to maintain its own tariff levels on imports from third countries. Without the CET, a good could be imported into a low-tariff member country (for example, an auto imported into the United States paying a 2.5 percent tariff) and transshipped to a higher-tariff country (for example, Mexico, with a tariff of six percent or higher). The only widely accepted method of discouraging transshipment among member countries in the absence of a common external tariff is to impose ROO, so that the export of a foreign auto imported into the United States from outside the region and transshipped to Mexico would be subject to payment of MFN tariffs upon entering Mexico.

---

42 See "Goldman Sachs to Move Hundreds of Staff Out of London Due to Brexit", *The Guardian* (21 March 2017), online: <www.theguardian.com/business/2017/mar/21/goldman-sachs-staff-london-brexit-frankfurt-paris>. See also Claire Jones & Katie Martin, "ECB in drive to control post-Brexit euro clearing", *Financial Times* (23 June 2017), online: <www.ft.com/content/8888e560-57e5-11e7-9fed-c19e2700005f>.

43 See e.g. Stefan Wagstyl & George Parker, "Cabinet Tension on Brexit Breaks Out into the Open", *Financial Times* (27 June 2017), online: <www.ft.com/content/db64f4ba-5b49-11e7-9bc8-8055f264aa8b>.

44 *General Agreement on Tariffs and Trade*, 30 October 1947, 55 UNTS 194, art XXIV:5 (entered into force 1 January 1948) [*GATT 1947*].

It can also be seen that the idea of one member of a traditional common market negotiating a trade agreement with a third country is not feasible, unless the bifurcated FCA approach is adopted. For example, if the United Kingdom were to remain in the existing CU, it could not negotiate a bilateral FTA with the United States because the United Kingdom, still bound by the CET, could not lower tariffs on imports from the United States, such as automobiles, which are currently subject to the European Union's 10 percent CET. In other words, in the area of tariffs, the United Kingdom would be legally incapable of agreeing to reductions in FTA negotiations. Even if the hybrid system were to be accepted and implemented by the European Union, the United Kingdom could offer its own lower tariffs to FTA partners only for goods destined for the United Kingdom, with a prohibition against transshipment and the need to trace separately components to be used in assembling finished products destined for the UK market and those destined for EU countries.

Whether third countries would be willing to conclude FTAs with the United Kingdom that provided clear access only to the UK market, with requirements for re-export of parts and components used for UK manufacturing being subject to various and possibly onerous non-circumvention requirements, remains to be seen.

All this being said, FTAs and CUs have historically provided the opportunity (although not necessarily success in the execution) of eliminating tariff and non-tariff barriers among willing parties, with FTAs accounting for about 80 percent of preferential trade agreements under GATT article XXIV, CUs for about 10 percent[45] and 10 percent under special rules for agreements solely among developing nations.[46] Thus, for the European Union and the United Kingdom, the challenge is both in the unwinding of the current relationship and moving in a sensible manner toward the creation of a new relationship that, in principle, is within the scope of that permitted in GATT article XXIV, along with a focus on simplifying customs and regulatory documentation.

Key Lessons from NAFTA Free Trade without Open Borders

NAFTA is one of the most successful FTAs ever negotiated in terms of the trade generated and the development of supply chains in North America that permit manufacturers there to compete with the European Union and Asia, where developed-country producers have easy access to lower labour-cost manufacturing for labour-intensive operations in neighbouring countries. Despite much criticism, NAFTA has led to significant advantages for all three parties, including:

- total goods and services trade approaches US$1.3 trillion annually;

- North America has one of the most efficient automotive production sectors in the world;

---

45 WTO, "List of all RTAs [regional trade agreements]" (27 June 2017), online: <http://rtais.wto.org/UI/PublicAllRTAList.aspx>.

46 WTO, "Differential and more favourable treatment reciprocity and fuller participation of developing countries" (28 November 1979), online: <www.wto.org/english/docs_e/legal_e/enabling1979_e.htm>.

- extensive trade in agricultural products is conducted among the parties, with Canada (US$21.8 billion) and Mexico (US$18.3 billion) representing the United States' first and third most important export destinations, respectively; and

- exports to Mexico alone are estimated to be responsible for 4.9 million US jobs.[47]

The areas of legal and practical experience in NAFTA that are most relevant to a UK-EU FTA are in ROO and other customs laws and procedures, including the common customs regulations required under Chapter 5 of NAFTA, and the practical simplifications for cross-border transit, such as the FAST and C-TPAT programs implemented by US Customs and Border Protection in close cooperation with Mexico and Canada.[48] Under NAFTA, such rules[49] have been adopted, along with the elimination of tariffs and non-tariff barriers on all originating goods.[50] All manufactured goods have traded duty free since January 1, 2008 (and most well before that date), whereas in the past many of them were subject to each party's MFN tariffs, currently averaging approximately 3.5 percent for the United States, 4.2 percent for Canada and 7.5 percent applied rate for Mexico (over 30 percent for bound tariffs).[51] However, such trade is subject to border inspection, even where such inspections are streamlined through the use of the latest technology.

This situation is in direct contrast to current trade relations between the European Union and the United Kingdom, with duty-free, tariff-free trade, without ROO and with free physical movement of goods within the Single Market. This will most likely be replaced with a trade relationship that requires ROO and border inspections of many or most shipments, even if those border requirements can be reduced by innovative electronic mechanisms agreed by the European Union and the United Kingdom, and by UK adoption of EU product standards for exports to the European Union.

Under NAFTA article 401, goods are considered to possess NAFTA origin in four ways:

- goods wholly obtained or produced in the NAFTA region;

- goods produced in the NAFTA region wholly from originating materials;

- goods meeting the Annex 401 origin rules; and

- unassembled goods and goods classified with their parts that do not meet Annex 401 ROO but that contain 60 percent regional value content using the transaction method, or 50 percent regional value using the net cost method.

---

47 See Melina Kolb & Cathleen Cimino-Isaacs, "A Guide to Renegotiating NAFTA" (19 June 2017), online: Peterson Institute for International Economics <https://piie.com/blogs/trade-investment-policy-watch/guide-renegotiating-nafta> (providing statistics on trade volumes, employment and other factors).

48 FAST, *supra* note 22.

49 See *NAFTA, supra* note 19, c 4–5, especially art 401.

50 *Ibid*, art 302, Annex 302.

51 See Mary Amiti & Carolyn Freund, "US Exporters Could Face High Tariffs without NAFTA" (18 April 2017), online: Peterson Institute for International Economics <https://piie.com/blogs/trade-investment-policy-watch/us-exporters-could-face-high-tariffs-without-nafta> (reporting that Mexican WTO-bound tariff rates average 35 percent, with applied rates averaging 7.4 percent compared to the US average of 3.7 percent).

Typically, the rules provide either for a change in tariff heading from a harmonized tariff system (HTS)[52] category applicable to parts and components to one applicable to the finished product, or to regional value content (usually but not always 60 percent using the "top-down" transaction value method, or 50 percent using the "bottom up" net cost method).[53] However, the only means to determine reliably the actual ROO applicable to each of the more than 6,000 individual goods listed in the HTS is to consult the voluminous NAFTA Annex 401, because the actual ROO vary considerably.

These calculations, usually focusing on the value of the non-originating goods that are part of the value of the product (for example, non-originating goods may be no more than 40 percent of the transaction value of the good), are complicated by the fact that component prices may vary from time to time because of cost increases or decreases and exchange rate fluctuations. In the euro zone, this problem is minimized, but in trade among the EU member countries, the exchange rates between the euro, other EU currencies such as the Czech crown and the British pound sterling will in some circumstances complicate ROO calculations, in particular where the aggregate originating parts and components are just above or just below the regional value content requirement, whether 50 percent, 60 percent, 62.5 percent (as in NAFTA for autos) or some other benchmark.

The enforcement of the ROO is governed in detail in Chapter 5 of NAFTA, including certificate of origin requirements; entry declarations based on the certificate of origin; the exporter's obligations relating to preparation of certificates of origin; retention of records relating to origin; and verification procedures for confirming that certificates of origin justifying duty-free importation are accurate.[54] Each party is also required to provide advance rulings to exporters and importers as to whether a particular good will meet NAFTA ROO requirements for duty-free trade.[55] It is also significant that at the time of its negotiation (1994), NAFTA provided that "the Parties shall establish, and implement through their respective laws or regulations by January 1, 1994, Uniform Regulations regarding the interpretation, application and administration of Chapter Four, this Chapter and other matters as may be agreed by the Parties."[56]

This system is similar in many respects to that incorporated into CETA,[57] which is said to follow standard EU product-specific origin rules, except for autos, textiles, fish and some agricultural products[58] Such product sectors are also subject to special treatment under NAFTA.[59] In contrast to NAFTA's regional value content calculations, CETA substitutes the concept of "sufficient production" occurring in the country alleging origin, but conceptually

---

52 World Customs Organization, "HS Convention", online: <www.wcoomd.org/en/topics/nomenclature/instrument-and-tools/hs_convention.aspx>. The harmonized system (HS) provides a uniform product classification system used by almost all the world's trading nations, including the 164 members of the WTO.

53 *NAFTA, supra* note 19, art 401; see also United States International Trade Commission, "Rules of Origin–Basic Principles", online: <www.usitc.gov/elearning/hts/media/2017/RulesofOrigina.pdf>.

54 *NAFTA, supra* note 51, arts 501, 502, 504, 505, 506.

55 *Ibid,* art 509.

56 *Ibid,* art 511.

57 Global Affairs Canada, "Protocol on rules of origin and origin procedures", online: <www.international.gc.ca/trade-commerce/assets/pdfs/ceta-rm-04-eng.pdf>.

58 European Commission, "CETA–Summary of the final negotiating results" at 6–7, online: <https://trade.ec.europa.eu/doclib/docs/2014/december/tradoc_152982.pdf>.

59 See e.g. *NAFTA, supra* note 19, Annexes 300-A (autos), 300-B (textiles and clothing).

the approaches seem similar, and both are subject to product-by-product ROO as the basis for actual determinations.[60]

NAFTA experience indicates that trade that is subject to the requirements of ROO can be managed economically, particularly for the major manufacturers that can systematically complete the required analyses and documentation, qualify for FAST and C-TPAT and have funds available for retaining customs lawyers and consultants, a process that adds an estimated two to three percent to landed product costs. One study alleges that NAFTA zero-tariff benefits for Mexico have been largely offset by the costs of complying with the NAFTA ROO.[61] With the average US MFN tariffs only three to four percent *ad valorem*, this conclusion does not seem unreasonable, even if a hybrid program, such as what the FCA paper advocates, might reduce these costs somewhat through self-calculation of customs duties by the exporter, as is the case in the United States, as well as greater automation and better use of data, but with a more extensive mechanism to enforce anti-circumvention rules.[62]

Still, where preferences are sought and ROO must be complied with, these costs will be passed on to customers, or where competition precludes this, will reduce profitability or even force producers to close. The burdens of ROO are most significant for SMEs, which often lack the resources for expert lawyers and consultants, and for start-up firms that are not subject to FAST and C-TPAT (or their UK equivalent, if available). In both situations, the additional costs of exporting resulting from ROO compliance may discourage such enterprises from exporting.[63] Experience under NAFTA also suggests that where US tariffs are under three percent or so, small importers are likely to forego duty-free treatment because the costs of complying are greater than the benefits of the tariff reductions.[64]

The demands of annually producing certificates of origin (legally required under NAFTA by the manufacturer[65]), and the various other documentation demanded for international trade transactions for presentation at the border crossing or retention by the importer, along with the record-keeping costs, may also contribute to border delays under NAFTA for people and goods. These have generally been avoided in the European Union under the Single Market rules (goods) and the Schengen Agreement (people),[66] whereby borders have been abolished (although not fully for the United Kingdom and Ireland), avoiding a significant cost and inconvenience for traders. Preserving this openness as much as possible is the objective of the FCA hybrid approach, but as discussed throughout this chapter, anything approaching the status quo will be very difficult to achieve. Of course, additional challenges exist and have caused delays on the US-Mexico border, including illegal immigration and drug trade, along with inadequate staffing

---

60 Global Affairs Canada, *supra* note 57, Annex 5.

61 Olivier Cadot et al, "Assessing the Effect of NAFTA's Rules of Origin" (June 2002) at 20, online: <http://web.worldbank.org/archive/website00955A/WEB/PDF/CADOT_RU.PDF>.

62 FCA, *supra* note 3 at 9–10, paras 35, 41.

63 See Caroline Freund, "Streamlining Rules of Origin in NAFTA" in C Fred Bergsten & Monica de Bolle, eds, *A Path Forward for NAFTA*, online: Peterson Institute for International Economics <https://piie.com/publications/piie-briefings/path-forward-nafta> at 113, 119.

64 Cadot et al, *supra* note 61 at 2. Inaccurate claims for duty-free treatment could subject the importer of record after audit to payment of the additional duties, interest on the duties since the time of original importation, and negligence or more severe penalties for failing to submit accurate entry documentation. See 19 USC § 1592.

65 *NAFTA*, *supra* note 19, art 501.

66 See EUR-Lex, "The Schengen Area and Cooperation", online: <http://eur-lex.europa.eu/legal-content/EN/TXT/?uri=URISERV%3Al33020>.

of customs ports of entry.[67] Since the 9/11 attacks, terrorism concerns have further delayed border crossings, not only between Mexico and the United States, but between the United States and Canada as well.[68]

It may be hoped that the future UK-EU trade arrangements could avoid some of the excesses of NAFTA ROO, which cover more than 150 pages of text.[69] As noted earlier, complex rules impose a disproportionate burden on SME exporters and importers, who may be encouraged to forego the benefits of duty-free trade — benefits that they currently enjoy while the United Kingdom is a member of the European Union — with the likely results of lower volumes of exports and imports and reduced employment. It may be that the more modern CETA rules can be adapted to UK-EU trade under an FTA. However, the fact that the CETA rules protocol comprises 229 pages, including the product-specific Annex 5, is an indication of the additional complications to which trade between the EU27 and the United Kingdom will be subject under an FTA.

Some experts on the NAFTA ROO have urged that in the context of the NAFTA renegotiation, the existing rules be greatly simplified, with the current complex product-by-product rules abandoned in favour of a 40 percent or 50 percent regional value content approach.[70] Incorporating a *de minimis* threshold, whereby low-tariff products do not have to be certified for ROO compliance, would also reduce compliance costs, in particular for SME importers and exporters.[71] It would be productive for both UK and EU traders to simplify ROO where they are required, and to focus efforts to streamline the clearance process with common electronic customs procedures throughout the region. Border congestion is, after all, not solely a product of complex regulations. Transit times can be reduced through maintaining additional customs officials on duty and conducting security inspections electronically, as at the NAFTA member countries' borders.[72] It remains unclear why the US authorities have been reluctant to build and equip border crossings that would further reduce wait times. This objective is primarily a function of personnel and funds.

Most major EU and UK exporters and importers are already coping with ROO in much of their trade with non-EU member states, since such rules are applicable in the majority of FTAs between the European Union and other nations,[73] as they will be under CETA as discussed above. As the European Commission notes, "If you are intending to import under a preferential regime into the EU a product from a beneficiary or partner country, it is not enough that the product is exported from that country. The product needs to be originating in that country.

---

67   See Sandra Dibble, "For regular crossers of the U.S.-Mexico border, waiting is part of the routine", *Los Angeles Times* (16 July 2016), online: <www.latimes.com/local/lanow/la-me-border-wait-20160714-snap-story.html> (reporting on border delays and a needed expansion of the San Ysidro crossing to be completed in 2019).

68   *Ibid*. Dibble writes, "since its creation in 2003 under the Department of Homeland Security, the agency's No. 1 task has been securing the U.S. border from potential terrorists."

69   See United States International Trade Commission, "Harmonized Tariff Schedule" (2017), online: <https://hts.usitc.gov/current> (incorporating NAFTA and other FTA ROO).

70   See Freund, *supra* note 63 at 123 (suggesting desired improvements in the current NAFTA rules).

71   *Ibid*.

72   See FAST, *supra* note 22.

73   See European Commission, "Rules of Origin," *Export Helpdesk*, online: <http://exporthelp.europa.eu/thdapp/display.htm?page=cd/cd_RulesOfOrigin.html&docType=main&languageId=EN>.

The rules of origin will tell you if indeed your product may be considered originating in that concrete country and therefore receive the preference."[74]

Thus, many traders in the other EU countries and the United Kingdom already have some, perhaps considerable, experience in meeting ROO requirements, even if currently those rules are not applicable to the largest volume of their trade, i.e., UK trade with the European Union. The problem may be one of magnitude, rather than meeting new and different legal concepts, and UK exporters that sell entirely in other EU member nations will not have dealt with ROO in the past. As well, these skills should be relatively easy to adapt to any new and streamlined procedures that arise from UK-EU negotiations.

A Key Example: The Automotive Industry

The automotive industry (finished vehicles and parts) is the single most important manufacturing industry in North America, accounting for an estimated 25 percent of total merchandise trade within NAFTA.[75] The large volume is partially explained by the fact that major parts and sub-assemblies may cross a national border as many as eight times before they are finally assembled into a finished automobile.[76] As well, automobiles produced in Mexico typically incorporate a US value content of about 40 percent.[77]

In the United Kingdom, the automotive industry and automotive trade are also economically significant, with an estimated 77 percent of the vehicles produced in the United Kingdom exported, and a net positive trade balance (exports over imports) of £70 million, with at least 33 vehicle and engine manufacturing facilities located in the United Kingdom.[78] In 2013, Nissan produced more than 500,000 cars in its Sutherland plant, of which 71 percent were exported to Europe (including Russia).[79] UK automakers directly source about 35 percent of components from the European Union, not counting the parts suppliers' sourcing,[80] but may seek to obtain more parts at home after Brexit,[81] in particular if components from the other EU members do not enter the United Kingdom duty free.

In both jurisdictions, trade in autos and auto parts is integrated, with well-established supply chains that typically permit some version of "just in time" manufacturing, despite border delays in North America. NAFTA replaced a situation whereby, in 1994, almost all auto and auto parts trade was already duty free between the United States and Canada under the 1965 United

---

74 *Ibid.*

75 United States Census Bureau, "U.S. Trade in Motor Vehicles and Parts by Selected Countries", (2016), online: <www.census.gov/foreign-trade/Press-Release/2016pr/12/exh18.pdf> (showing total motor vehicle trade between Canada and the United States, and Mexico and the United States at approximately US$263 billion).

76 Center for Automotive Research, "NAFTA Briefing: Trade benefits to the automotive industry and potential consequences of withdrawal from the agreement" (January 2017), online: <www.cargroup.org/wp-content/uploads/2017/01/nafta_briefing_january_2017_public_version-final.pdf>.

77 *Ibid* at 7–8.

78 KPMG, "The UK Automotive Industry and the EU" (April 2014), online: <www.smmt.co.uk/wp-content/uploads/sites/2/SMMT-KPMG-EU-Report.pdf> at 1 (2013 data).

79 *Ibid* at 5.

80 *Ibid* at 6.

81 See Peter Campbell & Michael Pooler, "Brexit triggers a great car parts race for UK auto industry", *Financial Times* (30 July 2017), online: <www.ft.com/content/b56d0936-6ae0-11e7-bfeb-33fe0c5b7eaa>.

States-Canada Automotive Products Agreement,[82] but was minimal between Canada and the United States with Mexico, because of Mexico's prohibitively high tariffs; the current five to six percent applied Mexican MFN tariff is relatively recent. (Canada's MFN duties on autos are 6.1 percent.)

NAFTA achieved growth in its auto and auto parts industry in significant part through strict ROO, where duty-free trade in finished autos occurs only when the North American (regional value) content is 62.5 percent, based on calculations relating to the net cost of the vehicle. Parts and components of major assemblies such as engines and transmissions are subject to further tracing with respect to sub-assembly origin.[83] These rules have strongly encouraged the sourcing of parts and components within North America, as noted above, even when they are available at lower cost elsewhere, to meet the 62.5 percent regional value content rule, as well as to facilitate shorter supply chains than those that are possible with more extensive reliance on Asian sources. However, studies have shown that because of generally low tariffs for US imports of components for transportation equipment, an estimated 23 percent of such trade is conducted under US MFN tariffs rather than NAFTA preferential tariffs,[84] presumably because the benefits from duty-free treatment under NAFTA are more than offset by the administrative costs of ROO compliance.

A UK-EU FTA would likely provide for duty-free, quota-free trade in autos and auto parts, based on an ROO that requires a significant percentage of total vehicle value to be regional (UK plus EU origin), even if the costs of complying with ROO are added. Otherwise, UK-EU trade in autos would be subject to the current prohibitive 10 percent *ad valorem* duty (approximately 4.5 percent for components).[85] The precise regional content would have to be agreed upon; in CETA, 50 percent regional content (increasing to 55 percent after seven years) is the established rule,[86] which could provide some guidance for a UK-EU negotiation. A more stringent ROO, such as the NAFTA 62.5 percent standard, would not likely be favoured by auto manufacturers in either the EU27 or the United Kingdom. It seems reasonable to assume that the negotiations would aim for preservation of the existing regional content of autos traded within the European Union as resulting from current MFN tariffs, so that autos assembled in the United Kingdom for export to the European Union would not be able to rely more extensively on less expensive Asian parts than has been the case pre-Brexit.

Clearly, the best solution, if the parties can agree, would be to maintain the equivalent of a CU between the other EU members and the United Kingdom for auto and auto component trade, even if it means that the United Kingdom will continue to be governed by EU standards and CJEU jurisdiction in that sector (and even if other sectors are subject to traditional FTA ROO). It may be that even if the hybrid approach is unacceptable for all originating trade between the EU27 and the United Kingdom, the mutual interest in the European auto and auto parts

---

82 *United States–Canada Automotive Products Agreement*, 16 January 1965, HR 6960 at 34, online: <www.stewartlaw.com/Content/Documents/HR%20-%20United%20States-Canada%20Automotive%20Products%20Agreement.pdf>.

83 *NAFTA, supra* note 19, Annex 300-A.

84 Freund, *supra* note 63 at 121.

85 Campbell & Pooler, *supra* note 81 at 1.

86 See Livingston, "A Closer Look at CETA, Part 2: Automotive Sector to Feel CETA's Impact", online: <www.livingstonintl.com/our-experts-speak/closer-look-ceta-part-2-automotive-sector-feel-cetas-impact/> (discussing the operation of automotive ROO in CETA).

sector would make special CU treatment of this sector politically acceptable and worth the complexities of dealing with potential circumvention problems.

Whether the status quo in the sector would be supported by central European auto producing members such as the Czech Republic, Hungary, Poland and Slovakia (where a new Jaguar/Land Rover plant is expected to open in Bratislava in 2018) is uncertain. Their governments may welcome any new trading relationship with the United Kingdom that makes it more expensive for multinational auto companies to produce in and export from the United Kingdom, as such restrictions (along with the lower wages in Eastern Europe) could encourage transfer of manufacturing facilities from the United Kingdom to Central Europe.[87]

Commentary, Conclusions and Recommendations

The Most Probable Option: A UK-EU FTA

For the reasons discussed earlier, unless there is a major shift in UK negotiating objectives toward more concern for preserving businesses and away from immigration control and greater sovereignty that independence from the CJEU would bring, regardless of cost, neither the Norway/EEA approach nor a CU is feasible under these circumstances. Thus, the only remaining option for a future permanent UK-EU trading relationship is an FTA. An FTA would provide a continuation of duty-free, quota-free trade in almost all manufactured goods that are considered to originate in the European Union or the United Kingdom, but with the additional requirements (compared to the Single Market) of an FTA, including ROO, customs declarations and other border controls, even if some streamlining of border procedures is achievable as advocated in the FCA paper.[88]

The concept of future customs arrangements combining a new CU for EU-UK trade and an FTA for UK trade with third countries is, on the surface, very attractive, but implementation in such a manner as to avoid border controls and circumvention seems highly problematic. The extent of damage an FTA would do to trade in goods compared to current UK membership in the Single Market and CU depends on the terms, in particular the agreed ROO and documentary requirements, and the extent to which the United Kingdom and European Union can agree on adequate border inspection facilities, and a very high level of automation, maintenance of common product standards through equivalency and day-to-day cooperation.

Even a favourable agreement would entail considerable costs compared to current trade within the Single Market and the CU. As discussed earlier, unless the EU CU is extended indefinitely, goods will be required to demonstrate that the traded goods meet the applicable ROO, with accompanying costs of analysis and document production, as has been the case for intra-NAFTA trade since 1994. These requirements would be accompanied by rules and regulations to enforce and monitor compliance, including border inspections upon entry of goods and periodic audits

---

87 See Neil Buckley, "Opportunities and risks for investors in central and east Europe", *Financial Times* (7 May 2017) at 4, 7-9, online: <www.ft.com/content/4248a712-07da-11e7-ac5a-903b21361b43> (reviewing the attractiveness of Eastern European EU members for investment, in particular in the auto industry).

88 FCA, *supra* note 3 at 7, para 27.

by the various customs services.[89] These burdens are probably similar to those that are currently applicable for goods entering from countries that are parties to FTAs with the European Union.

Such rules are manageable, and both governments and businesses that trade outside the European Union are familiar with them; the difference is that they would apply to virtually all trade between the EU27 and the United Kingdom, while at present they apply to almost none of it. Since approximately 44 percent of the United Kingdom's trade is with the EU nations, and eight to 18 percent of the European Union's trade is with the United Kingdom,[90] the added administrative burdens, no doubt amounting to billions of euros and pounds sterling in the aggregate, would be mostly passed on to consumers in both jurisdictions.

The significance of the additional costs will likely vary considerably among sectors and enterprises. Yet, it is reasonable to assume that some enterprises will either decide it is no longer feasible to produce goods for the EU market in the United Kingdom (and move some of their operations to EU member countries or forego such trade completely), or cease operations. The scope of such changes cannot be predicted now. It will likely take at least several years after the new trading relationships are in place to gauge the impact of the shift from Single Market/CU to FTA, but in some sectors, such as autos, it will be anything but negligible.

Benefits and Costs of Remaining in the CU

Even though it was rejected again by Theresa May in her Florence speech,[91] the possibility exists that during the initial two years of divorce negotiations, where the future trade relationship will also be on the table, UK officials will decide — perhaps under strong pressure from members of Parliament and an energized business lobby — that the adverse economic impact on enterprises and workers is simply too much to bear.[92] (Some EU members, in particular those who trade extensively with the United Kingdom, such as Germany, Spain, Belgium, the Netherlands and Ireland,[93] may well agree.) The FCA is clearly the first formal recognition by the UK government of the magnitude of the problem that would be created by UK withdrawal from the EU CU, even if the hybrid system proposed may not be acceptable to the European Union, and in any event, might not significantly reduce the additional costs of UK-EU trade.

Should the European Union reject the FCA proposals, or should both parties decide that they are unworkable, UK participation in the EU CU (but not the Single Market) is likely to be reconsidered, even though the FCA paper asserts, "As we leave the EU we will also leave the EU Customs Union."[94] CU participation (probably along the lines of the EU-Turkey Customs Union[95]) would have the advantages of *not* requiring the United Kingdom to accept the European Union's four freedoms (including freedom of intra-regional immigration) or the full jurisdiction

---

89 See *NAFTA, supra* note 19, arts 505 (record keeping), 506 (origin verifications).

90 Full Fact, "Everything you might want to know about the UK's trade with the EU" (15 August 2017), online: <https://fullfact. org/europe/uk-eu-trade/>.

91 May, *supra* note 4.

92 See Giles & Barker, *supra* note 27 at 4–14 (setting out the various hard and soft Brexit choices, from the most to the least disruptive).

93 Full Fact, *supra* note 90.

94 FCA, *supra* note 3 at 6, para 22.

95 *Agreement establishing an Association between the European Economic Community and Turkey*, 12 September 1963, No L 361/29 (entered into force 1 December 1964), online: <http://eur-lex.europa.eu/resource.html?uri=cellar:f8e2f9f4-75c8-4f62-ae3f-b86ca5842eee.0008.02/DOC_2&format=PDF>.

of the CJEU, and would greatly facilitate limited document export and import transactions. Issues of continued major financial contributions to the European Union, and continued operation under EU regulations and directives (including those relating to product standards) would have to be negotiated in a context where it is increasingly obvious that the failure of UK laws to mirror EU legislation could jeopardize some trade. For the United Kingdom, the only major downside to maintaining membership in the EU CU would be the inability of the United Kingdom to attempt to conclude bilateral FTAs with third countries in the future.

Politically, the legal authority of the United Kingdom to conclude separate FTAs is considered significant. Liam Fox would be principally responsible for negotiating such agreements; he would be out of a job if the future UK-EU relationship is a CU rather than an FTA. Providing Fox with a different portfolio would seem a much better solution than insisting on a 10- to 20-year odyssey of negotiating bilateral FTAs with dozens of countries. Still, while such negotiations could not formally begin until Brexit is complete, it appears that Fox has informally discussed a future FTA with US officials and perhaps others as well.[96] The next subsection assesses the practical benefits (or lack thereof) of such third-party FTAs.

Negotiation of New FTAs with Current EU Partners and with the United States

If the result of the UK-EU negotiations is a permanent FTA, or a hybrid agreement that leaves the United Kingdom free to negotiate FTAs governing trade between itself and other countries, the United Kingdom will be required, on an urgent basis, to negotiate FTAs with the more than 50 countries that have current agreements with the European Union. Until those agreements can be concluded, MFN tariffs will be applicable to British exports in place of the lower or zero tariffs applicable under EU FTAs, putting British exporters at a significant disadvantage, given that MFN tariffs applied by developing nations are generally higher than those among developed nations.[97]

Still, much attention has focused instead on a new agreement with the United States.[98] Politically, there are incentives on both sides to move quickly. May and Fox both seem eager to demonstrate that the United Kingdom, after detachment from the European Union, can successfully chart its own international economic policy through FTAs. In the United States, President Donald Trump is strongly committed to bilateral rather than multilateral FTAs, and "better" ones that are more beneficial to US interests.[99] After more than two centuries, the close British-US political, cultural and historical relationship remains almost sacred for many American and British citizens. However, while no one in the United States reasonably fears that a US-UK FTA would result in a significant shift of jobs, there are still many in both jurisdictions who resist all new trade liberalization.

---

96 See Darren Hunt, "Liam Fox laughs off allegations he's 'breaking the law' discussing future trade in the US", *Express* (20 June 2017), online: <www.express.co.uk/news/uk/818916/Brexit-latest-news-Liam-Fox-future-trade-US-Donald-Trump-European-Union-David-Davis> (where Fox defends his informal discussions).

97 The WTO reports that average tariffs applied by developing countries are approximately nine percent, while developed countries' applied tariffs average less than five percent. Developing country-bound tariffs average more than 40 percent. See WTO, "Trade and Tariffs: Trade Grows as Tariffs Decline" (2015), online: <www.wto.org/english/thewto_e/20y_e/wto_20_brochure_e.pdf>.

98 Hunt, *supra* note 96.

99 Don Lee, "Trump wants to cut bilateral trade deals, but what if nobody comes to the table?", *Los Angeles Times* (26 May 2017), online: <www.latimes.com/business/la-fi-trump-trade-strategy-20170526-story.html> (discussing the president's preference for bilateral agreements because he believes the United States has greater bargaining leverage).

As an example of the complexities of such negotiations, Fox appears to have been blindsided on his visit to Washington in July 2017. There, the principal topic of discussion was whether the United Kingdom, under an FTA with the United States, would be prepared to accept US chicken that had been subjected to a chlorinated wash process, currently banned by the European Union. While Fox suggested that the United Kingdom would be open to the prospect of allowing the entry of such chicken, Secretary of State for Environment, Food and Rural Affairs Michael Gove quickly dismissed the possibility.[100]

Fox and others who are strongly interested in the prospects of a future US-UK FTA should be paying close attention to the NAFTA renegotiation that began in August. It may provide signals as to what a Trump administration is seeking with regard to restricting current and future US investment in Mexico and, in particular, treatment of automotive trade within North America. As well, many suspect that US negotiators will try to expand already strong opportunities for US agricultural trade with Mexico (which is already relatively open) and Canada (which is restricted in such sectors as dairy and wheat), as well as different rules on sanitary and phytosanitary measures.[101] Similar efforts should be expected in a future US-UK FTA negotiation.

Unrelated factors could also complicate the possibility of early negotiations. Potential political complications exist for May in establishing closer US-UK relations, given concerns regarding US policies that are considered to weaken NATO[102] and the Trump administration's rejection of the Paris Agreement on climate change,[103] as well as the president's general unpopularity in the United Kingdom, as evidenced by the indefinite postponement of his state visit.[104]

Such an agreement would require careful legal structuring, as well as political sensitivity in the negotiations, regardless of the professed high level of interest in both the UK and US governments, even though bilateral trade is already substantial under WTO MFN duties (about US$109 billion), with the United States running a slight trade surplus.[105] The agreement probably would not be concluded until after the future UK-EU trade relationship were established, hopefully by the end of the transition period (2022). It would be unwise for the United States, even with the best of intentions, to conclude an FTA until the US government knows the scope of a post-Brexit UK-EU trade relationship, in particular if bilateral trade were to be complicated by aspects of the hybrid system advocated in the FCA paper.

---

100 See Kevin Rawlinson, "US-UK trade deal would not allow chlorinated chicken imports - Gove", *The Guardian* (25 July 2017), online: <www.theguardian.com/politics/2017/jul/26/uk-us-trade-deal-chlorinated-chicken-michael-gove-liam-fox> (noting that the disagreement "overshadowed Fox's trip to America").

101 See draft letter from United States Trade Representative Stephen Vaughn to United States Senate/United States House of Representatives (18 March 2017) at 3, online: KPMG <https://home.kpmg.com/content/dam/kpmg/us/pdf/2017/03/tnf-draft-nafta-letter.pdf> (on NAFTA negotiating objectives for Congress).

102 The president of the United States has equivocated with regard to providing a firm endorsement of the article 5 "attack against one is an attack against all" principle. See Rosie Gray, "Trump Declines to Affirm NATO's Article 5", *The Atlantic* (25 May 2017), online: <www.theatlantic.com/international/archive/2017/05/trump-declines-to-affirm-natos-article-5/528129/> (discussing Trump's continued refusal and the effect on European allies).

103 Michael D Shear, "Trump Will Withdraw U.S. From Paris Agreement", *New York Times* (1 June 2017), online: <www.nytimes.com/2017/06/01/climate/trump-paris-climate-agreement.html?_r=0>.

104 Patrick Wintour, "Trump's state visit to Britain put on hold", *The Guardian* (12 June 2017), online: <www.theguardian.com/us-news/2017/jun/11/donald-trump-state-visit-to-britain-put-on-hold>.

105 United States Census Bureau, "Trade in Goods with United Kingdom" (2016), online: <www.census.gov/foreign-trade/balance/c4120.html>.

A US-UK FTA might not be difficult to negotiate in some areas, given the mutual interest in such a relationship (an interest that likely would continue, regardless of who the US president is by then). Among other factors, the United States and the United Kingdom could:

- dispense with the controversies relating to ISDS, given the strength of both legal systems;

- use Trans-Pacific Partnership Agreement (TPP) language, any agreed provisions from a revised NAFTA, or what Transatlantic Trade and Investment Partnership language is available from those separate negotiations as the starting points on intellectual property, financial and other services, e-commerce, anti-competition, state-owned enterprises, SMEs, and possibly labour and environment; and

- limit immigration to the relatively non-controversial temporary visitors for business and professionals.

Areas of potential difficulty nevertheless exist. These include:

- Automotive trade, given the Trump administration's attacks on auto imports from Canada, Mexico, Korea, Japan and Germany,[106] even though auto trade has not been a large portion of bilateral US-UK trade in the past. Only 14.5 percent of UK auto exports are to the United States, despite the United States' MFN duty of only 2.5 percent, in contrast to 46 percent currently exported to the European Union duty free.[107] One can also speculate that even if the United States were reluctant to reduce its 2.5 percent MFN duty on autos except over an extended period of time, as with Japan in the TPP,[108] the United States would demand substantial reduction or elimination of the current EU-UK 10 percent tariff on imported autos and 4.5 percent on auto parts for exports to the United Kingdom.

- Agriculture, where US farmers (following whatever success or failure they achieve in a new NAFTA) will demand improved access to the British agricultural markets than is currently the case. This will be a sensitive issue for British farmers, who by then may have lost some or most of their generous EU subsidies, and the United States would likely seek UK acquiescence to imports of beef raised with hormones and products containing genetically modified organisms (GMOs), both long banned or heavily restricted under EU rules, along with chlorine-washed chicken.[109]

- The need to assure that any discussion of climate change initiatives be indirect, making it difficult to deal with environmental issues in the FTA, even though they are important to both national constituencies.

---

106 See e.g. Karen Gilchrist, "Trump reportedly calls Germans 'very bad,' threatens to end German car sales", CNBC (26 May 2017), online: <www.cnbc.com/2017/05/26/trump-calls-germans-very-bad-threatens-to-end-german-car-sales-reports.html> (detailing threats to block exports to the United States).

107 SMMT, *supra* note 10 at 3.

108 Under Chapter 3 of the TPP, Japanese autos would have entered the United States totally free of the United States' 2.5 percent MFN import duty only after 25 years.

109 See European Commission, "GMO legislation", online: <https://ec.europa.eu/food/plant/gmo/legislation_en> (discussing EU restrictions on GMOs); European Commission, "Hormones in Meat", online: <https://ec.europa.eu/food/safety/chemical_safety/meat_hormones_en> (discussing the EU prohibition on imports of meat raised with hormones). A three-month stay in Cambridge during the fall 2014 term convinced the author that British consumer reluctance to purchase GMO products or hormone-fed beef is as strong in the United Kingdom as in other EU nations.

- The ever-present ROO, which would not necessarily be the same as those applicable to UK-EU trade in an FTA or to EU-Canada trade under CETA.

Many other FTA options are feasible with sufficient time for complex negotiations and proper UK government staffing, but whether the long-term future potential of such agreements outweighs the considerable costs of insisting on an FTA with the European Union, rather than maintaining membership in the CU, is a decision the British government should carefully consider.

Conclusion

The UK government's choices for a permanent trade relationship with the remaining EU members range from the very adverse (reversion to WTO rules), to the less damaging (an FTA), to the more favourable but much less realistic (a hybrid system), to the even less politically likely (remain in the EU CU). Any closer relationship than a CU is impossible to achieve without a major change in UK policy, such as the willingness to agree to open EU immigration, EU rules on product standards (direct or through "equivalence") and the continued jurisdiction of the CJEU on a permanent basis. Given the constraints, NAFTA's approach to customs regulations and ROO in that FTA could provide useful lessons for the UK-EU negotiations. Still, given the continuing disarray of the UK government over Brexit policy, the possibility of major policy shifts may not be as far-fetched in October 2017 as they would have seemed prior to May's political weakening in June.[110]

---

110 See George Parker & Alex Barker, "UK government concedes transitional role for ECJ after Brexit", *Financial Times* (10 July 2017), online: <www.ft.com/content/815f56e4-655e-11e7-8526-7b38dcaef614>.

4

Trade Policy in the Age of Populism: Why the New Bilateralism Will Not Work

Thomas Cottier

Introduction: The New Bilateralism

In the wake of the Brexit vote of June 2016, the UK government announced its new trade policy in October 2017.[1] The new policy is based on the rules of the World Trade Organization (WTO), plurilateral agreements and a wide and new network of self-standing bilateral preferential agreements.[2] Upon leaving the European Union, the United Kingdom plans to enter into preferential agreements with its main trading partners, next to a comprehensive bilateral agreement with the European Union. About 100 agreements would be needed to replace the existing framework under the common commercial policy of the European Union.[3] Plans for a bilateral agreement with the United States (much welcomed by the new president), India (met

---

1   UK, Department for International Trade, "Preparing for our future UK trade policy" (9 October 2017), online: <www.gov. uk/government/publications/preparing-for-our-future-uk-trade-policy>.

2   *Ibid* at 29; see also "The six flavours of Brexit", *The Economist* (22 July 2017) at 25–27.

3   See Emily Lydgate, Jim Rollo & Rorden Wilkinson, "The UK Trade Landscape after Brexit" (2016) UK Trade Policy Observatory Briefing Paper 2, online: <http://blogs.sussex.ac.uk/uktpo/files/2017/01/Briefing-paper-2.pdf>.

with low interest and claims of labour market access), Australia, Canada, New Zealand and others (met with indifference), and Switzerland (met with interest) *inter alia* are contemplated. Rather than relying upon close integration within the European Union (which absorbs more than 44 percent of the United Kingdom's current international trade) and the European Union's global and growing network of currently 35 preferential trade agreements (PTAs), a vision to reassume an independent and leading role in trade policy carries the day in British politics.

While WTO membership and plurilateral agreements offer continuity, the plan to negotiate new bilateral agreements amounts to new territory for Britain in the twenty-first century. Other than the bilateral agreements concluded by Britain as a member of the European Union, the new generation of agreements no longer carry the weight of the largest global market. The plan exposes the United Kingdom to countries of diverging interests and different sizes and powers — some larger, some comparable and some smaller. It opens what may be called an era of new bilateralism.

With its foundations in WTO law, the new bilateralism of the United Kingdom does not entail a departure from traditional interests to preserve and foster free trade. It merely became a necessity due to the United Kingdom's leaving the EU common commercial policy and the need to find a replacement for the European Union's global relations. Trade policy has not been a main driver of Brexit. Rather, the challenge emerged after the vote. Brexit was mainly fuelled and motivated by issues of migration. But great hopes, on the one hand, were eventually created by hard-liners that the new bilateralism would be able to create jobs, mainly in the north of England, after long years of neo-liberal austerity. Critics and champions of a soft Brexit with close ties to the common market, on the other hand, argue in favour of staying in a Customs Union with the European Union and, thus, to continue to benefit from the common commercial policy. The issue has remained unresolved as of today. A resolution will depend strongly upon the terms of the divorce agreement.

The United Kingdom's trade policy is significantly different from that of the United States. While Donald Trump's presidency, inaugurated in January 2017, is equally built upon fears of migration, trade policy was — unlike in the United Kingdom — at the heart of the presidential campaign. It was motivated from the outset by fears of open markets and free trade, nurturing the promise and hope to bring industrial jobs back to the heartlands and rustbelts of the United States by abdicating plurilateral trade agreements, and possibly even the WTO. The multilateral system of the WTO and existing trade agreements are considered detrimental to US interests and are depicted as bad and unfair deals. The imbalance of trade in goods is deplored, without taking into account trade in services and the functions of the US dollar as the main currency in commodities. Remedying long-standing trade imbalances in industrial goods is at the centre of what the administration terms fair trade. The announced agenda places border taxes at its heart.[4] It departs from the traditional leadership and support for multilateralism and a rules-based system.

---

4   See e.g. "Trump reiterates border tax pledge in first post-election press conference", *Inside US Trade's World Trade Online* (13 January 2017), online: <https://insidetrade.com/inside-us-trade/trump-reiterates-border-tax-pledge-first-post-election-press-conference>.

The Trump administration immediately abandoned the recently negotiated Trans-Pacific Partnership Agreement[5] (TPP) with 10 Pacific countries.[6] Instead, it seeks new bilateral negotiations, mainly with Japan.[7] The administration first announced its intention to withdraw from and, then, to renegotiate the North American Free Trade Agreement[8] (NAFTA) with Canada and Mexico. Talks risk failing due to excessive demands being made, which would disturb regional value chains, in particular in the automotive sector. The fate of NAFTA remains unclear at this time. Work on the Transatlantic Trade and Investment Partnership (TTIP)[9] with the European Union has been suspended, and it remains unclear whether these negotiations will resume under this administration.[10] Instead, a new generation of bilateral agreements, including with Great Britain, following Brexit is contemplated.

The motives behind the new bilateralism in the United States seek to address and remedy the effects of allegedly unfettered globalization under the neo-liberal premises that successfully prevailed since the inception of the Uruguay Round of the General Agreement on Tariffs and Trade (GATT)[11] in 1986. The effort is essentially driven by job relocation and a long-standing trade deficit, in particular with China. The effort is based upon the idea of balanced trade in goods and should replace the existing framework in place.

In conclusion, it is important to note that the new bilateralism in the United Kingdom and United States significantly differ in foundations and motivations. While the United Kingdom continues to rely strongly upon the multilateral system of the WTO, the United States relies more strongly upon domestic trade policy and bilateral fair trade agreements. Yet, both seek a new generation of bilateralism, comparable to its inception in the Cobden-Chevalier agreement in the nineteenth century and the reciprocal trade agreements of the United States, established in the period from 1934 to 1942. These reciprocal agreements eventually formed the basis for the *Pax Americana*, which brought about twentieth-century multilateralism with the United Nations, the World Bank, the International Monetary Fund (IMF) and the GATT. GATT 1947[12] substituted for the failed Havana Charter and the Multilateral Trade Organization at the time.[13]

---

5   *Trans-Pacific Partnership Agreement*, 4 February 2016, online: Global Affairs Canada <www.international.gc.ca/trade-agreements-accords-commerciaux/agr-acc/tpp-ptp/text-texte/toc-tdm.aspx?lang=eng>.

6   "Trump directs USTR to formally withdraw from TPP", *Inside US Trade's World Trade Online* (23 January 2017), online: <https://insidetrade.com/content/trump-directs-ustr-formally-withdraw-tpp>.

7   "Report: Trump seeks early opportunity to talk with Abe about a bilateral deal", *Inside US Trade's World Trade Online* (27 January 2017), online: <https://insidetrade.com/trade/report-trump-seeks-early-opportunity-talk-abe-about-bilateral-deal>.

8   *North American Free Trade Agreement Between the Government of Canada, the Government of Mexico and the Government of the United States*, 17 December 1992, Can TS 1994 No 2, 32 ILM 289, 605 (entered into force 1 January 1994).

9   *Transatlantic Trade and Investment Partnership* [*TTIP*], online: European Commission <http://ec.europa.eu/trade/policy/in-focus/ttip/>.

10   *Cf* "Pro-trade House members reassure EU businesses of commitment to TTIP", *Inside US Trade's World Trade Online* (29 June 2017), online: <https://insidetrade.com/daily-news/pro-trade-house-members-reassure-eu-businesses-commitment-ttip>.

11   *General Agreement on Tariffs and Trade*, 15 April 1994, 1867 UNTS 187, 33 ILM 1153 (entered into force 1 January 1995).

12   *General Agreement on Tariffs and Trade*, 30 October 1947, 55 UNTS 194, TIAS 1700 (entered into force 1 January 1948).

13   For a historical account, see e.g. Thomas Cottier & Matthias Oesch, *International Trade Regulation: Law and Policy in the WTO, The European Union and Switzerland* (Bern, Switzerland & London, UK: Cameron May & Staempfli, 2005) at 9–32.

It is clear that multilateral trade policy, traditionally led by the United States since the end of World War II and strongly supported by the European Union, including the United Kingdom, in the WTO, is today without US support and leadership. The multilateral system is being undermined. Crucial institutions — in particular the WTO dispute settlement system — are being weakened by the United States, as the US administration seeks to condition the standard appointment of appellate body members to institutional reform and, thus, undermining the operation of a body critical to the rule of law and the work of the WTO as an international organization.[14] At the same time, China, strongly dependent on market access, increasingly assumes a leading role jointly with the European Union, Canada, Australia and other free-trading nations in a growing coalition of the willing and of friends of open trade.

The focus on bilateralism, of course, is not new. Ever since the breakdown of the Soviet Union in 1991, preferential agreements have mushroomed. There are more than 700 such agreements; those notified to the WTO only mark a fraction of the total.[15] While these agreements share the goal of open markets and reciprocally improving market access, many are not fully compatible with WTO rules. Yet, they are all founded upon the operation of the WTO. They complement existing multilateral disciplines, mainly by reducing and eliminating tariffs in goods, adding additional disciplines on intellectual property and government procurement, and introducing new chapters, such as competition law, labour standards and investment protection. With the law of the WTO, they form what this chapter refers to as the common law of international trade.[16] In crucial areas, such as food standards and technical barriers to trade (TBTs), they essentially refer to existing WTO rules. The same holds true for non-trade concerns and general exceptions. The 2017 EU-Canada Comprehensive Economic and Trade Agreement[17] (CETA) is a prominent and recent example in point.[18]

Except for regional integration, the economic impact of many of these existing preferential agreements beyond the effects of WTO rules is questionable for a number of reasons.[19] First, average bound tariffs in the WTO amount to not more than four percent, while PTAs operate on complex rules of origin in order to obtain zero-tariff treatment. The costs of obtaining certification often are higher than relying upon low Most Favoured Nation (MFN) tariffs. Second, these agreements often do not address non-tariff barriers beyond WTO rules, except for a few mutual recognition agreements in place. Third, liberalization and market access in services often do not extend beyond the General Agreement on Trade in Services[20] (GATS) standards. Some of them even limit and reverse existing commitments. Finally, dispute settlement in preferential agreements has remained weak. Countries prefer to use the WTO system.

---

14 "Pressure on U.S. mounts as it maintains link between Appellate Body seats, WTO reform", *Inside US Trade's World Trade Online* (15 September 2017), online: <https://insidetrade.com/daily-news/pressure-us-mounts-it-maintains-link-between-appellate-body-seats-wto-reform>.

15 See "Design of Trade Agreements (DESTA) Database", online: <www.designoftradeagreements.org/>; WTO, "Regional Trade Agreement Information System", online: <http://rtais.wto.org/UI/PublicMaintainRTAHome.aspx>.

16 Thomas Cottier, "The Common Law of International Trade and the Future of the World Trade Organization" (2015) 18 J Intl Econ L 3.

17 *Comprehensive Economic and Trade Agreement between Canada, of the one part, and the European Union [and its Member States...]*, 29 February 2016 [*CETA*], online: <http://trade.ec.europa.eu/doclib/docs/2016/february/tradoc_154329.pdf>.

18 *Ibid*, c XX.

19 *Cf* WTO, *World Trade Report 2011, The WTO and preferential trade agreements: From co-existence to coherence*, online: <www.wto.org/english/res_e/booksp_e/anrep_e/world_trade_report11_e.pdf>.

20 *General Agreement on Trade in Services*, 15 April 1994, 1869 UNTS 183, 33 ILM 1167 (entered into force 1 January 1995).

The new generation of bilateral agreements to be concluded by the United Kingdom upon Brexit is likely to build upon this tradition of preferential trade.[21] It is unclear to what extent this will also be true for the United States. Here, protectionist and mercantilist trade policies may produce substantial deviations from WTO obligations and result in violations of its rules.

The question is whether the new bilateralism in both the United States and the United Kingdom is suitable and able to bring about the results promised in populist campaigning: reclaiming sovereignty and self-determination, lowering immigration and creating new jobs in neglected areas suffering from deindustrialization. Leaving the European Union or dismantling the WTO dispute settlement system would respond to claims to restore sovereignty. Others would be less straightforward. While migration is largely addressed independently of trade, job creation is inherently linked to the structure of international trade. It cannot ignore the growth patterns of division of labour, of global value chains and the focus on non-tariff barriers in current trade rules without risking substantial welfare losses. These risks exist because the new bilateralism ignores basic facts of contemporary trade.

The Facts of International Trade and the Predominance of Regulatory Issues

Contemporary international trade is essentially characterized by trade in components. More than 60 percent of goods cross borders at least twice before reaching final consumers.[22] Complex products identifiable on a purely national basis are increasingly rare. Companies operate in global value chains, and operations are increasingly mixing goods and services in the age of information technology; trade in goods and services can no longer be neatly separated.[23] We speak of "servicification" of goods and their production. Moreover, trade is increasingly entangled with intellectual property, foreign direct investment and a complex web of technical standards relating to products and to modes of production. Trade increasingly depends upon close coordination of the legal rules of different countries trading with each other.

These structures and interdependencies evolved over time and are essential to the process of globalization and the modern division of labour. They are both a cause and a foundation of enhanced global welfare, but also of the accompanying problems and challenges addressed below. The structures are unlikely to return to previous patterns of domestic industrialization, albeit the implications of robotics and three-dimensional printing may cause repatriation and relocation to some extent.

Mercantilist trade policies fail to take these facts into account. The introduction of border measures and quantitative restrictions, advocated by President Trump's administration, will harm consumers, in particular the lower income strata. Such measures will reduce trade in components and will privilege more expensive domestic products, reducing the purchasing

---

21 UK, Department for International Trade, *supra* note 1.

22 In 2009, the total export share of final goods and services amounted to 34 percent (world) and 47 percent (China); Richard Baldwin & Javier Lopez-Gonzales, "Supply-Chain Trade: A Portrait of Global Patterns and Several Testable Hypotheses" (2013) National Bureau of Economic Research WP 18957 at 13, online: <www.nber.org/papers/w18957.pdf>.

23 See Deborah K Elms & Patrick Low, eds, *Global Value Chains in a Changing World* (Geneva, Switzerland: WTO Publications, 2013), online: <www.wto.org/english/res_e/booksp_e/aid4tradeglobalvalue13_e.pdf>.

power of domestic consumers. Border measures, moreover, will affect domestic jobs, as they hurt domestic industries dependent upon the export of incorporated imported components, as much as they harm companies exporting components, disrupting established value chains. Moreover, import restrictions do not take into account the importance and relevance of transnational services in running the supply chains. Restrictions on service providers will further disrupt value chains and modes of production. Mercantilist trade policies may seek to reduce or eliminate global value chains, but they are hardly able to bring back traditional structures and outsourced jobs, as they may impair the creation of new jobs in new industries, as access to competitive labour and components are restricted. Traditional trade policy instruments are largely unable to deliver the results promised in the US electoral and Brexit campaigns.

The challenges are elsewhere. They mainly lie in the field of regulatory cooperation, which is of key importance for growth and job creation, as production is based upon interdependent international markets and products.

Indeed, modern and waterfront trade policy today is mainly concerned with regulatory issues.[24] Except for trade in agriculture, where tariffs continue to play a dominant role, attention has mainly moved to non-tariff barriers, since the GATT Kennedy Round in the 1960s. It culminated in the Agreement on TBTs[25] (TBT agreement), the Agreement on the Application of Sanitary and Phytosanitary Measures[26] (SPS agreement), the inclusion of services (GATS), the Agreement on Trade-Related Aspects of Intellectual Property Rights[27] (TRIPS agreement) and of government procurement in the GATT Uruguay Round. All pillars of the WTO today focus mainly on domestic regulation, rather than on border measures and customs.[28] It should be noted that the importance of product standards for goods and services will increase further in the future. In the context of climate change mitigation and adaptation, production and process methods (PPMs) will take centre stage in distinguishing sustainably produced products from conventional like and substitutable products.[29] Future topics of international trade negotiations will focus on competition law, investment protection and labour standards. They all address what we call behind-the-border issues (BBIs).

BBIs address regulatory barriers inside of jurisdictions, traditionally pertaining to domestic affairs. Politically, they are highly sensitive to concerns of sovereignty and self-determination, the prerogatives of Parliament and the electorate. It is not a coincidence that international efforts to deal with these issues have been under attack by nationalist and populist movements for some time. These efforts impinge upon traditional perceptions of national sovereignty and independence. Modern standards also entail problems of extraterritorial effects to the extent that they address PPMs that leave no traces in the final product. At the same time, removing such barriers is essential for cross-border trade, in particular for small and medium enterprises that do not operate in vertically integrated value chains and private standards.

---

24 See WTO, *World Trade Report 2012, Trade and public policies: A closer look at non-tariff measures in the 21st century*, online: <www.wto.org/english/res_e/booksp_e/anrep_e/world_trade_report12_e.pdf>.

25 WTO, *Agreement on Technical Barriers to Trade*, online: <www.wto.org/english/docs_e/legal_e/17-tbt_e.htm>.

26 WTO, *Agreement on the Application of Sanitary and Phytosanitary Measures*, online: <www.wto.org/english/tratop_e/sps_e/spsagr_e.htm>.

27 *Agreement on Trade-Related Aspects of Intellectual Property Rights*, 15 April 1994, 1869 UNTS 299, 33 ILM 1197 [*TRIPS*].

28 Thomas Cottier, "International Economic Law in Transition from Trade Liberalization to Trade Regulation" (2014) 17 J Intl Econ L 671.

29 See Kateryna Holzer, *Carbon-Related Border Adjustment and WTO Law* (Cheltenham, UK: Edward Elgar, 2014).

The Limits of Bilateralism in Regulatory Affairs and the Impact of Dominant Markets

The WTO offers a robust and solid framework to address domestic regulations that limit market access without sufficient justification. The GATT and the TBT agreement offer legal guidance to discern what is excessive and protectionist from legitimate domestic regulations.[30] But neither of them requires mutual recognition or harmonization of domestic regulation. WTO law, generally, does not engage in prescribing recognition of foreign rules for market approval or in harmonizing domestic legal standards. An exception to this is the TRIPS agreement, which establishes minimum global standards for the protection of intellectual property rights (IPRs). Another exception is the SPS agreement for food standards, which operates in combination with binding World Health Organization/UN Food and Agriculture Organization (WHO/FAO) Codex Alimentarius standards, yet is subject to more restrictive domestic rules.[31] Finally, joint regulations of services in the GATS are still in their infancy, mainly codifying domestic standards in members' schedules of commitment. The Trade in Services Agreement[32] may bring some further progress to this effect.

It is important to note that most of the existing bilateral PTAs do not go much beyond multilateral non-tariff rules and standards.[33] BBIs are merely partly addressed in PTAs. The agreements essentially rely upon WTO rules or build upon them, if at all. TBTs going beyond WTO TBT disciplines are typically addressed in mutual recognition agreements (MRAs). They reciprocally allow testing market conformity with export destinations by home institutions and, thus, facilitate conformity assessment and the reduction of costs. Additional provisions on intellectual property rely upon the TRIPS agreement.

The essential reliance of BBIs upon multilateral rules is not a coincidence. The bilateral harmonization of rules and the extension of mutual recognition is of limited advantage as they are only applicable to the parties to the PTA. They are not extended to third parties and, thus, merely add to the complexity of production standards of a country. Or, they must be extended, as in the case of IPRs, on the basis of MFN obligations, yet without the third party obtaining privileges in return. Such limitations may be the prime reason why most bilateral agreements have remained of limited added value beyond WTO rules affecting BBIs.

Instead, BBIs are essentially addressed in non-reciprocal configurations of PTAs, which entail one large and dominant market to which others adjust. In particular, the European Union, the United States and, increasingly, China are in a position to impose and export their own domestic standards, due to market size and market power. While PTAs address non-tariff barriers and BBIs, they usually adopt the standards of the larger market. For example, Switzerland (and other European Free Trade Association [EFTA] members within the European Economic Area) largely align their rules to those of the European Union and ensure consistency with

---

30 See generally Peter van der Bossche & Werner Zdoug, *The Law and Policy of the World Trade Organization: Text, Cases and Materials*, 4th ed (Cambridge, UK: Cambridge University Press, 2017).

31 WHO/FAO, *Codex Alimentarius*, online: <www.fao.org/fao-who-codexalimentarius/en/>.

32 EC, Commission, *Trade in Services Agreement*, online: <http://ec.europa.eu/trade/policy/in-focus/tisa/>.

33 See Ana Cristina Molina & Vira Khoroshavina, "TBT Provisions in Regional Trade Agreements: To what extent do they go beyond the WTO TBT Agreement?" (2015) WTO Staff Working Paper ERSD-2015-09, online: <www.wto.org/english/res_e/reser_e/ersd201509_e.pdf>.

them in both preferential agreements and autonomous regulation.[34] Even in the absence of an obligation, a reliance on EU rules is chosen to avoid unnecessary trade barriers and burdens on production within the country.

The same holds true for Canada in relation to the United States under NAFTA rules. When Canada calls for greater regulatory cooperation in NAFTA talks,[35] it is likely to adjust to US standards in the end. The same would happen in the context of CETA, in relation to the European Union. In current preferential agreements, there is little genuine negotiation on new approaches to regulation and BBIs comparable to what was achieved, for example, in the TRIPS agreement's merging of European and American legal traditions. Instead, the PTAs normally follow a hub and spike approach. Compromise and new and innovative standards are the exception.

The new bilateralism stresses ideals of regulatory sovereignty ("America first" and, in the United Kingdom, release from the powers of the European Union and the European Court of Justice). In the case of the United States, it is, thus, rather a matter of imposing its own standards upon imports, rather than seeking mutual recognition or even common rules by means of partial or full harmonization in specific sectors. This is likely to deploy major disadvantages to those countries that are not in a position to impose their own standards as a hub. They will be forced to adjust to the different import regimes of different trading partners, which adds to costs and reduces competitiveness accordingly. Companies will need to produce in accordance with varied sets of standards for specific markets. This will amount to a particular problem of fragmentation for the United Kingdom upon leaving the European Union.

Britain will be able to maintain EU regulations and standards unilaterally and to adopt new rules unilaterally, an approach that, in Switzerland, is called "unilateral compliance."[36] Britain may be able to negotiate MRAs where reciprocity is required for recognition and market access. Given the relative size of the EU and UK economies, EU regulations and standards are likely to prevail.

The United Kingdom, upon Brexit, may also address BBIs in an agreement with the United States. Given the relative size of the economies, US regulations and standards are likely to prevail. Additional variants may result from additional bilateral agreements concluded with other trading partners around the world, in particular India and China, depending on market size and bargaining power. These countries alike need to avoid a proliferation of additional standards and will insist on their own rules. Others will refer to US or EU law. Canada, for example, will have to align to EU and/or US standards in dealing with the United Kingdom. Switzerland, in an agreement with the United Kingdom, will insist on adopted EU standards, avoiding duplications and conflict in domestic laws.

While the United States will be able to impose its own standards in the new bilateralism, the United Kingdom will very likely have to deal with diverging standards, aligning its standards to

---

34 See e.g. Thomas Cottier et al, *Die Rechtsbeziehungen der Schweiz und der Europäischen Union* (Bern, Switzerland: Staempfli, 2015).

35 "Canada pushing regulatory cooperation in second round of NAFTA talks", *Inside US Trade's World Trade Online* (3 September 2017), online: <https://insidetrade.com/daily-news/canada-pushing-regulatory-cooperation-second-round-nafta-talks>.

36 See Cottier et al, *supra* note 34 at 131–168 ("Integration durch autonomen Nachvollzug").

those of its larger and major trading partners. Different production standards will increase costs and, thus, render the United Kingdom less attractive as an industrial and financial location. The multitude of diverging standards, to which exports need to comply, will frustrate the creation of new jobs within the country.

It is here that the importance of TTIP for Britain, even after leaving the European Union, as well as for other NAFTA and EFTA states, becomes utterly clear.

The Importance of TTIP for Regulatory Convergence

The stalled TTIP is the most important contemporary project and effort in addressing BBIs, as the project covers approximately 30 percent of world trade and 46 percent of world GDP (2014).[37] The TTIP seeks to introduce enhanced regulatory cooperation between the European Union and the United States.[38] While the agreement includes traditional trade policy chapters from tariff reductions to non-tariff measures, services, intellectual property and investment protection, the most important innovation sought by the European Commission is enhanced regulatory cooperation. Originally proposing a standing transatlantic regulatory cooperation body, the effort was reduced to cooperation, due to US skepticism.[39] The framework is supposed to allow for incremental long-term approximation of divergent standards and regulatory practices on both sides of the Atlantic. The agreement also seeks to include regulations under subfederal levels.

It is premature to say to what extent these provisions would be able to trigger mutual recognition, equivalence or even harmonization in different sectors of the respective economies. Some sectors, such as automotive and pharmaceutical, strongly support closer governmental cooperation, as these industries are partly owned by the same multinational corporations operating on both sides of the Atlantic Ocean. But regulatory traditions differ substantially between Europe and the United States, and agreement will depend upon the possibility of establishing and preserving mutual trust in regulatory cooperation.

While the fate of these proposals is unclear under the new bilateralism, they clearly show and reflect contemporary needs of coordination, considering extensive value chains between the two trading blocks. Other than in unilateral adjustment to a hub and larger trading partner, EU-US standards would amount to new standards, which are able to obtain worldwide recognition, as exports to these large markets will need to comply with these standards. These standards are also of significant importance for non-parties.

---

37 Gilberto Gambini, Radoslav Istatkov & Riina Kerner, "USA-EU – international trade and investment statistics: EU and US form the largest trade and investment relationship in the world" (2015) *Eurostat* (31 percent of world exports, 27 percent of world imports [2013]), online: <http://ec.europa.eu/eurostat/statistics-explained/index.php/USA-EU_-_international_trade_and_investment_statistics?>; EC, Commission, *SIA in support of the negotiations on a Transatlantic Trade and Investment Partnership (TTIP): Final Report* (Brussels, Belgium: European Commission, 2017) at 15 (46 percent of world GDP), online: <http://trade.ec.europa.eu/doclib/docs/2017/april/tradoc_155464.pdf>; see also EC, Commission, "European Union, Trade in goods with USA", online: <http://trade.ec.europa.eu/doclib/docs/2006/september/tradoc_113465.pdf>.

38 See *TTIP*, *supra* note 9.

39 See EC, Commission, "EU negotiating texts in TTIP", online: <http://trade.ec.europa.eu/doclib/press/index.cfm?id=1230#institutions>.

TTIP regulations and standards would deploy significant global spillover effects and pave the way for subsequent formal global standards in international organizations, including the WTO, in the process of multilateralizing major PTAs. Studies suggest that an ambitious TTIP would produce benefits for third parties that align to the new standards, either by the third parties joining the agreement or by means of unilateral adjustment.[40] Producers in third countries, henceforth, would be able to manufacture or provide services based on transatlantic standards, avoiding duplications in production. For Britain, upon leaving the European Union, it will be essential that the TTIP succeeds in bridging the United States and the European Union, as much as this is important to EFTA and NAFTA states.

The new bilateralism of the United States and the United Kingdom ignores the importance of the TTIP. The Trump administration stalled negotiations on the TTIP. The United Kingdom, seeking bilateral agreements outside the EU commercial policy, ignores the importance of a common and balanced transatlantic framework, which a bilateral US-UK agreement will not be able to provide without the TTIP. Both countries seem to be informed by a past world of tariff concessions, trade remedies and domestic production, perfectly suitable for bilateral agreements of the twentieth century. As a result, the United States and the European Union will impose their own standards on the world. The United Kingdom will consequently fall into the trap of multiple production standards, further losing competitiveness vis-à-vis competitors who are able to produce under harmonized standards.

Addressing the Real Concerns

With hindsight, and taking into account the implications of the financial crisis and the great recession of 2007 to 2012, it is evident that liberal trade policy failed to take into account important concerns of domestic distributive justice. Populism has a point here. While WTO law contributed to a better balance between industrialized and developing countries (mainly thanks to China's growth) concerns of domestic inequality were left unattended. The benefits of trade liberalization do not necessarily trickle down at home. This much depends upon domestic economic and welfare policies, which are largely left to self-determination in international law.

Fuelled by neo-liberal policies of favouring markets, trade liberalization in the United States and the United Kingdom failed to be accompanied by sufficient flanking measures supporting the livelihood of people negatively affected by the process of globalization. The main challenges caused by globalization today lie outside the realm of trade policy, properly speaking, but remain inextricably interwoven with it. In particular, reducing unemployment is essentially linked to the system of education and training. European countries operating a dual system with structured apprenticeship clearly show lower levels of youth unemployment.[41] Unemployment benefits, trade adjustment programs and retraining for laid-off staff in regions highly affected offer

---

40 See Thomas Cottier & Joseph Francois, eds, *The Potential Impact of a EU-US Free Trade Agreement on the Swiss Economy and External Economic Relations* (Bern, Switzerland: World Trade Institute/Swiss State Secretariat for Economic Affairs, 2014), online: <www.newsd.admin.ch/newsd/message/attachments/35611.pdf>.

41 Virginia Hernandez & Juan F Jimeno, "Youth Unemployment in the EU" (2017) 18:2 CESifo Forum 3 ("A first group made up of Austria, Germany and Switzerland. These countries have been quite successful in keeping youth unemployment low, mostly because of their efficient use of vocational training and programmes targeted at disadvantaged youth. A second group includes France, Britain and Sweden. This group has been less successful, mainly due to employment protection and minimum wages, plus a partly dysfunctional education system" at 7), online: <www.econstor.eu/bitstream/10419/166711/1/cesifo-forum-v18-y2017-i2-p03-10.pdf>.

temporary relief and the potential to re-enter the job market. Permanent education takes centre stage in the new age of automation and robotics. Improving the quality of basic education in rural areas will do more than protectionist measures.

The framework of the WTO has not paid attention to these concerns.[42] Members failed to use existing policy spaces or governments hid behind existing rules; economists warned of increasing protectionism, irrespective of whether measures are lawful or not.[43]

The new US trade policy and the new bilateralism have their origins in frustration with the relocation (off-shoring) of industries, the loss of jobs and the failure of the capitalist system to provide appropriate opportunities for those working in rural areas and in traditional (mature) industries. The political success of populism and the promise of a new trade policy based on autonomous measures and bilateral agreements is commensurate with this decline and the frustrations it causes. The surge of populism can only be explained by fatal omissions in past domestic and international policy, and it would be expected that these omissions will be proactively addressed by the new bilateralism.

Yet, no recent evidence could be found to this effect. In the United States, enhanced worker adjustment programs and more generous unemployment benefits (much lower than in Europe) do not form part of the presidential agenda, nor do reforms of the educational system, or preparing young people for a changing world. Today, workers need to be able to adjust constantly and engage in permanent education, while relying upon a broad education that provides the foundations needed to master constant changes imposed. Plans to introduce a dual educational system with training and schooled apprentices, next to college education, as contemplated by the Obama administration, no longer seem to exist. In the United Kingdom, the May Cabinet, after the Brexit referendum, announced it would pay more attention to distributive justice and promoting a caring society; yet, it seems that no specific educational measures have been contemplated so far to offset losses in international trade and improve competitiveness. The trade policy contemplated will make such reforms even more unlikely, as it likely will further erode Britain's industrial base, for reasons discussed above.

Reworking Multilateral Trade Rules

To what extent do trade rules need to be changed to accommodate policies aimed at reducing unemployment and favouring job creation? Issues relating to income inequality and distributive justice need to be considered and adjustments made to rules, to the extent necessary to accommodate the non-trade concerns mentioned above. Environmental concerns and regulations have influenced trade rules over the last years, rebalancing market access and non-trade concerns. The most progress on these issues was achieved in WTO case law, and the challenge of climate change will further enhance the effort. Similar efforts need to be made in other areas. The 2015 to 2030 Sustainable Development Goals (SDGs) offer an important

---

42 But see recent and current discussions within the WTO Public Forum 2016 and 2017, respectively: WTO, "Public Forum 2017 – 'Trade: Behind the Headlines'", online: <www.wto.org/english/forums_e/public_forum17_e/public_forum17_e.htm>.

43 Cf Global Trade Alert, "Independent Monitoring of Policies that Affect World Commerce", online: <www.globaltradealert.org/>.

road map as to what should be achieved.[44] These goals apply to developing and industrialized countries alike. They include concerns that partly inspired the new mercantilist bilateralism and trade policy: the elimination of poverty, equality of opportunities in education, decent work and economic growth, reduction of inequalities and responsible cooperation. The SDGs provide an important yardstick for assessing to what extent the existing trade rules of the multilateral system need to be reviewed and examined and to what extent these rules are compatible with, and foster, the goals of sustainable development in industrialized and developing countries alike.

Enhanced regulatory cooperation among WTO members considering these challenges and goals will foster welfare and growth and, thus, help to generate the income to financially support appropriate flanking policies. The following areas may be briefly flagged in terms of examples: the GATT and TBT and SPS agreement rules should be reviewed and modified to foster multilateral cooperation and international standard setting. Rules relating to subsidies may need to be reviewed, as well as government procurement in terms of labour relations. Trade remedies need to accept more generous relief for restructuring, linked to development programs for regions affected. Intellectual property needs to bring about the true transfer of technology also to developing countries in need, implementing the goals of article 8 of the TRIPS agreement.[45] The production of sustainable energy in remote areas exposed to sun and wind will be able to generate sources of income, also in remote areas; transit rules and interconnection regimes need to be reviewed with a view to creating modern regional and even global grids.[46] GATS needs to increasingly address common regulation for services, rather than being limited to liberalization. Common disciplines in competition law and policy are necessary to offset strong monopoly powers based upon IPRs, in particular in the digital economy. Stronger linkages to labour standards and human rights are important to temper the negative impacts of open markets and of fierce competition to combat excessive domestic inequality. For similar reasons, investment protection needs to move toward investment cooperation with a much stronger role for home states in assuming responsibility for the activities of their companies abroad.

It is important to note that the resolution of most of these regulatory issues briefly alluded to cannot be achieved on the basis of bilateral agreements. Most such agreements will not be able to address these issues and will largely remain limited to enhancing market access and some cooperation. Most of them will follow the model of hub and spikes, adjusting to the rules of dominant large markets. Rather, the resolution may be achieved by means of plurilateral, regional agreements. The TTIP or the Regional Comprehensive Economic Partnership, perhaps the Comprehensive and Progressive Agreement for Trans-Pacific Partnership, given the size or number of countries involved, may deploy important effects due to market size. The effort of reform inherently needs to be undertaken in multilateral fora, and, thus, mainly in the WTO, the World Bank group, the IMF and the UN special agencies, perhaps including a new World Educational Organization, coordinating and supporting professional efforts to bringing about a well-coordinated dual system of vocational training and colleges that enables the workforce to

---

44 *Transforming Our World: The 2030 Agenda for Sustainable Development*, GA Res 70/1, UNGAOR, 70th Sess, UN Doc A/RES/70/1(2015), online: <www.un.org/ga/search/view_doc.asp?symbol=A/RES/70/1&Lang=E>; see also United Nations, "Sustainable Development Goals: 17 Goals to Transform our World", online: <www.un.org/sustainabledevelopment/development-agenda/>.

45 *TRIPS, supra* note 27, art 8.

46 See Thomas Cottier & Ilaria Espa, eds, *International Trade in Sustainable Electricity: Regulatory Challenges in International Economic Law* (Cambridge, UK: Cambridge University Press, 2017).

move nationally and internationally to where jobs can be found. Achieving the goals that were politically set forth to, and adopted by, electorates necessarily requires addressing these concerns in multilateral negotiations. It is tragic to note that the path and instruments chosen by populist governments will not be able to contribute to the achievement of such pressing and legitimate goals.

Finally, trade policy formulation needs to adjust to shifts in regulatory cooperation and become more inclusive in domestic policy making. Front-loading consultations on trade policy formulation to actively involve parliaments and stakeholders need to occur from the beginning. It is no longer sufficient to approve a treaty negotiated by the executive branch. With the shift toward regulation and cooperation, and away from classical border measures, alternative forms of consultations and decision making need to be found. In the United States, Congress assumes these functions and can build upon the 1974 trade act.[47] In Europe, where trade policy traditionally has been a prerogative of the executive branch, it will be necessary to expand the role of parliaments and civil society.[48] In the United Kingdom, the Great Repeal Bill risked extensively increasing the powers of the executive branch, moving trade policy in a wrong direction.[49] No efforts have been made by the Cabinet to render trade policy formulation more inclusive. To the contrary, it was defeated on December 13, 2017 by a narrow margin of 309 to 305 votes in the House of Commons, seeking to prevent Parliament from ruling on the final Brexit agreement.[50] The focus on classical tools and the difficulty in addressing regulatory issues in a bilateral context will build further pressures for institutional reforms toward greater inclusiveness in trade policy formulation and decision making.

Conclusion

The focus of modern trade policy on non-tariff barriers and regulatory BBIs renders isolated bilateralism largely ineffective, as such problems are not suitable for bilateral harmonization, unless one of the parties unilaterally adjusts to the existing standards of larger trading partners. Upon Brexit, the United Kingdom will be faced with different domestic standards to be applied to different trading partners, adding to the costs of production and reducing the competitiveness of exported products. Canada, today, faces similar problems in EU and US relations in CETA and NAFTA, respectively (for example, with the protection of geographical indications).

The avenue of bilateral agreements will not be effective in addressing these issues for the benefit of the UK economy, workers and consumers alike. Instead, Britain would be best served if it continued to strongly support the EU internal market harmonization, which amounts to some 44 percent of its exports. BBIs call for a multilateral approach. From the point of view of modern trade policy and the problem of BBIs, EU membership, avoiding Brexit in the first place, or at least a Customs Union with the European Union, including the TTIP, clearly offer the most advantageous solutions.

---

47 *Trade Act of 1974*, Pub L No 93-618, 88 Stat 1978 (codified at 19 USC 2101).

48 See Thomas Cottier, "Front-loading Trade Policy-Making in the European Union: Towards a Trade Act" (2017) Eur YB Intl Econ L 35.

49 Bill 5, *European Union (Withdrawal) Bill* [HL], 2017–2019 sess (1st reading 13 July 2017).

50 John Rentoul, "The Government defeat reveals the majority in the House of Commons for a soft Brexit", *Independent* (13 December 2017), online: <www.independent.co.uk/voices/brexit-amendment-7-dominic-grieve-eu-withdrawal-bill-vote-what-it-means-a8108666.html>.

Taking up the challenges of non-tariff barriers and regulatory cooperation inherently requires plurilateral or multilateral settings. The project of the TTIP remains of paramount importance, irrespective of whether Great Britain remains in the European Union. Britain should seek membership of the TTIP as a third country and work toward a plurilateral transatlantic agreement. Creating, in the long run, common product and production standards between the European Union and the United States would create level playing fields, which would also benefit non-EU members, NAFTA members, EFTA partners and Britain, in case of Brexit, by means of autonomous adjustment or membership. The TTIP may thus be developed post-Brexit into a new plurilateral transatlantic agreement, including the European Union, the United States, Britain, other NAFTA members (Canada and Mexico) and the EFTA states (Iceland, Liechtenstein, Norway and Switzerland). In sum, the idea of a plurilateral transatlantic trade agreement, as suggested by Armand de Mestral,[51] with the United States and the European Union at its heart will be necessary to address non-tariff and regulatory barriers. Such an agreement also offers the opportunity to draw lessons from past omission and to create favourable framework conditions for flanking policies needed to restore trust and confidence in the international trading system.

Foremost, Britain should proactively support and lead efforts to foster the harmonization of domestic standards in goods and services within the WTO and other international fora, independently of Brexit. The commitment made to support multilateralism by the UK government is of paramount importance. Within or outside the European Union, Britain shares an interest in multilateralizing a future TTIP and other plurilateral and regional agreements to secure global market access on the basis of common product and production standards for goods and services. At the same time, flanking policies that are able to offset the negative effects of open markets need to be developed. Political pressures for multilateral trade negotiations will increase in coming years, once the new bilateralism and nationalist Trump trade policy have been shown to be ineffective and disappointing to those they promised to serve, simply because these policies ignore the problem of BBIs and of modern trade. Britain and the world should prepare for enhanced multilateralism today.

Author's Note

I am indebted to the anonymous reviewers for their critical comments and valuable suggestions and to the editors of this volume.

---

51 See Armand de Mestral, "Squaring the Circle: The Search for an Accommodation between the European Union and the United Kingdom" in this volume.

Section Two

FINANCIAL SERVICES

5

Brexit and Financial Services: Navigating through the Complexity of Exit Scenarios

Maziar Peihani

Introduction

Brexit is certainly one of the most remarkable events in recent European history, marking the first time that an EU member state has decided to leave the bloc. In addition to important implications for European integration, Brexit has created significant uncertainty about a vast range of issues, including the rules that govern the United Kingdom's trade with the European Union and the rest of the world, the rights of EU workers in the United Kingdom and vice versa, and the resilience of the UK economy in coming years. Such uncertainty is perhaps most profound with respect to financial services, a globally oriented industry greatly reliant on unfettered access to European markets and infrastructure. EU financial exports account for 39 percent of the total EU financial services gross value added, with 22 percent of such trade occurring within the European Union. The United Kingdom is greatly involved in the intra-EU trade flows.[1] For example, it accounts for 78 percent of foreign exchange trading, 74 percent

---

1   PwC, *Planning for Brexit: Operational impacts on wholesale banking and capital markets in Europe* (2017) at 2, online: <www.afme.eu/globalassets/downloads/publications/afme-pwc-planning-for-brexit.pdf>.

of interest rate derivatives and 50 percent of fund management in Europe.[2] Once the United Kingdom has left the European Union, the financial intermediaries who have chosen London as their European base will lose their passports to conduct cross-border business.

The key question that therefore arises is how to govern future relations between the United Kingdom and the European Union in the realm of financial services. This chapter discusses three primary scenarios that may govern the parties' future relationship: European Economic Area (EEA) membership, third-country equivalence and a bespoke agreement. The chapter assesses each option, the opportunities and challenges they present, and the key legal and regulatory issues to which they give rise. It is argued that the EEA membership offers the greatest access to the Single Market, posing the least disruption to the smooth functioning of financial intermediation across Europe. At the same time, however, it poses the greatest political challenge for the UK government, which has opted for a Brexit vision that focuses on gaining back full control of immigration and staving off the jurisdiction of the Court of Justice of the European Union (CJEU).

The discussion on equivalence suggests that it is a relatively new regime only available under certain EU legislations. Not only does equivalence exclude important areas of financial activity, but its assessment and determination is a process administered by the European Commission, which can be influenced by politics. The commission can grant access on a partial or provisional basis and withdraw it altogether. Moreover, maintaining equivalence can be challenging as the two regimes will inevitably grow more divergent over time. Finally, the chapter discusses the concept of a bespoke arrangement and the agreements that the European Union has concluded with third countries such as Switzerland and Canada. It suggests that the existing arrangements do not offer good models for post-Brexit negotiations as they do not match the United Kingdom's trade profile, take significant time to conclude and offer relatively narrow access to the Single Market. The chapter also questions whether the United Kingdom can obtain preferential regulatory equivalence and access in a bespoke arrangement when it is adamant to leave the Single Market and the CJEU's jurisdiction.

The chapter starts with an overview of the United Kingdom's financial sector, and the freedoms and passport rights that UK financial institutions currently enjoy. It maps the passporting onto primary types of financial intermediation such as banking, insurance and asset management, and discusses how significant it is for each sector. The chapter then delves into possible options that may govern future relations between the United Kingdom and the European Union. It concludes the discussion by reflecting upon the path forward, outstanding transitional issues, and the possibility of the United Kingdom leaving the European Union without a deal and therefore falling back on the World Trade Organization (WTO) rules. The chapter stresses that it is in both parties' interests to find a workable solution to safeguard the valuable elements of the Single Market, such as passporting. However, it also warns that the United Kingdom's Brexit vision, as it currently stands, is founded on unrealistic and irreconcilable objectives, which risks driving the United Kingdom's economy off the cliff.

---

2   *Ibid.*

A Primer on the United Kingdom's Financial Sector, Single Market and Passporting

City of London

The United Kingdom, and the City of London in particular, has been a leading financial centre for centuries. Finance constitutes one of the most important areas of economic activity in the United Kingdom. The Office for National Statistics estimates the financial sector output to be eight percent of the United Kingdom's national output.[3] Some have argued that if relevant business services are included, this number could be as high as 12 percent.[4] The country's trade surplus in financial services was £63 billion in 2015, which is larger than the combined surpluses of the next three leading competitors, namely Luxembourg, Switzerland and the United States.[5]

The United Kingdom has one of the largest financial systems in the world. Standing at about £20 trillion, the sum of financial assets owned by UK financial institutions, excluding the Bank of England, is more than 10 times the United Kingdom's annual GDP.[6] Nearly a fifth of global banking activity is booked in the United Kingdom, and around half of the world's largest financial institutions, including banks, insurers and asset managers, have their European headquarters in the United Kingdom.[7] Four UK banks — HSBC, Barclays, Royal Bank of Scotland and Standard Chartered — have been designated as global systemically important banks.[8] The United Kingdom's insurance sector is the largest in Europe and third largest in the world.[9] In addition, the United Kingdom hosts the largest wealth management industry, as well as many of the important equity trading platforms in Europe.[10] More than half of euro-zone firms raise capital in London in the form of equity or debt. Finally, the United Kingdom is also a hub for securities and derivatives trading, hosting two of the largest central counterparties (CCPs) in the world.[11]

3   Gloria Tyler, *Financial services: contribution to the UK economy* (London, UK: House of Commons Library, 2015) at 1, online: <http://researchbriefings.parliament.uk/ResearchBriefing/Summary/SN06193>.

4   Angus Armstrong, "EU Membership, Financial Services and Stability" (2016) 236:1 Nat'l Inst Econ Rev at 31, online: <http://journals.sagepub.com/doi/abs/10.1177/002795011623600105?journalCode=nera>.

5   TheCityUK, "Key Facts about UK Financial and Related Professional Services 2016" (March 2016) at 9, online: <www.thecityuk.com/research/key-facts-about-uk-financial-and-related-professional-services-2016>.

6   International Monetary Fund (IMF), *United Kingdom: Financial Sector Assessment Program: Financial System Stability Assessment* (Washington, DC: IMF, 2016) at 9, online: <www.imf.org/en/Publications/CR/Issues/2016/12/31/United-Kingdom-Financial-Sector-Assessment-Program-Financial-System-Stability-Assessment-43978>.

7   *Ibid.*

8   Financial Stability Board, "2016 list of global systemically important banks (G-SIBs)" (November 2016) at 3, online: <www.fsb.org/2016/11/2016-list-of-global-systemically-important-banks-g-sibs/>.

9   IMF, *supra* note 6 at 9.

10 *Ibid.*

11 *Ibid.*

Table 1: Number of Firms with at Least One Passport under Each Directive

Directive	Outbound	Inbound
Alternative Investment Fund Managers Directive (AIFMD)	212	45
Insurance Mediation Directive	2,758	5,727
Markets in Financial Instruments Directive (MiFID)	2,250	988
Mortgage Credit Directive	12	0
Payment Services Directive	284	115
Undertakings for the Collective Investment in Transferable Securities (UCITS) Directive	32	94
Electronic Money Directive	66	27
Capital Requirements Directive IV (CRD IV)	102	552
Solvency II Directive	220	726

Source: Financial Conduct Authority, August 2016[12]

Passporting

In addition to the freedom of movement, which is a fundamental principle of EU law, the United Kingdom, as an EU member, enjoys freedom of movement of capital, as well as freedom of financial services.[12] Free movement of capital allows UK households and firms to borrow and invest abroad and make cross-border payments.[13] The free movement of financial services has two dimensions: the freedom to provide financial services and the freedom of establishment. While both freedoms date back to the Treaty of Rome (1957),[14] a key development in the free movement of financial services came in the 1990s when the European Union introduced the passporting regime. The concept of passporting relies on mutual recognition of prudential measures by member countries, coupled with minimum EU standards. It seeks to minimize legal, regulatory and operational barriers to cross-border provision of financial services in the EEA. A firm that is authorized by a regulator in one member state is therefore allowed to carry out the same permitted activities in another member state. It can do so by either directly providing cross-border financial services, or by setting up a branch in the other member state.[15]

Passporting has been introduced through several pieces of EU legislation for various financial activities and services.[16] Table 1 shows the EU laws that provide for passporting rights in financial services. It also shows the number of inbound and outbound passports that have been

---

12   *Treaty on the Functioning of the European Union*, 25 March 1957, C 326, Title IV Free Movement of Persons, Services and Capital (entered into force 1 January 1958) [*TFEU*].

13   Bank of England, *EU membership and the Bank of England* (October 2015) at 20, online: <www.bankofengland.co.uk/publications/Documents/speeches/2015/euboe211015.pdf>.

14   *Treaty Establishing the European Economic Community*, 25 March 1957, OJ, C 224, *Title I Free Movement of Goods, Title III Free Movement of Persons, Services and Capital* (entered into force 1 January 1958) [*Treaty of Rome*].

15   Bank of England, *supra* note 13 at 24.

16   *Ibid*.

issued under each piece of legislation. An outbound passport is issued by the United Kingdom's competent authorities, whereas an inbound passport is issued by an EU or EEA competent authority, which enables European firms to do business in the United Kingdom.

From the banking perspective, the CRD IV and MiFID are particularly important. The CRD allows banks based in the United Kingdom to lend directly to corporations based anywhere in the European Union, or conduct business through the establishment of branches.[17] These branches remain under the supervisory authority of the home country, namely, the United Kingdom. Important business activities covered by the CRD IV's passport include deposit taking, lending brokering, payment services, securities issuance and portfolio management.[18] The passport under the MiFID operates similarly to the CRD IV and covers the following business activities: executing orders for clients, as well as trading on one's own account, investment advice, underwriting, foreign exchange services and portfolio management.[19] Industry reports indicate that UK banks can lose up to 20 percent of their revenue if they lose access to the European Union's passport.[20]

For the investment fund industry, including asset managers, money market funds, hedge funds, private equity and venture capital, the passport is largely introduced through the AIFMD and the UCITS.[21] Together, these directives allow investment funds to market their products in any EU member state.[22] The passport regime for investment funds is less complete than banking, and therefore of less value. While services can be offered in any EU member state, the actual marketing of funds is still subject to national regulation.[23] Nonetheless, European business is still of significance to the United Kingdom's investment fund industry. The latest study published by the Investment Association suggests that UK firms managed £1.2 trillion in assets for European clients in 2015.[24] The loss of access to the EU Single Market can therefore have significant implications for the UK investment funds industry.

17 *Directive 2013/36/EU of the European Parliament and of the Council of 26 June 2013 on access to the activity of credit institutions and the prudential supervision of credit institutions and investment firms, amending Directive 2002/87/EC and repealing Directives 2006/48/EC and 2006/49/EC*, [2013] OJ, L 176/338, arts 33–34 [*CRD IV*]; *Directive 2004/39/EC of the European Parliament and of the Council of 21 April 2004 on markets in financial instruments amending Council Directives 85/611/EEC and 93/6/EEC and Directive 2000/12/EC of the European Parliament and of the Council and repealing Council Directive 93/22/EEC*, [2004] OJ, L 145, arts 32–34 [MiFID].

18 *CRD IV*, *supra* note 17, Annex I, List of Activities Subject to Mutual Recognition.

19 MiFID, *supra* note 17, Annex I, List of Services and Activities and Financial Instruments, s A–B.

20 For example, a recent Oliver Wyman study suggests that the UK banking sector's total revenue in 2015 was between £108 billion and £117 billion. Of this, between £23 billion and £27 billion were international and wholesale business related to the European Union. It therefore estimates that 21 percent to 23 percent of UK banks' revenue can be affected by the loss of passporting. See Oliver Wyman, *The Impact of the UK's Exit from the EU on the UK-Based Financial Services Sector* (2016) at 6, online: <www.oliverwyman.com/content/dam/oliver-wyman/global/en/2016/oct/Brexit_POV.PDF>.

21 *Directive 2011/61/EU of the European Parliament and of the Council of 8 June 2011 on Alternative Investment Fund Managers and amending Directives 2003/41/EC and 2009/65/EC and Regulations (EC) No 1060/2009 and (EU) No 1095/2010*, [2011] OJ, L 174, arts 31–32 [AIFMD]; *Directive 2009/65/EC of the European Parliament and of the Council of 13 July 2009 on the coordination of laws, regulations and administrative provisions relating to undertakings for collective investment in transferable securities*, OJ, L 302, art 16 [UCITS].

22 Vincenzo Scarpetta & Stephen Booth, *How the UK's financial services sector can continue thriving after Brexit*, (London, UK: Open Europe, 2016) at 23, online: <http://2ihmoy1d3v7630ar9h2rsglp.wpengine.netdna-cdn.com/wp-content/uploads/2016/10/0627_Digital_Pages-Open_Europe_Intel-Thriving_after_Brexit-V1.pdf?emailid=577bc2bcc0350c0300f8b09d&cftcamp=crm/email//nbe/Brexit/product>.

23 *Ibid* at 24.

24 The Investment Association, *Asset Management in the UK 2015–2016* (September 2016) at 16, online: <www.theinvestmentassociation.org/assets/files/research/2016/20160929-amsfullreport.pdf>.

For the insurance industry, the important legislation are Solvency II and the MiFID. The Insurance Mediation Directive II, which will be replaced by the Insurance Distribution Directive in February 2018, also has some significance as it governs the sale and disclosure of insurance products.[25] It has been argued that UK insurers do not use passporting as widely as the banks.[26] Open Europe, for example, estimates that 87 percent of the cross-border insurance business is conducted through subsidiaries and only 13 percent is done through branches.[27] One key reason behind this trend is that insurance firms prefer to keep risks isolated in separately capitalized subsidiaries. This business strategy is particularly common for retail insurance where a presence on the ground and local knowledge are especially important. Caution must be taken, however, in interpreting the numbers cited above. Lloyd's of London, which retains a significant share of the insurance market, relies significantly on passporting to provide underwriting services either directly or through branches in other member states. In 2015, the EU/EEA accounted for £2.9 billion, or 11 percent, of Lloyd's gross written premium.[28] As Huw Evans, director general of the Association of British Insurers, points out, the significance of this number is understood far better when it is noted that Lloyd's annual revenue in 2015 was £27 billion,[29] amounting to 64 to 69 percent of the United Kingdom's total insurance revenue.[30] Passporting is, therefore, far more important to the United Kingdom's insurance industry than is often noted in the quantitative studies on Brexit.

While there is a clear understanding that maintaining passporting rights is crucial to the United Kingdom's financial services, assessing the economic costs of losing such rights has proven difficult. Oliver Wyman estimates that a low access scenario could result in total revenue losses of about £18 to £20 billion.[31] The House of Lords' hearings on Brexit, however, suggest that it is difficult to read much into these numbers.[32] Neither the public authorities nor the financial industry seem to understand yet how passporting maps onto the business structure and the operation of financial institutions.[33] Indeed, it is difficult if not impossible to isolate various products and services and then quantify the impact of Brexit under different scenarios. While explanations can be offered on how financial institutions and markets operate, translating those explanations into impact

---

25 *Directive 2002/92/EC of the European Parliament and of the Council of 9 December 2002 on insurance mediation*, [2002] OJ, L 009; *Directive (EU) 2016/97 of the European Parliament and of the Council of 20 January 2016 on insurance distribution (recast) Text with EEA relevance*, [2016] OJ, L 26.

26 Dirk Schoenmaker, "The UK Financial Sector and EU Integration after Brexit: The Issue of Passporting", SSRN (October 2016) at 5, online: <https://papers.ssrn.com/sol3/papers.cfm?abstract_id=2844253>.

27 Scarpetta & Booth, *supra* note 23 at 27.

28 Michael Faulkner, "Lloyd's in talks to maintain EU licenses on Brexit", *Lloyd's List* (1 July 2016), online: <www.lloydslist.com/ll/sector/insurance/article529493.ece>.

29 House of Lords Select Committee on the European Union, Financial Affairs Sub-Committee, "Corrected oral evidence: Brexit and Financial Services in the UK" (12 October 2016) at Q 51, online: <http://data.parliament.uk/writtenevidence/committeeevidence.svc/evidencedocument/eu-financial-affairs-subcommittee/brexit-financial-services/oral/41228.html>.

30 These figures are the author's calculations based on the United Kingdom's total insurance revenue estimated by the European Parliament in December 2016. See European Parliament, *Brexit: the United-Kingdom and EU financial services*, (Briefing, PE 587.384, December 2016) at 1, online: <www.europarl.europa.eu/RegData/etudes/BRIE/2016/587384/IPOL_BRI(2016)587384_EN.pdf>.

31 The low access scenario means that the United Kingdom becomes a third country without receiving equivalence or preferential access on a bilateral basis. *Ibid* at 14.

32 House of Lords European Union Committee, *Brexit: financial services*, (9th Report of Session 2016–17, December 2016) at 13 [House of Lords EU Committee], online: <https://publications.parliament.uk/pa/ld201617/ldselect/ldeucom/81/81.pdf>.

33 *Ibid* at 15.

scenarios remains difficult.[34] Consequently, the impact of Brexit on the United Kingdom's financial ecosystem remains quite unclear, especially when no coherent information is yet available on the UK government's strategy or the direction of future negotiations.

Governing the UK-EU Future Relations: A Survey of Primary Options

The key question that has arisen since the Leave vote in the June 2016 referendum is how future relations between the United Kingdom and the European Union can be governed. While there are infinite Brexit scenarios, three options seem to be most relevant when it comes to governing the future relations of both parties: an EEA membership, equivalence or a bespoke arrangement. The first option offers the greatest access to the Single Market and the least disruption to the smooth functioning of financial institutions. The second option relies on specific EU laws that allow third countries to gain access to the Single Market on a case-by-case basis. Finally, the third option is a bespoke free trade agreement, which seeks to ensure that the United Kingdom maintains access to the Single Market.

At the time of writing, the third option seems the most favourable to the British government. The prime minister's speeches and a white paper on Brexit have repeatedly called for a bold and ambitious free trade agreement.[35] In spite of this preference, the other two options remain relevant and worthy of analysis. This is particularly the case as the government's proposed bespoke arrangement has elements of both the EEA membership and equivalence. The government not only seeks to conclude a free trade agreement, but also to maintain an EEA-type access to the Single Market, and ensure the continued equivalence of legal and regulatory regimes with the European Union.[36]

It is also important to be mindful of the United Kingdom's internal politics and that Brexit preferences can change over time. The Conservative government suffered a major defeat in a snap election that was supposed to seek a "strong Brexit mandate."[37] It currently holds a thin majority in Parliament, struggling to secure political backing for its vision of Brexit.[38] The principle of parliamentary sovereignty, which was upheld by the UK Supreme Court in the *Miller* case, requires the government to consult Parliament over Brexit.[39] Parliamentary debate and scrutiny can therefore pressure the government to re-evaluate and change its Brexit strategies and objectives. The following section will therefore discuss the legal and regulatory issues that arise under the three Brexit options.

---

34 House of Lords Select Committee on the European Union, Financial Affairs Sub-Committee, "Corrected oral evidence: Brexit and Financial Services in the UK" (19 October 2016) at Q 58, online: <http://data.parliament.uk/writtenevidence/committeeevidence.svc/evidencedocument/eu-financial-affairs-subcommittee/brexit-financial-services/oral/41565.html>.

35 Theresa May, "Theresa May's Brexit speech in full" (Speech delivered at Lancaster House, London, UK, 17 January 2017) *The Telegraph*, online: <www.telegraph.co.uk/news/2017/01/17/theresa-mays-brexit-speech-full/>; HM Government, *The United Kingdom's exit from and new partnership with the European Union* (February 2017) at 35 [Brexit White Paper], online: <www.gov.uk/government/publications/the-united-kingdoms-exit-from-and-new-partnership-with-the-european-union-white-paper>.

36 Brexit White Paper, *supra* note 35 at 42–43.

37 Steven Erlanger, "Theresa May Calls for New Election in Britain, Seeking Stronger 'Brexit' Mandate", *New York Times* (18 April 2017), online: <www.nytimes.com/2017/04/18/world/europe/uk-theresa-may-general-election.html>.

38 George Parker, "British election results: May's gamble backfires", *Financial Times* (9 June 2017), online: <www.ft.com/content/d50a9332-4c89-11e7-a3f4-c742b9791d43?mhq5j=e7>.

39 *R (Miller) v Secretary of State for Exiting the European Union* [2017] UKSC 5 at paras 110, 124.

EEA Membership

The EEA refers to a single market established between EU member states on one hand and the three members of the European Free Trade Association (EFTA), namely, Iceland, Liechtenstein and Norway.[40] These countries are commonly referred to as EEA EFTA members, and their relationship with the European Union is underpinned by the EEA Agreement.[41] Switzerland, another EFTA member, has its own agreement with the European Union, which will be discussed later in this chapter. The EEA Agreement grants virtually full access to the Single Market and provides for the four freedoms, namely, free movement of goods, services, capital and labour, in the same way as they are applicable within the European Union.[42] The EEA, however, is not a customs union and excludes agriculture, fisheries, common trade policy and foreign policy.

The EEA Agreement provides for the simultaneous application of EU rules on the internal market, state aid and competition within the EAA.[43] This is meant to ensure that the rules of the Single Market remain homogenous. The EU laws are imported as an annex to the EEA Agreement, and their implementation is monitored by the EFTA Surveillance Authority.[44] The decisions of the EFTA Surveillance Authority can be appealed to the EFTA Court. The EFTA Court can also hear actions against the Surveillance Authority, as well as disputes between the EFTA member states.[45] The EFTA Court takes into account the case law of the CJEU when interpreting the EEA Agreement, as well as EU treaties and laws.[46]

If the United Kingdom decides to join the EEA, disruptions to the financial sector will be minimized. UK financial institutions will continue to benefit from the passport regime by operating through branches or providing direct cross-border services. Non-EU financial institutions can also maintain their commercial presence in the United Kingdom and do not need to move their headquarters to other EU/EEA countries as the United Kingdom would remain the gateway to EU markets. In order to join the EEA, the United Kingdom needs to follow the procedures under article 108 of the EEA Agreement. Under this provision, any European state that seeks to become an EEA party should submit its application to the EEA Council, the highest decision-making authority in the EEA.[47] The terms and conditions of the accession need to be agreed upon by all contracting parties to the EEA Agreement, namely EU and EFTA member states. The agreement should then be submitted for ratification to the contracting parties under their domestic laws.[48]

However, while offering significant benefits, EEA membership comes with important costs and challenges. First, the United Kingdom is expected to make a contribution to the European

---

40 EFTA, "European Economic Area (EEA)/Relations with the EU", online: <www.efta.int/eea>.

41 *Agreement on the European Economic Area*, 2 May 1992, OJ, L 1 (entered into force 1 January 1994) [*EEA Agreement*].

42 *Ibid*, art 1.

43 *Ibid*, art 102.

44 *Ibid*, art 109.

45 *Ibid*, art 108.

46 *Agreement Between the EFTA States on the Establishment of a Surveillance Authority and a Court of Justice*, [1994] OJ, L 344, art 3.

47 *EEA Agreement*, *supra* note 41, art 90. The EEA Council consists of the EFTA governments, members of the EU Council, and representatives from the European Commission and European External Action Service.

48 *Ibid*, art 126.

Union's budget in return for access to the Single Market and other EU programs. Based on current estimates, this contribution will not significantly differ from what the United Kingdom is currently paying.[49] Second, in return for access to the Single Market, the United Kingdom needs to respect the four freedoms and submit to the jurisdiction of the EFTA Court, which closely follows the CJEU's precedent. The EEA Agreement allows member states to unilaterally adopt safeguard measures in case of "serious economic, societal or environmental difficulties."[50] As the language of article 112 indicates, however, these measures can only be adopted in exceptional circumstances and must be temporary and limited in scope. Moreover, the adoption of such measures entitles other contracting parties to take "proportionate rebalancing measures," which can mean restricting access to the Single Market.[51] Due to such restrictions, safeguard measures have been used in a limited manner. Norway, for example, has never used safeguard measures. While Liechtenstein has adopted safeguards to restrict the free movement of people, such measures have been reached by way of an agreement with the European Union, which Liechtenstein cannot amend unilaterally. More importantly, Liechtenstein's safeguards are very limited in scope and can be explained by its unique circumstances: a population of around 37,000 and a territory of around 160 square kilometres.[52] The final challenge has to do with the United Kingdom's influence over the EU rule-making process. As mentioned earlier, EU laws are transposed into the EEA legal order. Member states are expected to follow EU rules on core freedoms, state aid, competition and so on.[53] While the EFTA states can express their views on the proposed EU rules, they can have no vote on what is decided and can have only limited influence over the rule-making process.[54]

These challenges are of varying magnitude. For example, the issue of financial commitment seems to be of less concern, given that the UK government has recently expressed readiness to make some form of contribution to the EU budget in return for access to the internal market. Similarly, the United Kingdom's influence over the rule-making process can also be reinforced through greater emphasis on the EEA Agreement provisions, which seek to facilitate timely input from member states in the rule-making process.[55] Given the United Kingdom's significance as a major financial jurisdiction, it is likely that its views will have more influence over the European Union's rule-making process on financial services than other EFTA states. The second problem, however, seems to pose the greatest challenge to the viability of the EEA option. The UK prime minister expressly indicated that her country is not leaving the European Union to give up control of immigration or return to the jurisdiction of the CJEU.[56] If the United Kingdom seeks to resume full sovereignty over immigration and rule of law, EEA membership cannot be pursued as a realistic option.

49 Stephen Booth, "As the UK searches for a post-Brexit Plan, is the EEA a viable option?", *Open Europe* (4 August 2016) online: <http://openeurope.org.uk/intelligence/britain-and-the-eu/as-the-uk-searches-for-a-post-brexit-plan-is-the-eea-a-viable-option/>; Sam Ashworth-Hayes, "Norwegians pay about as much as Brits to access EU", *In Facts* (2 November 2016) online: <https://infacts.org/norwegians-pay-same-brits-eu-access/>.

50 *EEA Agreement, supra* note 41, art 112.

51 *Ibid*, art 114.

52 Booth, *supra* note 49.

53 *EEA Agreement, supra* note 41, part IV, c I–II.

54 Jean-Claude Piris, "If the UK votes to leave: The seven alternatives to EU membership", *Centre for European Reform* (12 January 2016) at 6, online: <www.cer.eu/sites/default/files/pb_piris_brexit_12jan16.pdf>.

55 *EEA Agreement, supra* note 41, arts 99–100.

56 Theresa May, "Prime Minister: Britain after Brexit: A Vision of a Global Britain" (Speech delivered at the Conservative Party conference at the ICC, Birmingham, UK, 2 October 2016), [May's Speech (October 2016)], online: <http://press.conservatives.com/post/151239411635/prime-minister-britain-after-brexit-a-vision-of>.

Third-country Equivalence

Certain EU financial laws allow a third country to gain access to the Single Market, provided that its legal and regulatory frameworks are recognized as equivalent to the European Union's. This recognition enables the European Union to rely on the foreign firms' compliance with an equivalent regulatory framework, allowing them access to the Single Market. The European Commission makes the decision on whether to grant equivalence. The decision is often based on the technical advice provided by the European Supervisory Authorities (ESA), although sometimes the commission itself does all the technical work.[57] The criteria for recognition of equivalence are set out in the relevant financial legislation. Typically, equivalence provisions require the third country to demonstrate to the regulatory regime that it meets three conditions: it has legally binding requirements in place; it exercises effective supervision; and it achieves the same results as the EU corresponding regime.[58]

The equivalence determination applies legislation by legislation. The following are some of the major activities that are covered by equivalence provisions of EU financial laws:

- provide cross-border investment services to professional clients and eligible counterparties (MiFID II/Markets in Financial Instruments Regulation [MiFIR]);

- establish CCPs and information-gathering trade repositories (European Market Infrastructure Regulation);

- provide access to trading venues, CCPs and benchmarks (MiFID II/MiFIR);

- provide access to trading venues for the purposes of trading obligations for derivatives and shares;

- provide marketing of AIFMD; and

- provide reinsurance (Solvency II).[59]

It must be noted that no equivalence decision can be taken yet under the MiFIR and MiFID II as these two legislations will not come into force until January 2018.[60] MiFID, which is currently the applicable legislation, does not provide for any common third-country regime.[61] Another important issue that can be discerned from the above list is that the equivalence regime does not cover the full range of financial services — deposit taking, lending, primary insurance, retail asset management and payment services are excluded.[62] Further, even when equivalence

---

57 European Commission, "Equivalence with EU Rules and Supervision", online: <http://ec.europa.eu/finance/general-policy/global/equivalence/index_en.htm#maincontentSec4>.

58 European Commission, "Recognition of non-EU financial frameworks (equivalence decisions)", online: <https://ec.europa.eu/info/business-economy-euro/banking-and-finance/international-relations/recognition-non-eu-financial-frameworks-equivalence-decisions_en>; House of Lords EU Committee, *supra* note 33 at 17.

59 European Commission, "Equivalence Decisions Taken by the European Commission (as at 21/12/2016)", (December 2016), online: <https://ec.europa.eu/info/sites/info/files/file_import/equivalence-table_en.pdf >.

60 *Ibid.*

61 Ernst & Young, *UK/EU: Working through uncertainty: Practical considerations for financial institutions,* (2016) at 8, online: <www.ey.com/Publication/vwLUAssets/EY-UK-EU-Working-through-uncertainty/$FILE/EY-UK-EU-Working-through-uncertainty-considerations-for-Financial-Institutions.pdf>.

62 House of Lords EU Committee, *supra* note 32 at 18, 21.

is allowed under a particular legislative scheme, equivalence can be granted only partially or provisionally. For example, there are three sets of criteria for equivalence under Solvency II: capital requirements, group supervision and reinsurance.[63] A third country's regulatory regime will only be reconciled as fully equivalent when all three criteria are met. To date, only Bermuda and Switzerland have achieved full equivalence with other third countries, such as Australia, Canada and Japan, achieving only provisional or partial equivalence.[64] Finally, even when granted, equivalence can be withdrawn on short notice.[65]

The equivalence regime's limited scope and legislation-specific nature make it a far less attractive option than an EEA-type passport. If the United Kingdom decides to pursue equivalence, it must apply to the commission under the relevant legislative scheme. Since the United Kingdom has been an EU member so far and plans to keep a significant portion of the EU legislation through the Great Repeal Bill,[66] achieving equivalence may not be technically difficult at the point of withdrawal. Politically, however, the process for achieving equivalence may prove slow and problematic. An interesting example in this respect is the commission's landmark decision on equivalence of US central clearing arrangements.[67] Simon Gleeson from Clifford Chance notes that while technical experts found the US regime broadly equivalent within six months, it took more than 30 months of discussion at the political level to grant equivalence. Yet, some have remained relatively optimistic that politics will not interfere with equivalence decisions. For example, University of Cambridge law scholar Eilis Ferran draws attention to the rise of the ESA and the strong technical expertise they bring to the equivalence process.[68] In her view, such technical input can shield against political interference. While there is merit to the observation that the ESA play an important role in technical determination, it is only the commission that can make the equivalence determination. It is hard to see why the commission's decision cannot be influenced by political considerations, especially when the EU members strongly stress the importance of safeguarding political unity and that the United Kingdom should not achieve a better deal than it currently enjoys as a member of the bloc.[69] The United Kingdom's withdrawal

---

63 *Directive 2009/138/EC of the European Parliament and of the Council of 25 November 2009 on the taking-up and pursuit of the business of Insurance and Reinsurance*, [2009] OJ, L 335, arts 227, 260, 172 [Solvency II].

64 *Commission Delegated Decision (EU) 2015/1602 of 5 June 2015 on the equivalence of the solvency and prudential regime for insurance and reinsurance undertakings in force in Switzerland based on Articles 172(2), 227(4) and 260(3) of Directive 2009/138/EC of the European Parliament and of the Council*, OJ, L 248, online: <http://eur-lex.europa.eu/legal-content/ EN/TXT/PDF/?uri=CELEX:32015D1602&from=EN>; *Commission Delegated Decision (EU) 2015/2290 of 12 June 2015 on the provisional equivalence of the solvency regimes in force in Australia, Bermuda, Brazil, Canada, Mexico and the United States and applicable to insurance and reinsurance undertakings with head offices in those countries*, OJ, L 323, online: <http:// eur-lex.europa.eu/legal-content/EN/TXT/PDF/?uri=CELEX:32015D2290&from=EN>; *Commission Delegated Decision (EU) 2016/310 of 26 November 2015 on the equivalence of the solvency regime for insurance and reinsurance undertakings in force in Japan to the regime laid down in Directive 2009/138/EC of the European Parliament and of the Council*, OJ, L 58, online: <http://eur-lex.europa.eu/legal-content/EN/TXT/PDF/?uri=CELEX:32016D0310&from=EN>.

65 European Parliament, "Third-country equivalence in EU banking legislation" (Briefing, PE 587.369, December 2016) at 2, online: <www.europarl.europa.eu/RegData/etudes/BRIE/2016/587369/IPOL_BRI(2016)587369_EN.pdf>.

66 See May's Speech (October 2016), *supra* note 56; Brexit White Paper, *supra* note 35 at 9.

67 See European Commission, Press Release, "European Commission adopts equivalence decision for CCPs in USA" (15 March 2016), online: <http://europa.eu/rapid/press-release_IP-16-807_en.htm>.

68 House of Lords Select Committee on the European Union, Financial Affairs Sub-Committee, "Corrected oral evidence: Brexit: Financial Services" (7 September 2016) at Q 5, online: <http://data.parliament.uk/writtenevidence/ committeeevidence.svc/evidencedocument/eu-financial-affairs-subcommittee/brexit-financial-services/oral/37866.html>; Eilis Ferran, "The UK as a Third Country Actor in EU Financial Services Regulation" (2016) University of Cambridge Faculty of Law Research Paper No 47/2016 at 20.

69 Tony Barber, "The EU 27's message to Brexit Britain", *Financial Times* (12 January 2017), online: <www.ft.com/content/ a6be290c-d8bd-11e6-944b-e7eb37a6aa8e?mhq5j=e7>.

from the European Union, coupled with its reluctance to accept the basic freedoms in return for market access, may adversely affect the prospect of achieving a favourable equivalence deal.[70]

Even if the United Kingdom can achieve equivalence in the short term, maintaining such equivalence may be challenging over the long run. It has yet to be seen whether the United Kingdom will choose to continue applying EU rules as a third country without any direct influence over EU regulatory design. If the country decides to break away from EU regulations, it will then find it difficult to maintain the level of equivalence required by EU law. To be sure, international standards continue to apply in both the United Kingdom and the European Union, providing some level playing field across jurisdictions. Such standards, however, lay out only minimum requirements, and considerable differences remain between jurisdictions in how they regulate and supervise financial markets. As Niamh Moloney notes, equivalence is not simply a matter of regulatory equivalence, but also how the authorities supervise firms and enforce the rules.[71] Equivalence assessments for supervision and enforcement are highly elusive. For example, a tougher or more lenient approach to enforcement on either side can easily diminish the prospect of equivalence.[72] The divergence between the UK and EU regimes is also likely to grow over time as both jurisdictions respond and adapt to fast-paced changes in their own markets. Thus, unless the United Kingdom closely follows the European Union's lead on financial regulation, losing equivalence will always be a present danger.

A Bespoke Free Trade Agreement

The third alternative to EU membership is a bespoke bilateral agreement. This option, which frequently appears in Brexit news and commentaries, seems most aligned with the UK government's Brexit priorities. In January 2017, UK Prime Minister Theresa May indicated that her government sought to pursue "a new, comprehensive, bold and ambitious free-trade agreement", with elements of Single Market arrangements in certain areas such as financial services.[73] The European Union currently has two important bilateral agreements that are relevant to financial services: the EU-Swiss agreement on insurance, and the Canada-European Union Comprehensive Economic and Trade Agreement (CETA).[74]

The EU-Swiss agreement is quite narrow in scope; it only covers direct insurance other than life insurance, with social insurance and reinsurance being excluded.[75] The agreement allows insurance firms that have been licensed by one contracting party to open a branch in the

---

70 Sara Hagemann, "Brexit – six months on: The rest of the EU", *The UK in a Changing Europe* (27 December 2016), online: <http://ukandeu.ac.uk/brexit-six-months-on-the-rest-of-the-eu/>.

71 Niamh Moloney, "Financial services, the EU, and Brexit: an uncertain future for the city?" (2016) 17 German LJ 75 at 79.

72 *Ibid.*

73 "Theresa May's blueprint for Brexit: full speech transcript", *Financial Times* (17 January 2017) [Theresa May's blueprint], online: <www.ft.com/content/589da76c-dcb3-11e6-9d7c-be108f1c1dce?mhq5j=e7>.

74 *Agreement between the European Economic Community and the Swiss Confederation on direct insurance other than life insurance,* [1991] OJ, L 205/4 [*EU-Swiss Agreement*], online: <http://eur-lex.europa.eu/legal-content/EN/TXT/?uri=CELEX%3A21991A0727%2801%29>; *Text of the Comprehensive Economic and Trade Agreement,* 30 October 2016, (not yet entered into force) [*CETA*], online: <www.international.gc.ca/trade-commerce/trade-agreements-accords-commerciaux/agr-acc/ceta-aecg/text-texte/toc-tdm.aspx?lang=eng>.

75 *EU-Swiss Agreement, supra* note 74, Annex 2 at para A.

territory of another contracting party.[76] The agreement, however, does not allow insurance firms to directly provide cross-border insurance services in the territory of the contracting party.[77]

CETA, as it appears from its title, is a much broader agreement than the EU–Swiss deal. The agreement, which took more than seven years of negotiation, has been praised as the most comprehensive trade agreement with the European Union. It consists of 30 chapters, with the thirteenth chapter specifically devoted to financial services.[78] CETA seeks to liberalize trade in financial services based on the four modes contained in the General Agreement on Trade in Services (GATS): cross-border supply, consumption abroad, commercial presence and presence of natural persons. It contains the principles of national treatment and Most Favoured Nation treatment, which prohibit contracting parties from discriminating against each other's businesses or treating them less favourably than a third country's firm. Market access under CETA is, however, quite limited as the contracting parties are under no obligation to permit foreign financial institutions to conduct or solicit business in their territory.[79] So, the cross-border provision or consumption of financial services will be subject to the same rules that each contracting party applies in its jurisdiction.[80] Similarly, with respect to commercial presence, financial institutions should comply with the rules that apply in the host jurisdiction. In fact, article 13.6(3)(a) expressly says that "a Party may impose terms, conditions, and procedures for the authorisation of the establishment and expansion of a commercial presence" if it does not lead to discrimination.[81] As a result, a European bank that seeks to operate in Canada has to comply with all the requirements imposed by the Canadian regulator, including the rule that foreign branches cannot accept deposits of less than CDN$150,000.[82] Similarly, a Canadian bank seeking to operate in the European Union has to comply with the EU directive on the taking up and pursuit of credit institutions' business.[83] In this respect, CETA bears resemblance to GATS, which also provides for a prudential carving-out: contracting parties can adopt all necessary regulatory and prudential measures even though they are incompatible with GATS freedoms.

As the above discussion suggests, the existing bespoke agreements do not represent good models for post-Brexit negotiations. The Swiss deal is narrow in scope, covering only a small segment of the insurance business. Its passport rights do not allow firms to directly engage in cross-border insurance business. Moreover, given that the insurance industry is not a major user of passport rights, a Swiss-type agreement would be of limited value to the United Kingdom's financial sector. CETA is also a poor policy choice, given the significant difference between the United Kingdom's and Canada's trade profiles. Trade in services is of much greater significance to the

76 *Ibid*, art 11.

77 *Ibid*, art 7.1, Annex 2 at para B.3.

78 Government of Canada, "Trade Negotiations and Agreements" (October 2016), online: <www.canadainternational.gc.ca/eu-ue/policies-politiques/trade_agreements-accords_commerciaux.aspx?lang=eng>.

79 Patrick Leblond, "CETA and Financial Services: What to Expect?" CIGI, CIGI Papers No 91, 12 February 2016 at 12.

80 *Ibid*.

81 *CETA*, *supra* note 74, art 13.6(3)(a).

82 Office of the Superintendent of Financial Institutions, "Guide to Foreign Bank Branching" at para 8(a), online: <www.osfi-bsif.gc.ca/Eng/fi-if/app/aag-gad/Pages/fbbguide.aspx>.

83 *Directive 2006/48/EC of the European Parliament and of the Council of 14 June 2006 relating to the taking up and pursuit of the business of credit institutions* (as amended), [2006] OJ, L 177, online: <http://eur-lex.europa.eu/legal-content/EN/TXT/?uri=CELEX%3A32006L0048>.

United Kingdom than to Canada, whose exports to Europe consist mainly of commodities.[84] In fact, the United Kingdom runs a substantial trade deficit in goods, which it can only seek to compensate with a surplus in services.[85] In contrast to an EU or EEA membership, CETA offers very little liberalization for trade in services. This is particularly the case with respect to the freedom to provide services and the right to establishment or commercial presence, which are crucial to the United Kingdom's financial institutions.

It has been argued that the aim of a bespoke agreement should be securing EU equivalence and passporting rights for the United Kingdom's financial institutions.[86] However, to what extent Brexit negotiations can secure such an aim has yet to be seen. European leaders have repeatedly emphasized that they will not allow cherry picking with respect to the Single Market. It is unlikely that a bespoke agreement can offer passport rights that are available only to EEA members that have accepted the core freedoms and surrendered to the applications of EU law in return for market access. Similar challenges will arise with respect to equivalence. As explained previously, the EU equivalence regime, which is administered by the European Commission, is relatively new and offers limited market access. Granting a preferential equivalence status and market access to the United Kingdom will require changing EU law on equivalence and will raise questions about the consistency of the European Union's approach to third countries. Such objectives will therefore be difficult to pursue, requiring extensive negotiations, and will depend on the European Union's negotiating position as well.

The Path Forward: Concluding Observations

Many unanswered questions remain about Brexit and how it will change the United Kingdom's future relationship with the European Union and the world. The surprising results of the June election have added to this uncertainty, as the UK government did not secure a strong Brexit mandate as it had hoped.

Particularly problematic is the fact that the United Kingdom still lacks a comprehensive and realistic strategy on how to govern its future relations with the European Union.[87] The only available document is the Brexit white paper, which came out in February 2017 after significant parliamentary pressure. The white paper calls for a new strategic partnership with the European Union, including a comprehensive trade agreement, and stresses the desire to maintain the deeply integrated trade and economic relationship.[88] However, it does not specify how such objectives ought to be achieved. Nor does it assess the tradeoffs involved, in particular with

---

84 In 2013, Canada's net export to the European Union was nearly CDN\$33.2 billion. Precious stones and metals accounted for \$10 billion and minerals for \$4.6 billion. In contrast, exports in services were just under \$14.5 billion for the same period. See Canadian Trade Commissioner Service, *Exporting to the EU: A Guide for Canadian Business* (2017) at para 1.4, online: <http://tradecommissioner.gc.ca/european-union-europeenne/market-facts-faits-sur-le-marche/0000256.aspx?lang=eng>.

85 For example, in 2014, the United Kingdom's trade deficit in goods was 6.7 percent of GDP, while its surplus in services for the same period was 4.7 percent. See Office for National Statistics, *UK Balance of Payments, The Pink Book: 2016* (2016), s 4 "Trade", online: <www.ons.gov.uk/economy/nationalaccounts/balanceofpayments/bulletins/unitedkingdombalanceofpaymentsthepinkbook/2016#trade>.

86 House of Lords EU Committee, *supra* note 32 at 33.

87 This problem has been admitted by UK government insiders as well. See e.g. Connor Murphy, "Brexit negotiations are not going well, says former top UK diplomat", *Politico* (7 August 2017), online: <www.politico.eu/article/brexit-negotiations-are-not-going-well-says-former-top-uk-diplomat/>.

88 Brexit White Paper, *supra* note 36 at 35.

respect to the free movement of people. The paper expressly indicates that the free movement directive will cease to apply following Brexit and that "the migration of EU nationals will be subject to UK law."[89]

Yet, maintaining the current level of economic and financial integration on the one hand and taking back full control of immigration on the other may prove to be irreconcilable objectives. Free movement of people is a founding principle of the EU project, enshrined in the EU treaties and case law.[90] With the exception of Liechtenstein, which is a very small country, none of the European countries with access to the Single Market have managed to impose restrictions on the flow of EU/EEA citizens. Even Switzerland, which has only partial access to the Single Market, has accepted the free movement of people.[91] It seems unrealistic to expect EU leaders to give the United Kingdom access to the Single Market without having to accept at least a mild form of free movement in return.

The lack of a Brexit strategy, combined with the daunting complexity of dismantling social and economic arrangements that were put in place over half a century ago, mean that the United Kingdom can crash out of the European Union without a deal. As set out in article 50 of the Treaty on European Union, the EU treaties will cease to apply to the United Kingdom when the withdrawal agreement comes into force, or two years from the day the article 50 notification has been made.[92] While there was initially some optimism that a deal could be achieved within two years, this outcome seems increasingly unlikely.[93] Free trade agreements are notoriously slow.[94] Consider CETA, for example, which took seven years to negotiate and has not yet come into force.[95] Indeed, CETA was relatively simple as it did not include the type of service provisions and non-trade tariff barriers that a large service economy such as the United Kingdom's needs to negotiate.[96] Significant time is also needed to agree upon important exit matters, such as the United Kingdom's exit bill, the rights of EU citizens in the United Kingdom and vice versa, and the future of EU agencies located in the United Kingdom.[97] Furthermore, it is possible that the

---

89 *Ibid* at 25.

90 Camino Mortera-Martinez & Christian Odendahl, "What free movement means to Europe and why it matters to Britain", *Centre for European Reform* (January 2017) at 3, online: <www.cer.eu/sites/default/files/pb_cmm_co_freemove_19jan17.pdf>.

91 *Ibid* at 6.

92 This is unless all 27 EU member states agree to extend the process. See *Treaty of Lisbon amending the Treaty on European Union and the Treaty establishing the European Community, signed at Lisbon*, 13 December 2007, OJ, C 306 art 50 (entered into force 1 December 2009), online: <http://eur-lex.europa.eu/legal-content/EN/TXT/?uri=celex:12007L/TXT>.

93 Peter Foster, "Brexit deal could be reached by October 2018, says lead EU negotiator Michel Barnier", *The Telegraph* (6 December 2016), online: <www.telegraph.co.uk/news/2016/12/06/eu-brexit-negotiator-michel-barnier-reiterate-no-cherry-picking/>; Brexit White Paper, *supra* note 36 at 65.

94 Caroline Freund & Christine McDaniel, "How Long Does It Take to Conclude a Trade Agreement With the US?", *Peterson Institute for International Economics* (21 July 2016), online: <https://piie.com/blogs/trade-investment-policy-watch/how-long-does-it-take-conclude-trade-agreement-us>.

95 Government of Canada, *supra* note 78.

96 Jon Henley & Dan Roberts, "Reality check: will it take 10 years to do a UK-EU trade deal post Brexit?" *The Guardian* (15 December 2016), online: <www.theguardian.com/politics/2016/dec/15/reality-check-will-it-take-10-years-to-do-a-uk-eu-trade-deal-post-brexit>.

97 *Ibid.*

future UK–EU agreement will be classified as a "mixed agreement" under EU law, which would then require the lengthy process of domestic ratification by all EU member states as well.[98]

To hedge against the risks of falling off the cliff, the United Kingdom needs a clear transition agreement that maintains access to the Single Market until a new partnership agreement has been put in place.[99] Yet, the prospect of a soft transitional agreement seems bleak if the UK government continues to pursue a hard Brexit strategy, stressing its determination to leave the Single Market.[100] In this regard, Michel Barnier, the European Union's lead negotiator, has noted that "the term transitional agreement only makes sense if it prepares the way for a future relationship."[101] This statement implies that the terms of the transitional deal need to be aligned with objectives and terms of the long-term agreement between the parties. If the parties cannot agree upon access to the Single Market in their post-Brexit partnership, passport rights risk disappearing altogether after the two-year limit when article 50 has been reached.[102]

If the United Kingdom leaves the European Union without a deal, its relationship with the European Union will then fall back on the WTO rules or, more specifically, on the schedules on goods and services, which set out the rights and obligations of the WTO members.[103] Currently, the United Kingdom's commitments are integrated into the EU schedules, which means that when the United Kingdom leaves the European Union, it needs to establish its own separate schedules.[104] Under the WTO rules, new schedules can only be established if other WTO members do not oppose them.[105] The UK government has indicated its plan to minimize any ground for objection by seeking to replicate the existing trade commitments that it currently shares with the European Union in the new schedules.[106] However, even if the United Kingdom supposedly succeeds at this mission, little access to the EU markets would follow. The EU Schedule Supplement on Financial Services, which has been submitted under GATS, offers

---

98 Trade agreements that contain provisions that fall under member states' responsibility are often referred to as mixed agreements. In addition to the European Union, individual member states also have to ratify mixed agreements according to their national ratification procedures. See European Commission, "Trade negotiations step by step" (September 2013) at 6, online: <http://trade.ec.europa.eu/doclib/docs/2012/june/tradoc_149616.pdf>. The CJEU is soon expected to rule on the legal classification of the EU-Singapore Free Trade Agreement (EUSFTA). In an opinion published on December 21, 2016, Advocate General Eleanor Sharpston found that the EUSFTA is a mixed agreement that can only be concluded by both the European Union and member states acting jointly. See CJEU, Press Release, No 147/16, "Advocate General's Opinion in Opinion procedure 2/15" (21 December 2016), online: <http://curia.europa.eu/jcms/upload/docs/application/pdf/2016-12/cp160147en.pdf>.

99 TheCityUK, "Brexit and UK-based financial and related professional services" (January 2017) at paras 6–7, online: <www.thecityuk.com/research/brexit-and-uk-based-financial-and-related-professional-services/>; House of Commons Treasury Committee, "The UK's future economic relationship with the EU inquiry" (10 January 2017) at Qs 302–306.

100 Theresa May's blueprint, *supra* note 73.

101 Alex Barker & Jim Brunsden, "Barnier urges UK to be realistic about trade terms for Brexit", *Financial Times* (6 December 2016).

102 Jennifer Rankin, "EU's Brexit negotiator wants to stop UK getting 'soft transitional deal'", *The Guardian* (29 November 2016), online: <www.theguardian.com/world/2016/nov/29/eus-brexit-negotiator-wants-to-stop-uk-getting-soft-transitional-deal-michel-barnier-access-single-market>.

103 In WTO terms, "These schedules contain the commitments made by individual WTO members allowing specific foreign products or service-providers access to their markets. The schedules are integral parts of the agreements." See WTO, "WTO legal texts: Members' schedules of commitments", online: <www.wto.org/english/docs_e/legal_e/legal_e.htm#schedules>.

104 *GATS, European Communities and Their Member States: Schedule of Specific Commitments*, GATS/SC/31 (1994), online: <www.wto.org/english/tratop_e/serv_e/telecom_e/sc31.pdf>.

105 See *General Agreement on Trade in Services*, 15 April 1994, 1869 UNTS 183, art XXI (entered into force 1 January 1995).

106 Julian Braithwaite, "Ensuring a smooth transition in the WTO as we leave the EU" (23 January 2017), *Foreign & Commonwealth Office* (blog), online: <https://blogs.fco.gov.uk/julianbraithwaite/2017/01/23/ensuring-a-smooth-transition-in-the-wto-as-we-leave-the-eu/#comment-78593>.

little market liberalization.[107] There is no passporting, and no business activities can be pursued in the European Union unless in accordance with EU laws, as well as any other national laws and requirements that apply in the member state in question.[108] Thus, dropping back to the WTO rules will be significantly detrimental to the United Kingdom's financial sector as they by no means constitute a satisfactory substitute to what is currently available under the Single Market regime.

It is undoubtedly in both parties' interests to preserve access to the Single Market in their transitional and long-term agreements. There are currently more than 8,000 EU firms that use passporting to access UK markets.[109] As mentioned previously, continental firms raise half their equity and debt through banks based in the United Kingdom. Further, the United Kingdom accounts for three-quarters of foreign exchange and derivative activity in the European Union.[110] Thus, losing access to the United Kingdom's deep capital markets would have severe consequences for the EU economy as well. Wolf-Georg Ringe sees this significance of the United Kingdom's financial markets as an important bargaining chip. He argues that while Brexit will inevitably come, it will be more in form than in substance.[111] In his analysis, economic realities and political constellations make such an outcome inevitable.[112] Along similar lines, a group of experts at the European think tank Bruegel have called for a new "continental partnership" that would allow the United Kingdom to participate in selected common market policies and maintain access to the Single Market.[113]

These assessments and proposals certainly have merit as they recognize that the economic stakes are too high for either party to allow a disorderly Brexit. Moreover, the bulk of negotiations are to be carried out by technocrats, who are less concerned with empty political ambitions than economic realities and practical solutions. Nevertheless, it must be borne in mind that the European Union is as much a political project as an economic one, and that maintaining political unity is currently of greatest importance to EU leaders. It is unrealistic to assume that the United Kingdom can pursue a hard version of Brexit, but at the same time simply copy and paste all the privileges of Single-Market membership into a tailor-made agreement. It is indeed possible that the UK government will moderate its stance regarding leaving the Single Market, staving off the jurisdiction of the CJEU and abolishing the free movement of EU citizens. However, if such statements are not just political rhetoric meant to please the Leave campaign, but rather true objectives and priorities, then a very rocky road to Brexit lies ahead.

---

107 *GATS, European Communities and Their Member States: Schedule of Specific Commitments, Supplement 4 on Financial Services,* GATS/SC/31/Suppl.4/Rev.1 (1999) [*EU Schedule Supplement*].

108 *Ibid* at 2, n 1.

109 Bailey letter, *supra* note 12 at 3.

110 Jill Treanor, "Mark Carney: European economies face hit if cut off from City of London", *The Guardian* (30 November 2016), online: <www.theguardian.com/business/2016/nov/30/mark-carney-european-economies-face-hit-if-cut-off-from-city-of-london>.

111 Wolf-Georg Ringe, "The Irrelevance of Brexit for the European Financial Market" (2017) Oxford Legal Studies Research Paper No 10/2017 at 28, online: <https://papers.ssrn.com/sol3/papers.cfm?abstract_id=2902715##>.

112 *Ibid* at 35.

113 Jean Pisani-Ferry et al, "Europe after Brexit: A proposal for a continental partnership", *Bruegel* (29 August 2016) at 6, online: <http://bruegel.org/2016/08/europe-after-brexit-a-proposal-for-a-continental-partnership/>.

6

How Does It Feel to Be a Third Country? The Consequences of Brexit for Financial Market Law

Matthias Lehmann and Dirk Zetzsche

Introduction

At the current stage, nobody can predict either what the legal status of the United Kingdom will be after it has left the European Union,[1] or what the consequences of Brexit will be for the European financial market.[2] Three basic scenarios can be envisaged: first, a close connection to the European Union, modelled on the European Economic Area (EEA), which would leave the United Kingdom with little autonomy and would ensure free movement of persons and

---

1   See e.g. John Armour et al, "Brexit and Corporate Citizenship" (2017) 18:2 Eur Bus Org Rev 225; Catharine Barnard, "Law and Brexit" (2017) 33 Oxford Rev Econ Pol'y S4; Peter Böckli et al, "The Consequences of Brexit for Companies and Company Law" (2017) Revue Trimestrielle de Droit Financier 16; Paul P Craig, "Brexit: A Drama in Six Acts" (2016) Eur L Rev 447; Pavlos Eleftheriadis et al, "Legal Aspects of Withdrawal from the EU: A Briefing Note" (2016) Oxford Legal Studies Research Paper No 47/2016.

2   For a pessimistic view, see e.g. Dirk Schoenmaker, "The UK Financial Sector and EU Integration after Brexit: The Issue of Passporting" in Nauro F Campos & Fabrizio Coricelli, eds, *The Economics of the UK-EU Relationship: From the Treaty of Rome to the Brexit Vote* (London, UK: Palgrave Macmillan, 2017). A quite optimistic view is adopted by Wolf-Georg Ringe, "The Irrelevance of Brexit for the European Financial Market" (2017) Oxford Legal Studies Research Paper No 10/2017.

services on an institutional level; second, a bilateral cooperation and partial Customs Union based on treaties, modelled on the relations of the European Union with Switzerland; and, finally, third-country status. None of these scenarios fulfills the promised triad created by Brexit promoters: greater legal autonomy, reduced immigration from Eastern Europe and continuous unlimited market access.[3] The promises are legally incompatible[4] and politically unrealistic,[5] as the European Union keeps emphasizing, given the European foreign trade and payments legislation.

This chapter addresses the legal consequences of Brexit for the European financial markets law by focusing on regulatory issues,[6] leaving aside the separate constitutional problems of EU treaties law.[7] It is based on the worst-case scenario that the United Kingdom and the European Union will fail to reach an agreement that deals with cross-border financial markets and services. This case is anything but unlikely, considering the short period of time for negotiations until March 29, 2019 and the complexity of financial markets law; in practical terms, it is also the only predictable case.

For the purposes of this chapter, the term "capital markets law" is meant to refer to corporate law for companies seeking capital investment. The focus will be on market abuse and prospectus liability law, legal duties to periodical and ad hoc information (for example, in case of changes

3   Jürgen Basedow, "Brexit und das Privat- und Wirtschaftsrecht" (2016) 24 Zeitschrift für Europäisches Privatrecht 567; Dörte Poelzig & Max Bärnreuther, "Die finanzmarktrechtlichen Konsequenzen des Brexit" in Malte Kramme, Christian Baldus & Martin Schmidt-Kessel, eds, *Brexit und die juristischen Folgen* (Baden-Baden, Germany: Nomos, 2016) at 154; Matthias Lehmann & Dirk Zetzsche, "Brexit and the Consequences for Commercial and Financial Relations between the EU and the UK" (2016) 27 Eur Bus LJ 99 [Lehmann & Zetzsche, "Brexit and the Consequences"].

4   *Cf* Lehmann & Zetzsche, "Brexit and the Consequences", *supra* note 3; Poelzig & Bärnreuther, *supra* note 3 at 154 et seq.

5   *Cf* the Prime Minister of Luxembourg Xavier Bettel, quoted in Siobhan Fenton, "Brexit: UK warned 'it cannot have its cake and eat it' following 'secret memo' leak", *The Independent* (29 November 2016), online: <www.independent.co.uk/news/uk/politics/brexit-latest-secret-memo-leak-plans-cake-and-eat-it-a7445231.html>; German Chancellor Angela Merkel is quoted in Peter Taylor, "Angela Merkel: Theresa May cannot 'cherry pick' Brexit terms", *The Independent* (6 December 2016), online: <www.independent.co.uk/news/world/europe/brexit-angela-merkel-theresa-may-cannot-cherry-pick-terms-latest-eu-uk-a7458486.html>.

6   *Cf* Miguel Tell Cremades & Petr Novak, "Brexit and the European Union: General Institutional and Legal Considerations" (2017) European Union Study for the AFCO Committee; Menelaos Markakis, "Legal Issues Arising from the Brexit Referendum: A UK and EU Constitutional Analysis" (2017) 45 Intl J Leg Info 1; Ulrich G Schroeter & Heinrich Nemeczek, "The (Uncertain) Impact of Brexit on the United Kingdom's Membership in the European Economic Area" (2016) 27:7 Eur Bus L Rev 921; Poelzig & Bärnreuther, *supra* note 3 at 156 et seq; Marc-Philippe Weller, Chris Thomale & Nina Benz, "Englische Gesellschaften und Unternehmensinsolvenzen in der Post-Brexit-EU" (2016) 69 Neue Juristische Wochenschrift 2378 at 2380.

7   *Cf* EC, Directorate-General for Internal Policies of the Union, "Implications of Brexit on EU Financial Services: Study for the ECON Committee" (June 2017); John Armour, "Brexit and Financial Services" (2017) 33:1 Oxf Rev Econ Pol'y 54; Eilis Ferran, "The UK as a Third Country Actor in EU Financial Services Regulation" (2017) 3:1 J Fin Reg 40; Poelzig & Bärnreuther, *supra* note 3 at 153 et seq; Schoenmaker, *supra* note 2.

in major shareholdings in a company or inside information)[8] and the law on takeovers. In terms of financial services covered, the chapter will focus on European regulation of markets for individual and collective investments and on the regulation of banks and insurances, including the role of counterparties.[9] Further, the chapter will consider financial regulation relating to the infrastructure of financial markets, such as central counterparties (CCPs) and central securities depositories (CSDs), as well as transaction registers or trade repositories.

Connecting factors and the consequences of European financial markets law will be elaborated, followed by the analysis of the four recognized ways of market access (equivalence, EU subsidiary, bilateral agreement and the use of passive fundamental freedom of services), against the assumption that the United Kingdom will become a third country.

How European Financial Markets Law Operates

Connecting Factors

The applicability of European financial markets law can arise from one of three connections: the location where an event takes place (the territoriality doctrine), the location where a transaction

---

8   *Regulation (EU) No 596/2014 of the European Parliament and of the Council of 16 April 2014 on market abuse (market abuse regulation) and repealing Directive 2003/6/EC of the European Parliament and of the Council and Commission Directives 2003/124/EC, 2003/125/EC and 2004/72/EC, [2014] OJ, L 173/1 [Market Abuse Regulation]; Directive 2003/71/EC of the European Parliament and of the Council of 4 November 2003 on the prospectus to be published when securities are offered to the public or admitted to trading and amending Directive 2001/34/EC, [2003] OJ, L 345/64, art 4(1)(3) [Prospectus Directive]; Regulation (EU) 2017/1129 of the European Parliament and of the Council of 14 June 2017 on the prospectus to be published when securities are offered to the public or admitted to trading on a regulated market, and repealing Directive 2003/71/EC, [2017] OJ, L 168/12 [Prospectus Regulation]; Directive 2004/109/EC of the European Parliament and of the Council of 15 December 2004 on the harmonisation of transparency requirements in relation to information about issuers whose securities are admitted to trading on a regulated market and amending Directive 2001/34/EC, [2004] OJ, L 390/38 [Transparency Directive]; Directive 2004/25/ EC of the European Parliament and of the Council of 21 April 2004 on takeover bids, [2004] OJ, L 142/12 [Takeover Directive]; Directive (EU) 2017/828 of the European Parliament and of the Council of 17 May 2017 amending Directive 2007/36/EC as regards the encouragement of long-term shareholder engagement, [2017] OJ, L 132/1 [Shareholder Rights Directive]. Additionally, Regulation (EU) No 236/2012 of the European Parliament and of the Council of 14 March 2012 on short selling and certain aspects of credit default swaps, [2012] OJ, L 86/1 [Short-selling Regulation] and Regulation (EU) 2016/1011 of the European Parliament and of the Council of 8 June 2016 on indices used as benchmarks in financial instruments and financial contracts or to measure the performance of investment funds and amending Directives 2008/48/EC and 2014/17/EU and Regulation (EU) No 596/2014, [2016] OJ, L 171/1 [Benchmark Regulation].*

9   *Directive 2013/36/EU of the European Parliament and of the Council of 26 June 2013 on access to the activity of credit institutions and the prudential supervision of credit institutions and investment firms, amending Directive 2002/87/EC and repealing Directives 2006/48/EC and 2006/49/EC, [2013] OJ, L 176/338 and Regulation (EU) No 575/2013 of the European Parliament and of the Council of 26 June 2013 on prudential requirements for credit institutions and investment firms and amending Regulation (EU) No 648/2012, [2013] OJ, L 176/1 [CRR]; Directive 2014/65/EU of the European Parliament and of the Council of 15 May 2014 on markets in financial instruments and amending Directive 2002/92/EC and Directive 2011/61/EU, [2014] OJ, L 173/349 [MiFID II] and Regulation (EU) No 600/2014 of the European Parliament and of the Council of 15 May 2014 on markets in financial instruments and amending Regulation (EU) No 648/2012, [2014] OJ, L 173/84 [MiFIR]; Regulation (EU) No 648/2012 of the European Parliament and of the Council of 4 July 2012 on OTC derivatives, central counterparties and trade repositories, [2012] OJ, L 201/1 [EMIR]; Directive 2011/61/EU of the European Parliament and of the Council of 8 June 2011 on Alternative Investment Fund Managers and amending Directives 2003/41/EC and 2009/65/EC and Regulations (EC) No 1060/2009 and (EU) No 1095/2010, [2011] OJ, L 174/1 [AIFMD]; Directive 2009/65/EC of the European Parliament and of the Council of 13 July 2009 on the coordination of laws, regulations and administrative provisions relating to undertakings for collective investment in transferable securities (UCITS), [2009] OJ, L 302/32 [UCITS Directive]; Directive 2013/36/EU of the European Parliament and of the Council of 26 June 2013 on access to the activity of credit institutions and the prudential supervision of credit institutions and investment firms, amending Directive 2002/87/EC and repealing Directives 2006/48/EC and 2006/49/ EC, [2013] OJ, L 176/338 [CRD IV].*

takes place (the market doctrine) or the location where a particular behaviour, relevant in terms of financial markets law, has consequences (the effects doctrine).[10]

The territoriality doctrine means that the authority at the seat or headquarters of the company[11] is competent for licensing and supervision.[12] It applies for the licensing of credit institutions, insurance companies, securities firms and funds. The market doctrine is followed with regard to market regulation,[13] including market integrity,[14] the distribution of financial products under the prospectus liability and investment law,[15] and takeover bids.[16]

The effects doctrine applies wherever events in third countries can have a negative impact on investor protection or the integrity and stability of financial markets, for instance, with regard to access to EU trade centres, central clearing systems and CCPs,[17] trade repositories, credit rating systems,[18] insider trading, short sales and shareholder transparency.[19] The connection to effects can be found, for instance, in the Market Abuse Regulation (MAR), the Short-selling Regulation and the Transparency Directive.[20] These acts apply to persons acting or located in a third country when they conclude a contract or transaction with EU parties, or when their activities generally interfere with the European market. Therefore, it is insignificant whether or not insider trading, short selling or the acquisition of controlling interests takes place in the European Union or the United Kingdom; EU law will have to be obeyed in Britain before and after Brexit.

---

10   Dirk Zetzsche, "Drittstaaten im Bank- und Finanzmarktrecht" in Gregor Bachmann & Burkhard Breig, *Finanzmarktregulierung zwischen Innovation und Kontinuität in Deutschland, Europa und Russland* (Tübingen, Germany: Mohr, 2014) at 92 et seq [Zetzsche, "Drittstaaten"]; Matthias Lehmann, *Münchener Kommentar zum BGB, IntFinMarktR*, 7th ed (Munich, Germany: CH Beck, 2017) at para 112 [Lehmann, *Münchener Kommentar*]; Poelzig & Bärnreuther, *supra* note 3 at 161 et seq.

11   See *European Parliament and Council Directive 95/26/EC of 29 June 1995 amending Directives 77/780/EEC and 89/646/ EEC in the field of credit institutions, Directives 73/239/EEC and 92/49/EEC in the field of non-life insurance, Directives 79/267/EEC and 92/96/EEC in the field of life assurance, Directive 93/22/EEC in the field of investment firms and Directive 85/611/EEC in the field of undertakings for collective investment in transferable securities (UCITS), with a view to reinforcing prudential supervision,* [1995] OJ, L 168/7, art 3.

12   *Cf CRD IV, supra* note 9, art 3(1)(39); *CRR, supra* note 9, art 4(1); *MiFID II, supra* note 9, arts 4(1)(55), 5(1), 67; *Regulation (EU) No 909/2014 of the European Parliament and of the Council of 23 July 2014 on improving securities settlement in the European Union and on central securities depositories and amending Directives 98/26/EC and 2014/65/EU and Regulation (EU) No 236/2012,* [2014] OJ, L 257/1, arts 2(1) (23), 10 [*CSDR*]; *AIFMD, supra* note 9, arts 4(1)(q), 6(1) (generally, statutory seat; in certain cases, state of reference).

13   *Cf CRD IV, supra* note 9, art 44 et seq; *MiFID II, supra* note 9, art 3 et seq; *MiFIR, supra* note 9. *Cf* Dirk Zetzsche & David Eckner, *Europäisches Kapitalmarktrecht: Grundlagen* in Martin Gebauer & Christoph Teichmann, *Enzyklopädie Europarecht,* vol 6 (Baden-Baden, Germany: Nomos, 2016), § 7A at para 155 et seq; Dirk Zetzsche & Christina Preiner, "Europäisches Kapitalmarktrecht: Intermediärsrecht" in Gebauer & Teichmann, *ibid,* § 7B at para 178 et seq.

14   Dirk Zetzsche, "Europäisches Kapitalmarktrecht: Marktintegrität/Marktmissbrauchsrecht" in Gebauer & Teichmann, *supra* note 13, § 7C at para 43 et seq [Zetzsche, "Marktintegrität/Marktmissbrauchsrecht"]; Dirk Zetzsche & Wilhelm Wachter, "Europäisches Kapitalmarktrecht: Unternehmenskapitalmarktrecht" in Gebauer & Teichmann, *supra* note 13, § 7D at para 102 et seq.

15   *Cf Prospectus Regulation, supra* note 8, art 29; *AIFMD, supra* note 9, art 31 et seq; *MiFID* II, *supra* note 9, recitals 39, 54, 71, arts 16(3), 24 et seq.

16   *Cf Takeover Directive, supra* note 8, art 4(2). The market doctrine applies because, in cases of a divergence between the statutory seat and the place of trading, the place of trading prevails; see Ulrich Noack & Timo Holzborn in Eberhard Schwark & Daniel Zimmer, eds, *Kapitalmarktrechts-Kommentar,* 4th ed (Munich, Germany: CH Beck, 2010), § 2 WpÜG at para 3.

17   *MiFIR, supra* note 9, arts 28(4), 38(1).

18   *Regulation (EU) No 462/2013 of the European Parliament and of the Council of 21 May 2013 amending Regulation (EC) No 1060/2009 on credit rating agencies,* [2013] OJ, L 146/1, art 4 [*Credit Rating Agency Regulation*]; *CSDR, supra* note 12, art 19(6); *EMIR, supra* note 9, arts 25, 75 et seq.

19   *Cf Short-selling Regulation, supra* note 8, art 1(1)(a); *Transparency Directive, supra* note 8, art 9(3)(2), as well as *Market Abuse Regulation, supra* note 8, arts 2(3), 2(4); Zetzsche, "Marktintegrität/Marktmissbrauchsrecht", *supra* note 14, § 7C at paras 5, 43 et seq.

20   *Cf Market Abuse Regulation, supra* note 8, art 2(4) ("The prohibitions and requirements in this Regulation shall apply to actions and omissions, in the Union and in a third country, concerning the instruments referred to in paragraphs 1 and 2"); *Transparency Directive, supra* note 8, art 9(2), on the acquisition or change of major holdings ("Where the issuer is incorporated in a third country, the notification be made for equivalent events").

Efficiency Benefits from EU Membership

Within the EU/EEA Single Market, the territoriality doctrine is overcome by European passports. In principle, an issuer or intermediary that is admitted in its state is required to hold a permit for distribution of its financial instruments or products abroad. Requiring these permits to be acquired for distribution in each and every foreign state would result in excessive costs. Therefore, under the so-called country of origin principle of EU law, admittance in the state of origin suffices for distribution throughout the European Union and the EEA. The admitting authority of the state of origin must merely notify the other member state before the financial firms can start activities in the latter.[21] Consequently, specialized financial services can be concentrated at the most suitable location. This has allowed the accumulation of banking in London (so far), Frankfurt and Paris, of funds management in Dublin and Luxembourg, of insurances in the United Kingdom, France, Germany, Italy and the Netherlands, and of stock market liquidity in Amsterdam, Milan and elsewhere. Issuers and intermediaries from third countries, in principle, do not enjoy these benefits as a consequence of the fact that their home countries are not members of the Single Market. These operators must apply for admission in each and every member state, which also results in the doubling up of supervisory law, save for a few exceptions, which will be addressed below.

Opportunities through Third-country Status

Being part of the EU financial market is not only a blessing; it also comes with obligations. In some areas, the opportunity for autonomous law making could be an advantage.

Financial Markets Law

In the area of financial markets law, three examples can be given in which EU law is particularly onerous. First, banks have to comply with complex regulation that covers the constitution, organization, day-to-day work and remuneration of boards of directors.[22] The impact of EU remuneration policy, especially the cap for variable parts, in other words, *boni*, to the equivalent of an annual fixed salary, reduces the attractiveness of the European Union as a financial market. Second, European fund managers have to comply with transparency requirements and the prohibition against asset stripping when acquiring companies not listed on a stock exchange.[23] The result is higher costs and complexity of private equity transactions. Third, the Shareholder Rights Directive[24] stipulates cost-intensive rules for portfolio managers, shareholder services and issuers. These onerous requirements apply to entities governed by EU law under the territoriality doctrine, for instance, where the adviser has his or her residence or branch in

---

21 *Cf MiFID II, supra* note 9, arts 34(2), 34(3); Zetzsche & Preiner, *supra* note 13, § 7B at para 99 et seq; Lehmann, *Münchener Kommentar, supra* note 10 at para 124; Poelzig & Bärnreuther, *supra* note 3 at 164 et seq.

22 *Cf CRD IV, supra* note 9, art 91 et seq; Luca Enriques & Dirk Zetzsche, "Quack Corporate Governance, Round III? – Bank Board Regulation Under the New European Capital Requirement Directive" (2015) 16:1 Theor Inq L 211; Guido Ferrarini, "Regulating Bankers' Pay in Europe: The Case for Flexibility and Proportionality" in Helmut Siekmann, ed, *Festschrift für Theodor Baums* (Tübingen, Germany: Mohr Siebeck, 2017) 401; Peter O Mülbert, "Corporate Governance von Banken: Ein europäisches Konzept?" (2014) 113 Zeitschrift für Vergleichende Rechtswissenschaft 520.

23 *Cf AIFMD, supra* note 9, art 25 et seq; Dirk Zetzsche, "Anteils- und Kontrollerwerb an Zielgesellschaften durch Verwalter alternativer Investmentfonds" (2012) 15 Neue Zeitschrift für Gesellschaftsrecht 1164; *Clerc* in Dirk Zetzsche, *The Alternative Investment Fund Managers Directive*, 2nd ed (Alphen aan Rijn, Netherlands: Wolters Kluwer, 2015) 649 [Zetzsche, *AIFMD*].

24 *Shareholder Rights Directive, supra* note 8.

the European Union, or where a listed company has its seat in the European Union and its shares are traded there.[25] The Shareholder Rights Directive, as amended, does not provide for a combination with the effects doctrine that is well-known in financial markets law. A firm can easily free itself from these and other duties connected to the company seat by maintaining or transferring its seat to the United Kingdom. This is an invitation to regulatory arbitrage.

Consequences for Investors

While a third-country investor usually becomes a shareholder or, in the case of trust, a beneficiary, it is also possible that the investor merely holds a contractual right called "securities entitlement." The difference between the two models matters, as shareholders are protected differently from co-contractors, who merely benefit from information duties (prospectus liability and incorrect advice) and not from genuine shareholder rights. In the future, this difference will become even more important because it is to be expected that the European Union and the United Kingdom will position themselves on the opposite sides of investor/shareholder protection. It cannot be excluded, however, that EU company law and trust law will take customers' interests into account by tightening the regulation.[26]

Third-country Access via the Principle of Equivalence

Some European legal instruments allow third-country companies to access the Single Market without the need for EU authorization, provided their home country subjects them to equivalent regulation and supervision. This equivalence mechanism[27] also exists — though in a very limited

---

25 *Cf* in particular *Directive 2017/828 (Shareholder Rights Directive II)*. Dirk Zetzsche, "Langfristigkeit im Aktienrecht? Der Vorschlag der Europäischen Kommission zur Reform der Aktionärsrechterichtlinie" (2014) Neue Zeitschrift für Gesellschaftsrecht 1121.

26 On the United Kingdom's options under the equivalence regime, see Ferran, *supra* note 7. For the possibility of lowering investor protection, see Poelzig & Bärnreuther, *supra* note 3 at 160 et seq.

27 *Cf* EC, Directorate-General for Internal Policies of the Union, *supra* note 7 at 23 et seq; Ferran, *supra* note 7; Matthias Lehmann, "Legal Fragmentation, Extraterritoriality and Uncertainty in Global Financial Regulation" (2017) 37:2 Oxford J Leg Studs 406 at 430 et seq; Niamh Moloney, "Brexit, the EU and its Investment Banker: Rethinking 'Equivalence' for the EU Capital Market" (2017) London School of Economics Legal Studies Working Paper No 5/2017 [Moloney, "Brexit, the EU and its Investment Banker]; Niamh Moloney, "Brexit: An Uncertain Future for the City?" (2016) 17 German LJ 75; Lucia Quaglia, "The Politics of 'Third Country Equivalence' in Post-Crisis Financial Services Regulation in the European Union" (2015) 38 Western Eur Pol 167; Rolf Sethe, "Das Drittstaatenregime von MiFIR und MiFID II" (2014) 86 Schweizer Zeitschrift für Wirtschaftsrecht 621 [Sethe, "Drittstaatenregime"]; Rolf Sethe & Rolf Weber, "Äquivalenz als Regelungskriterium im Finanzmarktrecht" (2014) 110 Schweizer Juristen-Zeitung 569; Eddy Wymmersch, "Brexit and the Equivalence of Regulation and Supervision" (2017) European Banking Institute Working Paper Series 2017 No 15, online: <https://papers.ssrn.com/sol3/papers.cfm?abstract_id=3072187>; Zetzsche, "Drittstaaten", *supra* note 10 at 60; Dirk Zetzsche, "Competitiveness of Financial Centers in Light of Financial and Tax Law Equivalence Requirements" in Ross P Buckley, Emilios Avgouleas & Douglas W Arner, eds, *Reconceptualising Global Finance and its Regulation* (Cambridge, UK: Cambridge University Press, 2016) 391 [Zetzsche, "Competitiveness"].

way — in US law, where it is known as substituted compliance.[28] Its function is to exempt cross-border trading companies from double regulation and supervision. At the same time, this mechanism grants domestic investors free access to third-country services providers, so that the investors can select their providers based solely on performance, rather than location. This fosters product innovation and competition. The requirement of EU equivalent regulation and supervision maintains a level playing field. It also reflects the intimate connection that exists between mutual recognition and minimum harmonization, which has long been known from the intra-EU context: states will open their markets to foreign firms only under the condition that the foreign firms' countries of origin submit them to a minimum of regulatory standards and supervision. In the international context, the degree of harmonization is less stringent. One could therefore speak of "regulatory alignment," rather than "regulatory harmonization." Nevertheless, this alignment is the quid pro quo of market access.

Scope

The equivalence mechanism has a long tradition in prospectus law with regard to transparency duties,[29] especially of foreign accounting standards and of respective auditing.[30] Beyond this area, equivalence has been promoted by the Financial Stability Board with regard to derivatives regulation,[31] where national fragmentation leads not only to additional costs and deficits of supervision, but also to risks for the stability of the financial system.[32]

Recently, the principle has become more widespread throughout EU financial markets law. It has been embraced, in particular, by the Alternative Investment Fund Managers Directive (AIFMD)[33] and the Markets in Financial Instruments Directive (MiFID II),[34] allowing equivalently regulated and supervised intermediaries from third countries to offer securities

---

28 On the determination of substituted compliance for certain swap regulations by the Commodity Futures Trading Commission (CFTC) under Title VII of the Dodd-Frank Act and CFTC regulations, see CFTC, "Cross-Border Application of Swaps Provisions", online: <www.cftc.gov/LawRegulation/DoddFrankAct/Rulemakings/Cross-Border ApplicationofSwapsProvisions/index.htm>. Howell E Jackson, "Substituted Compliance: The Emergence, Challenges, and Evolution of a New Regulatory Paradigm" (2015) 1:2 J Fin Reg 169; Sean J Griffith, "Substituted Compliance and Systemic Risk: How to Make a Global Market in Derivatives Regulation" (2014) 98 U Minn L Rev 1291 at 1293–94 ("Regulatory uniformity, in general, is a highly suspect means of addressing systemic risk" and "a better approach to derivatives regulation would be to adopt a more supple regulatory superstructure that encourages a diversity of approaches to achieve the objective of minimizing systemic risk"); *Deborah North, Noah Baer & Dustin Plotnick,* "The Regulation of OTC Derivatives in the United States of America" in Rüdiger Wilhelmi et al, eds, *Handbuch EMIR* (Berlin, Germany: Erich Schmidt Verlag, 2015) 618 [Wilhelmi, *EMIR*]. On the potential application to foreign broker dealers and exchanges, see Steven Davidoff Solomon, "Rhetoric and Reality: A Historical Perspective on the Regulation of Foreign Private Issuers" (2010) 79 U Cinn L Rev 619 at 633.

29 *Cf Prospectus Regulation, supra* note 8, art 29. On the previous law, see Pierre Schammo, *EU Prospectus Law* (Cambridge, UK: Cambridge University Press, 2011) at 142–92.

30 *Cf Commission Regulation (EC) No. 1569/2007 of 21 December 2007 establishing a mechanism for the determination of equivalence of accounting standards applied by third country issuers of securities pursuant to Directives 2003/71/EC and 2004/109/EC of the European Parliament and of the Council,* [2007] OJ, L 340/66; *Directive 2013/34/EU of the European Parliament and of the Council of 26 June 2013 on the annual financial statements, consolidated financial statements and related reports of certain types of undertakings, amending Directive 2006/43/EC of the European Parliament and of the Council and repealing Council Directives 78/660/EEC and 83/349/EEC,* [2013] OJ, L182/19, art 47 [*Financial Statements Directive*].

31 *Cf* Zetzsche, "Competitiveness", *supra* note 27 at 399 et seq. Transposed in the European Union in *EMIR, supra* note 9, art 25(6), 75.

32 *Cf* Rüdiger Wilhelmi & Benjamin Bluhm, "EMIR als Regulierung systemischer Risiken" in Wilhelmi, *EMIR, supra* note 28 at 21; Rüdiger Wilhelmi, "Grenzüberschreitende Derivate, zentrale Gegenparteien und EMIR" in Dirk Zetzsche & Matthias Lehmann, *Grenzüberschreitende Finanzdienstleistungen* (Tübingen, Germany: Mohr, 2018), § 10 at 315 [Zetzsche & Lehmann, *Finanzdienstleistungen*].

33 *AIFMD, supra* note 9, arts 36–42; Dirk Zetzsche & Thomas F Marte, "AIFMD versus MiFID II/MiFIR: Similarities and Differences" in Zetzsche, *AIFMD, supra* note 23 at 458.

34 *MiFID* II, *supra* note 9, arts 19(6), 24(4); *MiFIR, supra* note 9, arts 46–47.

and fund services for professional EU customers and investors. Another area in which the principle has been adopted is financial market infrastructure, especially in the European Market Infrastructure Regulation (EMIR), which grants third-country access to EU CCPs and trade repositories and allows EU parties the clearing through third-party CCPs,[35] the Credit Rating Agency Regulation, permitting the use of the rating by equivalently regulated rating agencies for regulatory purposes in the European Union,[36] and the Central Securities Depositories Regulation (CSDR), which allows CSDs from third countries to establish branches in the European Union and to form transnational holding chains with EU CSDs. The aim of opening up the Single Market for financial services toward third-country providers is twofold: first, to extend the range of offers, thereby to enhance competition,[37] and, second, to achieve greater resilience against smaller crises by establishing a global infrastructure system. The same motivation underlies the introduction of equivalence in the reinsurance market,[38] which is of particular relevance for the stability of the financial system as it allows for spreading major national risks globally.

By contrast, banks and primary insurers from third countries do not enjoy EU market access via equivalence. Instead, they need to set up a self-functioning EU/European Economic Community subsidiary, in terms of organization and capital, if they want to serve clients on the European continent. The only simplification is granted to cross-border groups by the consolidated supervision of the EU subsidiary and its third-country parent/associate companies; in particular, risk surcharges are not levied for group internal financial relations if the third-country law is equivalent to that of the European Union.[39]

In corporate law, the principle of equivalence applies to the transparency duties of issuers, although not in statutory law, but through special recognition by public authorities. Within the scope of EU law, the publication of insider information in the United States is itself not sufficient, but must be accompanied by a publication that fulfills the requirements of the MAR. Similarly, a takeover bid in the United States may have to comply with the conditions of the Takeover Directive,[40] which are different. Beneficial ownership disclosure and financial reporting under US securities law do not, in principle, satisfy the requirements of article 9 and others of the Transparency Directive. However, the competent authority can exempt a shareholder from the duties of the Transparency Directive if the third-country law provides for equivalent requirements.[41]

---

35 *EMIR, supra* note 9, arts 25, 75 et seq.

36 *Credit Rating Agency Regulation, supra* note 18, art 5(6).

37 *CSDR, supra* note 12, arts 25(1), 9.

38 *Cf Directive 2009/138/EC of the European Parliament and of the Council of 25 November 2009 on the taking-up and pursuit of the business of Insurance and Reinsurance,* [2009] OJ, L 335/1, art 172 et seq [*Solvency II*].

39 *Cf CRD IV, supra* note 9, arts 119 et seq, 127; *CRR, supra* note 9, arts 114(2), 115(4), 116(5), 405, 406; *Solvency II, supra* note 38, arts 135, 172 et seq, 227, 232. Zetzsche, "Drittstaaten", *supra* note 10 at 75 et seq; Dirk Looschelders & Lothar Michael, "Europäisches Versicherungsrecht" in Matthias Ruffert, *Enzyklopädie Europarecht vol 5 – Europäisches Sektorales Wirtschaftsrecht* (Baden-Baden, Germany: Nomos, 2013), § 11 at para 65.

40 *Takeover Directive, supra* note 8.

41 *Transparency Directive, supra* note 8, art 23(1).

Requirements

Establishing equivalence requires three conditions with differing goals. The requirement of equivalence protects investors and the financial system against risks created by insufficiently regulated or supervised market participants. The requirement of reciprocity creates a level playing field, allowing EU intermediaries the same market opportunities as intermediaries from third countries. The requirement of cooperation in fighting money laundering, terrorism financing and tax evasion protects important public interests, such as security and the functioning of social security systems.

Equivalence of Law and Supervision

First, the law and supervision must be equivalent; in other words, the functionally comparing third-country legal regime must be at least as effectively enforced as its EU counterpart.[42] The European Union has centralized essential parts of financial market regulation and supervision.[43] That also concerns the equivalence assessment: the European Supervisory Authorities (ESAs) — the European Banking Authority, the European Securities and Markets Authority (ESMA) and the European Insurance and Occupational Pensions Authority — as well as the European Commission have been declared exclusively competent for establishing third-country equivalence in some, but not all, areas.[44] This is a matter of sound economic policy: smaller member states would be disadvantaged in bilateral negotiations over market access with big third countries, while larger member states might try to take advantage of their superior market power. However, in some areas member states are either exclusively competent, or competent in the absence of the European Commission's equivalence assessment;[45] in this case, the ESAs must merely be informed about bilateral arrangements with third countries.[46] Where member-state authorities have such powers, a certain degree of regulatory arbitrage or political interference may be expected, depending on the member states' interests.[47] This is particularly true because the equivalence mechanism embedded in many EU legislative acts is as yet little tested in practice.

The term "equivalence" is a flexible one and subject to interpretation. It lends itself as a bargaining chip in political negotiations.[48] For instance, Switzerland was at first denied the equivalence of its clearing system after it had restricted the free movement of EU workers. This ultimately caused the Swiss to change their legal framework.[49]

---

42 *Cf Credit Rating Agency Regulation, supra* note 18, art 5(6); *CSDR, supra* note 12, art 25(9); *EMIR, supra* note 9, arts 25(2)(b), 25(6); *MiFIR, supra* note 9, arts 28(4), 47(1); *Prospectus Directive, supra* note 8, art 4(1)(3); *Short-selling Regulation, supra* note 8, art 7(2).

43 On EU external competence with regard to financial services, see Zetzsche, "Drittstaaten", *supra* note 10 at 66 et seq; Zetzsche & Eckner, *supra* note 13, § 7A at para 58 et seq. Generally, the conclusion of a free trade agreement by the European Union requires consent by the member states; see ECJ, Opinion 2/15 of 16 May 2017.

44 *Cf MiFIR, supra* note 9, arts 28(4), 33(2) (trading venues), 38(1) (CCPs), 47(1) (securities firms); *Credit Rating Agency Regulation, supra* note 18, art 5(6); *CSDR, supra* note 12, art 25(9); *EMIR, supra* note 9, arts 25(6) (CCP), 75 (trade repositories); *Financial Statements Directive, supra* note 30, recital 50, art 47. *Cf* also *Prospectus Regulation, supra* note 8, art 29(3); *AIFMD, supra* note 9, art 67(2).

45 See Wymmersch, *supra* note 27 at 3 et seq.

46 See e.g. *Transparency Directive, supra* note 8, art 25(4).

47 See Wymmersch, *supra* note 27 at 36 et seq.

48 *Cf* Zetzsche, "Drittstaaten", *supra* note 10 at 54 et seq, 127 et seq.

49 *Cf* European Commission, Press Release, "European Commission welcomes progress in relations between the European Union and Switzerland" (22 December 2016).

According to the European Commission, when taking decisions on equivalence, it exercises discretion; while it takes into account the goals of promoting the internal market for financial services and the protection of financial stability and market integrity, it also needs to factor in wider external policy priorities and concerns.[50] As a consequence of this view — assuming that it is correct — there would be no legal remedy against equivalence decisions; European Union and third-country intermediaries that are allegedly disadvantaged could not ask a court to review the decisions. For instance, an EU intermediary could not challenge the ESMA decision granting Switzerland and the United States equivalence status under the AIFMD, although the liability for assets in custody under Swiss and US law is limited to fault and is not strict liability, as it is under EU law. This difference results in serious cost advantages compared with EU custodians, yet, according to the European Commission, it cannot be remedied in court. Neither can an EU firm challenge the fact that Swiss and US collective investments managers are subject to less stringent requirements of their remuneration system than are those of EU alternative investment fund managers (AIFMs). Conversely, an asset manager from Hong Kong cannot request access to the Single Market by arguing that he or she is subject to equivalent regulation at home.

Reciprocity

The second requirement for access to the Single Market is reciprocity; in other words, the EU intermediaries must be permitted to offer their services in the third country.[51] This criterion is designed to level the competitive playing field. The European Union will open its market for the firms of another country only where foreign firms enjoy access to the market of the country in question. This avoids a situation in which European firms would have to deal with foreign competitors at home while not being able to compete with them on foreign markets. It is also an indirect tool to overcome entry barriers and the protectionist attitudes of some states.

The reciprocity criterion is, however, supported not only by the economic concern for a competitive level playing field, but also by the aim of avoiding an externalization of risks. As the service provider reaps the benefits, and the clients bear the risks of financial products, supervisors of the state of origin have little incentive to care for legal obedience of the service providers in the state of distribution. The situation is different if the risks are distributed symmetrically. The more likely it is that the risk will materialize in the firm's home state, the higher will be the willingness of the latter's financial authorities to cooperate.[52]

The reciprocity requirement has an impact especially on the relationship between the European Union and the United States. While the ESMA has, in principle, categorized the US legal framework and the supervision concerning AIFMs as being equivalent to their EU counterparts, the US-substituted compliance is restricted to the domain of derivatives and does not encompass

---

50 *Cf* European Commission, "Commission Staff Working Document – EU equivalence decisions in financial services policy: an assessment" (27 February 2017) SWD(2017) 102 at 9 et seq. In favour of a possible judicial review *de lege ferenda*, Zetzsche, "Drittstaaten", *supra* note 10 at 127, 136; *Moloney*, "Brexit, the EU and its Investment Banker", *supra* note 27).

51 *Cf* Zetzsche, "Drittstaaten", *supra* note 10 at 62 et seq.

52 *Cf ibid* at 60 et seq; Zetzsche, "Competitiveness", *supra* note 27 at 398 et seq.

investment funds.[53] As a consequence, managers of hedge or private equity funds may offer their products in the United States only with a separate US authorization. A logical reaction by the European Union would be to refuse US investment managers access to the Single Market.

Anti-money Laundering/Counter-terrorism Financing Rules and Tax Transparency

A further requirement is that the home country must comply with the regulation of money laundering and tax transparency. Specifically, it must not be part of the "blacklist" published by the Financial Action Task Force (FATF). It must also comply with the standards of the Organisation for Economic Co-operation and Development Model Tax Convention on Income and on Capital, and it must guarantee an effective information exchange in taxation matters according to article 26 of that convention.[54]

Legal Consequences

Once the aforementioned requirements are established, supervisory cooperation agreements are negotiated and approved either by the member states[55] — under coordination by the ESAs[56] — or by the ESAs themselves for legal areas for which they are directly competent.[57] This is followed by the recognition of the third-country intermediary by the competent authority. As far as the European financial market infrastructure is concerned, this authority is normally the ESMA[58] and, otherwise, the national authority in the intermediary's member state of reference.

On this basis, service providers from third countries can be granted a kind of European "passport" that is valid for the entire Single Market, allowing direct access by way of cross-border service or through the establishment of a branch offering services to professional customers and investors.[59] Member states may neither provide for additional requirements nor attempt to attract third-country companies by offering any privileges.[60]

ESMA keeps a register of all third-country corporations. Registration can be revoked if a corporation acts against investor interests in the European Union, if it threatens the functioning of the market or if there is evidence of "serious" infringements of the law of its state of origin.[61]

---

53 *Cf* ESMA, "ESMA's advice to the European Parliament, the Council and the Commission on the application of the AIFMD passport to non-EU AIFMs and AIFs" (12 September 2016) ESMA/2016/1140 at 26 ("ESMA is of the view that the market access conditions which would apply to U.S funds dedicated to professional investors in the EU in the event that the AIFMD passport is extended to the U.S would be different from the market access conditions applicable to EU funds dedicated to professional investors in the U.S. This is due to registration requirements under the U.S regulatory framework [which generate additional costs], and particularly in the case of funds marketed by managers involving public offerings").

54 *AIFMD, supra* note 9, arts 37(7)(e), 37(7)(f). *Cf* Zetzsche & Marte, *supra* note 33 at 463–65.

55 *Market Abuse Regulation, supra* note 8, art 26(2).

56 *Ibid*, art 26(1); *Prospectus Regulation, supra* note 8, art 30.

57 *Cf* for ESMA, *CSDR, supra* note 12, art 25(10); *Credit Rating Agency Regulation, supra* note 18, arts 4(3)(h), 5(7); *EMIR, supra* note 9, arts 25(7) (CCP), 76 (trade repositories); for the European Central Bank (ECB) in the context of its supervision of significant banks, *Regulation (EU) No 468/2014 of the European Central Bank of 16 April 2014 establishing the framework for cooperation within the Single Supervisory Mechanism between the European Central Bank and national competent authorities and with national designated authorities*, [2014] OJ, L 141/1, art 8.

58 *Cf CSDR, supra* note 12, art 25(6); *Credit Rating Agency Regulation, supra* note 18, art 5(6); *EMIR, supra* note 9, art 25 (CCP), 77(1) (trading repositories). On third-country CCP and trade repositories, Olaf Achtelik, "Zulassung und Anerkennung von CCPs" in Wilhelmi, *EMIR, supra* note 28 at 250 et seq; Dominik Zeitz, "Zulassungsverfahren für Transaktionsregister" in Wilhelmi, *EMIR, supra* note 28 at 333 et seq.

59 *MiFIR, supra* note 9, art 47(3).

60 *Ibid*, art 46(3).

61 *Ibid*, arts 48–49.

Contractual Obstacles Affecting Access via the Principle of Equivalence

The equivalence test operates on the level of interstate relations. In addition, third-country corporations must observe special duties when concluding a contract with an EU customer.

Information Duties

Third-country financial firms must inform their EU customers that they are not permitted to provide services for other customers other than eligible counterparties or professional clients (article 46[5][1] of the MiFIR). The purpose of this information duty remains unclear, the third-country passport being restricted anyway to eligible counterparties and professional clients. Probably the customer must assess whether it belongs to the target group, but this does not spare the third-country provider from making its own assessment. In case it does offer services to other than qualifying parties, the third-country provider risks sanctions by the EU supervisor, including the revocation of registration as a third-country corporation under article 46(5) of the MiFIR. Yet, this should be the *ultima ratio* and applies only in cases of serious and systematic infringement.[62] Private law consequences are doubtful. A right to damages[63] will rarely apply, as a violation of this information duty will hardly ever result in economic loss. Other private law consequences — for instance, rescission due to violation of pre-contractual duties could be considered — but the information and, accordingly, the infringement is of little importance, so that rescission is excluded, for instance, under German law[64] (see German Civil Code [BGB], § 323 at para 5).

Obligatory Offers for Dispute Settlement

According to article 46(6) of the MiFIR, a third-country corporation must, before performing its services for EU clients, offer to submit potential disputes in relation to its services to an EU/EEA court or arbitral tribunal. With this requirement, EU clients are protected from the need to go to a third-country court in order to have access to justice.

The scale and consequences of this provision are again doubtful. Some authors have interpreted it as meaning that choice-of-forum clauses in favour of third-country courts will no longer be permitted in financial service contracts with EU clients and will therefore be void after Brexit.[65] This construction fails to convince because the text requires the third-country corporation only to "offer" the dispute settlement before the court or arbitrator of a member state. This leaves open the possibility that, after such an offer is made, the parties decide for a third-state court or arbitrator.

The consequences of a violation of the duties arising from article 46(6) of the MiFIR are also uncertain. In particular, it is unclear whether the failure of the third-country service provider to offer dispute resolution via a court or an arbitral tribunal in a member state would result in any jurisdiction or arbitration clause in favour of a non-member state being void. It is true that

---

62 Jochen Eichhorn & Ulf Klebeck, "Drittstaatenregulierung der MiFID II und MiFIR. Aufsichtsrecht" (2014) 7 Recht der Finanzinstrumente 1 at 6.

63 See *MiFID* II, *supra* note 9, art 69(2)(3).

64 See in German law: BGB, §§ 323(1), 323(2)(3), 323(5)(2).

65 See Burkhard Hess & Marta Requejo-Isidro, "Brexit – Immediate Consequences on the London Judicial Market" (24 June 2016), *Conflict of Laws.net* (blog), online: <http://conflictoflaws.net/2016/brexit-immediate-consequences-on-the-london-judicial-market>.

according to article 25(1) of the Brussels Ia Regulation, choice-of-forum clauses are inoperative if they are null and void as to their substantive validity under the law of the chosen court. It is also true that article 2(3) of the New York Convention does not recognize arbitration agreements as far as they are "null and void, inoperative or incapable of being performed."[66] Arguably, however, these provisions presuppose voidness in terms of private law. Article 46(6) of the MiFIR is part of regulatory public law, so that an infringement does not per se result in the voidness of the dispute resolution clause in the sense of private law. Such voidness would be contrary to the interests of the EU clients that the provision aims to protect. They would be deprived of the possibility of invoking the choice-of-forum or arbitration clause against the third-state company. They may also fall victim to judicial conflicts between member-state courts and courts in third states that consider the dispute resolution clause as being valid. It is likely that courts outside the member states will not regard the agreement as null and void because of its violation of an EU regulation.

It is also not clear what is meant by "arbitral tribunal in a Member State" in article 46(6) of the MiFIR. *Per definitionem*, an arbitral tribunal does not belong to a state or member state. Yet, its seat may be located in a member state. This seat is to be distinguished from the arbitration institution that organizes the arbitration proceedings. If it is correct that (only) the arbitral tribunal must be based within the European Union, it would still be possible to have the proceedings organized by a third-state arbitration institution, such as the London Court of International Arbitration.

The matter is taken even one step further by article 37(13)(2) of the AIFMD. It requires that all disputes arising between the AIFM or the alternative investment funds (AIFs) and EU investors of the respective AIFs have to be settled according to the law of an EU/EEA member state and are subjected to its jurisdiction. The wording of this provision differs from that of article 46(6) of the MiFIR in several ways. It refers not only to jurisdiction, but also to the applicable law. Moreover, it is not confined to the necessity that an offer has to be made by the third-state company, but imposes the law of a member state and its jurisdiction as mandatory. In fact, the provision could be regarded as usurping, if it is understood as requiring that EU law and member-state courts should keep the upper hand over any dispute with EU clients.

Whether this strict consequence is intended remains uncertain, however. Hermeneutical difficulties start with the question of which member state the provision targets. Due to the lack of a definition in article 37(13)(2) of the AIFMD, one may speculate whether the member state should be determined by choice or in a different way, and in which way. The mandatory statutory determination of applicable law and jurisdiction would also be contrary to the general rules of EU private international law, which regularly allow the parties in business-to-business (B2B) relations to autonomously choose both the law and the court.[67] Finally, under a literal interpretation of the text, arbitration agreements envisaging a seat outside of the European

---

66 *Convention on the Recognition and Enforcement of Foreign Arbitral Awards*, 10 June 1958, 330 UNTS 38, 21 UST 2517, 7 ILM 1046, art 2(3) (entered into force 7 June 1959). Although a similar clause is missing, the situation is not different under the Lugano Convention: *Convention on Jurisdiction and the Enforcement of Judgments in Civil and Commercial Matters*, 16 September 1988, 28 ILM 620 (entered into force 1 January 1992); see Domenico Acocella, "Commentary on Art. 1-4, Vorbem. zu Art. 2, 5 Nr. 1-3, 18-21, 31, 57-58, 62 LugÜ" in Anton K Schnyder, ed, *Lugan-Übereinkommen zum internationalen Zivilverfahrensrecht* (Zurich, Switzerland: Schulthess, 2011), art 1 at paras 72, 133; Rainer Hausmann in Thomas Simons & Rainer Hausmann, ed, *Brüssel Ia-Verordnung* (Munich, Germany: IPR-Verlag, 2012), art 1 at para 110.

67 For details, see Dirk Zetzsche, "Das grenzüberschreitende Investmentdreieck" in Zetzsche & Lehmann, *Finanzdienstleistungen*, *supra* note 32 [Zetzsche, "Investmentdreieck"].

Union would be void. This would mean nothing less than a blunt interference with the general principles of international arbitration. One may doubt whether the drafters of the AIFMD, who were most likely experts in financial but not in·private international law, intended these outcomes or were even able to anticipate the problems.

Article 37 of the AIFMD was adopted earlier than article 46(6) of the MiFIR. The choice granted to EU customers by the latter seems to capture the intention in a more precise way than article 37(13)(2) of the AIFMD. One reasonable interpretation is, therefore, that the provision requires merely the offer of EU law and a member-state court, even though it must be admitted that the wording does not reflect this intention in an adequate manner.

Recognition of Judgments and Applicable Law

The fate of the Rome Regulation and the Brussels Ia Regulation after Brexit is far from clear.[68] The worst-case scenario would be that from March 30, 2019, and onwards the United Kingdom would have to be regarded as a third country in terms of private international law. This would make the enforcement of British court decisions much more difficult on the Continent.[69] For third-country companies, it would no longer be attractive to agree on the jurisdiction of British courts when contracting with EU customers. The lack of enforceability of British judgments in the European Union would probably be compensated through market mechanisms, for instance, through higher prepayments or margin payments. Both measures would make British legal services more expensive compared with those of EU competitors, as more capital or collateral would have to be provided for those transactions when compared to those where the recognition and enforcement of judgments is supported by harmonized European private international law and European civil procedure rules. Seizing a British court would still make sense for British financial service providers in defence against claims by EU customers. The possibility that a British court decision rejecting such claims might lack recognition in the European Union will not be detrimental if the British service provider has concentrated its assets in the United Kingdom.

Prospectuses and key investor information documents regularly contain references to the applicable law and jurisdiction.[70] Although so far, this reference serves merely a declaratory purpose, it may in the future become much more valuable and operate as the choice of law and court. The same applies to agreements designed to comply with provisions of the EU financial markets law requiring choice of law and court to be expressed in contracts.[71] Normally, these provisions do not require the choice of a certain court or law so that third-country courts and jurisdictions can be chosen. However, the effectiveness of such agreements would have to be reviewed against the background of EU law in general. For example, European private international law provides for a special role of court and jurisdiction at the consumer's habitual

---

68   Matthias Lehmann & Dirk Zetzsche, "Die Auswirkungen des Brexit auf das Zivil- und Wirtschaftsrecht" (2017) 72 Juristenzeitung 62 at 63 et seq [Lehmann & Zetzsche, "Die Auswirkungen des Brexit"].

69   *Ibid* at 62 et seq.

70   See *UCITS Directive, supra* note 9, Annex I, No 3.2; *AIFMD, supra* note 9, art 23(1)(c).

71   See e.g. *Commission Delegated Regulation (EU) 2016/438 of 17 December 2015 supplementing Directive 2009/65/EC of the European Parliament and of the Council with regard to obligations of depositaries*, [2016] OJ, L 78/11, art 2(5) for the contract between the management company and the depositary of a fund. For details, see Zetzsche, "Investmentdreieck", *supra* note 67.

residence.[72] British law might in the future depart from this view in a biased attempt to promote British service providers. This shows that it would be desirable also from the EU point of view to maintain the status quo of judicial cooperation in private international law.[73] However, in pursuing this goal the competence of the Court of Justice of the European Union (CJEU) to interpret European law is a pill that the British side will hardly be prepared to swallow in the Brexit negotiations.

Smaller obstacles are created by European financial markets law, where it abstains from regulating an issue and instead refers to member-state law. An example is article 11(2) of the Packaged Retail and Insurance-based Investment Products (PRIIPs) Regulation[74] on liability arising from a particularly faulty key information document. Terms such as "loss" or "damages," as used in this regulation, are to be interpreted and applied in accordance with the national law determined under the general rules of private international law (article 11[3] of the PRIIPs Regulation). After Brexit, the PRIIPs Regulation will no longer apply to the United Kingdom. It has to be assumed, though, that the regulation will continue to apply to already existing claims, and also that the EU rules of private international law apply.

Consequences

On the basis of equivalence decisions, UK companies will still be able to offer services and product delivery to professional counterparties and investors in the B2B reinsurer market, in the area of central financial market infrastructure and in capital and funds management for professional counterparties. This explains why alternative funds managers (hedge funds and private equity) in London make little effort to secure EU market access. As long as the United Kingdom does not completely change its law after Brexit, an equivalence decision should be within reach, provided that the United Kingdom in return grants market access to EU companies. The equivalence status might be threatened, though, if the British government decides to lower its standards in the area of money laundering and taxation cooperation. At present, this is not to be expected, as the United Kingdom has vested interests in a solid taxation basis and global coordination in the area of taxation. The same applies for financial market infrastructure. Changes may occur in clearing and settlement if — as it currently seems — the ECB will be successful in its plan to move euro clearing from the United Kingdom to the euro area.[75]

By contrast, the equivalence of law and supervision will not help banks and primary insurers much. This makes it invariably necessary for banks and insurers to establish independent subsidiaries in EU member states or subsidiaries to conduct business in the European Union;[76]

---

72 *Regulation (EC) No 593/2008 of the European Parliament and of the Council of 17 June 2008 on the law applicable to contractual obligations*, [2008] OJ, L 177/6, art 6; *Regulation (EU) No 1215/2012 of the European Parliament and of the Council of 12 December 2012 on jurisdiction and the recognition and enforcement of judgments in civil and commercial matters*, [2012] OJ, L 351/1, art 17 et seq [*Brussels Ia Regulation*].

73 See Lehmann & Zetzsche, "Die Auswirkungen", *supra* note 68 at 62, 64 et seq.

74 *Regulation (EU) No 1286/2014 of the European Parliament and of the Council of 26 November 2014 on key information documents for packaged retail and insurance-based investment products (PRIIPs)*, [2014] OJ, L 352/1.

75 *Cf* EC, Directorate-General for Internal Policies of the Union, *supra* note 7 at 46 et seq.

76 In the same sense, Heinrich Nemeczek & Sebastian Pitz, "The Impact of Brexit on Cross-Border Business of UK Credit Institutions and Investment Firms with German Clients" at sub 6 ("Conclusion"), online: <https://papers.ssrn.com/sol3/papers.cfm?abstract_id=2948944>; Norman Mugarura, "The 'EU Brexit' implication on a single banking license and other aspects of financial markets regulation in the UK" (2016) 58:4 Intl J L Mgmt 468.

this is a requirement from which especially France, Germany, Ireland, Luxembourg and the Netherlands will probably benefit.[77]

EU Subsidiary

British financial service providers could decide to offer services to EU clients through an EU subsidiary that is legally independent in terms of corporate law and supervision. This could be an interesting option, since a fully equipped and licensed EU subsidiary can exercise the freedom to provide services according to article 56 of the Treaty on the Functioning of the European Union *ex origine*; it can claim the benefits of the EU passport system and stay, or become even closer, to clients located in the European Union. At the same time, there are various means to reduce double costs. For instance, the group could benefit from a close interrelationship with the parent or sister companies in the same group through savings of prudential capital by booking transactions outright in group companies ("remote booking") or, at least, through hedge transactions using group companies as counterparties, such as by virtue of intragroup hedging through back-to-back hedges or split hedging arrangements where some sister (specialist) companies take certain (for example, currency) risks; for instance, a Japanese sister company may take all yen risks, while the Hong Kong sister company takes all Hong Kong dollar risk and so on. Another idea that could result in cost savings is dual hatting in which one fit and proper officer has multiple offices in the subsidiary, sister and parent companies. Or the group of companies seek to benefit from lower overall capital requirements by internal risk models that assume full group integration, for instance, by netting positions of parent, sister and EU-subsidiary companies.

Shareholder Vetting

Companies from third countries will be licensed in the European Union only after they have been thoroughly checked for any influence that could endanger the enforcement of European financial markets law.[78] Shareholders from countries notorious for corruption or for supporting terrorism give cause for concern, as do those that might withdraw customers' or equity assets from the EU subsidiary. Such danger should not arise with regard to British investors, as long as the United Kingdom maintains supervisory standards that are identical to EU law. The problem is that many intermediaries from countries outside the European Union used to organize their EU business via London. If this is to continue, the EU supervisory authorities will often have to look through the UK corporation in order to identify detrimental influences from third countries. However, banks and insurers from Asia and the United States may in the future take the direct route and hold shares in EU subsidiaries themselves.

More obstacles are looming on the horizon. Under some investment laws, third-country shareholders may be banned for public policy reasons (see, for example, sections 2[2], 5[2] of the German Foreign Trade and Payments Act). Where a shareholding conveys a "definite influence" on corporate governance, the CJEU reviews such laws exclusively against the freedom

---

77 *Cf* André Sapir, Dirk Schoenmaker & Nicolas Véron, "Making the best of Brexit for the EU27 Financial System" (2017) Bruegel Policy Brief Issue 1 at 1.

78 *Cf CRD IV*, *supra* note 9, art 14(3); *MiFID II*, *supra* note 9, arts 10(1), 10(2); *AIFMD*, *supra* note 9, art 8(3)(b); a similar practice exists with regard to insurance companies under *Solvency II*, *supra* note 38, art 24. See Zetzsche, "Drittstaaten", *supra* note 10 at 72 et seq.

of establishment, which is limited to member states of the European Union and EEA, and not against the freedom of capital, which is open to third countries.[79] These laws will therefore be applied in their full breadth to the United Kingdom once it has become a third country.[80] Even though nobody will regard the United Kingdom as a rogue state or an enemy, mergers and acquisitions between EU and British companies will take longer, as the recently prolonged auditing phase for takeovers illustrates.[81] Any delay in the sensitive transaction phase may, of course, create serious havoc.

Letter-box Companies

British companies could be tempted to avoid the complex transfer of staff, customers and offices by using EU subsidiaries that delegate the main services back to the UK parent. If the subsidiary is only minimally equipped, value creation will still mainly occur in the United Kingdom. Alternatively, British companies could transfer "secure" business to a registered EU intermediary, which then outsources or delegates some business back to the UK entity. Both strategies are possible because the legal framework of outsourcing is not fully harmonized; the European Union has adopted only some legal instruments concerning outsourcing on the financial market.[82] As a result, a competition seems to be developing between EU member states, which vie with each other to attract British subsidiaries (or branches in the area of MiFID II) by offering low requirements for capital, staff and material equipment.

In this context, ESMA has reminded member states of the need for the uniform application of EU law and of avoiding regulatory and supervisory arbitrage.[83] In particular, ESMA warns against too generous outsourcing to British headquarters, which enables the creation of letter-box companies from which the whole EU market is served. The warning is important, considering ESMA's coordinating function in applying the law and its power to solve disputes between national supervisors, especially in the area of asset management and market infrastructure.[84] Indeed, a race to the bottom with regard to substantial requirements would not only be detrimental for the national economy, but it would also undermine the efficiency of supervision if subsidiaries are so poorly equipped by their parents that the supervisory or resolution authorities cannot access assets and business links in a crisis.[85] The personnel of the subsidiary must be capable of coping with the subsidiary's operative business, as well as providing its internal control system (comprising compliance, risk management and internal

---

79 *Cadbury Schweppes plc and Cadbury Schweppes Overseas Ltd v Commissioners of Inland Revenue* (2006), C-196/04, ECR 2006, 7995 (CJEU) at para 31 et seq.

80 Accord Poelzig & Bärnreuther, *supra* note 3 at 157 et seq.

81 See from a German perspective, Christoph H Seibt & Sabrina Kulenkampf, "CFIUS-Verfahren und Folgen für M&A-Transaktionen mit Beteiligung deutscher Unternehmen" (2017) 39 Zeitschrift für Wirtschaftsrecht 1345.

82 See Zetzsche, "Drittstaaten", *supra* note 10.

83 *Cf* ESMA, "General principles to support supervisory convergence in the context of the UK withdrawing from the EU", 31 May 2017, ESMA 42-110-433.

84 *Cf Regulation (EU) No 1095/2010 of the European Parliament and of the Council of 24 November 2010 establishing a European Supervisory Authority (European Securities and Markets Authority), amending Decision No 716/2009/EC and repealing Commission Decision 2009/77/EC,* [2010] OJ, L 331/84 [*ESMA Regulation*], art 19; Zetzsche & Eckner, *supra* note 13, § 7A at para 92 et seq; Zetzsche & Preiner, *supra* note 13, § 7B at para 105.

85 For more details, see Zetzsche, "Drittstaaten", *supra* note 10 at 87 et seq.

audit[86]) independently of the parent company.[87] In addition, the efficient enforcement of EU law requires that the branch's data and servers work independently of the parent company and keep functioning in case of a breakdown in the parent company. This implies the need for a suitable hierarchy of reading and editing rights, a diversified selection of providers, as well as operation guarantees bespoke to EU countries, for instance, in the area of cloud computing.

Bilateral Market Access

As an alternative to equivalence-based access or the establishment of an EU subsidiary, third-country companies may opt to offer financial services in the European Union on the basis of a national licence. The companies could then access the market via cross-border offerings or via the establishment of dependent EU branches.

Bilateral Agreements of Market Access

For banks and primary insurers, the supervisory authorities of the EU member states are authorized to grant market access for their own territories. The EU member states also have the power to grant third-country providers market access for their territories under certain conditions, which are similar to the EU "third-country passport."[88]

This way may seem attractive to the United Kingdom, which in the past has often favoured a "divide and rule" strategy. However, the British government would have to deal separately with the 30 countries (27 remaining EU member states and three EEA members) and would be dependent on the decisions of their administrations. Such decisions might well be influenced by bilateral political conflicts, for instance, in the relationship with Spain by the status of Gibraltar and fishing rights in the North Sea, in Visegrad countries by the treatment of immigrants in Britain and so on. Linking market access with problematic areas of foreign policy is a no-go for financial intermediaries: in particular, the subsidiaries of US banks that are at present very active in the United Kingdom might prefer to access the EU Single Market directly from New York.[89]

Bilateral Market Access Based on MiFID II/MiFIR

Recent financial market reforms in the European Union have restricted national discretion on market access by establishing uniform access conditions. The MiFID II and MiFIR grant third-country service providers limited access to retail clients. A precondition is that essential conditions for the equivalence decision of the European Commission are fulfilled; these pertain to third-country registration and supervision, initial capital, participation in an investor protection system, consideration of FATF recommendations, cooperation agreements and tax

---

86 *Cf MiFID II, supra* note 9, arts 16(2), 16(5); *Commission Delegated Regulation (EU) 2017/565 of 25 April 2016 supplementing Directive 2014/65/EU of the European Parliament and of the Council as regards organisational requirements and operating conditions for investment firms and defined terms for the purposes of that Directive,* 31 March 2017, [2017] OJ, L 87/1, arts 22–24 (entered into force 20 April 2017).

87 ECB, "Relocating to the euro area" (2017), online: <www.bankingsupervision.europa.eu/banking/relocating/html/index.en.html> ("Banks in the euro area should be capable of managing all material risks potentially affecting them independently and at the local level, and should have control over the balance sheet and all exposures").

88 *Cf CRD IV, supra* note 9, recital 23; *Solvency II, supra* note 38, art 162(2); Zetzsche, "Drittstaaten", *supra* note 10 at 99 et seq; André Prüm, "Brexit: Options for Banks from the UK to Access the EU Market" (2017) European Banking Institute Working Paper Series 2017 No 7 at 3 et seq.

89 Armour, *supra* note 7 at 54 et seq.

transparency. Only the formal requirement of equivalence and its statement by the European Commission with regard to the law and supervision are missing. Without an EU equivalence decision, member states are able to maintain market access for traditionally close trade partners without the participation of EU authorities, which might benefit Britain.[90] Access could be achieved by establishing a branch or by cross-border trading.

Establishing a Branch

Member states are free to require that third-country service providers wishing to serve retail clients in their territory establish a branch in their country. Such a branch would not be granted an EU passport, meaning that it could only provide its products and services in the member state in which it had been established. For other member states, the third-country provider must observe the respective national requirements, including the establishment of an additional branch. The multiplication of national establishments would make access to the entire Single Market via dependent branches expensive and unattractive. British companies would probably concentrate on the markets of a few large member states.

Member states can decide on the operational conditions of the branch under articles 39 to 41 of the MiFID II. According to the same provisions, they are also free to grant market access without the establishment of a branch. The background of this latitude is a compromise between the European Commission and the European Parliament, on the one hand, and the member states, on the other hand: while the European institutions advocated for the general extension of EU equivalence requirements to retail clients, member states insisted on the need for autonomous national criteria, especially with regard to the requirement of a branch.[91] It should be noted that granting bilateral access might involve the loss of the third-country company's obligations arising from individual contracts.[92]

Cross-border Trade/Correspondence Services

Where British companies are spared from establishing branches in a certain member state, they may provide financial services by way of cross-border trading. They will be able to maintain the common practice of contacting clients and giving investment advice over the phone, in writing or via online platforms that is currently allowed under EU law.[93] This will be the case, for example, in Germany, which does not require the establishment of a branch to service retail clients in its territory (see section 2[4] of the German Banking Act [KWG] and section 96 of the German Securities Act, as amended by the Second Financial Market Reform Act, which permit the German Federal Financial Supervisory Authority [BaFin] to exempt third-country firms from mandatory organization required by these two acts, especially from the obligation to establish branches). The condition is that the company does not need supervision by BaFin because it is already supervised by the respective authority of its home country; the company must also fulfill the conditions of a statutory instrument adopted by the German Ministry of Finance (see section 53c of the KWG). If other member states also generously refrained from

---

90 *MiFID II, supra* note 9, art 39(1).
91 See Sethe, "Drittstaatenregime", *supra* note 27 at 620.
92 See especially article 46 of the MiFIR, *supra* note 9.
93 See Winfried Kluth in Christian Calliess & Matthias Ruffert, eds, *EUV/AEUV*, 5th ed (Munich, Germany: CH Beck, 2016), art 57 AEUV at para 32; Sethe, "Drittstaatenregime", *supra* note 27 at 617.

demanding the establishment of branches, market access under articles 39 to 41 of the MiFID II could become an attractive alternative to the EU passport in the area of investment services.

It remains to be seen how the member states and BaFin will chisel out the details of the legal framework for third-country access. In Germany, the text of section 53c of the KWG suggests that the conditions of the EU passport — equivalence of law and supervision, as well as reciprocity — also apply for market access to retail clients. This is understandable because, otherwise, risks would be imported and market opportunities would be given away. In addition, transactions between EU subsidiaries and parallel third-country branches should be closely monitored to prevent the circumvention of EU capital and other requirements.

Passive Use of the Freedom to Provide Services

Third-country status does not prevent EU citizens from using their freedom to passively receive services.[94] This can be done by so-called reverse solicitation,[95] in which the customer approaches the company abroad, rather than the other way around. In this case, the supervisory and private law of the company's home country applies. The passive use of the freedom of services is a consequence of the territoriality principle that is basically undisputed and partly set out in the secondary law of the European Union.[96]

Institutional Business

It is beyond doubt that EU citizens and companies may cross the border and order services by British providers in the United Kingdom. However, in contrast to the case of Switzerland, it is not to be expected that clients will travel to London with suitcases filled with cash. The London financial centre is dominant in the wholesale business with institutional clients; it is estimated that 90 percent of European institutional financial transactions take place in London.[97] This group of clients wants to be continuously counselled and taken care of, while the third-state company is interested in continually placing new derivatives and investment strategies with their customers.

The German financial supervisor BaFin follows a lenient interpretation of the passive use of the freedom of services. According to its view, customer-initiated "beauty contests," such as product offers to specific addressees or visits by sales staff of the third-state company to existing customers in Germany, would be covered.[98] This interpretation is favourable for British intermediaries engaged in this business. Large banks and investment firms probably have business contacts with almost every institutional investor. Where this is not the case, such contact could be arranged, if customers keep visiting the important financial centre of London several times a year. All in all,

---

94 See ECJ, *Luisi and Carbone v Ministero del Tesoro*, C-286/82, C-26/83, [1984] ECR 377 at para 10; *Decker v Caisse de maladie des employés privés, Kohll v Union des caisses de maladie*, C-120/95, C-158/96, [1998] ECR I-1831, I-1842 at para 29 et seq.

95 Sethe, "Drittstaatenregime", *supra* note 27 at 621 et seq; Kluth, *supra* note 93, art 57 at para 30.

96 *Cf MiFIR*, *supra* note 9, art 46(5)(3); *MiFID II*, *supra* note 9, art 42, which allow reverse solicitation and prohibit member states from imposing any limitations; see also Sethe, "Drittstaatenregime", *supra* note 27 at 621 et seq.

97 *Cf* Sapir, Schoenmaker & Véron, *supra* note 77 at 1.

98 *Cf* BaFin, "Merkblatt zur Erlaubnispflicht nach § 32(1) KWG und § 1(1) und (1a) KWG von grenzüberschreitend betriebenen Bankgeschäften und/oder grenzüberschreitend erbrachten Finanzdienstleistungen von April 2005", online: <www.bafin.de>.

the marketing of new products to institutional clients will remain possible after Brexit, perhaps with a few restrictions. The estimate that 60 percent of the European institutional business will remain in London even after Brexit, therefore, does not lack plausibility.[99]

Business with Retail Clients

The situation is different for business with retail clients.[100] Article 46(5)(3)(2) of the MiFIR and article 42(2) of the MiFID II restrict reverse solicitation: a customer-initiated approach does not entitle the third-country company to market *new* categories of investment products or securities services, if the customer has not explicitly ordered them. This makes it more difficult to reach retail clients, which may include high net worth individuals or smaller family offices.[101] This is why it will be necessary to define the limits of the passive use of the freedom of services, which are quite hazy in parts, for instance, in the marketing of funds shares.[102] Do activities such as the reward-based offer to EU banks and fund managers to join a marketing or an asset commission, the invitation of clients to sports events in the third country (with marketing intentions) or the publication of newspaper articles in the European Union constitute an extension of marketing activities to the European Union that requires the application of EU law? As long as these ambiguities exist, some British intermediaries will offer their services for EU customers in a grey area of law — just as some Swiss funds managers have done so far.

Conclusion

First, after Brexit, British issuers and financial intermediaries will be treated as being located in a third country. Regardless of the future status of the United Kingdom, UK financial intermediaries will be subject to those regulations of EU financial markets law that apply extraterritorially, covering countries with which EU intermediaries maintain financial trade relations.

Second, whether London can continue to fulfill a bundling function for the European business of many financial intermediaries from countries outside the European Union will depend on its future access to the Single Market. This access will most probably not be comprehensive. Rather, it will depend on the particular service or financial instrument offered, as well as the targeted customers.

Third, assuming that British regulation and supervision will be deemed to be equivalent to that of the European Union by a decision of the European Commission, UK firms will probably have market access in the area of public securities offerings, in the reinsurance business, in the area of market infrastructure and in funds management insofar as professional customers and investors are concerned. However, the situation will be different for the banking and primary insurance

---

99 See Sapir, Schoenmaker & Véron, *supra* note 77 at 1.

100 The rule applies to all individual clients, whether or not they have chosen to be professional clients, in the sense of *MiFID II*, *supra* note 9, Annex II, s II.

101 *Cf* Dirk Zetzsche, "Family Offices und Familienvermögen zwischen Recht und Regulierung" (2017) 38 Zeitschrift für Wirtschaftsrecht 945; Dirk Zetzsche, "Family Offices und Familienvermögen zwischen Recht und Regulierung" (2016) 45 Der Gesellschafter 370; Dirk Zetzsche, "Family Offices und Familienvermögen zwischen Recht und Regulierung" in Susanne Kalss, Holger Fleischer & Hans-Ueli Vogt, eds, *Gesellschafts- und Kapitalmarktrecht in Deutschland, Österreich und der Schweiz 2016* (Tübingen, Germany: Mohr, 2017).

102 For details, see Dirk Zetzsche & Thomas Marte, "The AIFMD's Cross-Border Dimension, Third-Country Rules and the Equivalence Concept" in Zetzsche, *AIFMD*, *supra* note 23 at 446 et seq.

businesses and for all financial services offered to retail clients. This could prompt global banking and insurance firms to relocate their European hub from London to the Continent.

Fourth, experience with the recognition practice of third-country equivalence is still lacking in the area of the MiFID II and the AIFMD (which are both important for the UK financial industry), but also in prospectus law and for shareholder transparency.[103] In spite of the European Commission's denial, political criteria may impact on the equivalence decisions. Further, as political decisions, equivalence assessments are not reviewable in court. As a result, UK financial services providers might be hanging in limbo for years.

Fifth, there is no EU passport for third-country companies in the area of banking and primary insurance business. This explains the hectic incorporation activities observed on the Continent since the United Kingdom has triggered the EU exit via article 50 of the Treaty on European Union. If the parent company is based in the United Kingdom, it is unlikely to move its headquarters into the European Union. In most cases, the parent company will try to establish a functionally independent, but minimally equipped, EU subsidiary, which takes advantage of the equivalence-based facilitation of capitalization and supervision.[104] This is why the question of minimal capitalization, staffing and equipment of EU subsidiaries (letter-box companies) deserves special attention by EU supervisors. In this area, crucial questions that need to be answered to achieve a harmonized approach include the availability of intragroup booking, hedging and risk calculation models, as well as the acceptance of dual hatting (in other words, officers functioning in more than one regulated entity at the same time).

Sixth, in the area of investment services to retail clients, member states retain some competences under articles 39 to 41 of the MiFID II. However, EU financial markets law requires third-country companies to fulfill a number of special and reporting duties in contract drafting. Questions of interpretation and application of these provisions, which so far have attracted little attention, are gaining in importance with Brexit and need to be clarified to allow for a smooth functioning of cross-border financial services.

Seventh, if EU investors make use of their right to receive services via reverse solicitation, the business with institutional clients could continue from London with few restrictions. Given the little degree of harmonization in this area, and the EU regulators' push for a harmonized approach vis-à-vis third countries that Brexit has brought about, some uncertainty remains as to the long-term availability of a reverse solicitation model. Among others, reciprocity may be one of the factors determining the future trajectory.

---

103 See also Armour, *supra* note 7 at 54 et seq.

104 *Cf* for insurances, *Solvency II*, *supra* note 38, arts 135, 172 et seq, 227, 232; for banks, *CRR*, *supra* note 9, arts 107, 114, 115, 116, 132, 142; *CRD IV*, *supra* note 9, art 116.

7

Cross-border Insolvencies after Brexit: Views from the United Kingdom and Continental Europe

Howard P. Morris, Gabriel Moss, Federico M. Mucciarelli
and Christoph G. Paulus

Introduction

On June 23, 2016, a small majority of voters engaged in a fit of collective madness and voted in a non-binding referendum to leave the European Union.[1] Despite the referendum being non-binding and purely advisory, the narrow margin of its result and a lack of ideas as to what was to replace EU membership, the UK government gave notice under article 50 of the Treaty

---

1   Between the death of Charlemagne in the ninth century and 1945, countries now in the European Union had taken part in more than 1,000 years of wars that killed many millions of people and devastated countries, cities and economies. Since the founding of the European Union, war between member states has become inconceivable. This can be contrasted with neighbours, such as the former Yugoslav states and the Ukraine. Joining the European Union has also made Western democracy (with some qualifications) permanent in countries that used to be fascistic (Spain, Portugal and Greece) and communist (former Eastern-bloc countries).

on European Union[2] in March 2017. This will potentially lead to the United Kingdom's[3] exit from the European Union in March 2019. Because the remaining 27 member states of the European Union (EU27) exported far more into the United Kingdom than vice versa, the apparent thinking was that the United Kingdom would by agreement be allowed to "have its cake and eat it"[4] — in other words, have all the benefits of EU membership with none of its disadvantages and costs. This, of course, is politically unacceptable to the EU27, who now have the better bargaining position.

As a matter of fact, the United Kingdom's economy is heavily interconnected to the EU Single Market. Such entanglement, which reflects the development of the forces of production in Europe, implies that British firms are often active on the territory of the European Union and that other European companies and firms have activities on the British territory. It goes without saying that the insolvency of firms active across national borders involves interests of stakeholders (creditors, employees and suppliers) situated in different member states. This situation makes it necessary to implement measures aimed at facilitating the mutual recognition and enforcement of insolvency procedures (and, possibly, in the future, the harmonizing of insolvency procedures at the EU level). Furthermore, over recent years, workout procedures, which aim at saving the firm and protecting stakeholders, have gained relevance in the insolvency practice of several member states; to some extent, such pre-insolvency workout proceedings are now included in the European Insolvency Regulation (EIR)[5] that entered into force in 2016.

This chapter is based on talks that the authors gave at a conference held in 2017.[6] Its aim is to address the main problems arising from the United Kingdom's decision to leave the European Union, and it discusses a number of issues in this context: the modes of recognition of foreign insolvency proceedings under British law and the likely impact of Brexit, the impact of Brexit on forum and law shopping, the reform proposal for British workout procedures and the use of British workout procedures by EU companies.

The Impact of Brexit on Recognition/Judicial Assistance in Cross-border Insolvencies

Currently, there are four means of recognition or judicial assistance available in the United Kingdom for foreign insolvency proceedings: first, the EIR; second, section 426 of the Insolvency Act 1986[7] (which applies mostly to Commonwealth countries only, plus Hong Kong and Ireland); third, the United Nations Commission on International Trade Law (UNCITRAL)

---

2   *Treaty of Lisbon Amending the Treaty on European Union and the Treaty Establishing the European Community*, 13 December 2007, [2007] OJ, C 306/01, art 50 (entered into force 1 December 2009).

3   Some self-governing law countries that are politically part of the United Kingdom, such as the Channel Islands and the Isle of Man, are already outside the European Union, but are not considered in this chapter. On the other hand, Gibraltar is treated as part of the United Kingdom for EU purposes.

4   "*Ils veulent le beurre, l'argent du beurre et baiser la fermiere.*" Kalypso Nicolaidis, "Brexit Arithmetics" in John Armour & Horst Eidenmüller, eds, *Negotiating Brexit* (London, UK: Beck/Hart, 2017) at 90.

5   *Regulation (EU) 2015/848 of the European Parliament and of the Council of 20 May 2015 on insolvency proceedings*, [2015] OJ, L 141/19, art 1(1) (entered into force 26 June 2016) [*EIR*].

6   "Cross-border insolvencies post Brexit" (Conference hosted by the British Institute of International and Comparative Law, London, UK, 23 May 2017).

7   *Insolvency Act 1986* (UK), c 45.

Model Law on Cross-border Insolvency (Model Law),[8] enacted in the United Kingdom as the Cross-Border Insolvency Regulations 2006[9] (CBIR); and, fourth, English common law (in England and Wales).

The concept of "recognition," properly so called, is restricted to the cases where the law of one country gives direct effect to the legal provisions of another country. For example, English law recognizes the appointment of a liquidator of a company in the country of its registration on the basis that the question of who is the authorized agent of a company is to be decided by the law of registration. A good statement of the narrow meaning of recognition can be found in the Court of Justice of the European Union (CJEU) decision in *Hoffmann v Krieg*[10]: "Recognition must have the result of conferring on judgments the authority and effectiveness accorded to them in the State in which they were given."[11] Recognition in this narrow sense can be contrasted with judicial assistance, which is the notion that the courts of one law country will use their own remedies to assist foreign proceedings or insolvency practitioners in or from another law country.

In the European Union, all member states are required to recognize/assist UK insolvency proceedings pursuant to the EIR, and some would recognize/assist in the absence of the EIR, pursuant to a local version of the UNCITRAL Model Law or domestic law.

The EIR

The EIR[12] lays down mandatory rules for the allocation of jurisdiction to open main and secondary proceedings between EU member states, mandatory choice of law rules and mandatory recognition and enforcement of insolvency proceedings. It applies to all EU member states, except Denmark, and applies only where the centre of main interests (COMI) of the debtor is in a member state. Jurisdiction to open main proceedings is based on the presence of COMI, and jurisdiction to open local (territorial or secondary) proceedings is based on the presence of an establishment.

In addition, the CJEU has taken jurisdiction in relation to insolvency law avoidance actions against defendants worldwide,[13] although recognizing that there may be problems of enforcement outside the European Union.

The EIR is mandatory EU law and, therefore, takes precedence over the other modes of recognition/assistance in all cases where there is a conflict. However, article 85(3)(b) of the EIR (formerly article 44[3][b] of the original regulation[14]), by way of exception to the overriding nature of the regulation, gives priority in the United Kingdom above the regulation "to the

---

8   UNCITRAL, *UNCITRAL Model Law on Cross-Border Insolvency with Guide to Enactment and Interpretation* (New York, NY: United Nations, 2014) [*Model Law*], online: <www.uncitral.org/pdf/english/texts/insolven/1997-Model-Law-Insol-2013-Guide-Enactment-e.pdf>.

9   *Cross-Border Insolvency Regulations 2006*, SI 2006/1030 [*CBIR*].

10   C-145/86, [1988] ECR I-00645.

11   *Ibid* at 10.

12   See generally Gabriel Moss, Ian E Fletcher & Stuart Isaacs, *The EU Regulation on Insolvency Proceedings*, 3rd ed (Oxford, UK: Oxford University Press, 2016).

13   *Schmid v Hertel*, C-328/12, [2014] ECLI:EU:C:2014:6 [*Hertel*].

14   *Council regulation (EC) No 1346/2000 of 29 May 2000 on insolvency proceedings*, [2000] OJ, L 160/1 (no longer in force) [*Original Regulation*].

extent that it is irreconcilable with the obligations arising in relation to bankruptcy and the winding up of insolvent companies from any arrangements with the Commonwealth"[15] existing at the time the original regulation entered into force. This rather oddly worded exception appears to be a reference to section 426 of the Insolvency Act 1986, but not every section-426 country was within the Commonwealth when the regulation came into effect. In particular, Ireland is within section 426, but not within the Commonwealth. Likewise, Hong Kong at the material date when the original regulation entered into force was within section 426, but outside the Commonwealth, having reverted to the People's Republic of China.

Section 426 of the Insolvency Act 1986

Section 426(4) creates judicial assistance between the UK insolvency courts and certain self-governing law countries that are politically part of the United Kingdom. The law countries specified in section 426(11) are the Channel Islands and the Isle of Man. Under section 426(11)(b), further countries were to be designated by statutory instrument.[16] These are mostly Commonwealth countries, with the exception of Hong Kong and the Republic of Ireland. The implicit theory in nominating all these law countries is that they provide reciprocal provisions mirroring section 426. That is not, in fact, correct, but assistance under section 426 is not conditional on reciprocity.

The use of the word "shall" in section 426 suggests that the granting of *some* assistance is mandatory, but that the type of assistance is discretionary. However, in *Hughes v Hannover*,[17] the court of appeal decided that there was no compulsion to give assistance and that the power to do so was discretionary. In that case, the granting of any assistance was refused. This decision is not altogether easy to reconcile with the subsequent case of *England v Smith*,[18] which stressed the need to give assistance under section 426, as long as it was a proper thing to do.

A necessary prerequisite for jurisdiction to give assistance under section 426 is the making of a request by the foreign court exercising insolvency jurisdiction. There does not seem to be any statutory basis in any section-426 country for sending the customary letter of request that fits into section 426, but it has been held in England that a court has inherent jurisdiction to send such a letter of request.[19]

By section 426(5), the UK courts have a discretion, in acceding to the request from the foreign court, as to whether to apply UK law or the law of the foreign court. The exercise of this discretion is informed by the following obscure sentence: "In exercising its discretion under this subsection, a court shall have regard in particular to the rules of private international law."[20]

A remarkable effect of section 426 is that it can empower the English courts to do something under English law on a request from the foreign court that the English court could not have

---

15   *EIR, supra* note 5, art 85(3)(b).

16   Currently, these are Anguilla, Australia, the Bahamas, Bermuda, Botswana, Canada, Cayman Islands, Falkland Islands, Gibraltar, Hong Kong, Republic of Ireland, Montserrat, New Zealand, St Helena, Turks and Caicos Islands, Tuvalu, British Virgin Islands, Malaysia, South Africa and Brunei.

17   *Hughes v Hannover Ruckversicherungs-Aktiengesellschaf*, [1997] EWCA Civ 857.

18   *England v Smith (Re Southern Equities Corp)*, [2001] Ch 419 (CA).

19   *Panayiotou v Sony Music Entertainment (UK) Ltd*, [1994] Ch 142, [1994] 1 All ER 755 (Nicholls LJ).

20   *Insolvency Act 1986, supra* note 7, s 426(5).

done simply under ordinary domestic insolvency law without a request. In the *Dallhold Estates*[21] case, the Australian court requested that the English court put an Australian company that owned an asset in the United Kingdom into administration. The English court assumed that under ordinary English law, it was not possible to make an administration order for a foreign company. Nevertheless, it made an administration order in respect of Dallhold using the powers given to the English court under section 426. In the *New Cap*[22] case, heard with *Rubin*,[23] one question was whether section 426 could be used to enforce an Australian insolvency judgment setting aside a voidable preference, against a Lloyd's syndicate in London. Although both at first instance and in the court of appeal, it was held that section 426 could be used in this way, the Supreme Court held that it could not.[24] Only the normal rules for the recognition of *in personam* judgments could apply in such a case. The Australian judgment was, in the end, only enforced because the syndicate had submitted to the Australian jurisdiction by lodging a proof in the liquidation and participating in creditors' meetings.

In the later Privy Council case of *Shell Pensioenfonds v Krys*,[25] just lodging a proof, even one that was, in fact, rejected, was held to be sufficient submission to the jurisdiction to enable an anti-suit injunction to be granted against a creditor taking proceedings in Holland to seize the assets in Ireland of a British Virgin Islands (BVI) company in liquidation. By lodging the proof, the defendant obtained a right to have his alleged claim considered for payment as a creditor. Having obtained this benefit, the defendant could not resist the burden of an equitable distribution of the debtor's assets under BVI law and the burden of not being able to disrupt such distribution.

The UNCITRAL Model Law and the UK CBIR

The Model Law, drafted under the auspices of UNCITRAL, is essentially based on a combination of two texts, namely the text of the failed draft convention on which the EIR is based and the now-repealed text of what used to be section 304 of the US Bankruptcy Code.[26] Section 304 permitted ancillary proceedings to be brought in the federal bankruptcy courts of the United States in order to assist foreign insolvency proceedings. Under section 304, the US federal courts applied foreign insolvency law avoidance provisions, such as voidable preferences, in order to assist the foreign insolvency proceeding. The Model Law was implemented in Great Britain[27] by the CBIR.

Differently from the US solution, in Great Britain, the implementation of the Model Law followed the text of article 7 of the Model Law and, thus, created an additional basis for assisting foreign insolvency proceedings, taking nothing away from any pre-existing modes of giving assistance, in particular assistance under common law.

---

21 *Re Dallhold Estates (UK) Pty Ltd*, [1992] BCLC 621 (Ch).
22 *New Cap Reinsurance Corp Ltd v Grant*, [2011] EWCA Civ 971 (Ch).
23 *Rubin v Eurofinance SA*, [2010] EWCA Civ 895, [2011] Ch 133.
24 *New Cap Reinsurance Corp Ltd v Grant*, [2012] UKSC 46.
25 *Shell Pensioenfonds v Krys*, [2014] UKPC 41 [*Shell Pensioenfonds*].
26 11 USC § 304.
27 The jurisdictions of England and Wales and Scotland.

By contrast, the US implementation replaced the former, very useful section 304, which applied to all foreign insolvency proceedings, and put in place something that narrowed the basis for assisting foreign insolvencies. By adopting the Model Law as, apparently, the sole basis for assistance, the US Congress appears unwittingly to have restricted assistance to foreign insolvency proceedings to those that took place in the place of COMI or in the place of an establishment. The COMI or establishment requirement was often difficult to satisfy in the case of offshore jurisdictions. Accordingly, at first, the US decisions under Chapter 15 refused to assist offshore liquidations even in uncontested cases and even where section 304 assistance would have been available. However, another line of US cases seems now to have provided a practical solution. These cases consider that the relevant date for judging where the COMI or establishment is located is not the date of opening of the foreign proceeding, but the date of filing the request for assistance in the United States, as long as any change was not a manipulation.[28]

Is this approach consistent with the approach under the EIR, under which the relevant time for judging COMI is the time of the request filed seeking an opening?[29] It has to be remembered that the EIR deals with jurisdiction *and* recognition/enforcement and uses the tests of COMI and establishment for the purposes of allocating jurisdiction, while the Model Law does not allocate jurisdiction to open insolvency proceedings, but only deals with so-called recognition (actually, judicial assistance). Thus, it is possible to have different approaches to the relevant time at which COMI and establishment are judged.

Great Britain (in other words, England and Wales and Scotland) implemented the Model Law fairly faithfully, but introduced special protections for secured creditors to protect them from the effects of the automatic stay following the so-called recognition. England and Wales remains a much more creditor-friendly jurisdiction than the United States.

Neither the British nor the American legislation of the Model Law requires reciprocity before assistance is given. Article 3 of Schedule 1 to the CBIR,[30] implementing the Model Law in Great Britain, makes it clear that the EIR prevails over the Model Law in case of a conflict. Article 7 of the CBIR, following the text of the UNCITRAL Model Law, provides that nothing in the CBIR limits the power of a court or insolvency office holder from providing additional assistance under other laws of Great Britain.[31] This would include section 426 (where applicable) and the common law.

Article 8 of the CBIR, on the subject of the approach to interpretation, also following the text of the Model Law, provides that regard is to be had to the international origin of the Model Law and the need to promote uniformity in its application.[32] Theoretically, therefore, the Model Law should be interpreted in the same way in every country that adopts it. In terms of the international origin, the terms such as "COMI" or "establishment," which were borrowed from the draft convention that became the EIR, should be interpreted in the same way as the interpretation laid down by the CJEU for the EIR.

---

28 *Re Fairfield Sentry Ltd*, 714 F (3d) 127 (2nd Cir 2013), 2013 US App Lexis 7608 [*Fairfield Sentry*].
29 *Interedil Srl, in liquidation v Fallimento Interedil Srl and Intesa Gestione Crediti SpA*, C-396/09, [2011] 2011 I-09915, ECLI:EU:C:2011:671 [*Interedil*].
30 *CBIR, supra* note 9, Schedule 1, art 3.
31 *Ibid*, art 7.
32 *Ibid*, art 8.

Under article 17 of the CBIR, the foreign proceeding "shall" be recognized.[33] The so-called recognition is recognition as a foreign main proceeding, if it is taking place in the location of COMI, or as a non-main proceeding, if it is taking place where there is an establishment. Thus, article 17 mirrors the system of main and secondary proceedings in the EIR.

In the spirit of the English maxim "justice delayed is justice denied," article 17(3) requires the application for the so-called recognition to be decided upon "at the earliest possible time."[34] Article 20 of the CBIR provides that upon recognition of a foreign main proceeding there is to be a stay, insofar as material, similar to the stay in winding up under the Insolvency Act 1986.[35] However, the English court has the usual powers to lift the stay.

There is an important variation in the standard Model Law in article 20 of the CBIR in that the taking of steps to enforce security over the debtor's property and in relation to similar rights is exempted from the automatic stay. This is perhaps the main difference between the original Model Law and the CBIR, reflecting the pro-secured-creditor nature of English and Scottish law.[36]

The article that perhaps caused the greatest controversy was article 21 of the CBIR. This lists a series of powers that the court can use at the request of the foreign representative to protect assets or to investigate the affairs of the company in the foreign proceedings. The list includes a power to entrust the administration or realization of all or part of the debtor's assets in Great Britain to the foreign representative.[37]

What has attracted controversy is the general introduction to the powers giving the court, at the request of the foreign representative, to "grant any appropriate relief."[38] Perhaps the most interesting question was whether these apparently very wide words included the ability to apply the foreign law, as in the case of section 426 of the Insolvency Act 1986.

The question of whether or not to enable the recognizing court to apply foreign law was debated by the working groups whose debates led to the formulation of the Model Law, and they decided against including any power to apply foreign law.

The inability to apply foreign law is consistent with the UK Supreme Court's decision in *Rubin*,[39] in holding that the apparently very wide words of article 21 do not permit the enforcement of foreign judgments. The question of recognition of foreign judgments, according to the UK Supreme Court, remains governed by the ordinary rules relating to *in personam* and *in rem* judgments to be found in *Dicey, Morris and Collins on the Conflict of Laws*.[40]

---

33 *Ibid*, art 17.

34 *Ibid*, art 17(3).

35 *Ibid*, art 20.

36 But note that Scottish domestic insolvency law has been "devolved" to the Scottish Parliament and, instead of the previous trend to convergence with English law, can now vary considerably from English law.

37 *CBIR*, *supra* note 9, Schedule 1, art 21.

38 *Ibid*.

39 *Rubin v Eurofinance SA*, [2013] 1 AC 236 (SC) [*Rubin*].

40 CGJ Morsel, David McClean & Lord Collins of Mapesbury, eds, *Dicey, Morris and Collins on the Conflict of Laws*, 15th ed (London, UK: Sweet & Maxwell, 2012) at c 14 [*Dicey, Morris and Collins*].

In relation to article 21 and the words "any appropriate relief,"[41] Judge Morgan held in the *Pan Ocean* case[42] that foreign law could not be applied. Judge Morgan refused to give effect to a bar on ipso facto clauses alleged to exist under South Korean law. Judge Morgan pointed to the negative indications regarding the idea of applying foreign law from the UK Supreme Court in *Rubin*. He did, however, give permission to appeal. The appeal has not been pursued.

Article 23 in the CBIR enables the foreign representative "upon recognition of a foreign proceeding"[43] to apply for avoidance orders relating to undervalues, voidable preferences and so on in Great Britain under British law. Article 23 also contains consequential adjustments to adapt the critical dates in the Insolvency Act 1986 to the critical dates in the foreign proceedings.

The CBIR does not prevent British proceedings being opened, notwithstanding the recognition of a foreign main proceeding. Articles 25 to 27, 29 and 30 of the CBIR provide for cooperation and communication between the courts of Great Britain and foreign courts or foreign representatives in order to coordinate proceedings. Where a British insolvency proceeding commences after the recognition of a foreign main proceeding, article 28 provides that the British proceedings will be restricted to assets located in Great Britain,[44] following the pattern of the original regulation,[45] set out in articles 3(2) and 27.

Article 31 of the CBIR parallels article 27 of the original regulation in that it provides for a presumption of insolvency, based on the recognition of a foreign main proceeding. However, the presumption in article 31 of the CBIR is a weaker provision, since it applies "in the absence of evidence to the contrary,"[46] whereas article 27 of the original regulation specifically states that the debtor's insolvency is not to be examined,[47] so that the presumption in the EIR is conclusive: *Bank Handlowy*.[48]

The hotchpot rule in article 20 of the original regulation finds a parallel in article 32 of the CBIR.

One of the early questions that arose in relation to the CBIR and the Model Law is whether the key concepts of COMI and establishment have the same meanings in the Model Law as they have in the EIR. In particular, some of the US case law on Chapter 15 of the US Bankruptcy Code seemed to develop a concept of COMI rather different from that put forward in Europe in the *Eurofood* case.

In the *Stanford* case,[49] in the UK Court of Appeal, some American fraudsters had set up a bank in Antigua as part of a pyramid, or in US terminology, a Ponzi scheme. Antiguan liquidators were appointed, as were Securities and Exchange Commission receivers in the United States.

---

41   *CBIR, supra* note 9, Schedule 1, art 21.
42   *Fibria Celulose S/A v Pan Ocean Co Ltd*, [2014] EWHC 2124.
43   *CBIR, supra* note 9, Schedule 1, art 23.
44   *Ibid*, art 28.
45   *Original Regulation, supra* note 14.
46   *CBIR, supra* note 9, Schedule 1, art 31.
47   *Original Regulation, supra* note 14, art 27.
48   *Bank Handlowy w Warszawie SA v Christianpol sp zoo*, C-116/11, ECLI:EU:C:2012:739.
49   *Re Stanford International Bank Ltd*, [2011] Ch 33 (CA) [*Re Stanford*].

One of several issues for the English courts was whether to recognize as main proceedings under the CBIR either the Antiguan or the US insolvency administrators. Antigua is not a section-426 country. The so-called recognition issue depended on whether the COMI of the bank was in Antigua, where its headquarters and apparent administration were, or in the United States, where the US fraudsters lived and from where they directed the frauds.

The UK court of appeal held that the COMI was in Antigua because the direction of the business from the United States was not ascertainable to creditors, following the emphasis on ascertainability in *Eurofood*.[50] The court of appeal took the view that COMI in the Model Law meant the same as COMI in the EIR.[51]

The most authoritative statement as to COMI under US Chapter 15 can now be found in the decision of the Second Circuit Court of Appeals in the *Fairfield Sentry* case.[52] This is the most highly respected US court, short of the Supreme Court. It adopts an approach based on the "head office functions" or "command and control" theories, without using such expressions. The test looks similar to that in *Interedil* in the CJEU.

The Common Law

An old example of common law judicial assistance lies in the doctrine of ancillary liquidation. Where, for example, there is a main liquidation in Australia and a further liquidation in England, in respect of a company that is registered in Australia, the English liquidation is in theory also a universal proceeding, but the case law since the nineteenth century says that the courts will assist the foreign proceeding by directing the English liquidator to act in a way that is ancillary to the main liquidation and, in particular, by directing the liquidator to transfer both assets and claims to the principal liquidation, net of secured and preferential claims. It is important to note that such a transfer avoids the application of normal English statutory rules of proving and distribution, but the old case law, in practice, was only applied to other English-law-based jurisdictions, which had similar rules of proof and distribution.

Common law judicial assistance was developed, mainly for English-law-based countries that had no legislative provisions on the subject, by internationalist-minded judges, in particular Lord Hoffmann.[53] The abolition of exchange controls in leading economies and the increasing internationalization of economies and markets required judge-led changes in the absence of international treaties and statutes affecting leading economies.

In the *Banque Indosuez* case,[54] there was a Chapter 11 bankruptcy, which under US law restrains realizations by secured creditors. A creditor claiming to be secured over certain assets in England

---

50 *Eurofood IFSC Ltd*, C-341/04, [2006] ECR-I 1078, ECLI:EU:C:2006:281 [*Eurofood*].

51 A majority of the court of appeal appeared to reject the "head office functions" test, which had been developed by the domestic case law in England, France, Germany, Hungary and elsewhere. This appears to have been based on a misunderstanding that the head office functions test was not based on objective and ascertainable facts as required by the *Eurofood*, *ibid*, decision. The head office functions test on the basis of objective and ascertainable facts has since been adopted, using slightly different language, in the *Interedil* case, *supra* note 29.

52 *Fairfield Sentry*, *supra* note 28.

53 *Banque Indosuez SA v Ferromet Resources Inc*, [1993] BCLC 112 [*Banque Indosuez*]; *Re HIH Casualty and General Insurance Ltd, McMahon v McGrath*, [2008] 1 WLR 852 (HL) [*HIH Casualty*]; *Cambridge Gas Transport Corp v Official Committee of Unsecured Creditors of Navigator Holdings Plc*, [2007] 1 AC 508 (PC) (in effect, overruled by subsequent cases: see *Singularis Holdings Ltd v PWC*, [2015] AC 1675 (PC) [*Singularis*]).

54 *Banque Indosuez*, *supra* note 53.

sought an injunction in England in relation to those assets. This was a claim against property of the debtor in Chapter 11 proceedings and subject to a stay under US bankruptcy law.

Judge Hoffman said as follows:

> This court is not of course bound by the stay under United States law but will do its utmost to co-operate with the United States Bankruptcy Court and avoid any action which might disturb the orderly administration of Inc in Texas under ch 11. This court has jurisdiction to make interlocutory orders for the preservation of Inc's property in this country by way of assistance to the United States Bankruptcy Court but no such assistance has been requested here. So far as the evidence shows, these proceedings are the individual act of a single creditor and, if successful, would enable that creditor to secure some of Inc's assets outside the United States bankruptcy process.[55]

In exercising the discretion whether or not to grant injunctive relief, Judge Hoffman took into account the fact that the proceedings had not been permitted by the US bankruptcy court by way of exception to their stay.

The *Banque Indosuez* case established two propositions. First, the Chapter 11 stay was not recognized by the English courts; in other words, the US statutory provision creating a mandatory worldwide stay would not be given direct effect in England. But, second, the English courts would provide judicial assistance to help the US bankruptcy proceedings and keep the assets subject to those proceedings intact and subject to the control of the US court. For the latter purpose, ordinary English law remedies such as injunctions could either be granted or refused. Note that granting an injunction is a statutory remedy.

While the result of common law judicial assistance looks similar to recognition in a narrow sense, there are fundamental differences. Recognition is automatic and subject to set rules. Judicial assistance is discretionary and is given on the basis of the principle of modified universalism.

In the *Rubin/New Cap* case,[56] Lord Collins describes common law judicial assistance as one of the four main methods for "assisting" insolvency proceedings in other jurisdictions. He gives examples of cases where common law judicial assistance has been granted: vesting of English assets in a foreign office holder, orders for examination in support of a foreign proceedings and orders for the remittal of assets to a foreign liquidation.[57]

In *Singularis*, Lord Sumption accepted the application of the principle of modified universalism by way of common law judicial assistance, "subject to local law and local public policy."[58]

Lord Sumption proceeded to ask the obvious corollary question, namely, what the limits are of the application of the principle of modified universalism. In particular, he referred to the issue of how far, in the absence of a relevant statutory power, it was appropriate to develop the common law so as to recognize an equivalent power. He said that this "does not admit of a single, universal answer. It depends on the nature of the power that the court is being asked to

---

55 *Ibid* at 117i–118b.
56 *Rubin, supra* note 39 at 25, 29.
57 *Ibid* at 31.
58 *Singularis, supra* note 53 at 19.

exercise."[59] The Privy Council confined itself to the particular form of assistance being sought in *Singularis*, namely, an order for production of information by an entity within the personal jurisdiction of the Bermuda court.

Lord Sumption identified the case of *Norwich Pharmacal*[60] as illustrating the capacity of the common law to develop a power in the court to compel the production of information when this is necessary to give effect to a recognized legal principle.[61] Lord Sumption considered that there was an analogous power of judicial assistance for foreign insolvency proceedings at common law.[62] The recognized legal principle which it gave effect to was the principle of modified universalism.[63] That, in turn, "is founded on the public interest in the ability of foreign courts exercising insolvency jurisdiction in the place of the company's incorporation to conduct an orderly winding up of its affairs on a worldwide basis, notwithstanding the territorial limits of their jurisdiction."[64]

Lord Sumption continued, "The basis of that public interest is not only comity, but a recognition that in a world of global business it is in the interest of every country that companies with transnational assets and operations should be capable of being wound up in an orderly fashion under the law of the place of their incorporation and on the basis that would be recognised as effective internationally."[65]

He then stated, rather helpfully, "The courts have repeatedly recognised not just a right but a duty to assist in whatever way they properly can."[66]

Lord Sumption, thus, appeared to be recognizing not merely a discretion to assist, but a positive duty to do so. He made the practical point that recognition by a domestic court of the status of the foreign liquidator would mean very little if it entitled the foreign liquidator to take possession of the company's assets "but left him with no effective means of identifying or locating them."[67]

Lord Sumption held that "[t]here is a power at common law to assist a foreign court of insolvency jurisdiction by ordering the production of information in oral or documentary form which is necessary for the administration of a foreign winding up."[68]

Lord Sumption, in the Privy Council *Shell Pensioenfonds v Krys*[69] case, applied the principle of modified universalism and common law principles to an "outgoing" case so as to prevent a creditor seizing assets outside the BVI of a BVI company in liquidation.

---

59 *Ibid.*

60 *Norwich Pharmacal Co v Customs & Excise Commissioners*, [1974] AC 133 [*Norwich Pharmacal*].

61 *Ibid* at 22–23.

62 *Ibid* at 23.

63 *Ibid.*

64 Note the reference to the place of incorporation. As Lord Hoffmann pointed out in *HIH Casualty*, *supra* note 53 at 31, this may now be out of date and courts should arguably look to the COMI instead.

65 *Norwich Pharmacal*, *supra* note 60 at 23.

66 *Ibid.*

67 *Ibid.*

68 *Ibid* at 25.

69 *Shell Pensioenfonds v Krys*, *supra* note 25.

The judgment concerned another aspect of the Fairfield Sentry liquidation which was referred to above.[70] A substantial amount of money was lodged with the Irish branch of a Dutch bank. Prior to the opening of Fairfield's liquidation, the pension fund claimed to be a creditor and obtained a pre-action freezing order over the money in a Dublin bank account from a Dutch court. After the opening of the BVI liquidation, it submitted a proof, which was rejected by the liquidators. Nevertheless, the pension fund was held to have submitted to BVI jurisdiction, as had occurred in *Rubin*. Lord Sumption pointed, as did Lord Collins in *Rubin*, to the benefit/ burden principle. The pension fund had the benefit of obtaining a right to have its claim considered, and it made no difference to the question of submission to the jurisdiction of the BVI court that the claim was rejected.[71]

On the basis of modified universalism, the Privy Council ruled that, in principle, any creditor subject to the jurisdiction who begins or continues foreign proceedings that will interfere with the statutory trusts over the assets of the company in insolvent liquidation will be subject to the grant of an injunction regardless of the residence or nationality of the creditor.[72] By contrast, there is no objection to invoking the merely adjudicatory jurisdiction of a foreign court as long as the litigation is not oppressive or vexatious.[73] Moreover, an injunction can be avoided if the creditor agrees to bring any assets realized in foreign proceedings into the insolvency.[74]

The Effect of Brexit on the above Regimes

The effect of Brexit on cross-border insolvencies depends on a number of potential variables.

The first variable is whether the United Kingdom will actually leave the European Union. Parliament will be able to vote on the terms of exit achieved by the negotiation. There is a possibility that the terms negotiated will not be accepted by Parliament, since the UK government only has a majority in the House of Commons with the help of the Democratic Unionist Party, a small sectarian Northern Irish party, that has special concerns relating to Ireland, and because of a risk posed by strongly pro-EU Conservative members of Parliament. The Conservatives also have no majority in the House of Lords, where the majority is strongly pro-European Union. There is also strong pressure for a second referendum on the actual terms of exit. These terms may be so unfavourable that a majority of people will prefer to stay in the European Union. Alternatively, there may be no deal at all if, for example, the UK government refuses to pay the substantial sums required by the EU27 for exit. Even government ministers have had to admit that leaving without a deal would be bad for the United Kingdom, and this could lead to a vote to stay in.

The second variable is whether the article 50 notice is irrevocable or not. The United Kingdom has assumed that it is irrevocable, but the legal position is unclear.

The third variable is whether there will be an interim deal or implementation period, pending the finalization of negotiations. Depending on whom one listens to, the existing situation, or something similar, could remain for a minimum of two years from March 2017 and possibly a

---

70 *Fairfield Sentry, supra* note 28 and accompanying text.
71 *Ibid* at 31.
72 *Ibid* at 39.
73 *Ibid* at 40.
74 *Ibid.*

number of years after that, as trade negotiations could take a number of further years, based on previous precedents, such as the EU deal with Canada.[75] Presumably, insolvency proceedings started under an EU or European Economic Area (EEA) law regime will continue to be governed by EU law even after exiting the European Union or the EEA.[76]

The fourth variable is whether, as well as leaving the European Union, the United Kingdom also leaves or rejoins the EEA. This is sometimes called the Norway option. It includes the further sub-issue of whether leaving the European Union automatically means that the United Kingdom leaves the EEA or not. According to a Clifford Chance analysis, the United Kingdom is an individual member of the EEA. The significance of the EEA is that the directives, although not the regulations, apply within the EEA to member states that are not part of the European Union, namely Norway, Liechtenstein and Iceland.

The fifth variable is whether, if the United Kingdom leaves the European Union and the EEA, the regulations and/or the directives are kept by means of treaty. The UK position paper seems to envisage this possibility, but UK-government policy seems to be against any role for the CJEU. It may be that a special solution can be found, such as the European Free Trade Association (EFTA) court, which applies to non-EU members of the EEA.

Assessment

Between 1995 and 2016, the United Kingdom, through the hard work of academics, judges and practitioners, had become the lead jurisdiction in all aspects of the EIR, and English has taken over entirely as the language in which the regulations are discussed throughout the European Union.[77] The vote to leave now threatens all the work, effort and success in relation to the regulations.

The repeal/withdrawal bill[78] promises, on the United Kingdom's leaving the European Union, to domesticate EU law and turn it into English law, capable of repeal or amendment as any other UK legislation. This would mean that the United Kingdom is bound, at least on day one, by the law contained in the regulations and the legislation implementing the directives. However, unless there is an agreement to the contrary, the EU27 and the further three countries of the EEA would not be bound, as far as the United Kingdom is concerned. This would be one-sided and would not make a great deal of sense. For example, if a French company entered French insolvency proceedings, England would be bound to recognize them in England as if the EIR applied, but there would be no reciprocity where an English company went into an English insolvency proceeding and sought recognition in France. The UK position paper suggests that relations should be based on reciprocity, so that in the absence of a treaty, the United Kingdom could expect an early repeal of the provisions of the regulations. The position on the directives may be more complicated, as the United Kingdom may wish to show "equivalence" in order to have access to the EU27 financial sectors.

---

75 The current government seems to be heading toward something like the Canada deal, rather than the EEA or Switzerland, whereas the opposition Labour Party appears to be sympathetic to a closer arrangement.

76 This is the sensible suggestion in the EU27 position paper.

77 The membership of the United Kingdom in the European Union and its designation of English as an official EU language have given Ireland and Malta the luxury of nominating Irish and Maltese as their official EU languages. If the United Kingdom leaves, Ireland and Malta will, in practice, probably have to request a change in EU rules to enable them to add English as an EU language in addition to Irish and Maltese.

78 Bill 5, *European Union (Withdrawal) Bill* [HL], 2017–2019 sess (1st reading 13 July 2017).

The UK policy is to leave the Single Market (and, thus, the EEA) and the Customs Union. Therefore, unless and to the extent that treaties are agreed on, the United Kingdom may well repeal the provisions derived from the regulations and possibly those derived from the directives. To some extent, the United Kingdom can fall back on the UNCITRAL Model Law and the common law. These may help incoming cases, but, of course, do not assist outgoing ones, except in the few EU member states that have adopted the UNCITRAL Model Law or where there are other ways of getting recognition for English insolvency proceedings. In some cases, it may be possible to have parallel proceedings and coordination/cooperation. Schemes of arrangement may also continue to work and be recognized on the basis of conflicts rules.

If the United Kingdom leaves the European Union without a treaty keeping the EIR, it will be in the same position as any other non-EU country, except in the few cases where the Model Law or domestic law comes to the rescue, and (it is thought) where an English scheme of arrangement can be used under English company law.

Impact of Brexit on Forum and Law Shopping

The Notion of Forum Shopping

The withdrawal of the United Kingdom from the European Union is likely to have an impact on debtors' ability to move from one jurisdiction to another in a search for the most suitable procedure (forum shopping). One of the goals of the EIR is to avoid "incentives for the parties to transfer assets or judicial proceedings from one member state to another, seeking to obtain a more favourable legal position to the detriment of the general body of creditors."[79] Forum shopping, therefore, is the situation whereby a debtor relocates relevant factors from his or her original country into another, with the aim of shifting the competence to hear the insolvency case and applying insolvency rules of the new country. In order to shift this competence, a debtor should relocate its COMI from one jurisdiction to another.[80] It is to be noted that, under the EIR, forum shopping is to be avoided only if detrimental for "the general body of creditors."

The rationale is that creditors must know in advance which insolvency rules and proceedings will apply in the event of a debtor's default. Therefore, at least in theory, in order to allow potential creditors to predict with absolute certainty which insolvency regime will apply should their debtors become insolvent, the latter must not be able to shift the relevant connecting factors after debts are incurred. Such a prohibition, however, would be in breach of the EU freedom of establishment and would be highly unrealistic in a globalized economy. Thus, the question is rather to what extent debtors should be allowed to shift their COMI from one jurisdiction to another and how to prevent fictive or merely exploitative relocations. Several scholars, indeed, have argued that a change of insolvency regime might produce efficient outcomes when the new applicable law increases the value of the firm and the likelihood of its workout.[81]

---

79 *EIR*, *supra* note 5, recital 5. See Moss, Fletcher & Isaacs, *supra* note 12; Reinhard Bork & Renato Mangano, *European Cross-Border Insolvency Law* (New York, NY: Oxford University Press, 2016).

80 *EIR*, *supra* note 5, art 3(1).

81 See Horst Eidenmüller, "Free Choice in International Insolvency Law" (2005) 6 Eur Bus Org L Rev 241; Sefa M Franken, "Three Principles of Transnational Corporate Bankruptcy Law: A Review" (2005) 11 Eur LJ 232; Wolf-Georg Ringe, "Forum shopping under the EU insolvency regulation" (2008) 9 Eur Bus Org L Rev 579; Gerard McCormack, "Jurisdictional Competition and Forum Shopping in Insolvency Proceedings" (2009) 68 Cambridge LJ 191.

Assessing when a debtor has actually shifted its COMI is, however, far from being an easy task and equally complex is assessing whether such a shift is detrimental for the general body of creditors. Until the United Kingdom eventually withdraws from the European Union, the answers to these questions are to be found by considering the EIR and by looking at the case law of the CJEU, while other sources of UK insolvency law (in particular, the Insolvency Act 1986 and the conflict of law rules based on common law) only play an ancillary function. The COMI, in particular, is a fact-sensitive criterion, which could be uncertain in the eyes of creditors at the moment when debts were incurred. To increase the predictability of a company's COMI, the EIR presumes that it is situated in the place of a company's registered office,[82] with the consequence that, unless such presumption is rebutted, the country of incorporation governs both company law issues and the insolvency proceeding.[83] Additionally, the insolvency regime of the member state where a debtor's COMI is situated should apply.[84] Regarding individuals exercising a business or a professional activity, the EIR presumes that their COMI is where their "principal place of business" is situated, unless the contrary is proven.[85] By contrast, the COMI of over-indebted private persons and consumers is presumed to be in the country of their habitual residence, unless the contrary is proven.

Companies' Insolvency Tourism

Companies and other legal entities can be incorporated in a member state and have all their assets, businesses and/or headquarters in any other member state, and member states cannot bar companies incorporated in other member states from having their entire activities or their headquarters on their territories, providing, however, that the state of incorporation allows this.[86] Regarding the relocation of a company's registered office, which normally leads to a change of applicable company law,[87] the case law of the CJEU has clarified that neither the country of arrival[88] nor the country of departure[89] can prohibit or unreasonably restrict these operations. In particular, freedom of establishment companies incorporated under the law of a member state can convert themselves into companies of another member state, regardless of whether any real establishment is transferred or not.

What is interesting, and quite ironic in light of the recent Brexit referendum, is that the United Kingdom has emerged as the winner of the regulatory competition among member states. In this regard, recent research conducted for the European Commission shows (with reference to private companies only) that the United Kingdom is by far the most popular target country for

---

82 *EIR, supra* note 5, art 3(1).

83 *Ibid*, art 7(1).

84 *Ibid*.

85 *Ibid*, art 3(1)(1). See Moss, Fletcher & Isaacs, *supra* note 12 at 446–47.

86 *Centros Ltd v Erhvervsog Selskabsstyrelsen*, C-212/97, [1999] ECR I-1459, ECLI:EU:C:1999:126; Überseering *BV v Nordic Construction Company Baumanagement GmbH*, C-208/00, [2002] ECR I-9919, CLI:EU:C:2002:632; *Kamer van Koophandel en Fabrieken voor Amsterdam v Inspire Art*, C-167/01, [2003] ECR I-1095, ECLI:EU:C:2003:512.

87 See Federico M Mucciarelli, "The Function of Corporate Law and the Effects of Reincorporations in the U.S. and the EU" (2012) 20 Tulane J Intl & Comp L 421; Carsten Gerner-Beuerle, Federico M Mucciarelli, Mathias Siems & Edmund-Philipp Schuster, "Cross-border reincorporations in the European Union: the case for comprehensive harmonisation" (2017) J Corp L Stud 1, online: <www.tandfonline.com/doi/abs/10.1080/14735970.2017.1349428?journalCode=rcls20>.

88 *VALE* Építési *kft*, C-378/10, [2012] ECLI:EU:C:2012:440 at 39 [*VALE*].

89 *Cartesio Oktato es Szolgaltato bt*, C-210/06, [2008] I-09641, ECLI:EU:C:2008:723 (obiter dictum); *Polbud v Wykonawstwo sp zoo*, C-106/16, ECLI:EU:C:2017:804.

incorporating pseudo-foreign companies.[90] The main reason for the United Kingdom's position is its adoption of a clear-cut incorporation theory[91] under the conflict of law standpoint. If the attention is shifted to COMI relocations, the United Kingdom would also be expected to be a popular target country for insolvency tourism and forum shopping.

First of all, companies incorporated in another member state might decide to relocate their headquarters, assets or activities onto the British territory, while keeping their registered offices in the countries of origin. This decision leads to a relocation of a company's COMI only by rebutting the presumption of coincidence with the company's registered office. In the *Eurofood* decision, the CJEU addressed the question of whether the COMI of Eurofood, an Irish subsidiary of the Italian group Parmalat, was located in Ireland or in Italy. The decision is significant in that the CJEU dismissed the notion that a debtor's COMI is in the place of its central administration, where the internal head office functions are carried out on a regular basis[92] and made it more burdensome to overcome the presumption that a company's COMI coincides with its registered office.

The *Eurofood* ruling, however, was not related to situations of *conflit mobile*, in which a shift of connecting factor also shifts applicable law. The CJEU addressed these cases some years later, in the decision rendered in the case, *Interedil*,[93] in which it provided an answer to the question of what the factual elements are that courts should consider in assessing a company's COMI after a cross-border relocation of its registered office. An Italian company (Interedil Srl) transferred its registered office to London and was henceforth removed from the local register.[94] Almost two years later, an important creditor filed for insolvency in Italy; the local court assessed that Interedil still owned assets and a bank account in Italy and concluded that its COMI was still in Italy. On Interedil's appeal, the Italian Corte di Cassazione referred to the CJEU for a preliminary ruling aiming at clarifying, among other things, which factual elements could rebut the presumption that a debtor's COMI coincides with a company's registered office in a situation where this registered office has been shifted from one country to another before the filing for insolvency. According to the CJEU, in these cases, the presumption that a company's COMI coincides with the new registered office can be rebutted if "a comprehensive assessment of all the relevant factors makes it possible to establish, in a manner that is ascertainable by third parties, that the company's actual centre of management and supervision and of the management of its interests is located in that other Member State."[95] The CJEU also held that if a company's headquarters actually coincides with its registered office in a way ascertainable by third parties, the presumption in that provision cannot be rebutted. The evidence to be provided to rebut the presumption is, however, still shrouded in uncertainties.

---

90 See Carsten Gerner-Beuerle, Federico M Mucciarelli, Mathias Siems & Edmund-Philipp Schuster, *Study on the law applicable to companies* (Luxembourg: Publications Office of the European Union, 2016), online: <https://publications.europa.eu/en/publication-detail/-/publication/259a1dae-1a8c-11e7-808e-01aa75ed71a1>.

91 According to the incorporation theory, companies are governed by the law of the country where they are incorporated or where their registered office is situated. See *Dicey, Morris and Collins, supra* note 40 at rule 173.

92 This solution was, however, followed by some British decisions. See e.g. *Re BRAC Rent-A-Car International Inc*, [2003] EWHC 128 (Ch); *Re Daisytek-ISA*, [2004] BPIR 30 (Ch); *Re MG Rover*, [2005] BWHC 874 (Ch); *Re Collins & Aikman Corp Group*, [2005] EWHC 1754 (Ch); *Re Lennox Holdings Ltd*, [2009] BCC 155 (Ch).

93 *Interedil, supra* note 29.

94 For a more detailed analysis of the facts (which are more complex than what they seem at first glance), see Federico Mucciarelli, "The Hidden Voyage of a Dying Italian Company: From the Mediterranean Sea to Albion" (2012) 9 Eur Co & Fin L Rev 571.

95 *Interedil, supra* note 29 at 53. This language will become part of the new recital 29 (see Insolvency Regulation Reform).

When a company incorporated in another member state shifts its headquarters or other physical elements onto the British territory, the question arises as to whether a British court would recognize that the presumption laid down in the EIR has been rebutted. In this regard, among other cases, two significant decisions can be mentioned.

In the first decision, a German company managed to convert into a British limited company, to whom all the assets and activities of the former were transferred.[96] Shortly thereafter, the company became insolvent and insolvency proceedings were simultaneously opened in Germany and in the United Kingdom. In that case, the British court recognized the COMI as being still in Germany, on the basis of quite evident factual elements that still linked the debtor's activity to that country. In particular, the insolvent company still had creditors and employees only in Germany, its bank account was still in Germany and, most importantly, all contracts were written in German.

The opposite conclusion was reached in the case, *Re Hellas Telecommunication*.[97] A Luxembourg company transferred its head office and its principal operating office to London before filing for insolvency. Judge Lewison considered the presumption of coincidence between registered office and COMI rebutted, on the basis that third parties could clearly ascertain that Hellas' COMI was in London. He maintained that creditors were aware that Hellas' head office functions were carried out in London for the following reasons: creditors "were notified of its change of address"; "an announcement was made by way of a press release that its activities were shifting to England"; Hellas has opened a bank account in London "and all payments are made into and from that bank account"; Hellas "has registered under the Companies Act in this country, although its registered office remains in Luxembourg and it may remain liable to pay tax in Luxembourg too"[98]; and "all negotiations between the company and its creditors have taken place in London."[99]

Eventually, the question of whether foreign EU companies can transfer their registered offices to the United Kingdom and convert into British companies should be addressed. Under the traditional UK conflicts of laws, neither domestic nor foreign companies can have a "domicile of choice." In the words of Judge Macnaughten, "the domicile of origin, or the domicile of birth, using with respect to a company a familiar metaphor, clings to it throughout its existence."[100] From the standpoint of English conflicts of laws rules, therefore, either a new company is incorporated in England or a company is registered in England as a foreign company having a place of business in England. Such an approach, however, when referred to inbound relocations of registered offices, is in breach of the freedom of establishment, as interpreted by the CJEU

---

96 *Hans Brochier Holding Ltd v Exner*, [2006] EWHC 2594. In theory, German companies cannot convert into foreign entities. A strategy, however, exists to circumvent this prohibition: the German company converts into a partnership, a GmbH & Co KG, one of whose partners is a newly formed foreign corporation (a British company in the *Brochier* case); thereafter, all German partners withdraw from the partnership with the result that all assets of the partnership accrue to the foreign shareholder under § 738 BGB (the German civil code).

97 *Re Hellas Telecommunication (Luxembourg) II SCA*, [2009] EWHC 3199 (Ch) [*Hellas*]; see Moss, Fletcher & Isaacs, *supra* note 12 at 56.

98 *Hellas*, *supra* note 97 at 4.

99 *Ibid* at 5.

100 *Gasque v Inland Revenue Commissioners*, [1940] 2 KB 80 at 84. See also *National Trust Co v Ebro Irrigation & Power Ltd*, [1954] DLR 326 (Ont H Ct J); *International Credit and Investment Co v Adham*, [1994] 1 BCLC 66 (Ch).

in *VALE*,[101] to the extent that it is applied to foreign companies incorporated in the EEA.[102] It is worth mentioning, however, that foreign companies can incorporate a shell company in England and merge into it under the Cross-Border Merger Directive.[103] Such a cross-border merger would lead to results quite similar to a cross-border conversion.

Individuals' Insolvency Tourism

Bankruptcy tourism of individuals is made more complex by the lack of any objective place or registration, such as companies' registered offices, and by the quite uncertain concepts of residence and place of business, which trigger the presumption of COMI under the EIR. Much more importantly, natural persons can relocate their activities or residences more easily than firms and companies; additionally, low-cost flights and fast transports throughout Europe (such as the Eurostar trains that connect London to Paris and Brussels) allow European citizens to dissociate their main residence from the place where they conduct their activities. Imagine that a professional is a resident on the Continent, for instance, in France or Germany, while conducting her professional activities mainly from London, where she, however, spends only three days a week, being able to work from home the other days of the week: where would her place of business be situated in case of default?

Individual bankruptcy tourism has been addressed by several decisions, yet two of them deserve to be analyzed more thoroughly. The seminal case, *Shierson v Vlieland-Boddy*, is to be addressed in the first place.[104] Shierson divorced his wife and then moved from the United Kingdom to Spain; after his divorce, he maintained a property in the United Kingdom, where he came regularly to visit his children. After Shierson's default, the question arose whether English courts had jurisdiction regarding the main insolvency proceeding. The registrar stated that "in order to give effect to the policy of the [EIR], the court must, in my judgment, have regard to the time at which the debt is incurred because that is the time at which the creditors need to assess the risks of insolvency." The registrar's opinion was coherently based upon creditors' request for predictability. This solution, however, is not compatible with the CJEU case law[105] and, therefore, the court of appeal reversed this decision.[106] The court of appeal, however, also maintained that historical facts could be considered in assessing a debtors' COMI. Indeed, Lord Justice Chadwick concluded that, although the COMI "is to be determined in the light of the facts as they are at the relevant time for determination...those facts include historical facts which have led to the position as it is at the time for determination [and that] it is important...

---

101 *VALE*, *supra* note 88.

102 Paul Davies & Sarah Worthington, *Gower: Principles of Modern Company Law*, 10th ed (Sweet and Maxwell, 2016) at 142.

103 *Directive 2005/56/CE, of 26 October 2005, on the cross-border mergers of limited liability companies*, [2005] OJ, L 310/1.

104 *Shierson v Vlieland-Boddy*, [2005] EWCA Civ 974 [*Shierson*].

105 The reference date to assess the COMI is the filing for insolvency: *Staubitz-Schreiber*, C-1/04, [2006] ECR I-00701.

106 The court of appeal denied competence to UK courts by stating that the relevant date to assess the COMI is the hearing date of the petition: *Shierson, supra* note 104 at 55. This part of the decision has been clearly overruled by the CJEU decisions in the cases *Staubitz-Schreiber*, and *Interedil, supra* note 29, which maintained that debtors' COMI are to be assessed at the date of the filing for insolvency: *O'Donnell v The Governor and Company of the Bank of Ireland*, [2012] EWHC 3749 (Ch) at para 36. See Gabriel Moss, "A very peculiar 'establishment'" (2006) 19:2 Insolvency Intelligence 20; David Petkovich, "The correct time to determine the debtor's COMI — case note and commentary on *Staubitz-Schreiber* and *Vlieland-Boddy*" (2006) 22 Insol L & Prac 76.

to have regard to the need, if the centre of main interests is to be ascertainable by third parties, for an element of permanence."[107]

Therefore, in order to prove that the new administrative seat has become permanent and is, therefore, ascertainable by third parties, courts shall also consider historical facts, but only to the extent that these facts have produced the position existing at the relevant time (the date of filing).

The second decision that deserves to be mentioned was rendered in the case, *Irish Bank Resolution v Quinn*.[108] Quinn, a professional resident in the Republic of Ireland, went bankrupt and claimed that his business was based in Northern Ireland, not far from the border with the Republic of Ireland. A court of Northern Ireland issued a bankruptcy order, which the High Court of Justice in Northern Ireland, however, reversed, recognizing that Quinn's COMI was in the Republic of Ireland. The court raised the question as to the circumstances under which a new head office is deemed "sufficiently accessible" to creditors. The criterion that the location of the COMI must be ascertainable by third parties "would indicate something different from being actually notified. If not made public, it must be 'sufficiently accessible.'...It should be reasonably or sufficiently ascertainable or ascertainable by a reasonably diligent creditor."[109]

In the court's view, in order to make the new head office ascertainable by third parties, it is necessary "to make the COMI available on the internet or through telephone directories or trade directories or otherwise generally available in the member state in which he has established his centre of main interest would make it public."[110] In that specific case, however, Quinn did not publish his telephone number in a public directory or his web page; hence, this location was not sufficiently ascertainable by third parties. In turn, had Quinn made his place of business publicly available, through telephone directories or online, the court would probably have reached a different conclusion.

Brexit and Forum Shopping

What has been described so far is likely to become outdated as soon as the United Kingdom withdraws from the European Union. At the moment, the final result of the withdrawal negotiation is unpredictable. Several scenarios might be imagined, ranging from a "soft" Brexit at the one extreme, to a "hard" Brexit at the other. A soft Brexit scenario might mirror, for example, the special agreements between the European Union and the member states with certain third countries, such as Switzerland. Under the opposite, hard Brexit, scenario, however, things are much more clear: both freedom of establishment (being an essential element of the Single Market) and the EIR will not apply to the United Kingdom anymore. The United Kingdom would be considered a third country by EU member states, which will apply their own private international law rules vis-à-vis the United Kingdom with regard to both company law and insolvency regime.

---

107 *Shierson, supra* note 104 at 55.
108 *Irish Bank Resolution Corp Ltd v Quinn*, [2015] IEHC 175, [2012] NICh 1, [2012] BCC 608.
109 *Ibid* at 28.
110 *Ibid.*

UK companies' private international law is based upon the incorporation theory.[111] Hence, not much will change regarding foreign EU companies: a company incorporated in an EU member state and having its assets or its headquarters on the British territory will continue to be automatically recognized in the United Kingdom as a foreign entity governed by the law of the country of incorporation. The country of incorporation, however, could follow different private international law criteria toward extra-EU countries (such as the United Kingdom in a hard Brexit scenario), ranging from a pure incorporation theory at the one extreme to a pure real seat theory at the other. If the country of origin follows the incorporation theory, a relocation of headquarters, assets or activities onto the British territory is perfectly acceptable and does not lead to the company's liquidation. By contrast, countries that follow the "real seat theory" are more likely to consider a relocation of headquarters as a shift of the relevant connecting factor, which should lead to a change of applicable law or to the company's liquidation.

The second issue that needs to be briefly addressed is how the hierarchy of sources will change in a hard Brexit scenario regarding insolvency law. The EIR will not apply in the United Kingdom, with the consequence that insolvencies of debtors having a cross-border relevance will be assisted by the Insolvency Act 1986, the UNCITRAL Model Law[112] and the conflict of law rules based on common law. The Insolvency Act 1986 provides for a quasi-automatic recognition and enforcement of foreign insolvency proceedings only from a list of countries designated by the Secretary of State;[113] in practice, such designated countries are only Commonwealth countries, among which the only EU member state is Ireland.[114] Unless all EU member states will be designated by the Secretary of State, therefore, section 486 of the Insolvency Act 1986 would not be of much help in sorting out cross-border insolvencies connected with other EU member states. The Model Law, by contrast, seems to be a much more promising instrument to deal with cross-border insolvencies, mostly so because the UK provisions do not include a reciprocity clause, which would have paralyzed its application due to the limited implementation of the UNCITRAL Model Law in other member states.[115] The fundamental idea of the Model Law is that, similarly to the EIR, foreign main proceedings should be recognized and enforced, based upon the criterion of COMI. Differently from the EIR, in the Model Law, it is not mentioned that a debtor's COMI should be ascertainable by third parties; British courts, however, seem to follow this criterion also with regard to cases regulated by the Model Law.[116]

---

111 See Dan Prentice, "The Incorporation Theory – The United Kingdom" (2003) 14 Eur Bus L Rev 1.

112 *CBIR, supra* note 9, Schedule 1.

113 *Insolvency Act 1986, supra* note 7, s 486.

114 See *The Co-operation of Insolvency Courts (Designation of Relevant Countries and Territories) Order 1986*, SI 1986/2123; *The Co-operation of Insolvency Courts (Designation of Relevant Countries) Order 1996*, SI 1996/253; *The Co-operation of Insolvency Courts (Designation of Relevant Country) Order 1998*, SI 1998/2766.

115 The UNCITRAL Model Law was implemented only in Greece, Slovenia, Romania, Poland and the United Kingdom.

116 *Re Stanford, supra* note 49.

Insolvency Law Reforms in the United Kingdom and Brexit

Slipping Down the Ladder

To climb the World Bank's *Doing Business* league table,[117] the United Kingdom must move closer to the best practices and rubrics of the World Bank in each of the areas on which it is scored. The United Kingdom has slipped down the insolvency ranking since the scoring system changed, and, to climb again, the United Kingdom must change, or close the distance to the frontier of best practices, as the World Bank describes it. That is why the reforms proposed last spring by the Insolvency Service in its *Review of the Corporate Insolvency Framework*[118] were so redolent of Chapter 11; certain elements of Chapter 11 are baked into the World Bank's (and UNCITRAL's) vision of best practices for an insolvency system.

The United Kingdom could stick with its very fine system, but other parts of the world are reforming like fury and are seeking to seize the United Kingdom's crown as the centre for international restructurings. Most recently, the European Commission has started a massive, heaving effort to modernize EU members' insolvency laws in order to push the European Union up those same World Bank rankings.[119] There is a deeper reason for embracing or, at least, accepting change and one that goes to the very philosophical heart of why nations need efficient insolvency systems. There is a pressing need for the United Kingdom to bring its insolvency laws closer into line with the World Bank's vision, all the more so as the United Kingdom aims to remain a leading capital market and economy after Brexit.

Changing Scales

In its 2015 rankings, the World Bank changed its approach to its "resolving insolvency" analysis. That year, the United Kingdom fell from seventh place to thirteenth place, where it has languished since. In contrast, the United States leapt from fourteenth place to fourth place and, for 2016 and 2017, it has ranked fifth for resolving insolvency. Until the 2015 rankings, the World Bank's assessment for resolving insolvency was calculated on the time, cost and outcome for creditors. The United Kingdom did, and still does, very well on these measures. But the World Bank introduced a new measure to determine the strength of an insolvency framework. This new metric assesses the extent to which the best practices championed by the World Bank and UNCITRAL are represented in the country's insolvency regime. The World Bank and UNCITRAL have been working on this topic for years. The World Bank has produced its "Principles for Effective Insolvency and Creditor/Debtor Regimes"[120] and UNCITRAL its

---

117 World Bank, *Doing Business*, online: <www.doingbusiness.org>.

118 *A Review of the Corporate Insolvency Framework* (London, UK: The Insolvency Service, 2016) [*Corporate Insolvency Framework*], online: <www.gov.uk/government/uploads/system/uploads/attachment_data/file/525523/A_Review_of_the_Corporate_Insolvency_Framework.pdf>.

119 EC, Commission, *Proposal for a REGULATION OF THE EUROPEAN PARLIAMENT AND OF THE COUNCIL amending Council Regulation (EC) No 1346/2000 on insolvency proceedings*, COM (2012) 744, online: <http://ec.europa.eu/justice/civil/files/insolvency-regulation_en.pdf>.

120 World Bank, *Principles for Effective Insolvency and Creditor and Debtor Regimes* (2015), online: <www.worldbank.org/en/topic/financialsector/brief/the-world-bank-principles-for-effective-insolvency-and-creditor-rights>.

Legislative Guide on Insolvency Law.[121] These have been married together in a World Bank publication, "Creditor Rights and Insolvency Standard."[122]

So, while the United Kingdom has scored nearly top marks since the 2015 table for the outcome of insolvency (sale as a going concern, as opposed to a piecemeal sale), on the commencement of proceedings, the management of the debtor's assets, the cost to the estate and the recovery rate, the United Kingdom scores much lower than the United States on the new measures of reorganization proceedings and creditor participation.

The World Bank uses a descriptor of overall performance called "distance to frontier," meaning the distance to the "best performance across all economies in the Doing Business sample since 2005." The United Kingdom's resolving insolvency, distance to frontier, with the new measures, fell from 95.33 to 82.04, while the United States (and other countries) went ahead of the United Kingdom. The United States went from a distance to frontier score of 87.72 to 89.20.

A big "so what?" is a perfectly natural response. In the United Kingdom, insolvency takes, on average, one year, as opposed to one and a half years in the United States; the cost to the estate is two percent less in the United Kingdom than in the United States and the return to creditors is 8.2 cents to the dollar higher. The British insolvency system, while not perfect, seems to be excellent if only the number of companies that flock to the United Kingdom from around the globe to restructure are considered. The obvious point here is that companies from abroad come to the United Kingdom to use the scheme of arrangement, which has nothing to do with the insolvency laws, and take advantage of the concentration of high-quality professional expertise of great integrity and a legal and judicial system that is held in the highest esteem worldwide. In other words, the attraction of the United Kingdom to foreign debtors and creditors does not lie in the administration procedure.

Chapter 11 in Disguise

In May 2016, the UK Insolvency Service put out consultation proposals for the reform of UK insolvency law. Of the four central proposals below, the government is pressing ahead with three: a moratorium procedure, with management remaining in control as debtor in possession; an extension of the essential suppliers regime, enabling debtors to specify contracts that then cannot be terminated by reason of the debtor's financial distress; a new plan of reorganization that goes further than any current UK procedure, including the scheme of arrangement, by permitting the cramming down of a whole class of creditors who do not support the plan; and super-priority rescue finance or debtor-in-possession lending. The fourth proposal, as was the case when it was previously canvassed in 2009, is not going forward.

There is, undoubtedly, something Chapter 11-ish about the proposals. In his foreword to the Insolvency Services' *Review of the Corporate Insolvency Framework*, Sajid Javid, the then-Secretary of State at the former Department for Business, Innovation and Skills, said, "To remain at the forefront of insolvency best practice we also need to ask what a 'good' regime looks like in 2016. An increasing international focus on company rescue has helped to shift the perceptions of what

121 UNCITRAL, *Legislative Guide on Insolvency Law* (New York, NY: United Nations, 2005), online: <www.uncitral.org/pdf/english/texts/insolven/05-80722_Ebook.pdf>.

122 World Bank, *Creditor Rights and Insolvency Standard* (2005), online: <http://siteresources.worldbank.org/GILD/ConferenceMaterial/20774191/ICR_Standard_21_Dec_2005_Eng.pdf>.

constitutes best practice; the UK needs to reflect this if our businesses, investors and creditors are to remain confident that the best outcomes can be achieved when things go wrong."[123]

In November 2016, the European Commission came forward with a new draft insolvency directive[124] that will require EU members to create, in their national laws, an insolvency framework meeting minimum standards. The framework is uncannily like that envisaged by the World Bank, UNCITRAL and the Insolvency Service.

There is a deeper reason for accepting, and actually welcoming, the Insolvency Service's proposals. The insolvency system, the law, the professionals who operate and police the system, and the courts that oversee and adjudicate the procedures and disputes are all part of the essential economic plumbing for an economy. The purpose of the European Commission's ambitious insolvency harmonization plan, something never attempted before, is to be an important part of creating Europe's single capital market. The "Five Presidents Report" of June 2015[125] lists "insolvency law among the most important bottlenecks preventing the integration of capital markets in the euro and beyond."[126]

If the system does not work efficiently and predictably, investors will choose some other place in which to invest. In deciding the attributes of the system — the emphasis and bias of the insolvency system toward the debtor or the creditor — there is no right or wrong answer other than the pragmatic one of what best promotes successful economic activity. The United Kingdom's insolvency regime is a product of the UK social and economic culture and, since the *Cork Report*,[127] has held a conscious and deliberate aim of fostering a rescue culture.

Capital providers are most at home, and find it easiest to price insolvency risk, when the insolvency regime is not only efficient, but also familiar. The capital markets are more international now than ever before, and money scours the world for investment opportunities. The hedge fund industry is a huge provider of capital for corporate restructurings, and the simple truth is that it, and a vast majority of the big sources of capital, are either US-based or have a strong US character[128]; it is the US restructuring and insolvency regime with which the hedge fund industry is most familiar. It is unlikely that an investor in a new deal will be attracted because the applicable insolvency regime is familiar, but an unfamiliar system can certainly deter an investor from putting up money or doing so at a keen price. Furthermore, in a world where enterprises have larger and far more complex capital structures than in the past, investors in all those different instruments and layers of debt want a system that gives them a voice in the restructuring. Our current administration procedure responds well to a secured creditor, but

---

123 *Corporate Insolvency Framework*, *supra* note 118 at 5.

124 EC, Commission, *Proposal for a Directive on preventive restructuring frameworks, second chance and measures to increase the efficiency of restructuring, insolvency and discharge procedures and amending Directive 2012/30/EU*, COM(2016) 723 final - 2016/0359 (COD).

125 EC, Commission, *The Five Presidents' Report: Completing Europe's Economic and Monetary Union* (2015), online: <http://ec.europa.eu/priorities/publications/five-presidents-report-completing-europes-economic-and-monetary-union_en>.

126 *Ibid* at 12.

127 UK, *Report of the Review Committee on Insolvency Law and Practice*, Cmnd 8558 (1982).

128 The United States remains the largest centre of investment, with US-based funds managing around 70 percent of global assets at the end of 2011, per TheCityUK, "Hedge Funds: March 2012" (2012). TheCityUK, "UK Fund Management: An Attractive Proposition for International Funds" (2014), online: <www.thecityuk.com/research/uk-fund-management-an-attractive-proposition-for-international-funds/>, reveals that UK assets under management reached a record £6.8 trillion at the end of 2014.

bondholders, unsecured lenders of different rankings, simply do not have the representation that they do in a Chapter 11 designed to accommodate an atomized constituency of creditors.

With so many countries reforming their insolvency laws to attract business and to smooth and enable the flow of capital, the United Kingdom, with Brexit imminent, and a fight on its hands to retain its position as a key capital market and centre for restructuring, must be at the forefront of reform to attract investors.

Insolvencies Post-Brexit: A Continental Perspective

The Impact of the CJEU

A few words should also be said about the future role of the courts, particularly the European ones (the CJEU and the EFTA court). It seems to have been one of the central issues of the Brexiteers to escape the dependency on the CJEU and to stop being affected by its decisions. That, however, might turn out to be a futile hope, as the EU27 are likely to play an essential role in the United Kingdom's future economic agenda. They are all governed by EU law, which is under the ultimate control and interpretation of the CJEU. As *The Economist*[129] has rightly pointed out, ask a company like Google or Microsoft whether they are ever affected by the CJEU. The answer in the positive[130] is also to be given when and if the United Kingdom should consider joining the EEA and thereby gain a seat in the EFTA court. As interesting as this court might be,[131] and as independent as it appears to be, de facto, there is a close interrelationship between those two European courts on the Kirchberg in Luxembourg. Accordingly, when and if the affectedness cannot be escaped from and is, anyway, reduced already to any indirect affect, the United Kingdom should — and certainly will — find a compromise to live and cope with this European power instrument.

Restructurings and Insolvencies in the United Kingdom and on the Continent Post-Brexit

As to restructuring and insolvency after March 29, 2019 (if no transitional deal is achieved), two scenarios need to be taken into account: the first is outbound, and the second inbound.

As to the previous one, the issue at stake is what the consequences are of a proceeding commenced in an EU member state, for instance, in Germany, with a debtor having assets or interests located in the United Kingdom. When and if the EIR should be adopted by the UK Parliament as a national piece of legislation, automatic recognition of the German proceeding would be guaranteed; assets, for instance, that are located in the United Kingdom and are subject to a right *in rem*, would be exempted from the reach of German insolvency law, pursuant to article 8 of the EIR. As a consequence of the CJEU judgment in the *Hertel* case,[132] the United Kingdom

---

129 "Britain cannot escape the long arm of European law" *The Economist* (26 August 2017), online: <www.economist.com/news/britain/21727039-though-government-may-pretend-otherwise-european-court-justice-will-have-role-after>.

130 *Cf* The Institute for Government, "Dispute Resolution after Brexit" (6 October 2017), online: <www.instituteforgovernment.org.uk/publications/dispute-resolution-after-brexit>.

131 Strongly advocating in favour of this option, Carl Baudenbacher, "After Brexit: is the EEA an option for the United Kingdom?" (2016) 4 Eur Law Rep 134.

132 *Hertel, supra* note 13; see also Christof Paulus, "The ECJ's Understanding of the Universality Principle" (2014) 27 Insolvency Intelligence 70.

would be qualified as a third state that can be subject to the outward reach of the insolvency laws of the EU27; but the British courts, under these circumstances, will have to thoroughly think through whether or not they should incorporate this decision into their reasoning.

In the opposite case, when and if there is a restructuring or insolvency proceeding in the United Kingdom, there will be no recognition automatism in the member states of the European Union, as the United Kingdom will no longer be one of them. This distortion — ongoing automatic recognition of EU proceedings in the United Kingdom but no automatism at all in the opposite case — is inescapable, despite its evident imbalance; it is hard to imagine that such a solution will be practised for a long time. It is rather to be assumed that the English courts will search for — and find — a justification for applying some sort of control, and be it in the way as the UNCITRAL Model Law foresees it with its distinction between main proceeding and non-main proceeding.

Turning to the German outbound cases, the EIR is applicable only to the degree of the abovementioned *Hertel* case. The United Kingdom will be a third country, accordingly, which implies that an avoidance action against an English national will be permitted before a German court; it remains to be seen, however, whether English courts will recognize a respective German judgment when an exequatur is requested for the purpose of enforcement.[133] Any argument by an English court, though, based on the assumption that the EIR violates the public order, article 33 of the EIR, should be barred due to the ongoing validity of this law as a national statute.

The biggest concern as of today, though, is the fate of the scheme of arrangement and its continuing use for EU companies. It is understood by the prevailing opinion to be a non-insolvency instrument, so that the EIR and its requirement of a COMI plays no role. Part of the scheme's attractivity in the other member states was and still is the automatic recognizability of a scheme. There are two options for recognition: the procedural side of the scheme qualifies as a judgment pursuant to article 36 of the Brussels I Regulation[134]; additionally, in several member states, a scheme qualifies as a contractual instrument, so that it is to be recognized under the Rome I Regulation[135] as well.[136] Brexit brings with it that the United Kingdom's use of automatic recognition ends in the United Kingdom as well — at least with regard to the Brussels I Regulation; with regard to the Rome I Regulation, things are different, since it implies applicability beyond the territory of the member states (see article 2 of the Rome I Regulation[137]).

It is to be feared, however, that recognizability of a scheme will be debated on a different level. That is where a reference to the above-mentioned comparison with a divorce rather than a clinical cut-off comes into play. Many practitioners have observed the growing prominence of the scheme grudgingly from the beginning on; there is a strong resentment that this binding

---

133 It is a nice corollary that the CJEU followed in its decision precisely the vote of the British Advocate General Eleanor V. E. Sharpston.

134 *Regulation (EU) No 1215/2012 of the European Parliament and of the Council of 12 December 2012 on jurisdiction and the recognition and enforcement of judgments in civil and commercial matters*, [2012] OJ, L 351/1, art 36.

135 *Regulation (EC) No 593/2008 of the European Parliament and of the Council of 17 June 2008 on the law applicable to contractual obligations (Rome I)*, [2008] OJ, L 177/6 [*Rome I*].

136 Christof Paulus, "Das englische Scheme of Arrangement — ein neues Angebot auf dem europäischen Markt für außergerichtliche Restrukturierungen" (2011) Zeitschrift für Wirtschaftsecht 1077.

137 *Rome I, supra* note 135, art 2.

effect of the creditors' majority vote outside of a formal insolvency proceeding is not entirely admissible under constitutional aspects. But some bad feelings seem to remain. Accordingly, a not unlikely development might be that practitioners in the European Union will give in to questioning a scheme's assessment of being non-insolvency. When reading the new article 1 of the EIR with its definition of the proceedings covered by this law, there are ways to come to the conclusion that a scheme is, as a matter of fact, an insolvency proceeding.

To the degree that this is a likely scenario, English scholarship might possibly be well advised to search for alternative ways to ensure a scheme's ongoing attraction on the Continent. To the degree that recognition is an issue, the obvious choice would be the New York Convention,[138] to which more than 150 states are members and which implies automatic recognition of arbitral awards. Because this legal consequence is exactly what the United Kingdom is looking for, the question needs to be discussed whether the term "court" in sections 895 and following of the English Companies Act[139] can be interpreted in a way that an arbitration panel or an arbiter is encompassed from the term "court." What might look on first sight somewhat strange is upon closer inspection not too far-fetched: after all, in the context of sections 315 and following of the German civil code (BGB), the court is entrusted with the task to judge under certain circumstances the fairness of a party's determination of contractual duties and to replace that determination when and if the court deems it to be unfair. Here, German scholarship and practice agrees that an arbitration panel can be interpreted as being a court in the meaning of this section.[140]

Just one remark deserves to be added. One of the great advantages of English scheme procedures is the highly developed expertise of English lawyers, accountants and financial experts over a long period of being involved in successful schemes, together with the deep knowledge and enthusiastic support of English judges. These benefits are not currently available in the EU27 or in new centres looking for business, such as Singapore. If continental companies seeking restructuring no longer felt that they could benefit from English schemes, this would be a "lose-lose" situation for both the United Kingdom and the EU27.

Conclusion

Whatever the outcome of the Brexit negotiations might be, it is possible that the United Kingdom will lose at least part of its attraction as a restructuring and insolvency hub for the EU27. And it is not unlikely that this gap will be filled one way or the other: the first option might be that the United States will try to step in with its Chapter 11 proceeding. Additionally, given the global nature of the modern economy, an alternative (or an additional) competitor might arise in Singapore. The other way of filling the Brexit gap could be a European instrument: the most recent development of a preventive restructuring framework has at least the potential (as of now) to develop into something like a pan-European scheme of arrangement.

---

138 *Convention on the Recognition and Enforcement of Foreign Arbitral Awards*, 10 June 1958, 330 UNTS 38, Can TS 1986 No 43 (entered into force 7 June 1959).

139 *Companies Act 2006* (UK), c 46.

140 *Cf* Markus Würdinger in *Münchener Kommentar zum Bürgerlichen Gesetzbuch*, 7th ed (Beck, 2016) at section 319, marginal no 26 with references to decisions of the German Supreme Court.

The common sense of all this might be that the United Kingdom and the EU27 (or, at least, the 26 remaining member states, excluding Denmark) will reproduce the EIR by treaty. While this is obviously common sense, there are significant problems. Firstly, the UK prime minister has said that she does not want to accept the jurisdiction of the CJEU, and it is difficult to see how the EIR can work without that. There is also a political problem in that the European Union is anxious to prevent other countries following the United Kingdom out of the European Union, and, therefore, the United Kingdom must be seen to be getting a worse deal than it had as an EU member. Depriving the United Kingdom of the benefits of recognition and enforcement under the EIR would be damaging to the United Kingdom. Countries remaining in the European Union would be seen to keep an advantage that the United Kingdom had lost by leaving. Of course, the United Kingdom could retaliate by legislating to refuse recognition to EU restructuring and insolvency proceedings.

There is now a very serious risk that the United Kingdom will lose all the benefits of the regulations and the directives. Current UK policy is to leave the Single Market (and, thus, the EEA) and the Customs Union. Therefore, unless the Brexit negotiations lead successfully to new treaties, the United Kingdom may well repeal the provisions derived from the regulations and possibly those derived from the directives. To some extent, the United Kingdom can fall back on the UNCITRAL Model Law and common law. These may help incoming cases, but, of course, do not assist outgoing ones, except in the few EU member states that have adopted the UNCITRAL Model Law, or where there are other ways of getting recognition for English insolvency proceedings. In some cases, it may be possible to have parallel proceedings and coordination/cooperation. Schemes of arrangement may also continue to work and be recognized on the basis of conflicts rules.

Prior to the original regulation, there was no satisfactory way of getting English insolvency proceedings recognized and enforced in continental Europe, and the United Kingdom may now be on the road to abandoning 14 years of progress and reverting to the completely unsatisfactory position before 2002.

Authors' Note

Although this article is based on common discussions, the authors should mention that Gabriel Moss drafted the "Impact of Brexit on Recognition/Judicial Assistance in Cross-border Insolvencies" section, Federico Mucciarelli drafted the "Impact of Brexit on Forum and Law Shopping" section, Howard Morris drafted the "Insolvency Law Reforms in the United Kingdom and Brexit" section and Christoph Paulus drafted the "Insolvencies Post-Brexit: A Continental Perspective" section.

8

Failing Financial Institutions: How Will Brexit Impact Cross-border Cooperation in Recovery, Reconstruction and Insolvency Processes?

Dorothy Livingston

Introduction

This chapter is directed at some important issues of cross-border recognition and assistance related to processes affecting financial institutions arising from the United Kingdom's decision to leave the European Union, commonly known as Brexit. Topics covered in this chapter include:

- the effects of Brexit on these issues in the United Kingdom and the European Union;

- consideration of whether Brexit represents a setback in efforts to create a robust approach to cross-border failure of systemically important financial institutions; and

- how Brexit will affect the recognition of recovery, reconstruction and insolvency proceedings with a cross-border element affecting financial institutions.

The chapter goes on to discuss the options open to the United Kingdom and the European Union in the context of the Basel Accords issued by the Basel Committee on Banking

Supervision (BCBS)[1] and the work of the Financial Stability Board (FSB),[2] which are aimed at increasing the stability of international financial systems. These international bodies, as well as the European Union and the United Kingdom, recognize the importance of the smooth operation of cross-border processes to financial stability in case of the failure of a systemically important financial institution.

The chapter also considers whether the General Agreement on Trade in Services (GATS)[3] has any bearing on the issues.

Finally, the chapter explores how far the courts can address any political and regulatory failures to preserve the existing levels of mutual recognition as between the United Kingdom and EU member states.

Inevitably, in the complex legislative and regulatory environment for financial services (much of it strengthened with new legislation following the 2007–2009 financial crisis), there is a good deal of scene setting to be done if we are to make sense of the key issues.

Principal Legislation and International Instruments

EU Legislation

The main pieces of EU legislation are directives. These require the EU member states to change their laws to meet the requirements of the directive and, in some circumstances, to refrain from action otherwise open to them. They are not directly effective (except in limited circumstances) in any member state and require national law to be changed to meet their requirements.

For the purpose of this chapter, it has not been necessary to look at national implementation, except in the United Kingdom, where further legislative measures are needed to prevent much of the implementing law from falling away when the United Kingdom leaves the European Union at the end of March 2019 (subject to agreement otherwise and to the application of transitional measures, which may apply EU law in the United Kingdom for a period after March 2019). The extent to which EU law, or UK law in the same terms, continues to apply is a policy matter, and the eventual outcome of the EU-UK negotiations under article 50 of the Treaty on European Union (TEU) will determine the matter.

---

1   Banking supervision accords are issued by the BCBS, a body made up of representatives of central banks and regulatory authorities of Group of Twenty (G20) countries (and other countries with major financial services centres such as Hong Kong, Luxembourg and Singapore). The committee is not underpinned by an international treaty and, although it is highly respected, it has no powers of enforcement. The European Union and the represented states among its members, including the United Kingdom, are highly supportive and follow its recommendations, including under the Bank Resolution and Recovery Directive (BRRD) discussed below.

2   The FSB is a body supported by the G20 states that plays an important part in coordinating at an international level the work of national financial authorities and international standard-setting bodies and promoting the implementation of effective policies in the interests of global financial stability. The FSB may also issue non-binding recommendations. It is currently chaired by Mark Carney, governor of the Bank of England.

3   *General Agreement on Trade in Services*, 15 April 1994, 1869 UNTS 183, 33 ILM 1167 (entered into force 1 January 1995) [*GATS*].

The BRRD[4] sets out the European Union's rules for the management of banks (known in EU law as credit institutions) and investment firms in financial difficulties. These rules may lead to a business in difficulty being recapitalized as a going concern, or to the transfer of its viable contracts and deposits to a "bridge bank," or directly to a solvent financial institution. A bridge bank is a newly established institution under the control of the resolution authorities in the relevant EU member state that will carry on the viable business of the failing bank, pending finding a purchaser for this business or the return of the bridge bank to independence as a fully capitalized entity wholly or partly owned by creditors of the failed bank whose claims have been "bailed in." These creditors principally will be holders of bonds issued by the failed institution. Where a viable business is transferred to a third party or bridge bank, the failing institution itself will become subject to an insolvency process and, ultimately, cease to exist as a legal entity.

As an EU directive, the BRRD requires EU member states to adjust their laws so as to meet its minimum requirements, which include requiring each of them to create certain structures (principally, the appointment of resolution authorities), as well as to put in place powers for the management of bank resolution and recovery. There are requirements and restrictions on the operation of the powers by member state resolution authorities and rules on the recognition of processes carried out in other member states. In its current form, the BRRD is fully or nearly fully implemented into UK law[5] and the law of most other EU member states. There are legislative proposals in Brussels to amend the BRRD, but it is not clear whether they will take effect before the United Kingdom leaves the European Union at the end of March 2019.

In addition, there are two principal older EU directives: the Credit Institutions Winding Up Directive (CIWUD) and Solvency II, concerned respectively with the insolvency of credit institutions and insurance companies.[6] These are fully implemented in the United Kingdom and in most other member states. An important feature of these directives is the recognition of insolvency processes carried out in other member states. A credit institution subjected to a resolution process in accordance with the BRRD, if it does not itself survive the process as a continuing legal entity with a viable business, will be wound up under a process that accords with CIWUD. The general European Insolvency Regulation (EIR)[7] does not apply to institutions subject to these directives.

This chapter will concentrate on the issues of recognition and conflict of laws arising under these three directives as a result of Brexit. It will not consider operational aspects of the directives, except where necessary to illustrate these issues.

---

4 *Directive 2014/59/EU of the European Parliament and of the Council of 15 May 2014 establishing a framework for the recovery and resolution of credit institutions and investment firms*, [2014] OJ, L 173 [*BRRD*].

5 This is achieved by the Banking Act 2009, as amended, and legislation under two statutory instruments under the European Communities Act 1972 and some rules of the Prudential Regulation Authority (PRA), which is controlled by the Bank of England.

6 *Directive 2001/24/EC of the European Parliament and of the Council of 4 April 2001 on the reorganisation and winding up of credit institutions*, [2001] OJ, L 125, commonly known as CIWUD; *Directive 2009/138/EC of the European Parliament and of the Council of 25 November 2009 on the taking-up and pursuit of the business of Insurance and Reinsurance*, [2009] OJ, L 335, Title IV [*Solvency II*]. The latter directive lays down a general framework for the regulation of insurance companies, including insolvency processes, while CIWUD is concerned only with the winding up of credit institutions, as other aspects of regulation are being dealt with in other EU laws.

7 *Regulation (EU) 2015/848 of the European Parliament and of the Council of 20 May 2015 on insolvency proceedings*, [2015] OJ, L 141 (the recast EIR from 26 June 2017), replacing *Council Regulation (EC) No 1346/2000 of 29 May 2000 on insolvency proceedings*, [2000] OJ, L 160.

International Instruments

The effect of the Agreement on the European Economic Area (EEA)[8] is that the EU legislation referred to above is all legislation with EEA relevance and the provisions referred to should, assuming implementation in Iceland, Liechtenstein and Norway, have the effect of treating those states, broadly speaking, in the same way as EU member states vis-à-vis EU countries and third countries. Those countries should apply the same approach as EU member states to the recognition of third-country processes.

The United Kingdom and some EU member states (Greece, Poland and Romania) have adapted their insolvency laws to the United Nations Commission on International Trade Law (UNCITRAL) Model Law on Cross-Border Insolvency, but the United Kingdom, at least, has chosen to exclude financial institutions from the application of this adaptation, so this has no immediate relevance to the issue of post-Brexit recognition of EU insolvency proceedings affecting banks and insurance companies.[9]

The Basel Accords issued by the BCBS are not specifically concerned with the issue of recognition of resolution and insolvency regimes. The accords concentrate on credit risk (Basel I) and capital adequacy (Basel II, as amended, and Basel III, issued since the financial crisis). Implementation in the European Union of the Basel capital adequacy standards is in part through the BRRD, and the subject of prudent regulation of banks is seen as closely linked to the question of effective resolution, should that be necessary.

The FSB has gone further than the BCBS in examining issues related to resolution, and in 2014, published an international standard for resolution regimes that are part of a set of policy measures arising from the November 2011 G20 summit meeting.[10] Chapters 7 to 9 of this *Key Attributes* document deal with the legal framework conditions, international crisis management groups and institution-specific, cross-border cooperation agreements. Chapter 7 encourages cooperation both between resolution authorities and legal mechanisms in different states. Paragraphs 7.5 and 7.6 are most pertinent:

> 7.5 Jurisdictions should provide for transparent and expedited processes to give effect to foreign resolution measures, either by way of a mutual recognition process or by taking measures under the domestic resolution regime that support and are consistent with the resolution measures taken by the foreign home resolution authority. Such recognition or support measures would enable a foreign home resolution authority to gain rapid control over the firm (branch or shares in a subsidiary) or its assets that are located in the host jurisdiction, as appropriate, in cases where the firm is being resolved under the law of the foreign home jurisdiction. Recognition or support of foreign measures should be provisional on the equitable treatment of creditors in the foreign resolution proceeding.[11]

---

8 · *Agreement on the European Economic Area*, 2 May 1992, [1994] OJ, L 1 (entered into force 1 January 1994). Chapter 3 removes restrictions on the supply of services and chapter 4 removes restrictions on the movement of capital.

9 See *Insolvency Act 1986* (UK) as supplemented by the *Cross-Border Insolvency Regulations 2006*, SI 2006/1030, Schedule 1 at para 2 (g)–(l).

10 FSB, *Key Attributes of Effective Resolution Regimes for Financial Institutions* (15 October 2014), online: <www.fsb.org/what-we-do/policy-development/effective-resolution-regimes-and-policies/key-attributes-of-effective-resolution-regimes-for-financial-institutions/>.

11 *Ibid* at para 7.5.

7.6 The resolution authority should have the capacity in law, subject to adequate confidentiality requirements and protections for sensitive data, to share information, including recovery and resolution plans (RRPs), pertaining to the group as a whole or to individual subsidiaries or branches, with relevant foreign authorities (for example, members of a CMG), where sharing is necessary for recovery and resolution planning or for implementing a coordinated resolution.[12]

The FSB *Key Attributes* document has not yet, however, led to any more formal international structure for the recognition of resolution or insolvency processes affecting financial institutions.[13]

Principal Provisions on Recognition and Conflict of Laws

BRRD: Recognition

The BRRD provides for cooperation both within the European Union and with third countries. Recital 102 states the general principle:

> Cooperation should take place both with regard to subsidiaries of Union or third-country groups and with regard to branches of Union or third-country institutions. Subsidiaries of third-country groups are enterprises established in the Union and therefore are fully subject to Union law, including the resolution tools laid down in this Directive. It is necessary, however, that Member States retain the right to act in relation to branches of institutions having their head office in third countries, when the recognition and application of third-country resolution proceedings relating to a branch would endanger financial stability in the Union or when Union depositors would not receive equal treatment with third-country depositors. In those circumstances, and in the other circumstances as laid down in this Directive, Member States should have the right, after consulting the national resolution authorities, to refuse recognition of third-country resolution proceedings with regard to Union branches of third-country institutions.[14]

Relations within the European Union in relation to resolution proceedings are dealt with by the amendment to CIWUD in article 117 (discussed below) and by provisions dealing with relations with third countries in articles 93 to 98. These articles lay down minimum powers that member states must have under their respective national laws in relation to foreign resolution processes and in relation to the resolution of branches of third-country entities established on their territory. They also deal with supervisory cooperation, such as sharing confidential information. These articles go on to provide for procedures that will shape whether a member state will recognize and assist third-country processes or be free to apply its own domestic processes instead.

---

12 *Ibid* at para 7.6.

13 See Matthias Lehmann, "BRRD, the SRM-Regulation and Private International Law: How to Make Cross-Border Resolution Effective" (Paper delivered at the European Banking Institute's inaugural workshop, Frankfurt, Germany, 27-28 January 2016) for a wide-ranging review of the issues.

14 *BRRD, supra* note 4, Recital 102.

Broadly speaking, this part of the BRRD (article 94) provides that, in the absence of a relevant international agreement between the European Union and a third country or, where there is neither an EU international agreement or a relevant bilateral agreement between a member state and the third country, that recognition of third-country resolution proceedings in relation to an institution (or its parent company) with branches or subsidiaries in the European Union regarded as significant by two or more member states, or having assets, rights or liabilities located in two or more member states, shall be decided by the relevant European resolution college (ERC) to be established under article 89. An ERC is an institution or group-specific body to be established by the regulators from the affected countries and chaired by the resolution authority of the member state where the consolidating supervisor[15] is located. In some circumstances, this function can be delegated to a similar body established under article 88. If an ERC decides to afford recognition, national resolution authorities should "seek the enforcement of the recognised third-country resolution proceedings in accordance with their national law."[16]

In the absence of an ERC or equivalent body and/or a recognition agreement, each member state can take its own decision whether to recognize and enforce foreign proceedings, but its decision must "give due consideration to the interests of each individual Member State where a third-country institution or parent undertaking operates, and in particular to the potential impact of the recognition and enforcement of the third-country resolution proceedings on the other parts of the group and the financial stability in those Member States."[17]

In circumstances set out in article 95, including national concerns about financial stability or fiscal implications, fair treatment of creditors or conflict with national law, a member state resolution authority can take a decision not to recognize foreign processes: this decision overrides the article 94 process.

In the absence of an international agreement, the European Banking Authority (EBA) can also conclude non-binding framework agreements with third-country authorities responsible for institutions operating in the European Union or their parent.[18] This type of agreement would principally be concerned with information sharing and coordination of public communications. Bilateral agreements are also possible. Information sharing must meet standards set out in article 98, including meeting EU data protection standards and equivalent standards of professional secrecy.

There are indications that a member state resolution authority may (indeed, should), even if not legally bound to give recognition, decide to give ad hoc recognition to a third-country process: for example, in the limitation in article 96 on using national processes in relation to a branch of a third-country institution, unless one of the circumstances in article 95 applies or there are no third-country processes in place.[19] Article 68 allows third-country resolution proceedings to be

15 For the purpose of *Directive 2013/36/EU of the European Parliament and of the Council of 26 June 2013 on access to the activity of credit institutions and the prudential supervision of credit institutions and investment firms*, [2013] OJ, L 176.
16 *BRRD, supra* note 4, art 94(2)
17 *Ibid*, art 94(3).
18 *Ibid*, art 97.
19 *Ibid*, arts 95-96

recognized as a "crisis measure" when they are recognized under article 94 "or otherwise where
a resolution authority so decides."[20]

BRRD: Conflicts

Article 45 *et seq.* deal with the identification of own funds and eligible liabilities, that is, broadly
speaking, equity, together with debt liabilities that can be treated as regulatory capital because
the holders are bound by law or agreement to accept that their debt is subject to bail-in (i.e.,
conversion to equity or write-off) in the event of a bank ceasing to have adequate capital.[21] This
section of the BRRD reflects parts of the Basel Accords.

There is concern that, if a debt is created under a contract governed by a foreign law, that legal
system (whose courts may well have jurisdiction over any dispute) may not recognize the bail-in
provisions of EU law. Article 55 of the BRRD, therefore, requires EU banks to include in foreign
law contracts creating a liability on their part a contractual term on the recognition of bail-in.
Article 45(5) allows resolution authorities to require institutions to demonstrate the effectiveness
of such an agreement (or that the bail-in arrangements will, in any event, be recognized under the
relevant third-country law) before the debt can be accepted for regulatory capital purposes.

It has been recognized for some time that the drafting and scope of article 55 is both uncertain
and impractically wide, so that it is extremely difficult for institutions to comply. In part, this is
because article 55 requires banks, at the time of a new contract, to have regard to tests set out
in article 44(2) that were designed to be applied at the time of an actual failure and containing
elements that can only be determined at that time. This is due partly to article 55 including every
type of liability in this obligation. The provision does not recognize the impracticality of expecting
certain third-country institutions (for example, a clearing system or exchange) to jeopardize their
own stability by entering into such an obligation. Current efforts at the EU level to change and
clarify the provision have not yet produced a draft that is a clear improvement, but it is to be
expected that this will have been achieved to a greater or lesser extent before Brexit and will be
reflected in UK implementation. This is not the place to discuss the details of this issue, but in
any event, the requirements of article 55 can be expected to continue to apply in respect of major
foreign law fundraising, such as bond issues or other large borrowing programs, regardless of
whether the issuing EU institution wishes to treat them as regulatory capital.

Once the United Kingdom leaves the European Union, EU-headquartered banks raising funds
through English law loan agreements, English law debt instruments (and possibly certain other
agreements) may consider seeking such clauses in English law contracts. This would not be
required by any EU bank whose home member state resolution authority had determined that the
liabilities or instruments can be subject to the write-down and conversion powers involved in bail-
in in accordance with the BRRD as a result of national law in the United Kingdom or of a binding
agreement with the United Kingdom made either by that member state or the European Union.

---

20 *Ibid*, art 68.

21 *BRRD, supra* note 4, art 45. The technical definition in article 2.1(71) is "liabilities and capital instruments that do not
qualify as Common Equity Tier 1, Additional Tier 1 or Tier 2 instruments of an institution or entity referred to in point
(b), (c) or (d) of Article 1(1) that are not excluded from the scope of the bail-in tool by virtue of Article 44(2)."

CIWUD: Recognition

CIWUD lays down a code for reorganization and winding up of credit institutions within the European Union and cooperation between member states in that process. This extends to processes under the BRRD, including those involving parent companies.[22] It assigns exclusive jurisdiction to the authorities of the home member state with regard to reorganization measures, including in relation to branches in other member states (article 3). The same article specifies that the law of that member state shall apply, except as otherwise provided in CIWUD and for recognition throughout the European Union. Articles 9 and 10 achieve the same in relation to a winding up.

Article 10 follows the EIR (which does not apply to credit institutions or insurance companies) in specifying the law applicable to various aspects of the winding up. Articles 20 to 27 and 30 to 31 deal with the application of a different law from that of the home member state in certain circumstances or for particular types of contract or legal right. In particular, article 21 follows the insolvency regulation in preserving the rights *in rem* of creditors in the member state where assets are situated. According to recital 21 and article 19, branches of third-country institutions are to be dealt with by the member state where they are established. Unlike in the BRRD, there are no specific provisions regarding third-country proceedings, recognition of which seems to be left to the national law of each member state.

Solvency II

Title IV of Solvency II deals with the reorganization and winding up of insurance and reinsurance companies in very similar terms to the way that CIWUD deals with the same issues for banks, except for provisions concerning the priority of insurance claims over other claims.[23] All the remarks made above in relation to CIWUD apply also in this context, except that there is no equivalent of BRRD article 117 extending the rules in Solvency II to reorganizations and windings-up involving parent companies.

UK Implementation of EU Law

The United Kingdom implements EU legislation such as directives, which are not directly effective, by statutory instruments relying on powers in section 2(2) of the European Communities Act 1972 (ECA 1972)[24] and may make other adjustments to comply with EU law in the same way. It may, however, in some cases use primary legislation or powers under existing UK legislation to achieve the same effect. In some cases, existing UK law may satisfy implementation requirements in whole or in part. To that extent, there may be no specific implementation in the form of UK legislation subsequent to the relevant EU legislation being passed.

The United Kingdom implemented CIWUD primarily by the Credit Institutions (Reorganisation and Winding Up) Regulations 2004.[25]

---

22 *BRRD, supra* note 4, art 117.
23 *Solvency II, supra* note 6, art 275.
24 *European Communities Act 1972* (UK), c 68, s 2(2) [*ECA 1972*].
25 *Credit Institutions (Reorganisation and Winding Up) Regulations 2004*, SI 2004/1045, made under ECA 1972, s 2.

As the winding-up provisions of Insolvency II reflect earlier EU legislation, and there have also been developments in national law, the provisions related to the winding up of insurance companies are scattered among the Insolvency Act 1986; the Financial Services and Markets Act 2000, as amended; the Insurers (Winding Up) Rules 2001; the Insurers (Reorganisation and Winding Up) Regulations 2004; and the Financial Services and Markets Act 2000 (Administration Orders Relating to Insurers) Order 2010. The 2004 regulations, made under ECA section 2(2), represent the primary piece of legislation implementing EU law.[26]

The BRRD is implemented in part by the Bank Resolution and Recovery Order 2014 and the Bank Resolution and Recovery Order 2016.[27] In addition, PRA rules deal with the supervision of compliance with article 55.[28] The legislative position in the United Kingdom is, however, a prime example of the situation where earlier UK legislation, in this case the Banking Act 2009 and statutory instruments made under it, already fulfill many of the implementation requirements of the BRRD. Indeed, many of the concepts in the BRRD are derived from the Banking Act 2009.

Leaving the European Union

Following the referendum in June 2016, the United Kingdom served notice under article 50 of the TEU to leave the European Union. The two-year notice period expires at the end of March 2019, unless extended by agreement. At the time of writing, extension seems highly unlikely, but it seems possible that there will be an implementation or transitional phase (possibly lasting about two years after Brexit) leading up to a new trading relationship. This may result in the United Kingdom being treated during the transition similarly to an EEA state, such as Norway, for the purposes of the legislation discussed in this chapter, or may otherwise smooth the effects of leaving the European Union, although there is no indication of what might be included in a "half-way house" transition, except that it may not include submitting to the jurisdiction of the Court of Justice of the European Union (CJEU) with regard to the interpretation and application of some or all EU and EU-derived law.

If treated similarly to an EEA state, such as Norway, during transition the United Kingdom could be essentially in the same position as it is currently in relation to any failure of a financial institution to which any of this legislation applies. If, however, the United Kingdom leaves the European Union without agreement of a new relationship that preserves mutual recognition of cross-border resolution and insolvency processes, then it will fall fully into third-country treatment regarding these matters, as well as being a third country for the purposes of BRRD article 55.

This chapter will consider the position on the basis that would arise if the United Kingdom leaves the European Union without relevant transitional provisions (or transitional provisions treating the United Kingdom like an EEA state expire without any relevant agreement). This gives a

---

26 *Insurers (Reorganisation and Winding Up) Regulations 2004*, SI 2004/353.

27 *Bank Resolution and Recovery Order 2014*, SI 2014/3329, and the *Bank Recovery and Resolution Order 2016*, SI 2016/1239, were both made primarily under the power given by section 2 of the ECA 1972 to implement EU legislation in the United Kingdom.

28 See Bank of England, "The contractual recognition of bail-in: amendments to Prudential Regulation Authority rules", Policy Statement 17/16, Consultation Paper 8/16 (29 June 2016), online: <www.bankofengland.co.uk/prudential-regulation/publication/2016/the-contractual-recognition-of-bail-in-amendments-to-pra-rules>.

starting point for discussions. At this point, the United Kingdom will cease to be a member state (or to be treated as an EEA state) for the purposes of this directive, and although the UK implementing laws may remain in force, the United Kingdom will no longer be automatically entitled to the recognition of its processes in EU and EEA states or the regulatory cooperation from EU and member state authorities afforded pursuant to the directive. This will involve the loss of extremely useful rights for the United Kingdom in the event of the insolvency of a financial institution headquartered in the United Kingdom with branches or subsidiaries elsewhere in the European Union/EEA. There would be a risk of parallel resolution or insolvency proceedings in one or more continuing EU member state where the UK institution had a branch or subsidiary. Equally, the United Kingdom might be able to open parallel proceedings in the case of the failure of an EU or EEA institution with branches or subsidiaries in the United Kingdom, where it previously might not have been free to do so.

This would be a backward step, having regard to the commitment of the G20 to effective cross-border resolution, and represent a falling away from the standards for cross-border insolvency espoused by the FSB. It would introduce, at least, inefficiencies and the risk of unequal treatment of creditors according to where their debts are dealt with. At worst, it could cause the failure of a systemically important institution that would have been saved if a single resolution authority could have dealt with its resolution or restructuring, significantly affecting financial stability because of its contagious effects.

It is to be expected that both the United Kingdom and the European Union, having regard to the fact that many of its continuing member states are G20 countries or participate in the BASEL and FSB processes, will seek to avoid that outcome, although, of course, politics may get in the way.

The UK Approach

Retention of EU Law

The UK government has taken a general decision with regard to EU law that is entirely consistent with its position as a member of the G20. It has decided to bring forward legislation, the European Union (Withdrawal) Bill (Withdrawal Bill),[29] which provides for EU law implemented in the United Kingdom up to "exit day" to be incorporated into the laws of the United Kingdom (this is known as "EU-derived domestic legislation") and for the incorporation of directly applicable EU legislation (such as regulations) into domestic legislation. Together with retained general principles of EU law and retained domestic and EU case law, these are described as "retained EU law."

At the time of writing, the Withdrawal Bill is at an early stage of passage through Parliament, and may be subject to significant change. Applying its provisions to the legislation that implements the relevant parts of the BRRD, CIWUD and Solvency II is thus something of a crystal-ball-gazing exercise, although it seems likely that the conceptual structure of the Withdrawal Bill, which incorporates EU law applicable in the United Kingdom before it leaves the European Union into domestic law after it leaves, will survive and become law.

---

29 Bill 5, *European Union (Withdrawal) Bill* [HC], 2017–2019 sess, 2017 (1st reading 13 July 2017) [*Withdrawal Bill*].

EU-derived domestic legislation includes enactments made under ECA section 2(2), such as the 2004 statutory instruments that largely implement CIWUD and Title IV of Solvency II, and the 2014 and 2016 instruments that implement the BRRD.[30] It also includes legislation not made under the ECA passed, made or operating:

(a) for the purpose of implementing any EU obligation of the United Kingdom, or enabling any such obligation to be implemented, or enabling any rights enjoyed or to be enjoyed by the United Kingdom under or by virtue of the Treaties to be exercised; or

(b) for the purpose of dealing with matters arising out of or related to any such obligation or rights or the coming into force, or the operation from time to time, of [Treaty provisions, directly effective EU legislation and decisions, as made directly applicable in the UK by ECA s 2(1)].[31]

In addition, the term includes enactments relating to legislation made under ECA section 2(2), anything falling within (a) and (b), above, to direct EU legislation preserved by clause 3(1) of the bill, and to EU legislation and decisions preserved by clause 4(1) of the bill and any other UK enactment "relating otherwise to the EU or the EEA."[32]

This means that, for example, insofar as the BRRD implementation by the Bank Resolution and Recovery Order 2016 is made both under powers in ECA section 2(2) and in the Small Business, Enterprise and Employment Act 2015 was for a purpose mentioned above or related otherwise to the European Union or the EEA, it may still be EU-derived domestic legislation.[33]

However, the position of older UK legislation, including parts of the Banking Act 2009 itself, that have been accepted as good implementation of the BRRD is unclear: the better view, having regard to the treatment of EU directives discussed below, would be that they are to be treated as purely domestic UK legislation, unless actually amended by one of the implementing orders.

Interpretation

EU-derived domestic legislation forms part of retained EU law and is subject to special rules of interpretation set out in clause 6 of the bill, which effectively, so long as the legislation is not modified by later UK legislation, allows for the application of CJEU decisions taken before exit day and the application of retained general principles of EU law as at that date. Later CJEU decisions are not binding at all, but may be considered. As currently drafted, clause 6 itself and related provisions scattered throughout the bill and its schedules provide for so many actual and potential disapplications of historic EU law that it is doubtful whether the UK courts will be able to follow their present approach to ECA section 2(2) statutory instruments, which would involve having regard to not just CJEU decisions, but a more purposive approach to

---

30 *ECA 1972, supra* note 24, s 2(2)(a).

31 *Ibid*, s 2(2)(b) applying *ECA 1972*, s 2(2)(a), (b).

32 *Ibid*, s 2(2)(c), (d).

33 The order refers to the *Small Business, Enterprise and Employment Act 2015*, c 26, s 28, 30. These sections relate to ministerial reviews of existing regulatory provision, and section 30(3) allows for the review to take account, *inter alia*, of how an EU obligation binding on the United Kingdom is implemented in other member states. The author does not express a concluded view on whether the 2016 order will be regarded wholly as EU-derived domestic legislation, but this is certainly a possible conclusion.

interpretation, taking account of the underlying directive so as to ensure consistent application. This is potentially an area of unnecessary legal uncertainty.

Position of Directives

Legal uncertainty is exacerbated by the failure of the Withdrawal Bill to give any status to the EU directives from which most EU-derived domestic legislation is derived. They are not direct EU legislation and their effect on EU-derived domestic legislation is severely limited because clause 4(2)(b) specifically excludes from the saving under clause 4(1) (and thus from the cross-reference into clause 4(1) in clause 2(2) of the bill): "any rights, powers, liabilities, obligations, restrictions, remedies or procedures in so far as they…arise under an EU directive…and are not of a kind recognised by the European Court [CJEU] or any court or tribunal in the United Kingdom in a case decided before exit day (whether or not it is an essential part of the decision in the case)." The effect of this would seem to be that directives are of no relevance in relation to retained EU law that is EU-derived, except insofar as their provisions are the subject of pre-exit judicial decisions of the CJEU or the UK courts.

If the courts take this exclusion to extend to issues of interpretation, the answer to the question whether the implementing statutory instruments relating to the BRRD, CIWUD or Title IV of Solvency II have, as a matter of UK law, to be interpreted consistently with the underlying directives would be something of a lottery, depending on whether the court regards any pre-exit case as determining this point. Will the courts have regard to cases of general principle, notably *Von Colson*[34] and *Marleasing*[35] that state the principle that a national court must interpret its implementing law (including earlier law treated as implementation) in the light of the wording and purpose of the underlying directive, or look only at cases with a bearing on the particular piece of implementing law at issue?

Given the United Kingdom's stated intention that "as a general rule, the same rules and laws will apply on the day after exit as on the day before,"[36] clause 4(2)(b) appears to introduce yet another layer of unnecessary legal uncertainty and to throw into question similar words in the February 2017 white paper, *The United Kingdom's exit from and new partnership with the European Union*,[37] as well as assurances that there will be legal certainty and continuity post-Brexit.

Legislative Outcome

It remains to be seen if the committee stages of the Withdrawal Bill will address these issues of legal uncertainty, in particular whether they will reinstate recognition of directives as part of the EU *acquis*, which should have a place in retained EU law after the United Kingdom leaves the European Union, and whether they will simplify the scheme for the application of CJEU decisions and the rules of interpretation for retained EU law. In the event that the bill were

---

34   Case 14/83, *Von Colson and Kamann*, [1984] ECR 1984-01891.

35   Case C-106/89, *Marleasing SA v La Comercial Internacional de Alimentacion SA*, [1990] ECR 1990 1-04135

36   UK, Department for Exiting the European Union (DEEU), *European Union (Withdrawal) Bill Explanatory Notes* (London, UK: House of Commons, 2017) at para 10 [DEEU, "*Explanatory Notes*"], online: <https://publications.parliament.uk/pa/bills/cbill/2017-2019/0005/en/18005en.pdf>. This echoes paragraph 11 of the February 2017 white paper.

37   UK, DEEU, *The United Kingdom's exit from and new partnership with the European Union*, (February 2017), online: <www.gov.uk/government/publications/the-united-kingdoms-exit-from-and-new-partnership-with-the-european-union-white-paper/the-united-kingdoms-exit-from-and-new-partnership-with-the-european-union--2>.

to pass into UK law in its present form, the courts will need to use their discretions to seek to maintain consistency of approach and limit unnecessary divergence of UK and EU law. In addition, it may be more difficult to obtain mutual recognition, while the extent to which the same laws will be interpreted in the same way in the United Kingdom as in the European Union remains unclear.

Amendment of Retained EU Legislation

It is evident that some retained legislation including EU-derived domestic law, such as the statutory instruments implementing the BRRD, CIWUD and Title IV of Solvency II, may require amendment to work effectively after Brexit. For example, they may refer to a role for the European Commission or the EBA. These roles may need to be assigned to a UK authority, such as the PRA or the Financial Conduct Authority.

The bill provides various methods for amendment by statutory instrument, some of which require a positive resolution of both Houses of Parliament, while others only require a negative procedure, whereby the legislation comes into effect unless voted down in Parliament within 40 days of it being made. These amendments may be applied to acts of Parliament, such as the Banking Act 2009, as well as to statutory instruments. The main process for dealing with deficiencies in the legislation, clause 7, is time limited to two years beginning with exit day, but clause 17, which deals with consequential, transitional, transitory and saving provisions does not appear to be so limited.[38] This aspect of the Withdrawal Bill is expected to be heavily debated in Parliament and further restrictions on these legislative powers seem possible, either by government concession or as a result of losing a vote in Parliament.

Objectively, the statutory instruments implementing the BRRD, CIWUD and Title IV of Solvency II seem unlikely to need substantive amendment. There is value in retaining a clear commitment to recognize and give effect to EU resolution and insolvency proceedings in the United Kingdom, although it has been suggested that amending powers could be used to remove recognition provisions if the European Union refuses to accord reciprocity.[39] Given the United Kingdom's commitment as a G20 country to the BASEL process and to the FSB standards, as well as its aim to be a leading modern international trading nation, it is to be hoped that the United Kingdom would not take this course, although it may have a case for allowing itself the protections of BRRD article 95 in relation to EU-headquartered institutions in the absence of EU reciprocity. Subject to considerations arising from the WTO GATS agreement discussed below, it would be questionable whether such a course was in accord with general principles of comity discussed below.

As regards BRRD article 55, as long as the United Kingdom will continue to recognize bail-in processes in the European Union, it ought to be possible to satisfy the EU regulators that they need not require EU-headquartered banks to add specific recognition clauses to their English law agreements, but ultimately, this will depend on the views of EU authorities at the EU or national level or, in the event of dispute, the decision of the CJEU.

---

38 *Withdrawal Bill, supra* note 29, cls 7, 17.
39 DEEU, "*Explanatory Notes*", *supra* note 36 at para 111.

The EU Approach

The EU approach is dictated by its general approach to the article 50 negotiations. Essentially that position is that on leaving the European Union, the United Kingdom ceases to be an EU or EEA state and therefore is a third country for the purposes of all EU legislation. Where there is a possibility of agreeing to mutual recognition or independently recognizing the equivalence of processes of third countries, neither the EU institutions or member states, where they have competency, should consider equivalence or recognition arrangements of a formal nature until after the United Kingdom has left the European Union.

There was, until December 2017, an unwillingness to discuss even the framework of any aspect of the future EU-UK relationship before there was agreement on the United Kingdom's financial contribution to the European Union, the treatment of EU citizens and the position on the Irish border. Progress has been made on these topics, and the next round of negotiations may give some indication whether the EU authorities will be prepared to continue recognition of UK resolution or insolvency processes after Brexit, given that they are currently accepted as compliant with EU law and are recognized throughout the European Union.

In the absence of a transition period, in which the United Kingdom is effectively treated as an EU member state even though it has left the European Union, there is a clear risk of a hiatus in which the European Union and its continuing member states would not recognize UK resolution or insolvency processes. The one exception would be if the general law of any particular member state might recognize UK resolution or insolvency processes. This would not assist in the cross-border resolution or winding up of a UK institution, unless its only EU operations were in member states that gave national recognition to the UK processes.

This situation could continue for a considerable time if there were no political will to resolve it, but it would not prevent a resolution college or an individual member state from providing recognition in an individual case. However, automatic recognition of UK resolution processes throughout the European Union would be lost.

Having regard to the commitments of many EU member states as members of the G20 and supporters of the FSB standards, it is to be hoped that politics will not get in the way of the European Union preserving its recognition of UK processes by reaching appropriate agreement on mutual recognition. This could happen in the context of an agreement on trade in services, or on the recognition of regulatory structures in the field of financial services. It could also occur by both the European Union and the United Kingdom adhering to a new international agreement related to resolution and insolvency processes to stand alongside the Hague Convention on Choice of Court (to which all parties should adhere after Brexit) and/or an agreement between the United Kingdom and the EU countries equivalent to the Brussels Regulation on civil proceedings.[40] Unwillingness to reach agreement in this area does not seem consistent with the international commitments of G20 EU states.

---

40 The Brussels Regulation may be replicated in whole or in part by the United Kingdom adhering to the Lugano Convention or making an ad hoc agreement with the EU member states with all the features of the Recast Brussels Regulation.

Negotiation with Third Countries

It is also the general position of the European Union that the United Kingdom cannot negotiate any agreements with third countries until after it leaves the European Union. This would apply in the area of trade policy generally, but it is to be noted[41] that under the BRRD, member states have considerable autonomy in deciding whether to recognize individual third-country proceedings and in making agreements with any third country, so long as there is no EU-wide agreement with that third country. It is also worth noting that article 33 of the European Banking Authority Regulation[42] preserves the right of member states to adopt bilateral or multilateral arrangements with third countries in the field of bank regulation. Insofar as these are trade-related matters, this appears to be a specific derogation, which may remove any inhibition to the UK proceeding with third-country negotiations in this field before Brexit.

The Way Forward: The GATS Dimension

As indicated above, there are many contexts in which a long-term provision for mutual recognition of resolution and insolvency provisions could be made, ranging from a new trade agreement that incorporated aspects of EU law, to an agreement limited to mutual recognition of resolution and insolvency provisions.

UK/EU Agreement

The obvious precedent for a trade agreement is the EEA Agreement, the services provisions of which apply, *inter alia*, to all EU financial services regulatory legislation, including the BRRD, CIWUD and Solvency II, but the question of decision making on interpretation and application may prove more of a stumbling block in the present climate than at the time of the EEA Agreement, when the European Union was prepared to recognize the role of an independent European Free Trade Agreement (EFTA) court. In the event that a free trade agreement was achieved between the United Kingdom and the European Union covering a wide range of services, using this as a vehicle to preserve the status quo related to the resolution and winding up of financial institutions would be entirely in accord with the requirements of GATS in relation to free trade agreements.[43]

Alternative arrangements are more limited agreements on mutual recognition of either financial regulation (including resolution and insolvency measures) or on the mutual recognition of resolution and insolvency measures in all contexts (that is, an agreement mirroring the general insolvency regulation, as well as the provisions for EU/EEA-wide recognition in the BRRD, CIWUD and Solvency II).

In considering alternative arrangements, the terms of the GATS specific to financial services need to be considered, in particular the provision on recognition:[44]

---

41 See *BRRD, supra* note 4, s 3 at paras 3.1–3.7.

42 *Regulation (EU) No 1093/2010 of the European Parliament and of the Council of 24 November 2010 establishing a European Supervisory Authority (European Banking Authority)*, [2010] OJ, L 331.

43 *GATS, supra* note 3, art v.

44 *GATS Schedule*, "Annex on Financial Services" at para 3 [*GATS Schedule*].

(a) A Member may recognize prudential measures of any other country in determining how the Member's measures relating to financial services shall be applied. Such recognition, which may be achieved through harmonization or otherwise, may be based upon an agreement or arrangement with the country concerned or may be accorded autonomously.

(b) A Member that is a party to such an agreement or arrangement referred to in subparagraph (a), whether future or existing, shall afford adequate opportunity for other interested Members to negotiate their accession to such agreements or arrangements, or to negotiate comparable ones with it, under circumstances in which there would be equivalent regulation, oversight, implementation of such regulation, and, if appropriate, procedures concerning the sharing of information between the parties to the agreement or arrangement. Where a Member accords recognition autonomously, it shall afford adequate opportunity for any other Member to demonstrate that such circumstances exist.

Thus, provided both the United Kingdom and the European Union, or (where they retain competency) the EU member states, are prepared to contemplate entering into similar arrangements with other WTO members, they may make an agreement between them covering mutual recognition across the full range of financial services regulation, which would include the BRRD, CIWUD and Solvency II provisions under discussion.

Finally, the parties might simply make an agreement on the recognition of each other's resolution and insolvency provisions. This would be a private international law treaty, similar in nature to the Lugano Convention (dealing with choice of court as between the EU and EFTA states) and the Rome and Brussels Conventions that preceded the European Union's Rome I and II Regulations on applicable law[45] and the Brussels regulation on choice of court.[46] This would arguably be outside the purview of the GATS altogether, as are UNCITRAL and other international-body-sponsored international agreements in this field. In particular, if it were open to additional members (as, for example, the Lugano Convention is) it would seem in any event not to go against GATS rules.

Unilateral Recognition

It should be noted that the GATS rule on the recognition of financial services regulation quoted above also covers the "autonomous" or unilateral recognition of another GATS member's regulatory regime. It is arguable that in making the recognition provisions of the BRRD, CIWUD and Solvency II part of UK law through the Withdrawal Bill, the United Kingdom is affording autonomous recognition to the European Union and EU member state regulation, and should comply with the rule that it should afford adequate opportunity for any other GATS member to demonstrate that its own legal position in relation to resolution and insolvency would warrant the United Kingdom giving similar recognition to its resolution and insolvency processes in relation to some or all financial institutions.

---

45 *Regulation (EC) No 593/2008 of the European Parliament and of the Council of 17 June 2008 on the law applicable to contractual obligations (Rome I)*, [2008] OJ, L 177 and *Regulation (EC) No 864/2007 of the European Parliament and of the Council of 11 July 2007 on the law applicable to non-contractual obligations (Rome II)*, [2007] OJ, L 199, respectively.

46 *Regulation (EU) No 1215/2012 of the European Parliament and of the Council of 12 December 2012 on jurisdiction and the recognition and enforcement of judgments in civil and commercial matters*, [2012] OJ, L 351 [*Recast Brussels Regulation*].

As a policy matter, this GATS rule would seem to be in line with the United Kingdom's general attitude to the rest of the world in relation to insolvency and other issues, as evidenced by its adoption of the UNCITRAL Model Law in relation to third-country insolvency proceedings relating to trading companies.[47]

There is one issue that would cause concern. Both before and after Brexit, the United Kingdom would be able to apply the provisions of BRRD article 95[48] to refuse recognition to third-country insolvency proceedings. After Brexit, EU countries (in the absence of reciprocal agreement) will be able to assert the right to apply those provisions against the recognition of UK processes, but the United Kingdom would not be able to use article 95 against EU processes. If any EU country has particularly protectionist processes or introduces them at a time when there is no reciprocal recognition arrangement in place, would the United Kingdom be justified in adapting its law so as to be able to refuse recognition and assistance? This issue would also arise in CIWUD and chapter IV of Solvency II, although these have not articulated the European Union's position on third-country processes.

To take an example, BRRD article 95 would allow the United Kingdom to take independent proceedings in relation to a failing institution headquartered in a third country if "creditors, including in particular depositors located or payable in a Member State, would not receive the same treatment as third-country creditors and depositors with similar legal rights under the third-country home resolution proceedings."[49] If, however, an EU member state adopted a provision that denied third-country nationals (including UK nationals) access to a deposit protection scheme in an EU member state, the United Kingdom would not be free to take action against assets in its jurisdiction of a failing institution headquartered in that member state, unless it modified its own retained EU law implementing the BRRD to some extent. Would it be justified in doing so? There is nothing in the GATS that would prevent it from doing so. Indeed, the GATS provides:[50] "Notwithstanding any other provisions of the Agreement, a Member shall not be prevented from taking measures for prudential reasons, including for the protection of investors, depositors, policy holders or persons to whom a fiduciary duty is owed by a financial service supplier, or to ensure the integrity and stability of the financial system. Where such measures do not conform with the provisions of the Agreement, they shall not be used as a means of avoiding the Member's commitments or obligations under the Agreement."

It may be argued the United Kingdom should apply article 95 to the EU member states in any event and add similar language to its implementation of CIWUD and chapter IV of Solvency II, if there is no agreement covering reciprocal arrangements at the time of Brexit and no transitional arrangement preserving the status quo. Article 95 is, of course, merely a qualification of recognition, and this would not remove the benefits of the detailed implementation of measures for the recognition of EU processes where none of the qualifying factors apply.

---

47 See "International Instruments" section, above, for more discussion.
48 See "BRRD Recognition" section, above, for more discussion.
49 *Ibid*, art 95.
50 *GATS Schedule*, *supra* note 44 at para 2(a).

The Courts: Can Comity Help at All?

The notion of comity in international law has a long history. Its origins lie in Dutch jurisprudence[51] and were taken up in the United Kingdom,[52] the United States and other common law jurisdictions widely and have been extensively applied in the context of insolvency processes.[53] The notion of comity has been expressed as follows:[54] "'Comity,' in the legal sense, is neither a matter of absolute obligation, on the one hand, nor of mere courtesy and good will, upon the other. But it is the recognition which one nation allows within its territory to the legislative, executive or judicial acts of another nation, having due regard both to international duty and convenience, and to the rights of its own citizens or of other persons who are under the protection of its laws."

The concept and application of comity has, however, found considerably less favour in the major civil law jurisdictions — and most of the continuing EU member states are civil law jurisdictions.[55] They are more inclined to look at rules, in their own or EU law, or specific international agreements to tell them what foreign processes they should or should not accept, and many have vestiges of preference for the interests of their own nationals when faced with a request to give effect to a foreign law or decision.[56] The CJEU would look to practice in the majority of member states if it had to consider what the approach of the EU courts would be and, as with legal professional privilege, it may be that the CJEU would give a disappointing and narrow answer from a common law perspective: declining to state a presumption of recognition in the absence of a policy-restricting recognition, or simply referring the matter to national rules of each member state to be applied on a case-by-case basis.

On the other hand, comity would support UK recognition of EU processes and might be a tool the English courts could use to make sense of the confusing interpretation rules for retained EU law proposed by the Withdrawal Bill, respecting and taking note of EU processes and EU and member state decisions so far as possible.

---

51 Ulrich Huber developed the idea of *comitas gentium* ("civility of nations"), leading to respect for and application of applicable foreign law, in the absence of prejudice in the place where that law is applied, so far as they do not cause prejudice to the powers or rights of such government or of their subjects.

52 Lord Mansfield is generally credited with developing the doctrine and setting its limits in English law, in particular in the *Case of James Sommersett* (1772), in which he refused to recognize the rights of an American slave owner in respect of his slave, on grounds that slavery was abhorrent to English public policy.

53 Most recently in *In re: Lehman Brothers Holdings Inc.*, 553 BR 476; *Belmont Park Investments PTY Limited v BNY Corporate Trustee Services Limited and Lehman Brothers Special Financing Inc*, [2011] UKSC 38; *Lehman Brothers Special Financing Inc v BNY Corporate Trustee Services Limited*, 422 BR 407 (Bankr SDNY 2010) when the English and US courts reached opposite conclusions on their similar provisions of insolvency law to uphold and overrule respectively a "flip clause" in an English law trust deed, which operated on an insolvency event of default, the US court considering that it would be contrary to the policies or prejudicial to the interests of the United States.

54 Justice Gray in the US Supreme Court case *Hilton v Guyot*, 159 US 113 (1895).

55 See the in-depth review in Joel R Paul, "Comity in International Law" (1991) 32 Harv Intl LJ 1; also touched upon in Joel R Paul, "Transformation of International Comity" (2008) 71 Law & Contemp Probs 19.

56 Overcome to a considerable extent by the EU rules in the Rome regulations and within the European Union by the rules in the Brussels Regulation.

Conclusion

The author is driven to the conclusion that Brexit represents a setback in international efforts to improve recognition of cross-border resolution and insolvency processes. While the European Union and the United Kingdom have the tools to preserve the status quo between them if they so choose, the need for wider international effort is clear, whether it be extension of the UNCITRAL model law or a more specialist convention to underpin the FSB key attributes recommendations.

Section Three

INTELLECTUAL PROPERTY

9

UK Patent Law and Copyright Law after Brexit: Potential Consequences

Luke McDonagh

Introduction

This chapter grapples with the slogan "take back control" — the signature claim of the pro-Brexit campaign that Britain's exit from the European Union, or "Brexit," would ensure the United Kingdom would take control of its own laws. Although intellectual property (IP) concerns were not front and centre during the referendum campaign, the idea of taking back control undoubtedly has resonance in the IP field.[1] This is the case, even though, unlike the areas of trademarks and designs explored by Marc Mimler's chapter in this book, neither patent law nor copyright law is fully "Europeanized." In fact, despite the lack of overarching harmonizing

---

1 Andreas Rahmatian, "Brief speculations about changes to IP law in the UK after Brexit" (2017) 12:6 J Intell Prop L & Pr 510; Trevor Cook, "'Brexit' and Intellectual Property Protection in the UK and the EU" (2016) 21:5–6 J Intell Prop Rts 355.

legislation, EU law has had a substantial effect on the protection of patented inventions and works of copyright in the United Kingdom.[2]

At the same time, it is important to recall that the UK legal system's protection of patents and copyrights predates the European Union. Even today, although compliant with EU law, UK patent and copyright laws are largely rooted in domestic legislation[3] and non-EU international agreements, such as the Berne Convention and the European Patent Convention.[4] Yet, the impact of EU law on IP means that Brexit will undoubtedly have a major impact on the United Kingdom's current legal framework and could, at least in theory, provide the opportunity for the United Kingdom to take back control.[5]

A so-called hard Brexit would sever all links with the EU *acquis*, including ending the European Court of Justice's (ECJ) jurisdiction in the United Kingdom. Nevertheless, the malleability of the common law system means that, post-Brexit, UK courts can continue to apply EU-derived principles within patent law and copyright law until new UK legislation provides otherwise. Moreover, UK courts will likely find ECJ judgments persuasive in cases involving EU law-derived definitions and terms.[6] By contrast, a soft Brexit, i.e., where the United Kingdom stays within the European Free Trade Agreement (EFTA) or the European Economic Area (EEA), would mean that many IP directives would remain valid.

Further to this, the guarantees of IP protection under the EU Charter on Fundamental Rights will not disappear entirely in the United Kingdom: post-Brexit, the United Kingdom will remain a member of the Council of Europe, and thus, will be subject to the European Convention on Human Rights (ECHR), which applies to UK courts under the Human Rights Act 1998.[7] The ECHR, like the EU Charter of Fundamental Rights, protects intellectual property, including patents and copyright, and the rulings of the two courts — the European Court of Human Rights and the ECJ — have always converged in the interpretation of these rights.[8]

At this delicate stage of the Brexit process, with negotiations ongoing at the time of writing, it is impossible to establish a definitive picture of what the law will look like in the years to come. However, it is possible to explain how EU law is integrated into the UK law of patents and copyright — the status quo — and to consider the possible directions the law may travel in the years to come. This chapter first examines how IP came to be integrated within the EU legal order, and then goes on to examine the specific cases of patent law and copyright law.

---

2   Marc Mimler, "The Effect of Brexit on Trademarks, Designs and Other 'Europeanized' Areas of Intellectual Property Law in the United Kingdom" in Oonagh E Fitzgerald & Eva Lein, eds, *Complexity's Embrace: The International Law Implications of Brexit* (Waterloo, ON: CIGI, 2018). See also Justine Pila, "Intellectual Property as a Case Study in Europeanization: Methodological Themes and Context" in Ansgar Ohly & Justine Pila, eds, *The Europeanization of Intellectual Property Law* (Oxford: Oxford University Press, 2013) 3.

3   *Patents Act 1977* (UK), c 37; *Copyright, Designs and Patents Act 1988* (UK), c 48.

4   *Berne Convention for the Protection of Literary and Artistic Works*, 9 September 1886 (amended 28 September 1979), online: <www.wipo.int/treaties/en/text.jsp?file_id=283698>; *European Patent Convention*, 5 October 1973 (amended 14 October 2015), online: <www.epo.org/law-practice/legal-texts/html/epc/2016/e/index.html> [*EPC*].

5   Benjamin Farrand, "Bold and newly Independent, or Isolated and Cast Adrift? The Implications of Brexit for Intellectual Property Law and Policy" (2017) 7:2 J Common Market Stud 1.

6   This may occur in a similar way to the current practice of UK courts with respect to European Patent Office Board of Appeals decisions: see e.g. *Conor v Angiotech* [2008] UKHL 49; *Human Genome Sciences v Eli Lilly* [2011] UKSC 51.

7   *Human Rights Act 1998* (UK), c 42.

8   Jonathan Griffiths & Luke McDonagh, "Fundamental Rights and European Intellectual Property Law: The Case of Art 17(2) of the EU Charter" in Christoph Geiger, ed, *Constructing European IP: Achievements and New Perspectives* (Cheltenham, UK: Edward Elgar, 2013) 75–93.

Finally, the chapter concludes by arguing that due to "the web of the international, regional and bilateral obligations that exist in the field of IP," "the benefits that this harmonization brings to the creative environment," and the "integration of markets that has occurred in part through the 60 years of the EU," the United Kingdom will likely take back control much less than the "Brexiteers" have imagined.[9]

EU Intellectual Property Law: A History of Ever-growing Integration

When the Treaty of Rome established the European Economic Community (EEC) in 1957, it did not grant the competence to legislate for IP.[10] The treaty rather stated in article 222 that EEC law would not "prejudice the system existing in Member States in respect of property."[11] For this reason, in the decades that immediately followed, IP legislative harmonization efforts took place at the international multilateral level.[12] One such measure was the 1975 Community Patent Convention, developed as a special agreement between member states of the then EEC.[13]

Nonetheless, over the past 50 years, as the EEC has transformed, first into the European Community (EC) and later the European Union, the ECJ has increasingly perceived that national rules for IP protection — and the variances therein — are capable of creating obstacles to the successful operation of key principles of the treaties.[14] Quite early on, from the 1960s onward, the ECJ began to scrutinize IP under the treaty rules — importantly, the court began to distinguish between the existence of IP rights, which were governed by national law, and their exercise, in particular as IP-relevant goods and services crossed borders within the European Union.[15] The ECJ perceived that the rules of the internal market required that the exercise of IP rights should fall under the shared scrutiny of both the member states and the European Union.[16] Initially, this concerned the impact of national IP rules on EU competition.[17] Soon, however, the focus shifted to the potentially adverse effects of IP rights on the free movement of goods.[18]

---

9   Graeme B Dinwoodie & Rochelle C Dreyfuss, "Brexit and IP: The Great Unraveling?" (2017) NYU School of Law Public Law & Legal Theory Research Paper Series Working Paper 17–26.

10   *Treaty Establishing the European Economic Community*, 25 March 1957, OJ, C 224 art 100 (entered into force 1 January 1958) [*Treaty of Rome*].

11   Additionally, article 36 states that the protection of industrial and commercial property could be regarded as exceptions for the prohibition of restrictions to the freedom of movement of goods.

12   Guy Tritton, *Tritton on Intellectual Property in Europe*, 4th ed (London: Sweet & Maxwell, 2014) at 1–21.

13   While the convention did not come into force, its provisions were used as templates for national patent laws: see e.g. *Patents Act 1977* (UK), c 37, s 130(7); "Resolution on the Adjustment of National Patent Law Records of the Luxembourg Conference on the Community patent 1975", *Records of the Luxembourg Conference on the Community patent 1975* (Luxembourg: Office for Official Publications of the European Communities, 1982) 332, online: <http://aei.pitt. edu/10329/1/10329.pdf>.

14   *Parke, Davis and Co. v Probel, Reese, Beintema-Interpharm and Centrafarm*, 29 February 1968, Case No 24/67, ECLI:EU:C:1968:11, 55, 71 [*Parke, Davis and Co.*], online: <http://eur-lex.europa.eu/legal-content/EN/ TXT/?uri=CELEX%3A61967CJ0024>.

15   Tritton, *supra* note 12.

16   Pila, *supra* note 2 at 10.

17   Peter Groves et al, *Intellectual Property and the Internal Market of the European Community* (London, UK: Graham & Trotman: 1993) at 5; see e.g. *Consten and Grundig v Commission of the EEC*, 13 July 1966, Case No 56/64, ECLI:EU:C:1966:41, online: <http://curia.europa.eu/juris/liste.jsf?num=C-56/64&language=en>; *Parke, Davis and Co.*, *supra* note 14.

18   Tritton, *supra* note 12.

Eventually, the European Union realized that it would be more efficient to resolve some of the discrepancies between treaty principles and national IP rights via harmonization. The European Commission did this primarily by enacting directives based on article 114(1) of the Treaty on the Functioning of the European Union (TFEU) and its predecessor,[19] concerning the establishment and functioning of the internal market.[20] In addition to harmonization via directives, unitary EU-wide IP rights have been enacted through regulations.[21] Such measures were initially based on article 352 of the TFEU,[22] however, the Treaty of Lisbon introduced article 118, which specifically provides for the introduction of EU-wide IP rights.[23] As this chapter shows, directives and regulations have had a substantial impact on the law of both patents and copyright.

Patents

The EU statute book reveals that there is much less EU legislation in this field than in the other IP areas. As a result, in theory patent law will be the IP area "where the UK will formally re-acquire the least sovereignty" post-Brexit.[24]

In fact, the key treaty on patenting in Europe — the European Patent Convention (EPC) of 1973 — was agreed outside the European Union and has a wider membership, including Iceland, Switzerland and Turkey, for example, as well as several other non-EU territories.[25] Via the EPC system, European patents (EPs) may be filed, prosecuted and administered at the European Patent Office (EPO), which has its main office in Munich, Germany. Yet, the EPO's "European patent" is actually a bundle of national patent rights that must be validated in the national territory. As such, UK EPs will continue to exist post-Brexit.[26]

Even though the primary governing law, the EPC, exists outside the European Union's authority, the European Union has, in fact, legislated in several areas relating to patents. The following pieces of EU legislation have a direct impact: Directive 98/44/EC (biotechnological inventions);[27] Regulation 2100/94 (plant variety rights);[28] Directive 2004/48/EC (enforcement

---

19 *Treaty on the Functioning of the European Union*, 13 December 2007, OJ, C 326/01 [*TFEU*]; *Treaty Establishing the European Community*, 25 March 1957, OJ, C 325 art 95 (entered into force 1 January 1958) [*EC Treaty*].

20 *Federal Republic of Germany v European Parliament and Council of the European Union*, C-376/98, [2000] ECLI:EU:C:2000:544 at paras 83–84.

21 Trevor Cook, *EU Intellectual Property Law* (Oxford, UK: Oxford University Press, 2010) at 4–5.

22 *EC Treaty*, *supra* note 19, art 308; *TFEU*, *supra* note 19, art 235.

23 *Treaty of Lisbon amending the Treaty on European Union and the Treaty establishing the European Community*, 13 December 2007, OJ, C 306 (entered into force 1 December 2009), online: <http://eur-lex.europa.eu/legal-content/EN/TXT/?uri=celex:12007L/TXT>.

24 Dinwoodie & Dreyfuss, *supra* note 9 at 8–10.

25 *EPC*, *supra* note 4.

26 Luke McDonagh, *European Patent Litigation in the Shadow of the Unified Patent Court* (Cheltenham, UK: Edward Elgar, 2016) at 1–10.

27 EC, *Directive 98/44/EC of the European Parliament and of the Council of 6 July 1998 on the legal protection of biotechnological inventions*, [1998] OJ, L 213/13.

28 EC, *Council Regulation (EC) No 2100/94 of 27 July 1994 on Community plant variety rights*, [1994] OJ, L 227. See also EC, *Council Regulation (EC) No 873/2004 of 29 April 2004 amending Regulation (EC) No 2100/94 on Community plant variety rights*, [2004] OJ, L 162.

directive);[29] Regulation 469/2009/EC (SPCs for medicinal products);[30] Directive 2001/82/EC (veterinary medicinal products);[31] Directive 2001/83/EC (medical products for human use);[32] Directive 2009/24/EC (computer programs);[33] Regulation 1257/2012 (unitary patent [UP] regulation);[34] and Regulation 1260/2012 (UP translation arrangements).[35] In addition, there is a regulation on IP border enforcement.[36]

For present purposes, the most significant pieces of EU legislation are the biotechnology directive (which governs the limits to biotechnological inventions), the supplementary protection certificates (SPCs) regulation (which allows an extension of up to five years' protection for patented medicines),[37] and the regulation establishing the UP. Keeping this in mind, this chapter will focus on the two most important elements of the relationship between patents and the European Union: ECJ jurisprudence, in particular in the areas of biotechnology and SPCs; and the implementation of the recent EU-led patent reforms, i.e., the Unified Patent Court (UPC) and the European Patent with Unitary Effect, including the UP regulation.

ECJ Case Law

It is beyond the scope of this chapter to give an authoritative overview of ECJ jurisprudence on patent case law — there is simply too much ground to cover. Rather, this chapter outlines two cases in the most significant areas of EU patent law — biotechnology and SPCs — in order to show the importance of EU law in the patent area.

The Biotechnology Directive

The biotechnology directive sets the terms for patenting inventions in the area of biotechnology. One of the most significant elements of the directive is that it restricts patentability for any invention that involves "uses of human embryos for industrial or commercial purposes." Yet, the directive does not provide a definition of what constitutes a "human embryo." It was therefore left to the ECJ in the 2011 *Brüstle* case to explain the meaning of a human embryo in this context.[38] The ECJ decided that article 6(2)(c) of the biotechnology directive must be interpreted as meaning the following: "The use of human embryos for scientific research purposes is not

---

29 EC, *Directive 2004/48/EC of the European Parliament and of the Council of 29 April 2004 on the enforcement of intellectual property rights*, [2004] OJ, L 195/22. A relevant UK case on the enforcement directive is *HTC Corporation v Nokia Corporation*, [2013] EWHC 3778 (Pat).

30 EC, *Regulation 469/2009/EC of the European Parliament and of the Council of 6 May 2009 concerning the supplementary protection certificate for medicinal products*, [2009] OJ, L 152.

31 EC, *Directive 2001/82/EC of the European Parliament and of the Council of 6 November 2001 on the Community code relating to veterinary medicinal products*, [2001] OJ, L 311.

32 EC, *Directive 2001/83/EC of the European Parliament and of the Council of 6 November 2001 on the Community code relating to medicinal products for human use*, [2001] OJ, L 311 [*Directive 2001/83/EC*].

33 EC, *Directive 2009/24/EC of the European Parliament and of the Council of 23 April 2009 on the legal protection of computer programs*, [2009] OJ, L 111.

34 *Regulation (EU) No 1257/2012 of the European Parliament and of the Council of 17 December 2012 implementing enhanced cooperation in the area of the creation of unitary patent protection*, [2012] OJ, L 361/1 [*UP Regulation*].

35 *Council regulation (EU) No 1260/2012 of 17 December 2012 implementing enhanced cooperation in the area of the creation of unitary patent protection with regard to the applicable translation arrangements* [2012] OJ, L 361/89 [*Translation Regulation*].

36 *Regulation (EU) No 608/2013 of the European Parliament and of the Council of 12 June 2013 concerning customs enforcement of intellectual property rights and repealing Council Regulation (EC) No 1383/2003*, [2013] OJ, L 181.

37 EC, *Directive 98/44/EC of the European Parliament and of the Council of 6 July 1998 on the legal protection of biotechnological inventions*, [1998] OJ, L 213/13.

38 *Brüstle v Greenpeace*, (2011) C-34/10, ECLI:EU:C:2011:669.

patentable. A 'human embryo' within the meaning of Union law is any human ovum after fertilisation or any human ovum not fertilised but which, through the effect of the technique used to obtain it, is capable of commencing the process of development of a human being."

The ECJ then referred the case back to the referring German court to decide the factual matter, giving account to available scientific evidence as to whether a stem cell obtained at the blastocyst stage from a human embryo falls within the definition of "human embryo."[39]

The ECJ's decision in *Brüstle* was hotly debated, with some considering the court to be an inappropriate place to determine questions of morality, while others wondering whether the European Union would be left at a competitive disadvantage with the United States, which does allow patenting under the *Brüstle* circumstances.[40] Either way, the impact of the ECJ's authority in this important area of patenting is undeniable. Further to this, even post-Brexit, the biotechnology directive will continue to carry influence on UK patent law via the United Kingdom's EPC membership, since the EPO pays regard to the directive and its interpretation by EU institutions.[41]

SPCs for Medicinal Products

A patentee can apply for an SPC to extend the life of a medicinal or pharmaceutical patent — beyond the usual 20 years — if there was a delay in the European Medicines Agency granting the marketing authorization allowing the patented medicine to be sold within the European Union's internal market.[42] Although the SPC regulation is a relatively short and seemingly unassuming piece of legislation, it has led to a great deal of ECJ case law.[43]

One significant example is the *Arne Forsgren* case.[44] Here, the ECJ analyzed the limits of SPC protection. The facts of the case were as follows: Protein D subsists in a vaccine called Synflorix, which has an important and lucrative pediatric use. Within Synflorix, Protein D acts as a "carrier protein" — one conjugated by covalent bonds. Yet, the actual application for an SPC referred to Protein D per se — not in the conjugated form.

The relevant Austrian authority therefore rejected the SPC application, stating that Protein D only subsists in Synflorix as a conjugate of other "active" ingredients and that Protein D is a mere excipient. Thus, in *Arne Forsgren* the ECJ was asked to analyze the following two questions: first, can an SPC be obtained with respect to a product per se in "separate" form, in a scenario involving a marketing authorization for a medicine in which the product is covalently bonded to other ingredients? Second, can the SPC rely on a marketing authorization that merely describes

---

39   Although the German Federal Court allowed the patent to continue as valid in amended form, the EPO later revoked the corresponding European patent. See European Patent Office, "EPO revokes patent in the 'Brüstle' case", (11 April 2013), online: <www.epo.org/news-issues/news/2013/20130411a.html>.

40   Alain Pottage & Claire Marris, "The cut that makes a part" (2012) 7:2 BioSocieties 103–114.

41   See European Patent Office, "EPO stays proceedings in certain biotechnology cases", (12 Dec 2016), online: <www.epo.org/news-issues/news/2016/20161212.html>; European Patent Office, "EPO clarifies practice in the area of plant and animal patents", (29 June 2017), online: <www.epo.org/news-issues/news/2017/20170629.html> (both EU provisions were issued in light of a Notice of the European Commission related to articles in the EU biotechnology directive).

42   Manthan Janodia, "Comparative Quantitative Analysis of Supplementary Protection Certificates (SPCs) in Europe" (2017) 22 J Intell Prop Rts 16 at 18–22.

43   David Brophy, "Another SPC referral: will we get clarity or more questions?", *The IPKat* (22 October 2012), online: <http://ipkitten.blogspot.co.uk/2012/10/another-spc-referral-will-we-get.html>.

44   *Arne Forsgren v Österreichisches Patentamt*, (2015) C-631/13, ECLI:EU:C:2015:13.

the product as a "carrier protein" and does not provide any information about an independent therapeutic effect?

In its 2015 decision, the ECJ answered the first question by stating that the "covalent bonding" issue should not prevent the granting of an SPC. In relation to the second question — whether the marketing authorization was sufficient to support the SPC — the ECJ held that for Protein D to be an "active ingredient" as required by the regulation, it needed to produce "a pharmacological, immunological or metabolic action of its own which is covered by the therapeutic indications of the marketing authorisation." Ultimately, the ECJ left that factual determination to the referring national authority. Yet, the ECJ's clear guidance is illustrative of its crucial role as the final arbiter of an important patent-related question: should an SPC be granted to extend the life of a particular patented medicine?

The Unified Patent Court

As noted earlier, the granting of EPs takes place at the EPO. However, patent litigation in Europe concerning, for example, infringement of EPs takes place at the national level.[45] It is national courts that deal with questions of patent infringement within their national territories. National courts can also consider issues of patent validity — although the EPO remains the final arbiter on patent validity via its opposition system.[46] Due to this overlap, national patent litigation and EPO opposition proceedings on the validity of the same patent can occur in parallel; furthermore, national courts are often quicker to decide questions of validity than the EPO Board of Appeals.[47] This can cause difficulties if the EPO rules that a patent is valid, when it has already been invalidated in a national territory. In addition, national courts in the United Kingdom and Germany, for example, can make divergent decisions on infringement (and validity), which can cause fragmented patenting across EU member states, impacting on competition within the internal market.[48]

With these problems in mind,[49] in February 2013, the United Kingdom and 24 other countries signed an intergovernmental agreement to create a UPC.[50] Effectively, the complete package establishes unitary patent protection and enforcement within the vast majority of the EU member states.[51] Total unification is not yet possible — Croatia, Poland and Spain are not yet

---

45 *EPC, supra* note 4. Even though at present a patentee can apply to the EPO for an EP with a single application in one of the three official EPO languages, once granted, a patent must be filed and translated into the other two official EPO languages. See also the *Agreement on the application of Article 65 of the Convention on the Grant of European Patents*, 17 October 2000, OJ EPO 549 (2001), online: <http://documents.epo.org/projects/babylon/eponet. nsf/0/7FD20618D28E9FBFC125743900678657/$File/London_Agreement.pdf>.

46 See generally EPO, *Patent Litigation in Europe: An overview of national law and practice in the EPC contracting states* (2016), online: <www.epo.org/learning-events/materials/litigation.html>.

47 McDonagh, *supra* note 26 at 1–16.

48 *Ibid.*

49 EPO Economic and Scientific Advisory Board, *Recommendations for improving the patent system* (Munich, Germany: EPO, 2012) at 1–5, online: <http://documents.epo.org/projects/babylon/eponot. nsf/0/835DA6DA218CB760C1257B2C004E809E/$FILE/ESAB_statement_en.pdf>.

50 *Agreement on a Unified Patent Court*, C 175/1 [*UPC Agreement*], online: <http://eur-lex.europa.eu/LexUriServ/ LexUriServ.do?uri=OJ:C:2013:175:0001:0040:EN:PDF>.

51 *UP Regulation, supra* note 34; *Translation Regulation, supra* note 35. For a further explanation of the changes, see the EPO website: <www.epo.org/law-practice/unitary.html>.

participants in the new system, although they may join at a later date. London is due to host one of the UPC's central divisions.[52]

Alongside the UPC Agreement, EU regulations were enacted to establish the European patent with unitary effect and the relevant UP translation arrangements.[53] The EU regulations were passed into law via the system of enhanced cooperation introduced by the Lisbon Treaty.[54] The UP is enabled by the EPC, which contains an option to allow validation of patents on a supranational basis.[55] In fact, the UP application and grant process will be the same as for the regular EPs. Thereafter, once the EPO grants the patent, the patentee will have the option to choose either the traditional EP or the new UP, which gives unitary protection across 25 EU member states.[56] Finally, the UPC will not only have exclusive jurisdiction to hear disputes concerning the validity and infringement of the new UPs, but also existing and prospective EPs (subject to the transition period, when jurisdiction over EPs will be shared with national courts, unless, during this period, EPs are opted out of the UPC in order to remain solely within the national system).[57]

The UPC and the UP Post-Brexit: Can the United Kingdom Still Participate?

Although the two EU regulations are technically already in force,[58] they will only apply once the UPC Agreement is ratified by Germany, France and the United Kingdom, as well as 10 more participating signatory states. As of September 2017, this ratification has yet to take place. Key to the delay has been Brexit (although that is not the only current stumbling block, as a recent German constitutional challenge demonstrates).[59]

The ECJ in Opinion 1/09 held that only states that accept the supremacy of EU law and the jurisdiction of the ECJ may sign up.[60] The reason this is important is that even though the UPC will have its own jurisdiction to rule with respect to most patent issues — such as patent infringement and validity — it must follow ECJ rulings in EU law matters, such as biotechnology, enforcement or SPCs. In this vein, article 21 of the UPC Agreement allows the UPC to refer EU law questions to the ECJ.[61] Therefore, the ECJ will have an impact on the law applied by the UPC, although not, apparently, on core patent-specific matters — a situation that is intended to differentiate the patents area from the field of trademarks, where the ECJ

---

52 Luke McDonagh, *supra* note 26 at 1–16. See also Luke McDonagh, *Exploring perspectives of the Unified Patent Court and the Unitary Patent within the Business and Legal Communities* (Newport, UK: Intellectual Property Office, 2014), online: <www.gov.uk/government/publications/exploring-perspectives-of-the-up-and-upc>.

53 *UP Regulation, supra* note 34; *Translation Regulation, supra* note 35.

54 *Treaty of Lisbon, supra* note 23.

55 *EPC, supra* note 4, arts 2, 142.

56 Reto Hilty, "The Unitary Patent Package: Twelve Reasons for Concern" (2012) Max Planck Institute for Intellectual Property & Competition Law Research Paper No 12-12.

57 Trevor Cook, "The Progress to date on the Unitary European Patent and the Unified Patent Court for Europe" (2013) 18 J Intell Prop Rts 584, 586.

58 *UP Regulation, supra* note 34, art 18(2); *Translation Regulation, supra* note 35, art 7(2).

59 Edward Nodder, "Further details on the German constitutional challenge to UPC legislation", Bristows UPS (17 August 2017), online: <www.bristowsupc.com/latest-news/further_details_on_german_constitutional_challenge_upc_legislation/>.

60 ECJ, Opinion 1/09, 8 March 2011, at para 82, online: <http://ec.europa.eu/dgs/legal_service/arrets/09a001_en.pdf>,

61 See also *UPC Agreement, supra* note 50, art 1(2); *Consolidated versions of the Treaty on European Union and the Treaty on the Functioning of the European Union*, C 326/01 (2012) art 267, online: <http://eur-lex.europa.eu/legal-content/EN/TXT/?uri=OJ:C:2012:326:TOC>.

has developed, and expanded upon, core EU legislation on trademarks, often to the chagrin of trademark experts.[62]

The ECJ's role makes the UPC an awkward court for the Brexit-focused United Kingdom to sign up to. Prime Minister Theresa May is on record as saying that the United Kingdom would, post-Brexit, end the jurisdiction of the ECJ, something repeated in the government's Brexit white paper.[63] If the UK government is determined to "escape" the ECJ's jurisdiction, then how can the United Kingdom participate in the UPC, which requires accepting the supremacy of patent-related EU law and ECJ jurisdiction on such questions? The answer is unclear. Yet, in November 2016, the UK government announced that it would ratify the UPC Agreement, despite the Brexit referendum result, since the UPC is "an international court," not an EU one. This continues to be the official policy at the time of writing.[64]

An optimistic view of the UK government's position on the UPC would be that, per the Brexit white paper (2.7–2.10), it accepts that the creation of new dispute resolution panels or tribunals will be a necessary element of any free trade agreement (FTA) between the United Kingdom and the European Union post-Brexit. It may even indicate that the United Kingdom would accept the authority of an "international court," such as the UPC, where it has the limited capacity to determine specific commercial law questions, i.e., patent matters that are common to the United Kingdom and its "new partnership with the European Union." A more pessimistic view would note that the United Kingdom's position is not the only factor: even if the UPC Agreement can be amended to allow the United Kingdom to participate as a non-EU member, it is uncertain whether the ECJ would be willing to accept this as valid.[65] Unless the United Kingdom demonstrates a sincere willingness to be bound by all the elements of EU law in this area, the prospect of UK UPC membership will remain a remote one.

At present, with the further delay caused by the German constitutional challenge, it is looking increasingly unlikely that UPC ratification will occur before Brexit takes place in March 2019. On the face of it, the seemingly endless delays, coupled with the awkwardness of the United Kingdom's position on the UPC/ECJ, puts continuing UK participation in serious doubt. This is not just a problem for UK legal services; it could have profound overall consequences for the United Kingdom's involvement in European patenting. Although the United Kingdom will remain an EPC member no matter what, unless it participates in the UPC system, the United Kingdom and UK judges will miss out on defining the future requirements of European patenting, since the UPC's decisions are likely to influence the jurisprudence of the EPC and its administrative appeals system.

If UK UPC participation is complicated, but legally possible, the UP is a different story. Created by an EU regulation, the UP is clearly an "EU IP right" — it cannot be considered a

---

62 See Jonathan Griffiths, "Constitutionalising or harmonising? The Court of Justice, the Right to Property and European Copyright Law" (2013) 38 Eur L Rev 65; Luke McDonagh, "From Brand Performance to Consumer Performativity: Assessing European Trade Mark Law after the Rise of Anthropological Marketing" (2015) 42 JL & Soc'y 611–636.

63 HM Government, *The United Kingdom's exit from and new partnership with the European Union* (London, UK: Williams Lea Group, 2017), online: <www.gov.uk/government/uploads/system/uploads/attachment_data/file/588948/The_United_ Kingdoms_exit_from_and_partnership_with_the_EU_Web.pdf>.

64 Katharine Stephens, Christopher de Mauny & Will Smith, "UK Government appoints new IP Minister, Jo Johnson MP, who provides an update on the UPC", *Bird & Bird* (12 January 2017), online: <www.twobirds.com/en/news/articles/2017/ uk/uk-government-appoints-new-ip-minister>.

65 Dinwoodie & Dreyfuss, *supra* note 9 at 19.

predominantly "international right." Further to this, the United Kingdom has not, as yet, given any indication of whether it would be willing to seek any accommodation with the European Union about how the UP might remain valid in the United Kingdom post-Brexit. Thus, even with so much uncertainty, it seems much more likely that the United Kingdom could remain part of the UPC system than the UP. If this strange situation were to occur, from the United Kingdom's perspective, only EPs valid in the United Kingdom could be litigated at the UPC, since the UP would apply only in the other 24 UPC signatory states.[66]

Copyright

There is no overarching unitary regulatory system for EU copyright. Despite this, key elements of substantive copyright law have been harmonized in the European Union. This has occurred via 10 EU directives that have been implemented in the United Kingdom: the Information Society (InfoSoc) Directive;[67] the Rental and Lending Directive;[68] the Artist's Resale Right Directive;[69] the Satellite and Cable Directive;[70] the Software Directive;[71] the Enforcement Directive (also relevant to patents, as noted earlier);[72] the Database Directive;[73] the Term Directive;[74] the Orphan Works Directive;[75] and the Collective Management of Copyright and Related Rights Directive.[76]

These directives have proven central to the adjudication of copyright law in Europe. In fact, in comparison with trademarks and designs, the harmonization of copyright law in the European Union has, to a great extent, been "the result of judicial interpretation by the Court of Justice, rather than comprehensive legislative intervention."[77] This body of ECJ case law will, post-Brexit, in principle cease to be binding on the United Kingdom (unless there is a transitional or longer-term agreement between the United Kingdom and the European Union that provides for the compulsory jurisdiction of the ECJ on copyright).

---

66 *Ibid* at 6–8.

67 EC, *Directive 2001/29/EC of the European Parliament and of the Council of 22 May 2001 on the harmonisation of certain aspects of copyright and related rights in the information society,* [2001] OJ, L 167/10 [*InfoSoc Directive*].

68 EC, *Directive 2006/115/EC of the European Parliament and of the Council of 12 December 2006 on rental right and lending right and on certain rights related to copyright in the field of intellectual property,* [2006] OJ, L 376/28.

69 EC, *Directive 2001/84/EC of the European Parliament and of the Council of 27 September 2001 on the resale right for the benefit of the author of an original work of art,* [2001] OJ, L 272/32 [*Directive 2001/84/EC*].

70 EEC, *Council Directive 93/83/EEC of 27 September 1993 on the coordination of certain rules concerning copyright and rights related to copyright applicable to satellite broadcasting and cable retransmission,* [1993] OJ, L 248/15.

71 EC, *Directive 2009/24/EC of the European Parliament and of the Council of 23 April 2009 on the legal protection of computer programs,* [2009] OJ, L 111/16.

72 EC, *Directive 2004/48/EC of the European Parliament and of the Council of 29 April 2004 on the enforcement of intellectual property rights,* [2004] OJ, L 157/45, *corrigendum* [2004] OJ, L 195/16.

73 EC, *Directive 96/9/EC of the European Parliament and of the Council of 11 March 1996 on the legal protection of databases,* [1996] OJ, L 77/20 [*Database Directive*].

74 EC, *Directive 2006/116/EC of the European Parliament and of the Council of 12 December 2006 on the term of protection of copyright and certain related rights,* [2006] OJ, L 372/12 (as amended by *Directive 2011/77/EU of the European Parliament and of the Council of 27 September 2011 amending Directive 2006/116/EC on the term of protection of copyright and certain related rights),* [2011] OJ, L 265/1.

75 EC, *Directive 2012/28/EU of the European Parliament and of the Council of 25 October 2012 on certain permitted uses of orphan works,* [2012] OJ, L 299/2.

76 EC, *Directive 2014/26/EU of the European Parliament and of the Council of 26 February 2014 on collective management of copyright and related rights and multi-territorial licensing of rights in musical works for online use in the internal market,* [2014] OJ, L 84.

77 Dinwoodie & Dreyfuss, *supra* note 9 at 3.

There is insufficient space here to consider all the areas of copyright involving EU law and ECJ jurisprudence — instead, this chapter focuses on perhaps the three most important areas: originality, exceptions to copyright protection and *sui generis* rights.

Originality

In the 2009 case of *Infopaq International A/S v Danske Dagblades Forening*,[78] the ECJ had the task of determining the scope of originality in the context of copyright infringement under the InfoSoc Directive in a case involving an online news aggregation service.[79] Crucially, the ECJ held that "intellectual creation" is the standard of originality that applies to all copyright works within the European Union. The ECJ considered that it is "only through the choice, sequence and combination of those words that the author may express his creativity in an original manner and achieve a result which is an intellectual creation."[80] This decision came as a surprise because the EU originality threshold of intellectual creation did not exist as a broad, wide-ranging standard in EU legislation;[81] it was merely the threshold for databases, photographs and computer programs, as stated in the relevant directives.[82] Nonetheless, the subsequent cases of *Murphy*[83] and *Painer*[84] confirm the ECJ's determination to enforce the criterion of intellectual creation as the uniform standard of originality for all works across the European Union.

One significant consequence of this is the end of the traditional UK originality test of "skill and labour"; following *Infopaq*, the test of intellectual creation applies in its place. Since intellectual creation appears to be a higher threshold than skill and labour, UK copyright judges have been forced to adjust.[85] The new ECJ-derived standard could mean that certain labour-intensive but uncreative works previously protected in the United Kingdom might no longer be given protection. Nevertheless, although UK courts have, post-*Infopaq*, adopted the new standard in cases such as *Meltwater*[86] and *SAS*,[87] it is still unclear whether any previously covered works are no longer covered by copyright.

Another important element of the *Infopaq* ruling is the ECJ's suggestion that there is virtually no limit on how short a copyright work might be in order for it to be considered sufficiently "original"; all that matters is that the work is considered to be the author's intellectual creation. The only limitation placed by the ECJ is that a single word "considered in isolation" could not be

---

78 *Infopaq International A/S v Danske Dagblades Forening* (2009), ECLI:EU:C:2009:465, online: <http://eur-lex.europa.eu/legal-content/EN/TXT/?uri=ecli:ECLI:EU:C:2009:465> [*Infopaq International*]. See also article 1(3) of *Council Directive 91/250/EEC of 14 May 1991 on the legal protection of computer programs* [*Council Directive 91/250/EEC*], online: <http://eur-lex.europa.eu/LexUriServ/LexUriServ.do?uri=CELEX:31991L0250:EN:HTML>. See also article 3(1) of *Database Directive, supra* note 73.

79 *InfoSoc Directive, supra* note 67.

80 *Infopaq International, supra* note 78.

81 See article 1(3) of *Council Directive 91/250/EEC, supra* note 78. See also article 3(1) of *Database Directive, supra* note 73.

82 *Infopaq International, supra* note 78.

83 Joined cases C-403/08, C-429/08 *Football Association Premier League and Others v QC Leisure and Others, Karen Murphy v Media Protection Services Ltd*, ECLI:EU:C:2011:631.

84 C-145/10 *Painer v Standard Verlags GmbH*, ECLI:EU:C:2011:798.

85 In this view, some non-creative works traditionally protected under UK copyright may no longer be protected as they are not able to satisfy the standard of intellectual creation. For commentary on this point, see C Handig, "*Infopaq International A/S v Danske Dagblades Forening* (C-5/08): is the term 'work' of the CDPA 1988 in line with the European Directives?" (2010) 32 Eur IP Rev 53 at 56.

86 *The Newspaper Licensing Agency Limited and others v Meltwater Holding BV and others*, [2010] EWHC 3099 (Ch).

87 *SAS Institute Inc v World Programming Ltd*, [2010] EWHC 1829 (Ch).

regarded as sufficient to be the intellectual creation of the author.[88] Therefore, while copyright in a single word was ruled out, the door was seemingly left wide open to copyright claims involving very short works of two or more words, or two or more musical notes.[89] This potentially fills gaps in UK national case law, opening up the possibility of a more liberal reading of what might be protected as a copyright work, and thus encouraging authors to make infringement claims over very small pieces of text or music.[90]

Finally, with the *Infopaq* case and the subsequent case of *BSA*,[91] the ECJ has seemingly put an end to the traditional UK "closed list" of works based on certain categories, i.e., literary work, musical work, dramatic work, etc. The UK approach was that anything, such as a TV show format, that fell outside the categories would not be given protection. However, this approach is in doubt since the ECJ's ruling that the sole criterion for copyright should be intellectual creation. This has led to suggestions that unusual creations such as perfumes and cheeses may be original enough to receive copyright protection in the United Kingdom.[92]

So, what about taking back control of the above elements of copyright? On the originality threshold, it is unknown at this stage whether the UK courts will revert to their old understanding of the originality test. The ECJ's intellectual creation standard has become part of the common law through its interpretation in cases such as *Meltwater*. So far, this has been unproblematic, but if any problems were to occur in difficult post-Brexit cases, the UK courts could decide to revert to skill and labour. The same is true of the ECJ's view that very small pieces of text or music can be protected, as well as the apparent end of the United Kingdom's closed list of categories of protected works — the United Kingdom could move away from the ECJ's approaches in both respects and return to the traditional UK views. Having said that, there may be reasons why the United Kingdom may wish to keep its originality principles in line with EU law. The terms of the future trading relationship between the European Union and the United Kingdom, along with any provisions on adjudication, will likely determine this.

Exceptions to Copyright Protection

Article 5 of the InfoSoc Directive mandates an exhaustive list of exceptions, limiting the ability of national legislatures to create new limitations to copyright protection. This means that exceptions that are not on the list cannot be brought into the law of an EU member state (and neither can a US-style broad "fair use" exception).[93] Post-Brexit, the United Kingdom could choose to legislate to break away from this closed set, and instead look to a broad US-style fair use approach.[94] The United Kingdom could also choose to bring back its narrow private copying exception, which was struck down in a 2015 judicial review action at the English High Court as being incompatible with EU law, as it was compensation-free, and rights holders argued they could have been negatively

---

88 *Infopaq International, supra* note 78.

89 Luke McDonagh, "Is the Creative Use of Musical Works Without a Licence Acceptable Under Copyright?" (2012) 4 Intl Rev IP & Competition L 401, 410–426.

90 *Ibid.*

91 *Bezpečnostní softwarová asociace v Ministerstvo kultury*, C-393/09, ECLI:EU:C:2010:816.

92 *The IPKat*, "Is there copyright in the taste of a cheese? Sensory copyright finally makes its way to CJEU" (24 May 2017), online: <http://ipkitten.blogspot.co.uk/2017/05/is-there-copyright-in-taste-of-cheese.html>.

93 *InfoSoc Directive, supra* note 67, art 5. See also the US fair use criteria in 17 USC § 107.

94 *Ibid.*

affected.[95] Although these are possible options, the UK government has, thus far, stressed the need for continuity of the law. New legislation on copyright may be some way off.

Even if the UK legislature does not bring in new legislation, and instead decides to keep a closed list of exceptions, the way these exceptions are interpreted by the national courts will be important. One exception that is permitted by the InfoSoc Directive is parody, which has been a part of UK copyright law since 2014.[96] Post-Brexit, the ECJ's definition of parody under this exception, as expressed in the *Deckmyn* case, will no longer be binding on the United Kingdom.[97] Nonetheless, UK courts will, even after Brexit, be free to continue to apply the EU-derived test for parody as part of the common law, although in time UK courts may begin to develop the parody definition in new ways. Yet, a grand deviation between the European Union and the United Kingdom on this issue seems unlikely — the *Deckmyn* decision was grounded in the EU Charter on Fundamental Rights, which has parallel provisions in the ECHR, to which the United Kingdom will remain a party.[98] For this reason, any new interpretation of parody taken by the UK courts is unlikely to stray far from *Deckmyn*.

Sui Generis Rights

In the context of Brexit, the EU-specific rights are of particular interest as they exist as a direct result of EU law. This means that once Brexit occurs, they will cease to apply in the United Kingdom (unless some reciprocal EU-UK agreement has been made by that time). One such right is the *sui generis* right for protection of databases.[99] Post-Brexit, this EU right would no longer be binding in the UK. The United Kingdom could enact national legislation to establish an equivalent UK *sui generis* right. Alternatively, UK courts may develop the United Kingdom's traditional form of protection of databases under copyright.[100]

Another important example of an EU-specific IP right linked to copyright is the artist's resale right.[101] This entitles authors of original art works to a royalty each time one of their works is resold via an art market professional. Like the database right, the artist's resale right would cease to be binding post-Brexit, and new UK legislation would be required to bring in a UK equivalent right. Although the European Union is on record as stating that such EU IP rights should be given equivalent protection in the United Kingdom, the United Kingdom has yet to respond at the time of writing.[102]

---

95 *BASCA and others v Secretary of State for Business, Innovation and Skills*, [2015] EWHC 1723 (Admin); [2015] EWHC 2041 (Admin).

96 *Copyright, Designs and Patents Act 1988* (UK), c 3, s 30A (added by Copyright and Rights in Performances [Quotation and Parody] Regulations 2014/2356).

97 *Johan Deckmyn and Vrijheidsfonds VZW v Helena Vandersteen and Others*, C-201/13, ECLI:EU:C:2014:2132.

98 Griffiths & McDonagh, *supra* note 8.

99 *Database Directive*, *supra* note 73.

100 See e.g. *Blair v Alan S Tomkins & Anor*, (1971) 21 QB 78; *Griggs Group Ltd and Others v Evans and Others*, [2003] EWHC 2914 (Ch).

101 *Directive 2001/84/EC*, *supra* note 69.

102 EC, *Position paper transmitted to EU27 on Intellectual property rights (including geographical indications)*, (2017), online: <https://ec.europa.eu/commission/publications/position-paper-transmitted-eu27-intellectual-property-rights-including-geographical-indications_en>.

Conclusion

There are cogent reasons to believe that the United Kingdom's post-Brexit taking back control of its IP laws will in fact lead to only minimal changes to patent law and copyright law. Regardless of Brexit, due to its WTO membership and the Agreement on Trade-Related Aspects of Intellectual Property Rights, the United Kingdom must abide by the minimum international IP standards in, for example, the Berne Convention and the Paris Convention, as well as fulfilling the requirements of its continuing membership of the EPC.

Although, post-Brexit, the United Kingdom can in theory immediately depart from EU-specific standards on originality and parody of copyright works, or the requirements of biotechnology patenting, in reality the UK government's proposed "Repeal Bill" aims to ensure continuity with EU law. Even before the Repeal Bill comes into play, it is worth recalling that several directives in the areas of copyright and patents have been implemented in the United Kingdom via national legislation, and the content of those directives has been analyzed through UK case law, embedding it within the common law system.

Moreover, the need for continuity in the IP field between the European Union and the United Kingdom will likely continue for the foreseeable future. The United Kingdom's attempt to participate in the UPC, notwithstanding Brexit, is an indicator of this (although it remains to be seen whether the United Kingdom will be successful in this regard). In addition, the most recent EU position paper on IP aims to establish reciprocity of protection of unitary IP rights within the United Kingdom post-Brexit, showing a determination, at least from the EU side, for convergence of IP protection.[103] Thus, there are certainly opportunities for continued cooperation between the European Union and the United Kingdom on IP issues — what is unknown is which route the UK government will take.

If the United Kingdom opts for a soft Brexit option, either as a transitional or permanent arrangement, such as joining the EEA or the EFTA, EU law will remain binding. The EFTA option even requires accepting the EFTA Court, which follows the ECJ's rulings on EU law. Even if the United Kingdom takes the hard Brexit route, leaving the internal market and Customs Union, and agreeing a mere EU-Canada style FTA with the European Union, EU law will remain highly relevant. Even if, as unlikely as it seems, the UK Intellectual Property Office seeks to align itself from a jurisprudential and administrative standpoint with other non-EU IP offices, such as with Commonwealth countries or the United States, every FTA that the European Union has with countries around the world includes a chapter on IP, requiring the other country under the FTA to comply with some features of EU law.

To conclude, a recurring theme of this chapter is that continuity in the IP field is both more likely and more beneficial than radical change. "Take back control" might sound comforting as a slogan, but the practice is likely to mean that patent law and copyright law in the United Kingdom remain much the same.

---

103 *Ibid.*

10

The Effect of Brexit on Trademarks, Designs and Other "Europeanized" Areas of Intellectual Property Law in the United Kingdom

Marc Mimler

Introduction

The wheels that may lead to the United Kingdom leaving the European Union after more than 40 years of membership have been turning relentlessly since the results of the EU referendum were announced in June 2016. The effects that Brexit may have on the various areas of UK law directly or indirectly influenced by more than four decades of EU membership are presently difficult to foresee. However, the effects of Brexit on intellectual property (IP) law in the United Kingdom will certainly be profound — simply because IP law represents the most Europeanized area of private law.[1] In addition, much vagueness and ambiguity remain over the shape and nature of Brexit. Whether a "hard," "soft" or "crash" Brexit[2] is ultimately applied will determine the extent to which UK IP law will disentangle itself from the EU IP law *acquis*. Since the

---

1 Justine Pila, "Intellectual Property as a Case Study in Europeanization: Methodological Themes and Context" in Ansgar Ohly & Justine Pila, eds, *The Europeanization of Intellectual Property Law* (Oxford, UK: Oxford University Press, 2013) 3.

2 Andreas Rahmatian, "Brief speculations about changes to IP law in the UK after Brexit" (2017) 12:6 J Intell Prop L & Prac 510 at 510.

ramifications for substantive and procedural IP law remain opaque, great uncertainty has arisen among IP right holders as to the situation post-Brexit.[3] In addition, the UK IP professions represented by the Chartered Institute of Patent Attorneys (CIPA) and the Chartered Institute of Trade Mark Attorneys (CITMA) have voiced their concerns, arguing strongly for continuing participation in European IP frameworks.[4]

However, the status quo will not change for the two-year period of the so-called "Article 50 procedure," subject to any additional transition period that may be the result of the ongoing negotiations. The scope and impact of Brexit will become clearer once these negotiations have progressed, and the future relationship of the United Kingdom with the European Union will largely depend on which form of Brexit is pursued.

Three possible scenarios, which will each have a different effect on the future of UK IP law, are generally discussed. A soft version of Brexit would entail the United Kingdom's membership in the European Economic Area (EEA), in which states such as Iceland, Liechtenstein and Norway are members, along with the European Union. Membership in the EEA would provide continued access to the Single Market of the European Union, but would oblige the United Kingdom to adhere to certain provisions of the EU treaties,[5] such as free movement of people[6] and goods.[7] Additionally, the United Kingdom would be required to implement certain EU directives and pay contributions to the EU budget,[8] without having the ability to significantly influence future legislation.[9] Another available option would involve a set of individual bilateral agreements between the United Kingdom and the European Union, similar to those established between the European Union and Switzerland, which is not a member of the EEA. This would, however, require a long and burdensome negotiation period[10] and would most probably also maintain some form of free movement of people.[11]

Finally, the United Kingdom could seek a completely new relationship with the European Union, which could be modelled along the lines of current free trade agreements (FTAs), such as the Comprehensive Economic and Trade Agreement (CETA) between Canada and the

---

3   This appears to be acknowledged by the United Kingdom Intellectual Property Office (UKIPO). See UKIPO, "IP and BREXIT: The facts" (2 August 2016), online: <www.gov.uk/government/news/ip-and-brexit-the-facts>. See also EC, Commission, "Position paper transmitted to EU27 on intellectual property rights (including geographical indications)" (6 September 2017) at 2 ["Position paper"], online: <https://ec.europa.eu/commission/sites/beta-political/files/position-paper-intellectual-property-rights_en.pdf>.

4   CITMA, "Our position on: Post-Brexit registered trade mark and design rights, and rights of representation" (July 2017) at 3.0 [CITMA, "Our position"], online: <www.citma.org.uk/membership/brexit/brexit_position_paper_v1>. See also Christopher Morcom, "The Implications of 'Brexit' for Trade Marks and for Practitioners in the UK: What Are the Likely Effects and What Needs to Happen Now?" (2016) 38:11 Eur IP Rev 657 at 659.

5   See e.g. EC, Commission, *European Economic Area Agreement*, [1994] OJ, L 1/3, art 1 (2) (entered into force 1 January 1994).

6   *Treaty on the Functioning of the European Union*, 13 December 2007, [2008] OJ, C 115/47, art 45 (entered into force 1 December 2009) [*TFEU*]. It has been argued that this fundamental freedom provided momentum for the Leave campaign; see Paul Craig, "Brexit: a drama in six acts" (2016) 41:4 Eur L Rev 447 at 455.

7   *TFEU*, *supra* note 6, arts 28–37.

8   Trevor Cook, "'Brexit' and Intellectual Property Protection in the UK and the EU" (2016) 21:5-6 J Intell Prop Rts 355 at 355.

9   Benjamin Farrand, "Bold and newly Independent, or Isolated and Cast Adrift? The Implications of Brexit for Intellectual Property Law and Policy" (2017) J Common Market Stud 1 at 7, DOI: <10.1111/jcms.12550>.

10   *Ibid* at 8.

11   Cook, *supra* note 8 at 356.

European Union.[12] This approach would not require the United Kingdom to adhere to freedom of movement of people and would only mandate adherence to the international IP norms of the World Trade Organization (WTO) and the World Intellectual Property Organization (WIPO), unless specific provisions were agreed on within a future agreement. In her January 2017 Lancaster House speech, UK Prime Minister Theresa May suggested that the United Kingdom would leave the internal market due to its nexus with free movement of people,[13] which would mean rejecting the first and second options discussed above.[14] Elements of such a hard Brexit approach have, however, been retracted more recently,[15] which means that more clarity will be provided only when the process of leaving the European Union has advanced.

The focus of this chapter is to analyze the effects of the United Kingdom's EU membership on the laws of trademarks and designs over the last decades and analyze the possible impact of Brexit. These fields of IP law are of particular interest because they have probably been Europeanized the most, and the different options of Brexit will directly impact the future of these areas of UK IP law. Additionally, the chapter scrutinizes a related area of law, the law regarding geographical indications (GIs), because, first, GIs are genuinely a child of EU law making, and, second, they are likely to be of great relevance in future trade negotiations between the United Kingdom and the European Union. Finally, the fate of the doctrine of exhaustion and the interface of IP and competition rules in the United Kingdom will be discussed, as both aspects derive from EU rules and jurisprudence.

Trademarks

European Harmonization

EU law has had a more profound impact on the national trademark laws of EU member states than on their patent and copyright law counterparts.[16] The current system of trademark law within the European Union and among its member states has been comprehensively redrafted and almost completely Europeanized by the European legislator.[17] This system is twofold: on the one hand, national trademark laws within EU member states have been harmonized by the Trade Marks Directive.[18] Further, the EU trademark as provided by the EU Trade Mark

---

12 EC, Commission, *Comprehensive Economic and Trade Agreement between Canada, of the one part, and the European Union [and its Member States…]*, 29 February 2016 [*CETA*], online: <http://trade.ec.europa.eu/doclib/docs/2016/february/tradoc_154329.pdf>.

13 Theresa May, "The government's negotiating objectives for exiting the EU" (Speech delivered on 17 January 2017), online: <www.gov.uk/government/speeches/the-governments-negotiating-objectives-for-exiting-the-eu-pm-speech>.

14 Richard Arnold et al, "IP Law post-BREXIT" (2017) 101:2 Judicature 65 at 65.

15 For instance, in a recently published paper, the British government spoke of ending the *direct* influence of the Court of Justice of the European Union (CJEU), hinting that an indirect influence remains possible. See UK, "Enforcement and dispute resolution: A Future Partnership Paper" (2017), online: <www.gov.uk/government/uploads/system/uploads/attachment_data/file/639609/Enforcement_and_dispute_resolution.pdf>. This statement needs to be contrasted with the statement in the Lancaster House speech that the version of Brexit pursued by the British government would put "an end to the jurisdiction of the European Court of Justice in Britain," which hints that any form of influence of the CJEU would end with Brexit. May, *supra* note 13.

16 Luke McDonagh, "UK Patent Law and Copyright Law after Brexit: Potential Consequences" in Oonagh E Fitzgerald & Eva Lein, eds, *Complexity's Embrace: The International Law Implications of Brexit* (Waterloo, ON: CIGI, 2018).

17 Lionel Bently & Brad Sherman, *Intellectual Property Law*, 4th ed (Oxford, UK: Oxford University Press, 2014) at 823.

18 EC, *First Council Directive 89/104/EEC of 21 December 1988 to approximate the laws of the Member States relating to trade marks*, [1989] OJ, L 40 [*Trade Marks Directive*].

Regulation[19] represents a federal and unitary trademark that is effective throughout the territory of the European Union.

The evolution of this system warrants some explanation. Prior to the initiatives undertaken by the European Union and its predecessors, the European Economic Community (EEC) and the European Communities (EC), national trademark systems differed substantially. These differences within national laws were perceived as posing obstacles for the creation of the Single Market, a goal enshrined within the EC treaty from its inception.[20] Hence, early European initiatives to tackle this issue can be traced back to the 1950s.[21] But true momentum for European integration was provided by the European Commission's memorandum on an EEC trademark from 1976. The memorandum showcased the motives behind the initiative to harmonize trademark protection: "There is as yet, to the disadvantage of consumers, distributors and manufacturers, no common market for branded goods and thus no internal market for a substantial proportion of goods for sale."[22]

The memorandum mooted the creation of a community trademark based on a regulation to ensure the free movement of branded goods. A mere approximation of national laws was held not to eliminate the barriers of territoriality.[23] The Community trademark regulation[24] was finally adopted in 1993 after some discussions as to its language regime and where its granting office would be located.[25] The regulation created a unitary Community trademark granted by the Office for Harmonisation in the Internal Market (OHIM), based in Alicante, Spain. This system was not meant to replace national trademarks, but rather to supplement them. After the entry into force of the Lisbon Treaty[26] in 2009, the EU trademark regulation replaced the Community trademark regulation in 2015 and changed some of the substantive law, but also relabelled Community trademarks as EU trademarks, and renamed the OHIM the European Union Intellectual Property Office (EUIPO).[27]

Aside from the creation of a unitary right, the harmonization of national laws was the second pillar in creating the European trademark *acquis*. The 1971 Benelux Trademarks Act[28] served as a model law for the Trade Marks Directive[29] that was adopted in 1988. The directive focused on

---

19   EC, *Council Regulation (EC) No 207/2009 of 26 February 2009 on the Community trade mark*, [2009] OJ, L 78/1 [*Trade Mark Regulation*].

20   Guy Tritton, *Tritton on Intellectual Property in Europe*, 4th ed (London, UK: Sweet & Maxwell 2014) at 3-035.

21   Alexander von Mühlendahl et al, *Trade Mark Law in Europe*, 3rd ed (Oxford, UK: Oxford University Press, 2016) at 2.03; Charles Gielen, "Harmonisation of trade mark law in Europe: the first trade mark harmonisation Directive of the European Council" (1992) 14:8 Eur IP Rev 262 at 262.

22   EC, Commission, *A Memorandum on a Creation of an EEC Trade Mark*, Bulletin of the European Communities, Supp 8/76 at 10.

23   *Ibid* at 34.

24   EC, *Council Regulation (EC) No 40/94 of 20 December 1993 on the Community trade mark*, [1993] OJ, L 011.

25   Thomas C Vinje, "Harmonising intellectual property laws in the European Union: past, present and future" (1995) 17:8 Eur IP Rev 361 at 369.

26   *Treaty of Lisbon Amending the Treaty on European Union and the Treaty Establishing the European Community*, 13 December 2007, OJ, C 306/1 (entered into force 1 December 2009).

27   EC, *Regulation (EU) 2015/2424 of the European Parliament and of the Council of 16 December 2015 amending Council Regulation (EC) No 207/2009 on the Community trade mark and Commission Regulation (EC) No 2868/95 implementing Council Regulation (EC) No 40/94 on the Community trade mark, and repealing Commission Regulation (EC) No 2869/95 on the fees payable to the Office for Harmonization in the Internal Market (Trade Marks and Designs)*, [2015] OJ, L 341/21, recital 2.

28   *Uniform Benelux Law on Marks*, online: WIPO <www.wipo.int/wipolex/en/text.jsp?file_id=128587>.

29   *Trade Marks Directive, supra* note 18. Anselm Kamperman Sanders, "Some frequently asked questions about the 1994 UK Trade Marks Act" (1995) 17:2 Eur IP Rev 67 at 67; Charles Gielen, *supra* note 21 at 264.

substantial provisions that could impede the creation and operation of the internal market, but did not intend a full-scale harmonization.[30] In practice, however, this means that the individual trademark statutes within the member states of the European Union now substantially resemble each other because the directive provided for mandatory provisions to be implemented and transformed into national laws. In the United Kingdom, the directive was implemented within the UK Trade Marks Act 1994.[31]

Trademark Law and the European Courts

The European trademark *acquis* of the Trade Mark Regulation and the Trade Marks Directive was supplemented by the case law of the European courts. IP cases are, indeed, a major subject of adjudication by the CJEU, as the 2016 annual report suggests,[32] and most of these IP-related cases are trademark cases.[33] The twofold approach within European trademark law, however, means that the European courts are involved in different stages of litigation. EU trademarks, which are granted by the EUIPO in Alicante, are enforced by national courts as courts of the European Union.[34] The General Court and the CJEU are directly involved in the adjudication of EU trademarks, arising from appeals from the EUIPO.[35] Additionally, the CJEU can be called upon by national courts seeking guidance on the interpretation of national provisions based on the Trade Marks Directive, through the system of preliminary rulings pursuant to article 267 of the Treaty on the Functioning of the European Union[36] (TFEU). The case law by the European courts with regard to the directive resulted in increasing harmonization of the trademark law within EU member states. This effect was increased by the fact that the substantive law in the directive and the regulation correspond to one another. As a result, decisions based on the directive can be applied when interpreting provisions of the regulation and vice versa.[37]

The case law of the European courts on aspects of trademark law is not always well received by national courts and commentators. The criticism revolves around the generalist nature of the court, which lacks expertise in a specialist subject matter such as trademark law. With regard to the United Kingdom, discontent with CJEU judgments can be seen in cases such as *Arsenal v Reed*,[38] in which Justice Hugh Laddie held that the CJEU had overstepped its competences by making findings of fact.[39] A more recent case along these lines was handed down by the Court of Appeal in *L'Oréal v Bellure*.[40] The case revolved around the referential use of L'Oréal's trademarks for perfumes in a comparison list for Bellure's range of smell-alike perfumes. The CJEU held that the defendant's use would amount to taking unfair advantage of the repute or the distinctiveness of L'Oréal's marks because Bellure would be riding on L'Oréal's

---

30 Gielen, *supra* note 21 at 262–63.

31 *Trade Marks Act 1994* (UK), c 26 [*Trade Marks Act 1994*].

32 CJEU, *Annual Report 2016: The Year in Review* (Brussels, Belgium: European Union, 2017) at 28, online: <https://curia.europa.eu/jcms/upload/docs/application/pdf/2017-04/ragp-2016_final_en_web.pdf>.

33 Graeme Dinwoodie, "The Europeanisation of Trade Mark Law" in Ohly & Pila, *supra* note 1 at 91.

34 *Trade Mark Regulation*, *supra* note 19, art 95.

35 *Ibid*, art 65.

36 *TFEU*, *supra* note 6.

37 Richard Arnold, "An Overview of European Harmonization Measures in Intellectual Property Law" in Ohly & Pila, *supra* note 1 at 31.

38 *Arsenal Football Club v Reed*, C-206/01, [2002] ECR I-10273.

39 *Arsenal Football Club v Reed* (No 2), [2002] EWHC 2695 (Ch) at 27.

40 *L'Oréal v Bellure*, [2010] EWCA Civ 535.

coattails without compensation.[41] After the CJEU's decision, the trial judge in *L'Oréal v Bellure* in the United Kingdom expressed concerns about this interpretation, but was bound to find for the claimants. The discomfort can be explained by the fact that the dilution provisions were a controversial element provided by the Trade Marks Directive.[42] The doctrine of dilution and the action against misappropriation do not fit seamlessly within UK trademark law, which traditionally focused more on the origin function of trademarks,[43] rather than on extending to non-origin functions, such as advertising.

The Impact of Brexit

Due to the high level of harmonization in trademark law within the European Union and its member states, Brexit will have a substantial effect on trademark protection in the United Kingdom. First, Brexit would mean that EU trademark protection would no longer extend to the United Kingdom. Not even an often-mooted membership of the EEA as a form of soft Brexit would enable the unitary right to extend to the United Kingdom,[44] since the unitary effect of EU trademarks currently has effect only within the EU member states.[45] This means that millions of trademarks registered at the EUIPO[46] would no longer extend to the United Kingdom after it leaves the European Union, while the trademarks would remain valid throughout the remaining 27 member states.[47] Additionally, UK proprietors of EU trademarks would have to consider whether their trademarks were being effectively used within the European Union in the future. An EU trademark can be revoked where there is no "genuine use in the Union in connection with the goods and services in respect of which it is registered" for a period of five years and where there is no proper reason for this non-use.[48] Use just within the territory of the United Kingdom may no longer suffice to challenge a request for revocation for non-use.[49]

Whether there is a possibility for current EU trademark registrations to extend to the United Kingdom post-Brexit depends largely on a future agreement between the United Kingdom and the European Union. CITMA devised a list of seven possible options that could apply with regard to EU trademarks after Brexit.[50] They range from the so-called "Jersey option," in which the United Kingdom would provide a piece of legislation declaring EU trademarks as having effect in the United Kingdom, to the "Conversion model"[51] of converting current EU trademarks into national trademark registrations.[52] The European Commission's position is that holders of an EU trademark should be provided with "an enforceable intellectual property right

---

41 *L'Oréal v Bellure*, C-486/07, [2009] ECR I-05185.

42 Hazel Carty, "Do marks with a reputation merit special protection?" (1997) 19:12 Eur IP Rev 684 at 684.

43 Ilanah Simon Fhima, "Exploring the roots of European dilution" (2012) 2012:1 IPQ 25 at 26.

44 Cook, *supra* note 8 at 357.

45 *Trade Mark Regulation*, *supra* note 19, art 1(2).

46 Arnold et al, *supra* note 14 at 66.

47 Morcom, *supra* note 4 at 658.

48 *Trade Mark Regulation*, *supra* note 19, art 51(1)(a).

49 Morcom, *supra* note 4 at 660; Arnold et al, *supra* note 14 at 66.

50 CITMA, "EU registered rights – trade marks", online: <www.citma.org.uk/membership/eu_resources/eu_brexit/eu_registered_rights_-_trade_marks>.

51 Rahmatian, *supra* note 2 at 514.

52 Luke McDonagh & Marc Mimler, "Intellectual Property Law and Brexit: A Retreat or a Reaffirmation of Jurisdiction?" in Michael Dougan, ed, *The UK after Brexit – Legal and Policy Challenges* (Cambridge, UK: Intersentia, 2017) at 165; Arnold et al, *supra* note 14 at 66.

in relation to the United Kingdom territory, comparable to the right provided by Union law."[53] Aside from the fate of EU trademarks, leaving the European Union would mean that UK courts would cease to be EU trademark courts[54] and could no longer be called on to enforce EU trademarks.[55] Additionally, rights of representation for trademark attorneys based in the United Kingdom before the EUIPO and the EU courts would require attention, since these are limited to those practitioners qualified and having their residence within the EEA.[56] CITMA has strongly urged that the rights of representation should continue post-Brexit.[57]

The uncertainties surrounding the future effect of EU trademarks in the United Kingdom could be the reason for an increase in national trademark registrations at the UKIPO.[58] Despite the great degree of harmonization that has been achieved so far, users of the system ought to acknowledge that some significant divergences between the EU trademark system and that of the United Kingdom remain. Applicants at the UKIPO, for instance, must demonstrate the use or the bona fide intention to use the trademark, while this is not necessary before the EUIPO.[59] Additionally, applicants for a UK trademark would need to show such use within the United Kingdom, and not just anywhere within the European Union, as under the EU trademark system. Conversely, this means that UK applicants who seek to expand their business into the continental European market could not rely on consumer recognition within the United Kingdom to receive an EU trademark.[60]

Beside the uncertainties that Brexit would create surrounding the future of EU trademarks within the United Kingdom, Brexit would also impact the United Kingdom's national trademark system. The extent of this effect would depend on what form of Brexit is finally taken. The current white paper on the Great Repeal Bill[61] foresees that current statutory trademark law would remain as is.[62] This would mean that the wording of the UK Trade Marks Act 1994, which derived from EU legislation, would remain unchanged. The UK Parliament, however, would be able to amend the law as it sees fit without considering future developments within the EU trademark *acquis*.

Depending on what type of Brexit is finally pursued, the United Kingdom may decide not to implement the recent Trade Marks Directive, which introduces some significant changes to the

---

53   "Position paper", *supra* note 3 at 2.

54   *Trade Mark Regulation, supra* note 19, art 95.

55   Julius Stobbs, Geoff Weller & Yana Zhou, "Overview of United Kingdom Trade Marks and Design Decisions 2016" (2017) 48:2 Intl Rev Intell Prop & Comp L 195 at 206.

56   *Trade Mark Regulation, supra* note 19, art 93(1)(a).

57   CITMA, "Our position", *supra* note 4.

58   CITMA, "Significant rise in UK trade mark and design registrations", online: <www.citma.org.uk/news/view?id=160&x[0]=/news/list>, referring to UKIPO, "Facts and figures: patent, trade mark, design and hearing data: 2016", online: <www.gov.uk/government/statistics/facts-and-figures-patent-trade-mark-design-and-hearing-data-2016>. Large US companies have already filed for UK trademarks; Arnold et al, *supra* note 14 at 67.

59   David Keeling et al, *Kerly's Law of Trade Marks and Trade Names,* 15th ed (London, UK: Sweet & Maxwell 2014) at 6-008.

60   Farrand, *supra* note 9 at 4. Generally, to prove acquired distinctiveness pursuant to the *Trade Mark Regulation, supra* note 19, art 7(3), the applicant would need to demonstrate that the trademark had been "used in the Community [now Union] as a whole or, at least, in a substantial part thereof"; *Ty Nant Spring Water Ltd's Application,* [1999] ETMR 974 at 15 (OHIM Third Board of Appeal).

61   Bill 5, *European Union (Withdrawal) Bill* [HL], 2017–2019 sess (1st reading 13 July 2017).

62   UK, Department for Exiting the European Union (DEEU), "Legislating for the United Kingdom's Withdrawal from the European Union" (March 2017) at 2.5 [DEEU, "Legislating"].

substantive law within EU member states.[63] For instance, the directive amends the functionality rules that bar from registration signs that consist exclusively of the shape of the goods that results from the nature of the goods or is necessary to achieve a technical result or gives substantial value to the goods. In the future, the functionality rules will extend to include characteristics other than shapes.[64] Additionally, the directive amends the "own name" and "descriptive" use defences — the former being limited to names of natural persons and the latter arguably being broadened.[65] Not adopting the new directive could create discrepancies between the law of the European Union member states and the United Kingdom. Trevor Cook, however, holds that due to the relatively minor nature of the changes posed by the new Trade Marks Directive, they would still be implemented into UK law.[66]

Additionally, the white paper states that case law by the CJEU pre-Brexit would acquire the same status as Supreme Court cases.[67] This means that CJEU cases up until Brexit would constitute precedents for lower courts and could only be overturned by the UK Supreme Court itself or through legislative amendment.[68] Post-Brexit, decisions by the CJEU would no longer need to be considered by UK courts, but may remain persuasive authorities.[69] Should the United Kingdom pursue a soft version of Brexit in the form of membership within the EEA, the links to the EU *acquis* would not be totally severed since adherence to the Trade Marks Directive would be required.[70] The case law of the CJEU would not be binding, as such, but the competent European Free Trade Association court could require the United Kingdom to amend legislation conflicting with the EEA agreement and decide cases in line with the CJEU decisions.[71]

Designs

The European legislator has been equally active in the designs field of IP law. Similar to the situation within trademark law, Brexit will have severe ramifications for the legal protection of designs in the United Kingdom.[72] Unitary EU rights have been created for registered and unregistered designs by the Community Design Regulation.[73] Such Community designs "have equal effect throughout the Community" and can only be transferred or declared invalid for the whole Community.[74] Registered Community designs can be applied for and are administered by the EUIPO,[75] while unregistered designs receive protection automatically through use.[76]

---

63 EC, *Directive (EU) 2015/2436 of the European Parliament and of the Council of 16 December 2015 to approximate the laws of the Member States relating to trade marks*, [2015] OJ, L 336/1.

64 *Ibid*, art 4, nr 1(e).

65 Stobbs, Weller & Zhou, *supra* note 55 at 206.

66 Cook, *supra* note 8 at 358–59. Additionally, the UK government has suggested that directives that should have been implemented by the day of Brexit will be implemented; Arnold et al, *supra* note 14 at 70.

67 DEEU, "Legislating", *supra* note 62 at 2.16.

68 Arnold et al, *supra* note 14 at 70.

69 Rahmatian, *supra* note 2 at 514.

70 Farrand, *supra* note 9 at 7.

71 *Ibid*.

72 Arnold et al, *supra* note 14 at 67.

73 EC, *Council Regulation (EC) No 6/2002 of 12 December 2001 on Community designs*, [2002] OJ, L3/1 [*Community Designs Regulation*].

74 *Ibid*, art 1(3).

75 *Ibid*, art 2.

76 *Ibid*, art 1(2)(a).

Additionally, the European legislator sought to harmonize the protection of registered national designs by means of the Design Directive.[77] However, these harmonization initiatives do not encompass national unregistered designs, which are available in EU member states. Finally, the complexity of the framework for protecting industrial designs is increased by the fact that the subject matter of design protection can overlap with that of copyright law.[78]

European Harmonization

The interest in harmonizing design protection within the then-EEC commenced in 1957, when the European Commission proposed the establishment of the Working Parties on Patent, Trade Mark and Design. The laws within the member states differed quite substantially at that time as to the scope and form of protection for industrial designs. As with the situation within trademark law, the belief was that these inconsistencies would impair trade between member states, thus distorting competition, and that uniform rules would help to alleviate this problem.[79]

The European Commission published the "Green Paper on the Legal Protection of Industrial Design"[80] in 1991. The paper mooted the creation of an autonomous community design right and finally established two instruments. On the one hand, the Design Directive was set to harmonize national registered design rights. On the other, an autonomous and unitary Community right with regard to registered and unregistered designs was created.[81] The Design Directive was implemented in the United Kingdom by an amendment to the Registered Designs Act 1949.[82] As mentioned, the directive did not affect national unregistered designs,[83] which are regulated within part III of the Copyright, Designs and Patents Act 1988.[84]

The Impact of Brexit

Similar considerations with regard to trademarks can be applied to the situation of Community-registered designs post-Brexit, since their protection does not extend to non-EU member states.[85] CITMA, again, provided a set of possible scenarios with regard to registered EU designs, largely resembling those provided for EU trademarks.[86] The fate of registered UK designs that derive from the Design Directive will depend largely on what future relationship the United Kingdom seeks with the European Union, mirroring the situation within trademark law.

---

77 EC, *Directive 98/71/EC of the European Parliament and of the Council of 13 October 1998 on the legal protection of designs*, [1998] OJ, L 289 [*Design Directive*].

78 Martin Howe, *Russel-Clarke and Howe on Industrial Designs*, 9th ed (London, UK: Sweet & Maxwell, 2016) at 1-001.

79 The divergent approaches within the substantive provisions of the law of the member states, in particular with regard to the definition of design, the criteria and term of protection, the nature of protection and the overlap of protection between design and other IP rights, was a main issue that needed to be addressed according to the working group on designs. See EC, Commission, *Legal review on industrial design protection in Europe – Under the contract with the Directorate General Internal Market, Industry, Entrepreneurship and SMEs* (Brussels, Belgium: European Union, 2016) at 131–134.

80 EC, Commission, "Green Paper on the Legal Protection of Industrial Design", EU Doc III/F/5131/91-EN (1991).

81 Note that the Community Designs Regulation still refers to "Community," in contrast to the recently amended EU trademark regulation that refers to the "EU."

82 *Registered Designs Act 1949* (UK), 12, 13, 14 Geo VI, c 88.

83 *Design Directive*, *supra* note 77, recital 7.

84 *Copyright, Designs and Patents Act 1988* (UK), c 48 [*CDP Act 1988*].

85 However, designs are not subject to revocation for non-use as trademarks are; Arnold et al, *supra* note 14 at 67.

86 CITMA, "EU registered rights – designs", online: <www.citma.org.uk/membership/eu_resources/eu_brexit/eu_registered_rights_-_designs>.

A genuinely different situation arises with regard to unregistered Community designs, for which the right automatically subsists when the design is first made available in the European Union.[87] After Brexit, when such a design is made available within the United Kingdom, it will no longer attract protection as an EU unregistered design right, but could be regarded as a UK unregistered design right. Since unregistered designs were not harmonized as their registered counterparts were, differences would remain between the protection provided to unregistered designs in the European Union and the United Kingdom. On the one hand, the UK right lasts significantly longer (15 years in comparison to three years),[88] but it does not protect surface decorations,[89] unlike the Community counterpart, on the other hand.[90] The protection for combinations of patterns and ornament surface decoration, however, proved to be useful for the fashion industry,[91] although copyright law may provide supplementary protection.[92] Additionally, the eligibility requirements under the UK unregistered design regime are more stringent than under the Community unregistered design right, which may make it necessary for current users to register for design protection within the United Kingdom.[93] All these issues warrant thorough consideration for the post-Brexit scenario.

Other IP-related Areas Affected by Brexit

GIs

An important field affected by Brexit, related to IP rights, is GIs and designations of origin. Both aim at protecting certain agricultural products and foodstuffs, deriving from particular geographical locations, that possess certain characteristics. Currently, both are protected as protected geographical indications (PGIs) and protected designations of origin (PDOs), along with traditional specialities guaranteed within an EU regulation.[94] This framework is part of the EU agricultural policy, as the production, manufacture and distribution of agricultural produce and foodstuffs play an important role within the European Union's economy.[95] The protected designations are protected first and foremost against any false or misleading use of the indication.[96]

Popular products, such as champagne, Roquefort cheese, Bavarian beer and Parma ham, are protected under this legislative framework. UK products currently protected under this framework include Welsh lamb, Stilton blue and white cheeses, Cornish pasties, Kentish ale and the Melton Mowbray pork pie.[97] After leaving the European Union, neither PGIs nor PDOs would have effect in the United Kingdom, similar to the situation with EU trademarks. Some voices have uttered

---

87 *Community Designs Regulation, supra* note 73, art 11(1).

88 *CDP Act 1988, supra* note 84, s 216.

89 *Ibid,* s 213(3)(c).

90 Additionally, the respective tests for infringement differ; Arnold et al, *supra* note 14 at 67.

91 Stobbs, Weller & Zhou, *supra* note 55 at 207.

92 Arnold et al, *supra* note 14 at 67.

93 *Ibid* at 68.

94 *Regulation (EU) No 1151/2012 of the European Parliament and of the Council of 21 November 2012 on quality schemes for agricultural products and foodstuffs,* [2012] OJ, L 343/1 [*Council Regulation (EU) No 1151/2012*].

95 Bertold Schwab, "The protection of geographical indications in the European Economic Community" (1995) 17:5 Eur IP Rev 242 at 242.

96 *Council Regulation (EU) No 1151/2012, supra* note 94, art 13(1).

97 UK, Department for Environment, Food and Rural Affairs, "Protected food name scheme: UK registered products", online: <www.gov.uk/government/collections/protected-food-name-scheme-uk-registered-products>.

fear that British producers could then freely use previously protected names.[98] Ironically, already registered UK products would not lose their registration as PGIs or PDOs in the remaining EU member states, since the regulation allows for the protection of products from non-EU states.[99]

UK law currently provides certain legal measures that could partially cover the protection provided by PDOs and PGIs post-Brexit. Supplementary protection could be provided by the common law action of "passing off." An extended form of this action allows groups of producers to file an action alleging misrepresentation by other traders. The producers of champagne used passing off successfully against producers labelling their beverage as "Spanish Champagne."[100] However, the scope of protection provided by passing off cannot be compared with that provided by the current system through registration as PGIs or PDOs, in which not only confusingly similar designations, but also designations that merely evoke the registered PGI or PDO, can be enjoined.[101] A successful claim of passing off, on the other hand, requires the claimant to demonstrate that there is a misrepresentation, meaning that consumers must have relied on the misrepresentation when purchasing the goods of the defendant.[102] Other national measures are certification[103] or collective marks,[104] which may provide a certain degree of protection for GIs.[105] Harris tweed[106] and Stilton cheese,[107] for example, are currently protected as certification marks in the United Kingdom.

Some form of protection for GIs will be necessary after the United Kingdom leaves the European Union, as this is mandated through the United Kingdom's membership in the WTO. Article 22 of the WTO's Agreement on Trade-Related Aspects of Intellectual Property Rights[108] (TRIPS) mandates that legal means to protect interested parties against misleading uses of GIs must be provided within the laws of WTO member states. However, because the provision's scope is limited, Cook suggests that the currently available forms of national protection within UK law may suffice to fulfill the requirements of the TRIPS agreement.[109] The European Commission, on the other hand, holds that "there is currently no domestic legislation in the United Kingdom on the protection of designations of origin and GIs as well as on other protected terms in relation to agricultural products."[110]

---

98 Daniel Boffey, "EU fears influx of 'British champagne' once Brexit ends food naming rules", *The Guardian* (15 February 2017), online: <www.theguardian.com/business/2017/feb/15/eu-fears-influx-of-british-champagne-once-brexit-ends-food-naming-rules>.

99 *Council Regulation (EU) No 1151/2012*, *supra* note 94, recital 24. For example, "Café de Colombia" has been protected as a geographical indication in the European Union since 2007: EC, *Commission Regulation (EC) No 1050/2007 of 12 September 2007 registering certain names in the Register of protected designations of origin and protected geographical indications (Mejillón de Galicia or Mexillón de Galicia (PDO) — Café de Colombia (PGI) — Castagna Cuneo (PGI) — Asparago Bianco di Bassano (PDO))*, [2007] OJ, L 240/7.

100 *Bollinger v Costa Brava Wine Co Ltd*, [1960] RPC 16 (Ch).

101 McDonagh & Mimler, *supra* note 52.

102 Christopher Wadlow, *The Law of Passing-Off*, 5th ed (London, UK: Sweet & Maxwell, 2016) at 7-178.

103 *Trade Marks Act 1994*, *supra* note 31, s 49.

104 *Ibid*, s 50.

105 Cook, *supra* note 8 at 357.

106 See Harris Tweed Authority, online: <www.harristweed.org/>.

107 See Stilton: Britain's Historic Blue, online: <www.stiltoncheese.co.uk/>.

108 *Agreement on Trade-Related Aspects of Intellectual Property Rights*, 15 April 1994, 1869 UNTS 299, 33 ILM 197, art 22 (entered into force 1 January 1995) [*TRIPS Agreement*].

109 Cook, *supra* note 8 at 357.

110 "Position paper", *supra* note 3 at 2, n 1.

Otherwise, the United Kingdom could provide a provision similar to article 22 of the TRIPS agreement within its law to be compliant with the agreement. This, however, may not prove sufficient, as any post-Brexit agreement with the European Union would be likely to include the protection of PGIs and PDOs. In the past, the European Union has placed great emphasis on its protection of PGIs and PDOs within its trade negotiations,[111] due to their financial value to producers, and has been successful in exporting its norms on many accounts.[112] An example is the recently negotiated and finalized CETA with Canada.[113] Consequently, the European Commission has said in a recent position paper that the United Kingdom should put "in place, as of the withdrawal date, the necessary domestic legislation" for the protection of PDOs and PGIs and that "such protection should be comparable to that provided by Union law."[114] This could mean that the United Kingdom might become a member of the Geneva Act of the Lisbon Agreement,[115] negotiated under the auspices of WIPO, which extends to GIs, aside from appellations of origin. The Geneva Act aims to broaden membership of the agreement by, *inter alia*, bridging the different approaches between common and civil law countries in protecting geographical names.[116]

The Interplay of IP and Competition Law

The interplay between EU competition law and IP law is important with regard to the exercise and enforcement of IP rights.[117] Superficially, both fields of law appear to have different aims — IP creates exclusive rights, while competition rules are intended to open markets. However, it is commonly held that both fields aim at enhancing consumer welfare, albeit by different means.[118] The relationship between IP and competition law within the European Union has constantly expanded since the creation of the EEC. Again, a main driver for this development was the logic of increasing integration of the Single Market.

European courts observed early on that national IP rules would impair the creation of the Single Market, which led European legislators to harmonize national IP laws to provide unitary IP rights. However, even earlier case law of the European courts[119] dealt with the conflict between IP rights and the competition rules of the EEC.[120] The EEC treaty did not touch on national regimes on industrial and commercial property[121] and left the existence of IP rights under the competence

---

111 Cook, *supra* note 8 at 357.

112 Farrand, *supra* note 9 at 10.

113 *CETA*, *supra* note 12, c 20, s C.

114 "Position paper", *supra* note 3 at 2.

115 *Geneva Act of the Lisbon Agreement on Appellations of Origin and Geographical Indications*, as adopted on 20 May 2015, WIPO, online: <www.wipo.int/publications/en/details.jsp?id=3983>.

116 Common law countries generally protect such subject matter by trademark law, while civil law countries would favour a *sui generis* system; see Daniel J Gervais & Matthew Slider, "The Geneva Act of the Lisbon Agreement: Controversial Negotiations and Controversial Results" in William van Caenegem & Jen Cleary, eds, *The Importance of Place: Geographical Indications as a Tool for Local and Regional Development* (Cham, Switzerland: Springer International, 2017) at 15; Danielle Dudding, "The Lisbon Agreement: Why the United States Should Stop Fighting the Geneva Act" (2015) 18:1 Vand J Ent & Tech L 167.

117 Cook, *supra* note 8 at 359.

118 Gustavo Ghidini, *Innovation, Competition and Consumer Welfare in Intellectual Property Law* (Cheltenham, UK: Edward Elgar, 2010) at 212.

119 See e.g. *Consten SaRL and Grundig GmbH v Commission*, C-56/64, 58/64, [1966] ECR 299; *Parke, Davis v Centrafarm*, C-24/67, [1968] ECR 55.

120 Peter Groves et al, *Intellectual Property and the Internal Market of the European Community* (London, UK: Graham & Trotman, 1993) at 5.

121 Now regulated within the *TFEU*, *supra* note 6, art 36.

of the national law of member states.[122] The European Union and its predecessors, on the other hand, had exclusive competence to legislate over such competition rules that are deemed necessary for the functioning of the internal market.[123] The exercise of IP rights, however, would fall under the shared scrutiny of the European Union and its member states,[124] which would pave the way for applying EU competition rules to the exercise of IP rights.

Articles 101 and 102 of the TFEU,[125] which constitute the core of EU competition law, have increasingly been used to sanction certain anti-competitive behaviours of IP right holders. Article 101 prohibits restrictive agreements that could prevent, restrict or distort competition within the internal market. In order to not restrict useful technology transfer agreements by this provision, the European Commission regularly provides for technology transfer block exemption regulations that specify which agreements would not fall foul of article 101 of the TFEU.[126] The idea behind the exemption is that technology transfer agreements would "improve economic efficiency and are pro-competitive."[127] Preventing the abuse of a dominant position in the market is the goal of article 102. In the IP context, such abuse can, under certain circumstances, occur when a dominant undertaking refuses to license an IP right to a competitor.[128]

Subject to any transitional agreements, Brexit will have a profound effect on this area of law. First, the substantive provisions within the UK Competition Act 1998[129] are based on EU competition law provisions.[130] In addition, section 60 of the Competition Act 1998 mandates that the interpretation of the act's provision ought to be "consistent with the treatment of corresponding questions arising in Community law in relation to competition within the Community."[131] Therefore, if a soft Brexit occurs, it can be expected that UK competition law practice would closely follow developments within EU practice. If, however, a hard Brexit is pursued, then it could be likely that section 60 of the UK Competition Act 1998 would be repealed to sever all remaining links to the European *acquis*[132] and, in particular, to the developing case law of the CJEU, as the court has been a main protagonist in the development of the interface between IP and competition law. Again, the extent of the exact impact remains opaque.

Finally, the future of the so-called "Euro defences" warrants attention. Defendants in IP infringement cases could argue that a positive finding of infringement would be a violation of articles 101 or 102 of the TFEU.[133] Such defences can be seen in cases concerning standard essential patents.[134] Brexit could undermine the defence's logic as stemming from the TFEU.

---

122 Richard Whish & David Bailey, *Competition Law*, 7th ed (Oxford, UK: Oxford University Press, 2012) at 768.

123 *TFEU, supra* note 6, art 3(1)(b).

124 Tritton, *supra* note 20 at 1-39.

125 *TFEU, supra* note 6.

126 EC, *Commission Regulation (EU) No 316/2014 of 21 March 2014 on the application of Article 101(3) of the Treaty on the Functioning of the European Union to categories of technology transfer agreements*, [2014] OJ, L 93/17, art 2(1).

127 Whish & Bailey, *supra* note 122 at 781.

128 *Radio Telefis Eireann v Commission (Magill)*, C-241 & 242/91P, [1995] ECR I-743.

129 *Competition Act 1998* (UK), c 41.

130 Marc Mimler, "United Kingdom" in Peter Chrocziel, Moritz Lorenz & Wolrad Prinz zu Waldeck und Pyrmont, eds, *Intellectual Property and Competition Law* (Alphen aan den Rijn, the Netherlands: Kluwer Law International, 2016) at 129.

131 *Competition Act 1998, supra* note 129, s 60.

132 Richard Whish, "Brexit and EU Competition Policy" (2016) 7:5 J Eur Comp L & Prac 297 at 297.

133 Mimler, *supra* note 130.

134 See e.g. *IPCom v Nokia*, [2012] EWHC 1446 (Ch).

Since the respective provisions of the chapter I and II prohibitions within the Competition Act 1998[135] mirror the TFEU's articles 101 and 102, a similar application in the future could, however, be applied.

Exhaustion

The doctrine of exhaustion would need to be reassessed after Brexit. This doctrine was developed by the case law of the CJEU as a response to the potential conflict of national IP rights and the fundamental principle of free movement of goods,[136] which is now contained within article 34 of the TFEU. To avoid a clash of IP rights with this fundamental freedom, the court held that once a product is placed on the market with the consent of the IP right holders, the right holders are no longer able to prevent further circulation, meaning that the rights have been exhausted.[137] This doctrine has found its way into EU IP legislation[138] and applies to states within the EEA, pursuant to protocol 28 of the EEA agreement.[139] This means that IP rights are no longer enforceable where, subject to certain exceptions, the products in question were put onto the market in the EEA by the right holder.

If the United Kingdom chooses the hard Brexit option, it would be free to apply whichever regime of exhaustion it wishes to pursue. The TRIPS agreement specifically leaves this matter largely to the discretion of WTO member states.[140] The United Kingdom could readopt the old rules in which it applied a regime of international exhaustion for trademarks and UK-only exhaustion for copyright.[141] If the United Kingdom were to apply a regime of international exhaustion, this would permit the importation of goods that have been placed onto the market anywhere in the world. This option would be in line with the ambitions of those who wish to make the United Kingdom a hub for global free trade post-Brexit and is said to benefit consumers due to lower prices for imported goods.[142] A system of national exhaustion, on the other hand, would arguably benefit IP right holders, as they would retain more control over the flow of their goods; as well, it would allow for more market segmentation.[143] It is therefore likely that affected industries would lobby for the latter option.[144] Should, however, the United Kingdom remain within the EEA, the current system would remain unchanged; the specific framework very much depends on the outcome of the Brexit negotiations.

---

135 *Competition Act 1998*, *supra* note 129, ss 2–16, 18–24.

136 Nicholas Macfarlane, "The tension between national intellectual property rights and certain provisions of EC law" (1994) 16:12 Eur IP Rev 525 at 525.

137 *Centrafarm BV et Adriaan de Peijper v Winthrop BV*, C-16/74, [1974] ECR 1183.

138 See e.g. *Community Designs Regulation*, *supra* note 73, arts 15, 21; *Design Directive*, *supra* note 77, art 15; *Trade Marks Directive*, *supra* note 18, art 15; *Trade Mark Regulation*, *supra* note 19, art 13.

139 With regard to trademarks, see *Silhouette International Schmied GmbH & Co KG v Hartlauer Handelsgesellschaft mbH*, C-355/96, [1998] ECR I-4799.

140 *TRIPS Agreement*, *supra* note 108, art 6.

141 Cook, *supra* note 8 at 358.

142 Kate O'Rourke & Olivia Gray, "Brexit: changes ahead for exhaustion of rights", online: World Intellectual Property Review <www.worldipreview.com/contributed-article/brexit-changes-ahead-for-exhaustion-of-rights>.

143 *Ibid.*

144 *Ibid.*

Conclusion

This chapter has shown the potential ramifications of Brexit on trademark and design protection, as well as on the fate of GIs. These areas require attention in order to provide right holders with legal certainty. But leaving the European Union will also require looking at the enforcement measures that were provided under the umbrella of the European Union, such as the EU regulation on customs enforcement of IP rights,[145] as well as the institutional support from the EUIPO and the European Union Agency for Law Enforcement Cooperation.[146] On the other hand, some flexibility in UK IP policy making can be attained after Brexit, as, for instance, in relation to the exhaustion regime.

As seen, EU law has had a profound impact on national IP laws within EU member states and has additionally provided for unitary IP rights within the European Union. The main driver for harmonizing IP rights in Europe was the detrimental effects that national IP rights would pose for the integration of the Single Market.[147] This logic would no longer apply after a hard Brexit, and IP law in the United Kingdom may develop in whatever way it may wish, subject to current international obligations. Even in such a case, it can be assumed that the United Kingdom would follow emerging trends within EU IP law. In addition, industry and professional bodies seek a close relationship with the current European frameworks; a total breakup does not appear likely.

More fundamentally, EU law and, through this, the impact of continental legal systems on the United Kingdom, have challenged the traditional approaches within UK IP law. This can be seen within copyright law, where the CJEU has arguably altered the traditional UK approach to assessing the originality of a work.[148] But it would be incorrect to say that the effects were only one-directional. The United Kingdom, with its traditional approach of protecting trademarks only against confusion, has been a moderating factor with regard to the scope of European dilution.[149] To this extent, the integration of IP laws within the European Union has been a fascinating and challenging project of a growing and expanding relationship and cross-fertilization. In the past, the impact of the UK approach to IP protection has been as an influential and authoritative voice within this project. Since the relationship was not always easy, notably with respect to trademark law, it remains to be seen which way the European Union's IP regime will go, once it loses its major common law jurisdiction with its often-pragmatic approach. For the United Kingdom, the hope remains that whatever form Brexit will take, if it actually occurs, it will not lead to a more inward-looking approach.[150]

---

145 EC, *Regulation (EU) No 608/2013 of the European Parliament and of the Council of 12 June 2013 concerning customs enforcement of intellectual property rights and repealing Council Regulation (EC) No 1383/2003*, [2013] OJ, L 181/15.

146 Farrand, *supra* note 9 at 6.

147 Whish & Bailey, *supra* note 122.

148 *Infopaq International A/S v Danske Dagblades Forening*, C-5/08, [2009] ECR I-6569.

149 Fhima, *supra* note 43 at 25.

150 Rahmatian, *supra* note 2 at 515.

Section Four

ENVIRONMENT

11

Brexit and Environmental Law: The Rocky Road Ahead

Markus Gehring and Freedom-Kai Phillips

Introduction

Concern over the inevitable lowering of UK environmental standards, or even the demise of regulation in some areas, following the Brexit vote was immediate and not without reason.[1] While much remains in flux and will probably depend on the eventual article 50 of the Treaty on European Union[2] (TEU) deal between the United Kingdom and the remaining 27 member states of the European Union (EU27), climate change — an area most important for environmental progress and collective action — is most likely not where the United Kingdom will aim its potential

---

1 Damian Carrington, "UK's out vote is a 'red alert' for the environment", *The Guardian* (24 June 2016), online: <www.theguardian.com/environment/damian-carrington-blog/2016/jun/24/uks-out-vote-is-a-red-alert-for-the-environment>; Fiona Harvey, "Brexit would damage UK environment, say experts", *The Guardian* (27 January 2016), online: <www.theguardian.com/politics/2016/jan/27/brexit-damage-uk-environment-rspb-national-trust>; Daniel Boffey, "MEPs in bid to force UK to meet environmental regulations after Brexit", *The Guardian* (31 January 2017), online: <www.theguardian.com/politics/2017/jan/31/european-parliament-force-uk-meet-environmental-regulations-after-brexit>.

2 *Treaty of Lisbon Amending the Treaty on European Union and the Treaty Establishing the European Community*, 13 December 2007, [2007] OJ, C 306/01, art 50 (entered into force 1 December 2009) [*TEU*].

deregulation efforts. In many ways, climate change as a crosscutting policy driver transcends EU membership, having broad impacts on trade, finance and product flows, and will heavily influence the post-Brexit environmental road map. This chapter argues that Brexit will have a largely negative impact on environmental law. Regulatory pressures from the current government pursuing its worldwide trade liberalization agenda will incite backlash when exporters have to comply with EU standards, despite the lack of UK influence, and could make it harder within the United Kingdom to agree on new laws. A more optimistic view is that, if a continued trading relationship with the EU27 is wanted, the external dimension of EU environmental law could have a lasting impact in the United Kingdom.[3] On the other hand, the United Kingdom also had a significant positive impact on EU environmental law. From the earliest introduction of rules protecting songbirds to the Integrated Pollution Prevention and Control (IPPC) Directive and the EU Emissions Trading System (ETS), many of the more recent EU environmental rules, in particular those with a dynamic element, were first tested in the United Kingdom.[4]

First, this chapter summarizes general considerations relating to trade and common socio-economic factors. Second, the EU legislative framework is outlined, highlighting the scope and basis of environmental governance. Third, the UK influence on EU environmental law is evaluated. Fourth, the breadth of EU influence on UK domestic environmental law is analyzed, and post-Brexit challenges are identified. Finally, the interface of climate change and UK environmental law is explored to illustrate key challenges.

Much as the early pillars of the common market were grounded in a recognition of the need to cooperate on issues of mutual interest, economic imperatives will heavily influence post-Brexit UK environmental law, invariably requiring policy stability, effective enforcement and continued influence in environmental reforms relating to shared natural resources.

General Considerations

Environmental governance requires cooperation and cohesive legislative and policy action at the national, regional and international levels. Early overtures of cooperation underpinning the creation of the European Union were based on similar principles of economic integration, but were initially silent on environmental policy.[5] The Treaty of Rome, which established the European Economic Community (EEC) in 1957, while lacking direct reference to environmental governance, provided flexibility through article 235 (now article 352 of the Treaty on the Functioning of the European Union [TFEU]) for the passage of "appropriate measures" to attain one of the objectives of the Community.[6] Early legislation, Directive 67/548 addressing

---

3   Elisa Morgera, ed, *The External Environmental Policy of the European Union: EU and International Law Perspectives* (Cambridge, UK: Cambridge University Press, 2012). Also, more recently, Robert Lee, "Always Keep a Hold of Nurse: British Environmental Law and Exit from the European Union" (2017) 29 J Envtl L 155; Colin Reid, "Brexit and the Future of UK Environmental Law" (2016) 34 J Energy & Nat Resources L 407.

4   See the summary by Chris Hilson, "Brexit and the Environment: The European Union and UK as Both Good and Bad Influences" (9 March 2017), *British Academy* (blog), online: <www.britac.ac.uk/blog/brexit-and-environment-eu-and-uk-both-good-and-bad-influences>.

5   Maria Lee, *EU Environmental Law, Governance and Decision-Making*, 2nd ed (London, UK: Hart, 2014) at 2; Jan H Jans & Hans HB Vedder, *European Environmental Law*, 3rd ed (Groningen, Netherlands: Europa Law, 2008) at 3.

6   *Treaty Establishing the European Economic Community*, 25 March 1957, art 235 (entered into force 1 January 1958), online: <http://ec.europa.eu/economy_finance/emu_history/documents/treaties/rometreaty2.pdf>; *TEU, supra* note 2; *Consolidated Version of the Treaty on the Functioning of the European Union*, 13 December 2007, [2012] OJ, C 326/47, art 352 (entered into force 26 October 2012) [*TFEU*].

the packaging and labelling of dangerous substances,[7] and Directive 70/157 pertaining to the exhaust systems of motorized vehicles,[8] was principally focused on economic integration and addressed environmental outcomes as a secondary, if not tertiary, aspect. Following the 1972 Stockholm Declaration on the Human Environment[9] and the growing recognition of the need for cooperative action to sustainably manage ecosystems, further efforts were made under provisions relating to the functions of the common market to address lead content in gasoline,[10] detergents,[11] exhaust systems,[12] aquatic pollution,[13] air pollution and hazards relating to industrial facilities[14] and toxic waste.[15]

Adoption of the Single European Act[16] (SEA) in 1986 saw inclusion of an explicit legal basis for governance of environmental matters through a supranational approach.[17] While, previously, environmental legislation had been passed pursuant to powers relating to essential objectives of the Community and was subsequently confirmed by the court,[18] integration of article 130(r) to (t) of the SEA (now articles 191 and 192 of the TFEU) provided a clear legal basis for environmental governance and, most importantly, legislated guiding principles for the environmental action of the European Union. Subsequent developments under the Treaty of Maastricht (1992) and the Treaty of Amsterdam (1997) increased the prominence of environmental factors, positioning economic integration in the context of sustainable development and increased environmental protection.[19] The principle of subsidiarity provides for the development of Community-wide

7   *Council Directive 67/548/EEC of 27 June 1967 on the approximation of laws, regulations and administrative provisions relating to the classification, packaging and labelling of dangerous substances*, [1967] OJ, L 196/1 (no longer in force), online: <http://eur-lex.europa.eu/LexUriServ/LexUriServ.do?uri=CELEX:31967L0548:EN:HTML>.

8   *Council Directive 70/157/EEC of 6 February 1970 on the approximation of the laws of the Member States relating to the permissible sound level and the exhaust system of motor vehicles*, [1970] OJ, L 42/16 [*Directive 70/157*], online: <http://eur-lex.europa.eu/legal-content/EN/TXT/?uri=CELEX%3A31970L0157>.

9   UN, "Stockholm Declaration on the Human Environment" (16 June 1972), online: <www.unep.org/Documents. Multilingual/Default.asp?documentid=97&articleid=1503>.

10   *Council Directive 85/210/EEC of 20 March 1985 on the approximation of the laws of the Member States concerning the lead content of petrol*, [1985] OJ, L 96/25 (no longer in force), online: <http://eur-lex.europa.eu/LexUriServ/LexUriServ. do?uri=CELEX:31985L0210:EN:HTML>.

11   *Council Directive 73/404/EEC of 22 November 1973 on the approximation of the laws of the Member States relating to detergents*, [1973] OJ, L 347/51 (no longer in force), online: <http://eur-lex.europa.eu/LexUriServ/LexUriServ. do?uri=CELEX:31973L0404:EN:HTML>.

12   *Directive 70/157, supra* note 8; *Council Directive 78/1015/EEC of 23 November 1978 on the approximation of the laws of the Member States on the permissible sound level and exhaust system of motorcycles*, [1978] OJ, L 349/21 (no longer in force), online: <http://eur-lex.europa.eu/legal-content/en/ALL/?uri=CELEX:31978L1015>.

13   *Council Directive 76/464/EEC of 4 May 1976 on pollution caused by certain dangerous substances discharged into the aquatic environment of the Community*, [1976] OJ, L 129/23 (no longer in force), online: <http://eur-lex.europa.eu/legal-content/ EN/TXT/?uri=CELEX%3A31976L0464>.

14   *Council Directive 84/360/EEC of 28 June 1984 on the combating of air pollution from industrial plants*, [1984] OJ, L 188/20 (no longer in force), online: <http://eur-lex.europa.eu/legal-content/EN/TXT/?uri=CELEX%3A31984L0360>; *Council Directive 82/501/EEC of 24 June 1982 on the major-accident hazards of certain industrial activities*, [1982] OJ, L 230/1 (no longer in force), online: <http://eur-lex.europa.eu/legal-content/EN/TXT/?uri=CELEX%3A31982L0501>.

15   *Council Directive 78/319/EEC of 20 March 1978 on toxic and dangerous waste*, [1978] OJ, L 84/43 (no longer in force), online: <http://eur-lex.europa.eu/legal-content/EN/TXT/?uri=CELEX%3A31978L0319>.

16   *Single European Act*, 17 February 1986, 1754 UNTS 3, 25 ILM 506, [1987] OJ, L 169/1 (entered into force 1 July 1987).

17   Lee, *supra* note 5 at 1, 3.

18   *Commission v Italy*, C-92/79, [1980] ECR I-1115; *Procureur de la République v Association de Défense des Brûleurs d'huiles Usagées*, C-240/83, [1985] ECR I-531 [*ADBHU*].

19   *Treaty on European Union, signed at Maastricht on 7 February 1992*, 29 July 1992, [1992] OJ, C 191/01, arts 2, 3, 130(r)–(t) (entered into force 1 November 1993) [*Treaty of Maastricht*], online: <http://eur-lex.europa.eu/legal-content/ EN/TXT/PDF/?uri=OJ:C:1992:191:FULL&from=EN>; *Treaty of Amsterdam Amending the Treaty on European Union, The Treaties Establishing the European Communities and Related Acts*, 10 November 1997, [1997] OJ, C 340/1, arts 2, 3 (entered into force 1 May 1999) [*Treaty of Amsterdam*], online: <http://eur-lex.europa.eu/legal-content/EN/ TXT/?uri=uriserv:OJ.C_.1997.340.01.0001.01.ENG&toc=OJ:C:1997:340:TOC>.

policy in cases where action by a single member state would be insufficient and concerted action by the Community is required.[20] Prioritization of policy harmonization to address transnational issues — in the environmental context including transboundary environmental pollution (both air and water), global climate change and preservation of biodiversity — practically aimed to foster social cohesion, provides for balanced competition and minimizes market distortions on trade.[21] Jointly, the principle of integration calling for environmental protection to be incorporated into broader Community policies[22] and subsidiarity endeavour to balance policy development, recognizing the interconnection of the European environment and providing for cohesive frameworks governing, among others, agriculture, transport, energy, habitats and wild birds.[23]

The EU Environmental Action Programme (EAP), first established in 1972 following the Stockholm Declaration and now on its seventh iteration,[24] has developed cooperatively to actualize core treaty principles, including the precautionary principle, the concept of sustainable development and the prioritization of the environment in policy making. Even during the early stages of the program, cooperation was identified as an essential element, given global economic interdependence.[25] The resulting patchwork of laws relating to the environment developed over nearly five decades of experience and, enforced by a highly evolved system of EU institutions, presents a range of complexities for the repatriation and administration of environmental policy within the United Kingdom post-Brexit.[26] While the recent House of Lords EU committee report doubted that the United Kingdom would opt to lower its own environmental standards, the House of Lords, in this chapter's view, rightly highlighted the impending enforcement deficit that will result if the United Kingdom does not rapidly establish significant regulatory and enforcement capacity.[27] The House of Lords highlighted the role of the European Court of Justice (ECJ) as a key institution, responsible for significant progress in the environmental field.[28]

Climate change, as a distinctly international challenge, similarly amplifies the complications inherent with a suggested disentanglement. The European Union has, since EAP 3 (1982–1986) and EAP 4 (1987–1992), stressed the need for policy integration and harmonization, in particular in fostering sustainable development and reductions in carbon dioxide (CO_2)

---

20 *Treaty of Maastricht, supra* note 19, art 3(b); *TEU, supra* note 2, art 5.

21 Jans & Vedder, *supra* note 5 at 10–13.

22 *Treaty of Maastricht, supra* note 19, art 130(r).

23 Jans & Vedder, *supra* note 5 at 16–17.

24 *Declaration of the Council of the European Communities and of the representatives of the Governments of the Member States meeting in the Council of 22 November 1973 on the programme of action of the European Communities on the environment*, [2012] OJ, C 112/1, online: <http://eur-lex.europa.eu/legal-content/EN/TXT/PDF/?uri=OJ:C:1973:112:FULL&from=EN> [*1st EAP*]; *Decision No 1386/2013/EU of the European Parliament and of the Council of 20 November 2013 on a General Union Environment Action Programme to 2020 "Living well, within the limits of our planet"*, [2013] OJ, L 354/171, online: <http://eur-lex.europa.eu/legalcontent/EN/TXT/PDF/?uri=CELEX:32013D1386&from=EN>.

25 *1st EAP, supra* note 24 at para 8.

26 UK, HL, "Brexit: environment and climate change", HL Paper 109, European Union Committee 12th Report of Session 2016–17 (14 February 2017) at 54 [HL Report], online: <www.publications.parliament.uk/pa/ld201617/ldselect/ldeucom/109/109.pdf>.

27 *Ibid.*

28 Alec Stone Sweet & Markus Gehring, "Environmental Protection" in Alec Stone Sweet, ed, *The Judicial Construction of Europe* (Oxford, UK: Oxford University Press, 2004) at 228–32.

emissions.[29] It is hoped — although it remains to be seen — that continued efforts by the United Kingdom to address climate change post-Brexit, notwithstanding ongoing international obligations and access to the European market, will be pursued in order to maintain a high degree of policy stability and alignment with policy efforts at the supranational level.

Legislative Framework

Where early environmental legislation was grounded in achieving the objectives of the common market, the inclusion of explicit powers relating to environmental policy development in the SEA galvanized decision-making priorities. The legal basis for the coordination of environmental protection at the EU level maintained a level of stability following the 2007 signing of the Treaty of Lisbon, which entered into force in 2009 and established the TEU[30] and the TFEU.[31] Key environmental provisions found in article 130(r) to (t) of the SEA were included in the TFEU, reinforcing the prominence of harmonized environmental governance.

Article 191 of the TFEU establishes the objectives and scope governing the environmental policy of the European Union. Environmental policy functions to preserve and improve environmental quality, protect human health, promote the rational use of natural resources and promote international measures to address environmental problems, including climate change.[32] Policy decisions are to foster a high level of environmental protection, consider national differences and be grounded in the precautionary and polluter-pays principles.[33] In establishing environmental policy, key factors include the use of available scientific data, the recognition of the environmental considerations of other regions in the European Union and the identification of the potential costs and benefits of both action and procrastination, as well as balanced economic and social development across the European Union.[34] Additionally, both the European Union and individual member states should cooperate with relevant jurisdictions and international organizations, subject to agreement, provided they comply with the EU treaties.[35] It must also be noted that the ECJ, in particular in the *Air Transport Association of America* decision,[36] has given EU legislators the competence to regulate environmental problems outside the application of the treaties, if these impact on the European Union itself.[37]

Any hope among commentators and scholars about an impending environmental paradise in Britain post-Brexit is largely tempered by the fact that, thus far, the United Kingdom has never adopted more stringent environmental measures. Article 193 authorizes member states to establish

---

29 Christian Hey, "EU Environmental Policies: A short history of the policy strategies" in Stefan Scheuer, ed, *EU Environmental Policy Handbook: A Critical Analysis of EU Environmental Legislation* (Utrecht, Netherlands: European Environmental Bureau and International Books, 2005) at 19–22.

30 *TEU*, *supra* note 2.

31 *TFEU*, *supra* note 6.

32 *Ibid*, art 191(1).

33 *Ibid*, art 191(2).

34 *Ibid*, art 191(3).

35 *Ibid*, art 191(4).

36 *Air Transport Association of America and others v Secretary of State for Energy and Climate Change*, C-366/10, [2011] ECR I-13755.

37 Markus Gehring, "Air Transport Association of America v. Energy Secretary: Clarifying Direct Effect and Providing Guidance for Future Instrument Design for a Green Economy in the European Union" (2012) 21:2 RECIEL 149.

more stringent protective measures[38] when implementing environmental policy at the national level.[39] This domestic deference allowing for higher levels of ambition is rarely used, and, arguably, the United Kingdom does not need Brexit to establish stricter environmental laws.

In addition, some of the most important norms, such as the protection of animal rights, integration of environmental concerns in economic decision making and all EU environmental law principles (article 191 of the TFEU), are contained only in the EU treaties. The concern is that the EU Withdrawal Bill,[40] as it currently stands, does not convert EU treaty norms into UK law unless the norms are directly effective. While this is the case (arguably) for all EU environmental law principles, it might not be the case for animal rights or other "newer" treaty norms. This has led to the suggestion that a failure to convert EU treaty norms might lessen environmental and animal rights protection post-Brexit.

Several prominent ECJ decisions have influenced and advanced EU environmental law, and, with Brexit, there will be a slow process of decoupling the direct influence of ECJ decisions on the UK version of EU environmental law, which could have profound impacts. EU environmental law has not been static over the last four decades, largely due to the ECJ. For example, the balancing of EU interests with the autonomy of member states has been a central theme of environmental jurisprudence. In *Danish Bottles*, the court considered a Danish beverage container preapproval process, which provided an exception for imported test products and a quantitative limitation on unapproved containers of 3,000 hectolitres per annum.[41] Following the holding in *ADBHU*, the court noted that environmental protection was an essential objective that could justify a trade-distorting bottle deposit and return system, but held that the preapproval process was discriminatory, as it disallowed otherwise reusable containers.[42] In effect, the decision placed a proportionality test on trade-distorting environmental measures. In *Commission v Belgium*, the court considered a Belgian prohibition on the dumping or storage of foreign or domestic waste in the region of Wallonia, other than waste originating in that region.[43] While the court noted the measure openly discriminated against imports, the court upheld the measure as having a clear objective to protect human health and the environment;[44] this decision reinforces the prominence of domestic environmental protection measures.

With the expansion of EU environmental regulatory powers came an increased need for the court to interpret statutory purpose, scope and definitions. A wide range of cases, often bringing about submissions from multiple member states, focused on clarifying whether the definition of "waste"

---

38 *TFEU*, *supra* note 6, art 193.

39 *Ibid*, art 258.

40 Bill 5, *European Union (Withdrawal) Bill* [HL], 2017–2019 sess, (1st reading 13 July 2017).

41 *Commission v Denmark*, C-302/86, [1988] ECR I-04607 [*Danish Bottles*].

42 *Ibid* at paras 20–22.

43 *Commission v Belgium*, C-2/90, [1992] ECR I-04431 [*Commission v Belgium*].

44 *Ibid* at para 50.

included reusable goods of economic value.[45] Illustrative of this trend, in *Commission v Germany*, the court reviewed the German legislation that exempted several categories of recyclable waste, finding this approach violated the EU-wide single definition of "waste."[46] In *Lappel Bank*, the court had to strike a balance between ecological and economic interests in the context of the Birds Directive (79/409)[47] and the Habitats Directive (92/43)[48] when considering the permissibility of a dike and reservoir adjacent to a protected area.[49] Concluding the works were justified on public interests grounds, as they improved the ecological situation by effectively managing flooding, the court, following *Leybucht Dykes*, cautioned that while economic justification could not be utilized in the establishment of a protected area, it could be considered in exceptional circumstances in examining the degree of encroachment on the ecosystem.[50] Similarly, in *Santoña Marshes*, the court noted that member states were under an obligation to treat waste in such a way as to ensure economic operations did not adversely impact protected areas,[51] clearly positioning environmental interests above economic interests. Overall, the court has supported EU environmental measures, favouring harmonization and supranational governance with exceptions grounded proportionally and economic influences positioned ancillary to the essential objective of environmental protection.

The current draft of the EU Withdrawal Bill is largely silent on the impact of ECJ jurisprudence post-Brexit. Most commentators assume that litigants will continue to use that body of law. Indeed, even the justice minister said publicly that the "UK will keep 'half an eye' on ECJ rulings."[52] In other words, legal developments interpreting identical norms in the European Union will continue to influence UK courts.[53]

---

45 *Criminal proceedings against Euro Tombesi and Adino Tombesi (C-304/94), Roberto Santella (C-330/94), Giovanni Muzi and others (C-342/94) and Anselmo Savini (C-224/95)* (joined), C-304/94, [1997] ECR I-03561; *Inter-Environnement Wallonie ASBL v Région wallonne*, C-129/96, [1997] ECR I-07411; *ARCO Chemie Nederland Ltd v Minister van Volkshuisvesting, Ruimtelijke Ordening en Milieubeheer (C-418/97) and Vereniging Dorpsbelang Hees, Stichting Werkgroep Weurt+ and Vereniging Stedelijk Leefmilieu Nijmegen v Directeur van de dienst Milieu en Water van de provincie Gelderland (C-419/97)* (joined), C-418/97, [2000] ECR I-04475; *The Queen, on the application of Mayer Parry Recycling Ltd, v Environment Agency and Secretary of State for the Environment, Transport and the Regions, and Corus (UK) Ltd and Allied Steel and Wire Ltd (ASW)*, C-444/00, [2003] ECR I-06163.

46 *Commission v Germany*, C-422/92, [1995] ECR I-01097 [*Commission v Germany*].

47 *Directive 79/409/EEC of 2 April 1979 on the conservation of wild birds*, OJ, L 103/1; *Directive 2009/147/EC of the European Parliament and of the Council of 30 November 2009 on the conservation of wild birds*, OJ, L 20/7, online: <http://eur-lex.europa.eu/legal-content/EN/TXT/PDF/?uri=CELEX:32009L0147&from=EN> [*Birds Directive*].

48 *Council Directive 92/43/EEC of 21 May 1992 on the conservation of natural habitats and of wild fauna and flora*, [1992] OJ, L 206/7 [*Habitats Directive*], online: <http://eur-lex.europa.eu/legal-content/EN/TXT/PDF/?uri=CELEX:31992L0043&from=EN>.

49 *Regina v Secretary of State for the Environment, ex parte: Royal Society for the Protection of Birds*, C-44/95, [1996] ECR I-03805 [*Lappel Bank*].

50 *Ibid* at paras 41–42.

51 *Commission v Spain*, C-355/90, [1993] ECR I-04221 at paras 53–56 [*Santoña Marshes*].

52 Jamie Grierson, Heather Stewart & Rowena Mason, "UK will keep 'half an eye' on ECJ rulings after Brexit, says justice minister", *The Guardian* (23 August 2017), online: <www.theguardian.com/law/2017/aug/23/uk-will-keep-half-an-eye-on-ecj-rulings-after-brexit-says-justice-minister>.

53 This will be different in other areas, such as citizenship rights. The UK courts will retain the right to make preliminary references to the ECJ for eight years and will be bound by ECJ interpretation as long as the rules exist.

The United Kingdom's Impact on EU Legislation

It is not easy to determine the positive or negative impact that the United Kingdom has had on EU environmental law. Some Brexit optimists have argued that the European Union has been so neo-liberal that its rules have neglected environmental values.[54] Many of the most strident neo-liberal EU reforms were driven by the United Kingdom, and one of the reasons many voted for Brexit was the argument that more economic dynamism could be developed outside the "ordo-liberal" reach of the European Union.

To be fair, the United Kingdom has been a driver behind some of the most sweeping environmental legal reforms in the European Union. The lifelong commentator on EU and UK environmental law and former editor of the *Journal of Environmental Law*, Chris Hilson, highlights five areas where the United Kingdom has had a distinctly positive impact on EU environmental policy: climate change targets and ETS, the common agricultural policy, fisheries, the IPPC Directive and early on with the Habitats Directive.[55] These are important contributions and, certainly, with one of four member states having a common law system leaving the European Union, overall, common law thinking will be less influential in the European Union. In other words, the United Kingdom will continue to develop its environmental laws post-Brexit and might well develop legal innovations that will have a significant impact on the European Union. However, if Switzerland and Norway are good examples, the situation may be different, as many of those countries' most progressive environmental rules were actually inspired by EU rules.[56]

Brexit and EU Environmental Legislation

While deference is given to member states relating to the method of implementation of EU environmental legislation, nearly five decades of EU law has had a profound influence on the substantive and procedural evolution of domestic law in the United Kingdom. Crucial legislation relating to habitats,[57] migratory birds,[58] air quality,[59] water resources and waste management,[60]

---

54 Lee, *supra* note 3.

55 Hilson, *supra* note 4.

56 EC, Commission, "EU and Switzerland join forces on emissions trading" (16 August 2017), online: <https://ec.europa.eu/clima/news/eu-and-switzerland-join-forces-emissions-trading_en>.

57 *Habitats Directive, supra* note 48.

58 *Birds Directive, supra* note 47.

59 EC, *Directive 2008/50/EC of the European Parliament and of the Council of 21 May 2008 on ambient air quality and cleaner air for Europe*, [2008] OJ, L 152/1.

60 EC, *Directive 2000/60/EC of the European Parliament and of the Council of 23 October 2000 establishing a framework for Community action in the field of water policy*, [2000] OJ, L 327/1, online: <http://eur-lex.europa.eu/resource.html?uri=cellar:5c835afb-2ec6-4577-bdf8-756d3d694eeb.0004.02/DOC_1&format=PDF>; EC, *Directive 2008/98/EC of the European Parliament and of the Council of 19 November 2008 on waste and repealing certain Directives*, [2008] OJ, L 312/3 [*Waste Directive*], online: <http://eur-lex.europa.eu/legal-content/EN/TXT/PDF/?uri=CELEX:32008L0098&from=EN>.

commercial trade in chemicals[61] and emissions trading,[62] along with common sectoral policies (in other words, agriculture and fisheries),[63] are cornerstones of both supranational and domestic environmental action. The full breadth and depth of the EU environmental *acquis* is difficult to fully ascertain, as there are more than 200 purely environmental instruments in place at the EU level, excluding internal market aspects — such as product standards and labelling, and governance of the agriculture, fisheries and energy sectors — where member states have shared competency; when areas of shared competency are included, more than 1,100 pieces of directly applicable legislation can be identified as falling under the remit of the UK Department for Environment, Food and Rural Affairs.[64] Overall, EU environmental and climate legislation, policies and jurisprudence are deeply embedded in the corpus of UK environmental law, which makes the task of directly transposing the entirety of the framework into domestic law a daunting and complex affair. It is, thus, not surprising that under the previous coalition government, the United Kingdom concluded, in a balance of competence review, that, by and large, the European Union possessed the right competences in this field and, if anything, was perhaps lacking further competences in the field of climate change.[65]

A crucial aspect of the common and harmonized environmental framework is to maintain a level playing field for intra-EU trade, while balancing the costs and benefits of administration. The EU market, accounting for 23.8 percent of the €58.7 trillion global GDP in 2014,[66] has benefited from the stability, continuity and climate-focused long-term perspective of regulations

---

61 EC, *Regulation (EC) No 1907/2006 of the European Parliament and of the Council of 18 December 2006 concerning the Registration, Evaluation, Authorisation and Restriction of Chemicals (REACH), establishing a European Chemicals Agency, amending Directive 1999/45/EC and repealing Council Regulation (EEC) No 793/93 and Commission Regulation (EC) No 1488/94 as well as Council Directive 76/769/EEC and Commission Directives 91/155/EEC, 93/67/EEC, 93/105/EC and 2000/21/EC,* [2006] OJ, L 396/1 [*REACH*].

62 EC, *Directive 2003/87/EC of the European Parliament and of the Council of 13 October 2003 establishing a scheme for greenhouse gas emission allowance trading within the Community and amending Council Directive 96/61/EC,* [2003] OJ, L 275/32 [*ETS Directive*], online: <http://eur-lex.europa.eu/legal-content/EN/TXT/PDF/?uri=CELEX:32003L0087&from=EN>.

63 EC, *Regulation (EU) 2015/812 of the European Parliament and of the Council of 20 May 2015 amending Council Regulations (EC) No 850/98, (EC) No 2187/2005, (EC) No 1967/2006, (EC) No 1098/2007, (EC) No 254/2002, (EC) No 2347/2002 and (EC) No 1224/2009, and Regulations (EU) No 1379/2013 and (EU) No 1380/2013 of the European Parliament and of the Council, as regards the landing obligation, and repealing Council Regulation (EC) No 1434/98,* [2015] OJ, L 133/1, online: <http://eur-lex.europa.eu/legal-content/EN/TXT/?uri=uriserv:OJ.L_.2015.133.01.0001.01.ENG>; EC, *Regulation (EU) No 1305/2013 of the European Parliament and of the Council of 17 December 2013 on support for rural development by the European Agricultural Fund for Rural Development (EAFRD) and repealing Council Regulation (EC) No 1698/2005,* [2013] OJ, L 347/487, online: <http://eur-lex.europa.eu/legal-content/EN/TXT/PDF/?uri=CELEX:32013R1305&from=en>; See also EC, *Regulation (EU) No 1306/2013 of the European Parliament and of the Council of 17 December 2013 on the financing, management and monitoring of the common agricultural policy and repealing Council Regulations (EEC) No 352/78, (EC) No 165/94, (EC) No 2799/98, (EC) No 814/2000, (EC) No 1290/2005 and (EC) No 485/2008,* [2013] OJ, L 347/549; EC, *Regulation (EU) No 1307/2013 of the European Parliament and of the Council of 17 December 2013 establishing rules for direct payments to farmers under support schemes within the framework of the common agricultural policy and repealing Council Regulation (EC) No 637/2008 and Council Regulation (EC) No 73/2009,* [2013] OJ, L 347/608; EC, *Regulation (EU) No 1308/2013 of the European Parliament and of the Council of 17 December 2013 establishing a common organisation of the markets in agricultural products and repealing Council Regulations (EEC) No 922/72, (EEC) No 234/79, (EC) No 1037/2001 and (EC) No 1234/2007,* [2013] OJ, L 347/671.

64 HL Report, *supra* note 26 at 9–10.

65 UK, "Review of the Balance of Competences between the United Kingdom and the European Union: Environment and Climate Change" (February 2014) at paras 2.13–2.18 [UK, "Balance of Competences"], online: <www.gov.uk/government/uploads/system/uploads/attachment_data/file/284500/environment-climate-change-documents-final-report.pdf>.

66 Eurostat, *The EU in the World: 2016 Edition* (Luxembourg: Publications Office of the European Union, 2016) at 79, online: <http://ec.europa.eu/eurostat/documents/3217494/7589036/KS-EX-16-001-EN-N.pdf/bcacb30c-0be9-4c2e-a06d-4b1daead493e>.

that drive innovation and create sufficient critical mass to allow for the broad development and deployment of low-carbon technologies.[67]

Rather than resulting in a higher level of environmental protection, Brexit is seen by some as an easy way to lower the administrative burden of compliance — in particular, organizational protocols, permitting, reporting and data sharing — with EU environmental and climate legislation.[68]

Following the Brexit vote, UK Prime Minister Theresa May announced plans to introduce a "Great Repeal Bill" that would repeal the European Communities Act 1972[69] and transpose EU law into the domestic law of the United Kingdom in accordance with bilateral and multilateral agreements.[70] The bill is currently being discussed in Parliament as the EU Withdrawal Bill, as mentioned above, and several environmentally inspired amendments have been tabled, notably by MP Caroline Lucas. The suggestion of such a "continuance," while desirable to foster continued market stability, also raises several challenges. First, decisions and regulations as direct-effect legislation are more direct to transpose than directives that require enabling legislation. For instance, the Registration, Evaluation, Authorisation and Restriction of Chemicals (REACH) framework[71] would be directly applicable, while conservation measures under the Habitats Directive would need legislative implementation, leaving potential room to manoeuvre. Second, wide use of "legislation by reference," or legislation that utilizes a definition or mechanism from another piece of legislation through direct integration, provides a range of unique complexities. For example, section 75 of the Environmental Protection Act 1990 incorporates definitions of "waste" and "hazardous waste" from the Waste Framework Directive and the Hazardous Waste Directive, respectively.[72] Third, core obligations and definitions have evolved through the interpretation and application of the ECJ. Admittedly, uncertainty remains as to the specific way past-ECJ jurisprudence will be incorporated into the common law on Brexit day with the UK Supreme Court in *Miller* concluding that judgments would be no more than "persuasive."[73] One commentator noted the potential for an interpretive approach that would allow UK courts to interpret and develop domestic law in accordance with the law of the European Union.[74] Moving forward, as the corpus of EU law would no longer be supreme, yet would continue to evolve, divergence poses a risk to compliance terms for continued market access.[75]

Fourth, where previously the ECJ and EU institutions played integral roles in maintaining the compliance of member states and domestic actors, Brexit leaves a gap in access to forms for

---

67 UK, "Balance of Competences", *supra* note 65.

68 Some Brexit supporters are also climate-change deniers, according to James Crisp, "Brexit campaign leadership dominated by climate-sceptics", *EurActiv* (24 May 2016), online: <www.euractiv.com/section/uk-europe/news/brexit-campaign-leadership-dominated-by-climate-sceptics/>.

69 *European Communities Act 1972* (UK), c 68.

70 Jack Simson Caird, "Legislating for Brexit: The Great Repeal Bill" (2017), House of Commons Briefing Paper 7793 at 8–9, online: <http://researchbriefings.files.parliament.uk/documents/CBP-7793/CBP-7793.pdf>.

71 *REACH, supra* note 61.

72 Caird, *supra* note 70 at 33; *Waste Directive, supra* note 60; *Environmental Protection Act 1990* (UK), c 43, s 75; EC, *Council Directive 91/689/EEC of 12 December 1991 on hazardous waste*, [1991] OJ, L 377/20 (no longer in force).

73 *R (on the application of Miller and another) v Secretary of State for Exiting the European Union*, [2017] UKSC 5 at para 80.

74 Thomas Horsley, "UK Courts and the Great Repeal Bill – Awaiting Fresh Instruction" (28 February 2017), *UK Constitutional Law Association* (blog), online: <https://ukconstitutionallaw.org/2017/02/28/thomas-horsley-uk-courts-and-the-great-repeal-bill-awaiting-fresh-instruction/>.

75 Caird, *supra* note 70 at 62–63.

accountability for national measures; this is a void that UK courts will struggle to fill adequately. The United Kingdom aims to establish an independent environmental watchdog to replace the European Commission's role. Many countries create environmental agencies that can effectively supervise governmental failings, or even establish separate environmental courts with special knowledge and experience in handling scientific advice. Perhaps the government should review whether special environmental courts will be necessary. Fifth, the departure from the European Union will include restrictions on access to funding programs supporting legislative implementation, research and innovation. Finally, any potential trade agreement with the European Union will include compliance with many environmental and market standards, such as REACH, utilized by partners in Asia and North America. The Comprehensive Economic and Trade Agreement[76] (CETA) between Canada and the European Union, for example, contemplates regulatory cooperation, but contains no precise rules on specific products. At the moment, Canadian chemical producers have to comply with the much stricter REACH standard if they wish to export to the European Union, despite CETA. In the future, there could be an agreement to accept the equivalent Canadian standard, but that is not currently the case, nor is it enshrined in the treaty itself. The United Kingdom may practically be required to comply with the EU environmental framework to maintain trade flows without having the ability to influence legal development, going forward. Finally, the government has made the comment that ministers will be allowed to unilaterally change or rescind EU laws under the EU Withdrawal Bill. While it is constitutionally doubtful whether such far-reaching authorizations could be given, it is clear that, while some continuity is intended, many parts of EU environmental law not currently transposed into UK law could face governmental repeal.

It should be noted that vast differences in environmental standards would not be acceptable to UK trading partners in the future. While the World Trade Organization (WTO) allows for certain variants in this regard, its aim remains a level playing field for international trade. Under the Agreement on the Application of Sanitary and Phytosanitary Measures[77] and the Agreement on Technical Barriers to Trade,[78] many international standards become de facto binding, and, if there is scientific proof for higher EU standards, those could also be justified, further increasing the regulatory pressure on the post-Brexit United Kingdom to comply with EU environmental law.[79] It is also likely that any EU-UK withdrawal agreement would contain an obligation, similar to that of CETA, not to lower environmental standards to attract investment or create business opportunities. This provision on "Upholding levels of protection" in article 24.5(1) of CETA reads, "The Parties recognise that it is inappropriate to encourage trade or investment by weakening or reducing the levels of protection afforded in their environmental law."[80]

---

76 *Comprehensive Economic and Trade Agreement between Canada, of the one part, and the European Union [and its Member States...]*, 29 February 2016 [CETA], online: <http://trade.ec.europa.eu/doclib/docs/2016/february/tradoc_154329.pdf>.

77 *Marrakesh Agreement Establishing the World Trade Organization*, 15 April 1994, UNTS Volume 1867, No 31874, Annex 1A: *Agreement on the Application of Sanitary and Phytosanitary Measures*, online: <www.wto.org/english/tratop_e/sps_e/spsagr_e.htm>.

78 *Marrakesh Agreement Establishing the World Trade Organization*, 15 April 1994, UNTS Volume 1867, No 31874, Annex 1A; *Agreement on Technical Barriers to Trade*, online: <www.wto.org/english/docs_e/legal_e/17-tbt_e.htm>. Marie-Claire Cordonier Segger & Markus W Gehring, *Sustainable Development in World Trade Law*, vol 9 (The Hague: Wolter Kluwer, 2005).

79 Cordonier Segger & Gehring, *supra* note 78. Markus W Gehring, Jarrod Hepburn & Marie-Claire Cordonier Segger, *World Trade Law in Practice* (London, UK: Globe Law and Business, 2006) at 164.

80 *CETA, supra* note 76, art 24.5(1).

Climate Change and Brexit

Where overtures around the EU Withdrawal Bill raise concerns about the complexity of such an undertaking and about its potential ramifications for the domestic UK market, existing climate change obligations, both internationally and domestically, perhaps show a slight silver lining in Brexit. Commitments established by the United Kingdom — not only the European Union — under the 2015 Paris Agreement,[81] the continued practical role of the EU ETS in providing a market measure for climate change mitigation and adaptation and domestic measures, including a carbon budget and long-term reduction targets, provide cornerstones for post-Brexit environmental priorities. Provided that climate deniers do not assume more power in the UK government, it is most likely that the United Kingdom will remain in the EU ETS.

Grounded in international obligations under the United Nations Framework Convention on Climate Change (UNFCCC) and the Kyoto Protocol,[82] the United Kingdom has progressively reduced its domestic basket of greenhouse gas (GHG) emissions, which, in 2015, totalled 495.7 million tonnes carbon dioxide equivalent (MtCO2e), representing a 38 percent reduction below the 1990 baseline.[83] The Paris Agreement, which entered into force less than a year following the twenty-first Meeting of the Conference of the Parties of the UNFCCC (COP 21) and includes intended nationally determined contributions (INDCs) submitted from 162 jurisdictions, covering 190 parties,[84] establishes a global goal to reduce global temperature rise to "well below 2°C."[85] EU member states collectively submitted an INDC committing to a minimum reduction of GHG emissions to 40 percent below 1990 levels by 2030.[86] Climate adaptation and mitigation measures in the European Union are guided by the EU strategy, which aims to promote member-state action, better informed decision making and adaptation in vulnerable sectors.[87] Eight core actions underpin the EU strategy, including encouraging the development of domestic adaptation strategies; providing funding for adaptation action; localizing climate actions through the Covenant of Mayors framework; overcoming knowledge gaps; further development of web resources (Climate-ADAPT);[88] adapting common policies relating to agriculture and fisheries to climate pressures; prioritizing climate-resilient infrastructure; and promoting insurance and financial products that foster climate-resilient investment and business decisions.[89] The House of Lords committee rightly expressed a concern that the level of ambition regarding climate change might be lowered, and that some of the most integrated

---

81 UNFCCC, *Adoption of the Paris Agreement*, 12 December 2015, Dec CP.21, 21st Sess, UN Doc FCCC/CP/2015/L.9 (entered into force 4 November 2016) [*Paris Agreement*].

82 *United Nations Framework Convention on Climate Change*, 9 May 1992, 1771 UNTS 107, 31 ILM 849 (entered into force 21 March 1994); *Kyoto Protocol to the United Nations Framework Convention on Climate Change*, 11 December 1997, 2303 UNTS 148, 37 ILM 22 (1998) (entered into force 16 February 2005).

83 UK, Department for Business, Energy and Industrial Strategy, "2015 UK Greenhouse Gas Emission, Final Figures: Statistical Release: National Statistics" (7 February 2017) at 8, online: <www.gov.uk/government/uploads/system/uploads/attachment_data/file/589825/2015_Final_Emissions_statistics.pdf> [UK Statistics 2017]. The Kyoto Protocol provides for a basket of GHGs: CO2, methane, nitrous oxide, hydrofluorocarbons, perfluorocarbons, sulphur hexafluoride and nitrogen trifluoride.

84 *Paris Agreement*, *supra* note 81.

85 *Ibid*, art 2(1).

86 EU, "Intended Nationally Determined Contribution of the EU and its Member States" (6 March 2015), online: <www4.unfccc.int/Submissions/INDC/Published%20Documents/Latvia/1/LV-03-06-EU%20INDC.pdf>.

87 EU, "An EU Strategy on adaptation to climate change", COM(2013) 216 final at 5–9, online: <http://ec.europa.eu/transparency/regdoc/rep/1/2013/EN/1-2013-216-EN-F1-1.Pdf>.

88 EU, "European Climate Adaptation Platform", online: <http://climate-adapt.eea.europa.eu/>.

89 *Ibid*.

climate policies with the European Union might be repealed. The United Kingdom would probably have to submit its own INDC post-Brexit under the Paris Agreement and orientate action in accordance with the Marrakech Action Proclamation agreed to at COP 22.[90] The ratification of the Paris Agreement by the United Kingdom provides prospects for hope. Such a submission could be the first litmus test as to the international environmental credibility of post-Brexit Britain.

A pillar of the EU climate change framework, Directive 2003/87/EC, establishes a scheme for GHG emission allowance trading, providing a market-based mechanism to positively incentivize decarbonization efforts.[91] The EU ETS covers CO_2, nitrous oxide and perfluorocarbons and includes power generation, energy intensive sectors — such as oil refineries, production of various metals, cement, glass, pulp and paper, cardboard, acids and bulk organic chemicals — and commercial aviation originating and arriving within the European Economic Area (EEA).[92] Carbon allowances are provided annually by auction under a single EU-wide target, with a total of 2,084 $MtCO_2e$ available for fixed installations over Phase III (2013–2020) and caps decreasing by 1.74 percent annually.[93] An additional 210 $MtCO_2e$ are provided for the aviation sector.[94] Article 6 of the Paris Agreement recognizes the importance of carbon markets, with the EU ETS exploring steps to link with other carbon markets within the EEA (Switzerland) and internationally (South Korea, Canada, California and China). The globalization of emissions trading increases the total percentage of global GDP generated under ETS-compliant jurisdictions. In early 2017, the European Parliament endorsed the expansion of the ETS to shipping.[95] The UK government has been critical of this move, potentially calling into question the United Kingdom's continued participation in the system. Of course, the United Kingdom has joined the coalition for the phase-out of coal,[96] while key EU member states, such as Germany, have not, so it is not entirely inconceivable that the United Kingdom might adopt stricter climate rules post-Brexit.

In 2008, the United Kingdom passed the Climate Change Act with the ambitious goal of reducing domestic GHG emissions by 80 percent below the 1990 baseline levels.[97] The scheme, which covers all six Kyoto GHGs,[98] establishes a carbon budget for each phase (2008–2012,

---

90 UNFCCC, "Marrakech Action Proclamation for Our Climate and Sustainable Development" (COP 22), online: <http://unfccc.int/files/meetings/marrakech_nov_2016/application/pdf/marrakech_action_proclamation.pdf>.

91 *ETS Directive*, *supra* note 62, Preamble.

92 *Ibid*, Annex I–II.

93 *Ibid*, art 10; EC, Commission, "Factsheet: The EU Emissions Trading System (EU ETS)" (September 2016), online: <https://ec.europa.eu/clima/sites/clima/files/factsheet_ets_en.pdf>; EC, Commission, "Emissions cap and allowances" [EC, "Emissions cap and allowances"], online: <https://ec.europa.eu/clima/policies/ets/cap_en>; *The Carbon Budgets Order 2009* (UK), No 1259, art 2, online: <www.legislation.gov.uk/uksi/2009/1259/pdfs/uksi_20091259_en.pdf>.

94 EC, "Emissions cap and allowances", *supra* note 93.

95 EC, *Regulation (EU) 2015/757 of the European Parliament and of the Council of 29 April 2015 on the monitoring, reporting and verification of carbon dioxide emissions from maritime transport, and amending Directive 2009/16/EC*, [2015] OJ, L 123/55, online: <http://eur-lex.europa.eu/legal-content/EN/TXT/PDF/?uri=CELEX:02015R0757-20161216&from=EN>; *Amendments adopted by the European Parliament on 15 February 2017 on the proposal for a directive of the European Parliament and of the Council amending Directive 2003/87/EC to enhance cost-effective emission reductions and low-carbon investments*, COM(2015)0337 – C8-0190/2015 – 2015/0148(COD), P8_TA(2017)0035, amendment 5, online: <www.europarl.europa.eu/sides/getDoc.do?pubRef=-//EP//NONSGML+TA+P8-TA-2017-0035+0+DOC+PDF+V0//EN>.

96 Powering Past Coal Alliance, "Powering Past Coal Alliance: Declaration" (16 November 2017), online: <www.gov.uk/government/uploads/system/uploads/attachment_data/file/660041/powering-past-coal-alliance.pdf>.

97 *Climate Change Act 2008* (UK), c 27, s 1, online: <www.legislation.gov.uk/ukpga/2008/27/pdfs/ukpga_20080027_en.pdf>.

98 *Ibid*, s 24.

2013–2017 and 2018–2022), which began at 26 percent below 1990 levels.[99] Calculation of the carbon budget comes from emission allowances under the EU ETS, emissions not covered by the EU ETS (non-traded GHGs) and emissions credits from other jurisdictions, with the current carbon budget sitting at 2,782 MtCO2e and moving to 1,725 MtCO2e for the fifth phase (2028–2032).[100] More than half of the emissions in the United Kingdom come from two sectors: energy supply (29 percent) and transportation (24 percent).[101] Sustainably focused legislative frameworks from the European Union in land use and waste management and the incorporation of renewable energy sources have supported continued GHG emission reductions in those sectors in the United Kingdom.[102] During this time, the UK economy has shown continued resilience despite global economic slow-downs in parallel with expanding climate legislation. Over the period of 2008–2016, the United Kingdom's GDP has grown steadily, annually, an average of 0.18 percent, demonstrating the second largest per capita income in comparison to population size within the European Union.[103]

Brexit and the Rocky Road Ahead

Global efforts to combat anthropogenic climate change achieved a crucial milestone at COP 21, not simply with the setting of global temperature increase goals (well below 2°C and striving for 1.5°C) and the rapid entry into force of the Paris Agreement, but also through the establishment of the Breakthrough Energy Coalition, a project spearheaded by Bill Gates to mobilize investment in clean energy technologies.[104] Apart from a promising trend in green business, the coalition marks a watershed moment in which private sector leaders recognized the strategic imperative of climate change adaptation on a global stage. The 2017 report "Better Business Better World," published by the Business and Sustainable Development Commission, identifies the UN Sustainable Development Goals as providing a transformative framework for business to foster sustainable development imperatives in our current and evolving economic system.[105] It is hoped that continued climate-conscious leadership, internationally and nationally, could be an imperative for the United Kingdom to foster economic growth and innovation through its first-mover advantage in GHG reductions.

International capital markets have also begun to respond to climate-related risk exposure. In December 2016, the Task Force on Climate-related Financial Disclosures — a 32-member task force established by Group of Twenty finance ministers and central bank governors under

---

99 *Ibid*, ss 4–5.

100 UK Statistics 2017, *supra* note 83 at 9–10.

101 *Ibid* at 19–24.

102 *Ibid* at 5, 19, 30, 36.

103 UK, Office for National Statistics, "Gross Domestic Product: chained volume measures: Seasonally adjusted £m" (23 November 2017), online: <www.ons.gov.uk/economy/grossdomesticproductgdp/timeseries/abmi/pn2>; UK, Office for National Statistics, "UK Perspectives 2016: The UK in a European context" (26 May 2016), online: <http://visual. ons.gov.uk/uk-perspectives-2016-the-uk-in-an-european-context/>. UK, Office for National Statistics, "Second estimate of GDP: Quarter 4 (Oct to Dec) 2016", Statistical Bulletin (22 February 2017), online: <www.ons.gov.uk/economy/ grossdomesticproductgdp/bulletins/secondestimateofgdp/quarter4octtodec2016>.

104 Breakthrough Energy Coalition, "Who we are", online: <www.b-t.energy/coalition/>; David Goldman, "The 30 rich and powerful people Bill Gates signed on to save the Earth", *CNN* (30 November 2015), online: <http://money.cnn. com/2015/11/30/technology/bill-gates-climate-change/>.

105 Business and Sustainable Development Commission, "Better Business Better World" (London, UK: Business and Sustainable Development Commission, 2017), online: <http://report.businesscommission.org/uploads/BetterBiz-BetterWorld.pdf>; *Transforming Our World: The 2030 Agenda for Sustainable Development*, GA Res 70/1, UNGAOR, 70th Sess, UN Doc A/RES/70/1 (2015), online: <www.un.org/ga/search/view_doc.asp?symbol=A/70/L.1&Lang=E>.

the Financial Stability Board and chaired by Michael Bloomberg — put forward guidelines for large-assets owners (banks, insurance companies and asset managers/owners) for publication of climate-related financial disclosure in public filings.[106] Coincidentally, in February 2017, Deutsche Bank announced it would halt all financing to coal-fired power plant construction as part of its commitments under the Paris Agreement and building on a 2014 step to pull financing from a proposed coal port that had impacts on the Great Barrier Reef.[107] This move mirrors an increasing trend in investment funds to divest fossil-fuel-intensive assets, with Arabella Advisors noting a committed divestment asset value of US$5.2 trillion in December 2016.[108] Prior to Brexit, the Bank of England issued the first comprehensive climate report, requesting that companies disclose their climate exposure.[109] It is doubtful whether the Bank of England would still trailblaze with the same vigour post-Brexit when the United Kingdom is seeking alignment with the current US administration to forge a comprehensive trade deal.

While Brexit uncertainty remains, climate change policy imperatives transcend EU membership and should inform plausible legal reforms to maintain economic growth. International responses to climate change are reaching an inflection point of mutual supportiveness, with a 2015 Grantham Research Institute study finding more than 850 climate laws and policies at the national level; by 2017, the database had increased to include 1,360 legislative or policy instruments [110] This strong global commitment promotes the continued prioritization of lower-carbon policies and appropriate legal and governance institutions to support innovation. Observers hope that climate change will remain a policy driver, if not because it is an environmental imperative but because to deviate from the global economic shift will leave UK-based organizations open to unfavourable exposure to otherwise avoidable climate-related risk. If the UK carbon budget continues to inform and prioritize policy decisions post-Brexit, the United Kingdom can maintain international influence and drive a domestic environmental agenda, emphasizing innovation in the green economy; this could mean that enhanced climate action could be an economic win for the United Kingdom post-Brexit.

In many areas, the United Kingdom, either through the EU Withdrawal Bill or because of export pressure, will continue to be a participant (perhaps spectator) in EU environmental law. While domestic pressure will aim to deregulate, exporters, traders, service providers and even the financial industry will try to keep environmental standards as close to the EU level as possible. While

---

106 Task Force on Climate-related Financial Disclosures, "Recommendations of the Task Force on Climate-related Financial Disclosures" (14 December 2016), online: <www.fsb-tcfd.org/wp-content/uploads/2016/12/16_1221_TCFD_Report_Letter.pdf>.

107 Agence France-Presse, "Deutsche Bank pulls out of coal projects to meet Paris climate pledge", *The Guardian* (1 February 2017), online: <www.theguardian.com/business/2017/feb/01/deutsche-bank-pulls-out-of-coal-projects-to-meet-paris-climate-pledge>; Australian Associated Press, "Germany's biggest bank pulls funding for Abbot Point coal terminal", *The Guardian* (23 May 2014), online: <www.theguardian.com/environment/2014/may/23/germanys-biggest-bank-pulls-funding-for-abbot-point-coal-terminal>.

108 Arabella Advisors, "The Global Fossil Fuel Divestment and Clean Energy Investment Movement" (December 2016), online: <www.arabellaadvisors.com/wp-content/uploads/2016/12/Global_Divestment_Report_2016.pdf>; Damian Carrington, "Fossil fuel divestment funds double to $5tn in a year", *The Guardian* (12 December 2016), online: <www.theguardian.com/environment/2016/dec/12/fossil-fuel-divestment-funds-double-5tn-in-a-year>.

109 Bank of England, *The impact of climate change on the UK insurance sector – A Climate Change Adaptation Report by the Prudential Regulation Authority* (London, UK: Prudential Regulation Authority, 2015), online: <www.bankofengland.co.uk/pra/Documents/supervision/activities/pradefra0915.pdf>.

110 Michal Nachmany et al, *The 2015 Global Climate Legislation Study: A Review of Climate Change Legislation in 99 Countries* (London, UK: Grantham Research Institute on Climate Change and the Environment, 2015), online: <www.lse.ac.uk/GranthamInstitute/wp-content/uploads/2015/05/Global_climate_legislation_study_20151.pdf>; Grantham Research Institute on Climate Change and the Environment & Sabin Center for Climate Change Law, *Climate Change Laws of the World*, online: <www.lse.ac.uk/GranthamInstitute/climate-change-laws-of-the-world/>.

changes in the areas of agriculture and fisheries were sold to the electorate as the great prospect of Brexit, in February 2017, the UK government announced that it will continue to comply with EU fisheries policies and quotas for the foreseeable future,[111] prioritizing trade within the European market as a Brexit imperative.[112] As such, it is fair to conclude that Brexit does not solve a single significant environmental problem, but rather makes the solution of those problems more complicated.

Authors' Note

We would like to thank our anonymous reviewer.

---

111 Daniel Boffey, "UK fishermen may not win waters back after Brexit, EU memo reveals", *The Guardian* (15 February 2017), online: <www.theguardian.com/environment/2017/feb/15/uk-fishermen-may-not-win-waters-back-after-brexit-eu-memo-reveals>.

112 UK, "The United Kingdom's exit from and new partnership with the European Union" (February 2017) at paras 35–40, online: <www.gov.uk/government/uploads/system/uploads/attachment_data/file/589191/The_United_Kingdoms_exit_from_and_partnership_with_the_EU_Web.pdf>.

12

Advancing Environmental Justice in a Post-Brexit United Kingdom

Damilola S. Olawuyi

Introduction

This chapter evaluates the possible implications of Brexit for achieving environmental justice in the United Kingdom. It discusses the need for a clear, committed and inclusive approach to environmental governance, if the United Kingdom is to maintain and advance recent progress on environmental justice matters post-Brexit.

The term "environmental justice" generally encapsulates the need for countries to mitigate sources of environmental pollution, and to approach development in a manner that respects, protects and fulfills the human rights of all sectors of society, especially populations already living in vulnerable situations.[1] As clarified by the United Nations, the ultimate aim of a human-rights-based approach (HRBA) is to mainstream five interconnected international human rights norms and principles into development planning and decision making.[2] These human rights norms are as follow: participation, accountability, non-discrimination and equality, empowerment and legality (PANEL principles).[3] By implementing the PANEL principles in the design, approval, finance and implementation of energy and climate projects, policy makers could better develop policies that tackle environmental problems and the uneven distribution of environmental benefits and burdens in a holistic and rights-based manner.[4]

Several studies have compiled the growing evidence of environmental injustice in, and caused by, the United Kingdom.[5] The alleged manifestations of environmental injustice in the United Kingdom include siting and concentrating development projects and factories in low-income communities,[6] uneven access to energy and food resources across the United Kingdom,[7] inadequate opportunities for stakeholder participation in project planning and implementation,[8]

---

1   See David Schlosberg, *Defining Environmental Justice: Theories, Movements and Nature* (Oxford, UK: Oxford University Press, 2007) at 1–15; see also Jonas Ebbesson, "Introduction: Dimensions of Justice in Environmental Law" in Jonas Ebbeson & Phoebe Okowa, eds, *Environmental Law and Justice in Context* (Cambridge, UK: Cambridge University Press, 2009) at 4–20; Benjamin K Sovacool et al, "Energy Decisions Reframed as Justice and Ethical Concerns" (2016) Nat Energy 16024. See also United Nations, Human Rights Council, *Human Rights and the Environment*, HRC Res 16/11, UNHRCOR, 16th Sess, UN Doc A/HRC/RES/16/11 (2011), stating in its preamble that environmental damage is felt most acutely by those segments of the population already in vulnerable situations.

2   See UN Practitioners' Portal on Human Rights Based Approaches to Programming, *The Human Rights Based Approach to Development Cooperation: Towards a Common Understanding Among UN Agencies*, online: <http://hrbaportal.org/the-human-rights-based-approach-to-development-cooperation-towards-a-common-understanding-among-un-agencies> [HRBA Portal]. See also Scottish Human Rights Commission, *A Human Rights Based Approach: An Introduction*, online: <www.scottishhumanrights.com/media/1409/shrc_hrba_leaflet.pdf>.

3   HRBA Portal, *supra* note 2.

4   *Ibid*. See also Damilola Olawuyi, *The Human Rights-Based Approach to Carbon Finance* (Cambridge, UK: Cambridge University Press, 2016) at 1–15 [Olawuyi, *Human Rights-Based Approach*]; Damilola Olawuyi, "Climate Justice and Corporate Responsibility: Taking Human Rights Seriously in Climate Actions and Projects" (2016) 34 J Energy & Nat Res L 27.

5   See United Nations Economic Commission for Europe (UNECE), *Draft decision VI/8k concerning compliance by the United Kingdom of Great Britain and Northern Ireland with its obligations under the Convention*, UN Doc ECE/MP.PP/2017/30 (28 July 2017) at paras 1–3 [*Draft decision VI/8k*], expressing concern that the United Kingdom has not yet met the requirements of the *Convention on Access to Information, Public Participation in Decision-Making and Access to Justice in Environmental Matters*, 28 June 1998, 2161 UNTS 447, 38 ILM 517 (entered into force 30 October 2001) [*Aarhus Convention*]; Ole W Pederson, "Environmental Justice in the UK: Uncertainty, Ambiguity and the Law" (2011) 31:2 J Leg Stud 279; Simin Davoudi & Elizabeth Brooks, *Environmental Justice and the City: Full Report* (Newcastle upon Tyne, UK: Global Urban Research Unit, Newcastle University, 2012) at 1–20; Carolyn Stephens, Simon Bullock & Alister Scott, *Environmental justice: Rights and means to a healthy environment for all* (ESRC Global Environmental Change Programme, 2001) at 1–20.

6   See Davoudi & Brooks, *supra* note 5; Stephens, Bullock & Scott, *supra* note 5; UK Department for Environment, Food and Rural Affairs (DEFRA), *Measuring Progress: Sustainable Development Indicators 2010* (London, UK: DEFRA, 2010) at 91–92, stating that populations living in low-income and deprived areas in the United Kingdom experience least favourable environmental conditions.

7   Studies indicate that more than 2.5 million homes in the United Kingdom live in energy poverty, while 20 percent of the population lack access to healthy food. See Department for Business, Energy and Industrial Strategy, *Annual Fuel Poverty Statistics Report, 2017 (2015 Data)* [BEIS Report], online: <www.gov.uk/government/uploads/system/uploads/attachment_data/file/639118/Fuel_Poverty_Statistics_Report_2017_revised_August.pdf>; see also Patrick Butler, "More than 8 million in UK struggle to put food on table, survey says", *The Guardian* (6 May 2016); Gordon Walker & Rosie Day, "Fuel Poverty as Injustice: Integrating Distribution, Recognition and Procedure in the Struggle for Affordable Warmth" (2012) 41 Energy Pol'y 69.

8   See Matthew Cotton, "Fair Fracking? Ethics and Environmental Justice in United Kingdom Shale Gas Policy and Planning" (2017) 22:2 Intl J Justice & Sustainability 185; Helen Chalmers & John Colvin "Addressing Environmental Inequalities in UK Policy: An Action Research Perspective" (2005) 10:4 Local Envt 333.

prohibitive costs for filing environmental cases[9] and legislative provisions that limit access to judicial remedies for victims of environmental pollution.[10] The United Kingdom has also been criticized for promoting international projects that stifle environmental justice, especially in developing countries. A good example is the Aguan clean development mechanism project, authorized by the UK government, in Honduras.[11] Failure by the UK government to promptly withdraw authorization of the project, amid petitions and protests within and outside of the United Kingdom, further accentuated gaps in the United Kingdom's domestic approach to environmental justice, in particular the lack of political commitment to integrate and safeguard human rights in energy and environmental decision making.[12]

However, the rise of a robust regional governance approach on environmental justice in the European Union over the last decade has made positive impacts and has provided hope for the future of environmental justice in the United Kingdom.[13] The European Union has one of the world's most comprehensive regimes on environmental justice and has, as a bloc, supported international environmental treaties that promote environmental justice.[14] For instance, the European Union has endorsed, and supported EU member states to implement, the UNECE's Convention on Access to Information, Public Participation in Decision-Making and Access to Justice in Environmental Matters (the Aarhus Convention).[15] Widely considered as the model for public participation in global environmental governance, the Aarhus Convention places legal obligations on countries to protect the rights of the public to environmental information, participation and access to justice in all environmental matters.[16] EU members are to take necessary legislative and regulatory measures to achieve the aims of the Aarhus Convention.[17] As a state party to the Aarhus Convention, and a member of the European Union, the United Kingdom has made some progress in aligning its domestic legislation and project-approval

---

9   In 2014, the Aarhus Convention Compliance Committee concluded that the cost of filing environmental actions in the United Kingdom was prohibitively expensive. See UNECE, *Draft Findings: ACCC/C/2008/33 with regard to compliance by the United Kingdom with its obligations under the Aarhus Convention* (2008), online: <www.unece.org/fileadmin/DAM/env/pp/compliance/C2008-27/Findings/C27DraftFindings.pdf>.

10 See Pederson, *supra* note 5; Chalmers & Colvin, *supra* note 8.

11 For comprehensive details of human rights violations by this project, see Damilola Olawuyi, "Aguan Biogas Project and the Government of the United Kingdom: Legal and International Human Rights Assessment" (2013) 4:3 Queen Mary LJ 37.

12 *Ibid.* More recently, the United Kingdom has also been accused of trying to lower environmental standards in Brazil. See "UK Trade Minister Lobbied Brazil on Behalf of Oil Giants", *The Guardian* (22 November 2017), online: <www.theguardian.com/environment/2017/nov/19/uk-trade-minister-lobbied-brazil-on-behalf-of-oil-giants>.

13 See Ian Johnston, "Will Brexit Help or Damage the Environment?", *The Independent* (27 May 2016).

14 *Ibid.* See also Chad Damro, Iain Hardie & Donald MacKenzie, "The EU and Climate Change Policy: Law, Politics and Prominence at Different Levels" (2008) 4:3 J Contemp Eur Res 179.

15 EC, Commission, *Council Decision of 17 February 2005 on the conclusion, on behalf of the European Community, of the Convention on access to information, public participation in decision-making and access to justice in environmental matters,* 17 May 2005, [2005] OJ, L 124/1 (in force) [*Council Decision of 17 February 2005*]. *Aarhus Convention, supra* note 5. See also EC, Commission, *Communication from the Commission of 24.4.2017: Commission Notice on Access to Justice in Environmental Matters,* C(2017) 2616 final, at para 24, stating that "the Aarhus Convention is an integral part of the EU legal order and binding on Member States under the terms of Article 216 (2) of the TFEU."

16 See Vera Rodenhoff, "The Aarhus Convention and its Implications for the 'Institutions' of the European Community" (2002) 11:3 Rev Eur Comp & Intl Env L 344.

17 *Council Decision of 17 February 2005, supra* note 15. See also article 19(1) of the *Treaty on European Union (Consolidated Version),* 7 February 1992, [2002] OJ, C 325/5 (entered into force 1 November 1993) [*TEU*], which requires that "Member States shall provide remedies sufficient to ensure effective legal protection in the fields covered by Union law."

frameworks with rights set out in the Aarhus Convention, in line with periodic directives and guidelines released by the European Union.[18]

The possible loss of the EU policy "backstop" on environmental justice post-Brexit raises fundamental questions about whether, and how, a stand-alone United Kingdom could guarantee and protect public rights to environmental justice with the same commitment, consistency and vigour as the European Union.[19] Furthermore, loss of the courageous and imaginative jurisprudence of the CJEU on fundamental questions relating to the PANEL principles could stifle environmental justice in the United Kingdom.[20] Despite these concerns, however, Brexit must not only be discussed in terms of challenges and complexities. As the UK government begins the process of clarifying how the United Kingdom's environmental law will look post-Brexit, there are significant opportunities to revise and revitalize environmental justice mechanisms in the United Kingdom to become clear, committed and inclusive.

This chapter evaluates the challenges and opportunities of Brexit for advancing environmental justice in the United Kingdom. It emphasizes the need for an inclusive governance approach, in other words, an approach that addresses barriers to the full realization and implementation of the PANEL principles, as an important aspect of consolidating progress already made on environmental justice issues in the United Kingdom.

The chapter is organized into four sections. The second section develops a profile of key environmental justice challenges raised by Brexit. These challenges include the potential loss of a coordinated regional approach on environmental issues, the untangling and loss of the robust jurisprudence of EU courts and bodies on environmental justice, and the loss of the integrated electricity and energy market. The third section discusses practical opportunities and pathways provided by Brexit for the United Kingdom to review and revitalize its environmental justice programs. These include opportunities to achieve greater efficiency in decision making on environmental issues, to integrate human rights safeguards into energy and climate change policies, and to reform environmental policies and programs to make them more inclusive. The chapter concludes in the fourth section.

---

18 See *Council Decision of 17 February 2005, supra* note 15 at para 24. Relevant provisions of the Aarhus Convention are implemented in England, Wales and Northern Ireland by the *Environmental Information Regulations 2004*, SI 2004/3391, and in Scotland by the *Environmental Information (Scotland) Regulations 2004*, SSI 2004/52.

19 The United Kingdom ratified the Aarhus Convention on February 23, 2005. Consequently, the United Kingdom's obligations as a state party to the Aarhus Convention will remain intact even after a departure from the European Union. However, one key question is whether a stand-alone United Kingdom, without any EU constraint, will have the appetite and courage to implement Aarhus provisions with the same consistency and vigour as the European Union. See David Baldock et al, *The Potential Policy and Environmental Consequences for the UK of a Departure from the European Union* (London, UK: Institute for European Environmental Policy, 2016) at 1–10; Janice Mophet, *Beyond Brexit? How to assess the UK's future* (Bristol, UK: The Policy Press, 2016) at 55–56.

20 See Francis Jacobs, "The Role of the European Court of Justice in the Protection of the Environment" (2006) 18:2 J Envtl L 185, rightly noting that "the Court has performed a difficult task, if not always coherently, nevertheless imaginatively, boldly and with broadly satisfactory results." See also Gunnar Beck, *The Legal Reasoning of the Court of Justice of the EU* (Oxford, UK: Hart, 2013) at 1–20.

Brexit and Environmental Justice Challenges

Brexit has opened a floodgate of questions about how the United Kingdom's commitment to environmental justice may weaken or change in the wake of the United Kingdom's exit from the European Union. This section discusses three key environmental justice challenges raised by Brexit.

Fragmentation and the Loss of a Coordinated Regional Framework on Environmental Issues

One of the most complex threats to environmental justice globally is the deep and growing divide between countries in international environmental treaty negotiations, which has, for many years, stifled and decelerated international cooperation in addressing serious global environmental challenges.[21] Due to divisions, bifurcations and political alignments at international levels, especially the North-North divide and the North-South divide, the process of consensus building at the international level, especially on complex issues of climate change and energy poverty, has been increasingly complicated.[22] Brexit, and the attendant possibility of the United Kingdom developing negotiation alignments and positions that could be at variance with EU countries, could further exacerbate this concern.[23]

The European Union has played a major role in deepening environmental multilateralism, not only by developing regional responses to global environmental problems, but also by promoting common and coordinated positions for EU members in multilateral environmental treaty negotiations.[24] A most recent example is the Paris Agreement,[25] under which the European Union submitted an intended nationally determined contribution (INDC) on behalf of its member states, acting jointly.[26] With the United Kingdom's impending departure from the European Union, a re-evaluation of the INDC will be needed. It is still unclear how the United Kingdom and the European Union will decide to move forward on this issue. Whatever the route taken, Brexit could create further divisions in calls for collective global and regional action to protect the environment.

---

21 The problem of fragmentation in international environmental law, and its implications for environmental justice, has been highlighted in several studies. See generally Carmen Gonzalez, "The North-South Divide in International Environmental Law: Framing the Issues" in Shawkat Alam et al, eds, *International Environmental Law and the Global South* (Cambridge, UK: Cambridge University Press, 2015) at 1–10; Sander Happaerts & Hans Bruyninckx, "Rising Powers in Global Climate Governance: Negotiating in the New World Order" (2013) Leuven Centre for Global Governance Studies Working Paper No 124; Radoslav Dimitrov, "Inside UN Climate Change Negotiations: The Copenhagen Conference" (2010) 27:6 Rev Pol'y Res 795.

22 Andrew Guzman describes this as the problem of getting to "yes" in international law. See Andrew Guzman, "Against Consent" (2012) 52:4 Virginia J Intl L 748; Carmen G Gonzalez, "Bridging the North-South Divide: International Environmental Law in the Anthropocene" (2015) 32 Pace Envtl L Rev 407; Dimitrov, *supra* note 21.

23 See S Karcher & T Forth, "Carbon Markets: Which Way Forward? Essentials on Cooperation with Developing Countries" (2013) Carbon Mechanisms Rev 4, where the authors argue that the ability to form a consensus in designing the future outlook of climate instruments has already reached its limits as far as climate change negotiations are concerned; see also Gonzalez, *supra* note 22.

24 See Gracia Marin-Duran, "The Role of the EU in Shaping the Trade and Environment Regulatory Nexus: Multilateral and Regional Approaches" in Bart Van Vooren, Steven Blockmans & Jan Wouters, eds, *The EU's Role in Global Governance: The Legal Dimension* (Oxford, UK: Oxford University Press, 2013) at 342.

25 United Nations Framework Convention on Climate Change (UNFCCC), *Adoption of the Paris Agreement*, 12 December 2015, Dec CP.21, 21st Sess, UN Doc FCCC/CP/2015/L.9 [*Paris Agreement*].

26 Latvian Presidency of the European Union, "Intended Nationally Determined Contribution of the EU and its 28 Member States" (6 March 2015), online: <www4.unfccc.int/submissions/INDC/Published%20Documents/Latvia/1/LV-03-06-EU%20INDC.pdf>.

Second, the loss of a regional watchdog on environmental issues raises questions about whether, and how, a stand-alone United Kingdom could implement, monitor and enforce public rights to environmental justice with the same consistency and vigour as the European Union. The European Union provides guardianship, monitoring and enforcement mechanisms aimed at ensuring that member states properly implement EU legislation and directives on environmental issues.[27] Pursuant to article 211 of the Treaty on European Union (TEU),[28] the European Commission (EC) is to ensure that EU members apply the provisions of the TEU on all matters.[29] Member states are to report to the EC their implementation and enforcement action taken at the national level to achieve environmental justice. The Treaty on the Functioning of the European Union (TFEU) also empowers the EC to investigate and initiate enforcement proceedings before the CJEU against members that fail to comply with EU environmental legislation and directives.[30] These enforcement and compliance mechanisms of the European Union have created strong checks and balances and have provided impetus for EU member states to properly implement all EU environmental legislation. Whether the UK government will have the appetite and courage to effectively and consistently implement safeguards on access to information, participation and access to justice without any EU constraint or oversight is a key question that will have to be monitored and evaluated post-Brexit.

Third, the European Union has provided a regional platform for the exchange of ideas, best practices and knowledge on environmental issues by EU countries. Regional cooperation can help promote expertise on environmental justice and the adoption of energy efficiency best practices. For example, EU regional centres and platforms, such as the European Union Network for the Implementation and Enforcement of Environmental Law and the Technical Platform for Cooperation on the Environment (TPCE), have provided robust platforms for policy makers, environmental inspectors and enforcement officers to exchange ideas and foster the development of enforcement structures and best practices.[31] It is still unclear how the United Kingdom and the European Union will decide to move forward on the issue of regional cooperation and knowledge sharing. If the United Kingdom adopts and domesticates EU environmental legislation, perhaps it could continue to access these regional centres in some capacity. In turn, the European Union may choose to restrict its platforms and resources to EU members. Another possibility is for the United Kingdom and the European Union to work together and agree to continued technical cooperation on environmental issues. In negotiating Brexit, the United Kingdom should try to avoid losing a vast network of regional knowledge-sharing platforms and institutions that have been available to it for more than 30 years.

---

27 According to the European Union, in addition to any implementation and enforcement action taken at the national level, the EC fulfills the role of "Guardian of the Treaty" to ensure that states comply with EU environmental legislation. See EC, Commission, *Communication on Improving the Delivery of Benefits from EU Environmental Measures: Building Confidence through Better Knowledge and Responsiveness*, online: <http://ec.europa.eu/environment/legal/implementation_en.htm>.

28 *TEU, supra* note 17.

29 EC, Commission, *supra* note 27.

30 See *Consolidated Version of the Treaty on the Functioning of the European Union*, 13 December 2007, [2012] OJ, C 326/47, art 253 (entered into force 26 October 2012), arts 258–60 [*TFEU*].

31 The TPCE was set up by the European Union's European Committee of the Regions' Commission for Environment to bring together environmental practitioners, experts and stakeholders from local and regional administrations in the European Union to foster cooperation, dialogue and knowledge exchange on key environmental issues. See EC, Commission, "Technical Platform for Cooperation on the Environment, DG Environment and the European Committee of the Regions", online: <http://ec.europa.eu/environment/legal/platform_en.htm>.

Untangling UK Courts from EU Jurisprudence on Access to Environmental Justice

Brexit raises two significant questions of whether and how UK courts will continue to refer to, and take into account, relevant decisions of and principles laid down in EU courts or entities, specifically with respect to access to environmental justice.

First, although not yet in effect, the UK withdrawal bill sheds some light on the future of EU legislation, regulations and decisions of the CJEU in the United Kingdom post-Brexit.[32] Section 6(1)(a) and (2) of the bill states that a UK court "is not bound by any principles laid down, or any decisions made, on or after exit day by the European Court" and that a UK court "need not have regard to anything done on or after exit day" by the CJEU or another EU entity or the European Union, "but may do so if it considers it appropriate to do so."[33] Section 6(4) of the bill also notes that UK courts will, in most cases, not be bound by any retained EU case law or domestic precedents based on EU law. These provisions effectively limit the continuous application and influence of CJEU principles and decisions in UK courts.[34] This means that the extensive jurisprudence of the CJEU, with respect to procedural justice in environmental matters, will only, at best, be of persuasive influence in UK courts.[35]

Despite its shortcomings, the imaginative and courageous jurisprudence of the CJEU has provided opportunities for non-governmental organizations (NGOs) and individuals to access justice, whenever justice was inaccessible or unaffordable domestically.[36] For example, in the Slovak Bears case,[37] the CJEU held that a national judge should interpret national procedural law in light of the Aarhus Convention, to the fullest extent possible so as to enable NGOs to challenge a government decision or action that is contrary to EU law. Similarly, in *European Commission v United Kingdom*, a case was brought by UK NGOs, persuading the EC to investigate UK environmental legal costs pursuant to article 9.4 of the Aarhus Convention.[38] This article provides that members of the public should be able to challenge environmental decisions, and the procedures for doing so shall be adequate and effective and "not prohibitively expensive." The NGOs argued that the practice of UK courts in requiring claimants to give "cross-undertakings" resulted in high financial costs for parties seeking justice on environmental issues.[39] After reviewing the substantive arguments and findings of the EC, the CJEU found that the UK courts' practice of requiring claimants to give cross-undertakings resulted in high financial costs and violated EU directives that mandate EU members to remove regulatory or legal provisions that make it difficult for citizens to access justice in environmental matters.

---

32 Bill 5, *European Union (Withdrawal) Bill* [HL], 2017–2019 sess (1st reading 13 July 2017), s 6 [*Withdrawal Bill*].

33 *Ibid.*

34 EU case law will be treated like all other decisions of national and international courts and will not be binding on UK courts. See UK, Department for Exiting the European Union, *Enforcement and Dispute Resolution: A Future Partnership Paper* (London, UK: HM Government, 2017) at 1–3.

35 *Ibid.*

36 See Jacobs, *supra* note 20 at 203, rightly noting that "the judicial system of the EU is, among all international and transnational courts, unique in its effectiveness."

37 *Lesoochranárske zoskupenie VLK v Ministerstvo* životného *prostredia Slovenskej republiky*, C-240/09 [2011] ECR I-01255.

38 *European Commission v United Kingdom of Great Britain and Northern Ireland*, C-530/11, [2014] 3 WLR 853.

39 *Ibid.*

As a result of this ruling, UK courts have, over the last few years, updated costs and expenses protection rules in environmental public law cases.[40] However, there is growing concern that Brexit may result in a reversal or dilution of progress made by UK courts in introducing cost caps that peg and limit the total costs of losing an environmental case in UK courts. These concerns have been fuelled by a decision of the UK government in February 2017 to scrap automatic cost caps provisions.[41] Under the changes, any person or organization wanting to bring a judicial review in environmental cases will not automatically receive the protection of a costs cap if the person or organization loses. According to the United Nations, these changes have moved the United Kingdom further away from achieving the tenets of environmental justice.[42] This procedural reversal by UK courts is one of the early warning signals that a stand-alone United Kingdom, without the constraints of the European Union's enforcement oversight, could trigger a fundamental reversal of some of the progress made in adhering to the PANEL principles under the European Union's regional umbrella.

Second, the provisions of the UK withdrawal bill could result in significant indeterminacy, which could further complicate environmental justice in the United Kingdom. Section 6(2) of the bill states that a UK court may only refer to anything done by EU courts or bodies post-Brexit "if it considers it appropriate to do so."[43] This provision is, however, silent on when and how judges should consult EU decisions post-Brexit. The lack of clarity on the status of decisions of post-Brexit EU courts presents complex challenges for environmental justice in the United Kingdom. In the absence of a clear and comprehensive framework that mandates judges to have regard to EU case law where the dispute concerns interpretation of EU law, which provides judges with the latitude to apply the CJEU ruling if they consider it appropriate to do so, the ability of an NGO to successfully invoke relevant and applicable EU rulings, especially in environmental justice matters, will rest squarely on the whims or liberality of the judge or court concerned. The problem of indeterminacy and "polycentricity" has been identified in several studies as a threat to access to justice.[44] For instance, one of the shortcomings of climate change litigation is that while some courts have recognized the failure of government to take action on climate change as a violation of human rights, other courts have failed to recognize or apply such an expansive view.[45] Brexit could result in a similarly uncertain and inconsistent approach to the interpretation or application of important EU-derived domestic legislation in UK courts. This could leave the chances of obtaining remedies for PANEL principles claims to the understanding or interpretation of the adjudicating court or judge.

---

40 The Aarhus Convention is now specifically applied to costs in judicial review proceedings in England and Wales by the *Civil Procedure (Amendment) Rules 2013*, SI 2013/262, part 45; in Northern Ireland by the *Costs Protection (Aarhus Convention) Regulations (Northern Ireland) 2013*, SR & O 2013/81, which sets out specific rules for fixed protective costs orders for proceedings to which the convention applies.

41 Under the *Civil Procedure (Amendment) Rules 2017*, 2017 No 95 (L 1), cost caps are no longer fixed, and cost limits will be determined by the courts on a case-by-case basis. See also Clive Coleman, "Fears for environment as automatic legal 'cost cap' scrapped", *BBC News* (28 February 2017), online: <www.bbc.com/news/uk-39109865>.

42 See *Draft decision VI/8k, supra* note 5 at para 1.

43 *Withdrawal Bill, supra* note 32, s 6(2).

44 See Clive Coleman, "UK Judges Need Clarity after Brexit – Lord Neuberger", *BBC News* (8 August 2017), online: <www.bbc.com/news/uk-40855526>, with Lord Neuberger, outgoing president of the UK Supreme Court, warning that "If [the government] doesn't express clearly what the judges should do about decisions of the European Court of Justice after Brexit, or indeed any other topic after Brexit, then the judges will simply have to do their best."

45 For a discussion of the problems of indeterminacy of environment and climate change litigation, see Francesco Francioni, "International Human Rights in an Environmental Horizon" (2010) 21:1 Eur J Intl L 55; William CG Burns & Hari M Osofsky, eds, *Adjudicating Climate Change: State, National, and International Approaches* (Cambridge, UK: Cambridge University Press, 2009).

It remains to be seen how the United Kingdom will deal with both the problem of untangling British courts from EU courts and precedents and the indeterminacy concern. One way forward is to put in place a clear legislative requirement that UK courts should refer to, and take into account, relevant decisions of and principles laid down in the CJEU, where a dispute concerns the interpretation of EU law. While this requirement would not make EU decisions automatically applicable or binding, it would go a long way in providing some measure of certainty that UK courts will take into account the relevant and applicable jurisprudence of EU courts. It could also provide greater opportunities for a uniform interpretation and application of EU precedents in the United Kingdom. A follow-up action would be to constitute a legal or judicial committee that would constantly review decisions of UK courts post-Brexit, especially decisions relating to EU-derived domestic legislation. Constant monitoring and surveillance of post-Brexit judicial interpretations could help eliminate uncertainty and divergence in how UK courts interpret and apply EU decisions.

Energy Poverty Concerns and the Loss of an Integrated Energy Market

Despite its challenges, the European Union has been rightly cited in several studies as a good example of the possibility and workability of an integrated regional electricity market.[46] The European Union internal energy market (IEM) was created to integrate the supply and distribution of energy across the European Union.[47] The aim of the IEM is to address energy poverty by facilitating the availability, affordability and accessibility of energy across the European Union.[48] Pursuant to article 194 of the TFEU,[49] the IEM aims to ensure the security of energy supply in the European Union, promote energy efficiency, energy saving and the development of new and renewable energy, and promote the interconnection of energy networks, so as to make it possible and easier for member states to rely on neighbour countries for the importation of the electricity they need.[50] To achieve these aims, the European Union's Directive 2009/72/EC calls on all EU countries to remove obstacles to cross-border interconnections and the sale of electricity on equal terms within the European Union.[51] The directive also calls on member countries to work together to develop social systems to tackle energy poverty. Further, the European Council, in October 2014, called on all member states to achieve interconnection of at least 10 percent of their installed electricity production capacity by 2020 as a primary way of addressing energy poverty.[52]

---

46 Peter D Cameron & Raphael J Heffron, *Legal Aspects of EU Energy Regulation: The Consolidation of Energy Law Across Europe* (Oxford, UK: Oxford University Press, 2016) at 1–20; Tim Boersma & Michael E O'Hanlon, "Why Europe's Energy Policy is a Strategic Success", *Brookings* (2 May 2016); Per Ove Eikeland, "EU Internal Energy Market Policy: Achievements and Hurdles" in Vicki L Birchfield & John S Duffield, eds, *Toward a Common European Union Energy Policy: Problems, Progress, and Prospects* (New York, NY: Springer, 2011) at 13–40.

47 Eikeland, *supra* note 46. See also *TFEU, supra* note 30, art 194.

48 European Parliament, *Fact Sheets on the European Union: Internal Energy Market*, online: <www.europarl.europa.eu/atyourservice/en/displayFtu.html?ftuId=FTU_2.1.9.html>.

49 *TFEU, supra* note 30, art 194.

50 European Parliament, *supra* note 48.

51 EC, Commission, *Directive 2009/72/EC of the European Parliament and of the Council of 13 July 2009 concerning common rules for the internal market in electricity and repealing Directive 2003/54/EC*, 14 August 2009, [2009] OJ, L 211/55.

52 Council of the European Union, *Transport, Telecommunications and Energy Council, 08/10/2014* (Luxembourg, October 2014), online: <www.consilium.europa.eu/en/meetings/tte/2014/10/08/>.

The United Kingdom has been one of the strongest voices in pushing for this integration, and has been increasing its level of dependence on imported energy in recent years.[53] In 2014, 45 percent of the United Kingdom's gas consumption and 6.5 percent of its electricity needs relied on imports.[54] Due to problems of uneven access to energy resources, the United Kingdom currently has one of the highest levels of energy poverty within the European Union.[55] Given this growing interdependence and the strong position that the United Kingdom has taken with regard to a unified energy market in the past, it is unlikely that the United Kingdom will want to unplug itself from the EU IEM. Isolating UK electricity systems from the integrated EU-wide energy market could exacerbate energy poverty in the United Kingdom.[56] Without integrated electricity infrastructure, it will be difficult for the United Kingdom to buy and sell electricity at competitive prices across borders. Brexit raises fundamental questions about whether, and how, a stand-alone United Kingdom could successfully address energy poverty challenges outside of the EU integrated energy market.[57]

It is still unclear how the United Kingdom and the European Union will decide to move forward on the issue of interconnection and integration of energy infrastructure. To maintain open access to its European market, the United Kingdom will have to stay compliant with a large portion of EU laws, including some environmental policy. Until an exit agreement is reached, the kind of model that will be put in place to govern the United Kingdom's future relationship with the European Union is open to speculation.[58] If the United Kingdom adopts and domesticates EU energy directives and legislation, perhaps it could continue to access these regional networks in some capacity. In turn, the European Union may choose to restrict its networks and resources to EU members. Another possibility is for the United Kingdom and the European Union to work together and agree to continued technical cooperation on energy integration to address energy poverty.[59] Brexit could result in the isolation of UK electricity systems, a situation that could further exacerbate energy poverty concerns in the United Kingdom. Incentives for the United Kingdom to remain integrated in a European energy scheme and the Single Market are high, and this will not be a reality unless the United Kingdom is willing to continue to comply with relevant EU policies to a significant degree.

Brexit raises substantial law and governance challenges that, if not properly addressed, could threaten progress in addressing environmental injustice in the United Kingdom, most especially

---

53   See UK, Department of Energy and Climate Change, "More Interconnection: Improving Energy Security and Lowering Bills" (17 December 2013), concluding that Great Britain's security of supply would be enhanced by further interconnection; see also UK, Department of Energy and Climate Change, "UK National Energy Efficiency Action Plan" (April 2014) at 1–5, online: <https://ec.europa.eu/energy/sites/ener/files/documents/2014_neeap_united-kingdom.pdf>.

54   UK, Office of National Statistics, "UK energy: how much, what type and where from?" (15 August 2016), online: <http://visual.ons.gov.uk/uk-energy-how-much-what-type-and-where-from/>.

55   See BEIS Report, *supra* note 7; Butler, *supra* note 7; Walker & Day, *supra* note 7.

56   See Michael Grubb & Stephen Tindale, "Brexit and Energy: Cost, Security and Climate Policy Implications" (May 2016), online: UCL European Institute <www.bartlett.ucl.ac.uk/sustainable/documents-news-events/brexit-and-energy>; Joint Declaration by a Group of Industry Associations, "2016, time to deliver...an ambitious power market reform" (April 2016), online: <https://windeurope.org/fileadmin/files/library/publications/position-papers/Joint-Declaration-by-a-Group-of-Industry-Associations.pdf>.

57   See Grubb & Tindale, *supra* note 56.

58   This arrangement could take a form similar to the relationship between Norway and the European Union. Another option would be to follow Switzerland's piecemeal approach of negotiating a multitude of agreements with the European Union on an issue-by-issue basis. See UK, *Alternatives to Membership: Possible Models for the United Kingdom Outside the European Union* (March 2016) at 16, online: <www.gov.uk/government/uploads/system/uploads/attachment_data/file/504661/Alternatives_to_membership_possible_models_for_the_UK_outside_the_EU_Accessible.pdf>.

59   *Ibid.*

with respect to energy poverty, access to judicial remedies and public participation in decision-making processes. However, Brexit also provides momentous opportunities for the United Kingdom to recalibrate and revitalize its environmental justice architecture to make it more inclusive, focused and committed. The next section reviews opportunities for the United Kingdom to advance environmental justice issues post-Brexit.

Advancing Environmental Justice in the United Kingdom Post-Brexit: Opportunities

Brexit has created an uncertain and complex outlook on the future of environmental justice in the United Kingdom. However, Brexit is not only about the United Kingdom untangling or isolating itself from the rest of the European Union. It provides the United Kingdom a chance to clarify, recalibrate and consolidate its domestic commitment to environmental justice issues post-Brexit. This section discusses three key opportunities for environmental justice created by Brexit.

Achieve Greater Inclusiveness and Transparency in Environmental Decision Making

Brexit will trigger a range of amendments or reforms to some of the United Kingdom's extant environmental legislation, to achieve a distinctive environmental regime for the country post-Brexit.[60] The ensuing legislative reform process provides a chance for the United Kingdom to emerge from the Brexit process with domestic laws and institutions that strengthen and protect the right of the UK public to environmental information, participation and access to justice in all environmental matters. Brexit provides an opportunity for the United Kingdom to integrate and reinforce some of the positive lessons learned from the European Union's environmental framework on the PANEL principles, by revitalizing decision-making processes on environmental issues to make them more transparent and inclusive.

The process of determining aspects of the EU environmental framework that will be transposed to the United Kingdom must itself be inclusive. How the United Kingdom will decide to move forward on the issue of revising its post-Brexit environmental policies and legislation is still a subject of speculation and debate.[61] One option is for the United Kingdom to review each piece of environmental legislation to remove or update references to EU standards in line with a UK focus. Another possibility is to keep UK domestic policies and legislation aligned with the European Union as much as is practicable to maintain consistency and to reduce market and policy instability. This would include transferring all EU legislation and directives into UK legislation, in order to ensure as much stability and continuity as possible. Whatever the route taken, the UK government must approach the task of revising its domestic environmental policy post-Brexit with as much transparency and stakeholder engagement as possible. Brexit provides a chance for the UK government to address social exclusion concerns by ensuring that

---

60 See Eloise Scotford & Megan Bowman, "Brexit and Environmental Law: Challenges and Opportunities" (2016) 27:3 Kings LJ 416; Robert G Lee, "Always Keep a Hold of Nurse: British Environmental Law and Exit from the EU" (2017) 29:1 J Envtl L 155, noting the significant workload that lies ahead in clarifying UK domestic environmental law; Colin Reid, "Brexit and the future of UK environmental law" (2016) 34:4 J Energy & Nat Res L 407.

61 Ibid.

all segments of society are given equal opportunities to take part in, and influence, decision-making processes on the future and outlook of UK environmental laws post-Brexit. It is only through an accountable and transparent approach that the positive implications of Brexit will be realized.

To achieve greater inclusiveness in decision-making processes on the future and outlook of UK environmental laws post-Brexit, a starting point is for the UK government to align its decision-making processes with provisions of the Aarhus Convention. This will include providing an open consultation process to ensure the voices of all members of the public can be heard. Article 2(4) of the Aarhus Convention defines the public to include individuals, NGOs, grassroots organizations, youth, women's groups, corporations and other business organizations that might be affected by environmental issues.[62] Article 3(9) of the Aarhus Convention also provides opportunities for the public to participate in decision making "without discrimination as to citizenship, nationality, domicile or seat of activities."[63] The United Kingdom can adopt this inclusive approach by publishing a schedule of when environmental laws and regulations will be reviewed and debated, and providing information on how members of the public can participate in the process.

Remove Procedural Barriers to Environmental Justice

As noted above, under the Aarhus Convention and the TEU, the United Kingdom undertook to ensure that members of the public would have access to procedures and processes that are fair, equitable, timely and not prohibitively expensive.[64] While Brexit raises challenges and questions of whether a stand-alone United Kingdom will continue to uphold this commitment, it also raises new opportunities for the United Kingdom to reform and revitalize its environmental justice institutions and processes to enhance their capabilities to deliver environmental remedies in a "fair, equitable, timely and inexpensive manner," as stipulated in article 9(4) of the Aarhus Convention. One important step is to holistically address and remove barriers to environmental public interest litigation in the United Kingdom, especially the costs regime of UK courts.

The fixed protective costs order (PCO) litigation cap that has recently been scrapped will further increase the cost of environmental litigation in the United Kingdom.[65] The PCO limits, at an early stage of litigation, the amount that a litigant will have to pay to the other side if the litigation is unsuccessful.[66] Removing the fixed-cost protection cap creates a possible situation whereby NGOs and individuals may have to expend personal resources to challenge environmental decisions, if the court decides to vary or remove costs limits. Unless this fixed cap is reinstated, the UK cost regime could make it expensive and difficult for individuals and NGOs to challenge processes and projects that affect environmental human rights. To achieve environmental justice, the United Kingdom must ensure that the allocation of costs in environmental matters is fair, consistent and not prohibitively expensive.

---

62 *Aarhus Convention, supra* note 5.

63 *Ibid*, art 3(9).

64 *Council Decision of 17 February 2005, supra* note 15. See also *TEU, supra* note 17, art 19(1), which requires that "Member States shall provide remedies sufficient to ensure effective legal protection in the fields covered by Union law."

65 *Supra* note 41.

66 See John Litton, *Protective Costs Orders in UK Environmental and Public Law Cases* (London, UK: Landmark Chambers, 2015) at 1–3.

Further, article 9(4) of the Aarhus Convention requires that procedures must be "timely."[67] One barrier to environmental justice in the United Kingdom is the lengthy delays in the administrative courts. Environmental cases in the United Kingdom often face a very slow process of determination, which makes it difficult for victims of environmental pollution to access justice in a timely manner.[68] Brexit provides an opportunity for the United Kingdom to reform and streamline its judicial processes to provide timely justice for victims of environmental pollution. One option is to establish specialist environmental tribunals and courts in the United Kingdom with jurisdiction to hear land use and environmental cases. Previous studies have examined the feasibility, in terms of the cost and impact, of establishing such specialist environmental courts in the United Kingdom.[69] Another proposal is to create a new environmental review jurisdiction for the Upper Tribunal to provide direct access for the timely resolution of environmental disputes.[70] Brexit provides fresh opportunities to revisit these proposals and consider how to address procedural delays in the process of obtaining redress for environmental harm in the United Kingdom.

Integrate Human Rights Standards in Climate and Energy Policies and Projects

Since the first World Climate Conference was organized by the World Meteorological Organization in 1979, the United Kingdom has established itself as a leader in international climate change diplomacy.[71] Apart from playing a major part in shaping the European Union's commitments to negotiations under the UNFCCC, the United Kingdom has frequently matched its international climate diplomacy with commendable domestic action.[72] However, one aspect of the UK climate change response that has yet to be aligned with the international climate regime is the requirement to address the human rights impacts of climate change mitigation and adaptation projects and policies.

The twenty-first Conference of the Parties to the UNFCCC in Paris recognized, in the Paris Agreement, that parties should, "when taking action to address climate change, respect,

---

67 Aarhus Convention, *supra* note 5, art 9(4).

68 See Richard Gordon, "What's Wrong with Judicial Review in the Aarhus Context?" (Public lecture delivered at the Centre for Law and Environment, University College London, 8 April 2015); see also Amy Street, *Judicial Review and the Rule of Law: Who is in Control?* (London, UK: The Constitution Society, 2013) at 54–56, online: <www.consoc.org.uk/wp-content/uploads/2013/12/J1446_Constitution_Society_Judicial_Review_WEB-22.pdf>.

69 See Malcolm Grant, *Environmental Court Project: Final Report (Report to the Department of Environment, Transport and the Regions)* at 3–5, stating that a specialist environmental court would have the ability to overcome problems of high costs associated with normal civil litigation; see also George Pring and Catherine Pring, *Environmental Courts and Tribunals: A Guide for Policy Makers* (United Nations Environment Programme, 2016) at iv–x.

70 The Upper Tribunal is an appellate body under the UK administrative justice system. It hears appeals against decisions of lower administrative tribunals in the United Kingdom and has the status of a superior court of record. The tribunal currently consists of four chambers, structured around subject areas of administrative appeals: tax and chancery, lands, and immigration and asylum. Creating a new environmental chamber could provide a timely and accessible path for the UK public to seek and obtain redress for environmental harm. See the *Tribunals, Courts and Enforcement Act 2007* (UK), c 15, ss 3–12; see also Gordon, *supra* note 68, arguing that the Upper Tribunal could provide a more effective forum for Aarhus legal challenges than conventional courts. See also Brian J Preston, "Benefits of Judicial Specialization in Environmental Law: The Land and Environment Court of New South Wales as a Case Study" (2012) 29 Pace Envtl L Rev at 396, 398, stating that a court with special expertise in environmental matters is best suited to advance environmental justice.

71 See John W Zillman, "A History of Climate Activities" (2009) 58:3 World Meteorological Org Bull; see also Clea Kolster & Sophie Smith, "The UK Post-Brexit: A Leader in Climate Change Diplomacy?" (2017) Imperial College London Discussion Paper at 1–2.

72 See Kolster & Smith, *supra* note 71.

promote and consider their respective obligations on human rights."[73] This includes the rights of Indigenous peoples, local communities and people in vulnerable situations.[74] Without an environmental justice perspective, projects and actions designed to combat climate change risk exacerbating social exclusions, land grabs and human rights concerns within the United Kingdom and internationally.[75]

Despite progress made in addressing climate change in the United Kingdom, several questions remain on the implications of energy and climate policies and projects on the enjoyment of fundamental human rights, especially in vulnerable and low-income communities. As noted earlier, human rights concerns, such as a lack of adequate information on climate policies and projects, inadequate stakeholder consultation and uneven access to energy and food resources across the United Kingdom are threats to environmental justice that must be holistically addressed.[76] Although the Department for Business, Energy and Industrial Strategy (BEIS)[77] and the Foreign & Commonwealth Office have provided great leadership in international climate change negotiations and diplomacy, more work needs to be done domestically to address human rights gaps in the design, approval and implementation of climate and energy projects in the United Kingdom.

Brexit provides an opportunity for the United Kingdom to revitalize and reform domestic climate change legislation and policies to incorporate robust human rights safeguards. The BEIS department must examine the implications of climate and energy policies and projects on human rights in the United Kingdom. Human rights standards and principles should inform and strengthen policy measures on climate change.[78] Decision-making processes that have excluded poor and vulnerable communities must be reformed to be more inclusive, based on the PANEL principles.[79]

The UK government could approach the task of revising UK climate change policy post-Brexit with equal or greater ambition than what is in place in the European Union. Climate change responses could reflect the renewed global consensus on the need to respect human rights in all climate actions. To advance this objective, the United Kingdom could develop robust legal and institutional frameworks that fully mainstream and integrate human rights standards into the design, approval, finance and implementation of energy projects.[80] This would ensure that

---

73 See *Paris Agreement*, *supra* note 25.

74 *Ibid.*

75 See Damilola Olawuyi, "Advancing Climate Justice in International Law: Potentials and Constraints of the United Nations Human Rights Based Approach" in Randall S Abate, ed, *Climate Justice: Case Studies in Global and Regional Governance Challenges* (Washington, DC: Environmental Law Institute Press, 2016) at 1–10; Robin Bronen, "Climate-Induced Community Relocations: Creating an Adaptive Governance Framework Based in Human Rights Doctrine" (2011) 35 NYU Rev L & Soc Change 357.

76 See *Draft decision VI/8k*, *supra* note 5; Pedersen, *supra* note 5; Davoudi & Brooks, *supra* note 5; Stephens, Bullock & Scott, *supra* note 5.

77 Formerly known as the Department of Energy and Climate Change.

78 Open letter from Navanethem Pillay, UN High Commissioner for Human Rights, to all permanent missions in New York and Geneva (30 March 2012), online: <www.ohchr.org/Documents/Issues/Development/OpenLetterHC.pdf> [Pillay Open Letter]; see also United Nations Regional Information Centre for Western Europe, "Pillay urges states to inject human rights into Rio+20" (19 April 2012), online: <www.unric.org/en/latest-un-buzz/27492-pillay-urges-states-to-inject-human-rights-into-rio20>.

79 Pillay Open Letter, *supra* note 78.

80 Olawuyi, *Human Rights-Based Approach*, *supra* note 4.

human rights and climate change obligations are coherently and systemically integrated, to avoid overlap, inefficiency and waste of resources.

As the United Kingdom evaluates and establishes its distinctive environmental policies and agenda post-Brexit, the ensuing legislative restructuring process provides great opportunities for the United Kingdom to develop and implement a clear, transparent and inclusive framework on environmental justice issues post-Brexit.[81] A good starting point is to provide transparent opportunities and a timetable for members of the public to take part in and influence decision-making processes on the future of UK environmental regulation post-Brexit. The UK government must also remove barriers to participation, such as a lack of easy access to meeting venues, complex voting processes or a lack of proper information on deliberations. A useful approach is to disclose a detailed agenda of how environmental legislation and regulations will be evaluated and then provide online platforms for stakeholders to participate in and influence final outcomes.

Similarly, legislative re-evaluations that will occur in the United Kingdom over the next few years as a result of Brexit provide excellent opportunities for the United Kingdom to generally reinvigorate its overall environmental legislation and programs with human rights safeguards and obligations, in accordance with the PANEL principles. Human rights could be integrated into the work, processes and budgets of UK environment and climate change institutions in order to address issues of social exclusion, energy poverty, costs barriers to environmental litigation and inadequate opportunities for low-income communities to participate in and influence decision-making processes. This could include integrating human rights safeguards into extant legislation and policies in the United Kingdom to reflect an emphasis on the importance of implementing climate and energy policies and projects in a manner that respects human rights.

Finally, an equally important step would be to establish an independent environmental standards watchdog to monitor and assess environmental justice issues in the United Kingdom post-Brexit.[82] An environmental watchdog, with a direct mandate, independence and funding to continually evaluate and report on how government agencies and departments are complying with the PANEL principles, could help identify and address social exclusion concerns in energy policies and projects. A good example is the Canadian Commissioner of the Environment and Sustainable Development, an independent environmental watchdog, housed within the Office of the Auditor General of Canada.[83] The commissioner has legislative powers to launch independent assessments as to whether federal government departments are meeting their sustainable development objectives. Consequently, incumbents have been able to pursue their mandates independently and address complaints from the public. To advance and deliver environmental justice programs in the United Kingdom post-Brexit, similar institutions could be established.

---

81 See also the 2017 UNECE decision calling on the United Kingdom to establish a clear, transparent and consistent framework to implement the provisions of the Aarhus Convention: *Draft decision VI/8k, supra* note 5.

82 The UK government will have to deliver on its promise to establish an environmental watchdog post-Brexit. See Charlotte Ryan, "U.K. Environment Secretary Promises Green Brexit With Watchdog", *Bloomberg* (12 November 2017), online: <www.bloomberg.com/news/articles/2017-11-12/u-k-environment-secretary-promises-green-brexit-with-watchdog>.

83 See Office of the Auditor General of Canada, Reports to Parliament, "Commissioner of the Environment and Sustainable Development Reports", online: <www.oag-bvg.gc.ca/internet/English/parl_lp_e_901.html>.

Conclusion

Brexit creates a complex and uncertain outlook on the future of environmental justice in the United Kingdom. However, the ensuing legislative re-evaluations that will occur in the United Kingdom over the next few years as a result of Brexit equally provide opportunities for the United Kingdom to develop and implement a clear, committed and inclusive framework on environmental justice issues post-Brexit. This approach will focus on removing legal and procedural barriers to the delivery of environmental justice programs in the United Kingdom. It will also mean clarifying how UK courts should approach and apply decisions of EU courts and bodies post-Brexit. Further, great emphasis could be placed on infusing energy and climate change policies and programs with robust human rights safeguards to prevent the execution of projects that could infringe upon human rights.

Revitalizing UK environmental laws and institutions to achieve environmental justice will come with considerable costs. This would include the cost of achieving wider public participation, establishing new institutions and expanding current institutions, including staffing, training and program funding.[84] To reduce the cost of an HRBA, the United Nations emphasizes the importance of eliminating institutional overlaps and fragmentation, improving institutional coordination and building on existing capacities and resources.[85] Further research is, therefore, necessary to understand how human rights and environment agencies in the United Kingdom can be restructured and strengthened to better monitor, assess and report on social exclusion issues in energy policies and projects in a coordinated manner. The Scottish Human Rights Commission, for example, is already spearheading significant efforts in mainstreaming a rights-based framework in decision making in various sectors in Scotland.[86] It will be important to examine how lessons learned from the Scottish human rights mainstreaming effort could inform and strengthen the robust implementation of the PANEL principles across the United Kingdom.

84 See Grant, *supra* note 69 at 3–5; Christopher McCrudden, "Mainstreaming Human Rights" in Colin Harvey, ed, *Human Rights in the Community: Rights as Agents for Change* (Oxford, UK: Hart, 2005) at 9–26.

85 HRBA Portal, *supra* note 2; United Nations Population Fund, "A Human Rights-Based Approach to Programming: Practical Implementation Manual and Training Materials" (2014) at 165, online: <http://hrbaportal.org/wp-content/files/UNFPA_HRBAto-Programming_2014.pdf>.

86 Scottish Human Rights Commission, "PANEL principles", online: <www.scottishhumanrights.com/rights-in-practice/human-rights-based-approach>.

13

Brexit and International Environmental Law

Richard Macrory and Joe Newbigin

Introduction

The United Kingdom is party to more than 40 international environmental treaties (and more than 100 international environmental agreements when protocols, amendments and so forth are also considered).[1] These agreements cover a broad range of matters, such as climate change, transboundary movement of hazardous waste, access to environmental information and nuclear safety.[2] Government ministers have repeatedly said that post-Brexit, the United Kingdom intends to remain bound by its international environmental obligations. For example, in a written statement to the House of Commons in September 2017, it was stated, "The UK will continue to be bound by international Multilateral Environmental Agreements (MEAs) to which it is party. We are committed to upholding our international obligations under these agreements

---

1 UK Environmental Law Association (UKELA), *Brexit and Environmental Law: The UK and International Environmental Law* (London, UK: UKELA, 2017) at 5 [UKELA, *Brexit and Environmental Law*].

2 *Ibid*, Annex.

and will continue to play an active role internationally following our departure from the EU."[3] The current Brexit policy is to ensure as much as possible that existing EU environmental law is rolled over after the United Kingdom's withdrawal from the European Union in the interests of regulatory stability until the opportunity for revaluation is taken.[4] The UK government's freedom to reshape national environmental law[5] in the future will be constrained by the international environmental treaties to which the United Kingdom is a party,[6] and in this sense, international environmental law could be seen to provide an important underpinning in terms of future national environmental obligations, rights and minimum standards.[7]

Post-Brexit international environmental law is therefore likely to assume increasing significance for the United Kingdom, but determining its potential impact and importance raises a number of issues, which are considered in this chapter. The first section addresses the question of which international agreements will bind the United Kingdom after Brexit. The UK government's statements that it will continue to honour its international environmental obligations raises the question of the extent of these obligations, since the European Union has been party to many of these agreements, and the legal position post-Brexit is not necessarily obvious. The next section considers how existing EU environmental law has implemented the international environmental agreements to which it is a party, the implications for national environmental law, and whether post-Brexit international environmental obligations will provide an equivalence in legal substance. Finally, the question of compliance and enforcement is considered. The EU has developed sophisticated mechanisms for the enforcement of EU obligations against member states, including those arising from international agreements, and it is questionable whether these will be replicated post-Brexit in relation to international agreements to which the United Kingdom is a party.

---

3   Written statement to the House of Commons by Thérèse Coffey, Parliamentary Under Secretary of State for the Department for Environment, Food and Rural Affairs, in response to written questions from Caroline Lucas, MP, "Environment: Treaties: Written question – 9691", (asked on 8 September 2017, answered on 18 September 2017) ["Environment: Treaties"], online: <www.parliament.uk/business/publications/written-questions-answers-statements/written-question/Commons/2017-09-08/9691/>; "Environment: EU External Relations: Written question – 9693", (asked on 8 September 2017, answered on 18 September 2017) ["Environment: EU External Relations"], online: <www.parliament.uk/business/publications/written-questions-answers-statements/written-question/Commons/2017-09-08/9693/>; UK, House of Commons Hansard, vol 628 (5 September 2017) (during debate on the first day of the second reading of the Withdrawal Bill, Steve Baker, MP, Parliamentary Under Secretary for the Department for Exiting the European Union, stated he would "put on the record again that we [the government] will uphold all our commitments to international law in relation to the environment" c 289); UK, Department for Exiting the European Union, "The United Kingdom's exit from and new partnership with the European Union" (2 February 2017) [Brexit White Paper] ("We will of course continue to honour our international commitments and follow international law" at para 2.13), online: <www.gov.uk/government/publications/the-united-kingdoms-exit-from-and-new-partnership-with-the-european-union-white-paper>.

4   Brexit White Paper, *supra* note 3 at para 2.7.

5   In this context, "government" will include the devolved administrations to the extent that environmental policy is fully devolved.

6   Richard Macrory, "Brexit unlikely to give UK free rein over green laws" (2016) 499 ENDS Report (September 2016) at 22–23.

7   See evidence of Maria Lee, House of Lords Select Committee on the European Union, Energy and Environment Sub-Committee, *Brexit: environment and climate change* (London, UK: 2016) at 156 [House of Lords], online: <www.parliament.uk/business/committees/committees-a-z/lords-select/eu-energy-environment-subcommittee/inquiries/parliament-2015/brexit-environment-and-climate-change/publications/>.

The United Kingdom's International Environmental Obligations after Brexit

Assessing the extent and nature of the United Kingdom's international environmental obligations post-Brexit is legally complex because of the distinct ways the European Union has been involved in the majority of environmental treaties to which the United Kingdom is currently bound. The European Union has legal personality[8] and it may conclude international treaties "where the Treaties so provide or where the conclusion of an agreement is necessary in order to achieve, within the framework of the Union's policies, one of the objectives referred to in the Treaties, or is provided for in a legally binding Union act or is likely to affect common rules or alter their scope."[9] But the exercise of these powers is critically dependent on considerations of the legal competence the European Union possesses in the substantive area of the treaty in question.[10] The provision in article 216 of the Treaty on the Functioning of the European Union (TFEU)[11] has been described as one that essentially codifies prior case law of the Court of Justice of the European Union (CJEU), which has played a critical role in defining and determining the extent of the Union's competence in the international field.[12] Even where no explicit external powers were provided under the treaty, the court in a series of cases, beginning in 1971 in *Commission of the European Communities v Council of the European Communities*,[13] was prepared to imply such external treaty-making powers. More recently, the court has noted that:

> [A] comprehensive and detailed analysis must be carried out to determine whether the Community has the competence to conclude an international agreement and whether that competence is exclusive. In doing so, account must be taken not only of the area covered by the Community rules and the provision of the agreement envisaged in so far as the latter are known, but also the nature and content of those rules and those provisions, to ensure that the agreement is not capable of undermining the uniform and consistent application of the Community rules and the proper functioning of the system which they establish.[14]

---

8   *Treaty on European Union (Consolidated Version)*, 7 February 1992, [2002] OJ, C 325/5 art 47 (entered into force 1 November 1993).

9   *Treaty on the Functioning of the European Union*, 13 December 2007, [2008] OJ, C 115/47 art 216(1) (entered into force 1 December 2009) [*TFEU*].

10 Geert De Baere, *Constitutional Principles of EU External Relations* (Oxford, UK: Oxford University Press, 2008) at 10.

11 *TFEU*, *supra* note 9, art 216.

12 Damian Chalmers, Gareth Davies & Giorgio Monti, *European Union Law: Cases and Materials* (Cambridge, UK: Cambridge University Press, 2010) at 640.

13 *Commission of the European Communities v Council of the European Communities: European Agreement on Road Transport*, C-22/70, [1971] ECR at 263.

14 *Convention on jurisdiction and the recognition and enforcement of judgments in civil and commercial matters (Lugano Convention)*, 30 October 2007, OJ, L 339 at para 133 (entered into force 1 January 2010).

In broad terms, three types of international agreements can be identified:

- international agreements in which member states retain exclusive competence to negotiate and ratify without the involvement of the Union;

- international agreements that are within the Union's exclusive competence and that only the Union may ratify; and

- international agreements in which the subject matter straddles the competences of both the Union and member states, and where both the Union and member states will therefore be parties.[15]

These so-called mixed agreements are frequently used to ensure member state support even in areas where the European Union strictly appears to have exclusive legal competence.[16]

When it comes to international environmental agreements, a recent study has identified 26 international environmental agreements where the European Union was not a party because it lacked competence, but which the United Kingdom had ratified.[17] These include the International Whaling Convention 1946[18] and the Convention on Wetlands of International Importance 1971 (the Ramsar Convention).[19] The United Kingdom will continue to be bound by these agreements post-Brexit, although there may be complexities because domestic implementation of these agreements has sometimes been achieved under EU environmental legislation, and care will be needed to ensure these legal provisions are maintained under national law.

International environmental agreements falling within the exclusive competence of the European Union are less common, but form an important element of the United Kingdom's current international commitments.[20] Currently, the United Kingdom is party to these agreements because article 216(2) of the TFEU states that international agreements entered into by the European Union alone bind the institutions of the Union and its member states. Such agreements may be implemented in the United Kingdom through a combination of directly applicable EU law and domestic law implementing EU directives.

Important subject areas include fisheries, where the United Kingdom's international obligations largely derive from agreements ratified by the European Union under exclusive competences.[21] Consideration should also be given to individual treaties, such as the 1992 Water Convention,

---

15 See generally Piet Eeekhout, *External Relations of the European Union: Legal and Constitutional Foundations* (Oxford, UK: Oxford University Press, 2004). For an early analysis relating to the environmental field, see Martin Hession & Richard Macrory, "The Legal Framework of European Community Participation in International Environmental Agreements" (1994) 2:1 New Europe L Rev at 59–136.

16 Joseph Weiler, *The Constitution of Europe* (Cambridge, UK: Cambridge University Press, 1999) at 177. See also Panos Koutrakos & Christophe Hillion, eds, *Mixed Agreements Revisited: The EU and its Member States in the World* (Oxford, UK: Hart, 2010).

17 UKELA, *The UK and International Environmental Law after Brexit* (London, UK: UKELA, 2017), Annex [UKELA, *The UK*].

18 *International Convention for the Regulation of Whaling*, 2 December 1946, 2124 UNTS 164 (entered into force 10 November 1948).

19 *Convention on Wetlands of International Importance especially as Waterfowl Habitat*, 2 February 1971, 14583 UNTS 996 (entered into force 21 December 1975) [*Ramsar Convention*].

20 Twelve such agreements have been identified. See UKELA, *Brexit and Environmental Law, supra* note 1.

21 The European Union is expressly granted exclusive competence in relation to conservation of marine biological resources under the common fisheries policy under article 3(1) of the TFEU.

governing crucial transboundary cooperation in relation to the waterways and lakes spanning the boundary between Northern Ireland and the Republic of Ireland, which the United Kingdom has signed but not ratified.[22] The 2013 Minamata Convention on Mercury, which recently came into force,[23] also falls into this category.

Upon leaving the European Union, the United Kingdom will no longer be bound by such treaties unless it decides to ratify them of its own accord. There are two main reasons for this. First, article 29 of the Vienna Convention sets out that a treaty is binding on a party in respect of its entire territory.[24] Therefore, where the European Union is the signatory to an international environmental agreement, the entire territory will most likely be interpreted as encompassing the combined territory of the European Union's member states; after Brexit, such an agreement will not encompass the territory of the United Kingdom.[25] Second, the inclusion of territorial application clauses in many EU external agreements restricts the agreement to territories where the EU treaties apply.[26] This will automatically end the United Kingdom's participation in such an agreement and preclude it from automatically becoming a party. After Brexit, the United Kingdom will no longer be bound by EU-only international environmental agreements and (to the extent that they are enforceable) the obligations and environmental protections contained within these agreements will no longer be effective in the United Kingdom.

The United Kingdom must decide which of these categories of international environmental agreements it will ratify, applying the procedure set out in section 20 of the Constitutional Reform and Governance Act 2010.[27] This provision requires that an agreement is laid before Parliament, alongside an explanatory memorandum, when it will be ratified if neither House resolves that it should not be ratified. The power proposed to be given to ministers by clause 8 of the Withdrawal Bill to remedy or prevent any breach of international obligations arising from Brexit does not appear (in its present form) to give the UK government power to displace or depart from the requirements of section 20.[28]

As yet, the UK government has not clarified which of these EU-only international environmental agreements it intends to ratify post-Brexit, and its position may be affected by the nature of any relationship it establishes with the European Union in the future. Although the UK government recently said that it "will give due consideration to the ratification of MEAs in the future to which the UK is not currently party in its own right, (recognising that some risks have no relevance to the UK)," this ambiguity appears contrary to the spirit of a commitment to honouring the United Kingdom's international commitments.[29]

---

22 *Convention on the Protection and Use of Transboundary Watercourses and International Lakes*, 17 March 1992, 1936 UNTS 269 (entered into force 6 October 1996) [*Water Convention*].

23 *Minamata Convention on Mercury*, 10 October 2013 (entered into force 16 August 2017).

24 *Vienna Convention on the Law of Treaties*, 23 May 1969, 1155 UNTS 331 (entered into force 27 January 1980).

25 Jed Odermatt, "Brexit and International Law" (4 July 2016), *Blog of the European Journal of International Law* (blog), online: <www.ejiltalk.org/brexit-and-international-law>.

26 Guillaume Van der Loo & Steven Blockmans, "The Impact of Brexit on the EU's International Agreements" (15 July 2016), *CEPS Commentary* (blog), online: <www.ceps.eu/publications/impact-brexit-eu%E2%80%99s-international-agreements>.

27 Arabella Lang, "Parliament's role in ratifying treaties" (17 February 2017) House of Commons Library Briefing Paper No 5855.

28 Bill 5, *European Union (Withdrawal) Bill* [HC], 2017–2019 sess, 2017 (1st reading 13 July 2017) clause 8.

29 See "Environment: Treaties", *supra* note 3; "Environment: EU External Relations", *supra* note 3.

The most common form of international environmental agreement is that which contains elements falling within both EU competence and member state competence. These mixed agreements, which both the United Kingdom and the European Union have ratified, represent 45 of the 101 international environmental agreements to which the United Kingdom is a party.[30]

What happens to these mixed agreements when the United Kingdom leaves the European Union? This question remains unresolved. A House of Commons Library briefing paper concluded that "[o]n balance, most analysts believe that both exclusive and mixed agreements will fall on exit day, and will have to be renegotiated after Brexit, or possibly in parallel with negotiations on the withdrawal agreement."[31] Others have argued that "leaving the EU would mean that the UK ceases to be bound by the 'EU-only' elements of mixed agreements,"[32] but this interpretation raises problems because, as Weiler notes, "most mixed agreements do not specify the demarcation between Community and Member States competences."[33]

The authors of this chapter favour the view that after withdrawing from the European Union, the United Kingdom will assume all the competences previously resting with the European Union and would be therefore bound automatically by all mixed agreements. This is also the view Thérèse Coffey held in 2016,[34] although her statements maintain an ambiguity as to both the extent of the United Kingdom's commitments after Brexit and the legal basis for her understanding.[35] The House of Lords Select Committee on the European Union, Energy and Environment Sub-Committee report on "Brexit: environment and climate change" acknowledged these "differing views within the legal community."[36] The report noted the concurrence among Coffey, Richard Macrory and Maria Lee that the United Kingdom would probably continue to be bound by agreements that the United Kingdom had signed and ratified, but it did not give an opinion as to the correctness of this position.[37] Nevertheless, it is apparent that these are uncharted legal waters and that legal views differ.

The UK government's statements to date contain ambiguities, and it would be welcomed if it published a more precise view of its understanding of the position and legal status of mixed agreements after Brexit, and whether it considers the United Kingdom to be automatically bound by the entirety of these mixed agreements, or would need to renegotiate with existing parties to

---

30 UKELA, *The UK*, *supra* note 17.

31 Vaughne Miller, "Legislating for Brexit: EU external agreements" (2017) House of Commons Library Briefing Paper No 7850 at 3. The paper does not detail the analyses relied upon. See also Sarah Priestly & Louise Smith, "Brexit and the environment" (2017) House of Commons Library Briefing Paper No CBP8132 at 24.

32 Van der Loo & Blockmans, *supra* note 26.

33 Weiler, *supra* note 16 at 177.

34 House of Lords, *supra* note 7 (Coffey stated, "It is my understanding that as the UK is already a party in its own right it absolutely will stick to the commitments, and is obliged to, once we leave" at 198). Coffey later said in response to a written question from MP Anne Main that "[t]he UK is a Party to 35 Multilateral Environmental Agreements (MEAs) in its own right. These are mixed agreements and we are bound by the obligations they contain; this will not change on exit from the EU. We are committed to continuing to play an active role internationally and will continue to be bound by the obligations under these MEAs after leaving the EU." See "Environment: Treaties: Written question – 64664" (asked on 20 February 2017, answered on 27 February 2017), online: <www.parliament.uk/business/publications/written-questions-answers-statements/written-question/Commons/2017-02-20/64664/>.

35 In response to a written question from MP Caroline Lucas, asking, "what the legal position will be of international environmental agreements ratified jointly by the EU and the UK after the UK leaves the EU," Coffey replied, "The UK will continue to be bound by international Multilateral Environmental Agreements (MEAs) to which it is party." See Environment: EU External Relations, *supra* note 3.

36 House of Lords Select Committee on the European Union, Energy and Environment Sub-Committee, *Brexit: environment and climate change* (London, UK: HL Paper 109, 2017) at para 48.

37 *Ibid.*

ensure it was bound. As Macrory said very recently, in evidence before the House of Commons' Environmental Audit Committee, "in an ideal world, one would have a joint statement from the Commission and the UK Government."[38] At the same hearing, Panos Koutrakos, noting that this would be consistent with statements made by the European Council, said that in the current climate a joint statement was "not as eccentric as it might appear."[39] Annalisa Savaresi concurred, suggesting such a joint statement may form the basis of a declaration issued with depositories of mixed agreement, or be formalized in a future collateral arrangement.[40]

Maintaining the Procedure and Substance of the United Kingdom's International Obligations

There are numerous areas of environmental law where EU legislation implementing international conventions has gone further than the actual terms of the treaty in question. Andy Jordan has noted that the European Union has not merely transposed international environmental agreements wholesale, but rather has added "hard edges" such as deadlines, timetables and defined standards.[41] He gives the example of how the 1979 Bern Convention[42] "gradually developed, evolved and transmogrified" into the nature conservation directives.[43]

Another salient example is the comparison of key provisions between the 1971 Ramsar Convention on Wetlands[44] and the provisions of the Habitats Directive.[45] Article 4.2 of the Ramsar Convention states: "[w]here a Contracting Party in its urgent national interest, deletes or restricts the boundaries of a wetland included in the List, it should as far as possible compensate for any loss of wetland resources, and in particular it should create additional nature reserves for waterfowl and for the protection, either in the same area or elsewhere, of an adequate portion of the original habitat."

The Habitats Directive reflects these provisions, but elaborates on assessment and compensation procedures where a member state wishes to interfere with a protected site for reasons of overriding public importance.[46] These are far more detailed, both in terms of substance and procedure, than the broad obligation under the convention.

---

38 See Joe Newbigin, "UKELA at Parliamentary Committee to Discuss Mixed Agreements" (5 December 2017), *UKELA Brexit Task Force Blog* (blog), online: <www.ukela.org/blog/Brexit-Task-Force/UKELA-at-Parliamentary-Committee-to-discuss-Mixed-Agreements> (oral evidence before the Environmental Audit Committee inquiry into UK progress on reducing fluorinated greenhouse gases [F-gas] emissions, Hansard unavailable at the time of writing).

39 *Ibid.*

40 *Ibid.*

41 House of Lords, *supra* note 7 at 156.

42 *Convention on the Conservation of European Wildlife and Natural Habitats*, 19 September 1979, 1284 UNTS 209 (entered into force 1 June 1982).

43 EC, *Council Directive 92/43/EEC of 21 May 1992 on the conservation of natural habitats and of wild fauna and flora*, [1992] OJ, L 206 [*Habitats Directive*]; EC, *Directive 2009/147/EC of the European Parliament and of the Council of 30 November 2009 on the conservation of wild birds*, [2009] OJ, L 20. The Habitats Directive was agreed some 13 years after the Bern Convention, but "takes it a step further, particularly by protecting certain types of habitats (often referred to in scientific terms as biotopes) for their own sake rather than because they harbor valued species." See Institute of European Environmental Policy, *Manual of European Environmental Policy* (Abingdon, UK: Routledge, 2011) at 725.

44 *Ramsar Convention*, *supra* note 19. The EU was not a party to the convention.

45 *Habitats Directive*, *supra* note 43.

46 *Ibid*, article 6(4); this is domestically implemented by Habitats Regulation Assessment requirements of *The Conservation of Habitats and Species Regulations 2010*, SI 2010/490.

The UK government intends that the existing provisions of EU law will be "rolled over" after Brexit in the interests of regulatory stability: "in order to achieve a stable and smooth transition, the Government's overall approach is to convert the body of existing EU law into domestic law, after which Parliament (and where appropriate, the devolved legislatures) will be able to decide which elements of that law to keep, amend or repeal once we have left the EU."[47] EU environmental law, such as the Habitats Directive, which has elaborated and extended international environmental treaties, will therefore continue to have legal force within the national system in the immediate future after Brexit. But when an opportunity is taken for reconsidering the substance of national law, the UK government will be faced with significant choices in respect of its international legal obligations. Taking the example of the Ramsar Convention, the United Kingdom could implement the broadly drawn obligations under article 4.2 with more elaborate procedural provisions equivalent to those in the Habitats Directive, or it could introduce a new domestic regime with different hard edges, while still remaining compliant with international environmental law.

In this context, it should be noted that the impact of the European Union is not only through the black letter of EU environmental legislation. The European Commission has published detailed guidance documents in a number of areas, such as habitat protection,[48] transfrontier shipment of waste[49] and environmental assessment,[50] designed to assist the interpretation and application of the legislation in question by member states. In respect of international environmental law, the United Kingdom will be reliant on guidance produced by secretariats or their equivalents to international conventions where, compared to the European Commission, practice as to the depth of guidance varies considerably.[51]

In the early days of EU environmental legislation, many countries (including Germany and the United Kingdom) transposed their EU obligations under environmental directives into their national system by means of government circular or similar administrative methods.[52] The terms of directives appear to give this option in that they typically require member states to bring into force "the laws, regulations and administrative provisions" necessary to comply with the obligations under the directive in question. But in a series of well-known cases in the 1980s and 1990s, the CJEU held that that transposition must be in the form of binding legislative or regulatory provision "in order to secure full implementation of directives in law and not only in

---

47 Department for Exiting the European Union, *Legislating for the United Kingdom's withdrawal from the European Union*, Cm 9446 (London, UK: Williams Lea Group, 2017) at 1.12.

48 European Commission, *Interpretation Manual of European Habitats – EUR 28* (Brussels, Belgium: 2013).

49 See European Commission, "Waste shipments: Correspondents' Guidelines and other guidance documents", online: <http://ec.europa.eu/environment/waste/shipments/guidance.htm>.

50 More than 15 guidance documents on environmental assessment have been published by the Commission. See European Commission, "Environmental Impact Assessment", online: <http://ec.europa.eu/environment/eia/eia-support.htm>.

51 For instance, the Council of Europe guidance on the Bern Convention on the Conservation of European Wildlife and Natural Habitats is far less detailed than the European Commission guidance on the Habitats Directive: <www.coe. int/en/web/bern-convention/monitoring>. In contrast, in respect of the 1991 Espoo Convention on Environmental Impact Assessment in a Transboundary Context, the United Nations Economic Commission for Europe (UNECE) has published fairly detailed guidance documents, agreed by the parties, on its implementation. See e.g. UNECE, *Good Practice Recommendations on Public Participation in Strategic Environmental Assessment* (Geneva, Switzerland: United Nations, 2016).

52 Ken Collins & David Earnshaw, "The Implementation and Enforcement of European Community Environmental Legislation" in David Judge, ed, *A Green Dimension for the European Community: Political Issues and Processes* (Abingdon, UK: Routledge, 1993) at 219–220; EC, *Eighth annual report to the European Parliament on Commission monitoring of the application of Community law*, [1990] OJ, 388, at 210, 215.

fact."[53] The underlying argument of the CJEU was that individuals and businesses needed legal certainty as to their rights and obligations under EU law.

When it comes to the domestic implementation of international conventions, no equivalent jurisprudence has been developed at the international level. Only where EU legislation has implemented an international environmental convention will the requirements for transposition into national law come into play. After Brexit, the UK government will have a free hand and could revert to far more informal means of implementing international obligations, such as circulars or policy statements. Examples can already be found in respect of conventions the United Kingdom has ratified without the participation of the European Union, where international obligations are currently implemented by administrative means rather than as legislative obligations. For instance, in respect of the Ramsar Convention, which was not ratified by the European Union, paragraph 118 of the National Planning Policy Framework[54] states that protection for wetland sites designated or proposed under the convention "should be given the same protection as European sites." These non-legislative means of implementation can easily be changed without parliamentary scrutiny, and if they become more common practice post-Brexit, could seriously weaken the effective implementation of international obligations within the domestic context.

An example of the sorts of legal uncertainties and difficulties that may arise can be found in a recent planning inspectorate appeal decision concerning a water abstraction licence, which potentially affected a site that was protected under both the Ramsar Convention and the Habitats Directive.[55] In respect to the Ramsar Convention, the inspector noted that the National Planning Policy Guidance applied only to planning decisions, and that previous guidance applying Ramsar protection to non-planning decisions had been withdrawn. The change was probably unintentional, and resulted from a policy of simplifying and reducing the amount of government planning guidance. The inspector concluded, "It has been Government's policy for many years that Ramsar sites should be afforded the [same] amount of protection as European sites and it seems to me there is nothing to indicate that the Government intends to change the position in relation to Ramsar sites affected by non-planning decisions. Nevertheless, there remains some uncertainty about the issue."[56]

In that case, the Habitats Directive and implementing regulations also applied and provided the necessary legal protection for the site in question. But it demonstrates the potential legal difficulties that can arise where reliance on solely administrative means of implementing legal obligations are employed. The UK government's post-Brexit policy on the domestic transposition of international environmental conventions has yet to be elaborated. EU requirements on transposition methods will no longer apply, but in the interests of legal clarity and certainty, legal rather than administrative means should be encouraged.

---

53 *Commission v Germany*, (1991) C-131/88, ECR I-825 at para 8. See also Ludwig Krämer, *EU Environmental Law*, 8th ed (London, UK: Sweet & Maxwell, 2015) at 12.03–12.07.

54 Department for Communities and Local Government, *National Planning Policy Framework* (London, UK: 2012).

55 Planning Inspectorate Appeal Decision, [2016] APP/WAT/15/316, online: <http://1exagu1grkmq3k572418odoooym-wpengine.netdna-ssl.com/wp-content/uploads/2016/09/GFQC-DM-DG-Inspectors-decision-Catfield.pdf>.

56 *Ibid* at para 131.

Emerging Issues with Enforcement Mechanisms

The enforcement mechanisms of the European Commission are a distinctive feature of the European legal landscape. Under article 17(1) of the Treaty on European Union, the Commission has a duty to ensure that EU law is applied, and possesses powers under article 258 of the TFEU to bring infringement proceedings against member states for failure to comply with their obligations under EU law. Infringement proceedings can relate both to the failure to faithfully transpose EU directives into national law, but also to the failure to apply EU law in practice. Infringement proceedings can eventually lead to action by the Commission before the CJEU, although, in practice, the majority are resolved without the need to do so. The CJEU has the power to impose financial penalties on member states that fail to comply with its judgments.[57]

These enforcement powers have applied to all sectors of EU law, but the environment field has consistently remained one of the areas in which the Commission has been especially active.[58] In relation to international environmental agreements, the Commission's practice is generally not to monitor the transposition and application by member states of international conventions that the European Union has ratified, whether on an exclusive or mixed-agreement basis. Only where an EU regulation or directive has implemented an international convention will the Commission use its enforcement powers against a member state in breach of its obligations to implement the EU law in question.

The view of the CJEU, however, is rather more expansive. It has held that mixed agreements concluded by the European Community, member states and non-member countries have the same status in the Community legal order as exclusive agreements concluded by the Community, so far as the provisions fall within Community competence,[59] and that as a result, member states have a duty to ensure compliance with those provisions.[60] In *Commission v France*,[61] the CJEU held that it followed from this case law that the Commission was entitled to bring infringement proceedings against a member state for failure to implement elements of a mixed agreement, the 1976 Convention for the Protection of the Mediterranean Sea Against Pollution,[62] even though there was as yet no Community legislation implementing those specific parts of the Convention:

> Since the Convention and the Protocol thus create rights and obligations in a field covered in large measure by Community legislation, there is a Community interest in compliance by both the Community and its Member States with the commitments

---

57   Since the Maastricht Treaty, the CJEU has had the power to impose a financial penalty on a member state that does not comply with its judgments, a power that was promoted by the British government at the time. For a more general exploration of this theme, see the report published by the UKELA, *Brexit and Environmental Law: Enforcement and Political Accountability Issues* (London, UK: UKELA, 2017) [UKELA, "*Enforcement*"].

58   At the end of 2016, there were 269 infringement cases open in the environment field, one less than the highest sector covering the internal market, entrepreneurship, and small and medium-sized enterprises. See EC, *Monitoring the application of European Union law: 2016 Annual Report*, (Brussels, Belgium: EC, 2017). See also Martin Hedemann-Robinson, *Enforcement of European Union Environmental Law* (Abingdon, UK: Routledge, 2007) part I; Pal Wenneras, *The Enforcement of EC Environmental Law* (Oxford, UK: Oxford University Press, 2007) c 6.

59   *Demirel v Stadt Schwäbisch Gmünd*, [1987] C-12/86, ECR 3719 at para 9.

60   *Commission v Ireland*, [2002] C-13/00, ECR I-2943 at para 14.

61   *Commission v France*, [2004] C-239/03, ECR I-9325.

62   *Convention for the Protection of the Mediterranean Sea Against Pollution*, 16 February 1976, 1102 UNTS NI-16908 (entered into force 12 February 1978).

entered into under those instruments. The fact that discharges of fresh water and alluvia into the marine environment, which are at issue in the present action, have not yet been the subject of Community legislation is not capable of calling that finding into question.[63]

This potential avenue for the supranational enforcement of international environmental conventions by the Commission will disappear after the United Kingdom withdraws from the European Union and any transition period expires. Modern international environmental agreements often contain fairly developed procedures for monitoring and reviewing non-implementation by parties, but ultimately, these supervision bodies generally rely upon the cooperation and acceptance of their findings by the parties involved.[64] While the CJEU possesses a general power to impose financial penalties on member states for non-compliance with its judgments,[65] there is little equivalent in relation to international environmental conventions. A small number do allow for penalties in the form of the suspension of rights (the Montreal Protocol[66] and the Convention on International Trade in Endangered Species of Wild Fauna and Flora [CITES][67] allow for trade restriction measures and suspension of specific rights and privileges, respectively), but this sort of provision is the exception.[68]

The 1993 North American Agreement on Environmental Cooperation provides a distinctive model.[69] The agreement contains obligations on the countries (Canada, Mexico and the United States) to effectively enforce their environmental laws and established a Commission for Environmental Cooperation that can hear citizen complaints.[70] It also provides for the establishment of an independent "arbitral panel" to investigate persistent patterns of failure to

---

63 *Ibid* at paras 29, 30. Krämer has argued that it follows that the Commission's general practice of not monitoring the implementation of international agreements in the absence of Community legislation is contrary to its general enforcement duties. See Krämer, *supra* note 53 at 13.21.

64 See e.g. the Aarhus Compliance Committee established under the 1998 Convention on Access to Information, Public Participation in Decision-Making and Access to Justice. The recent decision of the European Commission and Council to reject in whole or in part the Compliance Committee's findings in case ACCC/C/2008/32 that the European Union was in breach of Aarhus will be a significant test of the effectiveness of the compliance machinery. See *Draft Council Decision on the position to be adopted, on behalf of the European Union, at the sixth session of the Meeting of the Parties to the Aarhus Convention as regards compliance case ACCC/C/2008/32*, [2017] 11150/17, online: <data.consilium.europa.eu/doc/document/ST-11150-2017-INIT/en/pdf>; *Proposal for a Council Decision on the position to be adopted, on behalf of the European Union, at the sixth session of the Meeting of the Parties to the Aarhus Convention regarding compliance case ACCC/C/2008/32*, [2017] 10791/17, online: <data.consilium.europa.eu/doc/document/ST-10791-2017-INIT/en/pdf>.

65 *TFEU, supra* note 9, art 260. In respect of EU environmental law, substantial penalties have been imposed on member states in about a dozen cases since 2000. See Krämer, *supra* note 53 at 12.29–12.30.

66 *Montreal Protocol on Substances that Deplete the Ozone Layer*, 16 September 1987, 1522 UNTS 3, 26 ILM 1550 (entered into force 1 January 1989) [*Montreal Protocol*].

67 *Convention on International Trade in Endangered Species of Wild Fauna and Flora*, 3 March 1973, 27 UST 1087 (entered into force 1 July 1975) [*CITES*].

68 CITES does not include specific enforcement provisions, sanctions or penalties. However, article XIII and guidelines adopted by the Conference of the Parties provide for escalation up to and including trade bans. Article 8 of the Montreal Protocol similarly provides for the development of a non-compliance procedure by the Meeting of the Parties. The procedure developed is based on a non-confrontational, conciliatory and cooperative mechanism designed to encourage and assist parties to achieve compliance. See Legal Response Initiative, "Sanctions and penalties in environmental treaties", (19 July 2010), online: <http://legalresponseinitiative.org/legaladvice/sanctions-and-penalties-in-environmental-treaties>.

69 *North American Agreement on Environmental Cooperation Between the Government of Canada, the Government of the United Mexican States and the Government of the United States of America*, 32 ILM 1480 (entered into force 1 January 1994) [*North American Agreement on Environmental Cooperation*]; this is a parallel environmental agreement to the *North American Free Trade Agreement Between the Government of Canada, the Government of Mexico and the Government of the United States*, 17 December 1992, Can TS 1994 No 2, 32 ILM 289, 605 (entered into force 1 January 1994).

70 *North American Agreement on Environmental Cooperation, supra* note 69, arts 5–6.

enforce national environmental law,[71] and can impose financial penalties of up to $20 million where the matter has not been satisfactorily resolved.[72] No such penalties have yet been imposed, and because of the political sensitivities involved, the provisions may be more symbolic than a reality.[73] It is doubtful whether the United Kingdom will press for similar external enforcement mechanisms in international environmental conventions generally.

These mechanisms concern the enforcement of international law by external bodies, and will continue post-Brexit in relation to those conventions that the United Kingdom has ratified. As to the national machinery for ensuring compliance, the Environment Agency and other national and local regulatory bodies continue their enforcement activities against private parties and industry, but the real question concerns the duties of government and other public bodies. This has been the focus of the enforcement activity concerns of the European Commission. The UK government has stated that judicial review is a sufficient mechanism to hold government and other public bodies to legal account,[74] but let alone the question of costs and the availability of non-governmental organizations and individuals to bring cases, it is doubtful whether judicial review by itself can replicate the supervisory enforcement role of the European Commission. It may be a valuable long-stop, but the procedures are ill-suited to resolving issues in the way that the Commission has been able to do without bringing formal infringement proceedings. Other jurisdictions have recognized the peculiar vulnerability of the environment by establishing an environmental ombudsman to monitor public bodies or, in the case of New Zealand, a commissioner for the environment to review the implementation of environmental law and policy by central and local government, and report to Parliament.[75] Brexit provides an opportunity to consider the establishment of some similar independent body,[76] and the remit of such a body could include the international environmental obligations of the United Kingdom and whether there are failings in compliance.[77]

---

71 *Ibid*, art 24.

72 *Ibid*, art 34, Annex 34. Note also that there is an unusual provision in Annex 36A, which allows the Commission to bring a panel determination and penalty before the Canadian courts as an enforceable order by the national courts. Although this has never been used to date, it is an interesting feature to consider for the future.

73 See e.g. Joseph A McKinney, *Created from NAFTA: The Structure, Function, and Significance of the Treaty's Related Institutions* (Armonk, NY: ME Sharpe, 2000) at 223.

74 Letter from Thérèse Coffey, MP, Parliamentary Under Secretary of State, Department for Environment, Food and Rural Affairs, to Lord Teverson, EU Energy and Environment Sub-Committee (16 April 2017) at 4, online: <www.parliament.uk/documents/lords-committees/eu-energy-environment-subcommittee/Brexit-environment-climate-change/Gov-response-Brexit-env-climate.pdf>. In her letter, Coffey states, "The UK has always had a strong legal framework for environmental protection, and will continue to have a system of judicial review by UK judges after EU Exit. The judicial review mechanism enables any interested party to challenge the decisions of the Government of the day by taking action through the domestic courts."

75 UKELA, *"Enforcement"*, *supra* note 57 at paras 20–23.

76 See e.g. Robert G Lee, "Always Keep a Hold of Nurse: British Environmental Law and Exit from the European Union" (2017) 29:1 J Envtl L at 155–164; Maria Lee, "Brexit: environmental accountability and EU governance" (17 October 2016), *OUPblog* (blog), online, <https://blog.oup.com/2016/10/brexit-environment-eu-governance/>. This option appears to be gaining traction. See Environmental Audit Committee, *Oral Evidence: The Government's Environmental Policy, HC 544*, (1 November 2017), online: <http://data.parliament.uk/writtenevidence/committeeevidence.svc/evidencedocument/environmental-audit-committee/the-governments-environmental-policy/oral/72503.html>. Michael Gove, MP, Secretary of State, Department for Environment, Food and Rural Affairs, stated, "It is right we should take some time to reflect on what other countries provide for the appropriate level of protection to the environment and what the right balance is between ensuring people continue to have recourse to the courts through judicial review, continuing to ensure that bodies like this Select Committee can play a role, but also recognising that you may well need an agency, a body, a commission that has the power potentially to fine or otherwise hold Government to account and certainly to hold public bodies other than Government to account."

77 See UKELA, *"Enforcement"*, *supra* note 57, appendix 1 for examples of similar functions performed by environmental courts and tribunals in other jurisdictions.

Within the national court system, the dualist approach to international law is likely to continue. Provisions of international agreements that have not been implemented by domestic legislation are effectively non-justiciable and cannot be given direct legal effect, as doing so would create rights and obligations that Parliament has not conferred. In *R (SG) v Secretary of State for Work and Pensions*,[78] Lord Kerr doubted whether this doctrine should continue to apply in an action against a government that had ratified a convention relating to human rights but not transposed its provisions into national law.[79] But this was a dissenting opinion not followed by the majority, and the constitutional orthodoxy of the status of international law within the national system was reaffirmed in *R (Miller) v Secretary of State for Exiting the European Union*.[80]

Conclusion

Nevertheless, it is clear that international environmental law can have an influence within the domestic legal system in less direct ways, in particular in the interpretation of national legislation and the development of the common law.[81] Post-Brexit, international environmental law will undoubtedly assume greater national legal and policy significance as being the only source of supranational legal obligations on the United Kingdom. But how its legal impact will be felt in the future — and the extent to which this will differ from current practice — remains to be seen.

---

78 *R (SG) v Secretary of State for Work and Pensions*, [2015] UKSC 16, [2015] 1 WLR 1449.

79 *Ibid* at para 255. Lord Kerr stated, "the justification for refusing to recognise the rights enshrined in an international convention relating to human rights and to which the UK has subscribed as directly enforceable in domestic law is not easy to find. Why should a convention which expresses the UK's commitment to the protection of a particular human right for its citizens not be given effect as an enforceable right in domestic law?"

80 *R (Miller) v Secretary of State for Exiting the European Union*, [2017] UKSC 5, [2017] 2 WLR 583 at paras 55–57.

81 See James Maurici, "International law in domestic practice: advice for practitioners on how international and comparative law arises in domestic case law" (2016) 28 Envtl L & Mgmt 155.

14

Brexit, Brexatom, the Environment and Future International Relations

Stephen Tromans

Introduction

As in so many areas, in the field of environmental protection, views differ strongly as to the benefits of EU membership. EU membership could be seen as the European Commission and the Court of Justice of the European Union (CJEU) sticking their noses into matters of policy and practice that are the business of the United Kingdom. There could be allegations of hypocrisy in other EU states, castigating the United Kingdom as "the dirty man of Europe," while they pursue their own environmentally detrimental activities. EU environmental legislation could be portrayed as overly complex, bureaucratic and impractical, and the CJEU as handing down impenetrable judgments divorced from reality. On the other hand, it could be argued that the European Union has forced or cajoled the United Kingdom into dealing with some serious environmental problems that might otherwise have gone unaddressed, that EU law remains a vital tool and source of protection for citizens affected by environmental issues, and that the United Kingdom has benefited from some far-sighted legislative initiatives promoted by the European Union over the last 40 years.

What is clear is that the environment played a very minor role in the debates that preceded the referendum.[1] Leave campaigners did not formulate a serious attack on EU environmental law, although MP George Eustice reportedly described EU environmental directives as "spirit-crushing"[2] and as "a straitjacket that stifles innovation in environmental management."[3] As well, MP Boris Johnson is reported to have said that "[t]he more the EU does, the less room there is for national decision-making. Sometimes these EU rules sound simply ludicrous, like the rule that you can't recycle a teabag, or that children under eight cannot blow up balloons, or the limits on the power of vacuum cleaners."[4]

Regrettably, the key politicians on the Remain side failed to present the case as to the environmental benefits of EU membership. It was left to environmental groups such as Friends of the Earth,[5] the World Wide Fund for Nature (WWF)[6] and the Green Alliance[7] to make that case, which they did strongly. The narrow majority in favour of the Leave outcome has set the United Kingdom on a course that represents an unprecedented experiment in environmental law. What will be the outcome of releasing the UK government — or, more accurately, the governments of England, Northern Ireland, Scotland and Wales (environment being largely a devolved issue) — from the controlling influence of EU law, after a period of 40 years during which EU law has decisively shaped UK policy and law on the environment?

This chapter will, first, consider the impact of EU law on UK environmental law and policy. It will then look at the possible implications of the United Kingdom's exit from the European Union, and what this means for the environment. It will also consider the question of future relations between the United Kingdom, the European Union and the wider international community, in terms of any limits on the United Kingdom's autonomy to set its own environmental standards. It should be clear at the outset that this chapter is not intended as a detailed treatise on environmental law: much of the content will be quite familiar to environmental lawyers. Rather, it is intended to allow a reader with no particular knowledge of UK or EU environmental law to gain an understanding of the broad legal issues. There is still relatively little published in mainstream journals on the issue of Brexit and environmental law,[8] and it is therefore necessary, and indeed useful, to refer to other sources. In particular, there is a growing body of material

1   Loughborough University's Centre for Research in Communication and Culture analyzed all TV and news coverage of the referendum campaign and found the environment to be an issue that "barely registered." See Loughborough University, "Media coverage of the EU Referendum (report 1)" (23 May 2016), *Centre for Research in Communication and Culture* (blog), online: <http://blog.lboro.ac.uk/crcc/eu-referendum/media-coverage-eu-referendum-report-1/>.

2   "EU Referendum: The environmental arguments FOR and AGAINST Brexit", online: <www.edie.net/news/11/EU-Referendum--The-environmental-arguments-FOR-and-AGAINST-Brexit-/>.

3   Fiona Harvey, "MPs warn vote to leave EU would threaten UK environmental policy", *The Guardian* (19 April 2016), online: <www.theguardian.com/environment/2016/apr/19/vote-leave-eu-threaten-uk-environmental-policy-common-select-committee>.

4   Boris Johnson, "Boris Johnson exclusive: There is only one way to get the change we want — vote to leave the EU", *The Telegraph* (16 March 2016), online: <www.telegraph.co.uk/opinion/2016/03/16/boris-johnson-exclusive-there-is-only-one-way-to-get-the-change/>.

5   Charlotte Burns, "The EU Referendum and the Environment" (July 2015), online: Friends of the Earth <https://cdn.foe.co.uk/sites/default/files/downloads/eu-referendum-environment-81600.pdf>.

6   WWF, "EU Referendum: Think Environment", online: <http://assets.wwf.org.uk/custom/stories/euthinkenvironment/>.

7   Green Alliance, "The environmental case for staying in the EU", online: Inside Track <www.green-alliance.org.uk/resources/Inside_Track_36.pdf>.

8   For an exception, see Robert G Lee, "Always Keep a Hold of Nurse: British Environmental Law and Exit from the EU" (2017) 29:1 J Envtl L 155.

from parliamentary committees, and the UK Environmental Law Association (UKELA) is a very helpful resource, with a series of discussion papers on relevant topics.[9]

It was a trite observation from the early days following the referendum that "Brexit means Brexit." However, what was not clear at the time of the referendum — and indeed not until much later — was that Brexit also means leaving membership in the European Atomic Energy Community (Euratom), a separate legal entity, which, however, shares institutional features with the European Union. The implications of cessation of membership in Euratom were simply never explained or discussed, and arguably are still far from fully understood. The chapter will conclude with a discussion on this issue.

The Impact of EU Environmental Law in the United Kingdom

To fully understand the impact of EU environmental law in the United Kingdom, it is necessary to go back in time to the 1970s. The United Kingdom confirmed its membership in the common market in the 1975 referendum, but the role and implications of European Community (EC) law were far from understood. As a law student at the University of Cambridge in 1977, the author evinced interest in taking the short optional course that had recently become available on EC law, but was discouraged by being told that it was "all to do with regulating the size of beetroots." That was somewhat ironic, given the amount of time spent during the author's professional career as an environmental lawyer in advising on and arguing about EU law. However, the advice was understandable because, in the 1970s, EC environmental law was in its infancy, and, at times, it was a pretty sickly and unpromising infancy at that. As the Institute for European Environmental Policy (IEEP) has pointed out, the EC had, for many years, no environmental policy at all, and it was only in 1973 that the EC issued its first environmental action program and began to formulate the first environmental directives. The EC lacked a clear and unequivocal treaty base for such legislation, leading to criticism from states such as Germany and the United Kingdom.[10]

Since then, EU environmental law has burgeoned and has had a profound influence on UK law. A useful short summary of the development of EU environmental law and its impact is provided by the House of Lords European Union Committee in its February 2017 report, "Brexit: environment and climate change."[11] In evidence to that committee, the Department for Environment, Food and Rural Affairs indicated that more than 1,100 "core pieces of directly applicable EU legislation and national implementing legislation" had been identified as relating to policy areas falling within the remit of the department. That left aside legislation in areas such

---

9   UKELA, "UKELA's Work on Brexit", online: <www.ukela.org/brexitactivity>.

10 See AM Farmer, *Manual of European Environmental Policy: Environment in the Treaties* (London, UK: Routledge, 2012), online: <https://ieep.eu/uploads/articles/attachments/74389e41-868c-4906-9bdc-3f04addd0bf0/1.5_Environment_in_the_treaties_-_final.pdf?v=63664509873>.

11 UK, HL, European Union Committee, *Brexit: environment and climate change* (HL Paper 109) (London, UK: House of Lords, 2017) [HL Paper 109].

as energy falling within the ownership of other departments. It is hard, if not impossible,[12] to find examples of UK environmental legislation that do not have some EU connection.

It is obviously impossible within the constraints of this chapter to examine every aspect of environmental law that has been affected by the development of EU law over the period in question. Rather, the chapter proposes to deal with a number of selected areas to illustrate the point that the influence has been substantial and widespread. The chapter will focus on a limited number of areas that have been selected to provide an overall perspective on the different areas of EU law that have shaped the law on environmental protection in the United Kingdom, and that will provide the context for the discussion that follows on the implications of the United Kingdom's exit from the European Union. The chapter will provide, first, a quick overview of each of these areas, followed by a more detailed discussion.

- **Environmental Impact Assessment:** Environmental impact assessment (EIA) legislation is an example of overarching legislation that cuts across many areas of environmental protection and provides a framework to ensure that the environmental effects of projects are understood, that the public and relevant regulatory authorities have an opportunity to comment on those effects and that the resulting environmental information is taken into account in deciding whether to permit the project, and what mitigating measures are required.

- **Ambient Environmental Standards:** The European Union has, over the years, enacted important minimum standards to protect the environment and the public. Examples include drinking water quality, the quality of water suitable for freshwater fish and shellfish, the quality of bathing waters, and air quality in respect of pollutants such as nitrogen dioxide and particulate matter. This chapter will focus on the areas of bathing water quality and urban air quality for more detailed examination.

- **Emissions Standards:** Much of the legislation of the European Union is concerned with standards for emissions, whether from stationary installations, equipment or vehicles. In the case of equipment and vehicles, such standards obviously have important implications for trade and the free movement of goods. In the case of fixed plants, in some areas, the existence of such standards has produced significant shifts in UK practice, requiring massive investment or the closure of certain types of installation. The chapter will focus on two examples: the urban waste water treatment directive (waste water directive),[13] which has led to huge improvements in the treatment of waste water, and what is now the industrial emissions directive,[14] which has led to the virtual cessation of electricity generation by coal-fired power stations.

---

12 The prime example is probably the legislation dealing with contaminated land, in part IIA of the *Environmental Protection Act 1990* (UK), c 43, on which there is no specific EU law. However, even there the EU directive on environmental liability has some bearing in that its ambit includes damage to soil, at least where this presents a risk to human health. EC, *Directive 2004/35/EC of the European Parliament and of the Council of 21 April 2004 on environmental liability with regard to the prevention and remedying of environmental damage*, [2004] OJ, L 143/56. See Ugo Salanitro, "Directive 2004/35/EC on Environmental Liability" (Catania, Italy: European Union Action to Fight Environmental Crime, 2015), online: <www.ecologic.eu/sites/files/news/2015/efface_directive_2004_35_ec_on_environmental_liability.pdf>.

13 UK, Department for Environment, Food and Rural Affairs, *Waste Water Treatment in the UK — 2012: Implementation of the EU Urban Waste Water Treatment Directive* (London, UK: 2012) [*Waste Water Directive*], online: <www.gov.uk/government/uploads/system/uploads/attachment_data/file/69592/pb13811-waste-water-2012.pdf>.

14 EC, *Directive 2010/75/EU of the European Parliament and of the Council of 24 November 2010 on industrial emissions (integrated pollution prevention and control)*, [2010] OJ, L 334/17 [*Industrial Emissions Directive*].

- **Waste:** Waste management was an early focus of EU environmental law, with the waste framework directive,[15] followed by directives dealing with specific types of waste management, such as landfill and incineration, seeking to raise standards. A further development has been what is now called "the circular economy," encouraging waste minimization, reuse, recycling and resource recovery.[16] All of these have played an important part in shaping UK law and practice. Particularly striking examples are the landfill directive[17] and directives imposing producer responsibility for waste materials such as packaging, electrical and electronic equipment, and batteries.

- **Protection of Wildlife and its Habitats:** The approach of the European Union is to regard its wildlife and important areas of natural habitat as a common resource to be strictly protected from disturbance, damage and deterioration. The habitats directive[18] imposes stringent obligations and restrictions on activities, including projects, that may adversely affect such areas. As such, it has proven controversial throughout Europe,[19] the United Kingdom being no exception.

- **Renewable Energy:** EU energy policy and law is, of course, a vast and complex area in its own right and well beyond the modest scope of this chapter. However, it needs to be observed that legislation regarding renewable energy has had some impact on law in the United Kingdom, although the majority of the United Kingdom's energy policy and regulation remains determined at the domestic level.[20]

EIA

In assessing the impact of EU law on the United Kingdom, it is perhaps apt to start with the subject of EIA. This is so for a number of reasons. EIA has been one of the cornerstones of EU law[21] on the protection of the environment since the 1980s, and it encapsulates much of the EU philosophy and many of the principles on the environment, such as the principle of prevention. It has undoubtedly generated more case law in the UK courts than any other piece of EU environmental legislation, and continues to do so. It is probably the most potent legal weapon available to citizens concerned about the environmental implications of new projects, and its progeny, strategic environmental assessment, is becoming a worthy successor in that regard, when applied at the earlier stage of plans and programs.[22] EIA is much more powerful than the

---

15   EC, *Directive 2008/98/EC of the European Parliament and of the Council of 19 November 2008 on waste and repealing certain Directives*, [2008] OJ, L 312/3.

16   EC, "Closing the loop — An EU action plan for the Circular Economy", COM(2015) 614 final, online: <http://eur-lex. europa.eu/legal-content/EN/TXT/?uri=CELEX:52015DC0614>.

17   EC, *Council Directive 1999/31/EC of 26 April 1999 on the landfill of waste*, [1999] OJ, L 182/1 [*Landfill Directive*].

18   EC, *Council Directive 92/43/EEC of 21 May 1992 on the conservation of natural habitats and of wild fauna and flora*, [1992] OJ, L 206/7 [*Habitats Directive*].

19   See e.g. Mw M van Keulen, *The Habitats Directive: A Case of Contested Europeanization* (The Hague: WRR Scientific Council for Government Policy, 2007), online: <www.oapen.org/download?type=document&docid=439862>, referring to the perception in the Netherlands by some stakeholders of the directive as "undesired EU involvement into matters considered primarily a national or local competence" and its contribution to the "ridiculisation" of the European Union and its policies.

20   Gareth Baker & Gus Wood, "State of the Nation: The UK Renewables Sector" (2016) 6 Intl Energy L Rev 235.

21   Described as such by WR Sheate, "Amending the EC Directive on Environmental Impact Assessment" (1995) 4:3 Eur Energy & Envtl L Rev 77, online: <www.kluwerlawonline.com/abstract.php?area=Journals&id=EELR1995018>.

22   Gregory Jones & Eloise Scotford, eds, *The Strategic Environmental Assessment Directive: A Plan for Success?* (London, UK: Hart, 2017). See especially the discussion by Elizabeth Fisher in chapter 8 on strategic environmental assessment as "hot" law in terms of its structure and implications.

Aarhus Convention[23] on public participation, for the simple reason that it creates rights and duties that are directly enforceable in the UK courts in a way that the Aarhus Convention does not.

In the 1980s, when the European Commission was contemplating the introduction of EIA legislation, the United States was the world leader in the field. The United Kingdom had no legislation on EIA, and such rare and sporadic EIA as took place was done as a matter of practice. Despite this, the United Kingdom resisted the proposals on the baseless assertion that it would add little to UK practice, but the government did not wish to add procedural or legislative burdens to hard-pressed local authorities.[24] This was entirely wrong: while EIA applies only to a relatively small proportion of development projects, where it does apply, it has imposed a rigour in procedure on both promoters of development and authorities determining applications for development that would otherwise have been lacking. Indeed, it is strongly arguable that the process has become somewhat "gold-plated" and over-inflated in the United Kingdom, with environmental statements in some cases running to many thousands of pages.[25] Also, the law in the United Kingdom has become ludicrously complex. This is due to two factors. First, the EIA directive[26] has been back-fitted into pre-existing legislation, so that numerous consenting regimes each have their own set of regulations. Second, as a result of constitutional reform and devolution, England, Northern Ireland, Scotland and Wales each have their own separate EIA legislation, now with subtle — and in some cases substantial — divergences. The process of development of EIA law continues and, at the time of writing, the United Kingdom is in the course of transposing a further amendment of the directive, which will have significant implications for how EIA is undertaken.

Another important point is that the EIA regime has become one of the best illustrations in the environmental sphere of how the UK courts have embraced EU law as an integral part of the process of interpreting and applying the UK law that transposes it. A seminal early case was the decision of the House of Lords in *R v North Yorkshire County Council, ex p Brown*,[27] a case in which the relevant domestic law had failed to transpose adequately the requirements of the EIA directive to the procedures for updating the conditions attached to old mining permissions. The court had to determine whether the relevant UK procedures should be categorized as a "development consent" in the language of the directive and, hence, subject to EIA procedures. Lord Hoffmann, with whom the other members of the House of Lords agreed, emphasized that development consent was a concept of European law, and that to ascertain its meaning, it was necessary to "examine the language and in particular the purpose of the Directive."[28] Such examination involved consideration of, and deferral to, the seminal decisions of the CJEU, and

---

23 *Convention on Access to Information, Public Participation in Decision-Making and Access to Justice in Environmental Matters*, 28 June 1998, 2161 UNTS 447, 38 ILM 517 (entered into force 30 October 2001) [*Aarhus Convention*].

24 Stephen Tromans, *Environmental Impact Assessment*, 2nd ed (London, UK: Bloomsbury Professional, 2012) at paras 2.19–2.20.

25 Institute of Environmental Management and Assessment, "Environmental Statements — unfriendly giants" (2012), online: <http://transform.iema.net/article/environmental-statements-%E2%80%93-unfriendly-giants>.

26 The original directive was EC, *Council Directive 85/337/EEC of 27 June 1985 on the assessment of the effects of certain public and private projects on the environment*, [1985] OJ, L 175/40 (no longer in force). This has been replaced by EC, *Council Directive 2014/52/EU of the European Parliament and of the Council of 16 April 2014 amending Directive 2011/92/EU on the assessment of the effects of certain public and private projects on the environment*, [2014] OJ, L 124 at 1–18.

27 *R v North Yorkshire County Council, ex p Brown*, [2000] 1 AC 397.

28 *Ibid* at 401D.

EIA is almost certainly the leading area in environmental law in which CJEU decisions have influenced the UK courts.[29]

This raises the important general question of the continued status of current and future CJEU case law within the UK court system. Another facet of the EIA regime is the impact of EU law on the approach of the UK courts to remedies. EIA law is essentially procedural in nature — that is to say, it mandates a procedure, but not a specific outcome. Despite this, it has become a fertile basis for challenges — not always meritorious and not always successful — to decisions of local or central governments to grant planning permission for environmentally controversial schemes, such as wind farms and waste facilities. In some cases, the courts have reacted against this by stressing that litigants should not adopt an unduly legalistic approach to the requirements of the directive and domestic regulations, which should be interpreted in a "common sense way."[30]

The House of Lords established in *Berkeley v Secretary of State for the Environment*[31] that the normal discretion of the courts as to the granting or withholding of remedies in public law cases is severely curtailed by the obligation of the courts to provide cooperation in ensuring the fulfilment of the purposes of EU law. Subsequent decisions of the courts have in some cases queried this and have suggested a less absolutist and more characteristically UK pragmatic approach.[32] Once the Leave process is complete, and the courts are no longer bound by that ongoing obligation, it will be interesting to see how the important area of remedies develops, as discussed below.

Ambient Environmental Standards

It is not an unfair observation that before the United Kingdom's accession to the European Commission, the state of the United Kingdom's environment left much to be desired. During the 1970s and 1980s, the Royal Commission on Environmental Pollution, in a series of hard-hitting reports, was critical of the degraded and polluted condition of much of Britain's seas, coastline, waterways and air.[33] Serious water pollution had occurred from both industrial and domestic sewage; industrial and other emissions badly affected the air quality both of the United Kingdom and parts of the European continent. The quality of regulation, and indeed of public transparency as to the state of the environment and the polluting inputs to it, was poor. As one commentator put it, the closeness of the relationship between regulators and industry in many cases led to a "voluntaristic" approach: "policies were...implemented but targets were pitiably low, or where targets were breached legal action was rare."[34]

Beaches used for bathing and recreation were an example of such problems. Sewage was discharged, essentially untreated, through short sea outfalls or, in some cases, directly across the beach in the case of storm overflow sewers. The results were both aesthetically disgusting

---

29 Paul Stookes, "Environmental Judicial Review", online: <www.publiclawproject.org.uk/data/resources/151/Stookes_P_Env_JR_14_10_13.pdf>.

30 See e.g. *R (Blewett) v Derbyshire County Council*, [2003] EWHC 2775 (Admin).

31 *Berkeley v Secretary of State for the Environment*, [2001] 2 AC 603 at 608.

32 See e.g. *Walton v Scottish Ministers*, [2013] PTSR 51.

33 See, in particular, UK, Royal Commission on Environmental Pollution, *Tackling Pollution — Experience and Prospects*, Cmnd 9149 (London, UK: Her Majesty's Stationery Office, 1984), which drew together much of its previous 12 years' work.

34 Burns, *supra* note 5.

and hazardous to public health, as photographs shown in the Royal Commission's report demonstrate.[35] Numerous popular British beaches spectacularly failed to meet EC standards for maximum fecal coliforms in bathing water. The United Kingdom took an obstinately resistant approach to these requirements, to the extraordinary extent of seeking to argue before the CJEU that the archetypal pleasure resort of Blackpool need not be regarded as bathing waters.[36] However, the United Kingdom has gradually made efforts to come into compliance through enhanced sewage treatment and the provision of long sea outfalls, and its beaches and their users have benefited correspondingly.[37]

Air quality is another intractable area, and one where the United Kingdom remains in breach of what EU law requires (in fairness, so do many other member states).[38] Well before its membership in the European Union, the United Kingdom had taken steps to improve the most egregious impacts of coal burning in its cities, through the clean air acts,[39] prompted by the notorious London smog, such as in 1952. However, other problems — most notably the effects of emissions from vehicles in cities — have come to dominate the air quality agenda. Progress in compliance with EU legislation on ambient air quality has undoubtedly been made, but many urban areas remain in breach of requirements on nitrogen dioxide, a pollutant whose serious health impacts are gradually being understood. A series of cases brought against the UK government by the environmental non-governmental organization (NGO) ClientEarth have illustrated the inadequacy and unlawfulness of the government's plans to bring the situation into compliance.[40] Without that impetus, the government seems unlikely to display the requisite degree of urgency, no doubt because measures to restrict, or charge for, car use in cities would be unpopular with parts of the electorate, and, indeed, at the time of writing, further proceedings by ClientEarth are being threatened. In addition, an important and unresolved question is how far such non-compliance could affect approval of major infrastructure projects that impact air quality: the key current example is expansion at Heathrow Airport, where an application for expansion will almost certainly be met by an air quality challenge.[41] In fact, a fresh consultation has been opened regarding the draft national policy statement on airports, in light of new evidence on air quality and noise at Heathrow.[42] The updated work on air quality now suggests that while an expansion at Gatwick Airport by a second runway would present a low risk of

---

35   UK, Royal Commission on Environmental Pollution, *supra* note 33 at 133 ("Pellet of fat and faecal matter washed up on a Merseyside Beach").

36   *Commission of the European Communities v United Kingdom of Great Britain and Northern Ireland*, C-56/90, [1993] ECR I-04109.

37   To the extent that Blackpool was, in 2016, awarded a Blue Flag in recognition of its bathing water quality. See the report and photographs at Greenpeace UK, "Shifting sands: How EU membership helped transform Blackpool beach", online: Medium <https://medium.com/@GreenpeaceUK/shifting-sands-how-eu-membership-helped-transform-blackpool-beach-fa718f84d9d1>.

38   For a discussion of litigation in Germany raising issues very similar to those in the United Kingdom on compliance with limit values, see C Douhaire & R Klinger, "The breach of limit values under the Ambient Air Quality Directive: what is 'as short as possible'" (2016) 2 Envtl Liability 52.

39   *Clean Air Act, 1956* (UK), 4 & 5 Eliz II, c 52; *Clean Air Act 1968* (UK), c 62.

40   See e.g. *R (ClientEarth) v Secretary of State for the Environment, Food and Rural Affairs*, [2015] UKSC 28 [*ClientEarth 2015*]; *R (ClientEarth) v Secretary of State for the Environment, Food and Rural Affairs, (No 2)* [2016] EWHC 2740.

41   See e.g. the work of the Aviation Environment Federation, "Air Pollution", online: <www.aef.org.uk/issues/air-pollution/>.

42   Mattha Busby, "Heathrow third runway consultation reopened after new evidence", *The Guardian* (25 October 2017), online: <www.theguardian.com/environment/2017/oct/25/heathrow-third-runway-consultation-reopened-following-new-evidence>. See the consultation paper at UK, Department for Transport, "Open consultation: Heathrow expansion: revised draft Airports National Policy Statement", online: <www.gov.uk/government/consultations/heathrow-expansion-revised-draft-airports-national-policy-statement>.

impacting compliance with EU limit values, the proposed new runway at Heathrow presents a risk of delaying compliance.[43]

Emissions Standards

A significant body of EU law is concerned with the regulation of emissions from industrial and other installations, originally through directives dealing with specific issues such as large combustion plants and waste incinerators, and, subsequently, through the directive on integrated pollution prevention and control (IPPC directive),[44] now consolidated in the industrial emissions directive.[45] These operate in part by imposing quantitative limits on emissions of specified pollutants, such as sulphur dioxide or dioxins, and by requiring the application of best available techniques (whether by using particular abatement equipment or by modifying processes) to prevent or minimize pollution. Interestingly, this is an area where the United Kingdom led the way and where the European Union enthusiastically adopted the United Kingdom's approach.

During the 1980s, there was increasing awareness in the United Kingdom of the need to take an integrated approach to the control of pollution: a major industrial facility might be controlled by different regulators in respect of its emissions of gaseous waste to air, liquid effluent to water and solid waste to land. Decisions made in isolation on any of these could lead to adverse unintended consequences for other environmental media. Hence, the Royal Commission promoted the creation of an integrated system of pollution control,[46] which ultimately became embodied in part I of the Environmental Protection Act 1990.[47] The European Commission largely lifted the concept into the IPPC directive in 1996. However, the Commission has taken it to a new level with the creation of a sophisticated bureaucracy in which a European bureau based in Seville produces what are known as best available techniques reference documents (BREFs)for the various regulated industry sectors. It is relevant to consider, as this chapter will below, the implications of the United Kingdom no longer being involved in the Seville process of BREFs.

The practical implications of this body of law have been significant for many sectors of UK industry, but have nowhere been more profound than for the power generation sector. At the time of privatization of the Central Electricity Generating Board in 1989, huge coal-fired power stations (largely located in the major coal mining areas of the North Midlands and Yorkshire) formed the backbone of the United Kingdom's power generation capacity. The increasingly stringent requirements of EU law on emissions have meant that decisions have been taken to close these installations, engendering a long-term shift from coal to other sources of fuel, or to

---

43 UK, Department for Transport, "2017 Plan Update to Air Quality Re-Analysis", online: <www.gov.uk/government/uploads/system/uploads/attachment_data/file/653775/2017-plan-update-to-air-quality-re-analysis.pdf>.

44 EC, *Directive 2008/1/EC of the European Parliament and of the Council of 15 January 2008 concerning integrated pollution prevention and control (Codified version)*, [2008] OJ, L 24/8 (no longer in force).

45 *Industrial Emissions Directive, supra* note 14.

46 UK, Royal Commission on Environmental Pollution, "Air Pollution Control: An Integrated Approach", Cmnd 6371 (London, UK: Her Majesty's Stationery Office, 1976).

47 *Environmental Protection Act 1990* (UK), c 43. See Stephen Tromans, *The Environmental Protection Act 1990: Text and Commentary* (London, UK: Sweet & Maxwell, 1990).

renewables.[48] The first working day since the Industrial Revolution when coal-fired generation made a nil contribution to the national energy sources occurred in 2017,[49] a situation that would have been unthinkable in 1989.

Another area where EU law has had a major impact on utilities is that of the waste water directive.[50] In cities such as London, dependence has been placed on the well-engineered, but increasingly inadequate, network of sewers, pumping stations, treatment works and other infrastructure built by the Victorians. The waste water directive has required massive investment in more sophisticated forms of treatment and in increased capacity for sewers to contain their contents during episodes of heavy rain without discharging diluted raw sewage to rivers such as the Thames. The most striking example of improvement brought about by these requirements is the massive Thames Tideway project to intercept sewage outflows into the river, one of the largest and costliest engineering projects of the century so far.[51]

Waste

The United Kingdom's waste management practices have been heavily influenced by EU legislation. The United Kingdom had its own system for licensing the deposit of waste on land under the Control of Pollution Act 1974,[52] but licensing did little to raise standards significantly, as shown by the substantial number of closed landfills from that period and previously, which have presented serious problems in terms of generating hazardous landfill gas and polluting groundwater.[53] The European Union began by producing a framework directive on waste[54] (framework directive), addressing its disposal and recovery. The approach of the framework directive and the CJEU to defining waste by reference to the somewhat meaningless concept of "discard" has been a source of bemusement for UK judges and lawyers,[55] but it has meant that a wider approach to regulating materials has been taken than would have been the case without EU legislation.

It is probably in the field of the landfill of waste that EU law has had the greatest practical impact on UK waste management. Landfill was the United Kingdom's favoured method for disposal of both municipal and commercial waste for several reasons: the United Kingdom's geology in many areas was conducive to such disposal; mining and quarrying left many suitable voids to be

---

48 See the consultation paper, UK, Department for Business, Energy and Industrial Strategy, "Coal Generation in Great Britain: the pathway to a low-carbon future" (November 2016), online: <www.gov.uk/government/uploads/system/uploads/attachment_data/file/577080/With_SIG_Unabated_coal_closure_consultation_FINAL__v6.1_.pdf>. See also the summary of responses to the consultation, UK, Department for Business, Energy and Industrial Strategy, "Coal Generation in Great Britain: Summary of responses to consultation" (October 2017), online: <www.gov.uk/government/uploads/system/uploads/attachment_data/file/650476/unabated-coal-consultation-summary-of-responses.pdf>.

49 Georgia Brown, "British power generation achieves first ever coal-free day", *The Guardian* (22 April 2017), online: <www.theguardian.com/environment/2017/apr/21/britain-set-for-first-coal-free-day-since-the-industrial-revolution>.

50 *Waste Water Directive, supra* note 13.

51 Tideway, "The Tunnel", online: <www.tideway.london/the-tunnel/>.

52 *Control of Pollution Act 1974* (UK), c 40.

53 Stephen Tromans & Robert Turrall-Clarke, *Contaminated Land*, 2nd ed (London, UK: Sweet & Maxwell, 2007) at para 8.28. Many such landfills still provide a serious legacy problem, in particular for water quality: see Rachel Salvidge, "Landfill: What Lurks Beneath" (2016) 500 ENDS Rep 41.

54 EC, *Directive 2008/98/EC of the European Parliament and of the Council of 19 November 2008 on waste and repealing certain Directives*, [2008] OJ, L 312/3.

55 See e.g. *R (OSS Group Ltd) v Environment Agency*, [2007] EWCA Civ 611 [*OSS Group*], online: <www.bailii.org/ew/cases/EWCA/Civ/2007/611.html>.

filled; and it was a very cheap method of disposal. The landfill directive[56] not only imposed tough technical standards on landfill operators for gas control and groundwater protection, but also was an important first step in requiring the diversion of waste away from landfill into recycling and recovery — so much so that the House of Commons Select Committee on the Environment, in reporting on the proposed directive, noted a strong antipathy to landfill "seeping through the text."[57] EU law has reduced the quantity of waste landfilled, with local authorities under duties to achieve diversion targets. While landfill continues to play an important role for residual waste, it must be operated to strict standards, and is no longer the cheap and environmentally risky option that it once was. It seems most unlikely that such changes would have come about, to the extent they have, without the driving impetus of EU law. The House of Commons Environment, Food and Rural Affairs Committee expressed concern in its 2014 report, "Waste Management in England,"[58] as to a possible "stepping back" by the government from continued efforts toward a "zero waste" economy.

Protection of Wildlife and Its Habitats

The habitats directive[59] is one of those pieces of EU legislation that have tended to attract adverse popular comment, which is often misguided. For example, there is the "scourge of the building industry," the great crested newt, which can allegedly "halt a development in its tracks and add tens of thousands of pounds in costs."[60] This is perhaps not surprising, given the impact that the directive can have on preventing development of projects that may be important locally (such as roads or housing) or even nationally (such as ports or airports). Demonstrating that the habitats directive's high test of "imperative reasons of overriding public importance"[61] under article 6(4) is satisfied is notoriously difficult (no doubt as the legislation intends).[62] Traditional activities such as peat extraction have also been made subject to review under the directive and have been curtailed.[63] This may seem particularly objectionable where the habitat is designated because it is rare in the EU territory as a whole, but is relatively commonplace in the United Kingdom. As discussed below, the directive may, after the United Kingdom has left the European Union, be one of the prime areas where the government will be tempted to roll back the frontiers of EU regulation. As with EIA, the EU law on the protection of habitats has in recent years proved a

---

56 *Landfill Directive*, *supra* note 17.

57 UK, HC, Select Committee on the Environment, *The EC Draft Directive on the Landfill of Waste* (7th Report of Session 1990–1991) (London, UK: Her Majesty's Stationery Office, 1991).

58 UK, HC, Environment, Food and Rural Affairs Committee, *Waste Management in England* (4th Report of Session 2014–15) (London, UK: Her Majesty's Stationery Office, 2014), online: <https://publications.parliament.uk/pa/cm201415/cmselect/cmenvfru/241/241.pdf>.

59 *Habitats Directive*, *supra* note 18.

60 Emily Gosden, "Great crested newts will no longer block housing", *The Telegraph* (20 September 2015), online: <www.telegraph.co.uk/news/earth/11878624/Great-crested-newts-will-no-longer-block-housing.html>.

61 *Habitats Directive*, *supra* note 18, art 6(4).

62 See UK, Department for Environment, Food and Rural Affairs, "Habitats and Wild Birds Directives: guidance on the application of article 6(4)" (December 2012), online: <www.gov.uk/government/uploads/system/uploads/attachment_data/file/69622/pb13840-habitats-iropi-guide-20121211.pdf>.

63 See the proceedings by the Commission against Ireland in respect of ongoing peat cutting in raised bog special areas of conservation, described by the National Trust for Ireland as a "political and environmental time bomb." National Trust for Ireland, Press Release, "EU Legal Action on Peat bogs a 'Political and environmental time bomb'" (16 June 2011), online: <www.antaisce.org/articles/eu-legal-action-peat-bogs-political-and-environmental-time-bomb>.

fertile ground for legal challenges to controversial projects, and has sometimes been the subject of judicial comment that it should not be seen as an "obstacle course" for developers.[64]

Renewable Energy

EU law has consistently sought to promote the uptake of renewable energy through directives setting national targets. The United Kingdom has embraced these with relative enthusiasm, and the pace of development of wind, solar and biomass power has steadily increased. This is, however, perhaps an area where it can be said that EU law has not provided the sole impetus and that, even in the absence of EU law, the UK government would have acted to promote renewable energy for reasons of wider international obligations on climate change and for reasons of energy security. Nevertheless, while UK and EU objectives on energy policy are generally closely aligned, it is possible to find a number of areas of actual or potential tension in which EU law might be regarded as a constraint on the United Kingdom's freedom of action and on how the United Kingdom chooses to achieve its objectives, even when these are generally in line with the objectives of the European Union.[65]

Summary

Pausing here after what has necessarily been a brief and selective summary, it can be asserted with a good degree of confidence that EU environmental law has had a major influence in the United Kingdom. Ludwig Krämer has listed its achievements as having made standards for environmental protection enforceable, having led to the creation of environmental structures in member states, having conferred a degree of oversight on implementation and application of the law to the European Commission and, finally, having achieved the gradual transmission of information to EU citizens, with concomitant rights.[66] EU environmental law is not perfect, and has had its failures too, but overall it has benefited the environment in the United Kingdom and, consequently, UK citizens. In some respects, EU environmental law has had lasting effects that will not easily be expunged — for example, the infrastructure of waste and waste water management facilities. But, in other areas, continued vigilance and commitment are required if environmental standards are to be improved or, at least, not to slip. This is the subject of the next section of this chapter.

The Environmental Implications of the United Kingdom's Exit from the European Union

This section focuses on the difference Brexit is likely to make on environmental protection in the United Kingdom. There are three basic interconnected issues that provide a suitable framework. These are the substantive law, interpretation of that law by the courts and the accountability of government for adequate implementation. Together these are the central issues — there must be adequate law, the courts must interpret it in a way that is sympathetic

---

64 *Hart District Council v Secretary of State for Communities & Local Government*, [2008] EWHC 1204 (Admin). See also Gregory Jones, ed, *The Habitats Directive: A Developer's Obstacle Course* (London, UK: Hart, 2012).

65 Adam Brown, "Energy Brexit: Initial Thoughts" (2016) 5 Intl Envtl L Rev 209.

66 L Krämer, "EU environmental law and policy over the last 25 years: good or bad for the UK?" (2013) 25 Envtl L & Mgmt 48.

to the underlying objectives of environmental protection and there must be adequate means to hold the government and decision makers to account.

Substantive Law

It appears to be settled (insofar as anything can be regarded as settled within the current UK political framework) that EU legislation in force at the date of leaving will continue to have effect until such time as it is amended or repealed through UK legislative processes. This is the current effect of clauses 2 and 3 of the European Union (Withdrawal) Bill,[67] clause 2, dealing with EU-derived domestic legislation, and clause 3, dealing with incorporation of direct EU legislation. The principle of supremacy of EU law will, according to clause 4, continue to apply in respect of EU legislation as it applies immediately before "exit day," but will not apply in respect of UK legislation enacted after exit day, which will therefore be able to trump EU law. Exit day, itself, is proposed as a moveable feast, being defined in the bill as such a day as ministers may appoint in regulations. This, of course, may be important if — as seems possible, but by no means certain — the negotiations result in the establishment of a transitional period.

In terms of environmental law, the EU law is in the form of directives, although there are limited exceptions such as regulations on transfrontier shipment of waste. This is in line with the general approach to approximation of environmental laws in which member states have discretion as to how they reflect their EU obligations in national law, subject to compliance with the general principles of EU law.[68] The United Kingdom's approach to the transposition of environmental directives has moved away from the original technique of putting the EU law into British legislative drafting style and language, into an approach under which the relevant EU directive requirements are either copied out or are incorporated by reference, so that the reader can only make sense of the UK law by reading it side by side with the directive. This is not a very user-friendly approach[69] and is one that will appear increasingly untenable as the relevant directive, itself, is amended after the exit day.[70]

Amendment of EU-derived law may be necessary at exit in order to make it work: some provisions will simply not work legally or will not make sense because they are predicated on continued membership in the European Union. An example is section 8 of the Climate Change Act 2008,[71] which requires the Secretary of State to set carbon budgets with a view to (among other things) complying with the European obligations of the United Kingdom; another example is the power of the Secretary of State under section 122 of the Environment Act 1995[72] to give varied directions to the national environmental enforcement agencies for the purpose of implementing obligations of the United Kingdom under the EU treaties.

---

67 Bill 5, *European Union (Withdrawal) Bill* [HL], 2017–2019 sess (1st reading 13 July 2017) [*Withdrawal Bill*].

68 See EC, *Guide to the Approximation of European Union Environmental Legislation*, online: Europa <http://ec.europa.eu/environment/archives/guide/part1.htm>.

69 A research project in 2011 found significant examples of UK environmental legislation that were problematic in lacking coherence, integration and/or transparency: see UKELA & King's College, London, *The State of UK Environmental Legislation in 2011: an interim report by the UK Environmental Law Association and King's College London* (2011), online: <www.ukela.org/content/page/2957/Aim%205%20Interim%20report.pdf>.

70 A prime example of such "referential drafting" is *The Environmental Permitting (England and Wales) Regulations 2016*, SI 2016/1154. See Peter Kellett, "Better regulation, deregulation and environmental law" (2015) 27:5 Envtl Law & Mgmt 200.

71 *Climate Change Act 2008* (UK), c 27.

72 *Environment Act 1995* (UK), c 25.

Accordingly, the bill provides a power at clause 7 to make regulations to deal with "deficiencies" that arise from withdrawal. This is a controversial proposed power, since it is of a "Henry VIII" nature, allowing ministers to amend primary legislation. The ability of ministers to make such amendments is an inevitability, given the vast amount of primary and secondary legislation that will need to be subject to detailed and often technical amendment to accommodate the Brexit process. However, such powers can be abused, and they raise general constitutional issues. It will be interesting to see how the provisions may be amended during the parliamentary process to provide safeguards against misuse.[73] The UKELA has produced a useful paper, "Brexit and Environmental Law: Brexit, Henry VIII Clauses and Environmental Law,"[74] that identifies provisions that may be necessary or advisable to amend.

For other areas of law, the problems may be less easy to resolve, for example, where there is a European mechanism that underpins the law, such as an agency, institution or interactive process. Good examples are the regulation on registration, evaluation and approval of chemicals (REACH)[75] and the Seville process mentioned above, by which industrial environmental emissions standards are clarified and given substance. REACH has been the subject of a parliamentary enquiry and a report by the Commons Environmental Audit Committee, "The Future of Chemicals Regulation after the EU Referendum."[76]

The committee's stated key findings were that the EU REACH framework would be difficult to transpose into UK law directly, that certainty was essential and that establishing a United Kingdom stand-alone system would be very expensive for the taxpayer and for industry. The UKELA left the committee in no doubt that the legal process of retaining REACH would not be simple: "The Environmental Law Association told us that, because of the way that REACH operates and the terminology used in the Regulation, writing the REACH regulations into UK law could not sensibly be done simply by having a line in the 'Great Repeal Bill' (or one of its resulting statutory instruments) deeming REACH to apply in the United Kingdom. REACH was written from the perspective of participants being within the European Union, with much of it also relating to Member State co-operation and mutual obligations, oversight and controls, and freedom of movement of products."[77] It is therefore a prime example of a regulatory system that is dependent on continued interaction with EU institutions.

This is an area of great concern not only for the UK chemicals industry, but also for other industries using chemicals downstream.[78] The outcome will depend on where negotiations end up between the United Kingdom and the European Union on access to the Single Market, but the stakes are high, and the scope for serious cost and disruption is significant. The practical

---

73 One concern is that there will be a lack of transparency if changes are made by a series of negative statutory instruments, and that it may be difficult to assess properly what is being retained, what is being lost and how this may affect the shape of environmental protection: see Isabella Kaminski, "Government 'must offer' green Brexit guarantees" (2017) 508 ENDS Rep 26.

74 UKELA, "Brexit and Environmental Law: Brexit, Henry VIII Clauses and Environmental Law" (September 2017), online: <www.ukela.org/content/doclib/319.pdf>.

75 EC, *Regulation (EC) No 1907/2006 of the European Parliament and of the Council on the Registration, Evaluation, Authorisation and Restriction of Chemicals (REACH)*, [2006] OJ, L 396/1.

76 UK, Parliament, *The Future of Chemicals Regulation after the EU Referendum* (27 April 2017), online: <https://publications.parliament.uk/pa/cm201617/cmselect/cmenvaud/912/91203.htm>.

77 *Ibid.*

78 See e.g. the concerns of the furniture industry: Furniture Industry Research Association, "UK REACH alignment after Brexit" (18 April 2017), online: <www.fira.co.uk/news/article/uk-reach-alignment-after-brexit>.

issues are well set out in an excellent short article[79] written by experienced lawyers even before the results of the exit referendum were known. The article considered the various options open to the United Kingdom regarding continued participation in the REACH scheme and the disastrous implications of getting it wrong. As the authors put it: "Weighing the pros and cons of a possible exit from REACH, it would seem that the REACH implementation process is already far advanced and will continue at least in the near future, including in the UK. Any foreseeable benefit from the lessening of regulatory burden in the 'out-of-REACH' option would appear to be offset by the disadvantages of moving into a regulatory environment in the UK that would be partly compatible, and partly incompatible, with the EU single market."[80]

Finally, there is the issue of whether the United Kingdom will diverge over time from the EU standards applicable at exit and forge its own path in the areas discussed above, or others. The policy paper "Legislating for the UK's Withdrawal" indicated that over time, environmental legislation could become "outcome driven" and would deliver on the current Conservative Party commitment to "becoming the first generation to leave the environment in a better state than we found it"[81] (whatever these concepts might mean). Change might take either the form of setting additional or more stringent requirements, or lowering standards, or dispensing with some areas entirely. The wholesale reform of environmental law post-Brexit would be a massive task, and therefore any reforms seem likely to occur piecemeal.

The extent to which the United Kingdom is free to depart from EU norms will obviously depend on whether the United Kingdom accepts continuing commitments to EU standards as part of any trade agreement with the European Union. It seems unlikely that the European Union would be content to accord such rights, while leaving the United Kingdom the ability to give its industry a competitive advantage by lowering domestic standards. Further, the process of setting standards is itself not without cost, at least if done properly and in a fully participative manner: the default position may be to adopt a policy to keep pace with EU standards, although it is not necessarily attractive to have to abide by standards that the United Kingdom has no means of influencing or contributing to.

Are there any areas of EU environmental law that may be soft targets for domestic repeal or amendment after Brexit? Those already mentioned as being perceived as burdensome or irritating for the government are the areas of air quality and habitats. Given the economic cost and political unpopularity of achieving full compliance in accordance with EU law with ambient air quality in UK cities, it might not be surprising if a future government is tempted to row back on these obligations. Such action would itself be immensely controversial and would almost certainly lead to even further litigation on the topic. This raises the question of accountability, which is discussed below.

---

79 Riku Rinta-Jouppi & Keven Harlow, "Will Brexit mean avoiding the burden of REACH?" (May 2016), online: Chemical Watch <www.reachlaw.fi/wp-content/uploads/2016/06/Brexit-Article_CW.pdf>.

80 *Ibid*.

81 UK, Department for Exiting the European Union, "Legislating for the United Kingdom's Withdrawal from the European Union" (May 2017), online: <www.gov.uk/government/publications/the-repeal-bill-white-paper/legislating-for-the-united-kingdoms-withdrawal-from-the-european-union>.

Another area is habitats, which could be portrayed as presenting an undue burden on industry and development.[82] *The Telegraph*, in an article in March 2017, called for a "bonfire of EU red tape"[83] to "free the country from the shackles of Brussels"[84] and cited the habitats directive as an example: "Builders have been frustrated by rules on preserving newts, which are classed as 'endangered' in Europe even though they are thriving in the UK."[85] Such extreme populist sentiment could, of course, gain force in the event of a highly acrimonious and failed negotiation leading to a hard Brexit. However, again, an attempt to reduce the current level of protection would be highly controversial and hard fought. Indeed, various NGOs are already gearing up for the battle.[86]

Interpretation by the Courts

As discussed above, the UK courts have become accustomed to the citation and application of EU law in the environmental field: if not entirely second nature, it is not controversial. This extends to reading UK legislation against the background of EU law and its purposes as an important aid to interpretation, applying EU law directly where necessary under the principle of supremacy, and using the case law of the CJEU while sometimes criticizing the perceived lack of clarity and rigour in the court's reasoning, for example, in cases on the meaning of waste[87] and on the interpretation of concepts in the directive on strategic environmental assessment.[88] Also, the UK courts currently have the ability to refer questions to the European court: they have not always been keen to take this opportunity, but there have been some notable examples where this has been done and where the European court's ruling has had a dramatic and decisive effect.[89] As the exit bill is currently drafted, the defined exit day will mark an important watershed. Under clause 6,[90] previous EU case law will remain decisive, but later case law will only be taken into account if the court considers it appropriate to do so. The Supreme Court will have the power to depart from previous EU case law on the same basis that it may depart from its own decisions. Further, after exit day, there will no longer be the ability to refer questions to the CJEU.

It would be foolish and presumptuous to try to second guess how the courts will approach the formidable task of interpretation after exit. To take the example of EIA, the United Kingdom

---

82 See the helpful paper of the UKELA Nature Conservation Working Party, "Brexit and nature conservation fact sheet" (5 September 2017), which effectively debunks these "myths", online: <www.ukela.org/content/doclib/318.pdf>.

83 Gordon Rayner & Christopher Hope, "Cut the EU red tape choking Britain after Brexit to set the country free from the shackles of Brussels", *The Telegraph* (28 March 2017), online: <www.telegraph.co.uk/news/2017/03/27/cut-eu-red-tape-choking-britain-brexit-set-country-free-shackles/>.

84 *Ibid.*

85 *Ibid.*

86 ClientEarth, "What happens to EU nature laws after Brexit?" (10 November 2016), online: <www.clientearth.org/what-happens-to-eu-nature-laws-after-brexit/>; Royal Society for the Protection of Birds, "The EU Nature Directives are safe — so what next for protection of UK wildlife?" (8 December 2016), online: <www.rspb.org.uk/community/ourwork/b/martinharper/archive/2016/12/08/the-nature-directives-are-here-to-stay-so-what-next-for-protection-of-uk-wildlife.aspx>; Caroline Lucas, "Exiting the EU, Not the Environment" (2017), online: <www.carolinelucas.com/sites/carolinelucas.com/files/Safe%20Guarding%20Environment%20after%20Brexit.pdf>.

87 *OSS Group, supra* note 56.

88 *R (HS2 Action Alliance Ltd) v Secretary of State for Transport*, [2014] UKSC 3. For the strategic environmental assessment directive, see EC, *Directive 2001/42/EC of the European Parliament and of the Council of 27 June 2001 on the assessment of the effects of certain plans and programmes on the environment*, [2001] OJ, L 197/30.

89 See *ClientEarth* 2015, *supra* note 40, where the CJEU took a completely different view from that of the Court of Appeal as to the United Kingdom's obligations, leading in turn to further litigation, which shows no sign of abating.

90 *Withdrawal Bill, supra* note 67, s 6.

will, unless and until it chooses to change things, remain bound by the EIA directive, frozen in time as at the exit date. However, the CJEU will no doubt continue to generate relevant case law on the interpretation of the directive, which may well have a bearing on questions arising before UK courts. It seems unlikely that UK courts will simply choose to ignore that case law, and, unless they do so, they will have to develop principles as to the weight and deference they give to it.

One further problem arises from the fact that while EU law is underpinned by principles that may aid interpretation — the polluter pays, the precautionary principle and the principle of prevention — UK law is not. Such aims and objectives as are found in UK legislation, such as, for example, in respect of the Environment Agency in the Environment Act 1995 — are not really principles, but rather are akin to "operating instructions" for the agency.[91] This matters because principles have an important role to play in filling the interstices or plugging the gaps in law, which may be developing quickly or need to be applied to a changing factual context. In particular, the application of the precautionary principle — which is rarely explicitly formulated in UK legislation, but is a basic tenet of EU law and policy[92] — may come under attack, either from those who argue that the principle results in over regulation, or because it might conflict with trading relations with states that do not apply it, notably the United States.[93]

Accountability

In his book on the enforcement of EU environmental law, Martin Hedemann-Robinson points out that transposing and then implementing EU environmental law has been at times "a difficult legal and political pill to swallow," leading to a "low key and minimalist" approach.[94] He suggests that the approach to enforcement is undergoing a stage of transition, moving from a position in which the European Commission has a dominant role to one in which the Commission is also influenced by member state competent authorities and the public.[95] That trend has continued since the publication of Hedemann-Robinson's book in 2007. Currently, EU law imposes both political and legal accountability on the UK government. In many areas, systematic reporting to the European Commission on implementation is required. This will cease after Brexit (pending any arrangements made as part of trade agreements), and it will be important that the transparency and accountability provided by such reporting is not lost. Arrangements for reporting to Parliament and national devolved assemblies may have to be considered. Further, there will be a loss of the enforcement powers currently available to the European Commission and the important associated procedure in which citizens may make a complaint, informally and free of charge, to the Commission. This is a very valuable citizen's right.[96]

---

91 Jonathan Robinson, "Improving Environmental Law" (2009) 21:2 Envtl L & Mgmt 120 at 122.

92 The precautionary principle is referred to in article 191(2) of the Treaty on the Functioning of the European Union (ex article 174 of the European Treaty) as one of the bases for European Union policy on the environment. It seeks to provide a proportionate and structured basis for addressing risks to human health and the environment in the face of scientific uncertainty. See further, Communication from the Commission on the precautionary principle, COM/2000/0001 final, online: <http://eur-lex.europa.eu/legal-content/EN/TXT/?uri=LEGISSUM%3Al32042>.

93 "Precautionary Principle defended against Brexit cut" (2016) 502 ENDS Rep at 16.

94 Martin Hedemann-Robinson, *Enforcement of European Union Environmental Law: Legal Issues and Challenges* (London, UK: Routledge, 2007) at 3–4.

95 *Ibid* at 5.

96 Its value to the citizen was noted by the Court of Appeal in *R (England) v Tower Hamlets London Borough Council*, [2006] EWCA Civ 1742 at para 10.

As the UKELA pointed out in its July 2017 paper, "Brexit and Environmental Law: Enforcement and Political Accountability Issues,"[97] the majority of infringement proceedings against the United Kingdom have been brought in the environmental field, and for good reason: the environment lacks the commercial imperatives for enforcement and supervision found in relation to intellectual property, employment rights or competition law, and is dependent upon the intervention of concerned citizens if it is not to be at risk of "dying in silence."[98] Another significant paper by the IEEP and ClientEarth pointed out the worrying gap that will be created and calls both for new institutions in the United Kingdom that could replicate the role of the Commission and also for appropriate dispute resolution mechanisms in any future agreement between the United Kingdom and European Union, which would allow for the active participation of citizens and NGOs in monitoring compliance.[99] Whether a UK government would have any appetite for such mechanisms must be open to a degree of skepticism.

The government's position is that citizens will remain able to vindicate such rights by way of judicial review in the national courts: this is, however, an utterly unrealistic view in light of the formality and cost of the judicial review process, which is plainly not a substitute for the EU complaints procedure. As the UKELA observes, the loss of the European Commission's role as guardian of the treaty presents an opportunity to innovate and improve on domestic mechanisms for ensuring proper discharge of duties placed on government and public bodies.[100] The UKELA cites examples of environmental ombudsmen in jurisdictions such as Austria, Hungary, Kenya and Greece.[101] It is feared, however, that such reforms may be a low priority for a government preoccupied with the financial and economic implications of, and fallout from, the Brexit process. The House of Lords European Communities Committee has expressed worry about the removal of EU enforcement mechanisms and the complacency of the government view that the government will be able to effectively regulate itself: the committee stated that evidence it had heard strongly suggested that an effective and independent domestic enforcement mechanism would be necessary to fill the vacuum.[102] It appears that the current Secretary of State for the Environment, MP Michael Gove, now shares that view, according to very recent press reports.[103] However, whether this ambition will translate into real government action remains to be seen.

---

97 UKELA, "Brexit and Environmental Law: Enforcement and Political Accountability Issues" (July 2017) [UKELA, "Brexit, Enforcement"], online: <www.ukela.org/content/doclib/317.pdf>.

98 Sandra Laville, "Lawyers plan to stop UK dropping EU rules on environment after Brexit", *The Guardian* (3 July 2017), online: <www.theguardian.com/environment/2017/jul/03/lawyers-plan-to-stop-uk-dropping-eu-rules-on-environment-after-brexit-taskforce-protections-law>.

99 Martin Nesbit et al, *Ensuring compliance with environmental obligations through a future UK–EU relationship* (London, UK: IEEP, 2017), online: <https://ieep.eu/uploads/articles/attachments/b6cdff2e-3292-49e1-993f-cd39b3b897a4/Ensuring%20compliance%20with%20environmental%20law%20post%20-%2004%20October.pdf?v=63674328709>.

100 UKELA, "Brexit, Enforcement", *supra* note 97 at 3.

101 *Ibid* at 15.

102 HL Paper 109, *supra* note 11.

103 Michael Gove, "Outside the EU we will become the world-leading curator of the most precious asset of all: our planet", *The Telegraph* (11 November 2017), online: <www.telegraph.co.uk/news/2017/11/11/outside-eu-will-become-world-leading-curator-precious-asset/?WT.mc_id=tmg_share_em>.

International Obligations

A number of important and problematic issues arise here. These are essentially, first, the implications and relevance of existing commitments by the United Kingdom under international law, and, second, the possible implications of any ongoing trade arrangements between the United Kingdom and the European Union.

The first is an extremely complicated area, which is dissected in some detail by the UKELA paper, "Brexit and Environmental Law: The UK and International Environmental Law after Brexit."[104] Government policy — not surprisingly — is that, on withdrawal, the United Kingdom will continue to be bound by its existing international environmental obligations. These apply in important areas such as climate change, marine pollution, the transfrontier movement of waste, biodiversity and many others. Distinctions will need to be made between international agreements entered into by the European Union alone (which the United Kingdom will need to sign and/or ratify), mixed agreements entered into by both the United Kingdom and the European Union (where the legal position on whether the United Kingdom will remain bound in whole or in part may be obscure and will need to be clarified) and agreements entered into by the United Kingdom alone, where the position is relatively simple. This is a major exercise for government, yet to be undertaken. It is important because, after Brexit, such agreements may provide the only backstop against diminished standards of environmental protection. For example, in areas such as wildlife protection, the Ramsar Convention[105] on wetlands may represent an ongoing obligation. Similarly, the Aarhus Convention[106] on access to information, public participation and access to justice in environmental matters will be an important protection of the rights of citizens. The Aarhus Convention currently acquires much of its force in the UK legal system through the relevant EU secondary legislation implementing it, for example, on EIA.

Another important legal issue relating to international agreements is enforcement. Compared to the position under EU law, enforcement mechanisms in international agreements are generally weak, often relying on peer pressure rather than hard sanctions. As it has been put, "the implementation of treaty obligations is hampered by the fact that the vertical command and control structure governing domestic politics within states is conspicuously absent within the international legal order," and, in international environmental law, there is "no overarching pyramid of authority consisting of law-making, law-interpreting, law-implementing, or law-enforcing institutions."[107] The continued adherence of the UK courts to the dualist doctrine means that international agreements that have not been incorporated into UK law have very little value in judicial proceedings, other than as providing interpretative presumptions and in being a factor to be taken into account in the exercise of judicial discretion. This will be a question of huge importance in the future of UK environmental law after exit from the European Union.

---

104 UKELA, "Brexit and Environmental Law: The UK and International Environmental Law after Brexit" (September 2017), online: <www.ukela.org/content/doclib/320.pdf>.

105 *Convention on Wetlands of International Importance especially as Waterfowl Habitat*, 2 February 1971, 996 UNTS 245, TIAS 11084, 11 ILM 963 (entered into force 21 December 1975).

106 *Aarhus Convention, supra* note 23.

107 Lakshman Guruswamy & Mariah Leach, *International Environmental Law in a Nutshell*, 5th ed (St Paul, MN: West Academic, 2017) at 91.

The possibility of ongoing trade arrangements between the United Kingdom and the European Union after Brexit is, at the time of writing, entirely speculative, and, accordingly, difficult to discuss meaningfully. It would be possible to devote enormous effort to considering scenarios that never come about, given the current chaotic nature of the negotiations. There are, of course, various possible options ranging from Single Market access or the European Economic Area model, to membership in the European Free Trade Agreement, arrangements such as between Switzerland and the European Union, or some bespoke arrangement.[108] Compliance with EU environmental law seems likely to figure to some extent in any of these options, as the European Union's negotiating position is unlikely to countenance a complete exemption from requirements that apply to EU companies.

Brexit and Euratom

At the time of the referendum, no mention was made of Euratom and no thought was given to the implications of a Leave decision on the United Kingdom's membership in that community. Euratom and the European Union are linked through common institutions, but are constitutionally and juridically separate entities, and the leaving processes are also separate, notwithstanding the fact that the UK government chose to combine both notifications in a single letter to the president of the European Council. The implications of "Brexatom" have been most thoroughly considered in the UKELA paper, "Brexit and Environmental Law: Exit from the Euratom Treaty and its Environmental Implications."[109] The existence of underlying international instruments on nuclear safety and on the safety of spent fuel management and radioactive waste mean that little change to UK standards and regulation is likely to result. However, in the longer term, there may be the possibility for divergence between the United Kingdom and Euratom in terms of radiological protection standards, although, again, the existence of wider underpinning international standards reduces the possibility of this occurring. There is, however, a need for informed and timely action, in particular in the areas of the movement of radioactive substances and in external relations on nuclear cooperation. The arrangements for the supervision and control of shipments of radioactive waste and spent fuel, now covered by Directive 2006/117/Euratom,[110] will need to be given careful thought.

More urgently, a means will have to be found to avoid the interruption of shipments of radioactive sources, such as medical isotopes, currently undertaken under relatively light-touch arrangements within Euratom. Another potentially fraught area is that of international nuclear cooperation agreements that have been entered into by Euratom under article 101 of the Euratom treaty[111] and in respect of which replacement agreements will have to be made by the United Kingdom with the other parties, such as Brazil, Argentina, Canada and Japan. The ability to obtain vital nuclear services, material and know-how will depend on the continuity of such arrangements, and, for countries such as the United States, it will be a precondition

---

108 Some of the best current analyses are to be found in the summer 2017 journal of the Bar European Group, *European Advocate*, in particular the articles by Michael-James Clifton, "Road Map for Brexit," Ben Rayment, "Back from the Edge" and Evanna Fruithof, "Brexit Futures."

109 Stephen Tromans & Paul Bowden, "Brexit and Environmental Law: Exit from the Euratom Treaty and its Environmental Implications" (Dorking, UK: UKELA, 2017), online: <www.ukela.org/content/doclib/316.pdf>.

110 EC, *Council Directive 2006/117/Euratom of 20 November 2006 on the supervision and control of shipments of radioactive waste and spent fuel*, [2006] OJ, L 337/21.

111 *Consolidated version of the Treaty establishing the European Atomic Energy Community*, [2012] OJ, C 327/1, art 101.

that the United Kingdom has in place an acceptable system of safeguards, which are currently provided by Euratom. The UKELA paper's fundamental recommendation was that there was the need for a full "gap analysis"[112] of the United Kingdom's ability, post-withdrawal, to meet its international obligations in the nuclear safety field without interruption.

Whatever the ultimate position on the Brexit negotiations, it is clear that, in any event, the United Kingdom will need to retain a close and open future relationship with Euratom and its member states in order to be able to satisfy the wider international community and the public that the United Kingdom has the technical resources to continue to deliver nuclear safety. Such a relationship will need to apply in the areas of nuclear safety, waste management, radiological protection and emergency preparedness. The issue will be important if the United Kingdom is to realize its ambitions for substantial investment in nuclear power.

Summary and Conclusions

It is now possible to try to draw some of these threads together. EU environmental law is not perfect by any means, but it has achieved much in many important respects. These include measures to ensure that the environmental impact of projects and plans are properly assessed, that the public is informed and enabled to participate, that minimum standards are observed in respect of air and water, that the environmental safety of chemicals is assessed before they can be marketed, that industry observes consistent standards to abate harmful emissions, that products are designed with their environmental implications in mind, that waste is prevented or beneficially used — or where not so used, that it is disposed of in a responsible and environmentally sound manner — and that important wildlife habitats are protected from environmentally damaging activities.

All of these measures, as described above, have fed into and become embedded in UK law over the past decades. Governmental freedom of action has been constrained accordingly. Equally, citizens and NGOs have been able to use EU law as an effective tool in respect of non-compliance, whether in the courts or in the procedure for complaints to the European Commission.

With Brexit, the United Kingdom is moving into uncharted waters, or, to use another metaphor, embarking on a long-term experiment as to how a country (or, more accurately, four devolved countries) will develop its own distinctive body of environmental law when freed from the constraints of a legal regime imposed on a multilateral basis. This has caused concern among some environmental bodies; the concern is that Brexit may amount to a threat to environmental standards. This, of course, could potentially be the case, in particular if Brexit involves a harsher economic climate for the United Kingdom and international competitiveness becomes an important issue for future governments. However, there will also be long-term opportunities to improve environmental law and to achieve a system that benefits the UK environment, specifically. The risk is that the United Kingdom will lack the impetus provided by an energetic European Commission to continue to develop and improve environmental measures. There are precedents for the flourishing of domestic environmental law, but the last comprehensive review

---

112 Tromans & Bowden, *supra* note 109 at 8.

was in 1990 with the environment white paper of Margaret Thatcher's government,[113] and the Environmental Protection Act 1990, which was intended to provide the basic framework for pollution control well into the twenty-first century.[114]

The United Kingdom has, since then, essentially been a "taker" of EU law, which it has superimposed onto its domestic system, rather than an initiator of its own law — the Climate Change Act 2008 is one example to the contrary. The last major reform in 1990, as this chapter pointed out,[115] was the product of many years of policy development by bodies such as the Royal Commission on Environmental Pollution, and some particularly proactive parliamentary committees such as the House of Lords Committee on Science and Technology and the House of Commons Environment Select Committee. The challenge is going to be the recreation of such bodies that have the vision and political influence to direct future law along sound lines. The fact that the environment is a devolved competence will add another important layer of difficulty, which was not present in 1990.

To imagine that Brexit will mean that the United Kingdom disengages entirely from EU environmental standards is naïve. Companies based in the United Kingdom that wish to supply their goods and products to the EU market, in many cases, will still need to comply with such standards in practice, whatever the UK law may say. A good example is the ecodesign directive,[116] which provides consistent EU-wide rules for improving the environmental performance of products such as household appliances, and which sets out minimum mandatory requirements for the energy efficiency of these products. Companies selling energy-using products within the European Union must comply with the ecodesign directive's requirements and, consequently, with the standards and specifications set by the European Committee for Standardization (CEN), which are part of the EU system. For the United Kingdom to disengage from the CEN process, which includes non-EU countries such as Norway, Switzerland and Turkey, would be plainly disadvantageous.[117] Similarly, as pointed out above, UK engagement is likely to be desirable in the processes of the registration of chemicals under the Seville process for setting standards relating to industrial emissions, and in areas such as nuclear safety and the movement of radioactive sources and other nuclear materials.

In cases where there is no clear business or economic imperative to continue to play by EU rules, the position is less clear. There will still be constraints presented by international environmental law, through treaties such as the Aarhus and Ramsar conventions to which the United Kingdom is a party, and possibly through any ongoing trade arrangements with the European Union or indeed other countries (although these cannot be guaranteed and, in any event, may be a long way off). Such obligations are, however, not going to be a substitute for the legally enforceable obligations arising from EU law, certainly unless there is some sort of sea change in the attitude of the UK courts.

---

113 UK, Department of the Environment, "This Common Inheritance: Britain's Environmental Strategy", Cm 1200 (London, UK: Her Majesty's Stationery Office, 1990).

114 See the comment by Secretary of State Chris Patten introducing the bill: UK, HC, *Parliamentary Debates*, vol 165, col 6 (Chris Patten).

115 Tromans, *supra* note 47.

116 EC, *Directive 2009/125/EC of the European Parliament and of the Council of 21 October 2009 establishing a framework for the setting of ecodesign requirements for energy-related products*, [2009] OJ, L 285/10.

117 See Isabella Kaminski, "High Standards: A Better Way to Regulate?" (2017) 509 ENDS Rep 21.

The ability of citizens to challenge the government on environmental matters may well be affected by Brexit, with the loss of supremacy of EU law, but it seems probable that litigants will continue to attempt to rely on the future development of EU law as it emerges from the CJEU. What is much less clear is how the domestic courts will view the citation of such cases and the use of basic EU principles. This will be played out in the courts in the coming years.

These questions, and how the United Kingdom's environmental law will look a decade after it leaves the European Union, can only be matters for speculation. It is clear, however, that the United Kingdom is moving away from a situation that had become well understood, if not always well liked, and had, at least, to some extent provided UK businesses with certainty as to their environmental obligations, into a potentially quite new territory. It will be up to politicians, lawyers and the public to ensure that the best features of EU environmental law are not lost or eroded and that, in time, the United Kingdom develops its own environmental laws that are fit for purpose in a post-Brexit Britain.

Section Five

HUMAN RIGHTS

15

Lessons from Brexit: Reconciling International and Constitutional Aspirations

Oonagh E. Fitzgerald

Introduction

For some time, the myth of the Westphalian model of the sovereign equality of states defined by territory[1] has provided only a cracked and tarnished mirror to reflect the aspirations of minority populations or distinct peoples incorporated within nation-states. The Brexit vote and Britain's reversing trajectory from greater European integration to isolationism and extraction from the European Union draw into focus the expectations of minority populations and distinct peoples, and raise questions about their possible role in international and constitutional change affecting the nation-state. This paper examines the recent UK Supreme Court (UKSC) *Miller* decision[2] on the invocation of article 50 of the Treaty on European Union (TEU),[3] as well as

---

1   Stéphane Beaulac, "The Westphalian Model in Defining International Law: Challenging the Myth" (2004) 8:2 Austl J Leg Hist 181, online: <www.austlii.edu.au/au/journals/AJLH/2004/9.html>.

2   *R v Miller*, [2017] UKSC 5 [*Miller*].

3   *Treaty of Lisbon Amending the Treaty on European Union and the Treaty Establishing the European Community*, 13 December 2007, [2007] OJ, C 306/01, art 50 (entered into force 1 December 2009) [TEU].

the reasoning of the Supreme Court of Canada (SCC) in the *Reference re Quebec Secession*[4] to ascertain what can be learned about the subtle complexity of both sustaining and reforming a constitutional democracy.

The analysis suggests that majority rule is only one of a collection of core conventions, principles and laws that operate together to sustain constitutional democracy. Emphasizing majority rule above all other relevant conventions, principles and laws in pursuing the Brexit constitutional reform project risks undermining both feasibility and legitimacy. This chapter proceeds in three parts: The First Lesson: The *Miller* Decision and Constitutional Fundamentals; The Second Lesson: The Quebec *Secession Reference* and Constitutional Complexity; and The Third Lesson: Negotiating International and Constitutional Change, followed by a brief conclusion.

The First Lesson: The *Miller* Decision and Constitutional Fundamentals

The *Miller* decision,[5] issued by the UKSC on January 23, 2017, put to rest an important debate about who, under the British Constitution, has the authority to issue the notice under article 50[6] that would formally commence the withdrawal by the United Kingdom from the European Union. Not surprisingly, the court concluded that, because this notice would trigger a cascade of events that would lead to radical changes in UK law and, ultimately, withdrawal from the European Union, only the British Parliament through legislation, rather than the executive through prerogative action, could authorize the article 50 notice. Responding to the judgment, British Attorney General Jeremy Wright expressed disappointment, but undertook to seek parliamentary authorization.[7]

Two months later, the Theresa May government succeeded in getting a hurried bill through both Houses of Parliament, authorizing the government to invoke article 50, and, on March 29, 2017, the article was triggered by the prime minister writing to the European Council's President Donald Tusk.[8] With her hasty actions, the prime minister appears to have alienated Scottish

---

4   [1998] 2 SCR 217 [*Secession Reference*].
5   *Miller, supra* note 2. The majority judgment was delivered by Lord Neuberger, with whom Lady Hale, Lord Mance, Lord Kerr, Lord Clarke, Lord Wilson, Lord Sumption and Lord Hodge agreed.
6   *Ibid* at para 25:
    The Treaty of Lisbon introduced into the EU treaties for the first time an express provision entitling a member state to withdraw from the European Union. It did this by inserting a new article 50 into the TEU. This article (article 50) provides as follows:
    1.   Any member state may decide to withdraw from the Union in accordance with its own constitutional requirements.
    2.   A member state which decides to withdraw shall notify the European Council of its intention. In the light of the guidelines provided by the European Council, the Union shall negotiate and conclude an agreement with that state, setting out the arrangements for its withdrawal…
    3.   The Treaties shall cease to apply to the state in question from the date of entry into force of the withdrawal agreement or, failing that, two years after the notification referred to in paragraph 2, unless the European Council, in agreement with the member state concerned, unanimously decides to extend this period.
7   Owen Bowcott, Rowena Mason & Anushka Asthana, "Supreme court rules parliament must have vote to trigger article 50", *The Guardian* (24 January 2017), online: <www.theguardian.com/politics/2017/jan/24/supreme-court-brexit-ruling-parliament-vote-article-50>.
8   *European Union (Notification of Withdrawal) Act 2017* c 9, s 1(1) provides "The Prime Minister may notify, under Article 50(2) of the Treaty on European Union, the United Kingdom's intention to withdraw from the EU"; UK, Prime Minister's Office, "Prime Minister's letter to Donald Tusk triggering Article 50" (29 March 2017), online: <www.gov.uk/government/publications/prime-ministers-letter-to-donald-tusk-triggering-article-50>.

and Northern Irish populations, the majority of whom voted to remain in the European Union. Since then, an opportunistic election call that May expected would grant her a strong majority to lead the Brexit negotiation has backfired, resulting in an unstable minority government. The delivery of Brexit has become more complex and tenuous.

As the May government takes the United Kingdom ever closer to Brexit, and potentially its own dissolution, it is poignant to note that, in the *Miller* decision, the UKSC did not decide, but took as "common ground" between the parties, that article 50 notice was not revocable.[9] One gathers that there may be more debate on this in the future, and the powder may still be dry on this question. This is an important footnote to the *Miller* decision because, after considering the complexity, difficulty and cost of negotiating Brexit and establishing laws, institutions and international relationships to take the place of EU membership, it is conceivable that the British people might conclude that staying in the European Union is better than Brexit, on the terms being offered.

Constitutional democracy is far more subtle and complex than the advocates for Brexit allowed, and for all their nationalist fervour, their disregard for hallowed English constitutional principles was surprising. They acted as though majority rule was overriding, when constitutional democracy involves various nuanced relations between political convention and law. History has resulted in the evolution of the rule of law, the role of judges, the role of the executive and the role of Parliament. The Brexit question must contend with all of this, as well as with the legal requirements of the TEU.[10]

Citing A. V. Dicey, Sir Edward Coke, the Bill of Rights 1688[11] and the Claim of Right 1689,[12] the majority judgment in *Miller* provides a constitutional law primer to explain what should have been self-evident: parliamentary sovereignty means that the Crown in Parliament has the right to make and unmake any law, and neither the sovereign nor any branch of the executive can interfere with law so made.[13] The dualist system reinforces parliamentary sovereignty by constraining the royal prerogative to conduct foreign affairs, such that when "a proposed action on the international plane will require domestic implementation," the executive must seek

---

9   *Miller, supra* note 2 at para 26: "In these proceedings, it is common ground that notice under article 50(2)...cannot be given in qualified or conditional terms and that, once given, it cannot be withdrawn. Especially as it is the Secretary of State's case that, even if this common ground is mistaken, it would make no difference to the outcome of these proceedings, we are content to proceed on the basis that that is correct, without expressing any view of our own on either point."

10 One might ask whether the Brexit team was prepared for First Minister Nicola Sturgeon's calls for a referendum on Scottish independence prior to finalizing Brexit negotiations: "Nicola Sturgeon's consultation on a new Scottish independence referendum gets her out of a tight spot", *The Economist* (13 October 2016), online: <www.economist.com/blogs/bagehot/2016/10/canny-bluff>; Siobhan McFadyen, "Sturgeon public consultation on Referendum 2 — No 10 doesn't even waste time dismissing it", *Sunday Express* (20 October 2016), online: <www.express.co.uk/news/uk/723446/Sturgeon-independence-referendum-snubbed-by-Downing-Street>; Matt Broomfield, "Nicola Sturgeon's speech in full: SNP leader calls for second Scottish independence referendum", *Independent* (13 March 2017), online: <www.independent.co.uk/news/uk/politics/nicola-sturgeon-scottish-independence-speech-in-full-second-referendum-snp-leader-first-minister-a7627166.html>.

11 England, *Bill of Rights, 1688,* 1 William & Mary sess 2, c 2.

12 Scotland, *Claim of Right Act, 1689,* c 2.

13 *Miller, supra* note 2 at paras 43ff.

Parliamentary sanction.[14] Complete withdrawal from the European Union would "constitute as significant a constitutional change as that which occurred when EU law was first incorporated in domestic law by the 1972 Act."[15] Just as Parliament, through the 1972 Act,[16] gave effect to the United Kingdom's membership in what is now the European Union, "constitutional propriety" required "prior Parliamentary sanction for the process" of withdrawal.[17]

This meant that the executive branch did not have the power to change law, with or without the backing of a referendum. The executive could only try to persuade Parliament to change the law. A referendum could result in a change in law if Parliament provided for this by making the coming-into-force of a law conditional on obtaining a certain majority of votes in a referendum. As this was not done in the case of the Brexit referendum, the UKSC concluded that the referendum result was only advisory and could not usurp Parliament to become a new source of law-making authority.[18]

The judgment of the UKSC is circumspect and avoids commenting on the merits of the Brexit referendum. The majority explains that the court had to address the constitutional issues because of their importance, but implied EU membership itself was not one such issue: Some of the most important issues of law that judges have to decide concern questions relating to the constitutional arrangements of the United Kingdom, these proceedings being a case in point. These proceedings raise such issues. As already indicated, this is not because they concern the United Kingdom's membership of the European Union; it is because they concern "(i) the extent of ministers' power to effect changes in domestic law through exercise of their prerogative powers at the international level, and (ii) the relationship between the UK government and Parliament on the one hand and the devolved legislatures and administrations of Scotland, Wales and Northern Ireland on the other."[19]

It is noteworthy that these were the two issues distilled from the litigation under appeal, although the Leave vote was fundamentally about leaving the constitutional frame of the European Union. The manner in which the United Kingdom's domestic law and governance have been

---

14 *Ibid* at paras 54–57, citing Campbell McLachlan, *Foreign Relations Law* (Cambridge, UK: Cambridge University Press, 2014) at para 5.20. The majority also referred to the Ponsonby Convention, whereby it became standard practice to lay all treaties, including those that would not impact on domestic law, "before both Houses of Parliament at least 21 days before they were ratified, to enable Parliamentary objections to be heard" (*Miller, supra* note 2 at para 58). See also a blog by Jean Leclair in which he suggests "affording a role to Parliament in the triggering of Article 50 does not mean trumping the will of the people. Rather it amounts to complementing their will with a type of public deliberation for which the referendum campaign did not allow." Jean Leclair, "Brexit and the Unwritten Constitutional Principle of Democracy: A Canadian Perspective" (3 November 2016), *UK Constitutional Law Association* (blog), online: <https://ukconstitutionallaw.org/2016/11/03/jean-leclair-brexit-and-the-unwritten-constitutional-principle-of-democracy-a-canadian-perspective/>.

15 *Miller, supra* note 2 at para 81.

16 *European Communities Act 1972* (UK), c 68.

17 *Miller, supra* note 2 at para 100.

18 *Ibid* at para 124: "Thus, the referendum of 2016 did not change the law in a way which would allow ministers to withdraw the United Kingdom from the European Union without legislation. But that in no way means that it is devoid of effect. It means that, unless and until acted on by Parliament, its force is political rather than legal. It has already shown itself to be of great political significance."

19 *Ibid* at para 4.

shaped by EU law since 1972[20] is treated as mere background to inform the constitutional analysis, rather than as a core part of the constitutional order being scrutinized by the court. In other words, only the formal and non-substantive aspects of undoing 44 years of European political, legal, economic and social integration would be considered by the court. This may reflect a national psyche that, despite the depth, breadth and duration of integration, remains ambivalent and alienated from the European project. Not treating the United Kingdom's integration into the European Union as "constitutional" may seem at odds with the majority justices' characterization of the United Kingdom as not having "a constitution in the sense of a single coherent code of fundamental law which prevails over all other sources of law. Our constitutional arrangements have developed over time in a pragmatic as much as in a principled way, through a combination of statutes, events, conventions, academic writings and judicial decisions…[to be] 'the most flexible polity in existence.'"[21] One might wonder why more than 40 years of European integration had not become part of this evolving British Constitution.

The judgment addresses the question of the legal rights of devolved Parliaments in a minimalist way, noting the existence of the Sewel Convention[22] on consultation and referring to an SCC decision to point out that constitutional convention is neither legally binding nor enforceable in the courts. Popular media emphasized this point, provoking anxiety and legitimacy concerns for Remain voters in Northern Ireland and Scotland.

Citing the SCC's decision in the *Patriation Reference*,[23] Lord Neuberger, for the majority of the UKSC, asserted, "It is well established that the courts of law cannot enforce a political convention."[24] In support of this conclusion, he quoted the SCC majority judgment's comments on the nature of political questions: "The very nature of a convention, as political in inception and as depending on a consistent course of political recognition by those for whose benefit and

---

20 *Ibid* at paras 14–16:

On 22 January 1972, two days after that later debate, ministers signed a Treaty of Accession which provided that the United Kingdom would become a member of the EEC on 1 January 1973 and would accordingly be bound by the 1957 Treaty of Rome, which was then the main treaty in relation to the EEC, and by certain other connected treaties. As with most international treaties, the 1972 Accession Treaty was not binding unless and until it was formally ratified by the United Kingdom.

A Bill was then laid before Parliament, and after it had been passed by both Houses, it received Royal assent on 17 October 1972, when it became the European Communities Act 1972. The following day, 18 October 1972, ministers ratified the 1972 Accession Treaty on behalf of the United Kingdom, which accordingly became a member of the EEC on 1 January 1973.

The long title of the 1972 Act described its purpose as "to make provision in connection with the enlargement of the European Communities to include the United Kingdom." Part I of the 1972 Act consisted of sections 1 to 3, which contained its "General Provisions," and they are of central importance to these proceedings.

21 *Ibid* at para 40, citing AV Dicey, *Introduction to the Study of the Law of the Constitution*, 8th ed (London, UK: Macmillan, 1915) at 87.

22 *Miller, supra* note 2 at paras 137–138:

The convention takes its name from Lord Sewel, the Minister of State in the Scotland Office in the House of Lords who was responsible for the progress of the Scotland Bill in 1998…. The convention was embodied in a Memorandum of Understanding between the UK government and the devolved governments originally in December 2001 (Cm 5240). Para 14 of the current Memorandum of Understanding, which was published in October 2013, states:

"The UK Government will proceed in accordance with the convention that the UK Parliament would not normally legislate with regard to devolved matters except with the agreement of the devolved legislature. The devolved administrations will be responsible for seeking such agreement as may be required for this purpose on an approach from the UK Government."

23 *Reference re Resolution to Amend the Constitution*, [1981] 1 SCR 753 [*Patriation Reference*].

24 *Miller, supra* note 2 at para 141.

to whose detriment (if any) the convention developed over a considerable period of time is inconsistent with its legal enforcement."[25]

Lord Neuberger also relied on the dissenting judgment of Chief Justice Laskin and Justices Estey and MacIntyre, who pointed out that "a fundamental difference between the legal...and the conventional rules is that, while a breach of the legal rules...has a legal consequence in that it will be restrained by the courts, no such sanction exists for breach or non-observance of the conventional rules"; rather, "[t]he sanction for non-observance of a convention is political in that disregard of a convention may lead to political defeat, to loss of office, or to other political consequences, but will not engage the attention of the courts which are limited to matters of law alone. Courts, however, may recognize the existence of conventions."[26]

Lord Neuberger concludes this brief discussion by compartmentalizing constitutional convention as simply outside the purview of the courts. Asserting that the court does "not underestimate the importance of constitutional conventions, some of which play a fundamental role in the operation of our constitution," he concluded that "[t]he Sewel Convention has an important role in facilitating harmonious relationships between the UK Parliament and the devolved legislatures...[b]ut the policing of its scope and the manner of its operation does not lie within the constitutional remit of the judiciary, which is to protect the rule of law."[27]

The Second Lesson: The Quebec *Secession Reference* and Constitutional Complexity

Perhaps if there had been less political, public and media pressure directed at the judges and claimants in the Brexit cases, the UKSC might have considered guidance from another SCC decision, the 1998 *Reference re Quebec Secession*,[28] which could have shed more light on the subtle complexity of making momentous constitutional change. This case offers some important practical guidance and realism for future politicians, citizens, lawyers and courts in attempting to unravel the United Kingdom's relationship with Europe. The case has relevance to Brexit in two ways. First, it might help in understanding and addressing the dynamic within the United Kingdom after a divisive referendum revealed the polarized ambitions of its constituent nations. Second, it might assist in appreciating that through the United Kingdom's ratification of the TEU, the UK Parliament's implementing legislation and the resulting integration with Europe and European laws and regulations, a profound constitutional transformation occurred in both Europe and the United Kingdom, the undoing of which will be fraught with political, social, economic and legal risk.

---

25 *Patriation Reference, supra* note 23 at 774–775. See also *ibid* at 882–883: "It is because the sanctions of convention rest with institutions of government other than courts...or with public opinion and ultimately, the electorate, that it is generally said that they are political."

26 *Miller, supra* note 2 at para 142, citing from *Patriation Reference, supra* note 23 at 853.

27 *Miller, supra* note 2 at para 151.

28 *Secession Reference, supra* note 4.

Just as Britons were tensely awaiting the *Miller* ruling from the UKSC,[29] so were Canadians enthralled by the issues at stake in the *Secession Reference*. In the *Secession Reference*, the question was whether the Province of Quebec had a right to secede unilaterally from Canada in the event of a provincial referendum in favour of separation. Finding that the international law right of self-determination was not applicable to the people of Quebec because they enjoyed full political rights and representation in the provincial and federal governments,[30] the SCC focused its attention on secession in accordance with the Canadian Constitution.

Somewhat in contrast to the *Miller* decision's taciturnity, the unanimous judgment of the SCC is striking for its eloquence and profundity in dealing with the sensitive question of how to undo the Canadian state.[31] In the *Secession Reference*, the SCC observed that "the evolution of our constitutional arrangements has been characterized by adherence to the rule of law, respect for democratic institutions, the accommodation of minorities, insistence that governments adhere to constitutional conduct and a desire for continuity and stability."[32] The court identified "four foundational constitutional principles," "the vital unstated assumptions," these being "federalism, democracy, constitutionalism and the rule of law, and respect for minority rights," which "inform and sustain the constitutional text" and "function in symbiosis" such that no one principle can "trump or exclude the operation of any other."[33] The court explained the complex balance of these principles:

---

29   For an interesting English perspective on what hung in the balance, see Mark Elliot, "Brexit, Sovereignty, and the Contemporary British Constitution: four perspectives on *Miller*" (16 December 2016), *Public Law for Everyone* (blog), online: <https://publiclawforeveryone.com/2016/12/16/brexit-sovereignty-and-the-contemporary-british-constitution-four-perspectives/>.

30   *Secession Reference*, *supra* note 4 at para 138:
      In summary, the international law right to self-determination only generates, at best, a right to external self-determination in situations of former colonies; where a people is oppressed, as for example under foreign military occupation; or where a definable group is denied meaningful access to government to pursue their political, economic, social and cultural development. In all three situations, the people in question are entitled to a right to external self-determination because they have been denied the ability to exert internally their right to self-determination. Such exceptional circumstances are manifestly inapplicable to Quebec under existing conditions. Accordingly, neither the population of the province of Quebec, even if characterized in terms of "people" or "peoples", nor its representative institutions, the National Assembly, the legislature or government of Quebec, possess a right, under international law, to secede unilaterally from Canada.

31   As Warren J Newman notes, "The brilliance of the Supreme Court of Canada's ruling in the Quebec Secession Reference lies in the Court's having had the vision to wed the value of constitutional legality with that of political legitimacy." See Warren J Newman, "Reflections on the Tenth Anniversary of the Supreme Court's Opinion in the Quebec Secession Reference" (22 August 2008), *The Court* (blog), online: <www.thecourt.ca/reflections-on-the-tenth-anniversary-of-the-supreme-courts-opinion-in-the-quebec-secession-reference/>. See also Warren J Newman, "Grand Entrance Hall: Backdoor or Foundation Stone? The Role of Constitutional Principles in Construing and Applying the Constitution of Canada" (2001) 14 SCLR (2d) 197. See also Sébastien Grammond, "Canadian Constitutional Jurisprudence and the Brexit Process" (12 July 2016), *UK Constitutional Law Association* (blog) [Grammond, "Brexit Process"], online: <https://ukconstitutionallaw.org/2016/07/12/sebastien-grammond-canadian-constitutional-jurisprudence-and-the-brexit-process/>. Grammond suggests the court's generous constitutional interpretation "arguably filled gaps in the constitutional text, to ensure that those 'compacts' or 'historic bargains' between the country's constituent parts are upheld." There has been considerable commentary on the *Secession Reference*. The following is a sample: James T McHugh, "Making Public Law Public: An Analysis of the Quebec Reference Case and its Significance for Comparative Constitutional Analysis" (2000) 49:2 Intl Comp LQ 445 at 461–462; Jean Leclair, "Canada's Unfathomable Unwritten Constitutional Principles" (2002) 27 Queen's LJ 389; Richard S Kay, "The Secession Reference and the Limits of Law" (2003) 10 Otago LR 327; Stephen Tierney, *Constitutional Law and National Pluralism* (Oxford, UK: Oxford University Press, 2005); Hugh Mellon, "Secession and Constitutional Principles: Working with the Supreme Court's Statement of Principles" (2007) 20:2 Brit J Can Stud 211. Not all commentaries were laudatory. See e.g. Sujit Choudhry & Robert Howse, "Constitutional Theory and the Quebec Secession Reference" (2000) 13 Can JL & Jur 143 at 170, in which the authors express dissatisfaction with its "pragmatic perspective" and call for more clarity and justification for the judicial role in constitutional adjudication. The influence of the *Secession Reference* on constitutional developments in Eastern Europe, especially in Bosnia and Herzegovina, is also noteworthy: Zoran Oklopcic, "The Migrating Spirit of the Secession Reference in Southeastern Europe" (2011) 24 Can JL & Jur 347 at 348.

32   *Secession Reference*, *supra* note 4 at para 48.

33   *Ibid* at para 49.

The consent of the governed is a value that is basic to our understanding of a free and democratic society. Yet democracy in any real sense of the word cannot exist without the rule of law. It is the law that creates the framework within which the "sovereign will" is to be ascertained and implemented. To be accorded legitimacy, democratic institutions must rest, ultimately, on a legal foundation. That is, they must allow for the participation of, and accountability to, the people, through public institutions created under the Constitution. Equally, however, a system of government cannot survive through adherence to the law alone. A political system must also possess legitimacy, and in our political culture, that requires an interaction between the rule of law and the democratic principle. The system must be capable of reflecting the aspirations of the people. But there is more. Our law's claim to legitimacy also rests on an appeal to moral values, many of which are imbedded in our constitutional structure. It would be a grave mistake to equate legitimacy with the "sovereign will" or majority rule alone, to the exclusion of other constitutional values.

Finally, we highlight that a functioning democracy requires a continuous process of discussion. The Constitution mandates government by democratic legislatures, and an executive accountable to them, "resting ultimately on public opinion reached by discussion and the interplay of ideas" (*Saumur v. City of Quebec*, supra, at p. 330)…. No one has a monopoly on truth, and our system is predicated on the faith that in the marketplace of ideas, the best solutions to public problems will rise to the top. Inevitably, there will be dissenting voices. A democratic system of government is committed to considering those dissenting voices, and seeking to acknowledge and address those voices in the laws by which all in the community must live.[34]

The guidance provided by the SCC in these passages shows that a majority vote is an important indicator of the popular will, but taking action in furtherance of that expression is complex; it must be in accordance with the constitutional framework and take into account the other constitutional principles of accommodation of minority rights[35] and federalism or, in the case of the United Kingdom, regional interests.

The UKSC decision in *Miller* centred on the importance of following the constitutional framework, such that Crown prerogative was constrained by Parliamentary sovereignty. Thus, even though the executive could exercise Crown prerogative to negotiate, enter into and withdraw from treaties, it could not do this when it had the effect of making or unmaking domestic law. That could only be done by Parliament. The significance of this constitutional principle was highlighted by the fact that withdrawing from the European Union would result

---

34   *Ibid* at paras 67–68.

35   In a comment on the *Secession Reference*, Craig Scott noted, "Despite not having a definition given in his mandate, the [Organization for Security and Co-operation in Europe] OSCE High Commissioner on National Minorities in 1994 gave a speech that in effect gave a definition even while diplomatically characterizing it as a non-definition: 'The existence of a minority is a question of fact and not of definition….First of all, a minority is a group with linguistic, ethnic or cultural characteristics, which distinguish it from the majority. Secondly, a minority is a group which usually not only seeks to maintain its identity but also tries to give stronger expression to that identity.'" See Craig Scott, "The Québécois Form a Nation within a United Canada: No Help from International Law" (17 January 2007), *The Court* (blog), online: <www.thecourt.ca/the-quebecois-form-a-nation-within-a-united-canada-no-help-from-international-law/>.

in an unprecedented and massive unravelling of UK domestic law that had resulted from the 1972 Act, which enabled the flow-through of EU law into UK domestic law.[36]

The fundamental order of a constitutional democracy is usually maintained by techniques of entrenchment that make amendment more significant and difficult to achieve.[37] Entrenchment of the core rules of a society gives stability and relative permanence to those rules by imposing special requirements for their amendment. There is a passage in the *Secession Reference* on the entrenchment of rights in a Constitution that, on reflection, may have some relevance to the kind of "entrenchment" confirmed by the UKSC, by which article 50 of the TEU can only be invoked on the authority of an act of Parliament.[38] This may seem like an unusual kind of entrenchment, but it certainly has features of entrenchment: article 50 invocation cannot be done easily and certainly not by executive action; it must accord with domestic constitutional requirements; in particular Parliament must enact a law authorizing invocation — a vote on a Parliamentary motion is insufficient; then, the terms of separation must be successfully negotiated with the remaining EU countries.

The SCC in the *Secession Reference* stated, "An understanding of the scope and importance of the principles of the rule of law and constitutionalism is aided by acknowledging explicitly why a constitution is entrenched beyond the reach of simple majority rule."[39] The court identified three overlapping reasons: first, to safeguard fundamental human rights from government interference; second, to protect vulnerable minority groups from "assimilative pressures of the majority"; and, third, to allocate "political power amongst different levels of government."[40]

It is worth considering whether the 1972 Act bringing EU law into the United Kingdom, had these purposes and characteristics of entrenchment at the time of its passage, or whether it acquired this character of entrenchment over time. The majority in *Miller* is reluctant to go so

---

36 *Miller, supra* note 2 at paras 18–19:

> Section 2 of the 1972 Act was headed "General Implementation of Treaties." Section 2(1) of the 1972 Act was in these terms:
>
> > "All such rights, powers, liabilities, obligations and restrictions from time to time created or arising by or under the Treaties, and all such remedies and procedures from time to time provided for by or under the Treaties, as in accordance with the Treaties are without further enactment to be given legal effect or used in the United Kingdom shall be recognised and available in law, and be enforced, allowed and followed accordingly."
>
> Section 2(2) of the 1972 Act provided that "Her Majesty may by Order in Council, and any designated Minister or department may by regulations, make provision…for the purpose of implementing any Community [now EU] obligation of the United Kingdom," which is defined as any obligation "created or arising by or under the Treaties" or "enabling any rights…enjoyed…by the United Kingdom under or by virtue of the Treaties to be exercised," and for ancillary purposes, including "the operation from time to time of subsection (1)."

37 Peter Hogg, "Supremacy of the Canadian Charter of Rights and Freedoms" (1983) 61:1 Can Bar Rev 69 at 76–78, online: <http://digitalcommons.osgoode.yorku.ca/cgi/viewcontent.cgi?article=1638&context=scholarly_works>.

38 For some discussion of possible limitations on UK Parliamentary sovereignty, see *R (Jackson) v Attorney General*, [2005] UKHL 56, [2006] 1 AC 262.

39 *Secession Reference, supra* note 4 at para 73.

40 *Ibid* at para 74:

> First, a constitution may provide an added safeguard for fundamental human rights and individual freedoms which might otherwise be susceptible to government interference. Although democratic government is generally solicitous of those rights, there are occasions when the majority will be tempted to ignore fundamental rights in order to accomplish collective goals more easily or effectively. Constitutional entrenchment ensures that those rights will be given due regard and protection. Second, a constitution may seek to ensure that vulnerable minority groups are endowed with the institutions and rights necessary to maintain and promote their identities against the assimilative pressures of the majority. And third, a constitution may provide for a division of political power that allocates political power amongst different levels of government. That purpose would be defeated if one of those democratically elected levels of government could usurp the powers of the other simply by exercising its legislative power to allocate additional political power to itself unilaterally.

far, downplaying the complex constitutional implications of Brexit. While acknowledging that "in constitutional terms the effect of the 1972 Act was unprecedented"[41] and "[t]he content of the rights, duties and rules introduced into our domestic law as a result of the 1972 Act is exclusively a question of EU law,"[42] the majority considered that "the 1972 Act can be repealed like any other statute"[43] as "the constitutional processes by which the law of the United Kingdom is made is exclusively a question of domestic law."[44] Therefore, the *Miller* majority stated, "we would not accept that the so-called fundamental rule of recognition (i.e. the fundamental rule by reference to which all other rules are validated) underlying UK laws has been varied by the 1972 Act or would be varied by its repeal."[45] By suggesting that Brexit is just a matter of Parliament repealing and replacing domestic law, the UKSC misses the incommensurable and uncertain constitutional complexity alluded to in the *Secession Reference*.[46]

The Third Lesson: Negotiating International and Constitutional Change

Drawing analogies between the secession of a province from the Canadian federation and Brexit can make one's head spin, but there are points of comparison worth absorbing in order to understand what is at stake in the British government's current effort to withdraw from the European Union. To follow this analogy, one must imagine replacing the province of Quebec with the United Kingdom, to see whether the considerations relevant to the Cree Nation, and English and other minorities in Quebec are analogous to the perspectives of Northern Ireland, Scotland and Wales, and whether the interests of the rest of the provinces, territories and the federal government of Canada bear some resemblance to the interests of the remaining states of the European Union and Brussels.

The SCC in the *Secession Reference* described the process of constitutional change as beginning "with a political process undertaken pursuant to the Constitution itself....The federalism principle, in conjunction with the democratic principle, dictates that the clear repudiation of the existing constitutional order and the clear expression of the desire to pursue secession by the population of a province would give rise to a reciprocal obligation on all parties to Confederation to negotiate constitutional changes to respond to that desire."[47]

Consider how these words might apply by analogy to the situation in the United Kingdom. As Sébastien Grammond astutely observes, "the principles identified by the Court could apply, first at the level of the negotiations between the United Kingdom and the European Union, and second, within the United Kingdom."[48] At the international level, the expression by a majority of British voters of their desire to leave the European Union, and their government's

---

41 *Miller, supra* note 2 at para 60.

42 *Ibid* at para 62.

43 *Ibid* at para 60.

44 *Ibid* at para 62.

45 *Ibid* at para 60. See also the discussion at paras 61–63.

46 Brian Davey, "Brexit and complexity", Foundation for the Economics of Sustainability (Feasta) (10 May 2017), online: <www.feasta.org/2017/05/10/brexit-and-complexity/>.

47 *Secession Reference, supra* note 4 at para 88.

48 Grammond, "Brexit Process", *supra* note 31.

lawful invocation of article 50 gives rise to a concomitant duty on the other members of the European Union to negotiate in good faith. This is a political process undertaken pursuant to the Constitution of the European Union, that is, the TEU. At the domestic level, implementing the referendum result requires a negotiation with the constituent parts of the United Kingdom: the devolved governments, affected minorities and other stakeholders.

The SCC then explained that "[t]he corollary of a legitimate attempt by one participant in Confederation to seek an amendment to the Constitution is an obligation on all parties to come to the negotiating table....The clear repudiation by the people of Quebec of the existing constitutional order would confer legitimacy on demands for secession, and place an obligation on the other provinces and the federal government to acknowledge and respect that expression of democratic will by entering into negotiations and conducting them in accordance with the underlying constitutional principles already discussed."[49]

In that negotiation, all parties' conduct would be governed by the constitutional principles of "federalism, democracy, constitutionalism and the rule of law, and the protection of minorities."[50] These principles led the court to reject "absolutist propositions."[51] There was neither a legal right to unilateral secession nor a legal right to ignore the results of a clear referendum. The court reiterated that "[t]he democracy principle, as we have emphasized, cannot be invoked to trump the principles of federalism and rule of law, the rights of individuals and minorities, or the operation of democracy in the other provinces or in Canada as a whole."[52] Equally, the court observed, "The continued existence and operation of the Canadian constitutional order cannot remain indifferent to the clear expression of a clear majority of Quebecers that they no longer wish to remain in Canada."[53] As a consequence of these competing constitutional claims, "[n]egotiations would be necessary to address the interests of the federal government, of Quebec and the other provinces, and other participants, as well as the rights of all Canadians both within and outside Quebec."[54]

The court pointed out that, although the requirement to negotiate in good faith and adhere to constitutional principles would not determine whether or not secession in fact proceeded, the manner in which the negotiation occurred would substantially affect the legitimacy of the result whatever it might be, legitimacy being a crucial factor in both domestic and international acceptance of that result. A breach of the "constitutional duty" to engage in principled negotiation "undermines the legitimacy of a party's actions...and may have important ramifications at the international level....Thus, a failure of the duty to undertake negotiations and pursue them

---

49 *Secession Reference, supra* note 4 at para 88. See also David R Wingfield, "The Brexit Case: Does the Constitution Have a Place for Democracy?" (2016) 35 U Queensland LJ 343 at 348, emphasizing that the expression of democratic will obligates action by the executive and Parliament to take steps to leave the European Union:

   [S]hould the analysis of the Supreme Court of Canada be considered in the UK, the question raised before the Divisional Court might be answered quite differently. The answer would be that the executive branch of the Government has the political legitimacy and a corresponding constitutional duty to take those steps required under international law (which only the executive has the power to do) to bring about the departure of the UK from the various treaties that comprise its membership in the EU and Parliament has the political legitimacy and corresponding constitutional duty to take those steps required under domestic law (which only Parliament has the power to do) to remove EU law from the UK.

50 *Secession Reference, supra* note 4 at para 90.

51 *Ibid.*

52 *Ibid* at para 91.

53 *Ibid* at para 92.

54 *Ibid* at paras 92, 103.

according to constitutional principles may undermine that government's claim to legitimacy which is generally a precondition for recognition by the international community. Conversely, violations of those principles by the federal or other provincial governments responding to the request for secession may undermine their legitimacy."[55]

It is arguable that these dynamics are now playing out in the context of Brexit, within the United Kingdom and at the international level, with the launch of negotiations with the European Union. Majority rule is only part of constitutionalism, and those who fail to recognize this are unlikely to be effective negotiators in their own cause. The court's advice is deeply practical, as it explained the risks in allowing majority rule to trump all other constitutional values, which is what Quebec's assertion of a right to unilateral secession would do:

> Those who support the existence of such a right found their case primarily on the principle of democracy. Democracy, however, means more than simple majority rule. As reflected in our constitutional jurisprudence, democracy exists in the larger context of other constitutional values such as those already mentioned. In the 131 years since Confederation, the people of the provinces and territories have created close ties of interdependence (economically, socially, politically and culturally) based on shared values that include federalism, democracy, constitutionalism and the rule of law, and respect for minorities. A democratic decision of Quebecers in favour of secession would put those relationships at risk. The Constitution vouchsafes order and stability, and accordingly secession of a province "under the Constitution" could not be achieved unilaterally, that is, without principled negotiation with other participants in Confederation within the existing constitutional framework.[56]

This examination of the *Secession Reference* in the context of Brexit demonstrates that constitutional principles — including democratic principles that allow for the voices of distinct groups within a nation, relevant political conventions and rule of law, and respect for minorities — all need to be taken into account in negotiating Brexit. It is not a simple task, and the legitimacy of the outcomes will be judged by the way in which the processes adhere to these principles of inclusion. The judgment of the UKSC in *Miller* is clear that ministers are not legally compelled to consult the devolved governments. However, the guidance of the SCC in the *Patriation Reference*[57] and the *Secession Reference* indicates adherence to the Sewel Convention and other relevant democratic principles will be important for making constitutional changes that are viewed as legitimate within the United Kingdom and internationally. Reflecting on the *Secession Reference* years before the Brexit vote, Mark Walters considered what guidance is needed when legal systems become pathological:

> The [*Secession Reference*] confirms that these underlying constitutional principles are no less legal than the written ones they support, but that, as political allegiance to

---

55 *Ibid* at para 152. Speaking of legitimacy, a crucial but only obliquely addressed issue in the *Secession Reference* was the claim of the Cree Nation that a unilateral declaration of independence by Quebec would have drastic and deeply unjust consequences for them as it would force them out of Canada, dividing the Cree Nation between two countries. In their own referendum on the question, they had "overwhelmingly rejected (by over 95%) being separated from Canada without their consent." See Claude-Armand Sheppard, "The Cree Intervention in the Canadian Supreme Court Reference on Quebec Secession: A Subjective Analysis" (1999) 23 Vermont L Rev 845 at 850–851. If Quebec ever does try to negotiate an exit from Canada, how the issue of Cree sovereignty is addressed will likely be crucial in the quest for legitimacy.

56 *Secession Reference, supra* note 4 at para 149.

57 *Patriation Reference, supra* note 23.

positive sources of law begins to unravel and the idea of revolution is mooted seriously, adherence to the customary or unwritten constitution will become essential if peace and basic order in society is to be maintained. In other words, when the condition of a legal system is "pathological," only universal legal principles, not specific written ones from the system itself, will secure the ends of the rule of law.[58]

This prescription seems highly relevant in the aftermath of the Brexit vote. The early Brexit rhetoric was simplistic and polarized, implying that a majority vote was all that counted to move forward and even suggesting the courts had no role in guiding the process. This was both incorrect and inconsistent with the underlying historical and constitutional values that define the United Kingdom. Constitutional democracy and the rule of law could be victims of an inordinate emphasis on the referendum. Rather, the referendum should be treated as a first step, indicating a desire to engage in negotiation.

The terms of the negotiation, however, must address the full range of constitutional principles — respect for minorities, rule of law, constitutionalism and the democratic interests of distinct regions. To ignore these key points would sow seeds of conflict and disintegration within the United Kingdom. Fundamentally, the people of the United Kingdom need to ask whether they want separation at any cost, including to the integrity of the United Kingdom, or whether the trajectory of shared history and reconciliation that created the integrated United Kingdom is more important. If the latter, then much more political discussion needs to take place to set the negotiating terms for a new relationship with the European Union.

The European Union, in this analogy from the *Secession Reference*, is Canada, the remaining provinces and minorities within the province of Quebec. The European Union and its citizens, including Remain voters in the United Kingdom, have vested interests in the United Kingdom remaining within the European Union. They have organized their affairs confident in a future within the European Union. Their families, education, careers and businesses are now in a state of uncertainty and trepidation. These are the kind of minority rights and regional considerations that need to be addressed fairly if the Brexit process is to have legitimacy. After the disastrous election results, the UK government has started to confront the complexity of momentous constitutional change with stepped-up rhetoric about consultation with devolved governments and other affected stakeholders, such as internationally focused businesses and the consideration of EU workers.[59] The government has announced the contours of its Brexit negotiating plan,

---

58 Mark D Walters, "Nationalism and the Pathology of Legal Systems: Considering the Quebec Secession Reference and its Lessons for the United Kingdom" (1999) 62:3 Mod L Rev 371 at 384.

59 See e.g. UK, Department for Exiting the European Union (DEEU), News Release, "Minister Robin Walker visits the South West: Government engages with sectors at the heart of the region's economy" (31 July 2017), online: <www.gov.uk/government/news/minister-robin-walker-visits-the-south-west>; UK, DEEU, News Release, "Brexit Minister concludes two day tour of Scotland: the visit comes as the UK Government has stepped up its engagement with businesses from all parts of the UK" (28 July 2017), online: <www.gov.uk/government/news/brexit-minister-concludes-two-day-tour-of-scotland>; UK, Home Office, News Release, "The Home Secretary has today (27 July) commissioned the Migration Advisory Committee to examine the role EU nationals play in the UK economy and society" (27 July 2017), online: <www.gov.uk/government/news/home-secretary-commissions-major-study-on-eu-workers>. The government site offers the following helpful notice: "There is no need for EU citizens living in the UK to do anything now. There will be no change to the status of EU citizens living in the UK while the UK remains in the EU. If you would like to find out the latest information you can sign up for email updates." See UK, Home Office, UK Visas and Immigration, "Status of EU citizens in the UK: what you need to know", online: <www.gov.uk/guidance/status-of-eu-nationals-in-the-uk-what-you-need-to-know>.

including the Great Repeal Bill[60] and the rejection of the Charter of Fundamental Rights of the European Union[61] (the Charter), ostensibly on the grounds it created no new rights, freedoms or principles and added considerable complexity.[62] The Department for Exiting the European Union website reads like a community bulletin board in a (self-generated) state of emergency as it attempts to provide updates and answers to a wide array of increasingly anxious stakeholders.[63]

While the *Secession Reference* envisioned the possibility that good faith negotiations could fail to result in satisfactory terms of separation, article 50 suggests that even if negotiations fail, exit from the European Union may happen automatically. To state the obvious, there is no guarantee that the European Union will accept the terms that the United Kingdom proposes. The more the UK government adheres to constitutional principles of democracy, rule of law and respect for minorities, the more likely it will be able to ascertain whether Brexit is indeed a viable path for the United Kingdom, or whether it is a road leading toward the breakup of not only the European Union but also the United Kingdom itself. If, through a more inclusive negotiation process consistent with constitutional principles, the UK government finds a viable path for Brexit, the resulting departure from the European Union will also be more widely viewed as legitimate. With Brexit negotiations getting off to a rocky start, perhaps the last hope is that, as noted above, the UKSC did not decide, but took as "common ground" between the parties, that article 50 notice was not revocable. In other words, if the Brexit negotiations and the

---

60 UK, DEEU, "Factsheet 4: Power to implement the withdrawal agreement" in *Information about the Repeal Bill*, (London, UK: DEEU, 2017), online: <www.gov.uk/government/uploads/system/uploads/attachment_data/file/642864/Factsheets_-_Power_to_Implement_the_Withdrawal_Agreement.pdf>.

61 The Charter was given legal effect by the Lisbon Treaty on its entry into force in December 2009. Article 6(1) of the TEU provides for the Charter to have the same legal status as the EU treaties. See UK, DEEU, "Factsheet 6: Charter of Fundamental Rights" in *Information about the Repeal Bill* (London, UK: DEEU, 2017), online: <www.gov.uk/government/uploads/system/uploads/attachment_data/file/642866/Factsheets_-_Charter_of_Fundamental_Rights.pdf>. Other considerations for this decision may have been the Tory government's desire not to be subject to the European Court of Justice or to expand human rights. Meanwhile, a proposal to repeal the UK Human Rights Act was criticized as likely to have a negative impact in the "devolved nations": "Human rights are entrenched in the devolution settlements of Scotland, Wales and Northern Ireland in a way that they are not under the UK's constitution: acts of the devolved legislatures can, for example, be quashed by courts for non-compliance with the European Convention on Human Rights or the EU Charter." See UK, House of Lords European Union Committee, "The UK, the EU and a British Bill of Rights" HL Paper 139, 9 May 2016 at para 180, online: <https://publications.parliament.uk/pa/ld201516/ldselect/ldeucom/139/139.pdf>.

62 In the *UCL Brexit Blog*, Ronan McCrea opined:
    The most likely means through which a withdrawal agreement under Article 50 could be challenged is by means of a referral of the agreement to the Court of Justice under Article 218(11) of the Treaty on the Functioning of the European Union. Under this article, any Member State, the European Parliament, the Council and the Commission are all entitled under to seek the opinion of the Court of Justice "as to whether an agreement envisaged is compatible with the Treaties". The same Article makes it clear what occurs if incompatibility is found between the proposed agreement and the Treaties: "Where the opinion of the Court is adverse, the agreement envisaged may not enter into force unless it is amended or the Treaties are revised".
    As with so many elements of the Brexit process, the means by which the UK can attain what may have seemed rather clear objectives, are very unclear. Escaping from the control of the Court of Justice and avoiding the prospect of decisions of UK authorities being overturned on the basis that they violate EU fundamental rights norms was one of the key goals of those who supported Brexit....Compliance with EU fundamental rights, and indeed with the basic constitutional norms of the EU, will be part of any withdrawal agreement under Article 50.
    See Ronan McCrea, "Can a Brexit Deal Provide a Clean Break with the Court of Justice and EU Fundamental Rights Norms?" (17 October 2016), *UCL Brexit Blog* (blog), online: <https://ucl-brexit.blog/2016/10/17/ronan-mccrea-can-a-brexit-deal-provide-a-clean-break-with-the-court-of-justice-and-eu-fundamental-rights-norms/>. See also Albert Sanchez-Graells, "Why an Appeal of the High Court Parliamentary Approval of Brexit Judgment Will Bring the Litigation to CJEU" (3 November 2016), *How to Crack a Nut* (blog), online: <www.howtocrackanut.com/blog/2016/11/3/why-an-appeal-of-the-high-court-parliamentary-brexit>, in which Sanchez-Graells argues that "the UKSC has an absolute and inexcusable obligation to request a preliminary ruling on the interpretation of Article 50 TEU from the CJEU the moment the appeal against the High Court's Judgment (eventually) reaches its docket. Otherwise, the UKSC risks triggering an infringement of EU law and eventually creating liability in damages under the Kobler/Traghetti del Mediterraneo strand of case law on State liability."

63 UK, DEEU, online: <www.gov.uk/government/organisations/department-for-exiting-the-european-union>.

fraying relations with Northern Ireland, Scotland and Wales become too problematic, it may be necessary to explore the possibility of an exit from Brexit. After peering over the brink of Brexit at the complexity, difficulty, cost and acrimony that it entails, internal reconciliation with its own constituent nations and external reconciliation with the remaining EU nations may be a much-needed option for the United Kingdom to explore.

Conclusion

Pursuing momentous constitutional and international change such as the United Kingdom's exit from the European Union raises questions about whose voices will be included in the ensuing debate.[64] While the European project is a case study in pluralism, even its reluctant member, the United Kingdom, is not homogenous and gains both strength and vulnerability from its constituent communities. Recasting the lead characters in the *Secession Reference* allows access to a wealth of insights about the practical interplay of constitutional principles and conventions that could be useful for negotiators — whether for a devolved government, the United Kingdom or the European Union — to bear in mind. Casting the United Kingdom in the role of Quebec, one can imagine that the concerns of the Cree Nation and English and other minorities in Quebec bear some analogy to those of Northern Ireland, Scotland and Wales, and that the interests of the rest of the provinces, territories and the federal government of Canada are analogous to the interests of the remaining states of the European Union and Brussels. While there are many obvious legal and political differences in the facts underlying the *Secession Reference* and Brexit, this analysis suggests that, beyond the matters decided in *Miller*, there may be other constitutional issues to consider, such as the interests of devolved governments, Remain voters, European governments and European citizens.

James Tully illustrates the complexity and diversity that lurks beneath the surface of modern nation-states:

> Philosophers of multiculturalism, multinationalism, Indigenous rights and constitutional pluralism have elucidated struggles over recognition and accommodation of cultural diversity within and across the formally free and equal institutions of constitutional democracies. Theorists of empire, globalisation, globalisation from below, cosmopolitan democracy, immigration and justice-beyond-borders have questioned the accuracy of the inherited concepts of self-contained, Westphalian representative nation-states in representing the complex, multilayered global regimes of direct and indirect governance of new forms of inequality, exploitation, dispossession and violence, and the forms of local and global struggles by the governed here and now. Finally, post-colonial and post-modern scholars have drawn attention to how our prevailing logocentric languages of political reflection fail to do justice to the multiplicity of different voices striving for the freedom to have an effective democratic say over the ways they are governed.[65]

---

64 The subtleties have been missed by many. Ringo Starr probably spoke for a large swath of disgruntled Brexiters when he commented, "The people voted and, you know, they have to get on with it....Suddenly, it's like, 'Oh, well, we don't like that vote.' What do you mean you don't like that vote? You had the vote, this is what won, let's get on with it." See Harriet Gibsone, "Ringo Starr wants people of Britain to 'get on' with Brexit", *The Guardian* (14 September 2017), online: <www.theguardian.com/music/2017/sep/14/ringo-starr-wants-britain-to-get-on-with-brexit>.

65 James Tully, *Public Philosophy in a New Key*, vol 1 (Cambridge, UK: Cambridge University Press, 2008) at 19–20, online: <https://moodle.ufsc.br/pluginfile.php/1221563/mod_resource/content/1/Tully%20-%20Political%20Philosophy%20as%20Critical%20Activity.pdf>.

Tully outlines a "subaltern" school of political thought in which "questions of politics are approached as questions of freedom," where one asks "what are the possible practices of freedom in which free and equal subjects could speak and exchange reasons more freely over how to criticise, negotiate and modify their always imperfect practices," and in which it is a "permanent task" to ensure "practices of governance...do not become closed structures of domination under settled forms of justice but are always open to practices of freedom."[66]

There are difficult lessons to learn from Brexit about constitutional fundamentals, constitutional complexity and the interconnection between international and constitutional aspirations. Moments of dramatic international and constitutional change such as the Brexit project provide natural opportunities for dissent and discontent to be spoken out loud. The legitimacy of the Brexit project will in some measure be judged by how well the leaders heed these alternative voices and work to accommodate them in the new international and constitutional ordering.

Author's Note

This chapter originated as speaking notes for a presentation at a joint Conference on Brexit and International Law organized through the collaboration of the Centre for International Governance Innovation and the British Institute of International and Comparative International Law, held in London on January 31, 2017. The author thanks articling student Ryerson Neal for his assistance with research.

---

66 *Ibid* at 38.

16

Brexit and Human Rights

Colm O'Cinneide

Introduction

The potential impact of Brexit on human rights has attracted plenty of commentary since the Leave vote prevailed in the referendum of June 23, 2016. Much of this commentary has focused on the threats the Brexit process may pose to legal human rights protection in the United Kingdom. Thus, for example, Merris Amos has expressed concern that Brexit and, in particular, its legal implementation via the European Union (Withdrawal) Bill[1] (EU [Withdrawal] Bill) will open up a vacuum in rights protection.[2] Tobias Lock has argued that, even though the United Kingdom's exit from the European Union need not automatically result in a dilution of fundamental rights protection, Brexit is nevertheless likely to pose a risk to existing human rights protection.[3] Conor Gearty has dramatically suggested that Brexit is becoming Britain's Vietnam, partially in the sense

---

1   Bill 5, *European Union (Withdrawal) Bill* [HL], 2017–2019 sess (1st reading 13 July 2017) [*EU (Withdrawal) Bill*].

2   Merris Amos, "Red Herrings and Reductions: Human Rights and the EU (Withdrawal) Bill" (4 October 2017), *UK Constitutional Law Association* (blog), online: <https://ukconstitutionallaw.org/>.

3   Tobias Lock, "Human Rights Law in the UK after Brexit" (2017) Public Law, Brexit Special Extra Issue 117.

of becoming a policy quagmire that threatens the slow erosion of established human rights and civil liberties.[4] Colin Harvey and other commentators in Northern Ireland have been vocal in expressing the fear that Brexit will undermine the human rights framework that forms a key element of the Northern Irish peace settlement, laid out in the 1998 Good Friday Agreement.[5]

Nor have these concerns been confined to academic commentary. The Joint Committee on Human Rights (JCHR) of the UK Parliament has expressed concern that the process of Brexit could have a negative impact on human rights across a number of different areas, if careful action is not taken to alleviate its impact.[6] Similar concerns have been expressed in parliamentary debates on Brexit and, in particular, on the provisions of the EU (Withdrawal) Bill.[7]

In contrast, other commentators have argued that these concerns are radically overstated. For example, a response to the JCHR's report co-authored by a number of prominent law professors and published under the banner of the Judicial Power Project (a project funded by Policy Exchange, a leading centre-right think tank) argued that there is nothing intrinsic to the process of the United Kingdom exiting the European Union that necessarily leads to a reduction in the substantive protection of human rights.[8] The UK government has also argued that the legal adjustments required to give effect to Brexit will not lead to any diminution of the scope of core legal safeguards.[9] Indeed, some commentators even argue that leaving the European Union offers an opportunity for the United Kingdom to develop superior standards of rights protection than currently exist in British or European law — or, at least, to develop standards that better reflect British values and/or popular views as to the appropriate content of human rights norms.[10]

How are we to assess the merits of these competing claims, especially given the highly contested nature of Brexit and the charged political environment that surrounds it? As a first step, it is helpful to identify whether, how and to what extent the Brexit process creates a real risk that existing human rights standards may be eroded. Identifying the extent of any such risk then makes it possible to assess the potential impact of Brexit on rights — bearing in mind that Brexit is playing out against the background of the United Kingdom's particular political and constitutional culture, and Brexit's future impact will inevitably be shaped by this culture. In carrying out this assessment, the aim is not to make a polemical argument about the pros and cons of Brexit: instead, the objective of this analysis is to clarify Brexit's potential impact on human rights in the short- to medium-term future.

---

4   Conor Gearty, "A Happy Brexit? We should rather brace ourselves for a dramatic change in our democratic freedom — for the worse" (23 November 2017), *LSE Brexit* (blog), online: <http://blogs.lse.ac.uk/brexit/2017/11/23/a-happy-brexit-we-should-rather-brace-ourselves-for-a-dramatic-change-in-our-democratic-freedom-for-the-worse/>.

5   See e.g. Colin Harvey, "Brexit, Northern Ireland and Human Rights" (5 May 2017) *RightsNI* (blog), online: <http://rightsni.org/2017/05/brexit-northern-ireland-and-human-rights/>; "Brexit Implications for Human Rights Provisions to be Examined", *Belfast Telegraph* (13 February 2017), online: <www.belfasttelegraph.co.uk/news/republic-of-ireland/brexits-implications-for-human-rights-provisions-to-be-examined-35445599.html>.

6   UK, JCHR, *The Human Rights Implications of Brexit* (5th Report of Session 2016-17, HL Paper 88/HC 695) (London, UK: Parliament, 2016), online: <https://publications.parliament.uk/pa/jt201617/jtselect/jtrights/695/695.pdf>.

7   See e.g. Heather Steward, "'Great repeal bill' human rights clause sets up Brexit clash with Labour", *The Guardian* (13 July 2017), online: <www.theguardian.com/politics/2017/jul/13/great-repeal-bill-human-rights-clause-sets-up-brexit-clash-with-labour>.

8   Gunnar Beck et al, "What the JCHR gets Wrong about Fundamental Rights", *Judicial Power Project* (19 December 2016), online: <http://judicialpowerproject.org.uk/what-the-jchr-gets-wrong-about-fundamental-rights/>.

9   See the comments by Lord Keen of Elie, speaking for the government in the House of Lords debate on "Brexit: Human Rights": UK, HL, *Parliamentary Debates*, vol 787, col 1524 (12 December 2017).

10   See Beck et al, *supra* note 8.

The Risks of Brexit

The majority of the commentators expressing concern about the potential impact of Brexit on human rights have focused on how it may undermine existing legal methods of rights protection. Within this general strand of criticism, several different subthemes can be identified.

The Potential Impact of Brexit on Existing EU Legislative Protection for Human Rights

To start with, some commentators have highlighted the important role that EU primary and secondary legislation has come to play in securing certain human rights — which is particularly the case in areas such as discrimination law, workers' rights, environmental law, data protection and migrant rights.[11] In all of these contexts, EU law sets out minimum standards with which all EU member states must comply. Furthermore, the supremacy and direct effect of EU law means that these baseline standards cannot be overridden or diluted by national lawmakers. As a result, the protection these standards provide for human rights is relatively insulated against the vicissitudes of national politics. In addition, the purposive approach adopted by the Court of Justice of the European Union (CJEU) in interpreting EU law, and its willingness to read primary and secondary legislation with reference to the overarching human rights commitments that are supposed to underpin the EU legal order, have ensured that these rights-protective standards often have real teeth.

For example, the set of directives, treaty provisions and general principles that make up EU equality law requires states to prohibit discrimination on the grounds of age, disability, gender, race or ethnicity, religion or belief and sexual orientation in the area of employment and occupation (and, for gender and race, in access to goods and services and other areas of social advantage). By virtue of these legal standards, EU member states are obliged to ensure that their domestic laws provide effective protection against direct and indirect discrimination, harassment and victimization linked to one or more of the four protected grounds of non-discrimination set out in the EU equality directives. The CJEU has also given a purposive interpretation to the relevant EU legal norms in this context.[12] As a consequence, EU equality law provides strong protection against many forms of discrimination. This has had a substantial impact on UK law, which has had to be repeatedly modified and strengthened in response to its requirements.[13] Furthermore, the supremacy and direct effect of EU law has helped to give discrimination law a quasi-constitutional status in the United Kingdom, embedding it against attempts to dilute its requirements or water down its scope. In so doing, EU equality law provides substantive protection for the right to equality and non-discrimination as protected by article 14 of the European Convention on Human Rights[14] (ECHR) and other human rights

---

11 See Lock, *supra* note 3. See also Michael Ford, "Workers' Rights from Europe: The Impact of Brexit" (10 March 2016), online: <www.tuc.org.uk/sites/default/files/Brexit%20Legal%20Opinion.pdf> (advice prepared for the Trade Union Congress).

12 Colm O'Cinneide, *The Evolution and Impact of the Case-Law of the Court of Justice of the European Union on Directives 2000/43/EC and 2000/78/EC* (Brussels, Belgium: Migration Policy Group, 2012).

13 Colm O'Cinneide & Kimberly Liu, "Defining the Limits of Discrimination Law in the UK: Principle and Pragmatism in Tension" (2014) 15:1–2 Intl J Discrimination & L 239.

14 *European Convention on Human Rights*, 4 November 1950, ETS 5, 213 UNTS 221 (entered into force 3 September 1953) [*ECHR*].

treaty provisions: it acts as a backstop to the provisions of the Equality Act 2010[15] and other UK anti-discrimination legislation, ensuring that their provisions, and UK law more generally, give adequate effect to the principle of non-discrimination.[16]

The situation is similar when it comes to the other areas mentioned above where EU law protects human rights. The demanding requirements of EU data protection law, as interpreted by the CJEU with reference to the EU Charter of Fundamental Rights[17] (CFR), protects the rights to privacy and freedom of expression. The provisions of instruments such as the Working Time Directive[18] and the Part-time Workers Directive[19] help to secure core labour rights. EU law in the area of immigration, asylum and migrant rights, while at times problematic from a human rights perspective, also can take effect in a way that strengthens respect for the right to privacy, home and family life. EU environmental law has played a key role in protecting air quality and other essentials to human health and the right to life.[20]

However, after the United Kingdom exits the European Union, these standards will presumably no longer enjoy the benefit of supremacy/direct effect. Therefore, even though they will remain part of UK law by virtue of the provisions of the EU (Withdrawal) Act, the United Kingdom's withdrawal from the European Union creates the possibility that they may be diluted, amended or repealed by subsequent UK primary or secondary legislation. Furthermore, the purposive approach generally adopted by the CJEU in interpreting these standards may not be adopted by UK courts in the future as they might consider themselves constitutionally inhibited from following the CJEU's lead in this regard.

As a consequence, Brexit poses a potential threat to all these EU standards — and, by extension, to the specific and embedded forms of legal protection they afford to human rights. The extra layer of security currently provided by the supremacy and direct effect of EU law to many of the legal rules that help to secure equality and labour, environmental and migrants' rights at present will fall away — opening them up to the possibility of being watered down or substantially eroded.[21]

The Potential Impact of Brexit on the Legal Status of the General Principles of EU Law and the CFR

This concern is exacerbated by the likelihood that Brexit will dilute the impact of certain overarching aspects of EU law that serve to ensure the conformity of all aspects of EU law and national implementing measures with human rights — namely, the general principles of EU law and the CFR. Commentators have again focused upon this risk with concern, with some

---

15 *Equality Act 2010* (UK), c 15.

16 See Ford, *supra* note 11.

17 *Charter of the Fundamental Rights of the European Union*, [2000] OJ, C 364/01 [*CFR*].

18 *Directive 2003/88/EC of the European Parliament and of the Council of 4 November 2003 concerning certain aspects of the organisation of working time*, [2003] OJ, L 299/9.

19 *Council Directive 97/81/EC of 15 December 1997 concerning the Framework Agreement on part-time work concluded by UNICE, CEEP and the ETUC–Annex: Framework agreement on part-time work*, [1998] OJ, L 14/9.

20 For a general overview, see UK, JCHR, *supra* note 6.

21 See Ford, *supra* note 11.

identifying it as perhaps the most significant negative consequence of Brexit for human rights protection.[22]

The CJEU has recognized the existence of certain general principles that underpin the EU legal order. All EU law and national implementing measures must respect these general principles — which, since the early 1970s, have been interpreted by the court as requiring adherence to human rights that form part of the common constitutional tradition of EU member states or are recognized in international treaties, such as the ECHR, that have been ratified by all member states.[23]

The CFR was intended to specify these human rights obligations with more precision.[24] It sets out a wide-ranging list of fundamental rights and principles, extending to cover certain social and citizen rights that human rights instruments such as the ECHR do not cover. Since 2009, it has had the same legal status as the EU treaties, meaning that all EU law and national implementing measures must comply with its requirements.[25] As confirmed by the CJEU in the case of *NS*,[26] its provisions apply to the United Kingdom notwithstanding the provisions of protocol 30[27] to the Treaty on European Union, which affirm that nothing in the CFR extends the competency of the CJEU to set aside existing UK laws for incompatibility with fundamental rights principles: it appears as if the only legal impact of this protocol, often erroneously described as a UK opt-out from the CFR, may be to limit the application to UK law of certain social rights principles set out in the CFR.[28]

Taken together, the general principles and the CFR serve as human rights guarantors within the EU legal framework: the provisions of EU law and national implementing measures must be read subject to their requirements and can be set aside by the CJEU and national courts if they are incompatible with the rights they protect. Both the general principles and the CFR have been applied so as to reinforce fundamental rights protection by the CJEU and national courts (including the UK Supreme Court) — with particular impact in areas such as immigration and asylum, the application of EU sanctions, data protection and discrimination law.[29]

However, this constitutional layer of rights protection provided by the general principles and CFR is unlikely to be preserved in a post-Brexit United Kingdom. Once the United Kingdom leaves the European Union and the European Communities Act 1972[30] is repealed, the doctrine

---

22 See Amos, *supra* note 2.

23 *Nold v Commission*, C-4/73, [1974] ECR 491 at especially para 13. See generally Takis Tridimas, *The General Principles of EU Law*, 2nd ed (Oxford, UK: Oxford University Press, 2007).

24 As Young notes, "It can also be difficult to separate out Charter rights and general principles — the Charter and general principles are influenced by each other...developing in a coterminous manner." See Alison Young, "Oh, What a Tangled Web We Weave... The EU (Withdrawal) Bill 2017–19 and Human Rights post Brexit: Part 1" (15 August 2017) *Oxford Human Rights* (blog), online: <http://ohrh.law.ox.ac.uk/oh-what-a-tangled-web-we-weave-the-eu-withdrawal-bill-2017-19-and-human-rights-post-brexit-part-1>.

25 *Treaty on European Union (Consolidated Version)*, 7 February 1992, [2002] OJ, C 325/5, art 6 (entered into force 1 November 1993) [*TEU*].

26 *NS v Secretary of State for the Home Department*, Case C-411/10, [2012] 2 CMLR 9.

27 *Protocol (No 30) on the application of the Charter of Fundamental Rights of the European Union to Poland and to the United Kingdom*, 9 May 2008, [2008] OJ, C 115/313.

28 *Ibid* at para 2.

29 See e.g. *Kücükdevici*, C-555/07, [2010] I-00365, [2010] 2 CMLR 33; *Benkharbouche v Embassy of Sudan*, [2017] UKSC 62; *Walker v Innospec Ltd*, [2017] UKSC 47; *Google v Vidal-Hall*, [2015] EWCA Civ 311.

30 *European Communities Act 1972* (UK), c 68.

of parliamentary sovereignty will again take full effect: this means that national legislation will be immune from challenge on the basis of incompatibility with the general principles and/or the CFR, restricting the protection they currently afford to rights.

Furthermore, at the time of writing, the text of the EU (Withdrawal) Bill before Parliament provides that the CFR shall not remain part of UK law after Brexit.[31] This provision of the bill reflects the strongly negative views of many Conservative Party members of Parliament about the CFR and its wide-ranging set of human rights guarantees. It is not uncontroversial: the exclusion of the CFR from the carry-over provisions of the bill has been criticized by both the parliamentary opposition and the Equality and Human Rights Commission,[32] and the UK government has been forced to make the somewhat dubious argument that the provisions of the CFR add little or nothing to existing human rights protection.[33] However, absent from a significant shift in government policy, it is likely that the CFR will be uprooted from UK law on Brexit — taking with it the wide-ranging rights protection it currently offers within the scope of application of EU law.

This would leave the general principles of EU law still in play. While the general principles will not override parliamentary legislation post-Brexit, the UK courts will still be required to take them into account in interpreting those elements of EU law that will remain embedded in UK law. However, at the time of writing, the EU (Withdrawal) Bill provides that, from exit day onward, there will be no "right of action in domestic law…based on a failure to comply with any of the general principles of EU law."[34] This would prevent claims alleging a breach of the general principles being litigated in UK courts post-Brexit and limit the role of the general principles to being an interpretative aid. This particular government proposal risks destabilizing established EU law and, thus, generating legal uncertainty, so it may not survive the parliamentary debate on the withdrawal bill. However, as Alison Young has pointed out, the general principles lack specificity — meaning that, in the absence of the CFR, their usefulness as a source of rights protection post-Brexit may be limited.[35]

The EU (Withdrawal) Bill — Statutory Amendment by Executive Fiat?

Other concerns arise in relation to the legal mechanisms that the EU (Withdrawal) Bill provides for the UK government to amend or repeal the provisions of EU law that will continue to form part of UK law post-Brexit. The bill gives ministers wide-ranging powers to amend both transposed EU law and associated UK law via secondary legislation.[36] This means that ministers will have the power to amend or even repeal any aspect of EU law that protects human rights, along with any linked UK legislation, where necessary to give effect to the Brexit transition process. The use of such ministerial powers is open to scrutiny and veto by Parliament — but,

---

31 See *EU (Withdrawal) Bill, supra* note 1, cl 5(4).

32 Joe Watts, "UK government watchdog pushes for new British 'right to equality' to stop Brexit leading to more discrimination", *The Independent* (15 October 2017), online: <www.independent.co.uk/news/uk/politics/brexit-discrimination-laws-right-to-equality-uk-equalities-watchdog-eu-a7999461.html>.

33 UK Department for Exiting the European Union, "The Repeal Bill — Factsheet 6: EU Charter of Fundamental Rights" (13 July 2017), online: <www.gov.uk/government/uploads/system/uploads/attachment_data/file/642866/Factsheets_-_Charter_of_Fundamental_Rights.pdf>.

34 See *EU (Withdrawal) Bill, supra* note 1, Schedule 1, cl 3(1): see also (*ibid*) Schedule 1, cl 3(2) ("no court may disapply, quash, or decide that action is unlawful because it is incompatible with general principles of EU law").

35 Young, *supra* note 24.

36 See *EU (Withdrawal) Bill, supra* note 1, cl 9.

in reality, Parliament's capacity to exercise a meaningful rights protective role in this context is limited by the exigencies of time, a lack of expert knowledge and government control over the business of the House of Commons.

Many commentators have identified the scope of these ministerial powers as a real threat to the enjoyment of human rights post-Brexit, given that these powers make it possible for existing legal guarantees to be diluted, amended or repealed by the exercise of potentially unaccountable executive power.[37] At the time of writing, amendments have been tabled to the withdrawal bill to limit the extent to which these powers can be used to alter existing EU/UK law that impacts upon equality and human rights, and to impose greater parliamentary controls on their use more generally.[38] It remains to be seen what political compromises will be reached in this regard. However, it would appear inevitable that EU law, in general, once converted into UK law post-Brexit, will be open to being extensively amended by fast-track executive action — which, therefore, poses, by extension, a risk to the legal protection EU law currently provides for various fundamental rights.

Assessing the Brexit Risk to Human Rights

It is, therefore, possible to identify specific risks that Brexit poses to the protection of human rights. However, if a meaningful overview of Brexit's potential impact on human rights is to be devised, it is not enough merely to point to the existence of such risks. Brexit may make certain existing forms of rights protection vulnerable, but that does not necessarily mean that the protections are likely to be swept away: risks can be real, without ever coming to fruition. To make a full risk assessment about the impact of Brexit on human rights, some analysis is needed of the probability of existing rights protection being diluted — along with some critical engagement with the question of whether the current (EU) status quo should be regarded as a baseline worth retaining when it comes to human rights.

Starting with the probability of the above-mentioned risks coming to fruition, there are certain factors in play that suggest that Brexit is unlikely to result in a bonfire of rights-protective EU legislative instruments — at least, in the short to medium term. To start with, high levels of political disquiet have been expressed about the possibility of existing EU standards being diluted in fields such as equality law, labour rights and environmental protection. This has affected the political debate surrounding Brexit. For example, when she became prime minister in the wake of the referendum, Theresa May promised that there would be no dilution of existing workers' rights guaranteed through EU law.[39] Other government ministers have made similar remarks in respect of equality law and environmental protection.[40]

---

37 See e.g. Mark Elliott, "The EU (Withdrawal) Bill: Initial Thoughts" (14 July 2017) *Public Law For Everyone* (blog), online: <https://publiclawforeveryone.com/2017/07/14/the-eu-withdrawal-bill-initial-thoughts/>; UK, House of Lords Constitution Committee, *EU (Withdrawal) Bill: Interim Report* (3rd Report of Session 2017-18, HL Paper 19) (London, UK: Parliament, 2017).

38 See ECHR, "EU (Withdrawal) Bill: Second Reading, House of Commons, 7 September 2017", online: <www.equalityhumanrights.com/sites/default/files/briefing-eu-withdrawal-bill-second-reading.pdf>.

39 Theresa May, "Theresa May's Brexit speech in full", *The Telegraph* (17 January 2017), online: <www.telegraph.co.uk/news/2017/01/17/theresa-mays-brexit-speech-full/>.

40 Note that the UK government has confirmed that it only intends to make minor technical amendments to the Equality Act 2010 via the enabling powers conferred by the EU (Withdrawal) Bill: see UK, "Equality Legislation and EU Exit" (12 December 2017), online: <www.gov.uk/government/uploads/system/uploads/attachment_data/file/665442/171206_Equalities_SI_summary_FINAL_.pdf>.

The controversy that has surrounded the devolution dimension of Brexit — and in particular the issue of its impact on Northern Ireland — also makes it likely that both the current and future governments may feel the need to tread carefully when tinkering with EU baseline standards that help to secure human rights in politically sensitive areas such as equality law and environmental protection. There is also the possibility that the final withdrawal, transition and trade agreements to be negotiated with the European Union will require the United Kingdom to maintain regulatory alignment in various areas currently governed by EU law — with the trio of equality law, labour rights and environmental protection again being potential candidates for inclusion in this category.[41] In addition, there are areas where market forces will in all likelihood require the United Kingdom to continue to adhere to EU standards that are related to the enjoyment of human rights — such as data protection, where UK bulk holders of personal data that is sourced from a number of different EU states may need to maintain compliance with the EU data protection framework.

Having said that, there are also political factors in play which make it likely that there will be some departure from existing EU standards that currently help secure human rights. At present, both the Conservative and Labour parties are committed to changing EU free movement rules as they apply to the United Kingdom — meaning that migrant rights are likely to be diluted in the wake of the United Kingdom's exit from the European Union. Furthermore, various political factions within the broad pro-Leave coalition have supported the idea of the United Kingdom embracing a low-regulation economic model.[42] If implemented now or in the future, such an adjustment could entail substantial departures from the current EU regulatory framework in areas such as labour rights and environmental protection. In any case, it is likely that UK governments in the future will use the regulatory manoeuvre room left to them by the post-Brexit EU/UK trade agreement(s) to make adjustments to British law that will entail a departure from the existing (EU) status quo — which again could impact on the protection that status quo currently affords to human rights.

Therefore, while the risk of a radical dismantling of existing EU legislation that has a rights-protective function can be overstated, it is likely that Brexit will result in some adjustment of the status quo. In other words, Brexit will open existing EU rights-protecting standards to review, revision and potential repeal — and this is likely to result in changes to these standards, which are likely to be implemented through the potentially problematic secondary legislation mechanisms set out in the EU (Withdrawal) Bill. Thus, commentators who point to the risk of Brexit impacting upon human rights protection, and express fear that such changes will not be always subject to sustained parliamentary scrutiny, have a point.

Nonetheless, change is not inherently bad, even when it relates to the enjoyment of human rights. The EU standards under discussion in this chapter, which have conferred a degree of effective protection upon certain human rights in areas such as discrimination law, labour rights and migrant rights, are not the only way of securing such rights. Alternative modes of regulation might hypothetically confer equivalent or even superior levels of protection on such rights — or might protect rights in a way that resonates better with other values, such as democratic self-

---

41   See e.g. UK, "Joint Report on Progress during Phase 1 of Negotiations under Article 50 TEU on the United Kingdom's Orderly Withdrawal from the European Union" (8 December 2017) at para 53 (on rights protection in Northern Ireland: "The UK commits to ensuring that no diminution of rights is caused by [Brexit], including in the area of protection against forms of discrimination enshrined in EU law").

42   This is sometimes referred to as the Singapore model in Brexit debates. See e.g Patrick Collinson, "Billionaire Brexit Supporter says UK Should Emulate Singapore", *The Guardian* (12 May 2016), online: <www.theguardian.com/politics/2016/may/12/billionaire-brexit-supporter-says-uk-should-emulate-singapore>.

governance.[43] It is problematic to regard existing EU law that protects human rights — such as the CFR, or the equality directives — as sacred text: such instruments may be well-established features of the current European landscape of human rights protection, but that does not mean that replacing them with new legal frameworks need inevitably be a bad thing.

This is why some commentators downplay the risks Brexit poses to human rights, choosing instead to argue that the United Kingdom's exit from the European Union represents a positive opportunity to open up debate about how rights are protected through law and to rethink existing (EU) methods of protection.[44] However, there are problems with this perspective. When viewed in isolation, Brexit might seem a plausible opportunity to rethink existing modes of rights protection in the United Kingdom, free from the dead hand of EU orthodoxy. However, the potential consequences of Brexit for human rights cannot be assessed in isolation, detached from the background political and constitutional context. If this context is considered, then additional causes for concern about Brexit's impact on human rights enter the picture.

To start with, if EU standards in areas such as migrant rights or non-discrimination are to be replaced over time by UK regulation, this replacement process will inevitably play out against the divisive backdrop of acrimonious political debates about immigration, equality rights, devolution and the United Kingdom's continuing relationship with Europe. This creates a risk that new legal standards will be framed with an eye on achieving short-term political gains or to appease special interests or particular segments of the electorate, rather than with a fuller perspective centred around the assumption that human rights need to be given presumptive priority in law making.

Furthermore, this replacement process is likely to be channelled through law-making mechanisms that are often lacking in transparency and democratic accountability. For example, the executive has historically played a dominant role in framing UK immigration rules — and ministers and civil servants have regularly been accused of exercising too much authority over the shaping and application of British law in this regard, which is characterized by a high degree of complexity and non-transparent decision making.[45] Now, the Brexit process will give even greater powers to the executive in this regard, in particular due to the wide powers conferred on ministers by the provisions of the EU (Withdrawal) Bill. As a result, there are grounds for being concerned about how UK migration rules will be framed in the future — when ministers will, post-Brexit, be freed from the constraints of EU migration rules and the protective, rights-influenced jurisprudence of the CJEU.[46]

Furthermore, if the CFR is excluded from UK law post-Brexit, and the status of the general principles of EU law is watered down as discussed above, then the range of human rights that

---

43 For criticism of the CFR on the basis that it is incompatible with democratic values, see Richard Ekins, "The Charter of Fundamental Rights gives judges too much power, and is bad for accountable government", *Judicial Power Project* (22 July 2017), online: <https://judicialpowerproject.org.uk/richard-ekins-the-charter-of-fundamental-rights-gives-judges-too-much-power-and-is-bad-for-accountable-government/>.

44 See e.g. Beck et al, *supra* note 8.

45 See UK, House of Lords Constitutional Committee, *Immigration Bill* (7th Report of Session 2015-16, HL Paper 75) (London, UK: Parliament, 2016) at, in particular, paras 18–19.

46 See Joint Council for the Welfare of Immigrants (JCWI), "JCWI Response to the Exiting the European Union Inquiry on the UK's negotiating objectives for withdrawal from the EU" (20 March 2017), online: <www.jcwi.org.uk/sites/jcwi/files/2017-03/2017_03_20%20JCWI%20Response%20to%20the%20Exiting%20the%20European%20Union%20Inquiry.pdf>.

are directly enforceable within UK law will be considerably limited.[47] The Human Rights Act 1998[48] (HRA) will continue to apply after the United Kingdom's exit from the European Union. However, the fundamental rights protected by the HRA are much more limited in scope than those protected by the CFR or the general principles of EU law.[49] The HRA protects the core civil and political rights set out in the ECHR. However, the CFR's scope, in particular, is much greater, extending as it does to cover a wide range of dignitarian, social, equality and citizenship rights, in addition to the civil and political rights set out in the ECHR.[50] At present, the substance of many of these rights is not always clear, as the case law of the CJEU interpreting the CFR's provisions is still in embryonic form.[51] The extent to which respect for these rights is legally required as part of the general principles of EU law is also uncertain. Nevertheless, the requirements of the CFR, taken together with the general principles of EU law, considerably extend the range of individual rights claims that are directly enforceable before UK courts.[52] However, this will presumably change with Brexit. If the CFR is excluded from UK law post-Brexit, and the status of the general principles is diluted, then only the more limited range of rights protected by the HRA will be directly enforceable within UK law.[53]

Indeed, a Brexit-related shadow even hangs over this limited floor of protection afforded by the HRA. It transplants rights protected by the ECHR into UK law — and, therefore, attracts political controversy, in particular among many Brexit supporters, because the HRA is viewed as representing another instance of European supranational governance.[54] It may be the case that Brexit will divert attention and energy from the constant debates about the status and legitimacy of the HRA/ECHR, at least, in the short term. However, all forms of human rights law are likely to remain politically controversial — which means that any modification of existing EU rights-protective standards is likely to be carried out in a climate of intense rights skepticism, which is likely to extend even to the relatively narrow range of civil and political rights protected by the HRA.[55]

Some commentators have suggested that English common law could fill some of the gaps in rights protection left by the exclusion of the CFR and/or other post-Brexit dilution of European rights standards.[56] The UK courts have been willing to recognize the existence of certain common law rights, such as freedom of speech and the entitlement to a fair trial: public authorities cannot

---

47 Amos, *supra* note 2.

48 *Human Rights Act 1998* (UK), c 42.

49 Amos, *supra* note 2.

50 See especially *CFR*, *supra* note 17, Title 1 (Dignity), Title III (Equality), Title IV (Solidarity) and Title V (Citizens' Rights).

51 See generally Steve Peers et al, *The EU Charter of Fundamental Rights: A Commentary* (Oxford, UK: CH Beck/Hart/ Nomos, 2014).

52 See e.g. *Benkharbouche v Embassy of Sudan*, [2017] UKSC 62. The rights claim at issue in this case — the right to non-discrimination in the context of employment as protected by article 21 of the CFR — was enforceable in UK law as the provisions of the CFR were applicable (in other words, the issue concerned national measures coming within the scope of EU law). In contrast, the right to non-discrimination as protected by article 14 of the ECHR was not applicable in this context, as article 14 does not usually extend to cover employment issues. See generally Colm O'Cinneide, "The Principle of Equality and Non-discrimination within the Framework of the EU Charter and Its Potential Application to Social and Solidarity Rights" in Giuseppe Palmisano, ed, *Making the Charter of Fundamental Rights a Living Instrument* (Leiden, Switzerland: Brill, 2015) 199.

53 Amos, *supra* note 2.

54 Merris Amos, "Transplanting Human Rights Norms: The Case of the United Kingdom's Human Rights Act" (2013) 35:2 Hum Rts Q 386.

55 Lock, *supra* note 3.

56 See e.g. Mark Elliott, "Beyond the European Convention: Human Rights and the Common Law" (2015) 68:1 Current Leg Probs 85.

act in a manner that limits the enjoyment of these rights unless they are expressly or by necessary implication authorized to do so by parliamentary legislation.[57] These rights are widely regarded as constituting home-grown human rights standards, whose lineage can be traced back to the Magna Carta. In recent years, the UK Supreme Court has shown a willingness to develop the case law relating to these common law rights — perhaps reflecting the current political hostility directed toward transnational European standards in this field.[58] This expanding case law shows that these common law rights have some teeth. They will also remain unaffected by Brexit and, thereby, will continue to provide a degree of rights protection even if European standards are amended, diluted or repealed. However, the scope of these rights — like that of the HRA — is limited to a narrow range of civil and political rights.[59] Furthermore, the rights' content is uncertain and controversy persists as to whether judges should play an active role in developing such rights standards in the absence of clear parliamentary authorization to do so.[60] As a consequence, it is unlikely that common law rights can plug the gaps that Brexit may potentially generate in UK law relating to rights protection.

Given this background context, there are substantial reasons to be concerned about how the Brexit process will impact on human rights. There is the possibility that well-established human rights standards will be reviewed, revised and possibly even repealed — and this replacement process is likely to unfold in a political climate unfavourable to human rights concerns. This provides a reason to be concerned about Brexit's impact on rights, especially given the limited scope of the HRA and common law rights. This concern may prove unfounded: future UK adjustments to existing EU standards in this field may not turn out to be very damaging. However, as things stand at present, some sense of foreboding about the future is justified.

Qualifying the Brexit Risk to Human Rights — A Tentative Conclusion

As Lock has argued, Brexit is rights neutral when considered on its own terms.[61] However, Brexit makes it possible for certain EU rights-protective standards to be diluted, amended or repealed over time. Furthermore, the outcome of this process may be less than optimal when viewed from a human rights perspective, especially when it comes to the treatment of migrants and certain other vulnerable groups. Therefore, this risk assessment leads to the conclusion that Brexit poses a potential danger to rights. This danger may never materialize. However, the rights-negative background context against which Brexit is unfolding, and the limits of the non-EU forms of legal rights protection that currently exist in UK law, cannot be ignored. As a result, care needs to be taken that the United Kingdom's departure from the European Union will not lead to a diluted respect for human rights. Human rights activists, and indeed anyone concerned with the protection of civil liberties and fundamental rights within UK law and policy, will need to be vigilant in the post-Brexit era.

---

57 See e.g. *R v Home Secretary, Ex parte Simms*, [2000] 2 AC 115; *Osborn v The Parole Board*, [2013] UKSC 61; *Kennedy v Charity Commissioners*, [2014] UKSC 20.

58 See Elliott, *supra* note 56. See also Roger Masterman & Se-shauna Wheatle, "A Common Law Resurgence in Rights Protection?" [2015] Eur HRL Rev 56.

59 *Moohan v Lord Advocate*, [2014] UKHL 67.

60 Richard Clayton, "The Empire Strikes Back" [2015] Public Law 3.

61 *Ibid.*

17

Brexit: Can the United Kingdom Change Its Mind?

Helen Mountfield

Introduction: The Story So Far

On June 23, 2016, in a referendum held under the European Union (Referendum) Act 2015,[1] the British people were asked if they wanted to remain in the European Union or to leave. By a small, but significant, margin,[2] they indicated that they would prefer to leave. It is now apparent that the then-government had not banked on this result, and it had certainly not prepared for

---

1 *European Union Referendum Act 2015* (UK), c 36.
2 The Electoral Commission record is that 16,141,241 (in other words, 48.1 percent) of those voting in the referendum voted to remain, and 17,410,742 (51.9 percent) voted to leave, out of a total electorate of 46,500,001 (therefore, 12,948,018 expressed neither view).

it. No consistent government position was on the stocks as to what would happen next,[3] and, indeed, no clear or consistent UK negotiating position is yet in the public domain.

Following the referendum result on June 24, 2016, there have been a large number of political shocks. David Cameron immediately announced his intention to stand down as prime minister. The Conservative Party selected Theresa May, a leader who had ostensibly (albeit quietly) campaigned for the Remain cause during the referendum campaign, whose pitch for the leadership was nonetheless based on an assertion that she would deliver on the United Kingdom leaving the European Union as quickly and completely as possible because "Brexit means Brexit."

May and her newly appointed Secretary of State for Exiting the European Union David Davis also insisted that they did not need parliamentary authority to trigger the process of leaving the European Union. This was based on an argument that went as follows: because making and leaving treaties is a prerogative act of the Crown, a prerogative had taken the United Kingdom into the European Union, and there was also an act of prerogative discretion to take the United Kingdom out. On this argument, the European Communities Act 1972[4] was no more than a conduit through which the content of whatever EU treaties were or were not in force in the United Kingdom at any particular time could be given effect in national law, and that act could be emptied of any effective content by the stroke of a ministerial pen. The source of EU law would be cut off by the United Kingdom's withdrawal from all the treaties from which EU law was derived.

As is now history, that argument failed in the divisional court in the case of *Miller & Others v Secretary of State for Exiting the European Union*[5] (*Miller*) and failed again in the UK Supreme Court.[6] Sitting in a full eleven-judge court for the first and only time in its history, the UK Supreme Court held that since the European Communities Act 1972 had rendered EU law an enforceable system of law, as a matter of UK law, the Crown could not act so as to contradict the will of Parliament. Because Parliament had taken the United Kingdom into the EU system of law, as set out in the European treaties, only primary legislation passed by the legislature could authorize the government to withdraw from the treaties.[7]

The Supreme Court's judgment was handed down on January 24, 2017. Two days later, on January 26, 2017, the European Union (Notification of Withdrawal) Bill[8] was introduced (and was curiously followed, rather than preceded, by a white paper). Parliament passed this bill on March 13, 2017, and the bill received royal assent on March 16, 2017. Whatever the United

---

3   *The Conservative Party Manifesto 2015* promised an in-out referendum on membership of the European Union and to abide by the result of the referendum, but it also said, "We are clear about what we want from Europe. We say: yes to the Single Market." See Conservative Party, *The Conservative Party Manifesto 2015* at 74, online: <www.conservatives.com/manifesto2015>. Yet, in Theresa May's letter of March 29, 2017, to Donald Tusk, president of the European Council, notifying the United Kingdom's intention to leave the European Union, May recognized that this also meant leaving the Single Market because there could be "no cherry-picking." Letter from Theresa May to Donald Tusk (29 March 2017) [May, letter], online: <www.gov.uk/government/publications/prime-ministers-letter-to-donald-tusk-triggering-article-50>.

4   *European Communities Act 1972* (UK), c 68.

5   [2016] EWHC 2768 [*Miller* Div Ct].

6   [2017] UKSC 5 [*Miller* SC].

7   *Ibid* at paras 5, 82–83, 101, 111, 124.

8   Bill 132, *European Union (Notification of Withdrawal) Bill* [HL], 2017–2019 sess (1st reading 26 January 2017).

Kingdom thought Brexit is Brexit may have meant, and however many members of Parliament may have supported the Remain cause during the referendum campaign (at least 478 did so openly), there was a clear majority in favour of respecting the result of the referendum. The bill received little genuine opposition and no significant amendment.

The act's short title, European Union (Notification of Withdrawal) Act 2017, is a misnomer, because its only operative provision (section 1) gives the prime minister parliamentary authority to notify the United Kingdom's *intention* to withdraw from the European Union, "notwithstanding any provision made by or under the European Communities Act 1972 or any other enactment," rather than to withdraw the United Kingdom from the European Union. The act's long title more accurately describes it as "an Act to confer power on the Prime Minister to notify, under Article 50(2) of the Treaty on European Union, the United Kingdom's *intention* to withdraw from the EU."[9]

On January 17, 2017, the prime minister confirmed in her speech at Lancaster House that the government would put whatever deal it came up with "to a vote in both Houses of Parliament before it comes into force,"[10] but this was in the form of a political assurance only: no mechanism for seeking parliamentary approval of any deal before withdrawing from the European Union was put into the terms of the legislation itself.[11]

Those schooled in the Harvard Law School negotiating techniques[12] will know that successful negotiations depend on a party going into them with a clear idea of what it wants to achieve by agreement *and* a clear idea as to a bottom line, informed by a decision as to the best result that can be achieved unilaterally if negotiations work out: the best alternative to a negotiated agreement (BATNA). The prime minister talked tough on her Brexit BATNA: in her Lancaster House speech, she said that "no deal is better than a bad deal for Britain."[13] In other words, she contemplated leaving the European Union without any trade deal or other transitional arrangements in place if the remaining 27 member states of the European Union (EU27) did not give her a deal that she considered to be in Britain's interests, on terms she wanted.[14]

But the problem with this approach is that Britain is only one country, albeit an important one to the European Union. In a negotiation with a bloc of 27, the smaller party is unlikely to have a strong bargaining hand. And time for negotiating something other than a "no deal" Brexit was already running. On March 29, 2017, less than two weeks after the prime minister

---

9   *European Union (Notification of Withdrawal) Act 2017* (UK), c 9 [emphasis added].

10 Theresa May, "The government's negotiating objectives for exiting the EU: PM speech" (Speech delivered on 17 January 2017), online: <www.gov.uk/government/speeches/the-governments-negotiating-objectives-for-exiting-the-eu-pm-speech>. This assurance was repeated by Minister of State David Jones in the House of Commons on February 7, 2017. UK, HC, *Parliamentary Debates*, vol 621, col 264 (7 February 2017) (David Jones) [Jones, debates].

11 After a government defeat on an amendment proposed in debate by MP Dominic Grieve on December 13, 2017, during the passage of the European Union (Withdrawal) Bill, there will now be a parliamentary vote on the terms of any proposed withdrawal agreement before it is signed. But the legislative consequences if Parliament rejects any proposed agreement are not specified in the proposed amendment to the legislation, which, when this article went to press, was still in committee stage.

12 First articulated by Roger Fisher & William L Ury, "Getting to Yes: Negotiating Without Giving In", 3rd ed (New York, NY: Penguin Books, 2011).

13 May, *supra* note 10.

14 This was repeated in the text of the prime minister's letter to Donald Tusk on March 29, 2017, in which she said that if no satisfactory arrangement could be made, Britain would fall back on WTO terms for international trade. May, letter, *supra* note 3.

received authority to do so, the government gave notice to the European Union that it intended to leave. This triggered a two-year negotiation period, which will end on March 29, 2019. The government's position is that if there is no deal by then, or if Parliament rejects whatever deal the government proposes to it, then Britain will simply withdraw from the European Union with no transitional arrangements in place. If this is what happens, there will be the hardest of "hard" Brexits: the United Kingdom will simply cease to be a member of the European Union and will fall back on World Trade Organization (WTO) trading rules for its relationships with the European Union.[15] This is widely regarded as an economically catastrophic alternative to a negotiated solution of almost any kind.

With a relatively slim parliamentary majority, but with apparently strong authority, the prime minister sought to shore up her national position by calling a snap general election, which was announced on April 18, 2017. In another political shock, on June 8, 2017, she lost her majority. Further, at the time of writing, May's own future as prime minister remains in doubt. On October 1, 2017, at a Conservative Party conference event, the prime minister said that the relative success of the Labour Party led by Jeremy Corbyn indicated that the "consensus in Britain has changed" and urged her party to work to restore the old one.[16]

The period since the referendum has shown, if nothing else, that the political wind can change quickly. There may be a consensus that the economic and social consensus has changed (no one is quite sure how). However, in Britain, at the time of writing, there is still also a broad consensus that Brexit in some form or another will happen, come what may; the current political debate is not as to whether Brexit will happen, but as to the terms on which it will take place.

Even so, more than a quarter of the way through the notional two-year period envisaged by the text of article 50 of the Treaty on European Union (TEU) between notification of intention to withdraw and a member state ceasing to be a member,[17] there is no detailed indication of what a deal with the European Union might look like: no resolution is in prospect of a new free trade agreement with the European Union, the Irish border, EU citizens' rights or the EU financial settlement.

What if the political consensus changes? What if the European Union offers some compromise that makes the majority of parliamentarians inclined to advocate that membership is more attractive than leaving? As a matter of law, can the United Kingdom change its collective mind and decide, unilaterally, that it wants, after all, to stay in the European Union and instruct the government to notify the European Council that it does not, after all, wish to leave? Or, as a matter of EU law, is the die cast, and is the United Kingdom bound by the notification of March 29, 2017, to take whatever deal the EU27 may offer? Should the United Kingdom simply fall out of the European Union altogether?

---

15 Jones, debates, *supra* note 10, cols 272–273.

16 Theresa May, (Speech delivered at the reception for Conservative women activists, Conservative Party conference, Manchester, 1 October 2017).

17 *Treaty of Lisbon Amending the Treaty on European Union and the Treaty Establishing the European Community*, 13 December 2007, [2007] OJ, C 306/01, art 50 (entered into force 1 December 2009) [*TEU*]. This period — provided for in article 50(3) — is different from the potential for a further two-year "transition period," during which EU rules continue to apply in the United Kingdom, which may be agreed by member states as part of a withdrawal agreement. At the time of writing, the precise terms of this deal were still under negotiation.

However fast the political weathervane may change, a change of political mood on Brexit would be entirely irrelevant if, as a matter of law, the decision to leave the European Union has already been taken and cannot be unilaterally revoked without the agreement of the EU27 (which may not be forthcoming). This chapter addresses the question of whether Brexit is unstoppable. What — as a matter of law — would happen if, before March 29, 2019, Parliament concludes that the British people have changed their collective mind? There are two parts to this question. The first is whether a formal (and legally binding) decision to leave the European Union has already been taken as a matter of national constitutional law, or whether all that the prime minister has done so far, and all she has had statutory authority to do, is give notice of the present government's intention to leave. On this, this chapter's view is that a further act of Parliament, not just an indicative vote, is needed before a constitutionally valid decision can be taken to leave the European Union. If no such statutory authority is given before March 29, 2019, no constitutionally valid decision to withdraw has been made, and, in any event, the government could withdraw the notification of an intention to leave the European Union and decide to remain.

The second issue is whether, as a matter of EU law, a member state that has given notice of an intention to leave the European Union is bound to leave, or whether it can nonetheless withdraw the notice and decide, unilaterally, to remain. This question requires close consideration of the text of article 50, and what it might mean, (which has not been considered by the Court of Justice of the European Union [CJEU]), and close consideration of the *Miller* decision.

The Text of Article 50

Article 50 provides as follows:

1. Any Member State may decide to withdraw from the Union in accordance with its own constitutional requirements.

2. A Member State which decides to withdraw shall notify the European Council of its intention. In the light of the guidelines provided by the European Council, the Union shall negotiate and conclude an agreement with that State, setting out the arrangements for its withdrawal, taking account of the framework for its future relationship with the Union. That agreement shall be negotiated in accordance with Article 218(3) of the Treaty on the Functioning of the European Union. It shall be concluded on behalf of the Union by the Council, acting by a qualified majority, after obtaining the consent of the European Parliament.

3. The Treaties shall cease to apply to the State in question from the date of entry into force of the withdrawal agreement or, failing that, two years after the notification referred to in paragraph 2, unless the European Council, in agreement with the Member State concerned, unanimously decides to extend this period.

4. For the purposes of paragraphs 2 and 3, the member of the European Council or of the Council representing the withdrawing Member State shall not participate in the discussions of the European Council or Council or in decisions concerning it.

A qualified majority shall be defined in accordance with Article 238(3)(b) of the Treaty on the Functioning of the European Union.

5. If a State which has withdrawn from the Union asks to rejoin, its request shall be subject to the procedure referred to in Article 49.[18]

The Common Ground in *Miller*

It is an irony that the *Miller* litigation was founded on common ground whereby, for the purpose of the proceedings, all parties proceeded on the basis that the article 50 notification could not be given on a qualified or conditional basis, and that once it had been given, it could not be withdrawn, and so was effectively irreversible.[19]

As the Supreme Court put it: "If Ministers give Notice without Parliament having first authorised them to do so, the die will be cast before Parliament has become formally involved. To adapt Lord Pannick's metaphor, the bullet will have left the gun before Parliament has accorded the necessary leave for the trigger to be pulled. The very fact that Parliament will have to pass legislation once the Notice is served *and hits the target* highlights the point that the giving of the Notice will change the domestic law: otherwise there would be no need for new legislation."[20]

Given the intense legal controversy that has since arisen about this question, it is worth examining why the forensic consensus that article 50 was irreversible was advanced as a collectively underpinning presumption in the proceedings.

The consensus that article 50 was irreversible was a tactically convenient way of putting things from both parties' points of view. For the claimants, this position avoided tricky factual questions as to whether merely notifying the European Council of an intention to withdraw from the European Union actually changed anything. It avoided addressing the question of whether, if a later Parliament were to decide it did not wish to leave the European Union, the decision not to withdraw would have the effect of dodging the withdrawal bullet that was triggered by the article 50 notification, so that no authority was needed (in national law) simply to indicate an intention to withdraw. It avoided the possibility of a decision where, as a matter of national constitutional law, an indication of an intention to leave was reversible, and did not require statutory authority, but without a decision as to whether the CJEU would, in fact, accept the reversibility of article 50 as a matter of international law.

In the divisional court, the attorney general submitted on behalf of the secretary of state for exiting the European Union that he too was content to accept that once the notice trigger had been pulled, the Brexit bullet would hit the leave target, but for rather different reasons. He said that the Crown was prepared to accept this position because the legal possibility of the United Kingdom changing its mind was irrelevant. This was essentially a political concession made not

---

18 *Ibid*, art 50.
19 *Miller* SC, *supra* note 6; *Miller* Div Ct, *supra* note 5.
20 *Miller* SC, *supra* note 6 at para 94 [emphasis added]. Lord (David) Pannick was counsel for Miller.

as a matter of law, but because (according to the attorney general) as a matter of "firm policy," the United Kingdom's notification, once given, would not be withdrawn.[21]

For both parties and the court, this position avoided the politically unattractive possibility of referring the question (which was untested and could not have been regarded as *acte clair*) as to the meaning of article 50 to the CJEU on a preliminary reference under article 267 of the Treaty on the Functioning of the European Union.[22]

So it was that the Supreme Court examined the legality of the government's espoused intention to use prerogative powers to trigger article 50 on the assumption that a notification, once given, would not be withdrawn. It found that no such prerogative power existed, and the government lost the case.

This then left open the issues of whether separate parliamentary authority was needed for the Crown to decide to withdraw from the European Union, as well as to indicate an intention to do so, and whether the indication of intention could be withdrawn. Without a reference to the CJEU, no firm answer on the irreversibility premise, which remained unquestioned in *Miller*, could be given; however, this chapter asserts that the tactical *Miller* consensus was wrong as a matter of law.

The Constitutional Requirement of Parliamentary Authority

Article 50(1) of the TEU provides that the decision to withdraw from the European Union must be taken by a member state in accordance with "its own constitutional requirements."[23] What these are is a matter for the law of the member state, itself (see Lord Dyson in *Shindler v Chancellor of the Duchy of Lancaster*),[24] and, in the absence of a written constitution, the law is what the Supreme Court says it is.

In *Miller*, the Supreme Court reaffirmed an old constitutional principle, namely that primary legislation is the highest source of law in the Constitution, and the government does not have prerogative power to act in a way that would override the intention of Parliament, expressed through a statute. The court held, "The essential point is that if, as we consider, what would otherwise be a prerogative act would result in a change in domestic law, the act can only lawfully be carried out with the sanction of primary legislation enacted by the Queen in Parliament."[25]

The court also gave a rights-based rationale for precluding the use of Crown prerogative powers to withdraw from the European Union. EU law grants persons and businesses fundamental

---

21 *Miller* Div Ct, *supra* note 5 (Transcript of 17 October 2016 at 64).
22 *Consolidated Version of the Treaty on the Functioning of the European Union*, 13 December 2007, [2012] OJ, C 326/47, art 267 (entered into force 26 October 2012).
23 *TEU*, *supra* note 17, art 50(1).
24 [2016] EWCA Civ 469 at para 7.
25 *Miller* SC, *supra* note 6 at para 122.

rights, and fundamental rights can only be overridden by express statutory language. General or ambiguous words will not do.[26]

The European Union (Notification of Withdrawal) Act 2017 does not expressly say that rights in EU law can be withdrawn, nor does it give the government authority to take the United Kingdom out of the European Union. It does not remove any rights, nor does it, itself, expressly change domestic law. All it gives is express statutory authority for the government to notify the European Union of an *intention* to withdraw. If (as some have suggested) article 50(2) requires that a properly authorized decision to withdraw be taken *before* notice is given, then it is at least arguable that, on the basis of *Miller*, the notification of intention was not properly authorized in accordance with the United Kingdom's constitutional requirements.

The consequence of this lack of authorization is that, because article 50(1) only permits the actual decision to withdraw to be taken in accordance with the country's constitutional traditions, further statutory authority is required for the actual decision to withdraw. Such authority cannot be implied, because — at the point when the European Union (Notification of Withdrawal) Act 2017 was passed — Parliament may have known that some, but not which, fundamental EU law rights would be altered or amended if the United Kingdom fulfilled the intention to withdraw. Simple authority to remove a whole swath of fundamental rights without knowing which rights would be altered or repealed, or to what extent, is arguably contrary to the *Simms* principle of legality.[27] The Constitution does not allow for so sweeping an enabling law for the government to legislate as it will in uncertain future factual and legal circumstances.

The twin principles of parliamentary sovereignty and legality and the rule of law require that once the terms of withdrawal are known, but not until then, Parliament and *only* Parliament can take the decision as to whether to leave the European Union on the terms on offer, or to leave the European Union without any deal at all being agreed. The European Union (Notification of Withdrawal) Act 2017 does not set out any future mechanism by which Parliament could agree to terms of withdrawal;[28] only a statute would confer such parliamentary authority to depart from earlier legislation. Without such parliamentary authority, it is at least strongly arguable that the United Kingdom cannot lawfully leave the European Union as a matter of domestic law.

During the passage of the European Union (Notification of Withdrawal) Bill, the government said that parliamentary authority for abrogating from EU law rights that formerly existed would be granted by a so-called Great Repeal Bill,[29] which would repeal the European Communities Act and transpose much of the body of EU law into national law.

---

26 *Ibid* at paras 56–57, 83–87; *Miller* Div Ct, *supra* note 5 at para 83, in reliance on the *Simms* principle of legality: *R v Secretary of State for the Home Department ex parte Simms*, [2000] 2 AC 115 at 131 E-G [*Simms*].

27 Fisher & Ury, *supra* note 12.

28 The EU (Notification of Withdrawal) Act might have also given the prime minister authority actually to withdraw, once Parliament had approved the terms of withdrawal by a parliamentary motion; this mechanism would then have had the imprimatur of statutory authority, but — despite proposed opposition amendments suggesting that it should (which were not passed) — the act does not include any such device.

29 At the time of writing, legislation intended to achieve this object is before Parliament: Bill 5, *European Union (Withdrawal) Bill* [HL], 2017–2019 sess (1st reading 13 July 2017).

There are two objections to this argument. First, the terms of the European Union (Withdrawal) Bill (as the Great Repeal Bill is more prosaically called) are actually intended to give ministers power to enact secondary legislation to *retain* EU law, while only making some changes, subject to parliamentary oversight and sunset clauses. However, it is not yet clear how such powers — if conferred — would be used, and there are many rights that are enjoyed as a matter of EU law, which Parliament would not be able to replicate without the cooperation of other member states or the EU institutions. These include, for example, (reciprocal) rights of free movement or decisions that are referred to EU institutions in the event of disagreement.

Second, the Supreme Court in *Miller* rejected the suggestion that some kind of parliamentary "involvement" at a later stage would be adequate to fulfill the constitutional requirement for parliamentary authority to change the law.[30] It is not enough for Parliament to be given an opportunity to ratify (or not) what ministers may or may not have negotiated on the international plane after the fact, when it is too late in practical terms for them to change it. However, notwithstanding advice — including from claimant-side parties in the *Miller* litigation — to include some statutory parliamentary approval mechanism in the European Union (Notification of Withdrawal) Act 2017,[31] the government declined to do so. Therefore, the prime minister does not yet have any statutory authority to agree to any terms of withdrawal from the European Union, and she will require it, if she is to do so, because this would inevitably make significant changes to domestic law and the rights conferred by it.

As Lord Hope, the former deputy president of the Supreme Court, put it in the second reading debate of the European Union (Notification of Withdrawal) Bill in the House of Lords:

> There is a respectable argument...that only Parliament has the constitutional authority to authorise, by legislation, the concluding of an agreement with the EU or the act of withdrawal if that is what the Government decide that they have to do. As the Supreme Court said in Miller, at paragraph 123, a resolution of Parliament is an important political act, but it is not legislation and, "only legislation which is embodied in a statute will do".

> That was why the Court held that the change in the law that would result from commencing the Article 50 process must be made in the only way that our constitutional law permits: namely, through parliamentary legislation, which is where we are today. The argument that the Government may face is that the same reasoning must be applied to the final stage in the process, too.

> I...caution the Government against thinking that this Bill on its own will give them all the authority they need, or that obtaining approval for an agreement by resolution is the same thing as being given statutory authority to conclude that agreement. They could have provided for that in this Bill, perhaps using the same formula as in Clause 1, by saying that the Prime Minister may conclude an agreement with the EU if the agreement has been approved by both Houses — but it has not done so...they cannot

---

30   *Miller* SC, *supra* note 6 at para 94.

31   To make it clear that the United Kingdom would withdraw from the European Union when Parliament had legislated to authorize the terms of a withdrawal agreement. The text of the proposed amendment advanced by the People's Challenge parties in *Miller* (Pigney & Others) is available at "Proposed Amendment by the People's Challenge", online: <www.bindmans.com/uploads/files/documents/Peoples_Challenge_Amendment.pdf>.

escape from the effect of the Miller decision when we reach the end of the negotiation. It is all about respecting the sovereignty of Parliament. The law will see to that whatever the Government think, as it always does.[32]

In summary, the government does not yet have sufficiently clear and unambiguous parliamentary authority to withdraw from the European Union.

The current law is that the United Kingdom is part of the European Union, and that there has, as of yet, been no constitutionally valid decision by the United Kingdom (in other words, by Parliament) to leave the European Union, whether with or without a concluded withdrawal treatment. Thus far, Parliament has given the prime minister authority only to give the European Council notice of an *intention* to cease to be a member. This is not the same thing as the authority to withdraw. Ultimately, the decision to leave the European Union must be taken by Parliament, either by legislating to approve the terms of a withdrawal agreement or legislating to authorize the United Kingdom to leave without any agreement in place. This is because only Parliament can give effect to the removal or conferral of individual rights that will necessarily follow from that decision: this follows from the decision in *Miller*. Parliament is not yet in a position to do so because, without knowing whether or not there is any agreement between the United Kingdom and the European Union, or the terms of any such deal, it cannot know what rights of British citizens and businesses and of the nationals of other member states who are resident or established in the United Kingdom will be lost. Without such knowledge, Parliament cannot properly authorize the loss of these rights in sufficiently clear and unambiguous terms to comply with the legality principle.[33] In effect, therefore, the notice of an intention to leave the European Union that the prime minister addressed to the European Council on March 29, 2017, was given contingently on a future parliamentary decision to do so.

Can the Notice Given under Article 50(2) Be Given Conditionally, or Withdrawn?

It may be the position as a matter of national constitutional law that no valid decision to leave the European Union can be taken without express statutory authority, but notice has been given to the European Union that the United Kingdom intends to withdraw, and article 50(3) appears to suggest that this notice takes effect two years after the giving of notification, in the absence of an agreement by the rest of the European Union to extend that period. So there is an important question of EU law as to whether, even if the UK Parliament changes its mind and decides that it no longer wishes to follow through with the notice of an intention to withdraw, the European Union can or will regard notice of intention to withdraw as having been given on a constitutionally conditional basis. Moving forward to the end of the negotiation period, it is not clear what the position, as a matter of EU law, is as to whether the government can do no deal with the European Union or can do a deal that is politically unacceptable to a majority of the members of Parliament. In other words, having given the European Council notice of an intention to leave the European Union and having put the council to a lot of trouble in negotiating the terms of such a divorce,

---

32 UK, HL, *Parliamentary Debates*, vol 779, col 274 (20 February 2017) (Lord Hope).

33 Established in cases such as *R v Secretary of State for the Home Department ex parte Simms* [1990] 1 AC 109 per Lord Hoffmann at 131E–G.

can the United Kingdom decide to change its mind? If Parliament decides not to accept the terms of any deal the prime minister might come up with, but also declines to authorize withdrawal in the absence of such a deal, then the question, as a matter of EU law, is whether the notification of intention to withdraw from the European Union lapses or could be withdrawn by the United Kingdom acting unilaterally, without the consent or agreement of the EU27.

A wide range of views have been expressed on this question[34] and the language of article 50 does not give a clear answer. Of course, no country has ever before indicated an intention to leave the European Union on the basis of article 50, so this is also an untested question that would ultimately have to be determined by the CJEU. Although there are legal arguments both ways, the principles of EU law provide a strong indication that the European Union can treat the notification of intention to withdraw as conditional and that EU law would treat it as capable of being unilaterally withdrawn.

On the one hand, there is some support in the language of article 50(3) for the suggestion that article 50 is irrevocable. Article 50(3) provides that, in the absence of a concluded withdrawal agreement, the treaties "shall cease to apply" to the state in question two years after the notification given in article 50(2), unless the European Council unanimously agrees with the member state to extend that period.[35] It might be said that, read literally, this means that, once notification has been given, then either the treaties would cease to apply following the conclusion of a withdrawal agreement, or the treaties would automatically cease to apply two years after the notification, unless the European Council, acting unanimously, agreed with the member state to extend the two-year notice period. In other words, using Lord Pannick's metaphor from the *Miller* litigation, the triggering of article 50 set off an arrow or bullet that would inevitably meet the target of the United Kingdom leaving the European Union two years later, unless all other 27 member states agreed to extend the negotiation period.

34 See e.g. in favour of revocability: Charles Streeten, "Putting the Toothpaste Back in the Tube: Can an Article 50 Notification Be Revoked?" (13 July 2016), *UK Const Law Assoc* (blog); Alan Dashwood, "Revoking an Article 50" (18 July 2016), *InFacts*, online: <https://infacts.org/revoking-article-50/>; D Wyatt & D Edward, quoted in UK, HL, "Select Committee on the Constitution, 4th Report of Session 2016–2017: The Invoking of Article 50" (13 September 2016) at para 13, online: <https://publications.parliament.uk/pa/ld201617/ldselect/ldconst/44/44.pdf>; Aurel Sari, "Biting the Bullet: Why the UK is Free to Revoke its Withdrawal Notification under Article 50 TEU" (17 October 2016), *UK Const Law Assoc* (blog); Paul Craig, "Brexit: Foundational Constitutional and Interpretive Principles: II" (28 October 2016), *Oxford Hum Rts Hub*; Takis Tridimas, "Article 50: An Endgame without an End?" (2016) King's LJ 297; Aurel Sari, "Reversing a Withdrawal Notification under Article 50 TEU: Can the Member States Change their Mind?" (2016) Exeter Law School Working Paper Series; Piet Eeckhout & Eleni Frantziou, "Brexit and Article 50 TEU: A Constitutionalist Reading" (2016) UCL European Institute Working Paper. For those supporting a non-revocability interpretation, see e.g. Nick Barber, Tom Hickman & Jeff King, "Pulling the Article 50 'Trigger': Parliament's Indispensable Role" (27 June 2016), *UK Const Law Assoc* (blog); Jake Rylatt, "The Irrevocability of an Article 50 Notification: Lex Specialis and the Irrelevance of the Purported Customary Right to Unilaterally Revoke" (27 July 2016), *UK Const Law Assoc* (blog); Stijn Smismans, "About the Revocability of Withdrawal: Why the EU (Law) Interpretation of Article 50 Matters" (29 November 2016), *UK Const Law Assoc* (blog), online: <https://ukconstitutionallaw.org/2016/11/29/stijn-smismans-about-the-revocability-of-withdrawal-why-the-eu-law-interpretation-of-article-50-matters/>. For the views of EU officials, see e.g. Donald Tusk, (Speech 575/16 delivered at the European Policy Centre conference, 13 October 2016), online: <www.consilium.europa.eu/en/press/press-releases/2016/10/13/tusk-speech-epc/#>; Jean-Claude Piris, "Article 50 is not for ever and the UK could change its mind", *Financial Times* (1 September 2016); Jean-Claude Juncker, "Answer given by President Juncker on behalf of the Commission" in response to European Parliamentary question P-008603/2016 (17 January 2017), online: <www.europarl.europa.eu/sides/getAllAnswers.do?reference=P-2016-008603&language=EN>.

35 *TEU, supra* note 17, art 50(3).

But the CJEU tends toward a purposive interpretation of treaty provisions, and this reading does not accord with the apparent purpose of article 50 or other overriding principles of EU law. The better view, and apparently the view that the government's legal advice supports, is that article 50 is revocable.[36]

Notwithstanding the terms of article 50(3) discussed above, there are other indications in the language of article 50 that it is intended to be reversible. The text of article 50(1) (cited above) says that a decision to withdraw from the European Union must be in accordance with the member state's constitutional requirements.[37] As explained above, the constitutional requirement for the granting of irrevocable parliamentary authority to leave the European Union could not lawfully be given at the point when notice was given because Parliament would not, at that stage, have enough information to know what rights and laws would be abrogated by leaving.

The text of article 50(1) uses the language of "intention" (to leave) in article 50(2), and the present tense ("which decides," not "has decided") allows for the possibility that a member state could change its intention when the political consensus changes or if, for example, there is a change of government.[38] This is also in accordance with article 4 of the TEU,[39] which recognizes the inherent political and constitutional structures of member states, and the principle recognized in article 5 of the TEU[40] of subsidiarity and proportionality. If, following a democratic political change, the legislature of a member state wished to reach a constitutionally valid decision to withdraw an earlier notice of intention to withdraw from the European Union, it would be surprising if the CJEU were to say that this could not be done, which would, in effect, expel the member state against the will of its people as expressed through their elected representatives. To do so would be contrary to the shared democratic values of the European Union and the views on the role of parliaments, which are expressed in protocol 1 of the TEU on the role of national parliaments in the European Union. This states that "the way in which national parliaments scrutinize their governments in relation to the activities of the Union is a matter for the particular constitutional organization and practice of each member State."[41]

This protocol goes on to note that it is desirable for national parliaments to be involved in and able to express their views on matters of particular interest to them. Plainly, leaving the European Union is a matter of particular interest and concern to the UK Parliament.

A decision reached without satisfying a state's own constitutional requirements does not amount to a valid decision for the purposes of article 50(1). It is true that, in article 50(2), the treaty provides that a state that "decides" to withdraw "shall notify the European Council of its intention."[42] This could suggest that the decision to withdraw must have been taken before the notification is given, but this cannot be the correct interpretation. The decision to leave must

---

36 On October 8, 2017, the *Observer* reported that "two good sources" had suggested that the prime minister had been advised that article 50 notification could be withdrawn by the United Kingdom at any time before March 29, 2019, with the result that the United Kingdom could then choose to remain in the European Union with all its existing opt-outs in place: Toby Helm, "Come clean on right to Brexit Halt, May urged", *Observer* (7 October 2017), online: <www.theguardian.com/politics/2017/oct/07/theresa-may-secret-advice-brexit-eu>.

37 *TEU, supra* note 17, art 50(1).

38 *Ibid*, art 50(2).

39 *Ibid*, art 4.

40 *Ibid*, art 5.

41 *Ibid*, protocol 1.

42 *Ibid*, art 50(2).

be in accordance with constitutional requirements, and the requirement of sufficiently precise parliamentary authority cannot be met before Parliament has before it adequate information about the negotiated terms of withdrawal, which it is being invited to give statutory authorization. It follows that if Parliament decides to vote not to accept the terms of any deal agreed with the European Union, but does not pass legislation to authorize withdrawal in the absence of such a deal, there would be no constitutionally valid decision to leave the European Union at all.

The matter is not free from doubt, but it seems likely that the CJEU would accept, if the matter were to be challenged, that the notification of a decision to withdraw had simply lapsed. Provided that the United Kingdom had expressed a genuine intention to leave the European Union in good faith and in accordance with its own constitutional requirements, as it did on March 29, 2017, the notification would be treated as subject to any constitutionally valid change of heart within the notice period and subject to the national constitutional requirement that the terms of withdrawal must be authorized by any subsequent act of Parliament.

Moreover, there is no provision in article 50 that expressly precludes revocation of notice of withdrawal from the treaties. Since a treaty is, in effect, an international contract, in the absence of express language to the contrary, notice of a future intention to revoke could be unilaterally withdrawn at any time until the notice expires. Article 50 is a mechanism for the voluntary withdrawal of a member state from the European Union, not an expulsion mechanism. The *travaux preparatoires* indicate that those who drafted article 50 intended it to be revocable.[43] Article 50 has its origin in article I-60 of the proposed Treaty Establishing a Constitution for Europe (which did not in the event come into force), and the draft article I-60 was actually entitled "Voluntary Withdrawal from the Union."[44] Lord Kerr of Kinlochard, who, as permanent secretary of the Foreign and Commonwealth Office,[45] played a significant role in drafting article 50, has said in public that article 50 was intended to provide a procedural framework for the right, which already existed as a matter of public international law, for a member state to leave the European Union of its own free will. He is also of the view that a state's decision to leave is unilaterally revocable before the expiry of the notice period.[46]

By contrast, article 50(5) does expressly address the situation of a member state that has already withdrawn from the European Union, but later has a political change of heart and wishes to ask to rejoin. In those circumstances, article 50(5) sets out the formal constitutional mechanism through which such a request to rejoin is to be considered.[47] In effect, that is a request to make a new international law contract with the Union, and such a fresh agreement could not be entered into unilaterally, but would have to be entered into by agreement with all the remaining member states. The fact that there is no equivalent mechanism for a member state that has given notice of an intention to leave, but which decides not to leave, tends to suggest that there is no formal

---

43 Eeckhout & Frantziou, *supra* note 34. The authors' analysis of the *travaux* establishes that the respect for the constitutional requirements of the withdrawing state is key to a reading of article 50 that complies with EU law constitutional principles, and the broad discretion in article 50(1) is to be contrasted with the strict limitation on the negotiation period in article 50(3), the object of which is to prevent the withdrawing state from holding the Union to ransom during negotiations.

44 *Treaty establishing a Constitution for Europe*, 16 December 2004, OJ, C-310/1, art I-60 (unratified).

45 Lord Kerr is now a cross-bench peer and was active in the debates on the European Union (Notification of Withdrawal) Bill.

46 See e.g. Glenn Campbell, "Article 50 author Lord Kerr says Brexit not inevitable", *BBC News* (3 November 2016), online: <www.bbc.co.uk/news/uk-scotland-scotland-politics-37852628>.

47 *TEU, supra* note 17, art 50(5).

requirement for the agreement of the other member states if the state that had given notice decides not to follow through. The principles of respect for the democratic choices of member states and solidarity between member states also suggest that the European Union could not forcibly expel a member state simply for having expressed an intention to leave, which it later reconsiders. To expel a member state from the European Union would be to remove the rights as EU citizens and nationals from the citizens of a member state without good cause.

Circumstances may change. It seems most unlikely that it could be the case that if a member state recognized that there might be severe economic or security consequences of leaving the European Union, or if an election fought on whether the member state should remain in the European Union indicated a clear desire on the part of the people to remain, or even if the member state held a second referendum that indicated a clear desire to remain, the mere expression of an earlier intention to leave would result in expulsion. That would be contrary to the democratic principles that form the foundation of the European Union.[48]

Finally, a reading of article 50 that allows for the intention to leave to be withdrawn accords with the general provisions of the Vienna Convention on the Law of Treaties (Vienna Convention).[49] Article 65 of the Vienna Convention sets out a general notice procedure to be followed for (among other things) withdrawing from or suspending the operation of a treaty.[50] However, article 68 provides that notification of intention to withdraw may be revoked at any time before it takes effect.[51] It is true that article 50 of the TEU provides a special procedure for withdrawal from the European Union. Therefore, the clear terms of the Vienna Convention as to withdrawal from treaties in general are not determinative of the position of a state withdrawing from the EU treaties, in particular. However, they are a clear indication of the general position in international law that the giving of notice is not binding: the general position in international law is that while a state can get so far as indicating an intention to leave an agreement it has entered, until the moment it actually leaves, it may change its mind.

And So, Where Next?

It is true that, by a narrow margin, the British people expressed their view on the simple yes or no question of whether the United Kingdom should remain in the European Union in June 2016, but as the divisional court in *Shindler* and the Supreme Court in *Miller* reinforced, it is a long-established principle that the British courts do not recognize the will of the people, but only the will of the legislature that they choose to elect. An act of Parliament that calls for the holding of a referendum is only advisory unless and to the extent it provides for what will happen in the event of a particular result.[52]

---

48 See Craig, *supra* note 34.

49 *Vienna Convention on the Law of Treaties*, 23 May 1969, 1155 UNTS 331, 8 ILM 679 (entered into force 27 January 1980).

50 *Ibid*, art 65.

51 *Ibid*, art 68.

52 Contrast the terms of the *European Union Referendum Act 2015*, *supra* note 1, which provided only for a referendum to be held on a particular referendum question, with the terms of the *Parliamentary Voting System and Constituencies Act 2011* (UK), c 1, which provided for steps in the event of specific answers to the referendum question contained in that act.

Since Parliament has thus far chosen only to authorize the prime minister to notify the European Council of Britain's current intention to withdraw from the European Union, and has not authorized the withdrawal, itself, there is as yet no authority that accords with UK constitutional requirements for the prime minister to take the United Kingdom out of the European Union. The prime minister's statutory authority is thus far limited to the authority to negotiate a deal with this object, for Parliament to approve or not.

If Parliament ultimately declines to approve the deal the prime minister negotiates, or if there is a material change of circumstances, such as a significant shift in the public mood, detected by Parliament, or a change of government, or, if the prime minister is simply unable to negotiate acceptable terms for withdrawal, so that Parliament votes to reject a deal and also votes not to allow the United Kingdom to withdraw without one, there would be no constitutionally valid decision for the United Kingdom to leave the European Union. Article 50 would permit, and the British Constitution would require, the prime minister to inform the European Council that the United Kingdom's intention has changed, it withdraws its notice and it has decided to remain.

The aphorism attributed to John Maynard Keynes, "When the facts change, I change my mind," may not be precisely what he said,[53] but, as the events of recent months have shown, the consequences of leaving the European Union are becoming clearer, the facts are developing and public opinion can change with remarkable speed. If the political mood changes, as a matter of law, Parliament can change its mind.

---

53 There is no direct source for this well-known attributed statement. Paul Samuelson reported Keynes to have said, "When my information changes, I alter my conclusions. What do you do, sir?" This was in response to a criticism of Keynes' having changed his position on monetary policy during the Great Depression. Paul Samuelson, "The Keynes Centenary", *The Economist* (1983), later in Paul Samuelson, *The Collected Scientific Papers of Paul Samuelson*, vol 5 (Cambridge, MA: MIT Press, 1986) at 275.

Conclusion

Oonagh E. Fitzgerald and Eva Lein

The in-depth analysis by the contributors to this book points to a broad variety of issues that need to be discussed during the Brexit talks and shows the complexity of the consequences of Brexit. Two harsh realities emerge from the contributions to this book. The first is that a harder Brexit will inevitably result in many new legal barriers for businesses and citizens whose business and personal affairs extend beyond the United Kingdom. The second is that all versions of Brexit will reduce UK influence over rules that shape international commerce. As an EU member, the United Kingdom has considerable impact on the setting of EU policy and regulation, but as an outsider seeking to trade with the European Union, it will likely have to abide by these same standards without any influence on EU legislation. The United Kingdom will also no longer benefit from the European Union's heft in international negotiations and will need to build new alliances.

Brexit affects the international legal framework on more levels than even this collection could address. For example, leaving the European Union will affect cross-border civil and judicial cooperation, an area of great importance to practising lawyers and businesses who need certainty as to their future litigation risks. Concerns focus in particular on efficient cross-border enforcement of judgments — currently secured by EU law. The unanswered questions in this area are not limited to commercial relations. There is uncertainty over the future regimes for cross-border family law where various uniform EU rules presently regulate the areas of divorce, maintenance and parental responsibility. In addition, the rules on recognition of various professions likely will be affected.

Moreover, most consumers are not aware of the changes they may have to face in daily transactions. They appear not to consider that the huge body of UK consumer protection legislation derives from EU law implemented over the last decades into national law. EU law ranges from the protection of employees to the rules protecting consumers in sales, online transactions or in cross-border claims against foreign businesses. It also comprises the recent abolition of roaming fees, which makes travel across Europe so much easier. This body of consumer protection law might well be kept initially as domestic law, but ultimately there is no guarantee that it will not be cut down at the United Kingdom's discretion after Brexit has become effective. Everyday life is likely to be affected in many more ways, depending on the outcome of the Brexit negotiations, for instance, if the costs of imported cars or food from Europe increase.

Also, the contentious topics of free movement and immigration do not solely concern EU citizens in the United Kingdom. They equally concern UK citizens living or working in EU member states or who have holiday homes in the European Union. One could go on with questions concerning devolution, internal constitutional arrangements, foreign relations, aviation rights, agriculture and fishery policies, etc.

No doubt some of these questions will find their way into legal challenges. For example, a new crowd-funded case is being brought to challenge the UK notification under article 50 of the Treaty on European Union as not providing a sufficient legal basis for leaving the European Union.[1] As well, Scottish members of Parliament are seeking a ruling on the question of whether, if the United Kingdom decides to stay in the European Union, this would require a vote of all other EU members or would be automatically allowed.[2] Also, a group of UK citizens living in the Netherlands have brought a case where a referral to the European Court of Justice will be sought to rule on their right to free movement.[3]

While some of the issues have now become more prominent in public discourse, a plan for successfully tackling them has not yet been developed. At the time of writing, the Brexit negotiations, albeit advanced, have not yet given any reassurance that the above issues will be dealt with in a satisfactory way. The important and long-established economic and political links between the United Kingdom and the European Union should be able to facilitate a new comprehensive free trade agreement, a security partnership and guarantees of citizens' rights. Indeed, there is reason to believe that if the United Kingdom were to soften its approach and

---

1   Chloe Farand, "Brexit: Government facing High Court challenge to cancel Article 50", *The Independent* (22 December 2017), online: <www.independent.co.uk/news/uk/politics/brexit-latest-article-50-high-court-challenge-government-a8123626.html>.

2   This challenge is being brought by Scottish members of Parliament representing all parties except the Conservative Party: see Severin Carrell & Jennifer Rankin, "Legal action over whether UK can stop Brexit gets go-ahead," *The Guardian* (22 December 2017), online: <www.theguardian.com/politics/2017/dec/22/legal-action-uk-stop-brexit-go-ahead>.

3   Daniel Boffey & Lisa O'Carroll, "Britons in Netherlands take fight for their EU rights to Dutch court", *The Guardian* (16 January 2018), online: <www.theguardian.com/politics/2018/jan/16/britons-in-netherlands-take-fight-for-their-eu-rights-to-dutch-court>.

propose maintaining a very close relationship with the Single Market and Customs Union, the European Union likely would respond positively. For the moment, at least, positions remain far apart.

It is in both parties' interest to find a mutually satisfactory outcome to this negotiation that leaves them not weakened but strengthened, both at home and as players on the global stage. There will need to be some rethinking of Brexit strategy to facilitate such a smooth transformation of the relationship. It is hoped that the information in this book can contribute to these important reflections.

Contributors

Thomas Cottier is a member of the advisory committee of the International Law Research Program at CIGI, professor emeritus of European and international economic law at the University of Bern; senior research fellow at the World Trade Institute; and adjunct professor at the University of Ottawa Faculty of Law. He was the founder and managing director of the World Trade Institute from 1999 to 2015 and the National Centres of Competence in Research (international trade regulation). Prior to that, he was legal adviser to the Swiss External Economic Affairs Department and deputy director general of the Swiss Intellectual Property Office. He served on the Swiss negotiating team of the Uruguay Round and during European Economic Area negotiations. He has been a member and chair of numerous panels of the General Agreement on Tariffs and Trade and the World Trade Organization. He has published widely in international economic law and was also recently involved in training UK trade officials following the Brexit referendum.

Oonagh E. Fitzgerald is director of CIGI's International Law Research Program. She established and oversees CIGI's international law research agenda, which includes policy-relevant research on issues of international economic law, environmental law, intellectual property law and innovation, and Indigenous law.

She has extensive experience as a senior executive in the federal government, providing legal policy, advisory and litigation services, and strategic leadership in international law, national security, public law, human rights and governance.

As national security coordinator for the Department of Justice Canada from 2011 to 2014, Oonagh ensured strategic leadership and integration of the department's policy, advisory and litigation work related to national security. From 2007 to 2011, she served as the Department of National Defence and Canadian Forces legal adviser, leading a large, full-service corporate counsel team for this globally engaged, combined military and civilian institution. Before this, Oonagh served as acting chief legal counsel for the Public Law Sector of the Department of Justice and as special adviser for International Law.

Oonagh served as assistant secretary Legislation, House Planning/Counsel at the Privy Council Office from 2000 to 2003. Prior to this, she held various positions in the Department of Justice: senior general counsel and director general, Human Resources Development Canada Legal Services Unit; general counsel and director, International Law and Activities Section; senior counsel for Regulatory Reform; and legal adviser, Human Rights Law Section. She began her legal career at the Law Reform Commission of Canada, the Competition Bureau and the Immigration Appeal Board.

Oonagh has taught in the faculties of Law and Business Administration at the University of Ottawa, as well as in the Department of Law at Carleton University, l'Institut international du droit de l'homme and the International Institute of Humanitarian Law. She has written two books: *The Guilty Plea and Summary Justice* (Carswell, 1990) and *Understanding Charter Remedies: A Practitioner's Guide* (Carswell, 1994), and was chief editor for *The Globalized Rule of Law: Relationships between International and Domestic Law* (Irwin Law and Éditions Yvon Blais, 2006).

Oonagh has a B.F.A. (honours) from York University (1977). She obtained her LL.B. from Osgoode Hall Law School (1981) and was called to the Bar of Ontario in 1983. She obtained an LL.M. from the University of Ottawa (1990), an S.J.D. from the University of Toronto (1994) and an M.B.A. from Queen's University (2007).

David A. Gantz is the Samuel M. Fegtly Professor of Law and emeritus director of graduate law programs at the University of Arizona James E. Rogers College of Law. He teaches and writes in the areas of international trade and investment law, regional trade agreements, public international law, international business transactions and international environmental law. He was a visiting professor at Georgetown University in the fall 2016 semester. David previously served in the Office of the Legal Adviser, U.S. Department of State, and practised law in Washington, DC. He is the author or co-author of four books and more than 50 law review articles and book chapters. He has served as an arbitrator in multiple proceedings under Chapters 11, 19 and 20 of the North American Free Trade Agreement. David has an A.B. from Harvard College and a J.D. and J.S.M. from Stanford Law School.

Markus Gehring is a senior research fellow in the International Law Research Program at CIGI, as well as the Arthur Watts Fellow at BIICL. He is also a fellow at the Lauterpacht Centre for International Law at the University of Cambridge, where he teaches international and EU law. He also serves as lead counsel for trade law at the Centre for International Sustainable Development Law.

Valerie Hughes is a senior fellow with CIGI and teaches international trade law at Queen's University. She was director of the Legal Affairs Division of the World Trade Organization (WTO) from 2010 to 2016 and served as director of the WTO Appellate Body Secretariat from 2001 to 2005. Valerie held several positions with the Government of Canada, including assistant deputy minister at the Law Branch of the Department of Finance; general counsel of the Trade Law Division of the Department of Foreign Affairs and International Trade; and senior counsel, Constitutional and International Law Division of the Department of Justice. Valerie has also practised law in two large Canadian law firms, focusing mainly on international law.

Matthias Lehmann is a full professor and director of the Institute for Private International and Comparative Law at the University of Bonn. He holds doctoral degrees from the Friedrich Schiller University of Jena and Columbia University, as well as a *habilitation* from the University of Bayreuth. His main interest lies in international and comparative aspects of banking and financial law. He has published extensively on the subject in German, English, French and Spanish. Matthias is a member of the European Banking Institute.

Eva Lein is a professor at the University of Lausanne and senior research fellow at BIICL. Her fields of expertise are private international law, international dispute resolution and comparative law. She is also an honorary senior lecturer at Queen Mary University of London and at Queen Mary University of London, Institute in Paris, and was a visiting professor at various institutions, including the University Paris II (Panthéon-Assas). Eva is a qualified German lawyer. She has been lecturing in various countries and regularly speaks at conferences and seminars.

Eva has published extensively on topical issues of private international law, with a special focus on international litigation and European conflict of laws. Her Ph.D. focused on European, international and comparative contract law.

Since 2016, she has specialized on the legal consequences of Brexit and has been acting as an expert for the House of Commons and the Law Society on Brexit in a cross-border context. She was an expert for the UK Ministry of Justice, the UK Parliament, the European Commission, the European Parliament and Swiss Authorities and is engaged in international research projects in collaboration with foreign scientific institutions. She is also an advisory board member of the Yearbook of Private International Law.

Dorothy Livingston specializes in EU law and regulation. She was a partner at Herbert Smith LLP from 1980 to 2008, initially in the Finance Division and then in the Competition Regulation and Trade Department, where she is now a consultant of the enlarged firm, Herbert Smith Freehills LLP (HSF). Dorothy is one of the leaders of HSF's Brexit working group and has built up considerable expertise on the process of the United Kingdom leaving the European Union and what might follow, and on the possible consequences for business. Dorothy has spoken and written extensively on this subject, as well as on financial law and competition law. She has a unique combination of experience with her extensive background in financial and banking law and experience in EU law.

Dorothy is the chairman of the Financial Law Committee of the City of London Law Society (CLLS) and represents the CLLS on the Treasury Banking Liaison Panel appointed to consider important subsidiary legislation and the code of practice under the Banking Act 2009 related to the special resolution regime for failing banks. She is also a member of the CLLS Competition Law Committee and has commented on Brexit issues in this field.

Richard Macrory is a barrister at Brick Court Chambers and emeritus professor of environmental law at University College London (UCL), where he set up and was the first director of the Centre for Law and Environment. He established the Carbon Capture Legal Programme at UCL, and a second edition of his edited book *Carbon Capture and Storage: Emerging Legal and Regulatory Issues* will be published by Hart in early 2018.

Richard served as a board member of the Environment Agency in England and Wales between 1999 and 2004, and was a long-standing member of the Royal Commission on Environmental Pollution. He is a legal correspondent for the *ENDS Report*. In 2006, Richard led the Cabinet Office Review on Regulatory Sanctions, and his recommendations were reflected in part 3 of the Regulatory Enforcement and Sanctions Act 2008, which established the framework for civil sanctions in the regulatory field. More recently, he has been involved in reforming environmental statutory appeals procedures with the tribunal system. In 2016, Richard was appointed co-chair of the UK Environmental Law Association Brexit Task Force.

Luke McDonagh is a senior lecturer at the Law School at City, University of London. He has published widely on the subject of intellectual property in journals such as the *Modern Law Review*, *Journal of Law and Society* and *Intellectual Property Quarterly*. His first monograph, *European Patent Litigation in the Shadow of the Unified Patent Court*, was published in 2016 by Edward Elgar. He previously held the position of lecturer in law at Cardiff University (2013–2015) and was LSE Fellow at the London School of Economics (2011–2013). He has been a visiting lecturer at Keio University (2017) and a visiting scholar at Waseda University (2015 and 2017).

Armand de Mestral has been a CIGI senior fellow since November 2014. He leads a project addressing a central policy issue of contemporary international investment protection law: is investor-state arbitration suitable between developed liberal democratic countries?

An expert in international economic law, Armand is professor emeritus and Jean Monnet Chair in the Law of International Economic Integration at McGill University. He has taught constitutional law, law of the sea, public international law, international trade law, international arbitration, EU law and public international air law.

Armand's current research interest is the law of international economic integration. He has prepared books, articles and studies in English and French on international trade law and on Canadian and comparative constitutional and international law. He has served on World Trade Organization and North American Free Trade Agreement dispute settlements and public and private arbitration tribunals. He was made a member of the Order of Canada in December 2007. Armand was awarded the John E. Read Medal by the Canadian Council on International Law in November 2017.

Marc Mimler joined Bournemouth University in 2016 as a lecturer in law. He is a fully qualified German lawyer. After obtaining his undergraduate degree in law from the Ludwig-Maximilians-Universität München, he completed his bar school (Referendariat) at the Higher District Court of Munich. He then obtained a master's degree in intellectual property law. He defended his Ph.D. thesis in the field of patent law at Queen Mary Intellectual Property Research Institute.

Marc's research interests cover intellectual property law in general and its interfaces with human rights and international trade law, information technology law and competition law. Marc has a particular interest in exceptions to intellectual property rights from a doctrinal and practical perspective and is currently developing a monograph on this issue with Edward Elgar. He was also founding general editor of the *Queen Mary Journal of Intellectual Property*. Currently, Marc is the editor-in-chief of the *Interactive Entertainment Law Review*.

Howard P. Morris is head of the Business Restructuring & Insolvency Group at Morrison & Foerster in London. He has more than 20 years' experience in UK and international restructuring and insolvency work. He has acted for banks and other secured and unsecured creditors, committees of bondholders, trade creditors, debtors and acquirers of business and assets from insolvent companies. He has experience in international asset tracing and recovery, as well as a strong background in banking and finance. Howard's experience extends to matters involving the United Kingdom, the United States and a number of other jurisdictions, including continental Europe, Central Asia, Russia, Africa, the Middle East and offshore financial centres. He is a member of the Association of Business Recovery Professionals. Howard practised for a number of years at the bar before becoming a solicitor. He enjoyed a long career with Dentons, where he served two terms as chief executive and was most recently their global integration partner post-merger. He is an accredited Centre for Effective Dispute Resolution mediator, with a particular interest in mediating disputes arising from restructurings and insolvency proceedings.

Gabriel Moss, Q.C., graduated with a first-class honours degree in law and a master's level degree (B.C.L.) from the University of Oxford. He is also generally admitted to the bars of Gibraltar and the East Caribbean and has been specially admitted to the bars of Bermuda, Cayman Islands, Hong Kong and the Isle of Man for specific cases.

Gabriel specializes in international insolvency and restructuring in the United Kingdom, European Union and European Economic Area, as well as company, banking, financial services, commercial and offshore law and litigation. Gabriel sits part time as a deputy High Court judge of the Chancery Division and is a part-time visiting professor in corporate insolvency law at Oxford. He has provided expert evidence for cases in the United States, France, Germany, Australia, Denmark, Greece, the Netherlands, Italy, Iceland, Poland and Switzerland.

In the last few years, Gabriel has acted as leading counsel in 11 major Supreme Court, Privy Council, Court of Justice of the European Union and European Free Trade Association court cases involving insolvency, banking and commercial matters. He has been involved in most major insolvencies affecting the United Kingdom in recent years, including Lehman Brothers, Nortel, MF Global, Icelandic Banks, Irish Banks, Saad and Olympic Airlines. Gabriel has also been involved with major international restructurings, including the use of English schemes of arrangement, such as Bluebrook/IMO, British Vita Group, Deutsche Annington, PHS, Stemcor and Zodiac.

Helen Mountfield, Q.C., is a barrister in England, where she is a founder member of Matrix Chambers, which has a strong international presence. She specializes in constitutional and administrative law, and has appeared in many of the leading cases in the Supreme Court, the Court of Justice of the European Union and the European Court of Human Rights. These include being leading counsel for the Pigney group of claimants in *Gina Miller v Secretary of State for Exiting the European Union*. Helen is also an accredited mediator and sits as a deputy High Court judge. From September 2018, she will also be principal of Mansfield College, Oxford.

Federico M. Mucciarelli is a reader in law at the School of Finance and Management, SOAS University of London, and an associate professor in the Department of Economics at the University of Modena and Reggio Emilia. He has a J.D. from the University of Bologna (1996), an LL.M. from the University of Heidelberg (2000) and a Ph.D. in business law from the University of Brescia (2003). He was a visiting scholar in many research institutes and universities, such as the Max Planck Institute of Hamburg, the University of Oxford and the Institute of Advanced Legal Studies. He also worked at the Banca d'Italia (2000-2001). Federico has written several articles published in Italian and international journals on topics related to domestic and international company, insolvency and capital market law, with a particular focus on takeover regulation and international company law. He acted as one of the principal investigators for the *Study on the Law Applicable to Companies* drafted for the European Commission and published in 2016.

Joe Newbigin qualified as a barrister after completing pupillage at Francis Taylor Building, where he specialized in environmental and planning law. He previously worked for Richard Buxton Environmental & Public Law and sits on the advisory board for Public Interest Environmental Law.

Colm O'Cinneide is a professor of constitutional and human rights law at University College London (UCL). A graduate of University College Cork, the University of Edinburgh and King's Inns, he was called to the Irish Bar in 1997 and went on to work as a legal adviser in the UK House of Lords before joining UCL in 2001. He has published extensively in the field of comparative constitutional, human rights and anti-discrimination law. He has also acted as specialist legal adviser to the Joint Committee on Human Rights and the Women and Equalities Committee of the UK Parliament, and advised a range of international organizations, including the United Nations, the International Labour Organization and the European Commission. He was also a member of the European Committee on Social Rights of the Council of Europe from 2006 to 2016 and has been a member of the academic advisory board of Blackstone Chambers since 2008.

Damilola S. Olawuyi is an associate professor of petroleum, energy and environmental law at the Hamad Bin Khalifa University Law School and senior visiting research fellow at the Oxford Institute for Energy Studies, University of Oxford. He is also a chancellor's fellow at the Institute for Oil, Gas, Energy, Environment and Sustainable Development, Afe Babalola University.

A prolific and highly regarded scholar, Damilola has published several peer-reviewed articles, books and reports on climate finance, energy infrastructure and extractive resource governance.

His most recent publication is *The Human Rights-Based Approach to Carbon Finance* (Cambridge University Press, 2016).

Damilola was formerly deputy director, environmental law, of the International Law Research Program at CIGI. He also previously worked as an international energy lawyer at Norton Rose Fulbright Canada LLP, where he served on the firm's global committee on extractive resource investments in Africa. He has lectured on energy and environmental law in more than 20 countries, including Australia, Canada, China, Denmark, France, Greece, India, Jordan, Kenya, Kuwait, Nigeria, Qatar, Spain, the United Kingdom and the United States.

Damilola holds a doctoral degree in energy and environmental law from the University of Oxford, a master of laws degree from Harvard University, and a master's degree in natural resources, energy and environmental law from the University of Calgary.

Damilola was admitted to the bar in Alberta and Ontario, as well as in Nigeria. He serves on the executive committees and boards of the American Society of International Law (co-chair), the International Law Association and the Environmental Law Centre. He is vice-president of the International Law Association (Nigerian branch), editor-in-chief of the *Journal of Sustainable Development Law and Policy*, associate editor of the *Carbon and Climate Law Review* and associate fellow of the Centre for International Sustainable Development Law.

Christoph G. Paulus has been a professor of law at the Humboldt-Universität zu Berlin since 1994, holding a chair for civil law, civil procedure law, insolvency law and ancient Roman law. Before that, he taught, *inter alia*, at the universities of Heidelberg and of Saarland. He studied law at the University of Munich and earned his LL.M. at the University of California, Berkeley. As an expert primarily in insolvency law, Christoph has worked several times as a consultant for the International Monetary Fund and the World Bank. Moreover, from 2006 through 2011, he worked as an adviser for the German delegation on the United Nations Commission on International Trade Law insolvency law sessions. He has lectured worldwide and held guest professorships at various universities. In addition, he is a member of various international institutions such as the American College of Bankruptcy and the International Insolvency Institute (of which he was a vice-president until summer 2017).

Maziar Peihani is a post-doctoral fellow with CIGI's International Law Research Program. His research at CIGI is focused on international financial law and regulation, including sovereign debt resolution, international banking regulation, cross-border bank resolution and governance of climate-change-related financial risks. Prior to joining CIGI, Maziar was the inaugural post-doctoral fellow in the Centre for Banking & Finance Law at the National University of Singapore. He has a Ph.D. in law from the University of British Columbia, as well as an LL.M. and an LL.B. from Iran.

Freedom-Kai Phillips is a research associate in the International Law Research Program at CIGI. His research interests include international environmental law, with a focus on access and benefit sharing, governance of marine and terrestrial biodiversity, oceans and climate change interfaces, and governance of biodiversity beyond national jurisdictions. In addition, Freedom-Kai is a member of the International Union for Conservation of Nature World Commission on Environmental Law and a legal research fellow with the Centre for International Sustainable Development Law.

Freedom-Kai holds an LL.B. from the Schulich School of Law at Dalhousie University, an LL.M. from the University of Ottawa, an M.A. in international relations from Seton Hall University and an honours B.Sc. from Eastern Michigan University. Previously, he served as interim executive director of the Centre for Law, Technology and Society at the University of Ottawa Faculty of Law and was a legal researcher for the Ramsar Convention Secretariat.

Stephen Tromans, Q.C., is a barrister specializing in environmental, energy and infrastructure law. He practises from 39 Essex Chambers. He was previously a lecturer at the University of Cambridge and has practised as a solicitor. He is the author of a number of leading textbooks on topics such as contaminated land, nuclear law and environmental impact assessment, and was for many years the author and editor-in-chief of the *Encyclopedia of Environmental Law*. At the bar, he has been involved in some of the leading cases over the past decade and a half, appearing in the UK courts and in the European Court of Justice. He was a founder of the UK Environmental Law Association in 1986 and is a former chair of the association. He has acted as a parliamentary adviser to various committee inquiries in both Houses of Parliament, and currently sits on the Committee on Radioactive Waste Management, which advises the UK government.

Diana Wallis gained more than 15 years of professional experience as a litigation lawyer (solicitor), mainly in London, England, where she developed a European cross-border practice.

From 1999 to 2012, as a member of the European Parliament and particularly as a leading member of the Parliament's Legal Affairs Committee, Diana focused on European private international law (as rapporteur on Brussels I and Rome II); contract law, alternative dispute resolution (ADR) and mediation, collective redress, property rights and e-justice and was the author of a ground-breaking report on the role of the national judge in EU law. In 2007, she was elected to serve as vice-president of the European Parliament, with specific responsibility for transparency and access to documents

Since leaving the European Parliament in 2012, Diana has continued her activities in the European legal field, in particular as president of the European Law Institute from 2013 to 2017. She is a member of the Law Society's EU Committee, a trustee of the European Law Academy and a member of the Board of Trustees of BIICL.

Diana is also a senior fellow of the Law School at the University of Hull. She is an honorary associate of the Centre for Socio-legal Studies at the University of Oxford. She is a keen advocate of ADR and is an accredited mediator with the Centre for Effective Dispute Resolution and a member of the Charter Institute of Arbitrators.

Dirk Zetzsche is a full professor and holds the ADA Chair in Financial Law (Inclusive Finance) at the University of Luxembourg, as well as a non-executive directorship at the Center for Business and Corporate Law at the University of Düsseldorf. He holds a doctoral degree from the University of Düsseldorf, an LL.M. from the University of Toronto and a *habilitation* from the University of Düsseldorf. His main interest lies in international and comparative aspects of banking, financial, corporate, securities and private law. He has published extensively in German and English and advised various European, global and national regulators on the subject. Dirk is a member of the European Banking Institute.